Alexander Pope

THE

Poetical Works

OF

ALEXANDER POPE,

WITH

Notes by Warburton,

AND LIFE OF THE AUTHOR,

Pope and his Mother.

PHILADELPHIA.
WILLIS P. HAZARD, 190 CHESTNUT ST.

THE WORKS

OF

ALEXANDER POPE,

IN ONE VOLUME, COMPLETE,

WITH

NOTES

BY DR. WARBURTON,

AND

ILLUSTRATIONS ON STEEL

BY EMINENT ARTISTS.

FROM DESIGNS BY WEIGALL, HEATH, & OTHERS.

PHILADELPHIA:
WILLIS P. HAZARD, 190 CHESTNUT ST.
1856.

AUTHOR'S PREFACE.

I AM inclined to think that both the writers of books, and the readers of them, are generally not a little unreasonable in their expectations. The first seem to fancy that the world must approve whatever they produce, and the latter to imagine that authors are obliged to please them at any rate. Methinks, as on the one hand, no single man is born with a right of controling the opinions of all the rest; so on the other, the world has no title to demand, that the whole care and time of any particular person should be sacrificed to its entertainment. Therefore I cannot but believe that writers and readers are under equal obligations, for as much fame, or pleasure, as each affords the other.

Every one acknowledges, it would be a wild notion to expect perfection in any work of man: and yet one would think the contrary was taken for granted, by the judgment commonly passed upon Poems. A critic supposes he has done his part, if he proves a writer to have failed in an expression, or erred in any particular point: and can it then be wondered at, if the poets in general seem resolved not to own themselves in any error? For as long as one side will make no allowances, the other will be brought to no acknowledgments.

I am afraid this extreme zeal on both sides is ill-placed; poetry and criticism being by no means the universal concern of the world, but only the affair of idle men who write in their closets, and of idle men who read there.

Yet sure upon the whole, a bad author deserves better usage than a bad critic: for a writer's endeavour, for the most part, is to please his readers, and he fails merely through the misfortune of an ill judgment; but such a critic's is to put them out of humour; a design he could never go upon without both that and an ill temper.

I think a good deal may be said to extenuate the fault of bad poets. What we call a genius, is hard to be distinguished by a man himself, from a strong inclination: and if his genius be ever so great, he cannot at first discover it any other way, than by giving way to that prevalent propensity which renders him the more liable to be mistaken. The only method he has, is to make the experiment by writing, and appealing to the judgment of others: now if he happens to write ill (which is certainly no sin in itself) he is immediately made an object of ridicule. I wish we had the humanity to reflect that even the worst authors might, in their endeavour to please us, deserve something at our hands. We have no cause to quarrel with them but for their obstinacy in persisting to write; and this too may admit of alleviating circumstances. Their particular friends may be either ignorant, or insincere; and the rest of the world in general is too well bred to shock them with a truth, which generally their book-sellers are the first to inform them of. This happens not till they have spent too much of their time, to apply to any profession which might better fit their talents; and till such talents as they have are so far discredited as to be but of small service to them. For (which is the hardest care imaginable) the reputation of the man generally depends upon the first steps he makes in the world, and people will establish their opinion of us, from what we do at that season when we have least judgment to direct us.

On the other hand, a good poet no sooner communicates his works with the same desire of information, but it is imagined he is a vain young creature given up to the ambition of fame; when perhaps the poor man is all the while trembling with the fear of being ridiculous. If he is made to hope he may please the world, he falls under very unlucky circumstances; for, from the moment he prints, he must expect to hear no more truth, than if he were a prince or a beauty. If he has not very good sense (and indeed there are twenty men of wit, for one man of sense) his living thus in a course of flattery may put him in no small danger of becoming a coxcomb: if he has, he will consequently have so much diffidence as not to reap any great satisfaction from his praise; since, if it be given to his face, it can scarce be distinguished from flattery, and if in his absence, it is hard to be certain of it. Were he sure to be commended by the best and most knowing, he is as sure of being envied by the worst and most ignorant, which are the majority; for it is with a fine genius as with a fine fashion, all those are displeased at it who are not able to follow it: and it is to be feared that esteem will seldom do any man so much good, as ill-will does him harm. Then there is a third class of people who make the largest part of mankind, those of ordinary or indifferent capacities; and these (to a man) will hate, or suspect him: a hundred honest gentlemen will dread him as a wit, and a hundred innocent women as a satirist. In a word, whatever be his fate in poetry, it is ten to one but he must give up all the reasonable aims of life for it. There are indeed some advantages accruing from a genius to poetry, and they are all I can think of: the agreeable power of self-amusement when a man is idle or alone; the privilege of being admitted into the best company; and the freedom of saying as many careless things as other people, without being so severely remarked upon.

I believe, if any one, early in his life, should contemplate the dangerous fate of authors, he would scarce be of their number on any consideration. The life of a wit is a warfare upon earth; and the present spirit of the learned world is such, that to attempt to serve it (any way) one must have the constancy of a martyr, and a resolution to suffer for its sake. I could wish people would believe what I am pretty certain they will not, that I have been much less concerned about fame than I durst declare till this occasion, when methinks I should find more credit than I could heretofore: since my writings have had their fate already, and it is too late to think of prepossessing the reader in their favour. I would plead it as some merit in me, that the world has never been prepared for these trifles by prefaces, biassed by recommendations, dazzled with the names of great patrons, wheedled with fine reasons and pretences, or troubled with excuses. I confess it was want of consideration that made me an author; I wrote because it amused me; I corrected because it was as pleasant to me to correct as to write; and I published because I was told I might please such as it was a credit to please. To what degree I have done this I am really ignorant; I had too much fondness for my productions to judge of them at first, and too much judgment to be pleased with them at last. But I have reason to think they can have no reputation which will continue long, or which deserves to do so: for they have always fallen short not only of what I read of others, but even of my own ideas of poetry.

If any one should imagine I am not in earnest, I desire him to reflect, that the ancients (to say the least of them) had as much genius as we: and that to take more pains, and employ more time, cannot fail to produce more complete pieces. They constantly applied themselves not only to that art, but to that single branch of an art, to which their talent was most powerfully bent; and it was the business of their lives to correct and finish their works for posterity. If we can pretend to have used the same industry, let us expect the same immortality: though if we took the same care, we should still lie under a farther misfortune: they wrote in languages that became universal and everlasting, while ours are extremely limited both in extent and in duration. A mighty foundation for our pride! when the utmost we can hope, is but to be read in one Island, and to be thrown aside at the end of one age.

All that is left us is to recommend our productions by the imitation of the ancients: and it will be found true, that, in every age, the highest character for sense and learning has been obtained by those who have been most indebted to them. For, to say truth, whatever is very good sense, must have been common sense in all times; and what we call learning, is but the knowledge of the sense of our predecessors. Therefore they who say our thoughts are not our own, because they resemble the ancients, may as well say our faces are not our own, because they are like our fathers: and indeed it is very unreasonable, that people should expect us to be scholars, and yet be angry to find us so.

I fairly confess that I have served myself all I could by reading; that I made use of the judgment of authors dead and living;

that I omitted no means in my power to be informed of my errors, both by my friends and enemies: But the true reason these pieces are not more correct, is owing to the consideration how short a time they, and I, have to live: One may be ashamed to consume half one's days in bringing sense and rhyme together; and what critic can be so unreasonable, as not to leave a man time enough for any more serious employment, or more agreeable amusement?

The only plea I shall use for the favour of the public, is, that I have as great a respect for it, as most authors have for themselves and that I have sacrificed much of my own self-love for its sake, in preventing not only many mean things from seeing the light, but many which I thought tolerable. I would not be like those authors, who forgive themselves some particular lines for the sake of a whole poem, and *vice versa* a whole poem for the sake of some particular lines. I believe no one qualification is so likely to make a good writer, as the power of rejecting his own thoughts; and it must be this (if any thing) that can give me a chance to be one. For what I have published, I can only hope to be pardoned; but for what I have burned, I deserve to be praised. On this account the world is under some obligation to me, and owes me the justice in return, to look upon no verses as mine that are not inserted in this collection. And perhaps nothing could make it worth my while to own what are really so, but to avoid the imputation of so many dull and immoral things, as partly by malice, and partly by ignorance, have been ascribed to me. I must farther acquit myself of the presumption of having lent my name to recommend any miscellanies, or works of other men; a thing I never thought becoming a person who has hardly credit enough to answer for his own.

In this office of collecting my pieces, I am altogether uncertain, whether to look upon myself as a man building a monument, or burying the dead.

If time shall make it the former, may these poems (as long as they last) remain as a testimony, that their author never made his talents subservient to the mean and unworthy ends of party or self-interest; the gratification of public prejudices, or private passions; the flattery of the undeserving, or the insult of the unfortunate. If I have written well, let it be considered that it is what no man can do without good sense, a quality that not only renders one capable of being a good writer, but a good man. And if I have made any acquisition in the opinion of any one under the notion of the former, let it be continued to me under no other title than that of the latter.

But if this publication be only a more solemn funeral of my remains, I desire it may be known that I die in charity, and in my senses; without any murmurs against the justice of this age, or any mad appeals to posterity. I declare I shall think the world in the right, and quietly submit to every truth which time shall discover to the prejudice of these writings; not so much as wishing so irrational a thing, as that every body should be deceived merely for my credit. However, I desire it may then be considered, that there are very few things in this collection which were not written under the age of five and twenty: so that my youth may be made (as it never fails to be in executions) a case of compassion. That I was never so concerned about my works as to vindicate them in print, believing if anything were good it would defend itself, and what was bad could never be defended. That I used no artifice to raise or continue a reputation, depreciated no dead author I was obliged to, bribed no living one with unjust praise, insulted no adversary with ill language; or when I could not attack a rival's works, encourage reports against his morals. To conclude, if this volume perish, let it serve as a warning to the critics, not to take too much pains for the future to destroy such things as will die of themselves; and a *Memento mori* to some of my vain cotemporaries the poets, to teach them that, when real merit is wanting, it avails nothing to have been encouraged by the great, commended by the eminent, and favoured by the public in general.

Nov 10, 1716.

THE LIFE OF POPE

BY DR. JOHNSON.

ALEXANDER POPE was born in London, May 22, 1688, of parents whose rank or station was never ascertained: we are informed that they were of *gentle blood*; that his father was of a family of which the earl of Downe was the head; and that his mother was the daughter of William Turner, esquire, of York, who had likewise three sons, one of whom had the honour of being killed, and the other of dying, in the service of Charles the first; the third was made a general officer in Spain, from whom the sister inherited what sequestrations and forfeitures had left in the family.

This, and this only, is told by Pope; who is more willing, as I have heard observed, to shew what his father was not, than what he was. It is allowed that he grew rich by trade; but whether in a shop or on the Exchange was never discovered, till Mr. Tyers told, on the authority of Mrs. Racket, that he was a linen-draper in the Strand. Both parents were papists.

Pope was, from his birth, of a constitution tender and delicate; but is said to have shewn remarkable gentleness and sweetness of disposition. The weakness of his body continued through his life; but the mildness of his mind perhaps ended with his childhood. His voice, when he was young, was so pleasing, that he was called in fondness *the little nightingale*.

Being not sent early to school, he was taught to read by an aunt; and when he was seven or eight years old, became a lover of books. He first learned to write by imitating printed books; a species of penmanship in which he retained great excellence through his whole life, though his ordinary hand was not elegant.

When he was about eight, he was placed in Hampshire under Taverner, a Romish priest, who, by a method very rarely practised, taught him the Greek and Latin rudiments together. He was now first regularly initiated in poetry, by the perusal of Ogylby's *Homer*, and Sandys's *Ovid*. Ogylby's assistance he never repaid with any praise; but of Sandys he declared, in his notes to the *Iliad*, that English poetry owed much of its beauty to his translations. Sandys very rarely attempted original composition.

From the care of Taverner, under whom his proficiency was considerable, he was removed to a school at Twyford, near Winchester, and again to another school about Hyde-park corner; from which he used sometimes to stroll to the playhouse, and was so delighted with theatrical exhibitions, that he formed a kind of play from Ogylby's *Iliad*, with some verses of his own intermixed, which he persuaded his school-fellows to act, with the addition of his master's gardener, who personated Ajax.

At the last two schools he used to represent himself as having lost part of what Taverner had taught him; and on his master at Twyford he had already exercised his poetry in a lampoon. Yet under those masters he translated more than a fourth part of the *Metamorphoses*. If he kept the same proportion in his other exercises, it cannot be thought that his loss was great.

He tells of himself, in his poems, that he "lisp'd in numbers;" and used to say that he could not remember the time when he began to make verses. In the style of fiction, it might have been said of him, as of Pindar, that, when he lay in his cradle, "the bees swarmed about his mouth."

About the time of the revolution, his father, who was undoubtedly disappointed by the sudden blast of popish prosperity, quitted his trade, and retired to Binfield in Windsor forest, with about twenty thousand pounds; for which, being conscientiously determined not to intrust it to the government, he found no better use than that of locking it up in a chest, and taking from it what his expenses required; and his life was long enough to consume a great part of it, before his son came to the inheritance.

To Binfield Pope was called by his father, when he was about twelve years old; and there he had for a few months the assistance of one Deane, another priest, of whom he learned only to construe a little of *Tully's Offices*. How Mr. Deane could spend, with a boy who had translated so much of *Ovid*, some months over a small part of *Tully's Offices*, it is now vain to inquire.

Of a youth so successfully employed, and so conspicuously improved, a minute account must be naturally desired; but curiosity must be contented with confused, imperfect, and sometimes improbable intelligence. Pope, finding little advantage from external help, resolved thence-forward to direct himself, and at twelve formed a plan of study, which he completed with little other incitement than the desire of excellence.

His primary and principal purpose was to be a poet, with which his father accidentally concurred, by proposing subjects, and obliging him to correct his performances by many revisals; after which the old gentleman, when he was satisfied, would say, "these are good rhymes."

In his perusal of the English poets, he soon distinguished the versification of Dryden, which he considered as the model to be studied, and was impressed with such veneration for his instructor, that he persuaded some friends to take him to the coffee-house which Dryden frequented, and pleased himself with having seen him.

Dryden died May 1, 1701, some days before Pope was thirteen; so early must he therefore have felt the power of harmony, and the zeal of genius. Who does not wish that Dryden could have known the value of the homage that was paid him, and forseen the greatness of his young admirer?

The earliest of Pope's productions is his *Ode on Solitude*, written before he was twelve, in which there is nothing more than other forward boys have attained, and which is not equal to Cowley's performances at the same age.

His time was now wholly spent in reading and writing. As he

read the classics, he amused himself with translating them; and at fourteen made a version of the first book of the *Thebais*, which, with some revision, he afterwards published. He must have been at this time, if he had no help, a considerable proficient in the Latin tongue.

By Dryden's fables, which had then been not long published, and were much in the hands of poetical readers, he was tempted to try his own skill in giving Chaucer a more fashionable appearance, and put *January and May*, and the *Prologue of the Wife of Bath*, into modern English. He translated likewise the epistle of *Sappho to Phaon*, from Ovid, to complete the version which was before imperfect; and wrote some other small pieces, which he afterwards printed.

He sometimes imitated the English poets, and professed to have written at fourteen his poem on *Silence*, after Rochester's *Nothing*. He had now formed his versification, and the smoothness of his numbers surpassed his original: but this is a small part of his praise; he discovers such acquaintance both with human life and public affairs, as is not easily conceived to have been attainable by a boy of fourteen, in Windsor forest.

Next year, he was desirous of opening to himself new sources of knowledge, by making himself acquainted with modern languages; and removed for a time to London, that he might study French and Italian, which, as he desired nothing more than to read them, were by diligent application soon despatched. Of Italian learning he does not appear to have ever made much use in his subsequent studies.

He then returned to Binfield, and delighted himself with his own poetry. He tried all styles, and many subjects. He wrote a comedy, a tragedy, an epic poem, with panegyrics on all the princes of Europe; and, as he confesses, "thought himself the greatest genius that ever was." Self-confidence is the first requisite to great undertakings. He, indeed, who forms his opinion of himself in solitude, without knowing the powers of other men, is very liable to error: but it was the felicity of Pope to rate himself at his real value.

Most of his puerile productions were, by his maturer judgment, afterwards destroyed: *Alcander*, the epic poem, was burnt by the persuasion of Atterbury. The tragedy was founded on the legend of St. Genevieve. Of the comedy there is no account.

Concerning his studies, it is related that he translated Tully on *old age*; and that, besides his books of poetry and criticism, he read Temple's essays, and Locke on *human understanding*. His reading, though his favourite authors are not known, appears to have been sufficiently extensive and multifarious; for his early pieces shew, with sufficient evidence, his knowledge of books.

He that is pleased with himself easily imagines that he shall please others. Sir William Trumbull, who had been ambassador at Constantinople, and secretary of state, when he retired from business, fixed his residence in the neighbourhood of Binfield. Pope, not yet sixteen, was introduced to the statesman of sixty, and so distinguished himself, that their interviews ended in friendship and correspondence. Pope was, through his whole life, ambitious of a splendid acquaintance; and he seems to have wanted neither diligence nor success in attracting the notice of the great; for, from his first entrance into the world, and his entrance was very early, he was admitted to familiarity with those whose rank or station made them most conspicuous.

From the age of sixteen, the life of Pope, as an author, may be properly computed. He now wrote his pastorals, which were shewn to the poets and critics of that time: As they well deserved, they were read with admiration, and many praises were bestowed upon them and upon the preface, which is both elegant and learned in a high degree; they were, however, not published till five years afterwards.

Cowley, Milton, and Pope, are distinguished among the English poets, by the early exertion of their powers; but the works of Cowley alone were published in his childhood, and therefore to him only can it be certain that his puerile performances received no improvement from his maturer studies.

At this time began his acquaintance with Wycherley, a man who seems to have had among his contemporaries his full share of reputation, to have been esteemed without virtue, and caressed without good-humour. Pope was proud of his notice; Wycherley wrote verses in his praise, which he was charged by Dennis with writing to himself, and they agreed for a while to flatter one another. It is pleasant to remark how soon Pope learned the cant of an author, and began to treat critics with contempt, though he had yet suffered nothing from them.

But the fondness of Wycherley was too violent to last. His esteem of Pope was such, that he submitted some poems to his revision; and when Pope, perhaps proud of such confidence, was sufficiently bold in his criticisms, and liberal in his alterations, the old scribbler was angry to see his pages defaced, and felt more pain from the detection, than content from the amendment, of his faults. They parted; but Pope always considered him with kindness, and visited him a little time before he died.

Another of his early correspondents was Mr. Cromwell, of whom I have learned nothing particular, but that he used to ride a-hunting in a tye-wig. He was fond, and perhaps vain, of amusing himself with poetry and criticism; and sometimes sent his performances to Pope, who did not forbear such remarks as were now and then unwelcome. Pope, in his turn, put the juvenile version of *Statius* into his hands for correction.

Their correspondence afforded the public its first knowledge of Pope's epistolary powers; for his letters were given by Cromwell to one Mrs. Thomas; and she, many years afterwards, sold them to Curll, who inserted them in a volume of his miscellanies.

Walsh, a name yet preserved among the minor poets, was one of his first encouragers. His regard was gained by the pastorals, and from him Pope received the counsel by which he seems to have regulated his studies. Walsh advised him to correctness, which, as he told him, the English poets had hitherto neglected, and which therefore was left to him as a basis of fame; and, being delighted with rural poems, recommended to him to write a pastoral comedy, like those which are read so eagerly in Italy; a design which Pope probably did not approve, as he did not follow it.

Pope had not declared himself a poet; and, thinking himself entitled to poetical conversation, began at seventeen to frequent Will's, a coffee-house on the north side of Russel-street in Covent-Garden, where the wits of that time used to assemble, and where Dryden had, when he lived, been accustomed to preside.

During this period of his life he was indefatigably diligent, and insatiably curious; wanting health for violent, and money for expensive pleasures, and having excited in himself very strong desires of intellectual eminence, he spent much of his time over his books; but he read only to store his mind with facts and images, seizing all that his authors presented with undistinguishing voracity, and with an appetite for knowledge too eager to be nice. In a mind like his, however, all the faculties were at once involuntarily improving. Judgment is forced upon us by experience. He that reads many books must compare one opinion or style with another; and, when he compares, must necessarily distinguish, reject, and prefer. But the account given by himself of his studies was, that from fourteen to twenty he read only for amusement, from twenty to twenty-seven for improvement and instruction; that in the first part of his time he desired only to know, and in the second he endeavoured to judge.

The pastorals, which had been for some time handed about among poets and critics, were at last printed (1709) in Tonson's miscellany, in a volume which began with the pastorals of Philips, and ended with those of Pope.

The same year was written the *Essay on Criticism*; a work which displays such extent of comprehension, such nicety of distinction, such acquaintance with mankind, and such knowledge both of ancient and modern learning, as are not often attained by the maturest age and longest experience.

It was published about two years afterwards; and, being praised by Addison, in the Spectator, with sufficient liberality, met with so much favour as enraged Dennis, "who," he says, "found himself attacked, without any manner of provocation on his side, and attacked in his person instead of his writings, by one who was wholly a stranger to him, at a time when all the world knew he was persecuted by fortune; and not only saw that this was attempted in a clandestine manner, with the utmost falsehood and calumny, but found that all this was done by a little affected hypocrite, who had nothing in his mouth, at the same time, but truth, candour, friendship, good-nature, humanity, and magnanimity."

How the attack was clandestine is not easily perceived, nor how his person is depreciated; but he seems to have known

2

something of Pope's character, in whom may be discovered an appetite to talk too frequently of his own virtues.

The pamphlet is such as rage might be expected to dictate. He supposes himself to be asked two questions; Whether the essay will succeed? and, Who or what is the author?

Its success he admits to be secured by the false opinions then prevalent; the author he concludes to be "young and raw:"—

"First, because he discovers a sufficiency beyond his little ability, and hath rashly undertaken a task infinitely above his force. Secondly, while this little author struts, and affects the dictatorian air, he plainly shews, that at the same time he is under the rod; and, while he pretends to give laws to others, is a pedantic slave to authority and opinion. Thirdly, he hath, like school-boys, borrowed both from living and dead. Fourthly, he knows not his own mind, and frequently contradicts himself. Fifthly, he is almost perpetually in the wrong."

All these positions he attempts to prove by quotations and remarks; but his desire to do mischief is greater than his power. He has, however, justly criticised some passages. In these lines,

> There are whom Heaven has bless'd with store of wit,
> Yet want as much again to manage it;
> For wit and judgment ever are at strife—

it is apparent that wit has two meanings, and that what is wanted, though called wit, is truly judgment. So far Dennis is undoubtedly right; but, not content with argument, he will have a little mirth, and triumphs over the first couplet in terms too elegant to be forgotten. "By the way, what rare numbers are here! Would not one swear that this youngster had espoused some antiquated muse, who had sued out a divorce, on account of impotence, from some superannuated sinner; and, having been p-xed by her former spouse, has got the gout in her decrepit age, which makes her hobble so damnably?" This was the man who would reform a nation sinking into barbarity!

In another place, Pope himself allowed that Dennis had detected one of those blunders which are called bulls. The first edition had this line,

> What is this wit—
> Where wanted, scorn'd; and envied where acquir'd?

"How," says the critic, "can wit be *scorned* where it is not? Is not this a figure frequently employed in Hibernian land? The person that wants this wit may indeed be scorned, but the scorn shews the honour which the contemner has for wit." Of this remark Pope made the proper use, by correcting the passage.

I have preserved, I think, all that is reasonable in Dennis's criticism; it remains that justice be done to his delicacy. "For his acquaintance" (says Dennis) "he names Mr. Walsh, who had by no means the qualification which this author reckons absolutely necessary to a critic, it being very certain that he was, like this essayer, a very indifferent poet; he loved to be well-dressed; and I remember a little gentleman whom Mr. Walsh used to take into his company, as a double foil to his person and capacity. Inquire, between Sunninghill and Oakingham, for a young, short, squab gentleman, the very bow of the god of love, and tell me whether he be a proper author to make personal reflections ?—He may extol the ancients, but he has reason to thank the gods that he was born a modern; for had he been born of Grecian parents, and his father consequently had by law had the absolute disposal of him, his life had been no longer than that of one of his poems, the life of half a day.—Let the person of a gentleman of his parts be never so contemptible, his inward man is ten times more ridiculous; it being impossible that his outward form, though it be that of downright monkey, should differ so much from human shape, as his unthinking, immaterial part does from human understanding." Thus began the hostility between Pope and Dennis, which though it was suspended for a short time, never was appeased. Pope seems, at first, to have attacked him wantonly; but, though he always professed to despise him, he discovers, by mentioning him very often, that he felt his force or his venom.

Of this *Essay*, Pope declared, that he did not expect the sale to be quick, because "not one gentleman in sixty, even of liberal education, could understand it." The gentlemen, and the education of that time, seem to have been of a lower character than they are of this. He mentioned a thousand copies as a numerous impression.

Dennis was not his only censurer; the zealous papists thought the monks treated with too much contempt, and Erasmus too studiously praised; but to these objections he had not much regard.

The *Essay* has been translated into French by Hamilton, author of the *Comte de Grammont*, whose version was never printed; by Robotham, secretary to the king for Hanover; and by Resnel; and commented by Dr. Warburton, who has discovered in it such order and connection as was not perceived by Addison, nor, as is said, intended by the author.

Almost every poem, consisting of precepts, is so far arbitrary and immethodical, that many of the paragraphs may change places with no apparent inconvenience; for of two or more positions, depending upon some remote and general principle, there is seldom any cogent reason why one should precede the other. But for the order in which they stand, whatever it be, a little ingenuity may easily discover a reason. "It is impossible," says Hooker, "that, by long circumduction, from any one truth all truth may be inferred." Of all homogeneous truths, at least of all truths respecting the same general end, in whatever series they may be produced, a concatenation by intermediate ideas may be formed, such as, when it was once shewn, shall appear natural; but if this order be reversed, another mode of connection equally spacious may be found or made. Aristotle is praised for naming fortitude first of the cardinal virtues, as that without which no other virtue can steadily be practised; but he might, with equal propriety, have placed prudence and justice before it; since without prudence, fortitude is mad; without justice, it is mischievous.

As the end of method is perspicuity, that series is sufficiently regular that avoids obscurity; and where there is no obscurity, it will not be difficult to discover method.

In the Spectator was published the *Messiah*, which he first submitted to the perusal of Steele, and corrected in compliance with his criticisms.

It is reasonable to infer, from his letters, that the verses on the *unfortunate lady* were written about the time when his *Essay* was published. The lady's name and adventures I have sought with fruitless inquiry.

I can therefore tell no more than I have learned from Mr. Ruffhead, who writes with the confidence of one who could trust his information. She was a woman of eminent rank and large fortune, the ward of an uncle, who, having given her a proper education, expected, like other guardians, that she should make at least an equal match; and such he proposed to her, but found it rejected in favour of a young gentleman of inferior condition.

Having discovered the correspondence between the two lovers, and finding the young lady determined to abide by her own choice, he supposed that separation might do what can rarely be done by arguments, and sent her into a foreign country, where she was obliged to converse only with those from whom her uncle had nothing to fear.

Her lover took care to repeat his vows; but his letters were intercepted and carried to her guardian, who directed her to be watched with still greater vigilance, till of this restraint she grew so impatient, that she bribed a woman servant to procure her a sword, which she directed to her heart.

From this account, given from evident intention to raise the lady's character, it does not appear that she had any claim to praise, nor much to compassion. She seems to have been impatient, violent, and ungovernable. Her uncle's power could not have lasted long; the hour of liberty and choice would have come in time. But her desires were too hot for delay, and she liked self-murder better than suspense.

Nor is it discovered that the uncle, whoever he was, is with much justice delivered to posterity as "a false guardian;" he seems to have done only that for which a guardian is appointed; he endeavoured to direct his niece till she should be able to direct herself. Poetry has not often been worse employed than in dignifying the amorous fury of a raving girl.

Not long after, he wrote the *Rape of the Lock*, the most airy, the most ingenious, and the most delightful of all his compositions, occasioned by a frolic of gallantry, rather too familiar, in which Lord Petre cut off a lock of Mrs. Arabella Fermor's hair. This, whether stealth or violence, was so much resented, that the commerce of the two families, before very friendly, was interrupted. Mr. Caryl, a gentleman who, being secretary to king James's queen, had followed his mistress into France, and who, being the author of *Sir Solomon Single*, a comedy, and some translations, was entitled to the notice of a wit, solicited Pope to endeavour a reconciliation by a ludicrous poem, which might bring both the parties to a better temper. In compliance with Caryl's request, though his name was for a long time marked only by the first and last letter, C—l, a poem of two cantos was written, (1711), as is said, in a fortnight, and sent to the offended lady, who liked it well enough to shew it; and, with the usual process of literary transactions, the author, dreading a surreptitious edition, was forced to publish it.

The event is said to have been such as was desired, the pacification and diversion of all to whom it related, except Sir George Brown, who complained with some bitterness, that, in the character of Sir Plume, he was made to talk nonsense. Whether all this be true I have some doubt; for at Paris, a few years ago, a niece of Mrs. Fermor, who presided in an English convent, mentioned Pope's work with very little gratitude, rather as an insult than an honour; and she may be supposed to have inherited the opinion of her family.

At its first appearance it was termed by Addison *merum sal.* Pope, however, saw that it was capable of improvement; and having luckily contrived to borrow his machinery from the Rosicrucians, imparted the scheme with which his head was teeming to Addison, who told him that his work, as it stood, was "a delicious little thing," and gave him no encouragement to retouch it.

This has been too hastily considered as an instance of Addison's jealousy; for, as he could not guess the conduct of the new design, or the possibilities of pleasure comprised in a fiction in which there had been no examples, he might very reasonably and kindly persuade the author to acquiesce in his own prosperity, and forbear an attempt which he considered as an unnecessary hazard.

Addison's counsel was happily rejected. Pope foresaw the future efflorescence of imagery then budding in his mind, and resolved to spare no art, or industry of cultivation. The soft luxuriance of his fancy was already shooting, and all the gay varieties of diction were ready at his hand to colour and embellish it.

His attempt was justified by its success. The *Rape of the Lock* stands forward in the classes of literature, as the most exquisite example of ludicrous poetry. Berkeley congratulated him upon the display of powers more truly poetical than he had shewn before; with elegance of description and justness of precepts, he had now exhibited boundless fertility of invention.

He always considered the intermixture of the machinery with the action as his most successful exertion of poetical art. He indeed could never afterwards produce any thing of such unexampled excellence. Those performances which strike with wonder, are combinations of skilful genius with happy casualty; and it is not likely that any felicity like the discovery of a new race of preternatural agents, should happen twice to the same man.

Of this poem, the author was, I think, allowed to enjoy the praise for a long time without disturbance. Many years afterwards, Dennis published some remarks upon it, with very little force, and with no effect; for the opinion of the public was already settled, and it was no longer at the mercy of criticism.

About this time he published the *Temple of Fame*, which, as he tells Steele in their correspondence, he had written two years before; that is, when he was only twenty-two years old, an early time of life for so much learning, and so much observation as that work exhibits.

On this poem Dennis afterwards published some remarks, of which the most reasonable is, that some of the lines represent motion as exhibited by *sculpture*.

Of the epistle from *Eloisa to Abelard*, I do not know the date. His first inclination to attempt a composition of that tender kind arose, as Mr. Savage told me, from his perusal of Prior's *nut-brown maid*. How much he has surpassed Prior's work it is not necessary to mention, when perhaps it may be said with justice, that he has excelled every composition of the same kind. The mixture of religious hope and resignation gives an elevation and dignity to disappointed love, which images merely natural cannot bestow. The gloom of a convent strikes the imagination with far greater force than the solitude of a grove.

This piece was, however, not much his favourite in his latter years, though I never heard upon what principle he slighted it.

In the next year (1713) he published *Windsor Forest*; of which part was, as he relates, written at sixteen, about the same time as his pastorals; and the latter part was added afterwards: where the addition begins, we are not told. The lines relating to the peace confess their own date. It is dedicated to Lord Lansdowne, who was then high in reputation and influence among the tories; and it is said that the conclusion of the poem gave great pain to Addison, both as a poet and a politician. Reports like this are often spread with boldness very disproportionate to their evidence. Why should Addison receive any particular disturbance from the last lines of *Windsor Forest*? If contrariety of opinion could poison a politician, he would not live a day; and, as a poet, he must have felt Pope's force of genius much more from many other parts of his works.

The pain that Addison might feel it is not likely that he would confess; and it is certain that he so well suppressed his discontent, that Pope now thought himself his favourite; for, having been consulted in the revisal of *Cato*, he introduced it by a prologue; and, when Dennis published his remarks, undertook, not indeed to vindicate, but to revenge his friend, by a *narrative of the frenzy of John Dennis*.

There is reason to believe that Addison gave no encouragement to this disingenuous hostility; for, says Pope, in a letter to him, "indeed your opinion, that 'tis entirely to be neglected, would be my own in my own case; but I felt more warmth here than I did when I first saw his book against myself (though in two minutes it made me heartily merry)." Addison was not a man on whom such cant of sensibility could make much impression. He left the pamphlet to itself, having disowned it to Dennis, and perhaps did not think Pope to have deserved much by his officiousness.

This year was printed in the Guardian, the ironical comparison between the pastorals of Philips and Pope; a composition of artifice, criticism, and literature, to which nothing equal will easily be found. The superiority of Pope is so ingeniously dissembled, and the feeble lines of Philips so skilfully preferred, that Steele, being deceived, was unwilling to print the paper, lest Pope should be offended. Addison immediately saw the writer's design; and, as it seems, had malice enough to conceal his discovery, and to permit a publication which, by making his friend Philips ridiculous, made him for ever an enemy to Pope.

It appears that about this time Pope had a strong inclination to unite the art of *painting* with that of *poetry*, and put himself under the tuition of Jervas. He was near-sighted, and therefore not formed by nature for a painter: he tried, however, how far he could advance, and sometimes persuaded his friends to sit. A picture of Betterton, supposed to be drawn by him, was in the possession of Lord Mansfield: if this was taken from the life, he must have begun to paint earlier; for Betterton was now dead. Pope's ambition of this new art produced some encomiastic verses to Jervas, which certainly shew his power as a poet; but I have been told that they betray his ignorance of painting.

He appears to have regarded Betterton with kindness and esteem; and, after his death, published, under his name, a version into modern English of Chaucer's prologues, and one of his tales, which, as was related by Mr. Harte, were believed to have been the performance of Pope himself by Fenton, who made him a gay offer of five pounds, if he would shew them in the hand of Betterton.

The next year (1713) produced a bolder attempt, by which profit was sought as well as praise. The poems which he had hitherto written, however they might have diffused his name, had made very little addition to his fortune. The allowance which his father made him, though, proportioned to what he had, it might be liberal, could not be large; his religion hindered him from the occupation of any civil employment; and he complained that he wanted even money to buy books.

He therefore resolved to try how far the favour of the public extended, by soliciting a subscription to a version of the *Iliad*, with large notes.

To print by subscription was, for some time, a practice peculiar to the English. The first considerable work, for which this expedient was employed, is said to have been Dryden's *Virgil;* and it had been tried again with great success when the Tatlers were collected into volumes.

There was reason to believe that Pope's attempt would be successful. He was in the full bloom of reputation, and was personally known to almost all whom dignity of employment or splendour of reputation had made eminent; he conversed indifferently with both parties, and never disturbed the public with his political opinions; and it might be naturally expected, as each faction then boasted its literary zeal, that the great men, who on other occasions practised all the violence of opposition, would emulate each other in their encouragement of a poet who had delighted all, and by whom none had been offended.

With those hopes, he offered an English *Iliad* to subscribers, in six volumes in quarto, for six guineas; a sum, according to the value of money at that time, by no means inconsiderable, and greater than I believe to have been ever asked before. His proposal, however, was very favourably received; and the patrons of literature were busy to recommend his undertaking, and promote his interest. Lord Oxford, indeed, lamented that such a genius should be wasted upon a work not original; but proposed no means by which he might live without it. Addison recommended caution and moderation, and advised him not to be content with the praise of half the nation, when he might be universally favoured.

The greatness of the design, the popularity of the author, and the attention of the literary world, naturally raised such expectations of the future sale, that the booksellers made their offers with great eagerness; but the highest bidder was Bernard Lintot, who became proprietor, on condition of supplying at his own expense all the copies which were to be delivered to subscribers, or presented to friends, and paying two hundred pounds for every volume.

Of the quartos, it was, I believe, stipulated that none should be printed but for the author, that the subscription might not be depreciated; but Lintot impressed the same pages upon a small folio, and paper perhaps a little thinner; and sold exactly at half the price, for half-a-guinea each volume, books so little inferior to the quartos, that, by a fraud of trade, those folios, being afterwards shortened by cutting away the top and bottom, were sold as copies printed for the subscribers.

Lintot printed two hundred and fifty on royal paper in folio, for two guineas a volume; of the small folio, having printed seventeen hundred and fifty copies of the first volume, he reduced the number in the other volumes to a thousand.

It is unpleasant to relate, that the bookseller, after all his hopes and all his liberality, was, by a very unjust and illegal action, defrauded of his profit. An edition of the English *Iliad* was printed in Holland in duodecimo, and imported clandestinely for the gratification of those who were impatient to read what they could not yet afford to buy. This fraud could only be counteracted by an edition equally cheap and more commodious: and Lintot was compelled to contract his folio at once into a duodecimo, and lose the advantage of an intermediate gradation. The notes, which in the Dutch copies were placed at the end of each book, as they had been in the large volumes, were now subjoined to the text in the same page, and are therefore more easily consulted. Of this edition two thousand five hundred were first printed, and five thousand a few weeks afterwards; but indeed great numbers were necessary to produce considerable profit.

Pope, having now emitted his proposals, and engaged not only his own reputation, but in some degree that of his friends who patronized his subscription, began to be frighted at his own undertaking; and finding himself at first embarrassed with difficulties, which retarded and oppressed him, he was for a time timorous and uneasy, had his nights disturbed by dreams of long journeys, through unknown ways, and wished, as he said, "that somebody would hang him."

This misery, however, was not of long continuance; he grew by degrees more acquainted with Homer's images and expressions, and practice increased his facility of versification. In a short time he represents himself as dispatching regularly fifty verses a day, which would shew him, by an easy computation, the termination of his labour.

His own diffidence was not his only vexation. He that asks for a subscription soon finds that he has enemies. All who do not encourage him, defame him. He that wants money will rather be thought angry than poor; and he that wishes to save his money conceals his avarice by his malice. Addison had hinted his suspicion that Pope was too much a tory; and some of the tories suspected his principles, because he had contributed to the Guardian, which was carried on by Steele.

To those who censured his politics were added enemies yet more dangerous, who called in question his knowledge of Greek, and his qualifications for a translator of Homer. To these he made no public opposition; but, in one of his letters, escapes from them as well as he can. At an age like his, for he was not more than twenty-five, with an irregular education, and a course of life which much seems to have passed in conversation, it is not very likely that he overflowed with Greek. But when he felt himself deficient, he sought assistance; and what man of learning would refuse to help him? Minute inquiries into the force of words are less necessary in translating Homer than other poets, because his positions are general, and his representations natural, with very little dependence on local or temporary customs, or those changeable scenes of artificial life, which, by mingling original with accidental notions, and crowding the mind with images which time effaces, produces ambiguity in diction, and obscurity in books. To this open display of unadulterated nature, it must be ascribed, that Homer has fewer passages of doubtful meaning than any other poet, either in the learned or in modern languages. I have read of a man, who being, by his ignorance of Greek, compelled to gratify his curiosity with the Latin printed on the opposite page, declared, that, from the rude simplicity of the lines literally rendered, he formed nobler ideas of the Homeric majesty, than from the laboured elegance of polished versions.

Those literal translations were always at hand, and from them he could easily obtain his author's sense with sufficient certainty; and, among the readers of Homer, the number is very small of those who find much in the Greek more than in the Latin, except the music of the numbers.

If more help was wanting, he had the poetical translation of Eobanus Hessus, an unwearied writer of Latin verses; he had the French Homers of La Valterie and Dacier, and the English of Chapman, Hobbes, and Ogylby. With Chapman, whose work, though now totally neglected, seems to have been popular almost to the end of the last century, he had very frequent consultations, and perhaps never translated any passage till he had read his version, which indeed he has been sometimes suspected of using instead of the original.

Notes were likewise to be provided; for the six volumes would have been very little more than six pamphlets without them. What the mere perusal of the text could suggest, Pope wanted no assistance to collect or methodize; but more was necessary · many pages were to be filled, and learning must supply materials to wit and judgment. Something might be gathered from Dacier; but no man loves to be indebted to his contemporaries, and Dacier was accessible to common readers. Eustathius, was therefore necessarily consulted. To read Eustathius, of whose work there was then no Latin version, I suspect Pope, if he had been willing, not to have been able; some other was therefore to be found, who had leisure as well as abilities; and he was doubtless most readily employed who would do much work for little money.

The history of the notes has never been traced. Broome, in his preface to his poems, declares himself the commentator "in part upon the *Iliad*;" and it appears from Fenton's letter, preserved in the Museum, that Broome was at first engaged in consulting Eustathius; but that after a time, whatever was the reason, he desisted: another man of Cambridge was then employed, who soon grew weary of the work; and a third, that was recommended by Thirlby, is now discovered to have been Jortin, a man since well known to the learned world, who complained that Pope, having accepted and approved his performance, never testified any curiosity to see him, and who professed to have forgotten the terms on which he worked. The terms which Fenton uses are very mercantile: "I think at first sight that his performance is very commendable, and have sent word for him to finish the 17th book, and to send it with his demands for his trouble. I have here inclosed the specimen; if the rest come before the return, I will keep them till I receive your order."

Broome then offered his service a second time, which was probably accepted, as they had afterwards a closer correspondence. Parnell contributed the life of Homer, which Pope found so harsh, that he took great pains in correcting it; and by his own diligence, with such help as kindness or money could procure him, in somewhat more than five years he completed his version of the

Iliad, with the notes. He began it in 1712, his twenty-fifth year; and concluded it in 1718, his thirtieth year.

When we find him translating fifty lines a day, it is natural to suppose that he would have brought his work to a more speedy conclusion. The *Iliad*, containing less than sixteen thousand verses, might have been despatched in less than three hundred and twenty days, by fifty verses in a day. The notes, compiled with the assistance of his mercenaries, could not be supposed to require more time than the text.

According to this calculation, the progress of Pope may seem to have been slow; but the distance is commonly very great between actual performances and speculative possibility. It is natural to suppose, that as much as has been done to-day may be done to-morrow; but on the morrow some difficulty emerges, or some external impediment obstructs. Indolence, interruption, business, and pleasure, all take their turns of retardation; and every long work is lengthened by a thousand causes that can, and ten thousand that cannot, be recounted. Perhaps no extensive and multifarious performance was ever effected within the term originally fixed in the undertaker's mind. He that runs against *time* has an antagonist not subject to casualties.

The encouragement given to this translation, though report seems to have over-rated it, was such as the world has not often seen. The subscribers were five hundred and seventy-five. The copies, for which subscriptions were given, were six hundred and fifty-four: and only six hundred and sixty were printed. For these copies Pope had nothing to pay; he therefore received, including the two hundred pounds a volume, five thousand three hundred and twenty pounds four shillings without deduction, as the books were supplied by Lintot.

By the success of his subscription, Pope was relieved from those pecuniary distresses with which, notwithstanding his popularity, he had hitherto struggled. Lord Oxford had often lamented his disqualification for public employment, but never proposed a pension. While the translation of *Homer* was in its progress, Mr. Craggs, then secretary of state, offered to procure him a pension, which, at least during his ministry, might be enjoyed with secrecy. This was not accepted by Pope, who told him, however, that, if he should be pressed with want of money, he would send to him for occasional supplies. Craggs was not long in power, and was never solicited for money by Pope, who disdained to beg what he did not want.

With the product of this subscription, which he had too much discretion to squander, he secured his future life from want, by considerable annuities. The estate of the duke of Buckingham was found to have been charged with five hundred pounds a year, payable to Pope, which doubtless his translation enabled him to purchase.

It cannot be unwelcome to literary curiosity, that I deduce thus minutely the history of the English *Iliad*. It is certainly the noblest version of poetry which the world has ever seen; and its publication must therefore be considered as one of the great events in the annals of learning.

The original copy of the *Iliad* was obtained by Bolingbroke as a curiosity; it descended from him to Mallet, and is now, by the solicitation of the late Dr. Maty, reposited in the Museum.

The *Iliad* was published volume by volume, as the translation proceeded: the first four books appeared in 1715. The expectation of this work was undoubtedly high, and every man who had connected his name with criticism, or poetry, was desirous of such intelligence as might enable him to talk upon the popular topic. Halifax, who, by having been first a poet, and then a patron of poetry, had acquired the right of being a judge, was willing to hear some books while they were yet unpublished. Of this rehearsal Pope afterwards gave the following account:

"The famous Lord Halifax was rather a pretender to taste, than really possessed of it.—When I had finished the two or three first books of my translation of the *Iliad*, that lord desired to have the pleasure of hearing them read at his house.—Addison, Congreve, and Garth, were there at the reading. In four or five places, Lord Halifax stopt me very civilly, and, with a speech each time of much the same kind, 'I beg your pardon Mr. Pope; but there is something in that passage that does not quite please me. Be so good as to mark the place, and consider it a little at your leisure.—I am sure you can give it a little turn.'—I returned from Lord Halifax's with Dr. Garth, in his chariot; and, as we were going along, was saying to the doctor, that my lord had laid me under a great deal of difficulty by such loose and general observations; that I had been thinking over the passages almost ever since, and could not guess at what it was that offended his lordship in either of them. Garth laughed heartily at my embarrassment; said I had not been long enough acquainted with Lord Halifax to know his way yet; that I need not puzzle myself about looking those places over and over when I got home. 'All you need do (says he) is to leave them just as they are; call on Lord Halifax two or three months hence, thank him for his kind observations on those passages, and then read them to him as altered. I have known him much longer than you have, and will be answerable for the event.' I followed his advice; waited on Lord Halifax some time after; said, I hope he would find his objections to those passages removed; read them to him exactly as they were at first; and his lordship was extremely pleased with them, and cried out, 'Ay, now they are perfectly right: nothing can be better.'"

It is seldom that the great or the wise suspect that they are despised or cheated. Halifax, thinking this a lucky opportunity of securing immortality, made some advances of favour, and some overtures of advantage to Pope, which he seems to have received with sullen coldness. All our knowledge of this transaction is derived from a single letter, (Dec. 1, 1714), in which Pope says, "I am obliged to you, both for the favours you have done me, and those you intend me. I distrust neither your will nor your memory, when it is to do good: and if I ever become troublesome or solicitous, it must not be out of expectation, but out of gratitude. Your lordship may cause me to live agreeably in the town, or contentedly in the country, which is really all the difference I set between an easy fortune and a small one. It is indeed a high strain of generosity to think of making me easy all my life, only because I have been so happy as to divert you some few hours; but, if I may have leave to add it is because you think me no enemy to my native country, there will appear a better reason; for I must of consequence be very much (as I sincerely am) yours, &c."

These voluntary offers, and this faint acceptance, ended without effect. The patron was not accustomed to such frigid gratitude; and the poet fed his own pride with the dignity of independence. They probably were suspicious of each other. Pope would not dictate till he saw at what rate his praise was valued; he would be "troublesome out of gratitude, not expectation." Halifax thought himself entitled to confidence; and would give nothing, unless he knew what he should receive. Their commerce had its beginning in hope of praise on one side, and of money on the other, and ended because Pope was less eager of money than Halifax of praise. It is not likely that Halifax had any personal benevolence to Pope; it is evident that Pope looked on Halifax with scorn and hatred.

The reputation of this great work failed of gaining him a patron; but it deprived him of a friend. Addison and he were now at the head of poetry and criticism; and both in such a state of elevation, that, like the two rivals in the Roman state, one could no longer bear an equal, nor the other a superior. Of the gradual abatement of kindness between friends, the beginning is often scarcely discernible to themselves, and the process is continued by petty provocations, and incivilities sometimes peevishly returned, and sometimes contemptuously neglected, which would escape all attention but that of pride, and drop from any memory but that of resentment. That the quarrel of these two wits should be minutely deduced, is not to be expected from a writer to whom, as Homer says, "nothing but rumour has reached, and who has no personal knowledge."

Pope doubtless approached Addison, when the reputation of their wit first brought them together, with the respect due to a man whose abilities were acknowledged, and who, having attained that eminence to which he was himself aspiring, had in his hands the distribution of literary fame. He paid court with sufficient diligence by his prologue to *Cato*, by his abuse of Dennis, and with praise yet more direct, by his poem on the *dialogues on medals*, of which the immediate publication was then intended. In all this there was no hypocrisy; for he confessed that he found in Addison something more pleasing than in any other man.

It may be supposed, that, as Pope saw himself favoured by the world, and more frequently compared his own powers with those of others, his confidence increased, and his submission lessened;

and that Addison felt no delight from the advances of a young wit, who might soon contend with him for the highest place. Every great man, of whatever kind be his greatness, has among his friends those who officiously or insidiously quicken his attention to offences, heighten his disgust, and stimulate his resentment. Of such adherents Addison doubtless had many; and Pope was now too high to be without them.

From the emission and reception of the proposals for the *Iliad*, the kindness of Addison seems to have abated. Jervas the painter once pleased himself (Aug. 20, 1714) with imagining that he had re-established their friendship; and wrote to Pope that Addison once suspected him of too close a confederacy with Swift, but was now satisfied with his conduct. To this Pope answered, a week after, that his engagements to Swift were such as his services in regard to the subscription demanded, and that the tories never put him under the necessity of asking leave to be grateful. "But," says he, "as Mr. Addison must be the judge in what regards himself, and seems to have no very just one in regard to me, so I must own to you I expect nothing but civility from him."

In the same letter he mentions Philips, as having been busy to kindle animosity between them; but, in a letter to Addison, he expresses some consciousness of behaviour, inattentively deficient in respect.

Of Swift's industry in promoting the subscription there remains the testimony of Kennet, no friend to either him or Pope:—

"Nov. 2, 1713, Dr. Swift came into the coffee-house, and had a bow from every body but me, who, I confess, could not but despise him. When I came to the anti-chamber to wait, before prayers, Dr. Swift was the principal man of talk and business and acted as master of requests.—Then he instructed a young nobleman that the *best poet in England* was Mr. Pope (a papist), who had begun a translation of Homer into English verse, for which *he must have them all subscribe;* for, says he, the author *shall not* begin to print till *I have* a thousand guineas for him."

About this time, it is likely that Steele, who was, with all his political fury, good-natured and officious, procured an interview between these angry rivals, which ended in aggravated malevolence. On this occasion, if the reports be true, Pope made his complaint with frankness and spirit, as a man undeservedly neglected or opposed; and Addison affected a contemptuous unconcern, and, in a calm even voice, reproached Pope with his vanity; and, telling him of the improvements which his early works had received from his own remarks and those of Steele, said, that he being now engaged in public business, had no longer any care for his poetical reputation, nor had any other desire, with regard to Pope, than that he should not, by too much arrogance, alienate the public.

To this Pope is said to have replied with great keenness and severity, upbraiding Addison with perpetual dependence, and with the abuse of those qualifications which he had obtained at the public cost, and charging him with mean endeavours to obstruct the progress of rising merit. The contest rose so high, that they parted at last without any interchange of civility.

The first volume of *Homer* was (1715) in time published; and a rival version of the first *Iliad* (for rivals the time of their appearance inevitably made them) was immediately printed, with the name of Tickell. It was soon perceived that, among the followers of Addison, Tickell had the preference, and the critics and poets divided into factions. "I," says Pope, "have the town, that is, the mob, on my side; but it is not uncommon for the smaller party to supply by industry what it wants in numbers.—I appeal to the people as my rightful judges, and, while they are not inclined to condemn me, shall not fear the high-flyers at Button's." This opposition he immediately imputed to Addison, and complained of it in terms sufficiently resentful to Craggs, their common friend.

When Addison's opinion was asked, he declared the versions to be both good, but Tickell's the best that had ever been written; and sometimes said, that they were both good, but that Tickell had more of *Homer*.

Pope was now sufficiently irritated; his reputation and his interest were at hazard. He once intended to print together the four versions of Dryden, Maynwaring, Pope, and Tickell, that they might be readily compared, and fairly estimated. This design seems to have been defeated by the refusal of Tonson, who was the proprietor of the other three versions.

Pope intended, at another time, a rigorous criticism of Tickell's translation, and had marked a copy, which I have seen, in all places that appeared defective. But, while he was thus meditating defence or revenge, his adversary sunk before him without a blow; the voice of the public was not long divided, and the preference was universally given to Pope's performance.

He was convinced, by adding one circumstance to another, that the other translation was the work of Addison himself; but, if he knew it in Addison's lifetime, it does not appear that he told it. He left his illustrious antagonist to be punished by what has been considered as the most painful of all reflections, the remembrance of a crime perpetrated in vain.

The other circumstances of their quarrel were thus related by Pope:—

"Philips seemed to have been encouraged to abuse me in coffee-houses, and conversations: and Gildon wrote a thing about Wycherley, in which he had abused both me and my relations very grossly. Lord Warwick himself told me one day, that it was in vain for me to endeavour to be well with Mr. Addison; that his jealous temper would never admit of a settled friendship between us; and, to convince me of what he had said, assured me, that Addison had encouraged Gildon to publish those scandals, and had given him ten guineas after they were published. The next day, while I was heated with what I had heard, I wrote a letter to Mr. Addison, to let him know that I was not unacquainted with this behaviour of his; that if I was to speak severely of him in return for it, it should not be in such a dirty way; that I should rather tell him, himself, fairly of his faults, and allow his good qualities; and that it should be something in the following manner: I then adjoined the first sketch of what has since been called my satire on Addison. Mr. Addison used me very civilly ever after."

The verses on Addison, when they were sent to Atterbury, were considered by him as the most excellent of Pope's performances; and the writer was advised, since he knew where his strength lay, not to suffer it to remain unemployed.

This year (1715) being, by the subscription, enabled to live more by choice, having persuaded his father to sell their estate at Binfield, he purchased, I think only for his life, that house at Twickenham, to which his residence afterwards procured so much celebration, and removed thither with his father and mother.

Here he planted the vines and the quincunx which his verses mention; and, being under the necessity of making a subterraneous passage to a garden on the other side of the road, he adorned it with fossile bodies, and dignified it with the title of a grotto, a place of silence and retreat, from which he endeavoured to persuade his friends, and himself, that cares and passions could be excluded.

A grotto is not often the wish or pleasure of an Englishman, who has more frequent need to solicit than exclude the sun; but Pope's excavation was requisite, as an entrance to his garden; and, as some men try to be proud of their defects, he extracted an ornament from an inconvenience, and vanity produced a grotto, where necessity enforced a passage. It may be frequently remarked, of the studious and speculative, that they are proud of trifles, and that their amusements seem frivolous and childish:—whether it be that men, conscious of great reputation, think themselves above the reach of censure, and safe in the admission of negligent indulgencies; or, that mankind expect, from elevated genius, a uniformity of greatness, and watch its degradation with malicious wonder; like him who, having followed with his eye an eagle into the clouds, should lament that she ever descended to a perch

While the volumes of his *Homer* were annually published, he collected his former works (1717) into one quarto volume, to which he prefixed a preface, written with great sprightliness and elegance, which was afterwards reprinted, with some passages subjoined, that he at first omitted; other marginal additions of the same kind, he made in the later editions of his poems. Waller remarks, that poets lose half their praise, because the reader knows not what they have blotted. Pope's voracity of fame taught him the art of obtaining the accumulated honour, both of what he had published, and of what he had suppressed.

In this year his father died suddenly, in his seventy-fifth year, having passed twenty-nine years in privacy. He is not known but by the character which his son has given him. If the money with which he retired was all gotten by himself, he had traded very successfully, in times when sudden riches were rarely attainable.

The publication of the *Iliad* was at last completed in 1720. The splendour and success of this work raised Pope many enemies, that endeavoured to depreciate his abilities. Burnet, who was afterwards a judge of no mean reputation, censured him in a piece called *Homerides*, before it was published. Ducket likewise endeavoured to make him ridiculous. Dennis was the perpetual persecutor of all his studies. But, whoever his critics were, their writings are lost; and the names which are preserved are preserved in the *Dunciad*.

In this disastrous year (1720) of national infatuation, when more riches than Peru can boast were expected from the South sea, when the contagion of avarice tainted every mind, and even poets panted after wealth, Pope was seized with the universal passion, and ventured some of his money. The stock rose in its price; and for a while he thought himself the lord of thousands. But this dream of happiness did not last long; and he seems to have waked soon enough to get clear with the loss of what he once thought himself to have won, and perhaps not wholly of that.

Next year, he published some select poems of his friend Dr. Parnell, with a very elegant dedication to the earl of Oxford; who, after all his struggles and dangers, then lived in retirement, still under the frown of a victorious faction, who could take no pleasure in hearing his praise.

He gave the same year (1721) an edition of *Shakspere*. His name was now of so much authority, that Tonson thought himself entitled, by annexing it, to demand a subscription of six guineas for *Shakspere's Plays, in six quarto volumes*; nor did his expectation much deceive him, for, of seven hundred and fifty which he printed, he dispersed a great number at the price proposed. The reputation of that edition, indeed, sunk afterwards so low, that one hundred and forty copies were sold at sixteen shillings each.

On this undertaking, to which Pope was induced by a reward of two hundred and seventeen pounds twelve shillings, he seems never to have reflected afterwards without vexation; for Theobald, a man of heavy diligence, with very slender powers, first, in a book called *Shakspere Restored*, and then in a formal edition, detected his deficiencies with all the insolence of victory; and, as he was now high enough to be feared and hated, Theobald had from others all the help that could be supplied, by the desire of humbling a haughty character.

From this time Pope became an enemy to editors, collaters, commentators, and verbal critics; and hoped to persuade the world, that he miscarried in this undertaking only by having a mind too great for such minute employment.

Pope, in his edition, undoubtedly did many things wrong, and left many things undone; but let him not be defrauded of his due praise. He was the first that knew, at least the first that told, by what helps the text might be improved. If he inspected the early editions negligently, he taught others to be more accurate. In his preface, he expanded with great skill and elegance the character which had been given of Shakspere by Dryden; and drew the public attention upon his works, which, though often mentioned, had been little read.

Soon after the appearance of the *Iliad*, resolving not to let the general kindness cool, he published proposals for a translátion of the *Odyssey*, in five volumes, for five guineas. He was willing, however, now to have associates in his labour, being either weary with toiling upon another's thoughts, or having heard, as Ruffhead relates, that Fenton and Broome had already begun the work, and liking better to have them confederates than rivals.

In the patent, instead of saying that he had "translated" the *Odyssey*, as he said of the *Iliad*, he says, that he had "undertaken" a translation; and, in the proposals, the subscription is said to be not solely for his own use, but for that of "two of his friends, who have assisted him in this work."

In 1723, while he was engaged in this new version, he appeared before the lords, at the memorable trial of bishop Atterbury, with whom he had lived in great familiarity, and frequent correspondence. Atterbury had honestly recommended to him the study of the Popish controversy, in hope of his conversion; to which Pope answered in a manner that cannot much recommend his principles, or his judgment. In questions and projects of learning, they agreed better. He was called at the trial to give an account of Atterbury's domestic life and private employment, that it might appear how little time he had left for plots. Pope had but few words to utter, and in those few he made several blunders.

His letters to Atterbury express the utmost esteem, tenderness, and gratitude: "Perhaps," says he, "it is not only in this world that I may have cause to remember the bishop of Rochester." At their last interview in the Tower, Atterbury presented him with a bible.

Of the *Odyssey*, Pope translated only twelve books; the rest were the work of Broome and Fenton; the notes were written wholly by Broome, who was not over-liberally rewarded. The public was carefully kept ignorant of the several shares; and an account was subjoined at the conclusion, which is now known not to be true.

The first copy of Pope's books, with those of Fenton, are to be seen in the Museum. The parts of Pope are less interlined than the *Iliad;* and the latter books of the *Iliad* less than the former. He grew dexterous by practice, and every sheet enabled him to write the next with more facility. The books of Fenton have very few alterations by the hand of Pope. Those of Broome have not been found; but Pope complained, as it is reported, that he had much trouble in correcting them.

His contract with Lintot was the same as for the *Iliad*, except that only one hundred pounds were to be paid him for each volume. The number of subscribers were five hundred and seventy-four, and of copies eight hundred and nineteen; so that his profit, when he had paid his assistants, was still very considerable. The work was finished in 1725; and from that time he resolved to make no more translations.

The sale did not answer Lintot's expectation; and he then pretended to discover something of fraud in Pope, and commenced or threatened a suit in chancery.

On the English *Odyssey* a criticism was published by Spence, at that time prelector of poetry at Oxford; a man whose learning was not very great, and whose mind was not very powerful. His criticism, however, was commonly just; what he thought, he thought rightly; and his remarks were recommended by his coolness and candour. In him Pope had the first experience of a critic without malevolence, who thought it as much his duty to display beauties as expose faults; who censured with respect, and praised with alacrity.

With this criticism Pope was so little offended, that he sought the acquaintance of the writer, who lived with him from that time in great familiarity, attended him in his last hours, and compiled memorials of his conversation. The regard of Pope recommended him to the great and powerful; and he obtained very valuable preferments in the church.

Not long after, Pope was returning home from a visit in a friend's coach which, in passing a bridge, was overturned into the water; the windows were closed, and being unable to force them open, he was in danger of immediate death, when the postillion snatched him out by breaking the glass, of which the fragments cut two of his fingers in such a manner, that he lost their use.

Voltaire, who was then in England, sent him a letter of consolation. He had been entertained by Pope at his table, where he talked with so much grossness, that Mrs. Pope was driven from the room. Pope discovered, by a trick, that he was a spy for the court, and never considered him as a man worthy of confidence.

He soon afterwards (1727) joined with Swift, who was then in England, to publish three volumes of miscellanies, in which, amongst other things, he inserted the *Memoirs of a Parish Clerk*, in ridicule of Burnet's importance in his own history, and a *Debate upon Black and White Horses*, written in all the formalities of a legal process, by the assistance, as is said, of Mr. Fortescue, afterwards master of the rolls. Before these miscellanies is a preface signed by Swift and Pope, but apparently written by Pope; in which he makes a ridiculous and romantic complaint of the robberies committed upon authors by the clandestine seizure and sale of their papers. He tells, in tragic strains, how "the cabinets of the sick and the closets of the dead have been broken open and ransacked;" as if those violences were often committed for papers of uncertain and accidental value, which are rarely provoked by real treasures; as if epigrams and essays were in danger, where gold and diamonds are safe. A cat, hunted for his musk, is, according to Pope's account, but the emblem of a wit winded by booksellers.

His complaint, however, received some attestation; for, the same year, the letters written by him to Mr. Cromwell, in his youth, were sold by Mrs. Thomas to Curll, who printed them.

In these miscellanies was first published the *Art of Sinking in Poetry*, which, by such a train of consequences as usually passes in literary quarrels, gave, in a short time, according to Pope's account, occasion to the *Dunciad*.

In the following year, (1728), he began to put Atterbury's advice in practice; and shewed his satirical powers by publishing the *Dunciad*, one of his greatest and most elaborate performances, in which he endeavoured to sink into contempt all the writers by whom he had been attacked, and some others, whom he thought unable to defend themselves.

At the head of the *dunces* he placed poor Theobald, whom he accused of ingratitude: but whose real crime was supposed to be that of having revised *Shakspere* more happily than himself. This satire had the effect which he intended, by blasting the characters which it touched. Ralph, who, unnecessarily interposing in the quarrel, got a place in a subsequent edition, complained that for a time he was in danger of starving, as the booksellers had no longer any confidence in his capacity.

The prevalence of this poem was gradual and slow; the plan, if not wholly new, was little understood by common readers. Many of the illusions required illustration; the names were often expressed only by the initial and final letters, and, if they had been printed at length, were such as few had known or recollected. The subject itself had nothing generally interesting; for, whom did it concern to know that one or another scribbler was a *dunce*? If, therefore, it had been possible for those who were attacked to conceal their pain and their resentment, the *Dunciad* might have made its way very slowly in the world.

This, however, was not to be expected: every man is of importance to himself, and therefore, in his own opinion, to others; and, supposing the world already acquainted with all his pleasures and his pains, is perhaps the first to publish injuries or misfortunes, which had never been known unless related by himself, and at which those that hear them will only laugh; for no man sympathises with the sorrows of vanity.

The history of the *Dunciad* is very minutely related by Pope himself, in a dedication which he wrote to lord Middlesex, in the name of Savage:—

"I will relate the war of the *dunces*, (for so it has been commonly called), which began in the year 1727, and ended in 1730.

"When Dr. Swift and Mr. Pope thought it proper, for reasons specified in the preface to their miscellanies, to publish such little pieces of theirs as had casually got abroad, there was added to them the *Treatise of the Bathos*, or the *Art of Sinking in Poetry*. It happened that, in one chapter in this piece, the several species of bad poets were ranged in classes, to which were prefixed almost all the letters of the alphabet, (the greatest part of them at random): but such was the number of poets eminent in that art, that some one or other took every letter to himself: all fell into so violent a fury, that, for half a year or more, the common newspapers (in most of which they had some property, as being hired writers) were filled with the most abusive falsehoods and scurrilities they could devise; a liberty in no way to be wondered at in those people, and in those papers, that, for many years, during the uncontrolled license of the press, had aspersed almost all the great characters of the age; and this with impunity, their own persons and names being utterly secret and obscure.

"This gave Mr. Pope the thought, that he had now some opportunity of doing good, by detecting and dragging into light these common enemies of mankind; since, to invalidate this universal slander, it sufficed to shew what contemptible men were the authors of it. He was not without hopes that, by manifesting the dulness of those who had only malice to recommend them, either the booksellers would not find their account in employing them, or the men themselves, when discovered, want courage to proceed in so unlawful an occupation. This it was that gave birth to the *Dunciad*; and he thought it a happiness, that, by the late flood of slander on himself, he had acquired such a peculiar right over their names as was necessary to this design.

"On the 12th of March, 1729, at St. James's, that poem was presented to the king and queen, (who had before been pleased to read it), by the right honourable Sir Robert Walpole; and, some days after, the whole impression was taken and dispersed by several noblemen and persons of the first distinction.

"It is certainly a true observation, that no people are so impatient of censure as those who are the greatest slanderers, which was wonderfully exemplified on this occasion. On the day the book was first vended, a crowd of authors besieged the shop; entreaties, advices, threats of law and battery, nay cries of treason, were all employed to hinder the coming out of the *Dunciad*: on the other side, the booksellers and hawkers made as great efforts to procure it. What could a few poor authors do against so great a majority as the public? There was no stopping a torrent with the finger; so out it came.

"Many ludicrous circumstances attended it. The *dunces* (for by this name they were called) held weekly clubs, to consult of hostilities against the author; one wrote a letter to a great minister, assuring him Mr. Pope was the greatest enemy the government had; and another bought his image in clay, to execute him in effigy; with which sad sort of satisfaction the gentlemen were a little comforted.

"Some false editions of the book having an owl in their frontispiece, the true one, to distinguish it, fixed in its stead an ass laden with authors. Then, another surreptitious one being printed with the same ass, the new edition, in octavo, returned, for distinction, to the owl again. Hence arose a great contest of booksellers against booksellers, and advertisements against advertisements; some recommending the edition of the owl, and others the edition of the ass; by which names they came to b distinguished, to the great honour also of the gentlemen of the *Dunciad*."

Pope appears, by this narrative, to have contemplated his victory over the *dunces* with great exultation; and such was his delight in the tumult which he had raised, that for a while his natural sensibility was suspended, and he read reproaches and invectives without emotion, considering them only as the necessary effects of that pain which he rejoiced in having given.

It cannot however be concealed, that, by his own confession, he was the aggressor; for nobody believes that the letters in the *Bathos* were placed at random; and it may be discovered that, when he thinks himself concealed, he indulges the common vanity of common men, and triumphs in those distinctions which he had affected to despise. He is proud that his book was presented to the king and queen by the right honourable Sir Robert Walpole; he is proud that they read it before; he is proud that the edition was taken off by the nobility and persons of the first distinction.

The edition of which he speaks was, I believe, that which, by telling in the text the names, and in the notes the characters, of those whom he had satirised, was made intelligible and diverting. The critics had now declared their approbation of the plan, and the common reader began to like it without fear; those who were strangers to petty literature, and therefore unable to decipher initials and blanks, had now names and persons brought within their view; and delighted in the visible effect of those shafts of malice, which they had hitherto contemplated as shot into the air.

Dennis, upon the fresh provocation now given him, renewed the enmity which had for a time been appeased by mutual civilities; and published remarks, which he had till then suppressed, upon the *Rape of the Lock*. Many more grumbled in secret, or vented their resentment in the newspapers, by epigrams or invectives.

Ducket, indeed, being mentioned as loving Burnet, with "pious passion," pretended that his moral character was injured, and for some time declared his resolution to take vengeance with a cudgel. But Pope appeased him, by changing "pious passion" to "cordial friendship;" and by a note, in which he vehemently disclaims the malignity of meaning imputed to the first expression.

Aaron Hill, who was represented as diving for the prize, expostulated with Pope in a manner so much superior to all mean solicitation, that Pope was reduced to sneak and shuffle, sometimes to deny, and sometimes to apologize; he first endeavours to wound, and is then afraid to own that he meant a blow.

The *Dunciad*, in the complete edition, is addressed to Dr. Swift; of the notes, part were written by Dr. Arbuthnot; and an apologetical letter was prefixed, signed by Cleland, but supposed to have been written by Pope

After this general war upon *dulness*, he seems to have indulged himself awhile in tranquility; but his subsequent productions prove that he was not idle. He published (1731) a poem on *taste*, in which he very particularly and severely criticises the house, the furniture, the gardens, and the entertainments, of Timon, a man of great wealth and little taste. By Timon he was universally supposed, and by the earl of Burlington, to whom the poem is addressed, was privately said, to mean the duke of Chandos; a man perhaps too much delighted with pomp and show, but of a temper kind and beneficent, and who had consequently the voice of the public in his favour.

A violent outcry was therefore raised against the ingratitude and treachery of Pope, who was said to have been indebted to the patronage of Chandos for a present of a thousand pounds, and who gained the opportunity of insulting him by the kindness of his invitation.

The receipt of the thousand pounds Pope publicly denied; but, from the reproach which the attack on a character so amiable brought upon him, he tried all means of escaping. The name of Cleland was again employed in an apology, by which no man was satisfied; and he was at last reduced to shelter his temerity behind dissimulation, and endeavour to make that disbelieved which he never had confidence openly to deny. He wrote an exculpatory letter to the duke, which was answered with great magnanimity, as by a man who accepted his excuse, without believing his professions. He said, that to have ridiculed his taste, or his buildings, had been an indifferent action in another man; but that in Pope, after the reciprocal kindness that had been exchanged between them, it had been less easily excused.

Pope, in one of his letters, complaining of the treatment which his poem had found, "owns that such critics can intimidate him, nay almost persuade him to write no more, which is a compliment this age deserves." The man who threatens the world is always ridiculous; for the world can easily go on without him, and in a short time will cease to miss him. I have heard of an idiot, who used to revenge his vexations, by lying all night upon the bridge. "There is nothing," says Juvenal, "that a man will not believe in his own favour." Pope had been flattered till he thought himself one of the moving powers in the system of life. When he talked of laying down his pen, those who sat round him entreated and implored; and self-love did not suffer him to suspect that they went away and laughed.

The following year deprived him of Gay, a man whom he had known early, and whom he seemed to love with more tenderness than any other of his literary friends. Pope was now forty-four years old; an age at which the mind begins less easily to admit new confidence, and the will to grow less flexible; and when, therefore, the departure of an old friend is very acutely felt.

In the next year he lost his mother, not by an unexpected death, for she had lasted to the age of ninety-three: but she did not die unlamented. The filial piety of Pope was in the highest degree amiable and exemplary; his parents had the happiness of living till he was at the summit of poetical reputation, till he was at ease in his fortune, and without a rival in his fame, and found no diminution in his respect or tenderness. Whatever was his pride, to them he was obedient; and whatever was his irritability, to them he was gentle. Life has, among its soothing and quiet comforts, few things better to give than such a son.

One of the passages of Pope's life, which seems to deserve some inquiry, was a publication of letters between him and many of his friends, which falling into the hands of Curll, a rapacious bookseller of no good fame, were by him printed and sold. This volume containing some letters from noblemen, Pope incited a prosecution against him in the house of lords for a breach of privilege, and attended himself to stimulate the resentment of his friends. Curll appeared at the bar, and knowing himself in no great danger, spoke of Pope with very little reverence: "He has," said Curll, "a knack at versifying, but in prose I think myself a match for him." When the orders of the house were examined, none of them appeared to have been infringed; Curll went away triumphant; and Pope was left to seek some other remedy.

Curll's account was, that one evening a man in a clergyman's gown, but with a lawyer's band, brought and offered to sale a number of printed volumes, which he found to be Pope's epistolary correspondence; that he asked no name, and was told none, but gave the price demanded, and thought himself authorised to use his purchase to his own advantage.

That Curll gave a true account of the transaction it is reasonable to believe, because no falsehood was ever detected; and when, some years afterwards, I mentioned it to Lintot, the son of Bernard, he declared his opinion to be, that Pope knew better than any body else how Curll obtained the copies, because another parcel was at the same time sent to himself, for which no price had ever been demanded, as he made known his resolution not to pay a porter, and consequently not to deal with a nameless agent.

Such care had been taken to make them public, that they were sent at once to two booksellers; to Curll, who was likely to seize them as a prey; and to Lintot, who might be expected to give Pope information of the seeming injury. Lintot, I believe, did nothing: and Curll did what was expected. That to make them public was the only purpose may be reasonably supposed, because the numbers offered to sale by the private messengers, shewed that hope of gain could not have been the motive of the impression.

It seems that Pope, being desirous of printing his letters, and not knowing how to do, without imputation of vanity, what has in this country been done very rarely, contrived an appearance of compulsion; that, when he could complain that his letters were surreptitiously published, he might decently and defensively publish them himself.

Pope's private correspondence, thus promulgated, filled the

nation with praises of his candour, tenderness, and benevolence, the purity of his purposes, and the fidelity of his friendship There were some letters which a very good or a very wise man would wish suppressed; but, as they had been already exposed, it was impracticable now to retract them.

From the perusal of those letters, Mr. Allen first conceived the desire of knowing him; and with so much zeal did he cultivate the friendship which he had newly formed, that when Pope told his purpose of vindicating his own property by a genuine edition, he offered to pay the cost.

This however Pope did not accept; but in time solicited a subscription for a quarto volume, which appeared, (1737), I believe with sufficient profit. In the preface he tells, that his letters were reposited in a friend's library, said to be the earl of Oxford's, and that the copy thence stolen was sent to the press. The story was doubtless received with different degrees of credit. It may be suspected that the preface to the miscellanies was written to prepare the public for such an incident; and, to strengthen this opinion, James Worsdale, a painter, who was employed in clandestine negociations, but whose veracity was very doubtful, declared that he was the messenger who carried, by Pope's direction, the books to Curll.

When they were thus published and avowed, as they had relation to recent facts, and persons either then living or not yet forgotten, they may be supposed to have found readers; but as the facts were minute, and the characters, being either private, or literary, were little known, or little regarded, they awakened no popular kindness or resentment; the book never became much the subject of conversation; some read it as a contemporary history, and some perhaps as a model of epistolary language; but those who read it did not talk of it. Not much therefore was added by it to fame or envy; nor do I remember that it produced either public praise, or public censure.

It had, however, in some degree, the recommendation of novelty. Our language had few letters, except those of statesmen. Howel, indeed, about a century ago, published his letters, which are commended by Morhoff, and which alone, of his hundred volumes, continue his memory. Loveday's letters were printed only once; those of Herbert and Suckling are hardly known. Mrs. Phillips's [Orinda's] are equally neglected. And those of Walsh seem written as exercises, and were never sent to any living mistress or friend. Pope's epistolary excellence had an open field; he had no English rival, living or dead.

Pope is seen in this collection as connected with the other contemporary wits, and certainly suffers no disgrace in the comparison; but it must be remembered that he had the power of favouring himself; he might have originally had publication in his mind, and have written with care, or have afterwards selected those which he had most happily conceived, or most diligently laboured; and I know not whether there does not appear something more studied and artificial in his productions than the rest, except one long letter by Bolingbroke, composed with the skill and industry of a professed author. It is indeed not easy to distinguish affectation from habit; he, that has once studiously formed a style, rarely writes afterwards with complete ease. Pope may be said to write always with his reputation in his head; Swift, perhaps, like a man who remembered he was writing to Pope; but Arbuthnot, like one who lets thoughts drop from his pen as they rise into his mind.

Before these letters appeared, he published the first part of what he persuaded himself to think a system of ethics, under the title of an *Essay on Man*; which, if his letter to Swift (of Sept. 14, 1725), be rightly explained by the commentator, had been eight years under his consideration, and of which he seems to have desired the success with great solicitude. He had now many open, and doubtless many secret, enemies. The *dunces* were yet smarting with the war; and the superiority which he publicly arrogated, disposed the world to wish his humiliation.

All this he knew, and against all this he provided. His own name, and that of his friend to whom the work is inscribed, were in the first editions carefully suppressed; and the poem, being of a new kind, was ascribed to one or another, as favour determined, or conjecture wandered; it was given, says Warburton, to every man, except him only who could write it. Those who like only when they like the author, and who are under the dominion of a name, condemned it; and those admired it who are willing to scatter praise at random, which, while it is unappropriated, excites no envy. Those friends of Pope, that were trusted with the secret, went about lavishing honours on the new-born poet, and hinting that Pope was never so much in danger from any former rival.

To those authors whom he had personally offended, and to those whose opinion the world considered as decisive, and whom he suspected of envy or malevolence, he sent his essay, as a present, before publication, that they might defeat their own enmity by praises, which they could not afterwards decently retract.

With these precautions, (1733), was published the first part of the *Essay on Man*. There had been for some time a report that Pope was busy upon a system of morality; but this design was not discovered in the new poem, which had a form and a title with which its readers were unacquainted. Its reception was not uniform; some thought it a very imperfect piece, though not without good lines. While the author was unknown, some, as will always happen, favoured him as an adventurer, and some censured him as an intruder; but all thought him above neglect; the sale increased, and editions were multiplied.

The subsequent editions of the first epistle exhibited two memorable corrections. At first, the poet and his friend

> Expatiate freely o'er this scene of man,
> A mighty maze *of walks without a plan*;

For which he wrote afterwards

A mighty maze, *but not without a plan:*

for if there were no plan, it were in vain to describe or to trace the maze.

The other alteration was of these lines:

> And spite of pride, *and in thy reason's spite,*
> One truth is clear, whatever is, is right.

But having afterwards discovered, or been shewn, that the "truth" which subsisted "in spite of reason" could not be very "clear," he substituted

> And spite of pride, *in erring reason's spite.*

To such oversights will the most vigorous mind be liable, when it is employed at once upon argument and poetry.

The second and third epistles were published; and Pope was, I believe, more and more suspected of writing them; at last, in 1734, he avowed the fourth, and claimed the honour of a moral poet.

In the conclusion, it is sufficiently acknowledged, that the doctrine of the *Essay on Man* was received from Bolingbroke, who is said to have ridiculed Pope, among those who enjoyed his confidence, as having adopted and advanced principles of which he did not perceive the consequence, and as blindly propagating opinions contrary to his own. That those communications had been consolidated into a scheme regularly drawn, and delivered to Pope, from whom it returned only transformed from prose to verse, has been reported, but can hardly be true. The essay plainly appears the fabric of a poet; what Bolingbroke supplied could be only the first principles; the order, illustration, and embellishments, must all be Pope's.

These principles it is not my business to clear from obscurity, dogmatism, or falsehood; but they were not immediately examined; philosophy and poetry have not often the same readers; and the essay abounded in splendid amplifications and sparkling sentences, which were read and admired with no great attention to their ultimate purpose; its flowers caught the eye, which did not see what the gay foliage concealed, and for a time flourished in the sunshine of universal approbation. So little was any evil tendency discovered, that, as innocence is unsuspicious, many read it for a manual of piety.

Its reputation soon invited a translator. It was first turned into French prose, and afterwards by Resnel into verse. Both translations fell into the hands of Crousaz, who first, when he had the version in prose, wrote a general censure, and afterwards reprinted Resnel's version, with particular remarks upon every paragraph.

Crousaz was a professor of Switzerland, eminent for his treatise of *logic*, and his *Examen de Pyrrhonisme*; and, however little known or regarded here, was no mean antagonist. His mind was one of those in which philosophy and piety are happily united.

He was accustomed to argument and disquisition, and perhaps was grown too desirous of detecting faults; but his intentions were always right, his opinions were solid, and his religion pure.

His incessant vigilence for the promotion of piety disposed him to look with distrust upon all mataphysical systems of theology, and all schemes of virtue and happiness purely rational; and therefore he was not long before he was persuaded that the positions of Pope, as they terminated for the most part in natural religion, were intended to draw mankind away from revelation, and to represent the whole course of things as a necessary concatenation of indissoluble fatality; and it is undeniable, that, in many passages, a religious eye may easily discover expressions not very favourable to morals or to liberty.

About this time Warburton began to make his appearance in the first ranks of learning. He was a man of vigorous faculties, a mind fervid and vehement, supplied by incessant and unlimited inquiry, with wonderful extent and variety of knowledge, which yet had not oppressed his imagination, nor clouded his perspicacity. To every work he brought a memory full fraught, together with a fancy fertile of original combinations, and at once exerted the powers of the scholar, the reasoner, and the wit. But his knowledge was too multifarious to be always exact, and his pursuits too eager to be always cautious. His abilities gave him a haughty confidence, which he disdained to conceal or mollify; and his impatience of opposition disposed him to treat his adversaries with such contemptuous superiority as made his readers commonly his enemies, and excited against the advocate the wishes of some who favoured the cause. He seems to have adopted the Roman emperor's determination, *oderint dum metuant*; he used no allurements of gentle language, but wished to compel rather than persuade.

His style is copious without selection, and forcible without neatness; he took the words that presented themselves; his diction is coarse and impure; and his sentences are unmeasured.

He had, in the early part of his life, pleased himself with the notice of inferior wits, and corresponded with the enemies of Pope. A letter was produced, when he had perhaps himself forgotten it, in which he tells Concanen, "Dryden, I observe, borrows for want of leisure, and Pope for want of genius; Milton out of pride, and Addison out of modesty." And, when Theobald published *Shakspere*, in opposition to Pope, the best notes were supplied by Warburton.

But the time was now come when Warburton was to change his opinion; and Pope was to find a defender in him who had contributed so much to the exaltation of his rival.

The arrogance of Warburton excited against him every artifice of offence, and therefore it may be supposed that his union with Pope was censured as hypocritical inconstancy; but surely to think differently, at different times, of poetical merit may be easily allowed. Such opinions are often admitted, and dismissed, without nice examination. Who is there that has not found reason for changing his mind about questions of greater importance?

Warburton, whatever was his motive, undertook, without solicitation, to rescue Pope from the talons of Crousaz, by freeing him from the imputation of favouring fatality, or rejecting revelation; and from month to month continued a vindication of the *Essay on Man*, in the literary journal of that time called *The Republic of Letters*.

Pope, who probably began to doubt the tendency of his own work, was glad that the positions, of which he perceived himself not to know the full meaning, could by any mode of interpretation be made to mean well. How much he was pleased with his gratuitous defender, the following letter evidently shews,

"April 11, 1732.

"SIR,—I have just received from Mr. R. two more of your letters. It is in the greatest hurry imaginable that I write this; but I cannot help thanking you in particular for your third letter, which is so extremely clear, short, and full, that I think Mr. Crousaz ought never to have another answer, and deserved not so good a one. I can only say, you do him too much honour, and me too much right, so odd as the expression seems; for you have made my system as clear as I ought to have done, and could not. It is indeed the same system as mine, but illustrated with a ray of your own, as they say our natural body is the same still when it is glorified. I am sure I like it better than I did before, and so will every man else. I know I meant just what you explain; but I did not explain my own meaning so well as you. You understand me as well as I do myself; but you express me better than I could express myself. Pray, accept the sincerest acknowledgments. I cannot but wish these letters were put together in one book, and intend (with your leave) to procure a translation of part at least, or of all of them, into French; but I shall not proceed a step without your consent and opinion, &c."

By this fond and eager acceptance of an exculpatory comment, Pope testified, that, whatever might be the seeming or real import of the principles which he had received from Bolingbroke, he had not intentionally attacked religion; and Bolingbroke, if he meant to make him, without his own consent, an instrument of mischief, found him now engaged, with his eyes open, on the side of truth.

It is known that Bolingbroke concealed from Pope his real opinions. He once discovered them to Mr. Hooke, who related them again to Pope, and was told by him that he must have mistaken the meaning of what he heard; and Bolingbroke, when Pope's uneasiness incited him to desire an explanation, declared that Hooke had misunderstood him.

Bolingbroke hated Warburton, who had drawn his pupil from him; and a little before Pope's death they had a dispute, from which they parted with mutual aversion.

From this time Pope lived in the closest intimacy with his commentator, and amply rewarded his kindness and his zeal; for he introduced him to Mr. Murray, by whose interest he became preacher at Lincoln's-inn; and to Mr. Allen, who gave him his niece and his estate, and by consequence a bishopric. When he died, he left him the property of his works; a legacy which may be reasonably estimated at four thousand pounds.

Pope's fondness for the *Essay on Man* appeared by his desire of its propagation. Dobson, who had gained reputation by his version of Prior's *Solomon*, was employed by him to translate it into Latin verse, and was for that purpose some time at Twickenham; but he left his work, whatever was the reason, unfinished; and, by Benson's invitation, undertook the longer task of *Paradise Lost*. Pope then desired his friend, to find a scholar who should turn his essay into Latin prose; but no such performance has ever appeared.

Pope lived at this time *among the great*, with that reception and respect to which his works entitled him, and which he had not impaired by any private misconduct or factious partiality. Though Bolingbroke was his friend, Walpole was not his enemy; but treated him with so much consideration as, at his request, to solicit and obtain from the French minister an abbey for Mr. Southcot, whom he considered himself as obliged to reward, by this exertion of his interest, for the benefit which he had received from his attendance in a long illness.

It was said, that when the court was at Richmond, queen Caroline had declared her intention to visit him. This may have been only a careless effusion, thought on no more: the report of such notice, however, was soon in many mouths; and, if I do not forget or misapprehend Savage's account, Pope, pretending to decline what was not yet offered, left his house for a time, not, I suppose, for any other reason than lest he should be thought to stay at home in expectation of an honour which would not be conferred. He was therefore angry at Swift, who represents him as "refusing the visits of a queen," because he knew that what had never been offered had never been refused.

Beside the general system of morality, supposed to be contained in the *Essay on Man*, it was his intention to write distinct poems upon the different duties or conditions of life; one of which is the epistle to Lord Bathurst (1733) on the *use of riches*, a piece on which he declared great labour to have been bestowed.

Into this poem some hints are historically thrown, and some known characters are introduced, with others of which it is difficult to say how far they are real or fictitious; but the praise of Kyrl, the *man of Ross*, deserves particular examination, who, after a long and pompous enumeration of his public works and private charities, is said to have diffused all those blessings from *five hundred a-year*. Wonders are willingly told, and willingly heard. The truth is, that Kyrl was a man of known integrity and active benevolence, by whose solicitation the wealthy were persuaded to pay contributions to his charitable schemes. This influence he obtained by an example of liberality exerted to the utmost extent of his power, and was thus enabled to give more than he had. This account Mr. Victor received from the minister of the place; and I have preserved it, that the praise of a good man, being made more credible, may be more solid. Narrations of romantic and impracticable virtue will be read with wonder, but that which is unattainable is recommended in vain; that good may be endeavoured, it must be shewn to be possible.

This is the only piece in which the author has given a hint of his religion, by ridiculing the ceremony of burning the pope, and by mentioning with some indignation the inscription on the monument.

When this poem was first published, the dialogue, having no letters of direction, was perplexed and obscure. Pope seems to have written with no very distinct idea; for he calls that an *Epistle to Bathurst*, in which Bathurst is introduced as speaking.

He afterwards (1734) inscribed to Lord Cobham his *Characters of Men*, written with close attention to the operations of the mind and modifications of life. In this poem he has endeavoured to establish and exemplify his favourite theory of the *ruling passion*, by which he means an original direction of desire to some particular object; an innate affection. which gives all action a determinate and invariable tendency, and operates upon the whole system of life, either openly, or more secretly, by the intervention of some accidental or subordinate propension.

To the *Characters of Men*, he added soon after, in an epistle supposed to have been addressed to Martha Blount, but which the last edition has taken from her, the *Characters of Women*. This poem, which was laboured with great diligence, and in the author's opinion with great success, was neglected at its first publication, as the commentator supposes, because the public was informed, by an advertisement, that it contained *no character drawn from the life*; an assertion which Pope probably did not expect nor wish to have been believed, and which he soon gave his readers sufficient distrust, by telling them in a note that the work was imperfect, because part of his subject was *vice too high* to be yet exposed.

The time, however, soon came, in which it was safe to display the duchess of Marlborough under the name of *Atossa;* and her character was inserted, with no great honour to the writer's gratitude.

He published from time to time, (between 1730 and 1740), imitations of different poems of Horace, generally with his name, and once, as was suspected, without it. What he was upon moral principles ashamed to own, he ought to have suppressed. Of these pieces it is useless to settle the dates, as they had seldom much relation to the times, and perhaps had been long in his hands.

This mode of imitation, in which the ancients are familiarised, by adapting their sentiments to modern topics, by making Horace say of Shakspere what he originally said of Ennius, and accommodating his satires on Pantolabus and Nomentanus to the flatterers and prodigals of our own time, was first practised in the reign of Charles the second by Oldham and Rochester, at least I remember no instances more ancient. It is a kind of middle composition between translation and original design, which pleases when the thoughts are unexpectedly applicable, and the parallels lucky. It seems to have been Pope's favourite amusement; for he has carried it farther than any former poet.

He published likewise a revival, in smoother numbers, of Dr. Donne's satires, which was recommended to him by the duke of Shrewsbury and the earl of Oxford. They made no great impression on the public. Pope seems to have known their imbecility, and therefore suppressed them while he was yet contending to rise in reputation, but ventured them when he thought their deficiencies more likely to be imputed to Donne than to himself.

The epistle of Dr. Arbuthnot, which seems to be derived, in its first design, from Boileau's address *à son Esprit*, was published in January 1735, about a month before the death of him to whom it is inscribed. It is to be regretted, that either honour or pleasure should have been missed by Arbuthnot; a man estimable for his learning, amiable for his life, and venerable for his piety.

In this poem Pope seems to reckon with the public. He vindicates himself from censures; and with dignity, rather than arrogance, enforces his own claims to kindness and respect.

Into this poem are interwoven several paragraphs which had been before printed as a fragment, and among them the satirical lines upon Addison, of which the last couplet has been twice corrected. It was at first,

Who would not smile, if such a man there be?
Who would not laugh, if Addison were he?

Then,

Who would not grieve, if such a man there be?
Who would not laugh, if Addison were he?

At last it is,

Who but must laugh, if such a man there be?
Who would not weep, if Atticus were he?

He was at this time at open war with Lord Hervey, who had distinguished himself as a steady adherent to the ministry; and, being offended with a contemptuous answer to one of his pamphlets, had summoned Pulteney to a duel. Whether he or Pope made the first attack, perhaps cannot now be easily known: he had written an invective against Pope, whom he calls, "Hard as thy heart, and as thy birth obscure;" and hints that his father was a *hatter*. To this Pope wrote a reply in verse and prose; the verses are in this poem; and the prose, though it was never sent, is printed among his letters; but, to a cool reader of the present time, exhibits nothing but tedious malignity.

His last satires, of the general kind, were two dialogues, named, from the year in which they were published, *Seventeen Hundred and Thirty-eight*. In these poems many are praised, and many reproached. Pope was then entangled in the opposition; a follower of the prince of Wales, who dined at his house, and the friend of many who obstructed and censured the conduct of the ministers. His political partiality was too plainly shewn: he forgot the prudence with which he passed, in his early years, uninjured and unoffending, through much more violent conflicts of faction.

In the first dialogue, having an opportunity of praising Allen of Bath, he asked his leave to mention him as a man not illustrious by any merit of his ancestors, and called him in his verses "low-born Allen." Men are seldom satisfied with praise introduced or followed by any mention of defect. Allen seems not to have taken any pleasure in his epithet, which was afterwards softened into "humble Allen."

In the second dialogue, he took some liberty with one of the Foxes, among others; which Fox, in a reply to Lyttelton, took an opportunity of repaying, by reproaching him with the friendship of a lampooner, who scattered his ink without fear or decency, and against whom he hoped the resentment of the legislature would quickly be discharged.

About this time, Paul Whitehead, a small poet, was summoned before the lords for a poem called *Manners*, together with Dodsley his publisher. Whitehead, who hung loose upon society, skulked, and escaped; but Dodsley's shop and family made his appearance necessary. He was, however, soon dismissed; and the whole process was probably intended rather to intimidate Pope, than to punish Whitehead.

Pope never afterwards attempted to join the patriot with the poet, nor drew his pen upon statesmen. That he desisted from his attempts of reformation, is imputed, by his commentator, to his despair of prevailing over the corruption of the time. He was not likely to have been ever of opinion, that the dread of his satire would countervail the love of power or of money; he pleased himself with being important and formidable, and gratified sometimes his pride, and sometimes his resentment; till at last he began to think he should be more safe, if he were less busy.

The *Memoirs of Scriblerus*, published about this time, extend only to the first book of a work projected in concert by Pope, Swift, and Arbuthnot, who used to meet in the time of queen Anne, and denominated themselves the *Scriblerus Club*. Their purpose was to censure the abuses of learning, by a fictitious life of an infatuated scholar. They were dispersed; the design was never completed; and Warburton laments its miscarriage, as an event very disastrous to polite letters.

If the whole may be estimated by this specimen, which seems to be the production of Arbuthnot, with a few touches perhaps by Pope, the want of more will not be much lamented; for the follies which the writer ridicules are so little practised, that they are not known; nor can the satire be understood but by the learned: he raises phantoms of absurdity, and then drives them away. He cures diseases that were never felt.

For this reason, this joint production of three great writers has never obtained any notice from mankind; it has been little read, or, when read, has been forgotten, as no man could be wiser, better, or merrier, by remembering it.

The design cannot boast of much originality; for besides its general resemblance to *Don Quixote*, there will be found in it particular imitations of the *History of Mr. Ouffle*.

Swift carried so much of it into Ireland as supplied him with hints for his travels; and with those the world might have been contented, though the rest had been suppressed.

Pope had sought for images and sentiments in a region not known to have been explored by many other of the English writers: he had consulted the modern writers of Latin poetry, a class of authors whom Boileau endeavoured to bring into contempt, and who are too generally neglected. Pope, however, was not ashamed of their acquaintance, nor ungrateful for the advantages which he might have derived from it. A small selection from the Italians, who wrote in Latin, had been published at London, about the latter end of the last century, by a man who concealed his name, but whom his preface shews to have been well qualified for his undertaking. This collection Pope amplified by more than half, and (1740) published it in two volumes, but injuriously omitted his predecessor's preface. To these books, which had nothing but the mere text, no regard was paid; the authors were still neglected, and the editor was neither praised nor censured.

He did not sink into idleness; he had planned a work, which he considered as subsequent to his *Essay on Man*, of which he has given this account to Dr. Swift:—

"March 25, 1736.

"If ever I write any more epistles in verse, one of them shall be addressed to you. I have long concerted it, and begun it; but I would make what bears your name as finished as my last work ought to be, that is to say, more finished than any of the rest. The subject is large, and will divide into four epistles, which naturally follow the *Essay on Man*; viz. 1. Of the extent and limits of human reason and science. 2. A view of the useful, and therefore attainable; and of the unuseful, and therefore, unattainable, arts. 3. Of the nature, ends, application, and use, of different capacities. 4. Of the use of learning, of the science of the world, and of wit. It will conclude with a satire against the misapplication of all these, exemplified by pictures, characters, and examples."

This work in its full extent, being now afflicted with an asthma, and finding the powers of life gradually declining, he had no longer courage to undertake; but, from the materials which he had provided, he added, at Warburton's request, another book to the *Dunciad*, of which the design is to ridicule such studies as are either hopeless or useless, as either pursue what is unattainable, or what, if it be attained, is of no use.

When this book was printed, (1742), the laurel had been for some time upon the head of Cibber; a man whom it cannot be supposed that Pope could regard with much kindness or esteem, though in one of the imitations of Horace he has liberally enough praised the *Careless Husband.* In the *Dunciad,* among other worthless scribblers, he had mentioned Cibber; who, in his *Apology,* complains of the *great poet's* unkindness as more injurious, "because," says he, "I never have offended him."

It might have been expected that Pope should have been, in some degree, mollified by this submissive gentleness; but no such consequence appeared. Though he condescended to commend Cibber once, he mentioned him afterwards contemptuously in one of his satires, and again in his epistle to Arbuthnot; and, in the fourth book of the *Dunciad,* attacked him with acrimony, to which the provocation is not easily discoverable. Perhaps he imagined that, in ridiculing the laureat, he satirised those by whom the laurel had been given, and gratified that ambitious petulance with which he affected to insult the great.

The severity of this satire left Cibber no longer any patience. He had confidence enough in his own powers to believe that he could disturb the quiet of his adversary, and doubtless did not want instigators, who, without any care about the victory, desired to amuse themselves by looking on the contest. He therefore gave the town a pamphlet, in which he declares his resolution from that time never to bear another blow without returning it, and to tire out his adversary by perseverance, if he cannot conquer him by strength.

The incessant and unappeasable malignity of Pope he imputes to a very distant cause. After the *Three Hours after Marriage* had been driven off the stage, by the offence which the mummy and crocodile gave the audience, while the exploded scene was yet fresh in memory, it happened that Cibber played *Bayes* in the *Rehearsal*; and, as it had been usual to enliven the part by the mention of any recent theatrical transactions, he said, that he once thought to have introduced his lovers disguised in a mummy and a crocodile. "This," says he, "was received with loud claps, which indicated contempt of the play." Pope, who was behind the scenes, meeting him as he left the stage, attacked him, as he says, with all the virulence of a "wit out of his senses;" to which he replied, "that he would take no other notice of what was said by so particular a man, than to declare, that, as often as he played that part, he would repeat the same provocation."

He shews his opinion to be, that Pope was one of the authors of the play which he so zealously defended; and adds an idle story of Pope's behaviour at a tavern.

The pamphlet was written with little power of thought or language, and, if suffered to remain without notice, would have been very soon forgotten. Pope had now been enough acquainted with human life to know, if his passion had not been too powerful for his understanding, that from a contention like his with Cibber, the world seeks nothing but diversion, which is given at the expense of the higher character. When Cibber lampooned Pope, curiosity was excited; what Pope would say of Cibber nobody inquired; but in hope that Pope's asperity might betray his pain, and lessen his dignity.

He should therefore have suffered the pamphlet to flutter and die, without confessing that it stung him. The dishonour of being shewn as Cibber's antagonist could never be compensated by the victory. Cibber had nothing to lose; when Pope had exhausted all his malignity upon him, he would rise in the esteem both of his friends and his enemies. Silence only could have made him despicable; the blow which did not appear to be felt would have been struck in vain.

But Pope's irascibility prevailed, and he resolved to tell the whole English world that he was at war with Cibber; and, to shew that he thought him no common adversary, he prepared no common vengeance; he published a new edition of the *Dunciad*, (1743) in which he degraded Theobald from his painful pre-eminence, and enthroned Cibber in his stead. Unhappily the two heroes were of opposite characters, and Pope was unwilling to lose what he had already written; he has therefore depraved his poem by giving to Cibber the old books, the old pedantry, and the sluggish pertinacity of Theobald.

Pope was ignorant enough of his own interest, to make another change, and introduced Osborne contending for the prize among the booksellers. Osborne was a man entirely destitute of shame, without sense of any disgrace but that of poverty. He told me, when he was doing that which raised Pope's resentment, that he should be put into the *Dunciad*: but he had the fate of *Cassandra*; I gave no credit to his prediction, till in time I saw it accomplished. The shafts of satire were directed equally in vain against Cibber and Osborne; being repelled by the impenetrable impudence of one, and deadened by the impassive dulness of the other. Pope confessed his own pain by his anger; but he gave no pain to those who had provoked him. He was able to hurt none but himself; by transferring the same ridicule from one to another, he reduced himself to the insignificance of his own magpie, who from his cage calls cuckold at a venture.

Cibber, according to his engagement, repaid the *Dunciad* with another pamphlet, which Pope said, "would be as a dose of hartshorn to him;" but his tongue and heart were at variance. I have heard Mr. Richardson relate, that he attended his father, the painter, on a visit, when one of Cibber's pamphlets came into the hands of Pope, who said, "these things are my diversion." They sat by him while he perused it, and saw his features writhing with anguish; and young Richardson said to his father, when they returned, that he hoped to be preserved from such diversion as had been that day the lot of Pope.

From this time, finding his diseases more oppressive, and his vital powers gradually declining, he no longer strained his faculties with any original composition, nor proposed any other employment for his remaining life than the revisal and correction of his former works; in which he received advice and assistance from Warburton, whom he appears to have trusted and honoured in the highest degree.

He laid aside his epic poem, perhaps without much loss to mankind; for his hero was Brutus the Trojan, who, according to a ridiculous fiction, established a colony in Britain. The subject therefore was of the fabulous age; the actors were a race upon whom imagination had been exhausted, and attention wearied, and to whom the mind will not easily be recalled, when it is invited in blank verse, which Pope had adopted with great imprudence, and, I think, without due consideration of the nature of our language. The sketch is, at least in part, preserved by Ruffhead; by which it appears that Pope was thoughtless enough to model the names of his heroes with terminations not consistent with the time or country in which he places them.

He lingered through the next year; but perceived himself, as he expresses it, "going down the hill." He had for at least five years been afflicted with an asthma, and other disorders, which his physicians were unable to relieve. Towards the end of his life he consulted Dr. Thomson, a man who had, by large promises, and free censures of the common practice of physic, forced himself up into sudden reputation. Thomson declared his distemper to be a dropsy, and evacuated part of the water by tincture of jalap; but confessed that his belly did not subside. Thomson had many enemies, and Pope was persuaded to dismiss him.

While he was yet capable of amusement and conversation, as he was one day sitting in the air with lord Bolingbroke and lord Marchmont, he saw his favourite Martha Blount at the bottom of the terrace, and asked lord Bolingbroke to go and hand her up. Bolingbroke, not liking his errand, crossed his legs and sat still; but lord Marchmont, who was younger and less captious, waited on the lady, who, when he came to her, asked, "What! is he not dead yet?" She is said to have neglected him with shameful unkindness, in the latter time of his decay; yet, of the little which he had to leave she had a very great part. Their acquaintance began early; the life of each was pictured on the other's mind; their conversation therefore was endearing, for when they met, there was an immediate coalition of congenial notions. Perhaps he considered her unwillingness to approach the chamber of sickness as female weakness, or human frailty; perhaps he was conscious to himself of peevishness and impatience, or, though he was offended by her inattention, might yet consider her merit as overbalancing her fault; and if he had suffered his heart to be alienated from her, he could have found nothing that might fill her place; he could have only shrunk within himself; it was too late to transfer his confidence or fondness.

In May 1744, his death was approaching; on the 6th, he was all day delirious, which he mentioned four days afterwards as a sufficient humiliation of the vanity of man; he afterwards complained of seeing things as through a curtain, and in false colours; and one day, in the presence of Dodsley, asked what arm it was that came out of the wall. He said that his greatest inconvenience was inability to think.

Bolingbroke sometimes wept over him in this state of helpless decay; and, being told by Spence, that Pope, at the intermission of his deliriousness, was always saying something kind either of his present or absent friends, and that his humanity seemed to have survived his understanding, answered, "It has so:" and added, "I never in my life knew a man that had so tender a heart for his particular friends, or more general friendship for mankind." At another time he said, "I have known Pope these thirty years, and value myself more in his friendship than"—— His grief then suppressed his voice.

Pope expressed undoubting confidence of a future state. Being asked by his friend Mr. Hooke, a papist, whether he would not die like his father and mother, and whether a priest should not be called; he answered, "I do not think it is essential, but it will be very right; and I thank you for putting me in mind of it."

In the morning, after the priest had given him the last sacraments, he said, "There is nothing that is meritorious but virtue and friendship, and indeed friendship itself is only a part of virtue."

He died in the evening of the thirtieth day of May, 1744, so placidly, that the attendants did not discern the exact time of his expiration. He was buried at Twickenham, near his father and mother, where a monument has been erected to him by his commentator, the bishop of Gloucester.

He left the care of his papers to his executors; first to lord Bolingbroke, and, if he should not be living, to the earl of Marchmont; undoubtedly expecting them to be proud of the trust, and eager to extend his fame. But let no man dream of influence beyond his life. After a decent time, Dodsley the bookseller went to solicit preference as the publisher, and was told that the parcel had not been yet inspected; and, whatever was the reason, the world has been disappointed of what was "reserved for the next age."

He lost, indeed, the favour of Bolingbroke by a kind of posthumous offence. The political pamphlet called *The Patriot King* had been put into his hands that he might procure the impression of a very few copies, to be distributed, according to the author's direction, among his friends, and Pope assured him that no more had been printed than were allowed; but, soon after his death, the printer brought and resigned a complete edition of fifteen hundred copies, which Pope had ordered him to print, and retain in secret. He kept as was observed his engagement to Pope, better than Pope had kept it to his friend; and nothing was known of the transaction, till, upon the death of his employer, he thought himself obliged to deliver the books to the right owner, who, with great indignation, made a fire in his yard, and delivered the whole impression to the flames.

Hitherto nothing had been done which was not naturally dictated by resentment of violated faith; resentment more acrimonious, as the violator had been more loved or more trusted. But here the anger might have stopped; the injury was private, and there was little danger from the example.

Bolingbroke, however, was not yet satisfied; his thirst of vengeance excited him to blast the memory of the man over whom he had wept in his last struggles; and he employed Mallet, another friend of Pope, to tell the tale to the public with all its aggravations. Warburton, whose heart was warm with his legacy, and tender by the recent separation, thought it proper for him to interpose; and undertook, not indeed to vindicate the action, for breach of trust has always something criminal, but to extenuate it by an apology. Having advanced what cannot be denied, that moral obliquity is made more or less excusable by the motives that produce it, he inquires, What evil purpose could have induced Pope to break his promise? He could not delight his vanity by usurping the work, which, though not sold in shops, had been shewn to a number more than sufficient to preserve the author's claim; he could not gratify his avarice, for he could not sell his plunder till Bolingbroke was dead; and even then, if the copy was left to another, his fraud would be defeated, and if left to himself would be useless.

He brought some reproach upon his own memory by the petulant and contemptuous mention made in his will of Mr. Allen, and an affected repayment of his benefactions. Mrs. Blount, as the known friend and favourite of Pope, had been invited to the house of Allen, where she comported herself with such indecent arrogance, that she parted from Mrs. Allen in a state of irreconcilable dislike, and the door was for ever barred against her. This exclusion she resented with so much bitterness as to refuse any legacy from Pope, unless he left the world with a disavowal of obligation to Allen. Having been long under her dominion, now tottering in the decline of life, and unable to resist the violence of her temper, or perhaps, with the prejudice of a lover, persuaded that she had suffered improper treatment, he complied with her demand, and polluted his will with female resentment. Allen accepted the legacy, which he gave to the hospital at Bath, observing that Pope was always a bad accomptant, and that if to 150*l.* he had put a cipher more, he had come nearer to the truth.

The person of Pope is well known not to have been formed by the nicest model. He has, in his account of the *Little Club*, compared himself to a spider, and by another is described as protuberant behind and before. He is said to have been beautiful in his infancy; but he was of a constitution originally feeble and weak; and, as bodies of a tender frame are easily distorted, his deformity was probably in part the effect of his application. His stature was so low, that, to bring him to a level with common tables, it was necessary to raise his seat. But his face was not displeasing, and his eyes were animated and vivid.

By natural deformity, or accidental distortion, his vital functions were so much disordered, that his life was a "long disease." His most frequent assailant was the headach, which he used to relieve by inhaling the steam of coffee, which he very frequently required.

Most of what can be told concerning his petty peculiarities was communicated by a female domestic of the Earl of Oxford, who knew him perhaps after the middle of life. He was then so weak as to stand in perpetual need of female attendance; extremely sensible of cold, so that he wore a kind of fur doublet, under a shirt of very coarse warm linen, with fine sleeves. When he rose, he was invested in a bodice made of stiff canvas, being scarcely able to hold himself erect till they were laced, and he then put on a flannel waistcoat. One side was contracted. His legs were so slender, that he enlarged their bulk with three pair of stockings, which were drawn on and off by the maid; for he was not able to dress or undress himself, and neither went to bed nor rose without help. His weakness made it very difficult for him to be clean.

His hair had fallen almost all away; and he used to dine sometimes with Lord Oxford, privately, in a velvet cap. His dress of ceremony was black, with a tie-wig, and a little sword.

The indulgence and accommodation which his sickness required, had taught him all the unpleasing and unsocial qualities of a valetudinary man. He expected that every thing should give way to his ease or humour; as a child, whose parents will not hear her cry, has an unresisted dominion in the nursery.

> C'est que l'enfant toujours est homme,
> C'est que l'homme est toujours enfant.

When he wanted to sleep, he "nodded in company;" and once slumbered at his own table while the Prince of Wales was talking of poetry.

The reputation which his friendship gave procured him many invitations; but he was a very troublesome inmate. He brought no servant, and had so many wants, that a numerous attendance was scarcely able to supply them. Wherever he was, he left no room for another, because he exacted the attention, and employed the activity, of the whole family. His errands were so frequent and frivolous, that the footmen in time avoided and neglected him; and the earl of Oxford discharged some of the servants for their resolute refusal of his messages. The maids, when they had neglected their business, alleged that they had been employed by Mr. Pope. One of his constant demands was of coffee in the night, and to the woman that waited on him in his chamber he was very burthensome: but he was careful to recompense her want of sleep; and lord Oxford's servant declared, that in the house where her business was to answer his call, she would not ask for wages.

He had another fault, easily incident to those who, suffering much pain, think themselves entitled to whatever pleasures they can snatch. He was too indulgent to his appetite: he loved meat highly seasoned and of strong taste; and, at the intervals of the table, amused himself with biscuits and dry conserves. If he sat down to a variety of dishes, he would oppress his stomach with repletion; and though he seemed angry when a dram was offered him, did not forbear to drink it. His friends, who knew the avenues to his heart, pampered him with presents of luxury, which he did not suffer to stand neglected. The death of great men is not always proportioned to the lustre of their lives. Hannibal, says Juvenal, did not perish by the javelin or the sword; the slaughters of Cannæ were revenged by a ring. The death of Pope was imputed by some of his friends to a silver saucepan, in which it was his delight to heat potted lampreys.

That he loved too well to eat, is certain; but that his sensuality shortened his life will not be hastily concluded, when it is remembered that a conformation so irregular lasted six and fifty years, notwithstanding such pertinacious diligence of study and meditation.

In all his intercourse with mankind, he had great delight in artifice, and endeavoured to attain all his purposes by indirect and unsuspected methods. "He hardly drank tea without a stratagem." If, at the house of his friends, he wanted any accommodation, he was not willing to ask for it in plain terms, but would mention it remotely as some thing convenient; though, when it was procured, he soon made it appear for whose sake it had been recommended. Thus he teased Lord Orrery till he obtained a screen. He practised his arts on such small occasions, that lady Bolingbroke used to say, in a French phrase, that "he played the politician about cabbages and turnips." His unjustifiable impression of the *Patriot King*, as it can be imputed to no particular motive, must have proceeded from his general habit of secrecy and cunning; he caught an opportunity of a sly trick, and pleased himself with the thought of outwitting Bolingbroke.

In familiar or convivial conversation, it does not appear that he excelled. He may be said to have resembled Dryden, as being not one that was distinguished by vivacity in company. It is remarkable, that, so near his time, so much should be known of what he has written, and so little of what he has said: traditional memory retains no sallies of raillery, nor sentences of observation; nothing either pointed or solid, either wise or merry. One apophthegm only stands upon record. When an objection, raised against his inscription for Shakspere, was defended by the authority of Patrick, he replied—*horresco referens*—that "he would allow the publisher of a dictionary to know the meaning of a single word, but not of two words put together."

He was fretful and easily displeased, and allowed himself to be capriciously resentful. He would sometimes leave Lord Oxford silently, no one could tell why; and was to be courted back by more letters and messages than the footmen were willing to carry. The table was indeed infested by Lady Mary Wortley, who was the friend of Lady Oxford, and who, knowing his peevishness, could by no intreaties be restrained from contradicting him, till their disputes were sharpened to such asperity, that one or the other quitted the house.

He sometimes condescended to be jocular with servants or inferiors; but by no merriment, either of others or his own, was he ever seen excited to laughter.

Of his domestic character, frugality was a part eminently remarkable. Having determined not to be dependent, he determined not to be in want, and therefore wisely and magnanimously rejected all temptations to expense unsuitable to his fortune. This general care must be universally approved; but it sometimes appeared in petty artifices of parsimony, such as the practice of writing his compositions on the back of letters, as may be seen in the remaining copy of the *Iliad*, by which perhaps in five years five shillings were saved; or in a niggardly reception of his friends, and scantiness of entertainment, as, when he had two guests in his house, he would set at supper a single pint upon the table; and, having himself taken two small glasses, would retire, and say, "Gentlemen, I leave you to your wine." Yet he tells his friends, that "he has a heart for all, a house for all, and, whatever they may think, a fortune for all."

Of this fortune, which, as it arose from public approbation, was very honourably obtained, his imagination seems to have been too full; it would be hard to find a man, so well entitled to notice by his wit, that ever delighted so much in talking of his money. In his letters and in his poems, his garden and his grotto—his quincunx and his vines—or some hints of his opulence—are always to be found. The great topic of his ridicule is poverty; the crimes with which he reproaches his antagonists are their debts, their habitation in the Mint, and their want of a dinner. He seems to be of an opinion, not very uncommon in the world, that to want money is to want every thing.

Next to the pleasure of contemplating his possessions, seems to be that of enumerating the men of high rank with whom he was acquainted, and whose notice he loudly proclaims not to have been obtained by any practices of meanness or servility; a boast which was never denied to be true, and to which very few poets have ever aspired. Pope never set his genius to sale, he never flattered those whom he did not love, or praised those whom he did not esteem. Savage however remarked, that he began a little to relax his dignity when he wrote a distich for *his highness's dog*.

His admiration of the great seems to have increased in the advance of life. He passed over peers and statesmen to inscribe his *Iliad* to Congreve, with a magnanimity of which the praise had been complete, had his friend's virtue been equal to his wit. Why he was chosen for so great an honour, it is not now possible to know; there is no trace in literary history of any particular intimacy between them. The name of Congreve appears in the letters among those of his other friends, but without any observable distinction or consequence.

To his latter works, however, he took care to annex names

dignified with titles, but he was not very happy in his choice: for, except Lord Bathurst, none of his noble friends were such as that a good man would wish to have his intimacy with them known to posterity; he can derive little honour from the notice of Cobham, Burlington, or Bolingbroke.

Of his social qualities, if an estimate be made from his letters, an opinion too favourable cannot easily be formed; they exhibit a perpetual and unclouded effulgence of general benevolence and particular fondness. There is nothing but liberality, gratitude, constancy, and tenderness. It has been so long said as to be commonly believed, that the true characters of men may be found in their letters, and that he who writes to his friend lays his heart open before him. But the truth is, that such were the simple friendships of the *golden age*, and are now the friendships only of children.

If the letters of Pope are considered merely as compositions, they seem to be premeditated and artificial. It is one thing to write, because there is something which the mind wishes to discharge; and another, to solicit the imagination, because ceremony or vanity require something to be written. Pope confesses his early letters to be vitiated with *affectation and ambition*: to know whether he disentangled himself from these perverters of epistolary integrity, his book and his life must be set in comparison.

One of his favourite topics is contempt of his own poetry. For this, if it had been real, he would deserve no commendation; and in this he was certainly not sincere, for his high value of himself was sufficiently observed; and of what could he be proud but of his poetry? He writes, he says, when "he has just nothing else to do;" yet Swift complains that he was never at leisure for conversation, because he had "always some poetical scheme in his head." It was punctually required that his writing-box should be set upon his bed before he rose; and lord Oxford's domestic related, that, in the dreadful winter of forty, she was called from her bed by him four times in one night, to supply him with paper, lest he should lose a thought.

He pretends insensibility to censure and criticism, though it was observed, by all who knew him, that every pamphlet disturbed his quiet, and that his extreme irritability laid him open to perpetual vexation; but he wished to despise his critics, and therefore hoped that he did despise them.

As he happened to live in two reigns when the court paid little attention to poetry, he nursed in his mind a foolish disesteem of kings, and proclaims that "he never sees courts." Yet a little regard shewn him by the prince of Wales melted his obduracy; and he had not much to say when he was asked by his royal highness, "How he could love a prince while he disliked kings?"

He very frequently professes contempt of the world, and represents himself as looking on mankind, sometimes with gay indifference, as on emmets of a hillock, below his serious attention; and sometimes with gloomy indignation, as on monsters more worthy of hatred than of pity. These were dispositions apparently counterfeited. How could he despise those on whom he lived by pleasing, and on whose approbation his esteem of himself was superstructed? Why should he hate those to whose favour he owed his honour and his ease? Of things that terminate in human life, the world is the proper judge; to despise its sentence, if it were possible, is not just; and if it were just, is not possible. Pope was far enough from this unreasonable temper: he was sufficiently *a fool to fame,* and his fault was, that he pretended to neglect it. His levity and his sullenness were only in his letters; he passed through common life, sometimes vexed and sometimes pleased, with the natural emotions of common men.

His scorn of the great is too often repeated to be real; no man thinks much of that which he despises; and, as falsehood is always in danger of inconsistency, he makes it his boast at another time that he lives among them.

It is evident that his own importance swells often in his mind. He is afraid of writing, lest the clerks of the Post-office should know his secrets; he has many enemies; he considers himself as surrounded by universal jealousy: "after many deaths, and many dispersions, two or three of us," says he, "may still be brought together, not to plot, but to divert ourselves, and the world too, if it pleases:" and they can live together, and "shew what friends wits may be, in spite of all the fools in the world." All this while it was likely that the clerks did not know his hand; he certainly had no more enemies than a public character like his inevitably excites; and with what degree of friendship the wits might live, very few were so much fools as ever to inquire.

Some part of this pretended discontent he learned from Swift; and expresses it, I think, most frequently in his correspondence with him. Swift's resentment was unreasonable, but it was sincere, Pope's was the mere mimicry of his friend, a fictitious part which he began to play before it became him. When he was only twenty-five years old, he related that "a glut of study and retirement had thrown him on the world," and that there was danger lest "a glut of the world should throw him back upon study and retirement." To this Swift answered with great propriety, that Pope had not yet acted or suffered enough in the world to have become weary of it. And, indeed, it must have been some very powerful reason that can drive back to solitude him who has once enjoyed the pleasures of society.

In the letters both of Swift and Pope there appears such narrowness of mind, as makes them insensible of any excellence that has not some affinity with their own, and confines their esteem and approbation to so small a number, that whoever should form his opinion of the age from their representation, would suppose them to have lived amidst ignorance and barbarity, unable to find among their contemporaries either virtue or intelligence, and persecuted by those that could not understand them.

When Pope murmurs at the world, when he professes contempt of fame, when he speaks of riches and poverty, of success and disappointment, with negligent indifference, he certainly does not express his habitual and settled sentiments, but either wilfully disguises his own character, or, what is more likely, invests himself with temporary qualities, and sallies out in the colours of the present moment. His hopes and fears, his joys and sorrows, acted strongly upon his mind; and, if he differed from others, it was not by carelessness; he was irritable and resentful; his malignity to Philips, whom he had first made ridiculous, and then hated for being angry, continued too long. Of his vain desire to make Bentley contemptible, I never heard any adequate reason. He was sometimes wanton in his attacks; and, before Chandos, lady Wortley, and Hill, was mean in his retreat.

The virtues which seem to have had most of his affection were liberality and fidelity of friendship, in which it does not appear that he was other than he describes himself. His fortune did not suffer his charity to be splendid and conspicuous; but he assisted Dodsley with a hundred pounds, that he might open a shop; and, of the subscription of forty pounds a year that he raised for Savage, twenty were paid by himself. He was accused of loving money; but his love was eagerness to gain, not solicitude to keep it.

In the duties of friendship he was zealous and constant; his early maturity of mind commonly united him with men older than himself, and therefore, without attaining any considerable length of life, he saw many companions of his youth sink into the grave; but it does not appear that he lost a single friend by coldness or by injury; those who loved him once, continued their kindness. His ungrateful mention of Allen in his will, was the effect of his adherence to one whom he had known much longer, and whom he naturally loved with greater fondness. His violation of the trust reposed in him by Bolingbroke, could have no motive inconsistent with the warmest affection; he either thought the action so near to indifferent that he forgot it, or so laudable that he expected his friend to approve it.

It was reported, with such confidence as almost to enforce belief, that in the papers entrusted to his executors was found a defamatory life of Swift, which he had prepared as an instrument of vengeance, to be used if any provocation should be ever given. About this I inquired of the Earl of Marchmont, who assured me that no such piece was among his remains.

The religion in which he lived and died was that of the church of Rome, to which in his correspondence with Racine he professes himself a sincere adherent. That he was not scrupulously pious in some part of his life, is known by many idle and indecent applications of sentences taken from the scriptures; a mode of merriment which a good man dreads for its profaneness, and a witty man disdains for its easiness and vulgarity. But, to whatever levities he has been betrayed, it does not appear that his principles were ever corrupted, or that he ever lost his belief of revelation. The positions which he transmitted from Bolingbroke he seems not to have understood, and was pleased with an interpretation that made them orthodox.

A man of such exalted superiority, and so little moderation, would naturally have all his delinquencies observed and aggravated; those who could not deny that he was excellent, would rejoice to find that he was not perfect.

Perhaps it may be imputed to the unwillingness with which the same man is allowed to possess many advantages, that his learning has been depreciated. He certainly was, in his early life, a man of great literary curiosity; and, when he wrote his *Essay on Criticism*, had, for his age, a very wide acquaintance with books. When he entered into the living world, it seems to have happened to him as to many others, that he was less attentive to dead masters; he studied in the academy of Paracelsus, and made the universe his favourite volume. He gathered his notions fresh from reality, not from the copies of authors, but the originals of nature. Yet there is no reason to believe that literature ever lost his esteem; he always professed to love reading; and Dobson, who spent some time at his house translating his *Essay on Man*, when I asked him what learning he found him to possess, answered, "More than I expected." His frequent references to history, his allusions to various kinds of knowledge, and his images selected from art and nature, with his observations on the operations of the minds and the modes of life, shew an intelligence perpetually on the wing, excursive, vigorous, and diligent, eager to pursue knowledge, and attentive to retain it.

From this curiosity arose the desire of travelling, to which he alludes in his verses to Jervas, and which, though he never found an opportunity to gratify it, did not leave him till his life declined.

Of this intellectual character, the constituent and fundamental principle was good sense, a prompt and intuitive perception of consonance and propriety. He saw immediately, of his own conceptions, what was to be chosen, and what to be rejected; and in the works of others, what was to be shunned, and what was to be copied.

But good sense alone is a sedate and quiescent quality, which manages its possessions well, but does not increase them; it collects few materials for its own operations, and preserves safety, but never gains supremacy. Pope had likewise genius; a mind active, ambitious, and adventurous, always investigating, always aspiring; in its widest searches still longing to go forward, in its highest flights still wishing to be higher; always imagining something greater than it knows, always endeavouring more than it can do.

To assist these powers, he is said to have had great strength and exactness of memory. That which he had heard and read was not easily lost; and he had before him not only what his own meditations suggested, but what he had found in other writers that might be accommodated to his present purpose.

These benefits of nature he improved by incessant and unwearied diligence; he had recourse to every source of intelligence, and lost no opportunity of information; he consulted the living as well as the dead; he read his compositions to his friends, and was never content with mediocrity, when excellence could be attained. He considered poetry as the business of his life; and, however he might seem to lament his occupation, he followed it with constancy; to make verses was his first labour, and to mend them was his last.

From his attention to poetry he was never diverted. If conversation offered any thing that could be improved, he committed it to paper; if a thought, or perhaps an expression more happy than was common, rose to his mind, he was careful to write it; an independent distich was preserved for an opportunity of insertion; and some little fragments have been found containing lines, or parts of lines, to be wrought upon at some other time.

He was one of those few whose labour is their pleasure; he was never elevated to negligence, nor wearied to impatience; he never passed a fault unamended by indifference, nor quitted it by despair. He laboured his works first to gain reputation, and afterwards to keep it.

Of composition there are different methods. Some employ at once memory and invention, and, with little intermediate use of the pen, form and polish large masses by continued meditation, and write their productions only when, in their own opinion, they have completed them. It is related of Virgil, that his custom was to pour out a great number of verses in the morning, and pass the day in retrenching exuberances, and correcting inaccuracies. The method of Pope, as may be collected from his translation, was to write his first thoughts in his first words, and gradually to amplify, decorate, rectify, and refine them.

With such faculties, and such dispositions, he excelled every other writer in poetical prudence: he wrote in such a manner as might expose him to few hazards. He used almost always the same fabric of verse; and, indeed, by those few essays which he made of any other, he did not enlarge his reputation. Of this uniformity the certain consequence was readiness and dexterity. By perpetual practice, language had, in his mind, a systematical arrangement; having always the same use for words, he had words so selected and combined as to be ready at his call. This increase of facility he confessed himself to have perceived in the progress of his translation.

But, what was yet of more importance, his effusions were always voluntary, and his subjects chosen by himself. His independence secured him from drudging at a task, and labouring upon a barren topic; he never exchanged praise for money, nor opened a shop of condolence or congratulation. His poems, therefore, were scarcely ever temporary. He suffered coronations and royal marriages to pass without a song; and derived no opportunities from recent events, nor any popularity from the accidental disposition of his readers. He was never reduced to the necessity of soliciting the sun to shine upon a birth-day, of calling the graces and virtues to a wedding, or of saying what multitudes have said before him.

When he could produce nothing new, he was at liberty to be silent.

His publications were for the same reason never hasty. He is said to have sent nothing to the press till it had lain two years under his inspection; it is at least certain, that he ventured nothing without nice examination. He suffered the tumult of imagination to subside, and the novelties of invention to grow familiar. He knew that the mind is always enamoured of its own productions, and did not trust his first fondness. He consulted his friends, and listened with great willingness to criticism; and, what was of more importance, he consulted himself, and let nothing pass against his own judgment.

He professed to have learnt his poetry from Dryden, whom, whenever an opportunity was presented, he praised through his whole life with unvaried liberality; and perhaps his character may receive some illustration, if he be compared with his master.

Integrity of understanding and nicety of discernment were not allotted in a less proportion to Dryden than to Pope. The rectitude of Dryden's mind was sufficiently shewn by the dismission of his poetical prejudices, and the rejection of unnatural thoughts and rugged numbers. But Dryden never desired to apply all the judgment that he had. He wrote, and professed to write, merely for the people; and when he pleased others, he contented himself. He spent no time in struggles to rouse latent powers; he never attempted to make that better which was already good, nor often to mend what he must have known to be faulty. He wrote, as he tells us, with very little consideration; when occasion or necessity called upon him, he poured out what the present moment happened to supply, and, when once it had passed the press, ejected it from his mind; for, when he had no pecuniary interest, he had no further solicitude.

Pope was not content to satisfy; he desired to excel, and therefore always endeavoured to do his best; he did not court the candour, but dared the judgment, of his reader, and, expecting no indulgence from others, he shewed none to himself. He examined lines and words with minute and punctilious observation, and retouched every part with indefatigable diligence, till he had left nothing to be forgiven.

For this reason he kept his pieces very long in his hands, while he considered and reconsidered them. The only poems which can be supposed to have been written with such regard to the times as might hasten their publication, were the two satires of *Thirty-eight*; of which Dodsley told me that they were brought to him by the author, that they might be fairly copied. "Almost every line," he said "was then written twice over; I gave him a clean transcript, which he sent some time afterwards to me for the press, with almost every line written twice over a second time."

His declaration, that his care for his works ceased at their publication, was not strictly true. His parental attention never abandoned them; what he found amiss in the first edition, he silently corrected in those that followed. He appears to have revised the *Iliad*, and freed it from some of its imperfections; and the *Essay on Criticism* received many improvements after its first appearance. It will seldom be found that he altered without adding clearness, elegance, or vigour. Pope had perhaps the judgment of Dryden; but Dryden certainly wanted the diligence of Pope.

In acquired knowledge, the superiority must be allowed to Dryden, whose education was more scholastic, and who, before he became an author, had been allowed more time for study, with better means of information. His mind has a larger range, and he collects his images and illustrations from a more extensive circumference of science. Dryden knew more of man in his general nature, and Pope in his local manners. The notions of Dryden were formed by comprehensive speculation; and those of Pope by minute attention. There is more dignity in the knowledge of Dryden, and more certainty in that of Pope.

Poetry was not the sole praise of either; for both excelled likewise in prose; but Pope did not borrow his prose from his predecessor. The style of Dryden is capricious and varied; that of Pope is cautious and uniform. Dryden observes the motions of his own mind; Pope constrains his mind to his own rules of composition. Dryden is sometimes vehement and rapid; Pope is always smooth, uniform, and gentle. Dryden's page is a natural field, rising into inequalities, and diversified by the varied exuberance of abundant vegetation; Pope's is a velvet lawn, shaven by the scythe, and levelled by the roller.

Of genius, that power which constitutes a poet; that quality without which judgment is cold, and knowledge is inert; that energy which collects, combines, amplifies, and animates, the superiority must, with some hesitation, be allowed to Dryden. It is not to be inferred, that of this poetical vigour Pope had only a little, because Dryden had more; for every other writer since Milton must give place to Pope; and even of Dryden it must be said, that, if he has brighter paragraphs, he has not better poems. Dryden's performances were always hasty, either excited by some external occasion, or extorted by domestic necessity; he composed without consideration, and published without correction. What his mind could supply at call, or gather in one excursion, was all that he sought, and all that he gave. The dilatory caution of Pope enabled him to condense his sentiments, to multiply his images, and to accumulate all that study might produce, or chance might supply. If the flights of Dryden therefore are higher, Pope continues longer on the wing. If of Dryden's fire the blaze is brighter, of Pope's the heat is more regular and constant. Dryden often surpasses expectation, and Pope never falls below it. Dryden is read with frequent astonishment, and Pope with perpetual delight.

This parallel will, I hope, when it is well considered, be found just; and if the reader should suspect me, as I suspect myself, of some partial fondness for the memory of Dryden, let him not too

6

hastily condemn me; for meditation and inquiry may, perhaps, shew him the reasonableness of my determination.

The WORKS of POPE are now to be distinctly examined, not so much with attention to slight faults or petty beauties, as to the general character and effect of each performance.

It seems natural for a young poet to initiate himself by pastorals, which, not professing to imitate real life, require no experience; and, exhibiting only the simple operation of unmingled passions, admit no subtle reasoning or deep inquiry. Pope's pastorals are not however composed but with close thought; they have reference to the times of the day, the seasons of the year, and the periods of human life. The last, that which turns the attention upon old age and death, was the author's favourite. To tell of disappointment and misery, to thicken the darkness of futurity, and perplex the labyrinth of uncertainty, has been always a delicious employment of the poets. His preference was probably just. I wish, however, that his fondness had not overlooked a line in which the *zephyrs* are made *to lament in silence*.

To charge these pastorals with want of invention, is to require what was never intended. The imitations are so ambitiously frequent, that the writer evidently means rather to shew his literature than his wit. It is surely sufficient for an author of sixteen, not only to be able to copy the poems of antiquity with judicious selection, but to have obtained sufficient power of language, and skill in metre, to exhibit a series of versification, which had in English poetry no precedent, nor has since had an imitation.

The design of *Windsor Forest* is evidently derived from *Cooper's Hill*, with some attention to Waller's poem on *The Park*; but Pope cannot be denied to excel his masters in variety and elegance, and the art of interchanging description, narrative, and morality. The objection made by Dennis is the want of plan, of a regular subordination of parts terminating in the principal and original design. There is this want in most descriptive poems; because, as the scenes, which they must exhibit successively, are all subsisting at the same time, the order in which they are shewn must by necessity be arbitrary; and more is not to be expected from the last than from the first. The attention, therefore, which cannot be detained by suspense, must be excited by diversity, such as his poem offers to its reader.

But the desire of diversity may be too much indulged; the parts of *Windsor Forest* which deserve least praise, are those which were added to enliven the stillness of the scene—the appearance of father Thames, and the transformation of *Lodona*. Addison had, in his *Campaign*, derided the rivers that "rise from their oozy beds" to tell stories of heroes; and it is therefore strange that Pope should adopt a fiction not only unnatural but lately censured. The story of *Lodona* is told with sweetness; but a new metamorphosis is a ready and puerile expedient; nothing is easier than to tell how a flower was once a blooming virgin, or a rock an obdurate tyrant.

The *Temple of Fame* has, as Steele warmly declared, "a thousand beauties." Every part is splendid; there is great luxuriance of ornaments; the original version of Chaucer was never denied to be much improved; the allegory is very skilfully continued, the imagery is properly selected, and learnedly displayed; yet, with all this comprehension of excellence, as its scene is laid in remote ages, and its sentiments, if the concluding paragraph be excepted, have little relation to general manners or common life, it never obtained much notice, but is turned silently over, and seldom quoted or mentioned with either praise or blame.

That the *Messiah* excels the *Pollio* is no great praise, if it be considered from what original the improvements are derived.

The *verses on the unfortunate lady* have drawn much attention, by the illaudable singularity of treating suicide with respect; and they must be allowed to be written in some parts with vigorous animation, and in others with gentle tenderness; nor has Pope produced any poem in which the sense predominates more over the diction. But the tale is not skilfully told; it is not easy to discover the character of either the lady or her guardian. History relates that she was about to disparage herself by marriage with an inferior; Pope praises her for the dignity of ambition, and yet condemns the uncle to detestation for his pride; the ambitious love of a niece may be opposed by the interest, malice, or envy of an uncle, but never by his pride. On such an occasion a poet may be allowed to be obscure, but inconsistency never can be right.

The *Ode for St. Cecilia's Day* was undertaken at the desire of Steele: in this the author is generally confessed to have miscarried, yet he has miscarried only as compared with Dryden; for he has far outgone other competitors. Dryden's plan is better chosen; history will always take stronger hold of the attention than fable; the passions excited by Dryden are the pleasures and pains of real life; the scene of Pope is laid in imaginary existence; Pope is read with calm acquiescence, Dryden with turbulent delight; Pope hangs upon the ear, and Dryden finds the passes of the mind.

Both the odes want the essential constituent of metrical compositions, the stated recurrence of settled numbers. It may be alleged that Pindar is said by Horace to have written *numeris lege solutis*: but as no such lax performances have been transmitted to us, the meaning of that expression cannot be fixed; and perhaps the like return might properly be made to a modern Pindarist, as Mr. Cobb received from Bentley, who, when he found his criticisms upon a Greek exercise, which Cobb had presented, refuted one after another by Pindar's authority, cried out at last, "Pindar was a bold fellow, but thou art an impudent one."

If Pope's ode be particularly inspected, it will be found that the first stanza consists of sounds well chosen indeed, but only sounds.

The second consists of hyperbolical common-places, easily to be found, and perhaps without much difficulty to be as well expressed.

In the third, however, there are numbers, images, harmony, and vigour, not unworthy the antagonist of Dryden. Had all been like this—but every part cannot be the best.

The next stanzas place and detain us in the dark and dismal regions of mythology, where neither hope nor fear, neither joy nor sorrow, can be found: the poet, however, faithfully attends us: we have all that can be performed by elegance of diction, or sweetness of versification; but what can form avail without better matter?

The last stanza recurs again to common-places. The conclusion is too evidently modelled by that of Dryden; and it may be remarked that both end with the same fault; the comparison of each is literal on one side, and metaphorical on the other.

Poets do not always express their own thoughts; Pope, with all this labour in the praise of music, was ignorant of its principles, and insensible of its effects.

One of his greatest, though of his earliest works, is the *Essay on Criticism*, which, if he had written nothing else, would have placed him among the first critics and the first poets, as it exhibits every mode of excellence that can embellish or dignify didactic composition, selection of matter, novelty of arrangement, justness of precept, splendour of illustration, and propriety of digression. I know not whether it be pleasing to consider that he produced this piece at twenty, and never afterwards excelled it; he that delights himself with observing that such powers may be so soon attained, cannot but grieve to think that life was ever after at a stand.

To mention the particular beauties of the essay would be unprofitably tedious; but I cannot forbear to observe, that the comparison of a student's progress in the sciences with the journey of a traveller in the Alps, is perhaps the best that English poetry can shew. A simile, to be perfect, must both illustrate and ennoble the subject: must shew it to the understanding in a clearer view, and display it to the fancy with greater dignity; but either of these qualities may be sufficient to recommend it. In didactic poetry, of which the great purpose is instruction, a simile may be praised which illustrates, though it does not ennoble; in heroics, that may be admitted which ennobles, though it does not illustrate. That it may be complete, it is required to exhibit, independently of its references, a pleasing image; for a simile is said to be a short episode. To this antiquity was so attentive, that circumstances were sometimes added, which, having no parallels, served only to fill the imagination, and produced what Perrault, ludicrously called "comparisons with a long tail." In their similes, the greatest writers have sometimes failed; the ship-race, compared with the chariot-race, is neither illustrated nor aggrandised; land and water make all the difference: when Apollo, running after Daphne, is likened to a grey-hound chasing a hare there is nothing gained; the ideas of pursuit and flight are too plain to be made plainer; and a god, and the daughter of a god, are not represented much to their advantage by a hare and dog. The simile of the Alps has no useless parts, yet affords a striking picture by itself; it makes the foregoing position better understood, and enables it to take faster hold on the attention; it assists the apprehension, and elevates the fancy.

Let me likewise dwell a little on the celebrated paragraph, in which it is directed that "the sound should seem an echo to the sense;" a precept to which Pope is allowed to have observed beyond any other English poet.

This motion of representative metre, and the desire of discovering frequent adaptations of the sound to the sense, have produced, in my opinion, many wild conceits and imaginary beauties. All that can furnish this representation are the sounds of the words considered singly, and the time in which they are pronounced. Every language has some words framed to exhibit the noises which they express, as *thump, rattle, growl, hiss.* These however are but few, and the poet cannot make them more, nor can they be of any use but when sound is to be mentioned. The time of pronunciation was, in the dactylic measures of the learned languages, capable of considerable variety; but that variety could be accommodated only to motion or duration, and different degrees of motion were perhaps expressed by verses rapid or slow, without much attention of the writer, when the image had full possession of his fancy; but our language having little flexibility, our verses can differ very little in their cadence. The fancied resemblances, I fear, arise sometimes merely from the ambiguity of words; there is supposed to be some relation between a *soft* line and a *soft* couch, or between *hard* syllables and *hard* fortune.

Motion, however, may be in some sort exemplified; and yet it may be suspected that in such resemblances the mind often governs the ear, and the sounds are estimated by their meaning. One of their most successful attempts has been to describe the labour of Sisyphus:

With many a weary step, and many a groan,
Up a high hill he heaves a huge round stone;
The huge round stone, resulting with a bound,
Thunders impetuous down, and smokes along the ground.

Who does not perceive the stone to move slowly upward, and roll violently back? But, set the same numbers to another sense,

While many a merry tale, and many a song,
Cheer'd the rough road, we wish'd the rough road long;
The rough road then, returning in a round,
Mock'd our impatient steps, for all was fairy ground;

we have now surely lost much of the delay, and much of the rapidity.

But, to shew how little the greatest master of numbers can fix the principles of representative harmony, it will be sufficient to remark that the poet, who tells us, that

6*

When Ajax strives some rock's vast weight to throw,
The line too labours, and the words move slow;
Not so, when swift Camilla scours the plain,
Flies o'er th' unbending corn, and skims along the main;

when he had enjoyed for about thirty years the praise of Camilla's lightness of foot, he tried another experiment upon *sound* and *time*, and produced this memorable triplet;

Waller was smooth; but Dryden taught to join
The varying verse, the full resounding line,
The long majestic march, and energy divine.

Here are the swiftness of the rapid race, and the march of slow-paced majesty, exhibited by the same poet in the same sequence of syllables, except that the exact prosodist will find the line of *swiftness* by one time longer than that of *tardiness*.

Beauties of this kind are commonly fancied; and, when real, are technical and nugatory, not to be rejected, and not to be solicited.

To the praises which have been accumulated on the *Rape of the Lock*, by readers of every class, from the critic to the waiting-maid, it is difficult to make any addition. Of that which is universally allowed to be the most attractive of all ludicrous compositions, let it rather be now inquired from what sources the power of pleasing is derived.

Dr. Warburton, who excelled in critical perspicacity, has remarked that the preternatural agents are very happily adapted to the purposes of the poem. The heathen deities can no longer gain attention: we should have turned away from a contest between Venus and Diana. The employment of allegorical persons always excites conviction of its own absurdity; they may produce effects, but cannot conduct actions; when the phantom is put in motion, it dissolves; thus *discord* may raise a mutiny; but *discord* cannot conduct a march, or besiege a town. Pope brought into view a new race of beings; with powers and passions proportionate to their operation. The sylphs and gnomes act, at the toilet and the tea-table, what more terrific and more powerful phantoms perform on the stormy ocean, or the field of battle; they give their proper help, and do their proper mischief.

Pope is said, by an objector, not to have been the inventor of this petty nation; a charge which might with more justice have been brought against the author of the *Iliad*, who doubtless adopted the religious system of his country; for what is there but the names of his agents, which Pope has not invented. Has he not assigned them characters and operations never heard of before? Has he not, at least, given them their first poetical existence? If this is not sufficient to denominate his work original, nothing original ever can be written.

In this work are exhibited, in a very high degree, the two most engaging powers of an author. New things are made familiar, and familiar things are made new. A race of aërial people, never heard of before, is presented to us, in a manner so clear and easy, that the reader seeks for no further information, but immediately mingles with his new acquaintance, adopts their interests, and attends their pursuits, loves a sylph, and detests a gnome.

That familiar things are made new, every paragraph will prove. The subject of the poem is an event below the common incidents of common life; nothing real is introduced that is not seen so often as to be no longer regarded; yet the whole detail of a female-day is here brought before us, invested with so much art of decoration, that, though nothing is disguised, every thing is striking, and we feel all the appetite of curiosity for that from which we have a thousand times turned fastidiously away.

The purpose of the poet is, as he tells us, to laugh at "the little unguarded follies of the female sex." It is therefore without justice that Dennis charges the *Rape of the Lock* with the want of a moral, and for that reason sets it below the *Lutrin*, which exposes the pride and discord of the clergy. Perhaps neither Pope nor Boileau has made the world much better than he found it; but if they had both succeeded it were easy to tell who would have deserved most from public gratitude. The freaks, and humours, and spleen, and vanity of women, as they embroil families in discord, and fill houses with disquiet, do more to obstruct the happiness of life in a year than the ambition of the clergy in many centuries. It has been well observed, that the misery of man proceeds not from any single crush of overwhelming evil, but from small vexations continually repeated.

It is remarked by Dennis likewise, that the machinery is superfluous; that, by all the bustle of preternatural operation, the main event is neither hastened nor retarded. To this charge an efficacious answer is not easily made. The sylphs cannot be said to help or to oppose; and it must be allowed to imply some want of art, that their power has not been sufficiently intermingled with the action. Other parts may likewise be charged with want of connection; the game at *ombre* might be spared; but, if the lady had lost her hair while she was intent upon her cards, it might have been inferred that those who are too fond of play will be in danger of neglecting more important interests. Those perhaps are faults; but, what are such faults to so much excellence?

The epistle of *Eloise to Abelard* is one of the most happy productions of human wit: the subject is so judiciously chosen, that it would be difficult, in turning over the annals of the world, to find another which so many circumstances concur to recommend. We regularly interest ourselves most in the fortune of those who most deserve our notice. Abelard and Eloise were conspicuous in their days for eminence of merit. The heart naturally loves truth. The adventures and misfortunes of this illustrious pair are known from undisputed history. Their fate does not leave the mind in hopeless dejection; for they both found quiet and consolation in retirement and piety. So new and so affecting is their story, that it supersedes invention; and imagination ranges at full liberty without straggling into scenes of fable.

The story, thus skilfully adopted, has been diligently improved.

Pope has left nothing behind him which seems more the effect of studious p rseverance and laborious revisal. Here is particularly observable the *curiosa felicitas*, a fruitful soil and careful cultivation. Here is no crudeness of sense, nor asperity of language.

The sources from which sentiments, which have so much vigour and efficacy, have been drawn, are shewn to be the mystic writers, by the learned author of the *Essay on the Life and Writings of Pope;* a book which teaches how the brow of criticism may be smoothed, and how she may be enabled, with all her severity, to attract and to delight.

The train of my disquisition has now conducted me to that poetical wonder, the translation of the *Iliad*, a performance which no age or nation can pretend to equal. To the Greeks translation was almost unknown; it was totally unknown to the inhabitants of Greece. They had no recourse to the barbarians for poetical beauties, but sought for everything in Homer, where, indeed, there is but little that they might not find.

The Italians have been very diligent translators; but I can hear of no version, unless perhaps Anguilara's *Ovid* may be excepted, which is read with eagerness. The *Iliad* of Salvini every reader may discover to be punctiliously exact; but it seems to be the work of a linguist skilfully pedantic; and his countrymen, the proper judges of its power to please, reject it with disgust.

Their predecessors, the Romans, have left some specimens of translations behind them; and that employment must have had some credit in which Tully and Germanicus engaged: but, unless we suppose, what is perhaps true, that the plays of Terence were versions of Menander, nothing translated seems ever to have risen to high reputation. The French, in the meridian hour of their learning, were very laudably industrious to enrich their own language with the wisdom of the ancients; but found themselves reduced, by whatever necessity, to turn the Greek and Roman poetry into prose. Whoever could read an author could translate him. From such rivals little can be feared.

The chief help of Pope in this arduous undertaking was drawn from the versions of Dryden. Virgil had borrowed much of his imagery from Homer, and part of the debt was now paid by his translator. Pope searched the pages of Dryden for happy combinations of heroic diction; but it will not be denied that he added much to what he found. He cultivated our language with so much diligence and art, that he has left in his *Homer* a treasure of poetical elegancies to posterity. His version may be said to have tuned the English tongue; for since its appearance, no writer, however deficient in other powers, has wanted melody. Such a series of lines, so elaborately corrected, and so sweetly modulated, took possession of the public ear; the vulgar was enamoured of the poem, and the learned wondered at the translation.

But, in the most general applause, discordant voices will always be heard. It has been objected by some, who wish to be numbered among the sons of learning, that Pope's version of Homer is not Homerical; that it exhibits no resemblance of the original and characteristic manner of the *father of poetry*, as it wants his awful simplicity, his artless grandeur, his unaffected majesty. This cannot be totally denied, but it must be remembered that *necessitas quod cogit defendit*; that may be lawfully done which cannot be forborne. Time and place will always enforce regard. In estimating this translation, consideration must be had of the nature of our language, the form of our metre, and, above all, of the change which two thousand years have made in the modes of life and the habits of thought. Virgil wrote in language of the same general fabric with that of Homer, in verses of the same measure, and in an age nearer to Homer's time by eighteen hundred years; yet he found, even then, the state of the world so much altered, and the demand for elegance so much increased, that mere nature would be endured no longer; and perhaps, in the multitude of borrowed passages, very few can be shewn which he has not embellished.

There is a time when nations, emerging from barbarity, and falling into regular subordination, gain leisure to grow wise, and feel the shame of ignorance and the craving pain of unsatisfied curiosity. To this hunger of the mind plain sense is grateful; that which fills the void removes uneasiness, and to be free from pain for a while is pleasure; but repletion generates fastidiousness; a saturated intellect soon becomes luxurious, and knowledge finds no willing reception till it is recommended by artificial diction. Thus it will be found, in the progress of learning, that, in all nations, the first writers are simple, and that every age improves in elegance. One refinement always makes way for another: and what was expedient to Virgil was necessary to Pope.

I suppose many readers of the English *Iliad*, when they have been touched with some unexpected beauty of the lighter kind, have tried to enjoy it in the original, where, alas! it was not to be found. Homer doubtless owes to his translator many Ovidian graces not exactly suitable to his character; but to have added can be no great crime, if nothing be taken away. Elegance is surely to be desired, if it be not gained at the expense of dignity. A hero would wish to be loved, as well as to be reverenced.

To a thousand cavils one answer is sufficient; the purpose of a writer is to be read, and the criticism which would destroy the power of pleasing must be blown aside. Pope wrote for his own age and his own nation: he knew that it was necessary to colour the images and point the sentiments of his author; he therefore made him graceful, but lost him some of his sublimity.

The copious notes with which the version is accompanied, and by which it is recommended to many readers, though they were undoubtedly written to swell the volumes, ought not to pass without praise: commentaries which attract the reader by the pleasure of perusal have not often appeared; the notes of others are read to clear difficulties, those of Pope to vary entertainment.

It has however been objected, with sufficient reason, that there is in the commentary too much of unseasonable levity and affected gaiety; that too many appeals are made to the ladies, and the ease which is so carefully preserved is sometimes the ease of a trifler. Every art has its terms, and every kind of instruction its proper style: the gravity of common critics may be tedious, but is less despicable than childish merriment.

Of the *Odyssey* nothing remains to be observed; the same general praise may be given to both translations, and a particular examination of either would require a large volume. The notes were written by Broome, who endeavoured, not unsuccessfully, to imitate his master.

Of the *Dunciad* the hint is confessedly taken from Dryden's *Mac Flecknoe*; but the plan is so enlarged and diversified as justly to claim the praise of an original, and affords the best specimen that has yet appeared of personal satire ludicrously pompous

That the design was moral, whatever the author might tell either his readers or himself, I am not convinced. The first motive was the desire of revenging the contempt with which Theobald had treated his *Shakspere*, and regaining the honour which he had lost, by crushing his opponent. Theobald was not of bulk enough to fill a poem, and therefore it was necessary to find other enemies, with other names, at whose expense he might divert the public.

In this design there was petulance and malignity enough; but I cannot think it very criminal. An author places himself, uncalled, before the tribunal of criticism; and solicits fame, at the hazard of disgrace. Dulness or deformity are not culpable in themselves, but may be very justly reproached, when they pretend to the honour of wit, or the influence of beauty. If bad writers were to pass without reprehension, what should restrain them? *impune diem consumpserit ingens Telephus*; and upon bad writers only will censure have much effect. The satire which brought Theobald and Moore into contempt, dropped impotent from Bentley, like the javelin of Priam.

All truth is valuable, and satirical criticism may be considered as useful when it rectifies error and improves judgment; he that refines the public taste is a public benefactor.

The beauties of this poem are well known; its chief fault is the grossness of its images. Pope and Swift had an unnatural delight in ideas physically impure, such as every other tongue utters with unwillingness, and of which every ear shrinks from the mention.

But even this fault, offensive as it is, may be forgiven for the excellence of other passages; such as the formation and dissolution of Moore, the account of the *traveller*, the misfortune of the *florist*, and the crowded thoughts and stately numbers which dignify the concluding paragraph.

The alterations which have been made in the *Dunciad*, not always for the better, require that it should be published, as in the present collection, with all its variations.

The *Essay on Man* was a work of great labour and long consideration, but certainly not the happiest of Pope's performances. The subject is perhaps not very proper for poetry; and the poet was not sufficiently master of his subject: metaphysical morality was to him a new study; he was proud of his acquisitions, and, supposing himself master of great secrets, was in haste to teach what he had not learned. Thus he tells us, in his first epistle, that, from the nature of the Supreme Being, may be deduced an order of beings such as mankind, because Infinite Excellence can do only what is best. He finds out that these beings must be *somewhere*; and that "all the question is, whether man be in a wrong place?" Surely, if, according to the poet's Leibnitian reasoning, we may infer that man ought to be, only because he is, we may allow that his place is the right place, because he has it. Supreme Wisdom is not less infallible in disposing than in creating. But what is meant by *somewhere*, and *place*, and *wrong place*, it had been vain to ask Pope, who probably had never asked himself.

Having exalted himself into the chair of wisdom, he tells us much that every man knows, and much that he does not know himself; that we see but little, and that the order of the universe is beyond our comprehension; an opinion not very uncommon; and that there is a chain of subordinate beings "from infinite to nothing," of which himself and his readers are equally ignorant. But he gives us one comfort, which without his help he supposes unattainable, in the position "that though we are fools, yet God is wise."

The essay affords an egregious instance of the predominance of genius, the dazzling splendour of imagery, and the seductive powers of eloquence. Never were penury of knowledge and vulgarity of sentiment so happily disguised. The reader feels his mind full, though he learns nothing; and, when he meets it in its new array, no longer knows the talk of his mother and his nurse. When these wonder-working sounds sink into sense, and the doctrine of the essay, disrobed of its ornaments, is left to the powers of its naked excellence, what shall we discover? That we are, in comparison with our Creator, very weak and ignorant; that we do not uphold the chain of existence; and that we could not make one another with more skill than we are made. We may learn yet more: that the arts of human life were copied from the instinctive operations of other animals; that if the world be made for man, it may be said that man was made for geese. To these profound principles of natural knowledge are added some moral instructions equally new: that self-interest, well understood, will produce social concord; that men are mutual gainers by mutual benefits; that evil is sometimes balanced by good; that human advantages are unstable and fallacious, of uncertain duration, and doubtful effect; that our true honour is, not to have a great part, but to act it well; that virtue only is our own; and that happiness is always in our power.

Surely a man of no very comprehensive search may venture to say that he has heard all this before; but it was never till now recommended by such a blaze of embellishments, or such sweetness of melody. The vigorous contraction of some thoughts, the luxuriant amplification of others, the incidental illustrations, and sometimes the dignity, sometimes the softness of the verses, enchain philosophy, suspend criticism, and oppress judgment, by overpowering pleasure.

This is true of many paragraphs; yet, if I had undertaken to exemplify Pope's felicity of composition before a rigid critic, I should not select the *Essay on Man*; for it contains more lines unsuccessfully laboured, more harshness of diction, more thoughts imperfectly expressed, more levity without elegance, and more heaviness without strength, than will easily be found in all his other works.

The *Characters of Men and Women* are the product of diligent speculation upon human life: much labour has been bestowed upon them, and Pope very seldom laboured in vain. That his excellence may be properly estimated, I recommend a comparison of his *Characters of Women* with Boileau's satire; it will then be seen with how much more perspicacity female nature is investigated, and female excellence selected; and he surely is no mean writer to whom Boileau should be found inferior. The *Characters of Men*, however, are written with more, if not with deeper, thought, and exhibit many passages exquisitely beautiful. The *Gem and the Flower* will not easily be equalled. In the woman's part are some defects: the character of Atossa is not so neatly finished as that of Clodio; and some of the female characters may be found perhaps more frequently among men; what is said of Philomede was true of Prior.

In the epistles to Lord Bathurst and Lord Burlington, Dr. Warburton has endeavoured to find a train of thought which was never in the writer's head, and, to support his hypothesis, has printed that first which was published last. In one, the most valuable passage is perhaps the eulogy on *good sense*; and the other, the *end of the Duke of Buckingham.*

The epistle to Arbuthnot, now arbitrarily called *the prologue to the satires*, is a performance consisting, as it seems, of many fragments wrought into one design, which, by this union of scattered beauties, contains more striking paragraphs than could probably have been brought together into an occasional work. As there is no stronger motive to exertion than self-defence, no part has more elegance, spirit, or dignity, than the poet's vindication of his own character. The meanest passage is the satire upon Sporus.

Of the two poems which derived their names from the year, and which are called the *epilogue to the satires*, it was very justly remarked by Savage, that the second was in the whole more strongly conceived, and more equally supported, but that it had no single passages equal to the contention in the first for the dignity of *vice*, and the celebration of the triumph of *corruption.*

The imitations of Horace seem to have been written as relaxations of genius. This employment became his favourite by its facility; the plan was ready to his hand, and nothing was required but to accommodate as he could the sentiments of an old author to recent facts or familiar images; but what is easy is seldom excellent; such imitations cannot give pleasure to common readers, the man of learning may be sometimes surprised and delighted by an unexpected parallel; but the comparison requires knowledge of the original, which will likewise often detect strained applications. Between Roman images and English manners, there will be an irreconcilable dissimilitude, and the work will be generally uncouth and party-coloured; neither original nor translated, neither ancient nor modern.

Pope had, in proportions very nicely adjusted to each other, all the qualities that constitute genius. He had *invention*, by which new trains of events are formed, and new scenes of imagery displayed, as in the *Rape of the Lock*; and by which extrinsic and adventitious embellishments and illustrations are connected with a known subject, as in the *Essay on Criticism*: he had *imagination*, which strongly impresses on the writer's mind, and enables him to convey to the reader, the various forms of nature, incidents of life, and energies of passion, as in his *Eloisa*, *Windsor Forest*, and *Ethic Epistles*; he had *judgment*, which selects from life or nature what the present purpose requires; and, by separating the essence of things from its concomitants, often makes the representation more powerful than the reality: and he had *colours of language* always before him, ready to decorate his matter with every grace of elegant expression, as when he accommodates his diction to the wonderful multiplicity of Homer's sentiments and descriptions.

Poetical expression includes sound as well as meaning; "Music," says Dryden, "is inarticulate poetry:" among the excellencies of Pope, therefore, must be mentioned the melody of his metre. By perusing the works of Dryden, he discovered the most perfect fabric of English verse, and habituated himself to that only which he found the best; in consequence of which restraint, his poetry has been censured as too uniformly musical, and as glutting the ear with unvaried sweetness. I suspect this objection to be the cant of those who judge by principles rather than perception; and who would even themselves have less pleasure in his works, if he had tried to relieve attention by studied discords, or affected to break his lines and vary his pauses.

But, though he was thus careful of his versification, he did not oppress his powers with superfluous rigour. He seems to have thought with Boileau, that the practice of writing might be refined till the difficulty should overbalance the advantage. The construction of his language is not always strictly grammatical; with those rhymes which prescription had conjoined, he contented himself, without regard to Swift's remonstrances, though there was no striking consonance; nor was he very careful to vary his terminations, or to refuse admission, at a small distance, to the same rhymes.

To Swift's edict for exclusion of alexandrines and triplets he paid little regard; he admitted them, but, in the opinion of Fenton, too rarely; he uses them more liberally in his translation than his poems.

He has a few double rhymes; and always, I think, unsuccessfully, except once in the *Rape of the Lock*.

Expletives he very early ejected from his verses; but he now and then admits an epithet rather commodious than important. Each of the first six lines of the *Iliad* might lose two syllables with very little diminution of the meaning; and sometimes, after all his art and labour, one verse seems to be made for the sake of another. In his latter productions the diction is sometimes vitiated by French idioms, with which Bolingbroke had perhaps infected him.

I have been told that the couplet by which he declared his own ear to be most gratified was this:

> Lo, where Mæotis sleeps, and hardly flows
> The freezing Tanais through a waste of snows.

But the reason of this preference I cannot discover.

It is remarked by Watts, that there is scarcely a happy combination of words, or a phrase poetically elegant in the English language, which Pope has not inserted into his version of Homer. How he obtained possession of so many beauties of speech, it were desirable to know. That he gleaned from authors, obscure as well as eminent, what he thought brilliant or useful, and preserved it all in a regular collection, is not unlikely. When, in his last years, Hall's satires were shewn him, he wished that he had seen them sooner.

New sentiments and new images others may produce; but to attempt any farther improvement of versification will be dangerous. Art and diligence have now done their best, and what shall be added will be the effort of tedious toil and needless curiosity.

After all this, it is surely superfluous to answer the question that has once been asked, Whether Pope was a poet? otherwise than by asking in return, If Pope be not a poet, where is poetry to be found? To circumscribe poetry by a definition will only shew the narrowness of the definer, though a definition which shall exclude Pope will not easily be made. Let us look round upon the present time, and back upon the past; Let us inquire to whom the voice of mankind has decreed the wreath of poetry; let their productions be examined, and their claims stated, and the pretentions of Pope will be no more disputed. Had he given the world only his version, the name of *poet* must have been allowed him: if the writer of the *Iliad* were to class his successors, he would assign a very high place to his translator, without requiring any other evidence of genius.

THE

RAPE OF THE LOCK.

A HEROI-COMIC POEM.

CANTO I.

WHAT dire offence from amorous causes springs,
What mighty contests rise from trivial things,
I sing.—This verse to Caryl, Muse! is due:
This, ev'n Belinda may vouchsafe to view:
Slight is the subject, but not so the praise,
If she inspire, and he approve my lays.
Say what strange motive, goddess! could compel
A well-bred lord to assault a gentle belle?
O, say what stranger cause, yet unexplored,
Could make a gentle belle reject a lord?
In tasks so bold can little men engage?
And in soft bosoms dwells such mighty rage?
Sol through white curtains shot a timorous ray,
And oped those eyes that must eclipse the day:
Now lap-dogs give themselves the rousing shake,
And sleepless lovers, just at twelve awake;
Thrice rung the bell, the slipper knock'd the ground
And the press'd watch returned a silver sound.
Belinda still her downy pillow press'd,
Her guardian sylph prolong'd the balmy rest;
'Twas he had summon'd to her silent bed
The morning-dream that hover'd o'er her head;
A youth more glittering than a birth-night beau,
That ev'n in slumber caused her cheek to glow,
Seem'd to her ear his winning lips to lay,
And thus in whispers said, or seem'd to say:—
'Fairest of mortals, thou distinguish'd care
Of thousand bright inhabitants of air!
If e'er one vision touched thy infant thought,
Of all the nurse and all the priest have taught;
Of airy elves by moonlight shadows seen,
The silver token, and the circled green,

Or virgins visited by angel-powers
With golden crowns and wreaths of heavenly flowers;
Hear and believe; thy own importance know,
Nor bound thy narrow views to things below.
Some secret truths, from learned pride conceal'd,
To maids alone and children are revealed;
What though no credit doubting wits may give;
The fair and innocent shall still believe:
Know then, unnumber'd spirits round thee fly,
The light militia of the lower sky;
These, though unseen, are ever on the wing,
Hang o'er the box, and hover round the ring.
Think what an equipage thou hast in air,
And view with scorn two pages and a chair.
As now your own, our beings were of old,
And once enclosed in woman's beauteous mould;
Thence, by a soft transition, we repair
From earthly vehicles to these of air.
Think not, when woman's transient breath is fled,
That all her vanities at once are dead;
Succeeding vanities she still regards,
And though she plays no more, o'erlooks the cards.
Her joy in gilded chariots, when alive,
And love of ombre, after death survive.
For when the fair in all their pride expire,
To their first elements their souls retire;
The sprites of fiery termagants in flame
Mount up, and take a salamander's name.
Soft yielding minds to water glide away,
And sip, with nymphs, their elemental tea.
The graver prude sinks downward to a gnome,
In search of mischief still on earth to roam.
The light coquettes in sylphs aloft repair,
And sport and flutter in the fields of air.
'Know farther yet; whoever fair and chaste
Rejects mankind, is by some sylph embraced:
For spirits, freed from mortal laws, with ease
Assume what sexes and what shapes they please.
What guards the purity of melting maids,
In courtly balls, and midnight masquerades,
Safe from the treacherous friend, the daring spark,
The glance by day, the whisper in the dark,
When kind occasion prompts their warm desires,
When music softens, and when dancing fires?
'Tis but their sylph, the wise celestials know,
Though honour ... the word with men below.
'Some nymphs there are, too conscious of their face,
For life predestined to the gnomes' embrace.
These swell their prospects and exalt their pride,
When offers are disdain'd and love denied:

Then gay ideas crowd the vacant brain,
While peers, and dukes, and all their sweeping train,
And garters, stars, and coronets appear,
And in soft sounds, 'your grace' salutes their ear.
'Tis these that early taint the female soul,
Instruct the eyes of young coquettes to roll,
Teach infant cheeks a hidden blush to know,
And little hearts to flutter at a beau.
'Oft, when the world imagine women stray,
The sylphs through mystic mazes guide their way,
Through all the giddy circle they pursue,
And old impertinence expel by new.
What tender maid but must a victim fall
To one man's treat, but for another's ball?
When Florio speaks, what virgin could withstand,
If gentle Damon did not squeeze her hand?
With varying vanities, from every part,
They shift the moving toyshop of their heart;
Where wigs with wigs, with sword knots sword knots strive,
Beaux banish beaux, and coaches coaches drive.
This erring mortals levity may call:
O, blind to truth! the sylphs contrive it all.
'Of these am I, who thy protection claim,
A watchful sprite, and Ariel is my name.
Late, as I ranged the crystal wilds of air,
In the clear mirror of thy ruling star
I saw, alas! some dread event impend,
Ere to the main this morning sun descend,
But Heaven reveals not what, or how, or where:
Warn'd by the sylph, O pious maid, beware!
This to disclose is all thy guardian can:
Beware of all, but most beware of man!'
He said; when Shock, who thought she slept too long,
Leap'd up, and waked his mistress with his tongue;
'Twas then, Belinda, if report say true,
Thy eyes first open'd on a billet-doux:
Wounds, charms, and ardors were no sooner read,
But all the vision vanish'd from thy head.
And now, unveil'd, the toilet stands display'd
Each silver vase in mystic order laid.
First, robed in white, the nymph intent adores,
With head uncover'd, the cosmetic powers.
A heavenly image in the glass appears,
To that she bends, to that her eyes she rears;
The inferior priestess, at her altar's side,
Trembling begins the sacred rites of pride.
Unnumber'd treasures ope at once, and here
The various offerings of the world appear;
From each she nicely culls with curious toil,
And decks the goddess with the glittering spoil.

This casket India's glowing gems unlocks,
And all Arabia breathes from yonder box;
The tortoise here and elephant unite,
Transform'd to combs, the speckled, and the white.
Here files of pins extend their shining rows,
Puffs, powders, patches, bibles, billet-doux.
Now awful beauty puts on all its arms;
The fair each moment rises in her charms,
Repairs her smiles, awakens every grace,
And calls forth all the wonders of her face;
Sees by degrees a purer blush arise,
And keener lightnings quicken in her eyes.
The busy sylphs surround their darling care,
These set the head, and those divide the hair,
Some fold the sleeve, whilst others plait the gown:
And Betty's praised for labours not her own.

CANTO II.

Not with more glories, in the ethereal plain,
The sun first rises o'er the purpled main,
Then, issuing forth, the rival of his beams
Launch'd on the bosom of the silver Thames.
Fair nymphs and well-dress'd youths around her shone,
But every eye was fix'd on her alone.
On her white breast a sparkling cross she wore,
Which Jews might kiss and infidels adore.
Her lively looks a sprightly mind disclose,
Quick as her eyes, and as unfix'd as those;
Favours to none, to all she smiles extends;
Oft she rejects, but never once offends.
Bright as the sun, her eyes the gazers strike;
And like the sun, they shine on all alike.
Yet graceful ease, and sweetness void of pride,
Might hide her faults, if belles had faults to hide·
If to her share some female errors fall,
Look on her face, and you'll forget them all.
  This nymph, to the destruction of mankind,
Nourish'd two locks, which graceful hung behind
In equal curls, and well conspired to deck,
With shining ringlets, the smooth ivory neck.
Love in these labyrinths his slaves detains,
And mighty hearts are held in slender chains.
With hairy springes we the birds betray,
Slight lines of hair surprise the finny prey;
Fair tresses man's imperial race insnare,
And beauty draws us with a single hair.
  The adventurous baron the bright locks admired;
He saw, he wish'd, and to the prize aspired.
Resolved to win, he meditates the way,
By force to ravish, or by fraud betray;
For when success a lover's toil attends,
Few ask, if fraud or force attain'd his ends.
  For this, ere Phœbus rose, he had implored
Propitious Heaven, and every power adored,
But chiefly Love--to Love an altar built,
Of twelve vast French romances, neatly gilt.
There lay three garters, half a pair of gloves,
And all the trophies of his former loves;
With tender billet-doux he lights the pyre,
And breathes three amorous sighs to raise the fire;

Then prostrate falls, and begs with ardent eyes
Soon to obtain, and long possess the prize—
The powers gave ear, and granted half his prayer;
The rest the winds dispersed in empty air.
 But now secure the painted vessel glides,
The sun-beams trembling on the floating tides;
While melting music steals upon the sky,
And soften'd sounds along the waters die;
Smooth flow the waves, the zephyrs gently play,
Belinda smiled, and all the world was gay—
All but the sylph; with careful thoughts oppress'd,
The impending wo sat heavy on his breast.
He summons straight his denizens of air;
The lucid squadrons round the sails repair;
Soft o'er the shrouds aerial whispers breathe,
That seem'd but zephyrs to the train beneath.
Some to the sun their insect-wings unfold,
Waft on the breeze, or sink in clouds of gold;
Transparent forms, too fine for mortal sight,
Their fluid bodies half dissolved in light,
Loose to the wind their airy garments flew,
Thin glittering textures of the filmy dew,
Dipp'd in the richest tincture of the skies,
Where light disports in ever-mingling dies;
While every beam new transient colours flings,
Colours that change whene'er they wave their wings.
Amid the circle, on the gilded mast,
Superior by the head, was Ariel placed;
His purple pinions opening to the sun,
He raised his azure wand, and thus begun:—
 'Ye sylphs and sylphids, to your chief give ear!
Fays, fairies, genii, elves, and demons, hear!
Ye know the spheres and various tasks assign'd
By laws eternal to the aerial kind.
Some in the fields of purest ether play,
And bask and whiten in the blaze of day;
Some guide the course of wandering orbs on high,
Or roll the planets through the boundless sky;
Some less refined, beneath the moon's pale light
Pursue the stars that shoot athwart the night,
Or suck the mist in grosser air below,
Or dip their pinions in the painted bow,
Or brew fierce tempests on the wintry main,
Or o'er the glebe distil the kindly rain.
Others on earth o'er human race preside,
Watch all their ways, and all their actions guide;
Of these the chief the care of nations own,
And guards with arms divine the British throne.
 'Our humbler province is to tend the fair,
Not a less pleasing, though less glorious care;

To save the powder from too rude a gale,
Nor let the imprison'd essences exhale;
To draw fresh colours from the vernal flowers;
To steal from rainbows, ere they drop in showers,
A brighter wash; to curl their waving hairs,
Assist their blushes, and inspire their airs;
Nay, oft, in dreams, invention we bestow,
To change a flounce, or add a furbelow.
'This day black omens threat the brightest fair
That e'er deserved a watchful spirit's care;
Some dire disaster, or by force or slight;
But what or where, the fates have wrapp'd in night.
Whether the nymph shall break Diana's law,
Or some frail China jar receive a flaw,
Or stain her honour, or her new brocade;
Forget her prayers, or miss a masquerade;
Or lose her heart, or necklace, at a ball;
Or whether Heaven has doom'd that Shock must fall.
Haste then, ye spirits! to your charge repair:
The fluttering fan be Zephyretta's care:
The drops to thee, Brillante, we consign;
And, Momentilla, let the watch be thine;
Do thou, Crispissa, tend her favourite lock;
Ariel himself shall be the guard of Shock.
'To fifty chosen sylphs, of special note,
We trust the important charge, the petticoat:
Oft have we known that seven-fold fence to fail,
Though stiff with hoops, and arm'd with ribs of whale;
Form a strong line about the silver bound,
And guard the wide circumferance around.
'Whatever spirit, careless of his charge,
His post neglects, or leaves the fair at large,
Shall feel sharp vengeance soon o'ertake his sins,
Be stopp'd in vials, or transfixed with pins;
Or plunged in lakes of bitter washes lie,
Or wedged whole ages in a bodkin's eye;
Gums and pomatums shall his flight restrain,
While clogg'd he beats his silken wings in vain;
Or alum styptics with contracting power
Shrink his thin essence like a shrivel'd flower;
Or, as Ixion fix'd, the wretch shall feel
The giddy motion of the whirling mill;
In fumes of burning chocolate shall glow,
And tremble at the sea that froths below!'
He spoke; the spirits from the sails descend;
Some, orb in orb, around the nymph extend;
Some thread the mazy ringlets of her hair;
Some hang upon the pendents of her ear;
With beating hearts the dire event they wait;
Anxious, and trembling for the birth of fate.

CANTO III.

CLOSE by those meads, for ever crown'd with flowers,
Where Thames with pride surveys his rising towers,
There stands a structure of majestic frame,
Which from the neighbouring Hampton takes its name;
Here Britain's statesmen oft the fall foredoom
Of foreign tyrants, and of nymphs at home;
Here thou, great Anna! whom three realms obey,
Dost sometimes counsel take—and sometimes tea.
  Hither the heroes and the nymphs resort,
To taste awhile the pleasures of a court;
In various talk the instructive hours they pass'd,
Who gave the ball, or paid the visit last;
One speaks the glory of the British queen,
And one describes a charming Indian screen;
A third interprets motions, looks, and eyes;
At every word a reputation dies.
Snuff, or the fan, supply each pause of chat,
With singing, laughing, ogling, and all that.
  Meanwhile, declining from the noon of day,
The sun obliquely shoots his burning ray;
The hungry judges soon the sentence sign,
And wretches hang that jurymen may dine;
The merchant from th' Exchange returns in peace,
And the long labours of the toilet cease.
Belinda now, whom thirst of fame invites,
Burns to encounter two adventurous knights,
At ombre singly to decide their doom:
And swells her breast with conquests yet to come.
Straight the three bands prepare in arms to join,
Each band the number of the sacred Nine.
Soon as she spreads her hand, the aërial guard
Descend, and sit on each important card:
First Ariel perch'd upon a Matadore,
Then each according to the rank they bore:
For sylphs, yet mindful of their ancient race,
Are, as when women, wondrous fond of place.
  Behold, four kings, in majesty revered,
With hoary whiskers and a forky beard;
And four fair queens, whose hands sustain a flower,
The expressive emblem of their softer power;

Four knaves in garbs succinct, a trusty band,
Caps on their heads, and halberts in their hand;
And party-colour'd troops, a shining train,
Drawn forth to combat on the velvet plain.
  The skilful nymph reviews her force with care—
'Let spades be trumps!' she said, and trumps they were.
  Now move to war her sable Matadores,
In show like leaders of the swarthy Moors.
Spadillio first, unconquerable lord!
Led off two captive trumps, and swept the board;
As many more Manillio forced to yield,
And marched a victor from the verdant field:
Him Basto follow'd; but his fate, more hard,
Gain'd but one trump and one plebeian card.
With his broad sabre next, a chief in years,
The hoary majesty of Spades appears;
Puts forth one manly leg, to sight reveal'd;
The rest, his many-colour'd robe conceal'd.
The rebel Knave, who dares his prince engage,
Proves the just victim of his royal rage.
Ev'n mighty Pam, that kings and queens o'erthrew,
And mow'd down armies in the fights of Lu;—
Sad chance of war! now destitute of aid,
Falls undistinguished by the victor Spade;
  Thus far both armies to Belinda yield,
Now to the baron fate inclines the field,
His warlike Amazon her host invades,
The imperial consort of the crown of Spades.
The Clubs' black tyrant first her victim died,
Spite of his haughty mien and barbarous pride;
What boots the regal circle on his head,
His giant limbs, in state unwieldly spread;
That long behind he trails his pompous robe,
And, of all monarchs only grasps the globe?
  The baron now his Diamonds pours apace!
The embroider'd king, who shows but half his face,
And his refulgent queen, with powers combined,
Of broken troops, an easy conquest find.
Clubs, Diamonds, Hearts, in wild disorder seen,
With throngs promiscuous strew the level green.
Thus when dispersed a routed army runs,
Of Asia's troops, and Afric's sable sons,
With like confusion different nations fly,
Of various habit, and of various die;
The pierc'd battalions disunited fall,
In heaps on heaps; one fate o'erwhelms them all.
  The Knave of Diamonds tries his wily arts,
And wins (oh shameful chance!) the Queen of Hearts,
At this, the blood the virgin's cheek forsook,
A livid paleness spreads o'er all her look;

She sees, and trembles at th' approaching ill,
Just in the jaws of ruin, and Codille.
And now (as oft in some distemper'd state)
On one nice trick depends the general fate:
An ace of Hearts step forth: the king unseen
Lurk'd in her hand, and mourn'd his captive queen:
He springs to vengeance with an eager pace,
And falls like thunder on the prostrate ace.
The nymph, exulting, fills with shouts the sky;
The walls, the woods, and long canals reply.
O thoughtless mortals! ever blind to fate,
Too soon dejected, and too soon elate.
Sudden these honours sball be snatch'd away,
And curs'd for ever this victorious day.
For lo! the board with cups and spoons is crown'd,
The berries crackle, and the mill turns round;
On shining altars of Japan they raise
The silver lamp; the fiery spirits blaze;
From silver spouts the grateful liquors glide,
While China's earth receives the smoking tide:
At once they gratify their scent and taste,
And frequent cups prolong the rich repast.
Straight hover round the fair her airy band;
Some, as she sipp'd, the fuming liquor fann'd,
Some o'er her lap their careful plumes display'd,
Trembling, and conscious of the rich brocade.
Coffee (which makes the politician wise,
And see thro' all things with his half shut eyes)
Sent up in vapours to the baron's brain
New stratagems, the radiant lock to gain.
Ah cease, rash youth! desist ere 'tis too late;
Fear the just gods, and think of Scylla's fate!
Chang'd to a bird, and sent to flit in air,
She dearly pays for Nisus' injur'd hair!
But when to mischief mortals bend their will,
How soon they find fit instruments of ill!
Just then, Clarissa drew with tempting grace
A two-edg'd weapon from her shining case
So ladies, in romance, assist their knight,
Present the spear, and arm him for the fight.
He takes the gift with rev'rence, and extends
The little engine on his fingers' ends;
This just behind Belinda's neck he spread,
As o'er the fragrant steams she bends her head.
Swift to the lock a thousand sprites repair,
A thousand wings, by turns, blow back the hair;
And thrice they twitch'd the diamond in her ear;
Thrice she look'd back, and thrice the foe drew near.
Just in that instant, anxious Ariel sought
The close recesses of the virgin's thought

As on the nosegay in her breast reclin'd,
He watch'd the ideas rising in her mind,
Sudden he view'd, in spite of all her art,
An earthly lover lurking at her heart.
Amaz'd, confus'd, he found his pow'r expir'd!
Resign'd to fate, and with a sigh retired.
The peer now spreads the glitt'ring forfex wide,
T' inclose the lock; now joins it to divide.
E'en then, before the fatal engine clos'd,
A wretched sylph too fondly interpos'd:
Fate urg'd the sheers, and cut the sylph in twain
(But airy substance soon unites again:)
The meeting points the sacred hair dissever
From the fair head, for ever and for ever!
Then flash'd the living lightning from her eyes,
And screams of horror rend th' affrighted skies.
Not louder shrieks to pitying heav'n are cast,
When husbands, or when lap-dogs, breathe their last;
Or when rich China vessels, fall'n from high,
In glitt'ring dust and painted fragments lie!
'Let wreaths of triumph now my temples twine,'
The victor cried: 'the glorious prize is mine!
While fish in streams, or birds delight in air,
Or in a coach and six the British fair,
As long as Atalantis shall be read,
Or the small pillow grace a lady's bed,
While visits shall be paid on solemn days,
When num'rous wax-lights in bright order blaze,
While nymphs take treats, or assignations give,
So long my honour, name, and praise shall live!
What time would spare, from steel receives its date,
And monuments like men submit to fate!
Steel could the labour of the gods destroy,
And strike to dust the imperial tow'rs of Troy;
Steel could the works of mortal pride confound,
And hew triumphal arches to the ground.
What wonder then, fair nymph! thy hair should feel
The conq'uring force of unresisted steel?'

CANTO IV

But anxious cares the pensive nymph oppress'd,
And secret passions labour'd in her breast.
Not youthful kings in battle seized alive,
Not scornful virgins who their charms survive,
Not ardent lovers robb'd of all their bliss,
Not ancient ladies when refused a kiss,
Not tyrants fierce that unrepenting die,
Not Cynthia when her manteau's pinn'd awry,
E'er felt such rage, resentment, and despair,
As thou, sad virgin! for thy ravish'd hair.
  For, that sad moment, when the sylphs withdrew,
And Ariel weeping from Belinda flew,
Umbriel, a dusky, melancholy sprite,
As ever sullied the fair face of light,
Down to the central earth, his proper scene,
Repair'd to search the gloomy cave of Spleen.
Swift on his sooty pinions flits the gnome,
And in a vapour reached the dismal dome.
No cheerful breeze this sullen region knows,
The dreaded east is all the wind that blows.
Here in a grotto, shelter'd close from air,
And screen'd in shades from day's detested glare,
She sighs for ever on her pensive bed,
Pain at her side, and Megrim at her head.
  Two handmaids wait the throne: alike in place
But differing far in figure and in face.
Here stood Ill-nature like an ancient maid,
Her wrinkled form in black and white array'd:
With store of prayers, for mornings, nights, and noons,
Her hand is fill'd; her bosom with lampoons.
  There Affectation, with a sickly mien,
Shows in her cheek the roses of eighteen;
Practis'd to lisp, and hang the head aside,
Faints into airs and languishes with pride,
On the rich quilt sinks with becoming wo,
Wrapt in a gown, for sickness, and for show.
The fair ones feel such maladies as these,
When each new night-dress gives a new disease.
  A constant vapour o'er the palace flies;
Strange phantoms rising as the mists arise;

Dreadful as hermits' dreams in haunted shades,
Or bright as visions of expiring maids.
Now glaring fiends, and snakes on rolling spires,
Pale spectres, gaping tombs, and purple fires:
Now lakes of liquid gold, Elysian scenes,
And crystal domes, and angels in machines.
Unnumber'd throngs on ev'ry side are seen,
Of bodies chang'd to various forms by spleen.
Here living tea-pots stand, one arm held out,
One bent; the handle this, and that the spout;
A pipkin there, like Homer's tripod, walks;
Here sighs a jar, and there a goose-pie talks:
Men prove with child, as pow'rful fancy works
And maids, turn'd bottles, call aloud for corks.
Safe past the gnome through this fantastic band,
A branch of healing spleenwort in his hand.
Then thus address'd the pow'r—'Hail, wayward [Queen
Who rule the sex to fifty from fifteen:
Parent of vapours and of female wit,
Who gave th' hysteric or poetic fit,
On various tempers act by various ways,
Make some take physic, others scribble plays;
Who cause the proud their visits to delay,
And send the godly in a pet to pray:
A nymph there is that all thy power disdains,
And thousands more in equal mirth maintains.
But oh! if e'er thy gnome could spoil a grace,
Or raise a pimple on a beauteous face,
Like citron-waters matrons' cheeks inflame,
Or change complexions at a losing game;
If e'er with airy horns I planted heads,
Or rumpled petticoats, or tumbled beds,
Or caus'd suspicion when no soul was rude,
Or discomposed the head-dress of a prude,
Or e'er to costive lap-dogs gave disease,
Which not the tears of brightest eyes could ease;
Hear me, and touch Belinda with chagrin;
That single act gives half the world the spleen.'
The goddess, with a discontented air,
Seems to reject him, though she grants his pray'r.
A wondrous bag with both her hands she binds,
Like that where once Ulysses held the winds;
There she collects the force of female lungs,
Sighs, sobs, and passions, and the war of tongues.
A vial next she fills with fainting fears,
Soft sorrows, melting griefs, and flowing tears.
The gnome rejoicing bears her gifts away,
Spreads his black wings, and slowly mounts to day.
Sunk in Thalestries' arms the nymph he found,
Her eyes dejected, and her hair unbound

Full o'er their heads the swelling bag he rent,
And all the furies issued at the vent.
Belinda burns with more than mortal ire,
And fierce Thalestris fans the rising fire.
'O wretched maid!' she spread her hands, and cried,
While Hampton's echoes, 'wretched maid!' replied;
'Was it for this you took such constant care
The bodkin, comb, and essence to prepare;
For this your locks in paper durance bound?
For this with torturing irons wreath'd around?
For this with fillets strain'd your tender head?
And bravely bore the double loads of lead?
Gods! shall the ravishers display your hair,
While the fops envy, and the ladies stare!
Honour forbid! at whose unrivall'd shrine
Ease, pleasure, virtue, all our sex resign.
Methinks already I your tears survey,
Already hear the horrid things they say,
Already see you a degraded toast,
And all your honour in a whisper lost!
How shall I, then, your hapless fame defend?
'Twill then be infamy to seem your friend?
And shall this prize, the inestimable prize,
Expos'd through crystal to the gazing eyes,
And heighten'd by the diamond's circling rays,
On that rapacious hand for ever blaze?
Sooner shall grass in Hyde-park Circus grow,
And wits take lodgings in the sound of Bow;
Sooner let air, earth, sea, to chaos fall,
Men, monkies, lap-dogs, parrots, perish all!'
She said; then raging to Sir Plume repairs,
And bids her beau demand the precious hairs:
Sir Plume, (of amber snuff-box justly vain,
And the nice conduct of a clouded cane,)
With earnest eyes, and round unthinking face,
He first the snuff-box open'd, then the case,
And thus broke out—'My Lord, why, what the devil!
Z—ds! d—— the lock! 'fore Gad, you must be civil!
Plague on't! 'tis past a jest—nay, prithee, pox!
Give her the hair.'—He spoke and rapp'd his box.
'It grieves me much,' replied the peer again,
'Who speaks so well should ever speak in vain:
But by this lock, this sacred lock, I swear,
(Which never more shall join its parted hair,
Which never more its honours shall renew,
Clipp'd from the lovely head where late it grew,)
That, while my nostrils draw the vital air,
This hand, which won it, shall for ever wear.'
He spoke, and speaking, in proud triumph spread
The long-contended honours of her head.

But Umbriel, hateful gnome! forbears not so;
He breaks the vial whence the sorrows flow.
Then see! the nymph in beauteous grief appears,
Her eyes half languishing, half drown'd in tears;
On her heav'd bosom hung her drooping head,
Which with a sigh she rais'd, and thus she said—
'For ever curs'd be this detested day,
Which snatch'd my best, my fav'rite curl away!
Happy! ah ten times happy had I been,
If Hampton-Court these eyes had never seen!
Yet am not I the first mistaken maid,
By love of courts to num'rous ills betray'd.
Oh had I rather unadmir'd remain'd
In some lone isle, or distant northern land,
Where the gilt chariot never marks the way,
Where none learn ombre, none e'er taste Bohea!
There kept my charms conceal'd from mortal eye,
Like roses that in deserts bloom and die.
What mov'd my mind with youthful lords to roam?
O had I stay'd, and said my prayers at home!
'Twas this the morning omens seem'd to tell;
Thrice from my trembling hand the patch-box fell;
The tott'ring China shook without a wind;
Nay, Poll sat mute, and Shook was most unkind!
A sylph, too, warn'd me of the threats of fate,
In mystic visions now believ'd too late!
See the poor remnants of these slighted hairs!
My hands shall rend what e'en thy rapine spares:
These in two sable ringlets taught to break,
Once gave new beauties to the snowy neck;
The sister lock now sits uncouth, alone,
And in its fellow's fate foresees its own;
Uncurl'd it hangs; the fatal sheers demands,
And tempts once more thy sacrilegious hands
Oh hadst thou, cruel! been content to seize
Hairs less in sight, or any hairs but these.'

CANTO V.

She said: the pitying audience melt in tears;
But Fate and Jove had stopp'd the baron's ears
In vain Thalestris with reproach assails,
For who can move when fair Belinda fails?
Not half so fix'd the Trojan could remain
While Anna begg'd and Dido rag'd in vain.
Then grave Clarissa graceful waved her fan;
Silence ensued, and thus the nymph began:
'Say, why are beauties prais'd and honour'd most,
The wise man's passion, and the vain man's toast?
Why deck'd with all that land and sea afford,
Why angels call'd, and angel-like adored?
Why round our coaches crowd the white glov'd beaux?
Why bows the side-box from its inmost rows?
How vain are all these glories, all our pains,
Unless good sense preserve what beauty gains;
That men may say, when we the front-box grace,
Behold the first in virtue as in face!
Oh! if to dance all night, and dress all day,
Charm'd the small-pox, or chas'd old age away,
Who would not scorn what housewife's cares produce,
Or who would learn one earthly thing of use?
To patch, nay ogle, might become a saint;
Nor could it sure be such a sin to paint.
But since, alas! frail beauty must decay;
Curl'd or uncurl'd, since locks will turn to gray;
Since painted, or not painted, all shall fade,
And she who scorns a man must die a maid!
What then remains, but well our pow'r to use,
And keep good humour still whate'er we lose?
And trust me, dear! good humour can prevail,
When airs, and flights, and screams, and scolding fail.
Beauties in vain their pretty eyes may roll;
Charms strike the sight, but merit wins the soul.'
So spoke the dame, but no applause ensued;
Belinda frown'd, Thalestris call'd her prude.
'To arms, to arms!' the fierce virago cries,
And swift as lightning to the combat flies.
All side in parties, and begin the attack;
Fans clap, silks rustle, and tough whalebones crack;

Heroes' and heroines' shouts confus'dly rise,
And base and treble voices strike the skies.
No common weapons in their hands are found;
Like gods they fight, nor dread a mortal wound.
So when bold Homer makes the gods engage,
And heav'nly breasts with human passions rage;
'Gainst Pallas, Mars; Latona, Hermes arms;
And all Olympus rings with loud alarms;
Jove's thunder roars, heav'n trembles all around,
Blue Neptune storms, the bellowing deeps resound:
Earth shakes her nodding tow'rs, the ground gives way,
And the pale ghosts start at the flash of day!
Triumphant Umbriel, on a sconce's height,
Clapp'd his glad wings, and sat to view the fight;
Propp'd on their bodkin spears, the sprites survey
The growing combat, or assist the fray.
While through the press enrag'd Thalestris flies,
And scatters death around from both her eyes,
A beau and witling perish'd in the throng;
One died in metaphor, and one in song.
'O cruel nymph! a living death I bear,'
Cry'd Dapperwit, and sunk beside his chair.
A mornful glance Sir Fopling upwards cast,
'Those eyes are made so killing'—was his last
Thus on Mæander's flow'ry margin lies
Th' expiring swan, and as he sings he dies.
When bold Sir Plume had drawn Clarissa down,
Chloe stepp'd in, and kill'd him with a frown:
She smil'd to see the doughty hero slain,
But, at her smile, the beau reviv'd again.
Now Jove suspends his golden scales in air,
Weighs the mens' wits against the lady's hair:
The doubtful beam long nods from side to side;
At length the wits mount up, the hairs subside.
See fierce Belinda on the baron flies,
With more than usual lightning in her eyes;
Nor fear'd the chief th' unequal fight to try,
Who sought no more than on his foe to die.
But this bold lord, with manly strength endued,
She with one finger and a thumb subdued:
Just where the breath of life his nostrils drew,
A charge of snuff the wily virgin threw
The gnomes direct, to ev'ry atom just,
The pungent grains of titillating dust.
Sudden, with starting tears each eye o'erflows,
And the high dome re-echoes to his nose.
'Now meet thy fate,' incens'd Belinda cried,
And drew a deadly bodkin from her side.
(The same, his ancient personage to deck,
Her great grandsire wore about his neck,

In three seal-rings; which after, melted down,
Form'd a vast buckle for his widow's gown:
Her infant grandame's whistle next it grew,
The bells she gingled, and the whistle blew;
Then in a bodkin grac'd her mother's hairs,
Which long she wore, and now Belinda wears.)
'Boast not my fall,' he cried, 'insulting foe!
Thou by some other shall be laid as low.
Nor think to die dejects my lofty mind;
All that I dread is leaving you behind!
Rather than so, ah let me still survive,
And burn in Cupid's flames—but burn alive.'
'Restore the lock!' she cries; and all around
'Restore the lock!' the vaulted roofs rebound.
Not fierce Othello in so loud a strain
Roar'd for the handkerchief that caus'd his pain.
But see how oft ambitious aims are cross'd,
And chiefs contend till all the prize is lost!
The lock, obtain'd with guilt, and kept with pain,
In ev'ry place is sought, but sought in vain:
With such a prize no mortal must be blest,
So Heav'n decrees! with Heav'n who can contest?
Some thought it mounted to the lunar sphere,
Since all things lost on earth are treasured there.
There heroes' wits are kept in pond'rous vases,
And beaux in snuff-boxes and tweezer cases.
There broken vows and death-bed alms are found,
And lovers' hearts with ends of ribband bound,
The courtiers' promises, and sick men's prayers,
The smiles of harlots, and the tears of heirs.
Cages for gnats, and chains to yoke a flea,
Dried butterflies, and tomes of casuistry.
But trust the Muse—she saw it upward rise,
Though mark'd by none but quick poetic eyes:
(So Rome's great founder to the heav'ns withdrew,
To Proculus alone confess'd in view,)
A sudden star, it shot through liquid air,
And drew behind a radiant trial of hair,
Not Berenice's locks first rose so bright,
The heav'ns bespangled with dishevell'd light.
The sylphs behold it kindling as it flies,
And pleas'd pursue its progress through the skies.
This the beau monde shall from the Mall survey
And hail with music its propitious ray;
This the blest lover shall for Venus take,
And send up vows from Rosamonda's lake;
This Partridge soon shall view in cloudless skies,
When next he looks through Galilæo's eyes;

And hence the egregious wizzard shall foredoom
The fate of Louis and the fall of Rome.
  Then cease bright nymph! to morn thy ravish'd hair,
Which adds new glories to the shining sphere!
Not all the tresses that fair head can boast,
Shall draw such envy as the lock you lost.
For after all the murders of your eye,
When, after millions slain, yourself shall die;
When those fair suns shall set, as set they must,
And all those tresses shall be laid in dust;—
This lock the muse shall consecrate to fame,
And 'midst the stars inscribe Belinda's name.

ESSAY ON MAN.

THE DESIGN.

HAVING proposed to write some pieces on human life and manners, such as, to use my Lord Bacon's expression, 'come home to men's business and bosoms,' I thought it more satisfactory to begin with considering Man in the abstract, his nature and his state; since, to prove any moral duty, to enforce any moral precept, or to examine the perfection or imperfection of any creature whatsoever, it is necessary first to know what condition and relation it is placed in, and what is the proper end and purpose of its being.

The science of human nature is, like all other sciences, reduced to a few clear points: there are not many certain truths in this world: it is therefore in the anatomy of the mind as in that of the body; more good will accrue to mankind by attending to the large, open, and perceptible parts, than by studying too much such finer nerves and vessels, the conformations and uses of which will for ever escape our observation: the disputes are all on these last; and, I will venture to say, they have less sharpened the wits than the hearts of men against each other, and have diminished the practice, more than advanced the theory, of morality. If I could flatter myself that this Essay has any merit, it is in steering betwixt the extremes of doctrines seemingly opposite, in passing over terms utterly unintelligible, and in forming a temperate, yet not inconsistent, and a short, yet not imperfect, system of ethics.

This I might have done in prose; but I chose verse, and even rhyme, for two reasons: the one will appear obvious; that principles, maxims, or precepts so written, both strike the reader more strongly at first, and are more easily retained by him afterwards: the other may seem odd, but it is true: I found I could express them more shortly this way than in prose itself; and nothing is more certain, than that much of the force as well as grace of arguments or instructions depends on conciseness. I was unable to treat this part of my subject more in detail, without becoming dry and tedious; or more poetically, without sacrificing perspicuity to ornament, without wandering from the precision, or breaking the chain of reasoning: if a man can unite all these without diminution of any of them, I freely confess he will compass a thing above my capacity.

What is now published, is only to be considered as a general map of man, marking out no more than the greater parts, their extent, their limits, and their connexion, but leaving the particular to be more fully delineated in the charts which are now to follow: consequently these Epistles in their progress (if I have health and leisure to make any progress) will be less dry, and more susceptible of poetical ornament. I am here only opening the fountains, and clearing the passage: to deduce the rivers, to follow them in their course, and to observe their effects, may be a task more agreeable.

POPE.

EPISTLE I.

OF THE NATURE AND STATE OF MAN, WITH RESPECT TO THE UNIVERSE.

ARGUMENT.

Of Man in the abstract. I. That we can judge only with regard to our own system, being ignorant of the relations of systems and things. II. That man is not to be deemed imperfect, but a being suited to his place and rank in the creation, agreeable to the general order of things, and conformable to ends and relations to him unknown. III. That it is partly on his ignorance of future events, and partly upon the hope of a future state, that all his happiness in the present depends. IV. The pride of aiming at more knowledge, and pretending to more perfection, the cause of Man's error and misery. The impiety of putting himself in the place of God, and judging of the fitness or unfitness, perfection or imperfection, justice or injustice, of his dispensations. V. The absurdity of conceiting himself the final cause of the creation, or expecting that perfection in the moral world which is not in the natural. VI. The unreasonableness of his complaints against Providence, while, on the one hand, he demands the perfections of the angels, and, on the other, the bodily qualifications of the brutes: though to possess any of the sensitive faculties in a higher degree, would render him miserable. VII. That throughout the whole visible world, an universal order and gradation in the sensual and mental faculties is observed, which causes a subordination of creature to creature, and of all creatures to Man. The gradation of sense, instinct, thought, reflection, reason; that reason alone countervails all the other faculties. VIII. How much farther this order and subordination of living creatures may exend above and below us; were any part of which broken, not that part only, but the whole connected creation must be destroyed. IX. The extravagance, madness, and pride of such a desire. X. The consequence of all, the absolute submission due to Providence, both as to our present and future state.

AWAKE, my St. John! leave all meaner things
To low ambition and the pride of kings.
Let us (since life can little more supply
Than just to look about us and to die)
Expatiate free o'er all this scene of Man;
A mighty maze! but not without a plan;
A wild, where weeds and flow'rs promiscuous shoot;
Or garden, tempting with forbidden fruit.
Together let us beat this ample field,
Try what the open, what the covert yield;
The latent tracts, the giddy heights, explore,
Of all who blindly creep or sightless soar;

Eye Nature's walks, shoot Folly as it flies,
And catch the Manners living as they rise;
Laugh where we must, be candid where we can;
But vindicate the ways of God to Man.

I. Say, first, of God above, or Man below,
What can we reason but from what we know?
Of Man, what see we but his station here,
From which to reason, or to which refer?
Thro' worlds unnumber'd tho' the God be known,
'Tis ours to trace him only in our own.
He, who thro' vast immensity can pierce,
See worlds on worlds compose one universe,
Observe how system into system runs,
What other planets circle other suns,
What varied beings people ev'ry star,
May tell why Heaven has made us as we are.
But of this frame, the bearings and the ties,
The strong connections, nice dependencies,
Gradations just, has thy pervading soul
Look'd thro'? or can a part contain the whole?
Is the great chain that draws all to agree,—
And, drawn, supports—upheld by God or thee?

II. Presumptuous Man! the reason wouldst thou find,
Why form'd so weak, so little, and so blind;
First, if thou canst, the harder reason guess,
Why form'd no weaker, blinder, and no less:
Ask of thy mother Earth, why oaks are made
Taller or stronger than the weeds they shade:
Or ask of yonder argent fields above,
Why Jove's satellites are less than Jove.
Of systems possible, if 'tis confess'd
That Wisdom Infinite must form the best;
Where all must full, or not coherent be;
And all that rises, rise in due degree;
Then, in the scale of reas'ning life, 'tis plain
There must be, somewhere, such a rank as Man:
And all the question (wrangle e'er so long)
Is only this—if God has placed him wrong.
Respecting Man, whatever wrong we call,
May, must be right, as relative to all.
In human works, tho' labour'd on with pain,
A thousand movements scarce one purpose gain:
In God's, one single can its end produce;
Yet serves to second, too, some other use.
So Man, who here seems principal alone,
Perhaps acts second to some sphere unknown,
Touches some wheel, or verges to some goal;
'Tis but a part we see, and not a whole.

When the proud steed shall know why man restrains
His fiery course, or drives him o'er the plains,—
When the dull ox, why now he breaks the clod,
Is now a victim, and now Egypt's god,—
Then shall Man's pride and dulness comprehend
His actions', passions', being's, use and end;
Why doing, suff'ring, check'd, impell'd, and why
This hour a slave, the next a deity.
  Then say not Man's imperfect, Heav'n in fault,—
Say rather Man's as perfect as he ought:
His knowledge measur'd to his state and place,
His time a moment, and a point his space.
If to be perfect in a certain sphere,
What matter soon or late, or here or there?
The blest to-day is as completely so,
As who began a thousand years ago.

III. Heav'n from all creatures hides the book of fate,
All but the page prescrib'd, their present state;
From brutes what men, from men what spirits know:
Or who could suffer being here below?
The lamb thy riot dooms to bleed to-day,
Had he thy reason, would he skip and play?
Pleas'd to the last he crops the flow'ry food,
And licks the hand just rais'd to shed his blood.
O blindness to the future! kindly giv'n,
That each may fill the circle mark'd by Heav'n:
Who sees with equal eye, as God of all,
A hero perish, or a sparrow fall,
Atoms or systems into ruin hurl'd,
And now a bubble burst, and now a world.
  Hope humbly then; with trembling pinions soar;
Wait the great teacher Death, and God adore.
What future bliss he gives not thee to know,
But gives that hope to be thy blessing now.
Hope springs eternal in the human breast;
Man never is, but always to be blest:
The soul uneasy and confin'd from home,
Rests and expatiates in a life to come.

Lo, the poor Indian! whose untutor'd mind
Sees God in clouds, or hears him in the wind;
His soul proud Science never taught to stray
Far as the solar walk or milky way;
Yet simple Nature to his hope has giv'n,
Behind the cloud-topp'd hill, a humbler heav'n;
Some safer world in depth of woods embrac'd,
Some happier island in the wat'ry waste,
Where slaves once more their native land behold,
No fiends torment, no Christians thirst for gold!

To be, contents his natural desire;
He asks no angel's wing, no seraph's fire:
But thinks, admitted to that equal sky,
His faithful dog shall bear him company.

IV. Go, wiser thou! and, in thy scale of sense
Weigh thy opinion against Providence:
Call imperfection what thou fanciest such,—
Say, here he gives too little, there too much!
Destroy all creatures for thy sport or gust,
Yet cry, if Man 's unhappy, God 's unjust;
If Man alone ingross not Heav'n's high care,
Alone made perfect here, immortal there:
Snatch from his hand the balance and the rod,
Rejudge his justice, be the god of God.
In pride, in reas'ning pride, our error lies;
All quit their sphere and rush into the skies!
Pride still is aiming at the blest abodes,—
Men would be angels, angels would be gods.
Aspiring to be gods if angels fell,
Aspiring to be angels men rebel:
And who but wishes to invert the laws
Of Order, sins against th' Eternal Cause.

V. Ask for what end the heav'nly bodies shine,
Earth for whose use, Pride answers, " 'Tis for mine!
" For me kind Nature wakes her genial pow'r,
" Suckles each herb and spreads out ev'ry flow'r;
" Annual for me the grape, the rose renew
" The juice nectareous, and the balmy dew;
" For me the mine a thousand treasures brings;
" For me health gushes from a thousand springs;
" Seas roll to waft me, suns to light me rise;
" My footstool earth, my canopy the skies!"

But errs not Nature from this gracious end,
From burning suns when livid deaths descend,
When earthquakes swallow, or when tempests sweep
Towns to one grave, whole nations to the deep?
"No," 'tis replied, " the First Almighty Cause
" Acts not by partial, but by gen'ral laws;
" Th' exceptions few; some change since all began,
" And what created perfect?"—Why then Man?

If the great end be human happiness,
Then Nature deviates; and can Man do less?
As much that end a constant course requires
Of show'rs and sunshine, as of Man's desires:
As much eternal springs and cloudless skies,
As men for ever temperate, calm, and wise.

If plagues or earthquakes break not Heav'n's design,
Why then a Borgia, or a Catiline?
Who knows but He, whose hand the lightning forms,
Who heaves old Ocean, and who wings the storms;
Pours fierce ambition in a Cæsar's mind,
Or turns young Ammon loose to scourge mankind?
From pride, from pride our very reas'ning springs;
Account for moral, as for nat'ral things:
Why charge we Heav'n in those, in these acquit?
In both, to reason right, is to submit.
Better for us, perhaps, it might appear,
Were there all harmony, all virtue here;
That never air or ocean felt the wind;
That never passion discompos'd the mind.
But all subsists by elemental strife;
And passions are the elements of life.
The gen'ral Order since the whole began
Is kept in Nature, and is kept in Man.

VI. What would this Man? now upward will he soar,
And little less than angel, would be more!
Now looking downward, just as griev'd appears
To want the strength of bulls, the fur of bears.
Made for his use all creatures if he call,
Say what their use had he the pow'rs of all?
Nature to these, without profusion kind,
The proper organs, proper pow'rs assign'd;
Each seeming want compensated of course,
Here with degrees of swiftness, there of force:
All in exact proportion to the state;
Nothing to add, and nothing to abate.
Each beast, each insect, happy in its own:
Is Heav'n unkind to Man, and Man alone?
Shall he alone, whom rational we call,
Be pleas'd with nothing, if not bless'd with all?
The bliss of Man, (could Pride that blessing find)
Is not to think or act beyond mankind;
No pow'rs of body or of soul to share,
But what his nature and his state can bear.
Why has not Man a microscopic eye?
For this plain reason, Man is not a fly.
Say what the use were finer optics given?
T' inspect a mite, not comprehend the heav'n;
Or touch, if tremblingly alive all o'er,
To smart and agonize at ev'ry pore?
Or quick effluvia darting thro' the brain,
Die of a rose in aromatic pain?
If Nature thunder'd in his op'ning ears,
And stunn'd him with the music of the spheres,

How would he wish that Heav'n had left him still
The whisp'ring zephyr, and the purling rill!
Who finds not Providence all good and wise,
Alike in what it gives, and what denies?

VII. Far as creation's ample range extends,
The scale of sensual, mental pow'rs ascends:
Mark how it mounts to Man's imperial race,
From the green myriads in the peopled grass:
What modes of sight betwixt each wide extreme,
The mole's dim curtain, and the lynx's beam:
Of smell, the headlong lioness between,
And hound sagacious on the tainted green:
Of hearing, from the life that fills the flood,
To that which warbles thro' the vernal wood!
The spider's touch how exquisitely fine!
Feels at each thread, and lives along the line:
In the nice bee, what sense so subtly true
From pois'nous herbs extracts the healing dew?
How instinct varies in the grov'ling swine,
Compar'd, half-reas'ning elephant, with thine;
'Twixt that and reason what a nice barrier!
For ever sep'rate, yet for ever near!
Remembrance and reflection how allied,
What thin partitions sense from thought divide!
And middle natures, how they long to join,
Yet never pass th' insuperable line!
Without this just gradation could there be
Subjected these to those, or all to thee?
The pow'rs of all subdu'd by thee alone,
Is not thy reason all these pow'rs in one?

VIII. See, thro' this air, this ocean, and this earth,
All matter quick, and bursting into birth.
Above, how high progressive life may go!
Around, how wide! how deep extend below!
Vast chain of being! which from God began,
Natures ethereal, human, angel, man,
Beast, bird, fish, insect, what no eye can see,
No glass can reach—from infinite to thee,
From thee to nothing.—On superior pow'rs
Were we to press, inferior might on ours:
Or in the full creation leave a void,
Where, one step broken, the great scale 's destroy'd:
From Nature's chain whatever link you strike,
Tenth or ten thousandth, breaks the chain alike.
And, if each system in gradation roll
Alike essential to th' amazing whole,
The least confusion but in one, not all
That system only, but the whole must fall.

Let earth unbalanc'd from her orbit fly,
Planets and suns run lawless thro' the sky:
Let ruling angels from their spheres be hurl'd,
Being on being wreck'd, and world on world;
Heav'n's whole foundations to their centre nod,
And Nature trembles to the throne of God.
All this dread order break—for whom? for thee?
Vile worm!—oh madness! pride! impiety!

IX. What if the foot, ordain'd the dust to tread,
Or hand, to toil, aspir'd to be the head?
What if the head, the eye, or ear repin'd
To serve mere engines to the ruling mind?
Just as absurd for any part to claim
To be another in this general frame:
Just as absurd, to mourn the tasks or pains,
The great directing mind of all ordains.
All are but parts of one stupendous whole,
Whose body Nature is, and God the soul;
That, chang'd thro' all, and yet in all the same;
Great in the earth, as in th' æthereal frame;
Warms in the sun, refreshes in the breeze,
Glows in the stars, and blossoms in the trees,
Lives thro' all life, extends thro' all extent,
Spreads undivided, operates unspent;
Breathes in our soul, informs our mortal part,
As full, as perfect, in a hair as heart;
As full, as perfect, in vile Man that mourns,
As the rapt seraph that adores and burns:
To him no high, no low, no great, no small,
He fills, he bounds, connects, and equals all.

X. Cease then, nor Order Imperfection name:
Our proper bliss depends on what we blame.
Know thy own point: this kind, this due degree
Of blindness, weakness, Heav'n bestows on thee.
Submit.—In this, or any other sphere,
Secure to be as blest as thou canst bear:
Safe in the hand of one disposing Pow'r,
Or in the natal, or the mortal hour.
All Nature is but Art, unknown to thee;
All chance, direction, which thou canst not see.
All discord, harmony not understood,
All partial evil, universal good:
And, spite of pride, in erring reason's spite,
One truth is clear, whatever is, is right.

EPISTLE II.

OF THE NATURE AND STATE OF MAN, WITH RESPECT TO HIMSELF, AS AN INDIVIDUAL.

ARGUMENT.

I. The business of man not to pry into God, but to study himself. His middle nature; his powers and frailties. The limits of his capacity. II. The two principles of man, self-love and reason, both necessary. Self-love the stronger, and why. Their end the same. III. The passions, and their use. The predominant passion, and its force. Its necessity in directing men to different purposes. Its providential use in fixing our principle, and ascertaining our virtue. IV. Virtue and vice joined in our mixed nature; the limits near, yet the things separate and evident: what is the office of reason. How odious vice in itself, and how we deceive ourselves in it. VI. That, however, the ends of Providence and general good are answered in our passions and imperfections. How usefully these are distributed to all orders of men. How useful they are to society, and to individuals, in every state, and every age of life.

I. Know then thyself, presume not God to scan,
The proper study of mankind is Man.
Plac'd on this isthmus of a middle state,
A being darkly wise, and rudely great:
With too much knowledge for the sceptic side,
With too much weakness for the stoic's pride,
He hangs between: in doubt to act, or rest;
In doubt to deem himself a god, or beast;
In doubt his mind or body to prefer;
Born but to die, and reas'ning but to err;
Alike in ignorance, his reason such,
Whether he thinks too little, or too much:
Chaos of thought and passion, all confus'd;
Still by himself abus'd, or disabus'd;
Created half to rise, and half to fall;
Great lord of all things, yet a prey to all;
Sole judge of Truth, in endless Error hurl'd:
The glory, jest, and riddle of the world!
Go, wond'rous creature! mount where Science guides,
Go, measure earth, weigh air, and state the tides;
Instruct the planets in what orbs to run,
Correct old Time, and regulate the Sun;
Go, soar with Plato to the empyreal sphere,
To the first good, first perfect, and first fair;

Or tread the mazy round his followers trod,
And quitting sense call imitating God;
As Eastern priests in giddy circles run,
And turn their heads to imitate the Sun.
Go, teach Eternal Wisdom how to rule—
Then drop into thyself, and be a fool!
  Superior beings, when of late they saw
A mortal Man unfold all Nature's law:
Admir'd such wisdom in an earthly shape,
And shew'd a NEWTON as we shew an Ape.
  Could he, whose rules the rapid Comet bind,
Describe or fix one movement of his Mind?
Who saw it's fires here rise, and there descend,
Explain his own beginning, or his end?
Alas what wonder! Man's superior part
Uncheck'd may rise and climb from art to art;
But when his own great work is but begun,
What Reason weaves, by Passion is undone.
  Trace Science then, with Modesty thy guide
First strip off all her equipage of Pride;
Deduct what is but Vanity, or Dress,
Or Learning's Luxury, or Idleness;
Or tricks to shew the stretch of human brain,
Mere curious pleasure, or ingenious pain;
Expunge the whole, or lop th' excrescent parts
Of all our Vices have created Arts;
Then see how little the remaining sum,
Which served the past, and must the times to come

  II. Two Principles in human nature reign;
Self-love, to urge, and Reason, to restrain;
Nor this a good, nor that a bad we call,
Each works it's end, to move or govern all·
And to their proper operation still,
Ascribe all Good; to their improper, Ill.
  Self-love, the spring of motion, acts the soul,
Reason's comparing balance rules the whole.
Man, but for that, no action could attend,
And, but for this, were active to no end:
Fix d like a plant on his peculiar spot,
To draw nutrition. propagate, and rot;
Or, meteor-like, flame lawless thro' the void,
Destroying others, by himself destroy'd.
  Most strength the moving principle requires;
Active its task, it prompts, impels, inspires.
Sedate and quiet the comparing lies,
Form'd but to check, delib'rate, and advise.
Self-love still stronger, as its objects nigh;
Reason's at distance, and in prospect lie:

Reason itself but gives it edge and pow'r,
That sees immediate good by present sense;
Thicker than arguments, temptations throng,
At best more watchful this, but that more strong,
The action of the stronger to suspend
Reason still use, to Reason still attend.
Attention, habit and experience gains;
Each strengthens Reason, and Self-love restrains.
Let subtle schoolmen teach these friends to fight,
More studious to divide than to unite;
And Grace and Virtue, Sense and Reason split,
With all the rash dexterity of wit.
Wits just like Fools, at war about a name,
Have full as oft no meaning, or the same.
Self-love and Reason to one end aspire,
Pain their aversion, Pleasure their desire,
But greedy that, its object would devour,
This taste the honey, and not wound the flow'r
Pleasure, or wrong or rightly understood,
Our greatest evil, or our greatest good.

III. Modes of self-love the passions we may call;
'Tis real good, or seeming moves them all:
But since not ev'ry good we can divide,
And reason bids us for our own provide;
Passions, tho' selfish, if their means be fair,
List under reason, and deserve her care;
Those, that imparted, court a nobler aim,
Exalt their kind, and take some virtue's name.
In lazy apathy let stoics boast
Their virtue fix'd; 'tis fix'd as in a frost;
Contracted all, retiring to the breast;
But strength of mind is exercise, not rest:
The rising tempest puts in act the soul,
Parts it may ravage, but preserves the whole.
On life's vast ocean diversely we sail,
Reason the card, but passion is the gale;
Nor God alone in the still calm we find,
He mounts the storm, and walks upon the wind.
Passions, like elements, tho' born to fight,
Yet, mix'd and soften'd, in his work unite:
These 'tis enough to temper and employ;
But what composes Man, can Man destroy?
Suffice that Reason keep to Nature's road,
Subject, compound them, follow her and God.
Love, Hope, and Joy, fair Pleasure's smiling train,
Hate, Fear, and Grief, the family of Pain,
These mix'd with art, and to due bounds confin'd,
Make and maintain the balance of the mind:

The lights and shades, whose well-accorded strife,
Gives all the strength and colour of our life.
Pleasures are ever in our hands or eyes:
And when in act they cease, in prospect rise:
Present to grasp, and future still to find,
The whole employ of body and of mind.
All spread their charms, but charm not all alike;
On diff'rent senses diff'rent objects strike;
Hence diff'rent passions more or less inflame,
As strong or weak the organs of the frame;
And hence one master passion in the breast,
Like Aaron's serpent, swallows up the rest.
As man, perhaps, the moment of his breath
Receives the lurking principle of death;
The young disease, that must subdue at length,
Grows with his growth, and strengthens with his strength:
So, cast and mingled with his very frame,
The mind's disease, its ruling passion, came;
Each vital humour, which should feed the whole,
Soon flows to this, in body and in soul:
Whatever warms the heart, or fills the head,
As the mind opens, and its functions spread,
Imagination plies her dang'rous art,
And pours it all upon the peccant part.
Nature its mother, Habit is its nurse;
Wit, spirit, faculties but make it worse;
Reason, the future and the consequence.
As Heav'n's blest beam turns vinegar more sour.
We, wretched subjects tho' to lawful sway,
In this weak queen some fav'rite still obey.
Ah! if she lend not arms as well as rules,
What can she more than tell us we are fools?
Teach us to mourn our nature, not to mend.
A sharp accuser but a helpless friend!
Or from a judge turn pleader, to persuade
The choice we make, or justify it made;
Proud of an easy conquest all along,
She but removes weak passions for the strong:
So, when small humours gather to a gout,
The doctor fancies he has driven them out.
Yes Nature's road must ever be preferr'd;
Reason is here no guide, but still a guard:
'Tis hers to rectify, not overthrow,
And treat this passion more as friend than foe:
A mightier pow'r the strong direction sends,
And sev'ral men impels to sev'ral ends:
Like varying winds, by other passions toss'd,
This drives them constant to a certain coast.
Let pow'r or knowledge, gold or glory please;
Or (oft more strong than all) the love of ease:

Thro' life 'tis follow'd ev'n at life's expense;
The merchant's toil, the sage's indolence,
The monk's humility, the hero's pride;
All, all alike, find Reason on their side.
Th' Eternal Art, educing good from ill,
Grafts on this passion our best principle:
'Tis thus the mercury of man is fix'd,
Strong grows the virtue with his nature mix'd;
The dross cements what else were too refin'd,
And in one int'rest body acts with mind.
As fruits, ungrateful to the planter's care,
On savage stocks inserted learn to bear
The surest virtues thus from passions shoot,
Wild nature's vigour working at the root.
What crops of wit and honesty appear
From spleen, from obstinacy, hate or fear!
See anger, zeal, and fortitude supply:
Ev'n av'rice, prudence; sloth, philosophy;
Lust, thro' some certain strainers well refin'd,
Is gentle love, and charms all womankind;
Envy, to which th' ignoble mind 's a slave,
Is emulation in the learn'd or brave;
Nor virtue, male or female, can we name,
But what will grow on pride, or grow on shame
Thus Nature gives us (let it check our pride)
The virtue nearest to our vice allied;
Reason the bias turns to good from ill,
And Nero reigns a Titus if he will.
The fiery soul abhorr'd in Catiline,
In Decius charms, in Curtius is divine:
The same ambition can destroy or save,
And makes a patriot as it makes a knave.
This light and darkness in our chaos join'd,
What shall divide? The God within the mind.
Extremes in Nature equal ends produce;
In Man they join to some mysterious use;
Tho' each by turns the other's bounds invade,
As, in some well-wrought picture, light and shade
And oft so mix, the diff'rence is too nice,
Where ends the virtue, or begins the vice.
Fools! who from hence into the notion fall,
That vice or virtue there is none at all.
If white and black blend, soften, and unite
A thousand ways, is there no black or white?
Ask your own heart, and nothing is so plain;
'Tis to mistake them costs the time and pain.
Vice is a monster of so frightful mien,
As to be hated needs but to be seen;
Yet seen too oft, familiar with her face,
We first endure, then pity, then embrace.

But where th' extreme of vice was ne'er agreed:
Ask where's the North? at York, 'tis on the Tweed;
In Scotland, at the Orcades; and there,
At Greenland, Zembla, or the Lord knows where.
No creature owns it in the first degree,
But thinks his neighbour farther gone than he;
Ev'n those who dwell beneath its very zone,
Or never feel the rage, or never own;
What happier natures shrink at with affright,
The hard inhabitant contends is right.
Virtuous and vicious ev'ry man must be,
Few in the extreme, but all in the degree;
The rogue and fool by fits is fair and wise;
And ev'n the best, by fits, what they despise.
'Tis but by parts we follow good or ill;
For, vice or virtue, self directs it still;
Each individual seeks a several goal;
But Heaven's great view is one, and that the whole.
That counterworks each folly and caprice;
That disappoints the effect of every vice;
That, happy frailties to all ranks applied;
Shame to the virgin, to the matron pride,
Fear to the statesman, rashness to the chief,
To kings presumption, and to crowds belief:
That, virtue's ends from vanity can raise,
Which seeks no interest, no reward but praise,
And builds on wants, and on defects of mind,
The joy, the peace, the glory of mankind.
Heaven forming each on other to depend,
A master, or a servant, or a friend,
Bids each on other for assistance call,
Till one man's weakness grows the strength of all.
Wants, frailties, passions, closer still ally
The common interest, or endear the tie.
To these we owe true friendship, love sincere,
Each home-felt joy that life inherits here;
Yet from the same we learn, in its decline,
Those joys, those loves, those interests to resign;
Taught half by reason, half by mere decay,
To welcome death, and calmly pass away.
Whate'er the passions, knowledge, fame, or pelf,
Not one will change his neighbour with himself.
The learn'd is happy nature to explore,
The fool is happy that he knows no more;
The rich is happy in the plenty given,
The poor contents him with the care of Heaven,
See the blind beggar dance, the cripple sing
The sot a hero, lunatic a king;
The starving chemist in his golden views
Supremely bless'd, the poet in his Muse.

See some strange comfort every state attend;
And pride bestow'd on all, a common friend:
See some fit passion every age supply;
Hope travels through, nor quits us when we die.
Behold the child, by nature's kindly law,
Pleased with a rattle, tickled with a straw:
Some livelier plaything gives his youth delight,
A little louder, but as empty quite:
Scarfs, garters, gold, amuse his riper stage,
And beads and prayer-books are the toys of age:
Pleased with this bauble still, as that before,
Till tired he sleeps, and life's poor play is o'er.
Meanwhile opinion gilds with varying rays
Those painted clouds that beautify our days;
Each want of happiness by hope supplied,
And each vacuity of sense by pride:
These build as fast as knowledge can destroy;
In folly's cup still laughs the bubble, joy;
One prospect lost, another still we gain,
And not a vanity is given in vain;
Ev'n mean self-love becomes, by force divine,
The scale to measure others' wants by thine.
See! and confess, one comfort still must rise;
'Tis this, though man's a fool, yet God is wise.

EPISTLE III.

OF THE NATURE AND STATE OF MAN, WITH RESPECT TO SOCIETY.

ARGUMENT.

I. The whole universe one system of society. Nothing made wholly for itself, nor yet wholly for another. The happiness of animals mutual. II. Reason or instinct operate alike to the good of each individual. Reason or instinct operate also to society in all animals. III. How far society carried by instinct. How much farther by reason. IV. Of that which is called the state of Nature. Reason instructed by instinct in the invention of arts. And in the forms of society. V. Origin of political societies. Origin of monarchy. Patriarchal government VI. Origin of true religion and government, from the same prnciple of love. Origin of superstition and tyranny, from the same principle of fear. The influence of self-love operating to the social and public good. Restoration of true religion and government on their first principle. Mixed government. Various forms of each, and the true end of all.

I. Here then we rest: 'The Universal Cause
Acts to one end, but acts by various laws.'
In all the madness of superflous health,
The trim of pride, the impudence of wealth,
Let this great truth be present night and day;
But most be present if we preach or pray.
Look round our world; behold the chain of love
Combining all below and all above.
See plastic Nature working to this end,
The single atoms each to other tend.
Attract, attracted to, the next in place
Form'd and impell'd its neighbour to embrace.
See matter next, with various life endued,
Press to one centre still, the gen'ral good.
See dying vegetables life sustain,
See life dissolving vegetate again:
All forms thst perish other forms supply,
(By turns we catch the vital breath, and die)
Like bubbles on the sea of matter borne,
They rise, they break, and to that sea return
Nothing is foreign; parts relate to whole;
One all-extending, all-preserving soul
Connects each being, greatest with the least;
Made beasts in aid of man, and man of beast;

All serv'd, all serving: nothing stands alone;
The chain holds on, and where it ends unknown.
Has God, thou fool! worked solely for thy good,
Thy joy, thy pastime, thy attire, thy food?
Who for thy table feeds the wanton fawn,
For him as kindly spread the flow'ry lawn:
Is it for thee the lark ascends and sings?
Joy tunes his voice, joy elevates his wings;
Is it for thee the linnit pours his throat?
Loves of his own and raptures swell the note.
The bounding steed you pompously bestride,
Shares with his lord the pleasure and the pride:
Is thine alone the seed that strews the plain?
The birds of heav'n shall vindicate their grain:
Thine the full harvest of the golden year?
Part pays, and justly, the deserving steer:
The hog, that ploughs not nor obeys thy call,
Lives on the labours of this lord of all.
Know, Nature's children all divide her care;
The fur that warms a monarch warm'd a bear.
While man exclaims, 'See all things for my use!'
'See man for mine!' replies a pampered goose;
And just as short of reason he must fall,
Who thinks all made for one, not one for all.
Grant that the pow'rful still the weak control;
Be Man the wit, and tyrant of the whole:
Nature that tyrant checks; he only knows,
And helps another creature's wants and woes.
Say, will the falcon, stooping from above.
Smit with her varying plumage, spare the dove?
Admires the jay the insect's gilded wings?
Or hears the hawk when Philomela sings?
Man cares for all: to birds he gives his woods,
To beasts his pastures, and to fish his floods:
For some his int'rest prompts him to provide,
For more his pleasure, yet for more his pride:
All feed on one vain patron, and enjoy
Th' extensive blessing of his luxury.
That very life his learned hunger craves,
He saves from famine, from the savage saves;
Nay, feasts the animal he dooms his feast,
And, till he ends the being, makes it blest;
Which sees no more the stroke, or feels the pain,
Than favour'd Man by touch ethereal slain.
The creature had his feast of life before;
Thou too must perish, when thy feast is o'er!
To each unthinking being, Heav'n, a friend
Gives not the useless knowledge of its end:
To man imparts it; but with such a view
As, while he dreads it, makes him hope it too

The hour conceal'd, and so remote the fear,
Death still draws nearer, never seeming near.
Great standing miracle! that Heav'n assign'd
Its only thinking thing this turn of mind.

II. Whether with reason or with instinct bless'd,
Know all enjoy that power which suits them best;
To bliss alike by that direction tend,
And find the means proportion'd to their end.
Say, where full instinct is the unerring guide,
What pope or council can they need beside?
Reason, however able, cool at best,
Cares not for service, or but serves when press'd,
Stays till we call, and then not often near;
But honest instinct comes a volunteer,
Sure never to o'ershoot, but just to hit,
While still too wide or short is human wit;
Sure by quick nature happiness to gain,
Which heavier reason labors at in vain.
This too serves always, reason never long;
One must go right, the other may go wrong.
See then the acting and comparing powers
One in their nature, which are two in ours:
And reason raise o'er instinct as you can,
In this 'tis God directs, in that 'tis man.
Who taught the nations of the field and wood
To shun their poison, and to choose their food?
Prescient, the tides or tempests to wit stand,
Build on the wave, or arch beneath the sand?
Who made the spider parallels design,
Sure as Demoivre, without rule or line?
Who bid the stork, Columbus-like, explore
Heav'ns not his own and worlds unknown before
Who calls the council, states the certain day,
Who forms the phalanx, and who points the way?

III. God, in the nature of each being, founds
Its proper bliss, and sets its proper bounds;
But as he framed the whole, the whole to bless,
On mutual wants built mutual happiness:
So from the first, eternal order ran,
And creature link'd to creature, man to man.
Whate'er of life all-quickening ether keeps,
Or breathes through air, or shoots beneath the deeps,
Or pours profuse on earth, one nature feeds
The vital flame, and swells the genial seeds.
Not man alone, but all that roam the wood,
Or wing the sky, or roll along the flood,
Each loves itself, but not itself alone,
Each sex desires alike, till two are one.

Nor ends the pleasure with the fierce embrace;
They love themselves, a third time, in their race.
Thus beast and bird their common charge attend,
The mothers nurse it, and the sires defend:
The young dismiss'd to wander earth or air,
There stops the instinct, and there ends the care;
The link dissolves, each seeks a fresh embrace,
Another love succeeds, another race.
A longer care man's helpless kind demands;
That longer care contracts more lasting bands:
Reflection, reason, still the ties improve,
At once extend the interest, and the love;
With choice we fix, with sympathy we burn;
Each virtue in each passion takes its turn;
And still new needs, new helps, new habits rise
That graft benevolence on charities.
Still as one brood, and as another rose,
These natural love maintain'd, habitual those:
The last, scarce ripen'd into perfect man,
Saw helpless him from whom their life began:
Memory and forecast just returns engage;
That pointed back to youth, this on to age;
While pleasure, gratitude, and hope, combined,
Still spread the interest, and preserved the kind.

IV. Nor think, in nature's state they blindly trod;
The state of nature was the reign of God:
Self-love and social at her birth began,
Union the bond of all things, and of man.
Pride then was not; nor arts, that pride to aid;
Man walk'd with beast, joint-tenant of the shade;
The same his table, and the same his bed;
No murder clothed him, and no murder fed.
In the same temple, the resounding wood,
All vocal beings hymn'd their equal God:
The shrine with gore unstain'd, with gold undress'd,
Unbribed, unbloody, stood the blameless priest:
Heaven's attribute was universal care;
And man's prerogative to rule, but spare.
Ah! how unlike the man of times to come!
Of half that live the butcher and the tomb;
Who, foe to nature, hears the general groan;
Murders their species, and betrays his own.
But just disease to luxury succeeds,
And every death its own avenger breeds;
The fury-passions from that blood began,
And turn'd on man a fiercer savage, man.
See him from nature rising slow to art!
To copy instinct then was Reason's part:

Thus then to man the voice of Nature spake:—
'Go, from the creatures thy instructions take:
Learn from the birds what food the thickets yield;
Learn from the beasts the physic of the field:
Thy arts of building from the bee receive;
Learn of the mole to plough, the worm to weave;
Learn of the little nautilus to sail;
Spread the thin oar, and catch the driving gale:
Here too all forms of social union find,
And hence let reason, late, instruct mankind:
Here subterranean works and cities see;
There towns aerial on the waving tree:
Learn each small people's genius, policies,
The ants' republic and the realm of bees;
How those in common all their wealth bestow,
And anarchy without confusion know;
And these for ever, though a monarch reign,
Their separate cells and properties maintain.
Mark what unvaried laws preserve each state;—
Laws wise as nature, and as fix'd as fate.
In vain thy reason finer webs shall draw;
Entangle justice in her net of law;
And right, too rigid, harden into wrong,
Still for the strong too weak, the weak too strong.
Yet go! and thus o'er all the creatures sway;
Thus let the wiser make the rest obey;
And for those arts mere instinct could afford,
Be crown'd as monarchs, or as gods adored.'

V. Great Nature spoke; observant men obey'd;
Cities were built, societies were made:
Here rose one little state; another near
Grew by like means, and join'd through love or fear.
Did here the trees with ruddier burdens bend,
And there the streams in purer rills descend?
What war could ravish, commerce could bestow;
And he return'd a friend, who came a foe.
Converse and love mankind may strongly draw,
When love was liberty, and nature law:
Thus states were form'd; the name of king unknown,
Till common interest placed the sway in one
'Twas Virtue only, or in arts or arms,
Diffusing blessings, or averting harms;
The same which in a sire the sons obey'd,
A prince the father of a people made.

VI. Till then, by Nature crown'd, each patriarch sate,
King, priest, and parent of his growing state;
On him, their second Providence, they hung;
Their law his eye, their oracle his tongue.

He from the wondering furrow call'd the food;
Taught to command the fire, control the flood;
Draw forth the monsters of the abyss profound,
Or fetch the aerial eagle to to the ground;
Till drooping, sickening, dying, they began
Whom they revered as god to mourn as man
Then, looking up from sire to sire, explored
One great first Father, and that first adored.
Or plain tradition that this all begun,
Convey'd unbroken faith from sire to son;
The worker from the work distinct was known,
And simple reason never sought but one:
Ere wit oblique had broke that steady light,
Man, like his Maker, saw that all was right;
To virtue in the paths of pleasure trod,
And own'd a father when he own'd a God.
Love all the faith and all the allegiance then;
For nature knew no right divine in men,
No ill could fear in God; and understood
A sovereign being but a sovereign good.
True faith, true policy, united ran
That was but love of God, and this of man.
Who first taught souls enslaved, and realms undone
The enormous faith of many made for one;
That proud exception to all Nature's laws,
To invert the work, and counterwork its cause?
Force first made conquest, and that conquest law
Till superstition taught the tyrant awe;
Then shared the tyranny, then lent it aid,
And gods of conquerors, slaves of subjects made:
She, 'midst the lightning's blaze and thunder's sound
When rock'd the mountains, and when groan'd the
She taught the weak to bend, the proud to pray, [ground
To Power unseen, and mightier far than they:
She, from the rending earth and bursting skies,
Saw gods descend, and fiends infernal rise:
Here fix'd the dreadful, there the bless'd abodes;
Fear made her devils, and weak hope her gods;—
Gods partial, changeful, passionate, unjust,
Whose attributes were rage, revenge, or lust;
Such as the souls of cowards might conceive;
And, form'd like tyrants, tyrants would believe.
Zeal then, not charity, became the guide;
And hell was built on spite, and heaven on pride:
Then sacred seem'd the ethereal vault no more;
Altars grew marble then, and reek'd with gore:
Then first the flamen tasted living food;
Next his grim idol smear'd with human blood;
With Heaven's own thunders shook the world below,
And play'd the god an engine on his foe.

So drives self-love, through just and through unjust
To one man's power, ambition, lucre, lust:
The same self-love, in all, becomes the cause
Of what restrains him, government and laws:
For, what one likes if others like as well,
What serves one will, when many wills rebel?
How shall we keep, what, sleeping or awake,
A weaker may surprise, a stronger take?
His safety must his liberty restrain:
All join to guard what each desires to gain.
Forced into virtue thus by self-defence,
Ev'n kings learn'd justice and benevolence:
Self-love forsook the path it first pursued,
And found the private in the public good.
'Twas then, the studious head or generous mind,
Follower of God or friend of human-kind,
Poet or patriot, rose but to restore
The faith and moral Nature gave before;
Relumed her ancient light, not kindled new;
If not God's image, yet his shadow drew;
Taught power's due use to people and to kings;
Taught not to slack nor strain its tender strings;
The less or greater set so justly true,
That touching one must strike the other too;
Till jarring int'rests of themselves create
Th' according music of a well-mix'd state.
Such is the world's great harmony, that springs
From order, union, full consent of things:
Where small and great, where weak and mighty made
To serve, not suffer, strengthen, not invade;
More pow'rful each as needful to the rest,
And in proportion as it blesses, blest;
Draw to one point, and to one centre bring
Beast, man, or angel, servant, lord, or king.
For forms of government let fools contest;
Whate'er is best administer'd is best:
For modes of faith let graceless zealots fight;
His can't be wrong whose life is in the right:
In faith and hope thee world will disagree,
But all mankind's concern is charity:
All must be false that thwart this one great end;
And all of God, that bless mankind, or mend.
Man, like the gen'rous vine, supported lives:
She strength he gains is from th' embrace he gives
On their own axis as the planets run,
Yet make at once their circle round the sun;
So two consistent motions act the soul;
And one regards itself, and one the whole.
Thus God and Nature link'd the gen'ral frame.
And bade self-love and social be the same.

EPISTLE IV

OF THE NATURE AND STATE OF MAN, WITH RESPECT TO HAPPINESS

ARGUMENT.

I. False notions of happiness, philosophical and popular, answered. II. It is the end of all men, and attainable by all. God intends happiness to be equal; and to be so, it must be social, since all particular happiness depends on general, and since he governs by general, not particular laws. As is is necessary for order, and the peace and welfare of society, that external goods should be unequal, happiness is not made to consist in these. But notwithstanding that inequality, the balance of happiness among mankind is kept even by Providence, by the two passions of hope and fear. III. What the happiness of individuals is, as far as is consistent with the constitution of this world; and that the good man has here the advantage. The error of imputing to virtue what are only the calamities of nature, or of fortune. IV. The folly of expecting that God should alter his general laws in favour of particulars. V. That we are not judges who are good; but that whoever they are they must be happiest. VI. That external goods are not the proper rewards, but often inconsistent with, or destructive of, virtue. That even these can make no man happy without virtue: instanced in riches, in honours, nobility, greatness, fame, superior talents, with pictures of human infelicity in men possessed of them all. VII. That virtue only constitutes a happiness, whose object is universal, and whose prospect eternal. That the perfection of virtue and happiness consists in a conformity to the order of Providence here, and resignation to it here and hereafter.

O happiness! our being's end and aim,
Good, pleasure, ease, content! whate'er thy name:
That something still which prompts th' eternal sigh;
For which we bear to live, or dare to die;
Which still so near us, yet beyond us lies,
O'erlook'd, seen double by the fool and wise:
Plant of celestial seed! if dropp'd below,
Say in what mortal soil thou deign'st to grow?
Fair op'ning to some court's propitious shine,
Or deep with diamonds in the flaming mine?
Twin'd with the wreaths Parnassian laurels yield,
Or reap'd in iron harvests of the field?
Where grows?—where grows it not? If vain our toil,
We ought to blame the culture, not the soil:
Fix'd to no spot is Happiness sincere,
'Tis no where to be found, or ev'ry where:

'Tis never to be bought, but always free;
And, fled from monarchs, St. John! dwells with thee.
Ask of the learn'd the way, the learn'd are blind;
This bids to serve, and that to shun mankind;
Some, place the bliss in action, some in ease,
Those call it pleasure, and contentment these;
Some, sunk to beasts, find pleasure end in pain;
Some, swell'd to gods confess e'en virtue vain;
Or, indolent, to each extreme they fall,
To trust in ev'ry thing, or doubt of all.
Who thus define it, say they more or less
Than this, that Happiness is Happiness?
Take Nature's path, and mad Opinion's leave;
All states can reach it and all heads conceive;
Obvious her goods, in no extreme they dwell;
There needs but thinking right, and meaning well;
And mourn our various portions as we please,
Equal is common sense, and common ease.
Remember, man, 'the Universal Cause
Acts not by partial, but by gen'ral laws;'
And makes what happiness we justly call
Subsist not in the good of one, but all.
There's not a blessing individuals find,
But some way leans and hearkens to the kind:
No bandit fierce, no tyrant mad with pride,
No cavern'd hermit rests self-satisfied:
Who most to shun or hate mankind pretend,
Seek an admirer or would fix a friend:
Abstract what others feel, what others think,
All pleasure sicken, and all glories sink:
Each has his share; and who would more obtain,
Shall find the pleasure pays not half the pain.
Order is Heav'n's first law; and this confess'd
Some are, and must be, greater than the rest,
More rich, more wise; but who infers from hence
That such are happier, shocks all common sense.
Heav'n to mankind impartial we confess,
If all are equal in their happiness:
But mutual wants this happiness increase,
All Nature's diff'rence keeps all Nature's peace.
Condition, circumstance is not the thing;
Bliss is the same in subject or in king,
In who obtain defence, or who defend,
In him who is, or him who finds a friend:
Heav'n breaths thro' ev'ry member of the whole
One common blessing, as one common soul.
But Fortune's gifts if each alike possess'd,
And each were equal, must not all contest?
If then to all men happiness was meant,
God in externals could not place content

Fortune her gifts may variously dispose,
And these be happy call'd, unhappy those;
But Heaven's just balance equal will appear,
While those are placed in hope, and these in fear:
Not present good or ill, the joy or curse;
But future views of better or of worse.
O sons of earth! attempt ye still to rise,
By mountains piled on mountains, to the skies?
Heaven still with laughter the vain toil surveys,
And buries madmen in the heaps they raise.
Know, all the good that individuals find,
Or God and nature meant to mere mankind,
Reason's whole pleasure, all the joys of sense,
Lie in three words,—health, peace, and competence.
But health consists with temperance alone;
And peace, O Virtue! peace is all thy own.
The good or bad the gifts of Fortune gain;
But these less taste them, as they worse obtain.
Say, in pursuit of profit or delight,
Who risk the most, that take wrong means, or right?
Of vice or virtue, whether bless'd or cursed.
Which meets contempt, or which compassion first?
Count all the advantage prosperous Vice attains,
'Tis but what Virtue flies from and disdains:
And grant the bad what happiness they would,
One they must want, which is, to pass for good.
O, blind to truth, and God's whole scheme below,
Who fancy bliss to vice, to virtue woe!
Who sees and follows that great scheme the best,
Best knows the blessing, and will most be bless'd:
But fools the good alone unhappy call,
For ills or accidents that chance to all.
See Falkland dies, the virtuous and the just!
See godlike Turenne prostrate on the dust!
See Sidney bleeds amid the martial strife!
Was this their virtue or contempt of life?
Say, was it virtue, more though Heaven ne'er gave,
Lamented Digby! sunk thee to the grave?
Tell me, if virtue made the son expire,
Why, full of days and honour, lives the sire?
Why drew Marseilles' good bishop purer breath,
When Nature sicken'd, and each gale was death?
Or why so long, in life if long can be,
Lent Heaven a parent to the poor and me?
What makes all physical or moral ill?
There deviates nature, and here wanders will.
God sends not ill, if rightly understood;
Or partial ill is universal good,
Or change admits, or nature lets it fall;
Short, and but rare, till man improved it all.

We just as wisely might of Heaven complain
That righteous Abel was destroy'd by Cain,
As that the virtuous son is ill at ease
When his lewd father gave the dire disease.
Think we, like some weak prince, the Eternal Cause
Prone for his favourites to reverse his laws?
Shall burning Etna, if a sage requires,
Forget to thunder, and recall her fires?
On air or sea new motions be impress'd,
O blameless Bethel! to relieve thy breast?
When the loose mountain trembles from on high,
Shall gravitation cease if you go by?
Or some old temple, nodding to its fall,
For Chartres' head reserve the hanging wall?
But still this world, so fitted for the knave,
Contents us not. A better shall we have?
A kingdom of the just then let it be:
But first consider how those just agree.
The good must merit God's peculiar care;
But who but God can tell us who they are?
One thinks on Calvin Heaven's own spirit fell·
Another deems him instrument of hell:
If Calvin feel Heaven's blessing or its rod,
This cries there is, and that there is no God:
What shocks one part will edify the rest,
Nor with one system can they all be bless'd.
The very best will variously incline,
And what rewards your virtue punish mine.
'Whatever is, is right.'—This world, 'tis true,
Was made for Cæsar, but for Titus too:
And which more bless'd? who chain'd his country? say
Or he whose virtue sigh'd to lose a day?
'But sometimes virtue starves, while vice is fed.'
What then? Is the reward of virtue bread?
That vice may merit; 'tis the price of toil;
The knave deserves it, when he tills the soil;
The knave deserves it, when he tempts the main,
Where folly fights for kings, or dives for gain.
The good man may be weak, be indolent;
Nor is his claim to plenty, but content.
But grant him riches, your demand is o'er?
'No; shall the good want health, the good want power?
Add health, and power, and every earthly thing.
'Why bounded power? why private? why no king?'
Nay, why external for internal given?
Why is not man a god, and earth a heaven?
Who ask and reason thus, will scarce conceive
God gives enough, while he has more to give:
Immense the power, immense were the demand:
Say, at what part of nature will they stand?

What nothing earthly gives or can destroy,
The soul's calm sunshine, and the heartfelt joy,
Is Virtue's prize: a better would you fix?
Then give Humility a coach and six,
Justice a conq'ror's sword, or Truth a gown,
Or Public Spirit its great cure, a crown.
Weak, foolish man! will Heav'n reward us there
With the same trash mad mortals wish for here?
The boy and man an individual makes,
Yet sigh'st thou now for apples and for cakes?
Go, like the Indian, in another life
Expect thy dog, thy bottle, and thy wife:
As well as dream such trifles are assign'd,
As toys and empires, for a god-like mind.
Rewards, that either would to Virtue bring
No joy, or be destructive of the thing:
How oft by these at sixty are undone
The virtues of a saint at twenty-one!
To whom can riches give repute, or trust,
Content, or pleasure, but the good and just?
Judges and senates have been bought for gold;
Esteem and love were never to be sold.
O fool! to think God hates the worthy mind,
The lover and the love of human kind,
Whose life is healthful, and whose conscience clear
Because he wants a thousand pounds a-year.
Honour and shame from no condition rise;
Act well your part, there all the honour lies.
Fortune in men has some small difference made,
One flaunts in rags, one flutters in brocade;
The cobler apron'd, and the parson gown'd,
The friar hooded, and the monarch crown'd.
'What differ more,' you cry, 'than crown and cowl?
I'll tell you, friend! a wise man and a fool.
You'll find, if once the monarch acts the monk,
Or, cobler-like, the parson will be drunk,
Worth makes the man, and want of it the fellow;
The rest is all but leather or prunella.
Stuck o'er with titles, and, hung round with strings
That thou may'st be by kings, or whores of kings,
Boast the pure blood of an illustrious race.
In quiet flow from Lucrece to Lucrece:
But by your father's worth if your's you rate,
Count me those only who were good and great.
Go! if your ancient, but ignoble, blood
Has crept thro' scoundrels ever since the flood,
Go! and pretend your family is young;
Nor own your fathers have been fools so long.
What can ennoble sots, or slaves, or cowards?
Alas! not all the blood of all the Howards.

Look next on greatness; say where greatness lies?
'Where, but among the heroes and the wise?'
Heroes are much the same, the point's agreed,
From Macedonia's madman to the Swede;
The whole strange purpose of their lives to find
Or make an enemy of all mankind!
Not one looks backward, onward still he goes,
Yet ne'er looks forward farther than his nose.
No less alike the politic and wise;
All sly, slow things, with circumspective eyes:
Men in their loose, unguarded hours they take;
Not that themselves are wise, but others weak.
But grant that those can conquer, these can cheat;
'Tis phrase absurd to call a villain great:
Who wickedly is wise, or madly brave,
Is but the more a fool, the more a knave.
Who noble ends by noble means obtains,
Or failing, smiles in exile or in chains,
Like good Aurelius let him reign, or bleed
Like Sociates, that man is great indeed.
What 's fame? a fancied life in others' breath;
A thing beyond us, ev'n before our death.
Just what you hear, you have; and what's unknown
The same, my lord! if Tully's or your own.
All that we feel of it begins and ends
In the small circle of our foes or friends;
To all beside as much an empty shade
A Eugene living as a Cæsar dead:
Alike or when or where they shone or shine,
Or on the Rubicon, or on the Rhine.
A wit 's a feather, and a chief a rod;
An honest man 's the noblest work of God.
Fame but from death a villain's name can save,
As justice tears his body from the grave;
When what to oblivion better were resign'd,
Is hung on high, to poison half mankind.
All fame is foreign, but of true desert;
Plays round the head, but comes not to the heart
One self-approving hour whole years outweighs
Of stupid starers and of loud huzzas;
And more true joy Marcellus exiled feels,
Than Cæsar with a senate at his heels.
In parts superior what advantage lies!
Tell, for you can, what is it to be wise?
'Tis but to know how little can be known;
To see all others' faults, and feel our own:
Condemn'd in business or in arts to drudge,
Without a second, or without a judge:
Truths would you teach, or save a sinking land?
All fear, none aid you, and few understand.

Painful pre-eminence! yourself to view
Above life's weakness, and its comforts too.
Bring then these blessings to a strict account
Make fair deductions; see to what they mount;
How much of other each is sure to cost;
How each for other oft is wholly lost;
How inconsistent greater goods with these;
How sometimes life is risk'd, and always ease:
Think, and if still the things thy envy call,
Say, wouldst thou be the man to whom they fall.
To sigh for ribands if thou art so silly,
Mark how they grace lord Umbra, or sir Billy.
Is yellow dirt the passion of thy life?
Look but on Gripus, or on Gripus' wife.
If parts allure thee, think how Bacon shined,
The wisest, brightest, meanest of mankind:
Or ravish'd with the whistling of a name,
See Cromwell, damn'd to everlasting fame!
If all, united, thy ambition call,
From ancient story learn to scorn them all:
There, in the rich, the honour'd, famed and great,
See the false scale of happiness complete.
In hearts of kings, or arms of queens who lay,
How happy—those to ruin, these betray!
Mark by what wretched steps their glory grows,
From dirt and sea-weed as proud Venice rose;
In each how guilt and greatness equal ran,
And all that raised the hero sunk the man:
Now Europe's laurels on their brows behold,
But stain'd with blood, or ill exchanged for gold
Then see them broke with toils, or sunk in ease,
Or infamous for plunder'd provinces.
O wealth ill-fated! which no act of fame
E'er taught to shine, or sanctified from shame!
What greater bliss attends their close of life?
Some greedy minion, or imperious wife,
The trophied arches, storied halls invade.
And haunt their slumbers in the pompous shade.
Alas! not dazzled with their noontide ray,
Compute the morn and evening to the day:
The whole amount of that enormous fame,
A tale, that blends their glory with their shame!
Know then this truth, enough for man to know,—
'Virtue alone is happiness below.'
The only point where human bliss stands still,
And tastes the good without the fall to ill;
Where only merit constant pay receives,
Is bless'd in what it takes and what it gives;
The joy unequall'd if its end it gain;
And if it lose, attended with no pain:

Without satiety, though e'er so bless
And but more relish'd as the more distress'd
The broadest mirth unfeeling folly wears,
Less pleasing far than virtue's very tears:
Good from each object, from each place acquired,
For ever exercised, yet never tired;
Never elated, while one man's oppress'd;
Never dejected, while another's bless'd;
And where no wants, no wishes can remain;
Since but to wish more virtue is to gain.
 See the sole bliss Heaven could on all bestow!
Which who but feels can taste, but thinks can know:
Yet poor with fortune, and with learning blind,
The bad must miss; the good, untaught, will find;
Slave to no sect, who takes no private road,
But looks through nature up to nature's God;
Pursues that chain which links the immense design,
Joins heaven and earth, and mortal and divine;
Sees, that no being any bliss can know,
But touches some above, and some below;
Learns from this union of the rising whole,
The first, last purpose of the human soul;
And knows where faith, law, morals, all began,
All end, in love of God, and love of man.
 For him alone hope leads from goal to goal,
And opens still, and opens on his soul;
'Till lengthen'd on to faith, unconfined,
It pours the bliss that fills up all the mind.
He sees, why nature plants in man alone
Hope of known bliss, and faith in bliss unknown:
(Nature, whose dictates to no other kind
Are given in vain, but what they seek they find)
Wise is her present; she connects in this
His greatest virtue with his greatest bliss;
At once his own bright prospect to be bless'd
And strongest motive to assist the rest.
 Self-love thus push'd to social, to divine,
Gives thee to make thy neighbour's blessing thine.
Is this too little for the boundless heart?
Extend it, let thy enemies have part:
Grasp the whole worlds of reason, life, and sense,
In one close system of benevolence:
Happier as kinder, in whate'er degree,
And height of bliss but height of charity.
 God loves from whole to parts: but human soul
Must rise from individual to the whole.
Self-love but serves the virtuous mind to wake,
As the small pebble stirs the peaceful lake;
The centre mov'd, a circle straight succeeds,
Another still, and still another spreads;

Friend, parent, neigbour, first it will embrace;
His country next; and next all human race;
Wide and more wide th' o'erflowings of the mind
Take ev'ry creature in of ev'ry kind;
Earth smiles around, with boundless bounty bless'd,
And Heav'n beholds its image in his breast.
Come then, my friend! my genius! come along,
O master of the poet and the song!
And while the Muse now stoops, or now ascends,
To man's low passions or their glorious ends,
Teach me, like thee in various nature wise,
To fall with dignity, with temper rise;
Form'd by thy converse, happily to steer
From grave to gay, from lively to severe;
Correct with spirit, eloquent with ease,
Intent to reason, or polite to please.
Oh! while along the stream of time thy name
Expanded flies, and gathers all its fame,
Say, shall my little bark attendant sail,
Pursue the triumph, and partake the gale?
When statesman, heroes, kings, in dust repose,
Whose sons shall blush their fathers were thy foes,
Shall then this verse to future age pretend
Thou wert my guide, philosopher, and friend?
That urg'd by thee, I turn'd the tuneful art
From sounds to things, from fancy to the heart;
For Wit's false mirror held up Nature's light;
Show'd erring Pride, WHATEVER IS, IS RIGHT;
That Reason, Passion, answer one great aim;
That true Self-love and Social are the same;
That Virtue only makes our bliss below;
And all our knowledge is, OURSELVES TO KNOW.

SAPPHO TO PHAON.

THE ARGUMENT

PHAON, a youth of exquisite beauty, was deeply enamoured of Sappho, a lady of Lesbos, from whom he met with the tenderest returns of passion; but his affection afterwards decaying, he left her, and sailed for Sicily. She, unable to bear the loss of her lover, hearkened to all the mad suggestions of despair; and seeing no other remedy for her present miseries, resolved to throw herself into the sea, from Leucate, a promontory of Epirus, which was thought a cure in cases of obstinate love, and therefore had obtained the name of the lover's leap. But before she ventured upon this last step, entertaining still some fond hope that she might be able to reclaim her inconstant, she wrote him this epistle, in which she gives him a strong picture of her distress and misery, occasioned by his absence; and endeavours, by artful insinuations and moving expressions she is mistress of, to sooth him to softness and a mutual feeling.

SAY, lovely youth, that dost my heart command,
Can Phaon's eyes forget his Sappho's hand?
Must then her name the wretched writer prove,
To thy remembrance lost, as to thy love?
Ask not the cause that I new numbers choose,
The lute neglected, and the lyric muse;
Love taught my tears in sadder notes to flow,
And tun'd my heart to elegies of woe.
I burn, I burn, as when through ripened corn
By driving winds the spreading flames are borne
Phaon to Ætna's scorching fields retires,
While I consume with more than Ætna's fires!
No more my soul a charm in music finds;
Music has charms alone for peaceful minds.
Soft scenes of solitude no more can please;
Love enters there, and I'm my own disease.
No more the Lesbian dames my passions move,
Once the dear objects of my guilty love;
All other loves are lost in only thine,
Oh youth, ungrateful to a flame like mine!
Whom would not all those blooming charms surprise
Those heav'nly looks, and dear deluding eyes?
The harp and bow would you like Phœbus bear,
A brighter Phœbus Phaon might appear;
Would you with ivy wreath your flowing hair,
Not Bacchus' self with Phaon could compare:
Yet Phœbus lov'd, and Bacchus felt the flame;
One Daphne warm'd, and one the Cretan dame;

Nymphs that in verse no more could rival me,
Than e'en those gods contend in charms with thee.
The muses teach me in their softest lays,
And the wide world resounds with Sappho's praise
Though great Alcæus more sublimely sings,
And strikes with bolder rage the sounding strings,
No less renown attends the moving lyre
Which Venus tunes, and all her loves inspire;
To me what nature has in charms denied,
Is well by wit's more lasting flames supplied.
Though short my stature, yet my name extends
To heav'n itself, and earth's remotest ends,
Brown as I am, an Ethiopian dame
Inspir'd young Perseus with a gen'rous flame;
Turtles and doves with different hues unite,
And glossy jet is pair'd with shining white.
If to no charms thou wilt thy heart resign,
But such as merit, such as equal thine,
By none, alas! by none thou canst be mov'd;
Phaon alone by Phaon must be loved!
Yet once thy Sappho could thy cares employ,
Once in her arms you centered all your joy:
No time the dear remembrance can remove,
For oh! how vast a memory has love?
My music, then, you could for ever hear,
And all my words were music to your ear.
You stopp'd with kisses my enchanting tongue,
And found my kisses sweeter than my song.
In all I pleas'd, but most in what was best;
And the last joy was dearer than the rest.
Then with each word, each glance, each motion fired,
You still enjoy'd, and yet you still desired.
'Till, all dissolving, in the trance we lay,
And in tumultuous raptures died away.
The fair Sicilians now thy soul inflame;
Why was I born, ye gods! a Lesbian dame?
But ah, beware, Sicilian nymphs! nor boast
That wand'ring heart which I so lately lost;
Nor be with all those tempting words abus'd
Those tempting words were all to Sappho us'd
And you that rule Sicilia's happy plains,
Have pity, Venus, on your poet's pains!
Shall fortune still in one sad tenor run,
And still increase the woes so soon begun?
Inur'd to sorrow from my tender years,
My parents' ashes drank my early tears;
My brother next, neglecting wealth and fame
Ignobly burn'd in a destructive flame:
An infant daughter late my griefs increas'd,
And all a mother's cares distract my breast.

Alas! what more could fate itself impose,
But thee, the last, and greatest of my woes?
No more my robes in waving purple flow,
Nor on my hand the sparkling di'monds glow;
Nor more my locks in ringlets curl'd diffuse
The costly sweetness of Arabian dews,
For braids of gold the varied tresses bind,
That fly disorder'd with the wanton wind:
For whom should Sappho use such arts as these
He's gone whom only she desir'd to please!
Cupid's light darts my tender bosom move,
Still is there cause for Sappho still to love:
So from my birth the Sisters fix'd my doom,
And gave to Venus all my life to come;
Or, while my muse in melting notes complains,
My yielding heart keeps measure to my strains.
By charms like thine, which all my soul have won,
Who might not—ah! who would not be undone?
For those, Aurora Cephalus might scorn,
And with fresh blushes paint the conscious morn:
For those, might Cynthia lengthen Phaon's sleep,
And bid Endymion nightly tend his sheep:
Venus for those had rapt thee to the skies,
But Mars on thee might look with Venus' eyes.
O scarce a youth, yet scarce a tender boy!
O useful time for lovers to employ!
Pride of thy age, and glory of thy race,
Come to these arms, and melt in this embrace!
The vows you never will return, receive;
And take at least the love you will not give.
See, while I write, my words are lost in tears!
The less my sense, the more my love appears.
Sure 'twas not much to bid one kind adieu:
At least, to feign was never hard to you.
'Farewell, my Lesbian love!' you might have said;
Or coldly thus,—'Farewell O Lesbian maid!'
No tear did you, no parting kiss receive,
Nor knew I then how much I was to grieve.
No lover's gift your Sappho could confer;
And wrongs and woes were all you left with her.
No charge I gave you, and no charge could give,
But this,—'Be mindful of our loves, and live.'
Now by the Nine, those powers adored by me;
And Love, the god that ever waits on thee;—
When first I heard (from whom I hardly knew)
That you were fled, and all my joys with you,
Like some sad statue, speechless, pale I stood;
Grief chill'd my breast, and stopp'd my freezing blood;
No sigh to rise, no tear had power to flow,
Fix'd in a stupid lethargy of woe;

But when its way the impetuous passion found,
I rend my tresses, and my breast I wound;
I rave, then weep; I curse, and then complain;
Now swell to rage, now melt in tears again.
Not fiercer pangs distract the mournful dame,
Whose first-born infant feeds the funeral flame.
My scornful brother with a smile appears,
Insults my woes, and triumphs in my tears;
His hated image ever haunts my eyes;
And why this grief? thy daughter lives, he cries.
Stung with my love, and furious with despair,
All torn my garments, and my bosom bare,
My woes, thy crimes, I to the world proclaim;
Such inconsistent things are love and shame;
'Tis thou art all my care and my delight,
My daily longing, and my dream by night:
Oh night more pleasing than the brightest day,
When fancy gives what absence takes away:
And, dress'd in all its visionary charms,
Restores my fair deserter to my arms!
Then round your neck in wanton wreaths I twine;
Then you, methinks, as fondly circle mine:
A thousand tender words I hear and speak;
A thousand melting kisses give and take:
Then fiercer joys, I blush to mention these;
Yet, while I blush, confess how much they please.
But when, with day, the sweet delusions fly,
And all things wake to life and joy but I,
As if once more forsaken, I complain,
And close my eyes to dream of you again:
Then frantic rise, and like some fury rove
Through lonely plains, and through the silent grove,
As if the silent grove, and lonely plains,
That knew my pleasures, could relieve my pains.
I view the grotto, once the scene of love,
The rocks around, the hanging roofs above,
That charm'd me more, with native moss o'ergrown,
Than Phrygian marble, or the Parian stone.
I find the shades that veil'd our joys before;
But, Phaon gone, those shades delight no more.
Here the press'd herbs with bending tops betray
Where oft entwin'd in am'rous folds we lay;
I kiss that earth which once was press'd by you,
And all with tears the withering herbs bedew
For thee the fading trees appear to mourn,
And birds defer their songs till thy return:
Night shades the groves, and all in silence lie,
All but the mournful Philomel and I:
With mournful Philomel I join my strain;
Of Tereus she of Phaon I complain.

A spring there is, whose silver waters show
Clear as a glass, the shining sands below:
A flow'ry lotos spreads its arms above,
Shades all the banks, and seems itself a grove;
Eternal greens the mossy margin grace,
Watch'd by the sylvan genius of the place.
Here as I lay, and swell'd with tears the flood,
Before my sight a wat'ry Virgin stood:
She stood, and cry'd, 'O you that love in vain!
Fly hence and seek the fair Leucadian main;
There stands a rock, from whose impending steep,
Apollo's fane surveys the rolling deep;
There injur'd lovers, leaping from above,
Their flames extinguish, and forget to love.
Deucalion once with hopeless fury burn'd,
In vain he lov'd, relentless Pyrrah scorn'd:
But when from hence he plung'd into the main,
Deucalion scorn'd, and Pyrrah lov'd in vain.
Haste, Sappho, haste, from high Leucadia throw
Thy wretched weight, nor dread the deeps below!
She spoke, and vanish'd with the voice—I rise,
And silent tears fall trickling from my eyes.
I go, ye nymphs! those rocks and seas to prove;
How much I fear, but ah, how much I love!
I go, ye nymphs! where furious love inspires;
Let female fears submit to female fires.
To rocks and seas I fly from Phaon's hate,
And hope from seas and rocks a milder fate.
Ye gentle gales, beneath my body blow,
And softly lay me on the waves below!
And thou, kind love, my sinking limbs sustain,
Spread thy soft wings, and waft me o'er the main,
Nor let a lover's death the guiltless flood profane!
On Phœbus' shrine my harp I'll then bestow,
And this inscription shall be placed below:
'Here she who sung, to him that did inspire,
Sappho to Phœbus consecrates her lyre:
What suits with Sappho, Phœbus, suits with thee;
The gift, the giver, and the god agree.'
But why, alas! relentless youth, ah! why
To distant seas must tender Sappho fly?
Thy charms than those may far more pow'rful be,
And Phœbus' self is less a god to me.
Ah! canst thou doom me to the rocks and sea?
Oh far more faithless and more hard than they!
Ah! canst thou rather see this tender breast
Dash'd on these rocks than to thy bosom press'd?
This breast which once, in vain! you lik'd so well;
Where the loves play'd, and where the muses dwell,

Alas! the muses now no more inspire;
Untun'd my lute, and silent is my lyre;
My languid numbers have forgot to flow,
And fancy sinks beneath a weight of woe.
Ye Lesbian virgins, and ye Lesbian dames,
Themes of my verse, and objects of my flames,
No more your groves with my glad songs shall ring,
No more these hands shall touch the trembling string:
My Phaon's fled, and I those arts resign;
(Wretch that I am, to call that Phaon mine!)
Return, fair youth, return, and bring along
Joy to my soul, and vigour to my song:
Absent from thee, the poet's flame expires;
But ah! how fiercely burns the lover's fires?
Gods! can no pray'rs, no sighs, no numbers move
One savage heart, or teach it how to love?
The winds my pray'rs, my sighs my numbers bear,
The flying winds have lost them all in air;
Oh when, alas! shall more auspicious gales
To these fond eyes restore thy welcome sails!
If you return—ah why these long delays?
Poor Sappho dies while careless Phaon stays.
O launch thy bark, nor fear the watery plain;
Venus for thee shall smooth her native main.
O launch thy bark, secure of prosp'rous gales;
Cupid for thee shall spread the swelling sails.
If you will fly—(yet ah! what cause can be,
Too cruel youth, that you should fly from me?)
If not from Phaon I must hope for ease,
Ah let me seek it from the raging seas:
To raging seas unpitied I'll remove,
And either cease to live or cease to love!

ELOISA TO ABELARD.

ARGUMENT.

ABELARD and Eloisa flourished in the twelfth century; they were two of the most distinguished persons of their age in learning and beauty, but for nothing more famous than for their unfortunate passion. After a long course of calamities, they retired each to a several convent, and consecrated the remainder of their days to religion. It was many years after this separation that a letter of Abelard's to a friend, which contained the history of his misfortune, fell into the hands of Eloisa: this, awakening all her tenderness, occasioned those celebrated letters, out of which the following is partly extracted; which give so lively a picture of the struggles of grace and nature, virtue and passion.—POPE.

IN these deep solitudes and awful cells,
Where heavenly pensive contemplation dwells,
And ever musing melancholy reigns,
What means this tumult in a vestal's veins?
Why rove my thoughts beyond this last retreat?
Why feels my heart its long forgotten heat?
Yet, yet I love:—From Abelard it came,
And Eloisa yet must kiss the name.
  Dear fatal name! rest ever unreveal'd,
Nor pass these lips, in holy silence seal'd;
Hide it, my heart, within that close disguise,
Where mix'd with God's, his lov'd idea lies:
O write it not my hand—The name appears
Already written—wash it out, my tears!
In vain lost Eloisa weeps and prays,
Her heart still dictates, and her hand obeys.
  Relentless walls! whose darksome round contains
Repentant sighs, and voluntary pains:
Ye rugged rocks! which holy knees have worn!
Ye grots and caverns, shagg'd with horrid thorn!
Shrines, where their vigils pale-eyed virgins keep,
And pitying saints, whose statues learn to weep!
Though cold like you, unmoved and silent grown,
I have not yet forgot myself to stone.
All is not Heaven's while Abelard has part;
Still rebel nature holds out half my heart;
Nor prayers, nor fasts its stubborn pulse restrain,
Nor tears for ages taught to flow in vain.

Soon as thy letters trembling I unclose,
That well-known name awakens all my woes.
O, name for ever sad, for ever dear!
Still breathed in sighs, still usher'd with a tear.
I tremble too, where'er my own I find;
Some dire misfortune follows close behind.
Line after line my gushing eyes o'erflow,
Led through a sad variety of woe:
Now warm in love, now withering in my bloom,
Lost in a convent's solitary gloom!
There stern Religion quench'd the unwilling flame;
There died the best of passions, Love and Fame.
Yet write, O, write me all, that I may join
Griefs to thy griefs, and echo sighs to thine.
Nor foes nor fortune take this power away;
And is my Abelard less kind than they?
Tears still are mine, and those I need not spare;
Love but demands what else were shed in prayer:
No happier task these faded eyes pursue;
To read and weep is all they now can do.
Then share thy pain; allow that sad relief;
Ah, more than share it, give me all thy grief.
Heaven first taught letters for some wretch's aid,
Some banish'd lover, or some captive maid;
They live, they speak, they breathe what love inspires,
Warm from the soul, and faithful to its fires;
The virgin's wish without her fears impart,
Excuse the blush, and pour out all the heart;
Speed the soft intercourse from soul to soul,
And waft a sigh from Indus to the pole.
Thou know'st how guiltless first I met thy flame,
When love approach'd me under friendship's name;
My fancy form'd thee of angelic kind,
Some emanation of the all-beauteous Mind.
Those smiling eyes, attempering every ray,
Shone sweetly lambent with celestial day:
Guiltless I gazed; heaven listen'd while you sung;
And truths divine came mended from that tongue.
From lips like those what precept fail'd to move?
Too soon they taught me 'twas no sin to love:
Back, through the paths of pleasing sense, I ran,
Nor wish'd an angel whom I loved a man.
Dim and remote the joys of saints I see;
Nor envy them that heaven I lose for thee.
How oft, when press'd to marriage, have I said,
Curse on all laws but those which love has made!
Love, free as air, at sight of human ties,
Spreads his light wings, and in a moment flies.
Let wealth, let honour wait the wedded dame,
August her deed, and sacred be her fame:

Before true passion all those views remove;
Fame, wealth, and honour! what are you to Love?
The jealous god, when we profane his fires,
Those restless passions in revenge inspires;
And bids them make mistaken mortals groan,
Who seek in love for aught but love alone.
Should at my feet the world's great master fall,
Himself, his throne, his world, I'd scorn them all:
Not Cæsar's empress would I deign to prove;
No, make me mistress to the man I love:
If there be yet another name more free,
More fond than mistress, make me that to thee.
O, happy state! where souls each other draw,
When love is liberty, and nature law:
All then is full, possessing and possess'd,
No craving void left aching in the breast:
Ev'n thought meets thought, ere from the lips it part;
And each warm wish springs mutual from the heart.
This sure is bliss, if bliss on earth there be;
And once the lot of Abelard and me.
  Alas, how changed! what sudden horrors rise!
A naked lover bound and bleeding lies!
Where, where was Eloise? her voice, her hand,
Her poinard had opposed the dire command.
Barbarian, stay! that bloody stroke restrain;
The crime was common, common be the pain.
I can no more: by shame, by rage suppress'd,
Let tears and burning blushes speak the rest.
  Canst thou forget that sad, that solemn day,
When victims at yon altar's foot we lay?
Canst thou forget what tears that moment fell,
When, warm in youth, I bade the world farewell?
As with cold lips I kiss'd the sacred veil,
The shrines all trembled, and the lamps grew pale.
Heaven scarce believed the conquest it survey'd,
And saints with wonder heard the vows I made:
Yet then, to those dread altars as I drew,
Not on the cross my eyes were fix'd, but you;
Not grace or zeal, love only was my call;
And if I lose thy love, I lose my all.
Come, with thy looks, thy words, relieve my woe;
Those still at least are left thee to bestow:
Still on that breast enamour'd let me lie,
Still drink delicious poison from thy eye,
Pant on thy lip, and to thy heart be press'd:
Give all thou canst—and let me dream the rest.
Ah, no! instruct me other joys to prize;
With other beauties charm my partial eyes;
Full in my view set all the bright abode,
And make my soul quit Abelard for God.

Ah! think at least thy flock deserves thy care,
Plants of thy hand, and children of thy pray'r.
From the false world in early youth they fled,
By thee to mountains, wilds, and deserts led.
You rais'd these hallow'd walls; the desert smil'd,
And paradise was open'd in the wild,
No weeping orphan saw his father's stores
Our shrines irradiate, or emblaze the floors
No silver saints, by dying misers giv'n,
Here brib'd the rage of ill-requited Heav'n;
But such plain roofs as piety could raise,
And only vocal with the maker's praise.
In these lone walls (their days eternal bound)
These moss-grown domes with spiry turrets crown'd,
Where awful arches make a noon-day night,
And the dim windows shed a solemn light;
Thy eyes diffused a reconciling ray,
And gleams of glory brighten'd all the day.
But now no face divine contentment wears;
'Tis all blank sadness, or continual tears.
See how the force of others' pray'rs I try,
(Oh pious fraud of am'rous charity!)
But why should I on others' pray'rs depend?
Come thou, my father, brother, husband, friend!
Ah let thy handmaid, sister, daughter move,
And all those tender names in one, thy love!
The darksome pines, that o'er yon rocks reclin'd,
Wave high, and murmer to the hollow wind;
The wand'ring streams, that shine between the hills;
The grots, that echo to the tinkling rills;
The dying gales, that, pant upon the trees
The lakes, that quiver to the curling bree
No more these scenes my meditation aid,
Or lull to rest the visionary maid:
But o'er the twilight groves and dusky caves,
Long-sounding aisles and intermingled graves,
Black melancholy sits, and round her throws
A death-like silence and a dread repose:
Her gloomy presence saddens all the scene.
Shades every flower, and darkens every green,
Deepens the murmur of the falling floods,
And breathes a browner horror on the woods.
Yet here for ever ever must I stay;
Sad proof how well a lover can obey!
Death, only death can break the lasting chain;
And here, e'en then, shall my cold dust remain;
Here all its frailties, all its flames resign;
And wait till 'tis no sin to mix with thine.
Ah, wretch! believed the spouse of God in vain,
Confess'd within the slave of love and man!

Assist me, Heaven! but whence arose that prayer?
Sprung it from piety or from despair?
Ev'n here, where frozen chastity retires,
Love finds an altar for forbidden fires.
I ought to grieve, but cannot what I ought
I mourn the lover, not lament the fault;
I view my crime, but kindle at the view;
Repent old pleasures, and solicit new;
Now turn'd to heaven, I weep my past offence
Now think of thee, and curse my innocence.
Of all affliction taught a lover yet,
'Tis sure the hardest science to forget!
How shall I lose the sin, yet keep the sense?
And love the offender, yet detest the offence?
How the dear object from the crime remove?
Or how distinguish penitence from love?
Unequal task! a passion to resign,
For hearts so touch'd, so pierced, so lost as mine.
Ere such a soul regains its peaceful state,
How often must it love, how often hate!
How often hope, despair, resent, regret,
Conceal, disdain,—do all things but forget!
But let Heaven seize it; all at once 'tis fired;
Not touch'd, but rapt; not waken'd, but inspired!
O, come! O, teach me nature to subdue,
Renounce my love, my life, myself—and you:
Fill my fond heart with God alone, for he
Alone can rival, can succeed to thee.
How happy is the blameless vestal's lot!
The world forgetting, by the world forgot:
Eternal sunshine of the spotless mind!
Each prayer accepted, and each wish resign'd;
Labour and rest, that equal periods keep;
'Obedient slumbers, that can wake and weep;'
Desires composed, affections ever even;
Tears that delight, and sighs that waft to heaven:
Grace shines around her with serenest beams,
And whispering angels prompt her golden dreams:
For her the unfading rose of Eden blooms,
And wings of seraphs shed divine perfumes;
For her the spouse prepares the bridal ring;
For her white virgins hymeneals sing;
To sounds of heavenly harps she dies away,
And melts in visions of eternal day.
Far other dreams my erring soul employ,
Far other raptures of unholy joy.
When, at the close of each sad, sorrowing day,
Fancy restores what vengeance snatch'd away,
Then conscience sleeps, and leaving nature free,
All my loose soul unbounded springs to thee.

O, cursed, dear horrors of all-conscious night!
How glowing guilt exalts the keen delight!
Provoking demons all restraint remove,
And stir within me every source of love.
I hear thee, view thee, gaze o'er all thy charms,
And round thy phantom glue my clasping arms.
I wake:—no more I hear, no more I view;
The phantom flies me, as unkind as you.
I call aloud; it hears not what I say:
I stretch my empty arms; it glides away.
To dream once more I close my willing eyes;
Ye soft illusions, dear deceits, arise!
Alas, no more! methinks we wandering go
Through dreary wastes, and weep each other's woe,
Where round some mouldering tower pale ivy creeps,
And low-brow'd rocks hang nodding o'er the deeps.
Sudden you mount, you beckon from the skies;
Clouds interpose, waves roar, and winds arise.
I shriek, start up, the same sad prospect find,
And wake to all the griefs I left behind.
For thee the fates, severely kind, ordain
A cool suspense from pleasure and from pain;
Thy life a long dead calm of fix'd repose;
No pulse that riots, and no blood that glows:
Still as the sea, ere winds were taught to blow,
Or moving spirit bade the waters flow;
Soft as the slumbers of a saint forgiven,
And mild as opening gleams of promised heaven.
Come, Abelard! for what hast thou to dread?
The torch of Venus burns not for the dead.
Nature stands check'd; religion disapproves;
Ev'n thou art cold—yet Eloisa loves.
Ah, hopeless, lasting flames! like those that burn
To light the dead, and warm the unfruitful urn.
What scenes appear where'er I turn my view!
The dear ideas, where I fly, pursue,
Rise in the grove, before the altar rise,
Stain all my soul, and wanton in my eyes.
I waste the matin lamp in sighs for thee;
Thy image steals between my God and me;
Thy voice I seem in every hymn to hear;
With every bead I drop too soft a tear.
When from the censer clouds of fragrance roll,
And swelling organs lift the rising soul,
One thought of thee puts all the pomp to flight;
Priest, tapers, temples, swim before my sight;
In seas of flame my plunging soul is drown'd,
While altars blaze, and angels tremble round.
While prostrate here in humble grief I lie,
Kind, virtuous drops just gathering in my eye;

While praying, trembling, in the dust I roll,
And dawning grace is opening on my soul;
Come, if thou dar'st, all charming as thou art!
Oppose thyself to Heaven; dispute my heart:
Come, with one glance of those deluding eyes
Blot out each bright idea of the skies;
Take back that grace, those sorrows, and those tears
Take back my fruitless penitence and prayers;
Snatch me, just mounting, from the bless'd abode;
Assist the fiends, and tear me from my God!
No, fly me, fly me, far as pole from pole;
Rise Alps between us, and whole oceans roll!
Ah, come not, write not, think not once of me;
Nor share one pang of all I felt for thee.
Thy oaths I quit, thy memory resign;
Forget renounce me, hate whate'er was mine.
Fair eyes, and tempting looks, which yet I view!
Long loved, adored ideas, all adieu!
O, grace serene! O, virtue heavenly fair!
Divine oblivion of low-thoughted care!
Fresh-blooming hope, gay daughter of the sky
And faith, our early immortality!
Enter, each mild, each amicable guest:
Receive, and wrap me in eternal rest!
  See in her cell sad Eloisa spread,
Propp'd on some tomb, a neighbour of the dead.
In each low wind methinks a spirit calls,
And more than echoes talk along the walls.
Here, as I watched the dying lamp around,
From yonder shrine, I heard a hollow sound.
'Come, sister, come;' it said, or seem'd to say;
'Thy place is here; sad sister, come away!
Once, like thyself, I trembled, wept, and pray'd;
Love's victim then, though now a sainted maid:
But all is calm in this eternal sleep;
Here grief forgets to groan, and love to weep;
E'en superstition loses every fear:
For God, not man, absolves our frailties here.'
  I come, I come! prepare your roseate bow'rs,
Celestial palms, and ever-blooming flow'rs.
Thither, where sinners may have rest I go,
Where flames refin'd in breasts seraphic glow.
Thou Abelard! the last sad office pay,
And smooth my passage to the realms of day:
See my lips tremble, and my eye-balls roll,
Suck my last breath, and catch my flying soul!
Ah, no—in sacred vestments may'st thou stand,
The hallow'd taper trembling in thy hand,
Present the cross before my lifted eye,
Teach me at once, and learn of me to die,

Ah then, thy once lov'd Eloisa see;
It will be then no crime to gaze on me;
See from my cheek the transient roses fly!
See the last sparkle languish in my eye!
'Till ev'ry motion, pulse, and breath be o'er;
And e'en my Abelard be lov'd no more.
Oh death, all-eloquent! you only prove
What dust we dote on, when 'tis man we love.
  Then too, when fate shall thy fair frame destroy,
(That cause of all my guilt, and all my joy,)
In trance ecstatic may thy pangs be drown'd,
Bright clouds descend, and angels watch thee round;
From op'ning skies may streaming glories shine,
And saints embrace thee with a love love like mine.
  May one kind grave unite each hapless name,
And graft my love immortal on thy fame!
Then, ages hence, when all my woes are o'er,
When this rebellious heart shall beat no more;
If ever chance two wandering lovers brings
To Paraclete's white walls and silver springs,
O'er the pale marble shall they join their heads,
And drink the falling tears each other sheds;
Then sadly say, with mutual pity moved,—
'O, may we never love as these have loved!'
From the full choir when loud hosannas rise,
And swell the pomp of dreadful sacrifice;—
Amid that scene, if some relenting eye
Glance on the stone where our cold relics lie,
Devotion's self shall steal a thought from Heav'n,
One human tear shall drop, and be forgiv'n.
  And sure if fate some future bard shall join,
In sad similitude of griefs to mine,
Condemn'd whole years in absence to deplore,
And image charms he must behold no more;
Such if there be, who loves so long, so well;
Let him our sad, our tender story tell!
The well-sung woes will soothe my pensive ghost;
He best can paint them who shall feel them most.

WINDSOR FOREST.

TO THE RIGHT HON. GEORGE LORD LANSDOWN.

THY forest, Windsor! and thy green retreats,
At once the Monarch's and the Muses' seats,
Invite my lays. Be present, sylvan maids!
Unlock your springs, and open all your shades,
Granville commands: your aid, O Muses! bring:
What Muse for Granville can refuse to sing?
The groves of Eden, vanish'd now so long,
Live in description, and look green in song:
These, were my breast inspir'd with equal flame,
Like them in beauty, should be like in fame.
Here hills and vales, the woodland and the plain,
Here earth and water seem to strive again;
Not chaos-like, together crush'd and bruis'd,
But, as the world, harmoniously confus'd;
Where order in variety we see,
And where, though all things differ, all agree.
Here waving groves a chequer'd scene display,
And part admit and part exclude the day;
As some coy nymph her lover's warm address
Nor quite indulges, nor can quite repress.
There interspers'd in lawns and op'ning glades,
Thin trees arise that shun each other's shades.
Here in full light the russet plains extend;
There, wrapt in clouds, the bluish hills ascend.
E'en the wild heath displays her purple dyes,
And 'midst the desert fruitful fields arise,
That, crown'd with tufted trees and springing corn,
Like verdant isles, the sable waste adorn.
Let India boast her plants, nor envy we
The weeping amber or the balmy tree,
While by our oaks the precious loads are borne,
And realms commanded which those trees adorn,
Not proud Olympus yields a nobler sight,
Tho' gods assembled grace his towering height,
Than what more humble mountain offer here,
Where, in their blessings all those gods appear.

See Pan with flocks, with fruits Pomona crown'd
Here blushing Flora paints th' enamell'd ground
Here Ceres' gifts in waving prospect stand,
And nodding tempt the joyful reaper's hand;
Rich industry sits smiling on the plains,
And peace and plenty tell, a Stuart reigns.
Not thus the land appear'd in ages past,
A dreary desert and a gloomy waste,
To savage beasts and savage laws a prey,
And kings more furious and severe than they
Who claim'd the skies, dispeopled air and floods;
The lonely lords of empty wilds and woods:
Cities laid waste, they storm'd the dens and caves,
(For wiser brutes were backward to be slaves.)
What could be free when lawless beasts obey'd,
And e'en the elements a tyrant sway'd?
In vain kind seasons swell'd the teeming grain,
Soft show'rs distill'd and suns grew warm in vain
The swain with tears his frustrate labour yields,
And famish'd dies amidst his ripen'd fields.
What wonder then a beast or subject slain
Where equal crimes in a despotic reign?
Both doom'd alike, for sportive tyrants bled;
But while the subject starv'd the beast was fed.
Proud Nimrod first the bloody chase began,
A mighty hunter, and his prey was man;
Our haugty Norman boasts that barb'rous name,
And makes his trembling slaves the royal game.
The fields are ravish'd from th' industrous swains,
From men their cities, and from gods their fanes:
The levell'd towns with weeds lay cover'd o'er,
The hollow winds thro' naked temples roar;
Round broken columns clasping ivy twin'd;
O'er heaps of ruin stalk'd the stately hind;
The fox obscene to gaping tombs retires,
And savage howlings fill the sacred quires.
Aw'd by his nobles, by his commons curs'd,
Th' oppressor rul'd tyranic where he durst,
Stretch'd o'er the poor and church his iron rod,
And serv'd alike his vassals and his God.
Whom e'en the Saxon spar'd, and bloody Dane,
The wanton victims of his sport remain.
But see the man, who spacious regions gave
A waste for beasts, himself denied a grave!
Stretch'd on the lawn his second hope survey,
At once the chaser, and at once the prey:
Lo Rufus, tugging at the deadly dart,
Bleeds in the forest like a wounded hart.
Succeeding monarchs heard the subjects' cries,
Nor saw displeas'd the peaceful cottage rise:

Then gath'ring flocks on unknown mountains fed,
O'er sandy wilds were yellow harvests spread;
The forest wonder'd at th' unusal grain,
And secret transports touch'd the conscious swain.
Fair Liberty, Brittania's goddess, rears
Her cheerful head, and leads the golden years.
Ye vig'rous swains! while youth ferments your blood
And purer spirits swell the sprightly flood,
Now range the hills, the gameful woods beset,
Wind the shrill horn, or spread the waving net.
When milder autumn summer's heat succeeds,
And in the new-shorn fie d the partridge feeds;
Before his lord the ready spaniel bounds;
Panting with hope, he tries the furrow'd grounds;
But when the tainted gales the game betray.
Couch'd close he lies, and meditates the prey;
Secure they trust th' unfaithful field beset,
'Til' hov'ring o'er them sweeps the swelling net.
Thus (if small things we may with great compare)
When Albion sends her eager sons to war,
Some thoughtless town, with ease and plenty blest
Near, and more near, the closing lines invest;
Sudden they seize th' amaz'd defenceless prize,
And high in air Britannia's standard flies.
See! from the brake the whirring pheasant springs,
And mounts exulting on triumphant wings:
Short is his joy; he feels the fiery wound,
Flutters in blood, and panting beats the ground.
Ah! what avail his glossy, varying dyes,
His purple crest, and scarlet-circled eyes,
The vivid green his shining plumes unfold,
His painted wings, and breast that flames with gold?
Nor yet, when moist Arcturus clouds the sky,
The woods and fields their pleasing toils deny.
To plains with well-breath'd beagles we repair,
And trace the mazes of the circling hare:
(Beasts, urg'd by us, their fellow beasts pursue,
And learn of man each other to undo.)
With slaught'ring guns th' unweared fowler roves,
When frosts have whiten'd all the naked groves,
Where doves in flocks the leafless trees o'ershade,
And lonely woodcocks haunt the wat'ry glade.
He lifts the tube, and levels with his eye;
Straight a short thunder breaks the frozen sky
Oft, as in airy rings they skim the heath,
The clam'rous lapwings feel the leaden death:
Oft, as the mounting larks their notes prepare,
They fall, and leave their little lives in air.
In genial spring, beneath the quiv'ring shade,
Where cooling vapours breath along the mead,

The patient fisher takes his silent stand
Intent, his angle trembling in his hand;
With looks unmov'd, he hopes the scaly breed,
And eyes the dancing cork and bending reed.
Our plenteous streams a various race supply;
The bright-ey'd perch, with fins of Tyrian dye;
The silver eel, in shining volumes roll'd;
The yellow carp, in scales bedropp'd with gold;
Swift trouts, diversified with crimson stains;
And pikes, the tyrants of the wat'ry plains.
Now Cancer glows with Phœbus' fiery car,
The youth rush eager to the sylvan war,
Swarm o'er the lawns, the forest walks surround,
Rouse the fleet hart, and cheer th' op'ning hound.
Th' impatient courser pants in ev'ry vein,
And, pawing, seems to beat the distant plain:
Hills, vales, and floods, appear already cross'd,
And ere he starts a thousand steps are lost.
See the bold youth strain up the threat'ning steep.
Rush through the thickets, down the valleys sweep,
Hang o'er the coursers' heads with eager speed,
And earth rolls back beneath the flying steed.
Let old Arcadia boast her ample plain,
The immortal huntress, and her virgin train;
Nor envy, Windsor! since thy shades have seen
As bright a goddess, and as chaste a queen;
Whose care, like her's, protects the sylvan reign,
The earth's far light, and empress of the main
Here too, 'tis sung, of old, Diana stray'd,
And Cynthus' top forsook for Windsor shade;
Here was she seen o'er airy wastes to rove,
Seek the clear spring, or haunt the pathless grove:
Here, arm'd with silver bows, in early dawn,
Her buskin'd virgins trac'd the dewy lawn.
Above the rest a rural nymph was fam'd,
Thy offspring, Thames! the fair Lodona nam'd;
(Lodona's fate, in long oblivion cast,
The Muse shall sing, and what she sings shall last.)
Scarce could the goddess from her nymph be known,
But by the crescent and the golden zone.
She scorn'd the praise of beauty, and the care;
A belt her waist, a fillet binds her hair;
A painted quiver on her shoulder sounds,
And with her dart the flying deer she wounds.
It chanc'd, as eager of the chase, the maid
Beyond the forest's verdant limits stray'd,
Pan saw and lov'd, and, burning with desire,
Pursu'd her flight; her flight increas'd his fire.
Not half so swift the trembling doves can fly
When the fierce eagle cleaves the liquid sky,

Not half so swiftly the fierce eagle moves
When thro' the clouds he drives the trembling doves,
As from the god she flew with furious pace,
Or as the god, more furious, urg'd the chase.
Now fainting, sinking, pale, thy nymph appears;
Now close behind his sounding steps she hears;
And now his shadow reach'd her as she run,
His shadow, lengthen'd by the setting sun;
And now his shorter breath, with sultry air,
Pants on her neck, and fans her parting hair
In vain on father Thames she calls for aid,
Nor could Diana help her injur'd maid.
Faint, breathless, thus she pray'd, nor pray'd in vain;
'Ah, Cynthia! ah—tho' banish'd from thy train,
Let me, O let me, to the shades repair,
My native shades—there weep, and murmur there.'
She said, and melting as in tears she lay,
In a soft silver stream dissolv'd away.
The silver stream her virgin coldness keeps,
For ever murmurs, and for ever weeps:
Still bears the name the hapless virgin bore,
And bathes the forest where she rang'd before.
In her chaste current oft the goddess laves,
And with celestial tears augments the waves.
Oft in her glass the musing shepherd spies
The headlong mountains and the downward skies;
The wat'ry landscape of the pendant woods,
And absent trees that tremble in the floods:
In the clear azure gleam the flocks are seen,
And floating forests paint the waves with green.
Thro' the fair scene roll slow the ling'ring streams,
Then foaming pour along, and rush into the Thames.
Thou, too, great father of the British floods!
With joyful pride survey'st our lofty woods;
Where tow'ring oaks their growing honours rear,
And future navies on thy shores appear.
Not Neptune's self from all his streams receives
A wealthier tribute than to thine he gives.
No seas so rich, so gay no banks appear,
No lake so gentle, and no spring so clear.
Nor Po so swells the fabling poets lays,
While led along the skies his current strays,
As thine, which visits Windsor's fam'd abodes,
To grace the mansion of our earthly gods;
Nor all his stars above a lustre show
Like the bright beauties on thy banks below;
Where Jove, subdu'd by mortal passions still,
Might change Olympus for a nobler hill.
Happy the man whom this bright court approves,
His sov'reign favours, and his country loves:

Happy next him, who to these shades retires,
Whom nature charms, and whom the Muse inspires;
Whom humbler joys of home-felt quiet please,
Successive study, exercise and ease.
He gathers health from herbs the forest yields,
And of their fragrant physic spoils the fields;
With chemic art exalts the min'ral pow'rs,
And draws the aromatic souls of flow'rs:
Now marks the course of rolling orbs on high;
O'er figur'd worlds now travels with his eye;
Of ancient writ unlocks the learned store,
Consults the dead, and lives pasts ages o'er:
Or wand'ring thoughtful in the silent wood,
Attends the duties of the wise and good,
T' observe a mean, be to himself a friend,
To follow Nature, and regard his end;
Or looks on Heav'n with more than mortal eyes,
Bids his free soul expatiate in the skies,
Amid her kindred stars familiar roam,
Survey the region, and confess her home!
Such was the life great Scipio once admir'd.
Thus Atticus, and Trumball thus retir'd.
  Ye sacred Nine! that all my soul posses,
Whose raptures fire me, and whose visions bless,
Bear me, oh bear me to sequester'd scenes,
The bow'ry mazes, aud surrounding greens;
To Thames's banks, which fragrant breezes fill,
Or where ye Muses sport on Cooper's Hill.
(On Cooper's Hill eternal wreaths shall grow,
While lasts the mountain, or while Thames shall flow.)
I seem through consecrated walks to rove,
I hear soft music die along the grove:
Led by the sound, I roam from shade to shade,
By godlike poets venerable made:
Here his first lays majestic Denham sung;
There the last numbers flow'd from Cowley's tongue.
O early lost! what tears the river shed,
When the sad pomp along his banks was led!
His drooping swans on ev'ry note expire,
And on his willows hung each muse's lyre.
  Since Fate relentless stopp'd their heav'nly voice,
No more the forests ring, or groves rejoice:
Who now shall charm the shades where Cowley strung
His living harp, and lofty Denham sung?
But hark! the groves rejoice, the forest rings!
Are these reviv'd? or is it Granville sings?
'Tis yours, my Lord, to bless our soft retreats,
And call the Muses to their ancient seats;
To paint anew the flow'ry sylvan scenes,
To crown the forests with immortal greens;

Make Windsor-hills in lofty numbers rise,
And lift her turrets nearer to the skies;
To sing those honours you deserve to wear,
And add new lustre to her silver star.
  Here noble Surrey felt the sacred rage;
Surrey, the Granville of a former age:
Matchless his pen, victorious was his lance,
Bold in the lists, and graceful in the dance:
In the same shades the Cupids tun'd his lyre,
To the same notes of love and soft desire:
Fair Geraldine, bright object of his vow,
Then filled the groves, as heavenly Mira now.
  Oh wouldst thou sing what heroes Windsor bore,
What kings first breath'd upon her winding shore,
Or raise old warriors, whose ador'd remains
In weeping vaults her hallow'd earth contains!
With Edward's acts adorn the shining page,
Stretch his long triumphs down through ev'ry age,
Draw monarchs chain'd, and Cressy's glorious field,
The lilies blazing on the regal shield:
Then from her roofs when Verrio's colours fall,
And leave inanimate the naked wall,
Still in thy song should vanquish'd France appear,
And bleed for ever under Britain's spear.
  Let softer strains ill-fated Henry mourn,
And palms eternal flourish round his urn.
Here o'er the martyr king the marble weeps,
And, fast beside him, once fear'd Edward sleeps·
Whom not th' extended Albion could contain,
From old Belerium to the northern main.
The grave unites; where e'en the great find rest,
And blended lie th' oppressor and th' oppress'd!
  Make sacred Charles's tomb for ever known;
(Obscure the place, and uninscrib'd the stone,)
Oh fact accurs'd! what tears has Albion shed!
Heav'ns! what new wounds! and how her old have bled!
She saw her sons with purple deaths expire,
Her sacred domes involved in rolling fire,
A dreadful series of intestine wars,
Inglorious triumphs, and dishonest scars,
At length great Anna said, 'Let discord cease!'
She said; the world obey'd, and all was peace!
  In that blest moment from his oozy bed
Old father Thames advanc'd his reverend head;
His tresses dropp'd with dews, and o'er the stream
His shining horns diffused a golden gleam:
Grav'd on his urn appear'd the moon, that guides
His swelling waters, and alternate tides;
The figur'd streams in waves of silver roll'd,
And on her banks Augusta rose in gold.

Around his throne the sea-born brothers stood,
Who swell with tributary urns his flood:
First the fam'd authors of his ancient name,
The winding Isis, and the fruitful Thame:
The Kennett swift, for silver eels renown'd;
The Loddon slow, with verdant alders crown'd;
Cole, whose dark streams his flow'ry islands lave;
And chalky Wey, that rolls a milky wave:
The blue transparent Vandalis appears;
The gulphy Lee his sedgy tresses rears;
And sullen Mole, that hides his diving flood;
And silent Darent, stain'd with Danish blood.
High in the midst, upon his urn reclin'd
(His sea-green mantle waving with the wind,)
The god appear'd; he turn'd his azure eyes
Where Windsor domes and pompous turrets rise;
Then bow'd and spoke; the winds forget to roar
And the hush'd waves glide softly to the shore.
Hail, sacred Peace! hail, long expected days,
That Thames's glory to the stars shall raise!
Though Tyber's streams immortal Rome behold,
Though foaming Hermus swells with tides of gold;
From Heav'n itself though sevenfold Nilus flows,
And harvest on a hundred realms bestows;
These now no more shall be the Muses' themes,
Lost in my fame, as in the sea their streams.
Let Volga's banks with iron squadrons shine,
And groves of lances glitter on the Rhine.
Let barb'rous Ganges arm a servile train,
Be mine the blessings of a peaceful reign.
No more my sons shall dye with British blood
Red Iber's sands, or Ister's foaming flood:
Safe on my shore each unmolested swain
Shall tend the flocks, or reap the bearded grain;
The shady empire shall retain no trace
Of war or blood, but in the sylvan chace;
The trumpet sleep, while cheerful horns are blown,
And arms employ'd on birds and beast alone.
Behold th' ascending villas on my side
Project long shadows o'er the crystal tide;
Behold! Augusta's glittering spires increase,
And temples rise, the beauteous works of peace.
I see, I see, where two fair cities bend
Their ample bow, a new Whitehall ascend!
There mighty nations shall inquire their doom,
The world's great oracle in times to come;
There kings shall sue, and supplaint states be seen
Once more to bend before a British Queen.
Thy trees, fair Windsor! now shall leave their woods,
And half thy forests rush into the floods,

Bear Britain's thunder, and her cross display
To the bright regions of the rising day;
Tempt icy seas, where scarce the waters roll,
Where clearer flames glow round the frozen pole:
Or under southern skies exalt their sails,
Led by new stars, and borne by spicy gales!
For me the balm shall bleed, and ambar flow,
The coral redden, and the ruby glow,
The pearly shell its lucid globe unfold,
And Phœbus warm the rip'ning ore to gold.
The time shall come, when, free as seas or wind,
Unbounded Thames shall flow for all mankind,
Whole nations enter with each swelling tide,
And seas but join the regions they divide;
Earth's distant ends our glory shall behold,
And the new world launch forth to seek the old.
Then ships of uncouth form shall stem the tide,
And feather'd people crowd my wealthy side,
And naked youths and painted chiefs admire
Our speech, our colour, and our strange attire!
Oh stretch thy reign, fair peace! from shore to shore,
Till conquest cease, and slav'ry be no more;
Till the freed Indians in their native groves
Reap their own fruits, and woo their sable loves;
Peru once more a race of kings behold,
And other Mexicos be roof'd with gold.
Exil'd by thee, from earth to deepest hell,
In brazen bonds, shall barb'rous discord dwell:
Gigantic pride, pale terror, gloomy care,
And mad ambition, shall attend her there:
There purple vengeance, bath d in gore, retires,
Her weapons blunted, and extinct her fires:
There hateful envy her own snakes shall feel,
And persecution mourn her broken wheel:
There faction roar, rebelion bite her chain,
And gasping furies thirst for blood in vain.
 Here cease thy flight, nor with unhallow'd lays
Touch the fair fame of Albion's golden days:
The thoughts of gods let Granville's verse recite,
And bring the scenes of op'ning fate to light.
My humble muse, in unambitious strains,
Paints the green forests and the flow'ry plains,
Where Peace descending bids her olives spring,
And scatters blessings from her dove like wing.
E'en I more sweetly pass my careless days,
Pleased in the silent shade with empty praise;
Enough for me, that to the listening swains
First in these fields I sang the sylvan strains.

THE DUNCIAD.

TO DR. JONATHAN SWIFT.

BY AUTHORITY.

By virtue of the Authority in us vested by the act for subjecting poets to the power of a licence, we have revised this piece; where, finding the style and appellation of King to have been given to a certain pretender, pseudo-poet, or phantom, of the name of Tibbald; and apprehending the same may be deemed in some sort a reflection on majesty, or at least an insult on that legal authority which has bestowed on another person the crown of poesy: We have ordered the said pretender, pseudo-poet, or phantom, utterly to vanish and evaporate out of this work; and to declare the said throne of poesy from henceforth to be abdicated and vacant, unless duly and lawfully supplied by the Laureate himself. And it is hereby enacted, that no other person do presume to fill the same.

BY THE AUTHOR.

A DECLARATION.

Whereas certain haberdashers of points and particles, being instigated by the spirit of pride, and assuming to themselves the name of critics and restorers, have taken upon them to adulterate the common and current sense of our glorious ancestors, poets of this realm, by clipping, coining, defacing the images, mixing their own base alloy, or otherwise falsifying the same; which they publish, utter, and vend as genuine; the said haberdashers having no right thereto, as neither heirs, executors, administrators, assigns, or in any sort related to such poets, to all or any of them. Now we, having carefully revised this our Dunciad, beginning with the words 'The Mighty Mother,' and ending with the words 'buries all,' containing the entire sum of one thousand seven hundred and fifty-four verses, declare every word, figure, point and comma, of this impression to be authentic; and do therefore strictly enjoin and forbid any person or persons whatsoever, to erase, reverse, put between hooks, or by any other means, directly or indirectly, change or mangle any of them. And we do hereby earnestly exhort all our brethern to follow this our example, which we heartily wish our great predecessors had heretofore set, as a remedy and prevention of all such abuses; provided always, that nothing in this declaration shall be construed to limit the lawful and undoubted right of every subject of this realm to judge, censure, or condemn, in the whole, or in part, any poem or poet whatsoever.

Given under our hand at London, this third day of January, in the year of our Lord one thousand seven hundred and thirty-two.

Declarat' cor' me,
JOHN BARBER, **Mayor.**

THE DUNCIAD

TO DR. JONATHAN SWIFT.

BOOK I.

THE ARGUMENT.

The Proposition, the Invocation, and the Inscription. Then the original of the great Empire of Dulness, and cause of the continuance thereof. The College of the Goddess in the city, with her private academy for poets in particular; the governors of it, and the four cardinal virtues. Then the poem hastes into the midst of things, presenting her, on the evening of a Lord Mayor's day, revolving the long succession of her sons, and the glories past and to come. She fixes her eyes on Bayes, to be the instrument of that great event which is the subject of the poem. He is described pensive among his books, giving up the cause, and apprehending the period of her empire. After debating whether to betake himself to the church, or to gaming, or to party-writing, he raises an altar of proper books, and (making first his solemn prayer and declaration) purposes thereon to sacrifice all his unsuccessful writings. As the pile is kindled, the Goddess, beholding the flame from her seat, flies and puts it out, by casting upon it the poem of Thule. She forthwith reveals herself to him, transports him to her temple, unfolds her arts, and initiates him into her mysteries; then announcing the death of Eusden the Poet Laureate, anoints him, carries him to court, and proclaims him successor.

The mighty mother, and her son, who brings
The Smithfield muses to the ear of kings,
I sing. Say you, her instruments, the great!
Called to this work by Dulness, Jove, and Fate;
You by whose care, in vain decried and curs'd,
Still Dunce the second reigns like Dunce the first;
Say how the goddess bade Britannia sleep,
And poured her spirit o'er the land and deep.
  In eldest time, ere mortals writ or read,
Ere Pallas issued from the Thunderer's head,
Dulness o'er all possessed her ancient right,
Daughter of Chaos and eternal Night:
Fate in their dotage this fair idiot gave,
Gross as her sire, and as her mother grave;

Laborious, heavy, busy, bold, and blind,
She ruled, in native anarchy, the mind.
Still her old empire to restore she tries,
For, born a goddess, Dulness never dies.
O thou! whatever title please thine ear,
Dean, Drapier, Bickerstaff, or Gulliver!
Whet er thou choose Cervantes' serious air,
Or laugh and shake in Rabelais' easy chair,
Or praise the court, or magnify mankind,
Or thy grieved country's copper chains unbind;
From thy Bœotia though her power retires,
Mourn not, my Swift! at ought our realm acquires.
Here pleased behold her mighty wings outspread
To hatch a new Saturnian age of lead.
Close to those walls where Folly holds her throne,
And laughs to think Monroe would take her down,
Where o'er the gates, by his famed father's hand
Great Cibber's brazen, brainless brothers stand,
One cell there is, concealed from vulgar eye,
The cave of poverty and poetry:
Keen hollow winds howl through the black recess,
Emblem of music caused by emptiness:
Hence bards, like Proteus long in vain tied down,
Escape in monsters, and amaze the town;
Hence miscellanies spring, the weekly boast
Of Curl's chaste press, and Lintot's rubric post:
Hence hymning Tyburn's elegiac lines;
Hence journals, medleys, Merc'ries, magazines:
Sepulchral lies, our holy walls to grace,
And New-year odes, and all the Grub-street race.
In clouded majesty here Dulness shone;
Four guardian virtues, round, support her throne:
Fierce champion Fortitude, that knows no fears
Of hisses, blows, or want or loss of ears:
Calm Temperance, whose blessings those partake
Who hunger and who thirst for scribbling sake;
Prudence, whose glass presents the approaching jail
Poetic Justice, with her lifted scale,
Where, in nice balance, truth and gold she weighs,
And solid pudding against empty praise.
Here she beholds the chaos dark and deep,
Where nameless somethings in their causes sleep,
'Till genial Jacob, on a warm third day,
Call forth each mass, a poem or a play:
How hints, like spawn, scarce quick in embryo lie,
How new-born nonsense first is taught to cry,
Maggots half-formed in rhyme exactly meet,
And learn to crawl upon poetic feet.
Here one poor word an hundred clenches makes,
And ductile Dulness new meanders takes:

There motley images her fancy strike,
Figures ill-paired, and similies unlike.
She sees a mob of metaphors advance,
Pleased with the madness of the mazy dance;
How tragedy and comedy embrace;
How farce and epic get a jumbled race;
How Time himself stands still at her command,
Realms shift their place, and ocean turns to land
Here gay description Egypt glads with showers,
Or gives to Zembla fruits, to Barca flowers;
Glittering with ice here hoary hills are seen,
There painted vallies of eternal green;
In cold December fragrant chaplets blow,
And heavy harvests nod beneath the snow.
All these, and more, the cloud-compelling queen
Beholds through fogs that magnify the scene.
She, tinsel'd o'er in robes of varying hues,
With self-applause her wild creation views;
Sees momentary monsters rise and fall,
And with her own fools-colours gilds them all
'Twas on the day when T***d rich and grave,
Like Cimon, triumph'd both on land and wave:
Pomps without guilt, of bloodless swords and maces,
Glad chains, warm furs, broad banners, and broad faces.
Now night descending, the proud scene was o'er,
But liv'd in Settle's numbers one day more.
Now mayors and shrieves all hush'd and satiate lay,
Yet eat, in dreams, the custard of the day;
While pensive poets painful vigils keep,
Sleepless themselves to give their readers sleep.
Much to the mindful queen the feast recalls
What city swans once sung within the walls;
Much she revolves their arts, their ancient praise,
And sure succesion down from Heywood's days.
She saw with joy the line immortal run,
Each sire impress'd and glaring in his son:
So watchful Bruin forms, with plastic care
Each growing lump, and brings it to a bear.
She saw old Pryn in restless Daniel shine,
And Eusden eke out Blackmore's endless line;
She saw slow Philips creep like Tate's poor page,
And all the mighty mad in Dennis rage.
In each she marks her image full express'd,
But chief in Bayes's monster-breeding breast;
Bayes, formed by Nature stage and town to bless,
And act and be a coxcomb with success.
Dulnees with transport eyes the lively dunce,
Remembering she herself was pertness once.
Now (shame to fortune!) an ill run at play
Blank'd his bold visage, and a thin third day:

Swearing and supperless the hero sate,
Blasphemed his gods, the dice, and damned his fate;
Then gnawed his pen, then dashed it on the ground,
Sinking from thought to thought a vast profound!
Plunged for his sense, but found no bottom there
Yet wrote and floundered on in mere despair
Round him much embryo, much abortion lay
Much future ode, and abdicated play;
Nonsense precipitate, like running lead,
Then slipp'd through cracks and ziz-zags of the head;
All that on folly frenzy could beget,
Fruits of dull heat, and sooterkins of wit.
Next o'er his books his eyes began to roll,
In pleasing memory of all he stole;
How here he sipp'd, how there he plundered snug,
And sucked all o'er like an industrious bug.
Here lay poor Fletcher's half-eat scenes, and here
The frippery of crucified Moliere;
There hapless Shakspeare, yet of Tibbald sore,
Wished he had blotted for himself before.
The rest on outside merit but presume,
Or serve, like other fools, to fill a room;
Such with their shelves as due proportion hold,
Or their fond parents dressed in red and gold;
Or where the pictures for the page atone,
And Quarles is saved by beauties not his own.
Here swells the shelf with Ogilby the great;
There, stamped with arms, Newcastle shines complete.
Here all his suffering brotherhood retire,
And 'scape the martyrdom of jakes and fire:
A Gothic library! of Greece and Rome
Well purged, and worthy Settle, Banks, and Broome.
  But, high above, more solid learning shone,
The classics of an age that heard of none:
There Caxton slept, with Wynkyn at his side,
One clasped in wood, and one in strong cow-hide;
There, saved by spice, like mummies many a year,
Dry bodies of divinity appear
De Lyra there a dreadful front extends,
And here the groaning shelves Philemon bends.
  Of these twelve volume, twelve of amplest size,
Redeemed from tapers and defrauded pies,
Inspired he seizes: these an altar raise;
An hecatomb of pure unsullied lays
That altar crowns; a folio common-place
Founds the whole pile, of all his works the base:
Quartos, octavos, shape the lessening pyre,
A twisted birth-day ode completes the spire.
  Then he, great tamer of all human art!
First in my care, and ever at my heart

Dulness! whose good old cause I yet defend,
With whom my muse began, with whom shall end,
E'er since Sir Fopling's periwig was praise,
To the last honours of the butt and bays:
Oh thou! of business the directing soul!
To this our head, like bias to the bowl,
Which, as more ponderous, made its aim more true
Obliquely waddling to the mark in view:
Or! ever gracious to perplexed mankind,
Still spread a healing mist before the mind;
And, lest we err by wit's wild dancing light,
Secure us kindly in our native night.
Or, if to wit a coxcomb make pretence,
Guard the sure barrier between that and sense;
Or quite unravel all the reasoning thread,
And hang some curious cobweb in its stead!
As, forced from wind-guns, lead itself can fly,
And ponderous slugs cut swiftly through the sky;
As clocks to weight their nimble motions owe,
The wheels above urged by the load below;
Me Emptiness and Dulness could inspire,
And were my elasticity and fire.
Some demon stole my pen (forgive the offence)
And once betrayed me into common sense,
Else all my prose and verse were much the same;
This prose on stilts, that poetry fallen lame.
Did on the stage my fops appear confined?
My life gave ampler lessons to mankind.
Did the dead letter unsuccessful prove?
The brisk example never failed to move.
Yet sure, had Heaven decreed to save the state,
Heaven had decreed these works a longer date.
Could Troy be saved by any single hand,
This gray-goose weapon must have made her stand.
What can I now! my Fletcher cast aside,
Take up the Bible, once my better guide?
Or tread the path by venturous heroes trod;
This box my thunder, this right hand my God?
Or, chaired at White's, amidst the doctors sit,
Teach oaths to gamesters, and to nobles wit?
Or bidst thou rather party to embrace?
(A friend to party thou, and all her race;
'Tis the same rope at different ends they twist;
To Dulness Ridpath is as dear as Mist.)
Shall I, like Curtius, desperate in my zeal,
O'er head and ears plunge for the commonweal?
Or rob Rome's ancient geese of all their glories,
And cackling save the monarchy of Tories?
Hold—to the minister I more incline;
To serve his cause, O queen! is serving thine.

And see! thy very Gazetters give o'er;
E'en Ralph repents, and Henley writes no more.
What then remains? Ourself Still, still remain,
Cibberian forehead, and Cibberian brain.
This brazen brightness, to the 'squire so dear;
This polished hardness, that reflects the peer;
This arch absurd, that wit and fool delights;
This mess, tossed up of Hockley-hole and White's;
Where dukes and butchers join to wreathe my crown;
At once the bear and fiddle of the town.
O born in sin, and forth in folly brought!
Works damned, or to be damned! (your fathers's fault)
Go, purified by flames, ascend the sky,
My better and more Christian progeny!
Unstained, untouched, and yet in maiden sheets,
While all your smutty sisters walk the streets.
Ye shall not beg, like gratis-given Bland,
Sent with a pass, and vagrant through the land;
Nor sail with Ward to ape-and-monkey climes,
Where vile Mundungus trucks for viler rhymes:
Not, sulphur-tipp'd, emblaze an ale-house fire!
Nor wrap up oranges to pelt your sire!
O! pass more innocent, in infant state,
To the mild limbo of our father Tate:
Or, peaceably forget, at once be bless'd
In Shadwell's bosom with eternal rest!
Soon to that mass of nonsense to return,
Where things destroyed are swept to things unborn.
With that, a tear (portentous sign of grace!)
Stole from the master of the sevenfold face;
And thrice he lifted high the birth-day brand,
And thrice he dropp'd it from his quivering hand;
Then lights the structure with averted eyes;
The rolling smoke involves the sacrifice.
The opening clouds disclose each work by turns,
Now flames the Cid, and now Perolla burns;
Great Cæsar roars and hisses in the fires:
King John in silence modestly expires;
No merit now the dear Nonjuror claims,
Moliere's old stubble in a moment flames.
Tears gushed again, as from pale Priam's eyes,
When the last blaze sent Il.on to the skies.
Roused by the light, old Dulness heaved the head,
Then snatched a sheet of Thule from her bed;
Sudden she flies, and whelms it o'er the pyre;
Down sinks the flames, and with a hiss expire.
Her ample presence fills up all the place;
A veil of fogs dilates her awful face:
Great in her charms! as when on shrieves and mayors
She looks, and breathes herself into their airs.

She bids him wait her to her sacred dome:
Well pleased he entered, and confessed his home.
So spirits, ending their terrestial race,
Ascend, and recognise their native place.
This the great mother dearer held than all
The clubs of quidnuncs, or her own Guildhall:
Here stood her opium, here she nursed her owls,
And here she planned the imperial seat of fools.
Here to her chosen all her works she shows,
Prose swelled to verse, verse loitering into prose:
How random thoughts now meaning chance to find,
Now leave all memory of sense behind:
How prologues into prefaces decay,
And these to notes are frittered quite away:
How index-learning turns no student pale,
Yet holds the eel of science by the tail:
How, with less reading than makes felons 'scape,
Less human genius than God gives an ape,
Small thanks to France, and none to Rome or Greece,
A past, vamped, future, old revived, new piece,
'Twixt Platus, Fletcher, Shakespeare, and Corneille,
Can make a Cibber, Tibbald, or Ozell.
The goddess then o'er his anointed head,
With mystic words, the sacred opium shed.
And, lo! her bird (a monster of a fowl,
Something betwixt a heideggre and owl,)
Perched on his crown. 'All hail! and hail again.
My son! the promised land expects thy reign.
Know Eusden thirsts no more for sack or praise;
He sleeps among the dull of ancient days;
Safe where no critics damn, no duns molest,
Where wretched Withers, Ward, and Gildon rest.
And high-born Howard, more majestic sire,
With Fool of Quality complete the quire.
Thou, Cibber! thou his laurel shalt support;
Folly my son, has still a friend at court.
Lift up your gates, ye princes, see him come!
Sound, sound, ye viols, be the cat-call dumb!
Bring, bring the madding bay, the drunken vine;
The creeping, dirty, courtly ivy join.
And thou! his aid-de-camp, lead on my sons,
Light armed with points, antitheses and puns.
Let bawdry, Billingsgate, my daughters dear,
Support his front and oaths bring up the rear.
And under his, and under Archer's wing,
Gaming and Grub-street skulk behind the king.
'O! when shall rise a monarch all our own,
And I, a nursing mother, rock the throne;
'Twixt prince and people close the curtain draw,
Shade him from light, and cover him from law

Fatten the courtier, starve the learned band,
And suckle armies, and dry-nurse the land:
'Till senates nod to lullabies divine,
And all be sleep, as at an ode of thine!'
  She ceased. Then swells the chapel-royal throat;
God save king Cibber! mounts in every note.
Familiar White's, God save king Colley! cries;
God save king Colley! Drury-lane replies:
To Needham's quick the voice triumphal rode,
But pious Needman dropp'd the name of God;
Back to the Devil the last ech .es roll,
And Coll! each butchers roars at Hockley-hole.
So when Jove's block descended from on high
(As sings thy great forefather Ogilby)
Loud thunder to its bottom shook the bog,
And the hoarse nation croak'd, 'God save king Log!'

BOOK II.

THE ARGUMENT

THE king being proclaimed, the solemnity is graced with public games and sports of various kinds; not instituted by the hero, as by Æneas in Virgil, but for greater honour by the goddess in person (in like manner as the games Pithia, Ishmia, &c. were anciently said to be ordained by the gods; and as Thetis herself appearing, according to Homer, Odyssey xxiv proposed the prizes in honour of her son Achilles). Hither flock the poets and critics, attended, as is but just, with their patrons and booksellers. The goddess is first pleased, for her disport, to propose games to the booksellers, and setteth up the phantom of a poet, which they contend to overtake. The races described, with their divers accidents. Next the game for a poetess. Then follow the exercises for the poets, of tickling, vociferating, diving: the first holds forth the arts and practices of dedicators, the second of disputants and fustian poets, the third of profound, dark, and dirty party-writers. Lastly, for the critics, the goddess proposes (with great propriety) an exercise, not of their parts, but their patience, in hearing the works of two voluminous authors, one in verse and the other in prose, deliberately read, without sleeping; the various effects of which, with the several degrees and manners of their operation, are here set forth, till the whole number, not of critics only, but of spectators, actors, and all present, fall fast asleep; which naturally and necessarily ends the games.

HIGH on a gorgeous seat, that far out-shone
Henley's gilt tub, or Fleckno's Irish throne,
Or that where on her Curlls the public pours,
All bounteous, fragrant grains and golden show'rs,
Great Cibber sat: the proud Parnassian sneer,
The conscious simper, and the jealous leer,
Mix on his look: all eyes direct their rays
On him, and crowds turn coxcombs as they gaze.
His peers shine round him with reflected grace,
New edge their dulness, and new bronze their face.
So from the sun's broad beam, in shallow urns,
Heaven's twinkling sparks draw light, and point their horns.
  Not with more glee, by hands pontific crown'd,
With scarlet hats wide waving circled round,
Rome in her Capitol saw Querno sit,
Thron'd on seven hills, the Antichrist of wit.
  And now the queen, to glad her sons, proclaims
By herald hawkers, high heroic games.
They summon all her race: an endless band
Pours forth, and leaves unpeopled half the land.

A motley mixture! in long wigs, in bags,
In silks, in crapes, in garters, and in rags,
From drawing-rooms, from colleges, from garrets,
On horse, on foot, in hacks, and gilded chariots:
All who true Dunces in her cause appear'd,
And all who knew those Dunces to reward.
Amid that area wide they took their stand,
Where the tall may-pole once o'erlook'd the Strand,
But now, so Anne and piety ordain,
A church collects the saints of Drury-lane.
With authors, stationers obey'd the call;
The field of glory is a field for all!
Glory and gain the industrous tribe provoke,
And gentle Dulness ever loves a joke.
A poet's form she placed before their eyes,
And bade the nimblest racer seize the prize:
No meagre, muse-rid mope, adust and thin,
In a dun night-gown of his own loose skin;
But such a bulk as no twelve bards could raise,
Twelve starveling bards of these degenerate days.
All as a partridge plump, full-fed and fair,
She form'd this image of well-bodied air;
With pert flat eyes she window'd well its head,
A brain of feathers, and a heart of lead;
And empty words she gave, and sounding strain,
But senseless, lifeless; idol void and vain!
Never was dash'd out, at one lucky hit,
A fool, so just a copy of a wit;
So like, that critics said, and courtiers swore,
A wit it was, and call'd the phantom More.
All gaze with ardour: some a poet's name.
Others a sword-knot and laced suit inflame:
But lofty Lintot in the circle rose,
'This prize is mine, who tempt it are my foes;
With me began this genius, and shall end.'
He spoke, and who with Lintot shall contend?
Fear held them mute. Alone untaught to fear,
Stood dauntless Curll: 'Behold that rival here!
The race by vigour, not by vaunts, is won;
So take the hindmost, Hell!' He said, and run.
Swift as a bard the bailiff leaves behind,
He left huge Lintot, and outstripp'd the wind.
As when a dab-chick waddles through the copse
On feet and wings, and flies, and wades, and hops;
So labouring on, with shoulders, hands, and head,
Wide as a windmill all his figure spread,
With arms expanded, Bernard rows his state,
And left-legg'd Jacob seems to emulate.
Full in the middle way there stood a lake,
Which Curll's Corinna chanc'd that morn to make:

Such was her wont, at early dawn to drop
Her evening cates before his neighbour's shop;
Here fortuned Curll to slide; loud shout the band;
And 'Bernard! Bernard!' rings through all the Strand.
Obscene with filth the miscreant lies bewray'd,
Fallen in the plash his wickedness had laid:
Then first, if poets aught of truth declare,
The caitiff vaticide conceived a prayer:—
'Hear, Jove! whose name my bards and I adore,
As much at least as any god's, or more;
And him and his, if more devotion warms,
Down with the Bible, up with the Pope's arms.'
A place there is betwixt earth, air, and seas,
Where from ambrosia, Jove retires for ease.
There in his seat, two spacious vents appear;
On this he sits, to that he leans his ear,
And hears the various vows of fond mankind;
Some beg an eastern, some a western wind:
All vain petitions, mounting to the sky,
With reams abundant this abode supply:
Amused he reads, and then returns the bills,
Sign'd with that ichor which from gods distills.
In office here fair Cloacina stands,
And ministers to Jove with purest hands.
Forth from the heap she pick'd her votary's prayer,
And placed it next him, a distinction rare!
Oft had the goddess heard her servant's call,
From her back grottos near the temple wall,
Listening delighted to the jest unclean
Of link-boys vile, and watermen obscene;
Where, as he fish'd her nether realms for wit,
She oft had favoured him, and favours yet.
Renewed by ordure's sympathetic force,
As oil'd with magic juices for the course,
Vigorous he rises; from the effluvia strong,
Imbibes new life, and scours and stinks along;
Repasses Lintot, vindicates the race,
Nor heeds the brown dishonours of his face.
And now the victor stretched his eager hand
Where the tall nothing stood, or seemed to stand;
A shapeless shade, it melted from his sight,
Like forms in clouds, or visions of the night.
To seize his papers, Curll, was next thy care;
His papers light, fly diverse, toss'd in air;
Songs, sonnets, epigrams, the winds uplift,
And whisk them back to Evans, Young, and Swift.
The embroidered suit at least he deem'd his prey,
That suit an unpaid tailor snatch'd away.
No rag, no scrap, of all the beau, or wit,
That once so fluttered, and that once so writ.

Heaven rings with laughter: of the laughter vain,
Dulness, good Queen, repeats the jest again.
Three wicked imps, of her own Grub-street choir,
She deck'd like Congreve, Addison, and Prior
Mears, Warner, Wilkins run: delusive thought!
Breval, Bond, Besaleel, the varlets caught.
Curll stretches after Gay, but Gay is gone;
He grasps an empty Joseph for a John:
So Proteus, hunted in a nobler shape,
Became, when seized, a puppy, or an ape.
To him the Goddess: 'Son! thy grief lay down,
And turn this whole illusion on the town.
As the sage dame, experienced in her trade,
By names of toasts retails each battered jade;
(Whence hapless Monsieur much complains at Paris
Of wrong from duchesses and Lady Maries;)
Be thine, my stationer! this magic gift;
Cook shall be Prior; and Concanen, Swift:
So shall each hostile name become our own,
And we, too, boast our Garth and Addison.'
With that she gave him (piteous of his case,
Yet smiling at his rueful length of face)
A shaggy tapestry, worthy to be spread
On Codrus' old or Dunton's modern bed.
Instructive work! whose wry-mouth'd portraiture
Display'd the fates her confessors endure.
Earless on high stood unbash'd De Foe,
And Tutchin flagrant from the scourge below.
There Ridpath, Roper, cudgelled might ye view,
The very worsted still looked black and blue.
Himself among the storied chiefs he spies,
As, from the blanket, high in air he flies,
'And oh!' he cried, 'what street, what lane but knows
Our purgings, pumpings, blanketings, and blows?
In every loom our labours shall be seen,
And the fresh vomit run for ever green!'
See in the circle next Eliza placed,
Two babes of love close-clinging to her waist;
Fair as before her works she stands confessed,
In flowers and pearls by bounteous Kirkall dressed.
The goddess then: "Who best can send on high
The salient spout, far-streaming to the sky,
His be yon Juno of majestic size,
With cow-like hudders, and with ox-like eyes.
This China jordan let the chief o'ercome
Replenish, not ingloriously, at home.'
Osborne and Curll accept the glorious strife;
(Though this his son dissuades, and that his wife.)
One on his manly confidence relies,
One on his vigour and superior size.

First Osborne leaned against his lettered post;
It rose and labour'd to a curve at most.
So Jove's bright bow displays its watery round,
(Sure sign that no spectator shall be drowned.)
A second effort brought but new disgrace,
The wild meander washed the artist's face;
Thus the small jet, which hasty hands unlock,
Spirts in the gardener's eyes who turns the cock.
Not so from shameless Curll; impetuous spread
The stream, and smoking flourish'd o'er his head
So (famed like thee for turbulence and horns)
Eridanus his humble fountain scorns;
Through half the heavens he pours the exalted urn
His rapid waters in their passage burn.
  Swift as it mounts, all follow with their eyes;
Still happy impudence obtains the prize.
Thou triumph'st, victor of the high-wrought day,
And the pleased dame, soft smiling, lead'st away.
Osborne, through perfect modesty o'ercome,
Crowned with the jordan, walks contented home,
  But now for authors nobler palms remain:
Room for my lord! three jockies in his train;
Six huntsmen with a shout precede his chair:
He grins, and looks broad nonsense with a stare.
His honour's meaning Dulness thus expressed:
'He wins this patron who can tickle best.'
  He chinks his purse, and takes his seat of state;
With ready quills the dedicators wait;
Now at his head the dexterous task commence,
And, instant, fancy feels the imputed sense;
Now gentle touches wanton o'er his face,
He struts Adonis, and affects grimace:
Rolli the feather to his ear conveys;
Then his nice taste directs our operas:
Bentley his mouth with classic flattery opes,
And the puffed orator bursts out in tropes.
But Welsted most the poet' healing balm
Strives to extract from his self-giving palm.
Unlucky Welsted! thy unfeeling master,
The more thou ticklest gripes his fist the faster.
  While thus each hand promotes the pleasing pain,
And quick sensations skip from vein to vein,
A youth unknown to Phœbus, in despair,
Puts his last refuge all in heaven and prayer.
What force have pious vows! The queen of love
Her sister sends her votress from above.
As taught by Venus, Paris learnt the art
To touch Achilles' only tender part;
Secure through her, the noble prize to carry,
He marches off, his grace's secretary.

'Now turn to different sports,' the goddess cries,
'And learn, my sons, the wond'rous power of noise,
To move, to raise, to ravish every heart.
With Shakspeare's nature, or with Johnson's art,
Let others aim; 'tis yours to shake the soul
With thunder rumbling from the mustard bowl;
With horns and trumpets now to madness swell,
Now sink in sorrows with a toiling bell!
Such happy arts attention can command
When fancy flags, and sense is at a stand.
Improve we these. Three cat-calls be the bribe
Of him, whose chattering shames the monkey tribe;
And his this drum, whose hoarse heroic bass
Drowns the loud clarion of the braying ass.'
Now thousand tongues are heard in one loud din;
The monkey-mimics rush discordant in;
'Twas chattering, grinning, mouthing, jabbering all,
And noise and Norton, brangling and Breval,
Dennis and dissonance, and captious art,
And snip-snap short, and interruption smart,
And demonstration thin, and theses thick,
And major, miner, and conclusion quick.
'Hold,' cried the queen, 'a cat-call each shall win;
Equal your merits! equal is your din!
But that this well-disputed game may end,
Sound forth, my brayers, and the welkin rend.'
As when the long-ear'd milky mothers wait
At some sick miser's triple-bolted gate,
For their defrauded, absent foals they make
A moan so loud, that all the guild awake;
Sore sighs Sir Gilbert, starting at the bray,
From dreams of millions, and three groats to pay:
So swells each wind-pipe; ass intones to ass,
Harmonic twang! of leather, horn, and brass;
Such as from labouring lungs the enthusiast blows,
High sound, attempered to the vocal nose;
Or such as bellow from the deep divine;
There Webster! pealed thy voice, and Whitefield! thine
But far o'er all sonorous Blackmore's strain,
Walls, steeples, skies, bray back to him again,
In Totenham-fields the brethren, with amaze,
Prick all their ears up, and forget to graze!
Long Chancery-lane retentive rolls the sound,
And courts to courts return it round and round;
Thames wafts it thence to Rufus' roaring hall,
And Hungerford re-echoes bawl for bawl.
All hail him victor in both gifts of song,
Who sings so loudly and who sings so long.

This labor past, by Bridewell all descend,
(As morning prayers and flagelation end)
To where Fleet-ditch, with disemboguing streams,
Rolls the large tribute of dead dogs to Thames,
The king of dykes! than whom no sluice of mud
With deeper sable blots the silver flood.
'Here strip, my children! here at once leap in,
Here prove who best can dash through thick and thin;
And who the most in love of dirt excel,
Or dark dexterity of groping well:
Who flings most filth, and wide pollutes around
The stream, be his the weekly journals bound;
A pig of lead to aim who dives the best;
A peck of coals a-piece shall glad the rest.'
In naked majesty Oldmixon stands,
And, Milo-like, surveys his arms and hands;
Then sighing, thus, 'And am I now threescore?
Ah, why, ye gods! should two and two make four?'
He said, and climbed a stranded lighter's height,
Shot to the black abyss, and plunged downright:
The senior's judgment all the crowd admire,
Who but to sink the deeper rose the higher.
Next Smedely dived; slow circles dimpled o'er
The quaking mud, that closed and oped no more.
All look, all sigh, and call on Smedly lost;
Smedly in vain resounds through all the coast.
Then essayed; scarce vanish'd out of sight,
He buoys up instant, and returns to light;
He bears no tokens of the sabler streams.
And mounts far off among the swans of Thames.
True to the bottom, see Concanen creep,
A cold, long-winded, native of the deep;
If perseverance gains the diver's prize,
Not everlasting Blackmore this denies;
No noise, no stir, no motion canst thou make,
The unconscious stream sleeps o'er thee like a lake
Next plunged a feeble but a desperate pack,
With each a sickly brother at his back:
Sons of a day! just buoyant on the flood,
Then numbered with the puppies in the mud.
Ask ye their names? I could as soon disclose
The names of these blind puppies as of those.
Fast by, like Niobe (her children gone)
Sits mother Osborne, stupified to stone!
And monumental brass this record bears,
'These are, ah no! these were, the Gazetteers!'
Not so bold Arnall; with a weight of skull
Furious he dives, percipitately dull.

Whirlpools and storms his circling arm invest,
With all the might of gravitation bless'd.
No crab more active in the dirty dance,
Downward to climb, and backward to advance;
He brings up half the bottom on his head,
And loudly claims the journals and the lead.
  The plunging prelate, and his ponderous grace,
With holy envy gave one layman place.
When lo! a burst of thunder shook the flood,
Slow rose a form in majesty of mud;
Shaking the horrors of his sable brows,
And each ferocious feature grim with ooze.
Greater he looks, and more than mortal stares!
Then thus the wonders of the deep declares.
  First he relates how, sinking to the chin,
Smit with his mien, the mud nymphs sucked him in;
How young Lutetia, softer than the down,
Nigrina black, and Merdamante brown,
Vied for his love in jetty bowers below,
As Hylas fair was ravished long ago.
Then sung, how shown him by the nut-brown maids,
A branch of Styx here rises from the shades,
That, tinctured as it runs with Lethe's streams,
And wafting vapours from the land of dreams,
(As under seas Alpheus' secret sluice
Bears Pisa's offerings to his Arethuse,)
Pours into Thames; and hence the mingled wave
Intoxicates the pert and lulls the grave:
Here brisker vapours o'er the Temple creep:
There all from Paul's to Aldgate drink and sleep.
  Thence to the banks where reverend bards repose,
They led him soft; each reverend bard arose;
And Milbourn chief, deputed by the rest,
Gave him cossack, surcingle, and vest.
'Receive,' he said, 'these robes which once were mine;
Dulness is sacred in a sound divine.'
He ceased, and spread the robe; the crowd confess
The reverend flamen in his lengthened dress.
Around him wide a sable army stand,
A low-born, cell-bred, selfish, servile band,
Prompt or to guard or stab, to saint or damn;
Heaven's Swiss, who fight for any god or man. [Fleet,
  Through Lud's famed gates, along the well-known
Rolls the black troop, and overshades the street,
Till showers of sermons, characters, essays,
In circling fleeces whiten all the ways:
So clouds, replenish'd from some bog below,
Mount in dark volumes, and descend in snow.

Here stopp'd the goddess; and in pomp proclaims
A gentler exercise to close the games.
'Ye critics! in whose heads, as equal scales,
I weigh what author's heaviness prevails;
Which most conduce to soothe the soul in slumbers,
My H—ley's periods, or my Blackmore's numbers;
Attend the trial we propose to make:
If there be man, who o'er such works can wake,
Sleep's all-subduing charm: who dares defy,
And boasts Ulysses' ear with Argus' eye;
To him we grant our amplest powers, to sit
Judge of all present, past, and future wit;
To cavil, censure, dictate, right or wrong,
Full and eternal privilege of tongue.'
Three college sophs, and three pert templars came
The same their talents, and their tastes the same;
Each prompt to query, answer, and debate,
And smit with love of poesy and prate.
The ponderous books two gentle readers bring;
The heroes sit, the vulgar form a ring.
The clamorous crowd is hushed with mugs of mum,
Till all, tuned equal, send a general hum.
Then mount the clerks, and in one lazy tone
Through the long, heavy, painful page drawl on:
Soft creeping, words on words, the sense compose,
At every line they stretch, they yawn, they doze.
As to soft gales top-heavy pines bow low
Their heads, and lift them as they cease to blow;
Thus oft they rear, and oft the head decline,
As breathe, or pause, by fits, the airs divine.
And now to this side, now to that they nod,
As verse, or prose, infuse the drowsy god.
Thrice Budgel aimed to speak, but, thrice suppress'd
By potent Arthur, knocked his chin and breast.
Toland and Tindal, prompt at priests to jeer,
Yet silent bowed to 'Christ's no kingdom here.'
Who sat the nearest, by the words o'ercome,
Slept first; the distant nodded to the hum,
Then down are roll'd the books; stretched o'er them lies
Each gentle clerk, and muttering seals his eyes.
As when a Dutchman plumps into the lakes,
One circle first, and then a sec nd makes;
What Dulness dropp'd among her sons impress'd
Like motion from one circle to the rest:
So from the midmost the nutation spreads
Round and more round, o'er all the sea of heads.
At last Centlivre felt her voice to fail,
Motteux himself unfinished left his tale.

Boyer the state, and Law the stage gave o'er,
Morgan and Mandevil could prate no more;
Norton, from Daniel and Ostrœa sprung,
Blessed with his father's front and mother's tongue,
Hung silent down his never-blushing head;
And all was hushed, as folly's self lay dead.
  Thus the soft gifts of sleep conclude the day,
And stretched on bulks, as usual, poets lay.
Why should I sing, what bards the nightly muse
Did slumbering visit, and convey to stews;
Who prouder marched, with magistrates in state,
To some famed round-house, ever-open gate?
How Henley lay inspired beside a sink,
And to mere mortals seemed a priest in drink:
While others, timely, to the neighbouring Fleet
(Haunt of the muses) make their safe retreat?

BOOK III.

THE ARGUMENT.

After the other persons are disposed in their proper places of rest, the goddess transports the king to her temple, and there lays him to slumber with his head on her lap; a position of marvellous virtue, which causeth all the visions of wild enthusiasts, projectors, politicians, inamoratos, castle-builders, chemist, and poets. He is immediately carried on the wings of fancy, and led by a mad poetical sibyl to the Elysian shade; where, on the banks of Lethe, the souls of the dull are dipped by Bavius, before their entrance into this world. There he is met by the ghost of Settle, and by him made acquainted with the wonders of the place, and with those which he himself is destined to perform. He takes him to a Mount of Vision, from whence he shows him the past triumphs of the Empire of Dullness, then the present, and lastly the future; how small a part of the world was ever conquered by science, how soon those conquests were stopped, and those very nations again reduced to her dominion. Then distinguishing the island of Great Britain, he shows by what aids, by what persons, and by what degrees, it shall be brought to her empire. Some of the persons he causes to pass in review before his eyes, describing each by his proper figure, character and qualifications. On a sudden the scene shifts, and a vast number of miracles and prodigies appear, utterly surprising and unknown to the king himself, till they are explained to be the wonders of his own reign now commencing. On this subject Settle breaks into a congratulation, yet not unmixed with concern, that his own times were but the types of these. He prophecies how first the nation shall be over-run with farces, operas, and shows; how the throne of Dulness shall be advanced over the theatres, and set up even at court; then how her sons shall preside in the seats of arts and sciences; giving a glimpse or Pisgah sight, of the future fulness of her glory, the accomplishment whereof is the subject of the fourth and last book.

But in her temple's last recess inclosed,
On Dulness' lap the anointed head reposed.
Him close she curtains round with vapours blue,
And soft besprinkles with Cimmerian dew:
Then raptnres high the seat of sense o'erflow,
Which only heads refined from reason know.
Hence from the straw where Bedlam's prophet nods,
He hears loud oracles, and talks with gods:
Hence the fool's paradise, the statesman's scheme,
The air-built castle, and the golden dream,
The maid's romantic wish, the chemist's flame,
And poet's vision of eternal fame.
And now, on fancy's easy wing conveyed,
The king descending, views the Elysian shade.

A slip-shod Sibyl led his steps along,
In lofty madness meditating song;
Her tresses staring from poetic dreams,
And never washed but in Castalia's streams.
Taylor, their better Charon, lends an oar,
(Once swan of Thames, though now he sings no more.)
Benlowes, propitious still to blockheads, bows;
And Shadwell nods, the poppy on his brows.
Here in a dusky vale, where Lethe rolls,
Old Bavius sits, to dip poetic souls,
And blunt the sense, and fit it for a skull
Of solid proof, impenetrably dull:
Instant, when dipp'd, away they wing their flight,
Where Brown and Meers unbar the gates of light,
Demand new bodies, and in calf's array,
Rush to the world, impatient for the day.
Millions and Millions on these banks he views,
Thick as the stars of night or morning dews,
As thick as bees o'er vernal blossoms fly,
As thick as eggs at Ward in pillory.
  Wondering he gazed; when, lo! a sage appears,
By his broad shoulders known, and length of ears,
Known by the band and suit which Settle wore
(His only suit) for twice three years before:
All as the vest appeared the wearer's frame,
Old in new state, another yet the same.
Bland and familiar, as in life begun
Thus the great father to the greater son:
Oh! born to see what none can see awake!
Behold the wonders of the oblivious lake!
Thou, yet unborn, has touched this sacred shore:
The hand of Bavius drenched thee o'er and o'er.
But, blind to former as to future fate,
What mortal knows his pre-existent state?
Who knows how long thy transmigrating soul
Might from Bœotian to Bœotian roll?
How many Dutchmen she vouchsafed to thrid?
How many stages through old monks she rid?
And all who since, in mild benighted days,
Mix'd the owl's ivy with the poet's bays.
As man's meanders to the vital spring
Roll all their tides, then back their circles bring
Or whirligigs, twirled round by skilful swain,
Suck the thread in, then yield it out again;
All nonsense thus, of old or modern date,
Shall, in the centre, from thee circulate.
For this, our queen unfolds to vision true
Thy mental eye, for thou hast much to view:
Old scenes of glory, times long cast behind,
Shall, first recalled, rush forward to thy mind:

Then stretch thy sight o'er all her rising reign,
And let the past and future fire thy brain.
Ascend this hill, whose cloudy point commands
Her boundless empire over seas and lands.
See round the poles where keener spangles shine,
Where spices smoke, beneath the burning line,
(Earth's wide extremes) her sable flag displayed,
And all the nations covered in her shade!
Far eastward cast thine eye, from whence the sun
And orient science their bright course begun:
One godlike monarch all that pride confounds,
He, whose long wall the wandering Tartar bounds;
Heavens! what a pile! whole ages perish there,
And one bright blaze turns learning into air.
Thence to the south extend thy gladdened eyes;
There rival flames with equal glory rise;
From shelves to shelves see greedy Vulcan roll,
And lick up all their physic of the soul.
How little, mark! that portion of the ball,
Where, faint at best, the beams of science fall:
Soon as they dawn, from hyperborean skies
Embodied dark, what clouds of Vandals rise!
Lo! where Mæotis sleeps, and hardly flows
The freezing Tanais through a waste of snows,
The north by myriads pours her mighty sons,
Great nurse of Goths, of Alans, and of Huns!
See Alaric's stern port! the martial frame
Of Genseric! and Attila's dread name!
See, the bold Ostrogoths on Latium fall;
See, the fierce Visigoths on Spain and Gaul!
See, where the morning gilds the palmy shore
(The soil that arts and infant letters bore)
His conquering tribes the Arabian prophet draws,
And saving ignorance enthrones by laws.
See Christans, Jews, one heavy sabbath keep,
And all the western world believe and sleep.
Lo! Rome herself, proud mistress now no more
Of arts, but thundering against heathen lore;
Her gray-haired synods damning books unread,
And Bacon trembling for his brazen head,
Padua, with sighs, beholds her Livy burn,
And e'en th' Antipodes Virgilius mourn.
See, the Cirque falls, the unpillared temple nods,
Streets paved with heroes, Tyber choked with gods;
Till Peter's keys some christened Jove adorn,
And Pan to Moses lends his Pagan horn;
See Graceful Venus to a virgin turned,
Or Phidias broken, and Apelles burned,
Behold yon isle, by palmers, pilgrims trod,
Men bearded, bald, cowled, uncowled, shod, unshod'

Peeled, patched, and piebald, linsey-wolsey, brothers,
Grave mummers! sleeveless some and shirtless others.
That once was Britain—Happy! had she seen
No fiercer sons, had Easter never been.
In peace, great goddess ever be adored;
How keen the war, if Dulness draw the sword!
Thus visit not thy own! on this blessed age
O spread thy influence, but restrain thy rage.
  And see, my son! the hour is on its way
That lifts our goddess to imperial sway;
This favorite isle, long severed from her reign,
Dove-like she gathers to her wings again.
Now look through fate! behold the scene she draws!
What aids, what armies, to assert her cause!
See all her progeny, illustrious sight?
Behold; and count them as they rise to light.
As Berecynthia, while her offspring vie
In homage to the mother of the sky,
Surveys around her, in the blessed abode,
An hundred sons, and every son a god:
Not with less glory mighty Dulness crowned,
Shall take through Grub-street her triumphant round;
And, her Parnassus glancing o'er at once,
Behold a hundred sons, and each a dunce.
  Mark first that youth who takes the foremost place,
And thrusts his person full into your face.
With all thy father's virtues blessed, be born!
And a new Cibber shall the stage adorn.
  A second see, by meeker manners known,
And modest as the maid that sips alone;
From the strong fate of drams if thou get free,
Another D'Urfey, Ward; shall sing in thee.
Thee shall each alehouse, the each gillhouse mourn,
And answering gin-shops sourer sighs return.
Jacob, the scourge of grammar, mark with awe;
Nor less revere him, blunderbus of law.
Lo, P—p—le's brow, tremendous to the town,
Horneck's fierce eye, and Roome's funereal frown.
Lo! sneering Goode, half malice and half whim,
A fiend in glee, ridiculously grim.
Each cygnet sweet, of Bath and Tunbridge race,
Whose tuneful whistling makes the waters pass;
Each songster, riddler every nameless name,
All crowd, who foremost shall be d——d to fame.
Some strain in rhyme; the muses, on their racks,
Scream like the winding of ten thousand jacks;
Some, free from rhyme or reason, rule or check,
Break Priscian's head, and Pegasus's neck;
Down, down the larum, with impetuous whirl,
The Pindars and the Miltons of a Curll.

Silence, ye wolves? while Ralph to cynthia howls
And makes night hideous—Answer him, ye owls!
Sense, speech, and measure, living tongues and dead,
Let all give way—and Morris may be read.
Flow, Welsted, flow! like thine inspirer, beer,
Though stale, not ripe; though thin, yet never clear;
So sweetly mawkish, and so smoothly dull;
Heady, not strong; o'erflowing, though not full,
Ah, Dennis! Gildon, ah! what ill-starred rage
Divides a friendship long confirmed by age?
Blockheads with reason wicked wits abhor.
But fool with fool is barbarous civil war.
Embrace, embrace, my sons! be foes no more!
Nor glad vile poets with true critics' gore.
Behold yon pair, in strict embraces joined;
How like in manners, and how like in mind!
Equal in wit, and equally polite,
Shall this a Pasquin, that a Grumbler write;
Like are their merits, like rewards they share,
That shines a consul, this commissioner.
'But who is he, in closet closely pent,
Of sober face, with learned dust besprent?'
Right well mine eyes arede the myster wight,
On parchment scrapes y-fed, and Wormius hight.
To future ages may thy dulness last,
As thou preservest the dulness of the past!
There, dim in clouds, the poring scholiasts mark:
Wits, who, like owls, see only in the dark;
A lumber-house of books in every head,
For ever reading, never to be read!
But, where each science lifts its modern type
History her pot, divinity his pipe,
While proud philosphy repines to show,
Dishonest sight! his breeches rent below;
Imbrowned with native bronze, lo! Henley stands,
Tuning his voice, and balancing his hands,
How fluent nonsense trickles from his tongue!
How sweet the periods, neither said nor sung!
Still break the benches, Henley! with thy strain,
While Sherlock, Hare, and Gibson, preach in vain.
Oh great restorer of the good old stage,
Preacher at once, and zany of thy age!
Oh worthy thou of Egypt's wise abodes,
A decent priest, where monkeys where the gods!
But fate with butchers placed thy priestly stall,
Meek modern faith to murder, hack, and maul:
And bade thee live, to crown Brittannia's praise,
In Toland's, Tindal's, and in Woolston's days.
Yet, oh, my sons! a father's words attend,
(So may the fates preserve the ears you lend:

'Tis yours, a Bacon or a Locke to blame,
A Newton's genius, or a Milton's flame:
But oh! with One, immortal One, dispense,
The source of Newton's light, of Bacon's sense.
Content, each emanation of his fires
That beams on earth, each virtue he inspires,
Each art he prompts, each charm he can create,
Whate'er he gives are given for you to hate.
Persist, by all divine in man unawed,
But 'Learn, ye Dunces! not to scorn your God.'
Thus he, for then a ray of reason stole
Half through the solid darkness of his soul;
But soon the cloud returned—and thus the sire:
See now, what Dulness and her sons admire!
See what the charms that smite the simple heart,
Not touched by Nature and not reached by art.
His never-blushing head he turned aside,
(Not half so pleased when Goodman prophesied;)
And looked, and saw a sable scorcerer rise,
Swift to whose hand a winged volume flies:
All sudden, gorgons hiss, and dragons glare,
And ten-horned fiends and giants rush to war.
Hell rises, heaven descends, and dance on earth;
Gods, imps, and monsters, music, rage, and mirth,
A fire, a jig, a battle, and a ball,
Till one wide conflagration swallows all.
Thence a new world, to Nature's laws unknown,
Breaks out refulgent, with a heaven its own:
Another Cynthia her new journey runs,
And other planets circle other suns.
The forests dance, the rivers upward rise,
Whales sport in woods, and dolphins in the skies;
And last, to give the whole creation grace,
Lo! one vast egg produces human race.
Joy fills his soul, joy innocent of thought;
'What power,' he cries, 'what power these wonders wrought?'
Son, what thou seek'st is in thee! Look and find
Each monster meets his likeness in thy mind.
Yet wouldst thou more? in yonder cloud behold,
Whose sarsenet skirts are edged with flaming gold.
A matchless youth! his nod these worlds controlls,
Wings the red lightning, and the thunder rolls;
Angel of Dulness, sent to scatter round
Her magic charms o'er all unclassic ground:
Yon stars, yon suns, he rears at pleasure higher,
Illumes their light, and sets their flames on fire.
Immortal Rich! how calm he sits at ease,
'Midst snows of paper, and fierce hail of peas!
And, proud his mistress' orders to perform,
Rides in the whirlwind, and directs the storm.

But, lo! to dark encounter in mid air
New wizards rise; I see my Cibber there!
Booth in his cloudy tabernacle shrined,
On grinning dragons thou shalt mount the wind.
Dire is the conflict, dismal is the din,
Here shouts all Drury, there all Lincoln's-inn;
Contending theatres our empire raise;
Alike their labours, and alike their praise.
  And are these wonders, son, to thee unknown?
Unknown to thee! these wonders are thy own.
These fate reserved to grace thy reign divine,
Foreseen by me, but ah! witheld from mine.
In Lud's old walls though long I ruled, renowned.
Far as loud Bow's stupendous bells resound;
Though my own alderman conferred the bays,
To me committing their eternal praise,
Their full-fed heroes, their pacific mayors
Their annual trophies, and their monthly wars:
Though long my party built on me their hopes,
For writing pamphlets, and for roasting popes;
Yet lo! in me what authors have to brag on!
Reduced at last to hiss in my own dragon.
Avert it, Heaven! that thou, my Cibber, e'er
Shouldst wag a serpent-tail in smithfield fair!
Like the vile straw that's blown about the streets,
The needy poet sticks to all he meets,
Coached, carted, trod upon, now loose, now fast,
And carried off in some dog's tail at last.
Happier thy fortunes! like a rolling stone,
Thy giddy dulness still shall lumber on,
Safe in its heaviness, shall never stray,
But lick up every blockhead in the way.
Thee shall the patriot, thee the courtier taste,
And every year be duller than the last.
Till, raised from booths, to theatre, to court,
Her seat imperial Dulness shall transport.
Already opera prepares the way,
The sure forerunner of her gentle sway:
Let her thy heart, next drabs and dice, engage,
The third mad passion of thy doting age.
Teach thou the warbling Polypheme to roar,
And scream thyself as none e'er screamed before!
To aid our cause, if heaven thou canst not bend,
Hell thou shalt move; for Faustus is our friend;
Pluto with Cato thou for this shalt join,
And link the Mourning Bride to Proserpine.
Grub-street! thy fall should men and gods conspire,
Thy stage shall stand, ensure it but from fire.
Another Æschylus appears! prepare
For new abortions, all ye pregnant fair!

In flames, like Semele's, be brought to bed,
While opening hell spouts wild-fire at your head.
Now, Bavius, take the poppy from thy brow,
And place it here! here all ye heroes bow!
'This, this is he, foretold by ancient rhymes,
The Augustus born to bring Saturnian times.
Signs following signs lead on the mighty year!
See! the dull stars roll round and re-appear.
See, see, our own true Phœbus wears the bays!
Our Midas sits lord chancellor of plays!
On poets' tombs see Benson's titles writ!
Lo! Ambrose Philips is preferred for wit!
See under Ripley rise a new Whitehall,
While Jones' and Boyle's united labours fall;
While Wren with sorrow to the grave descends
Gay dies unpensioned with a hundred friends.
Hibernian politics, O Swift! thy fate;
And Pope's, ten years to comment and translate,
Proceed, great days! till learning fly the shore,
Till birch shall blush with noble blood no more;
Till Thames see Eton's sons for ever play,
Till Westminster's whole year be holiday;
Till Isis' elders reel, their pupils' sport,
And *alma mater* lie dissolved in port!
'Enough! enough!' the raptured monarch cries!
And through the ivory gate the vision flies.

BOOK IV.

THE ARGUMENT.

The poet being, in this book, to declare the completion of the prophecies mentioned at the end of the former, makes a new invocation, as the greater poets are wont, when some high and worthy matter is to be sung. He shows the goddess coming in her majesty, to destroy order and science, and to substitute the kingdom of the dull upon earth; how she leads captive the sciences, and silences the Muses; and what they be who succeed in their stead. All her children, by a wonderful attraction, are drawn about her, and bear along with them divers others, who promote her empire by connivance, weak resistance, or discouragement of arts; such as half-wits, tasteless admirers, vain pretenders, the flatterers of dunces, or the patrons of them: all these crowd around her; one of them, offering to approach her, is driven back by a rival; but she commends and encourages both. The first who speak in form are the geniuses of the schools, who assure her of their care to advance her cause by confining youth to words, and keeping them out of the way of real knowledge: their address, and her gracious answer; with her charge to them and the universities. The universities appear by their proper deputies, and assure her that the same method is observed in the progress of education: the speech of Aristarchus on this subject. They are driven off by a band of young gentlemen returned from travel with their tutors; one of whom delivers to the goddess, in a polite oration, an account of the whole conduct and fruits of their travels; presenting to her at the same time a young nobleman perfectly accomplished: she receives him graciously, and endues him with the happy quality of want of shame. She sees loitering about her a number of indolent persons abandoning all business and duty, and dying with laziness: to these approaches the antiquary Annius, entreating her to make them virtuosos, and assign them over to him; but Mummius, another antiquary, complaining of his fradulent proceeding, she finds a method to reconcile their difference. Then enter a troop of people fantastically adorned, offering her strange and exotic presents: among them, one stands forth and demands justice on another, who had deprived him of one of the greatest curiosities in nature: but he justifies himself so well, that the goddess gives them both her approbation; she recommends to them to find proper employment for the indolents beforementioned, in the study of butterflies, shells, birds-nests, moss, &c., but with particular caution, not to proceed beyond trifles, to any useful or extensive views of nature, or of the Author of nature. Against the last of these apprehensions, she is secured by a hearty address from the minute philosophers and free-thinkers, one of whom speaks in the name of the rest. The youth, thus instructed and principled, are delivered to her in a body by the hands of Silenus; and then admitted to taste the cup of the Magus her high priest, which causes a total oblivion of all obligations, divine, civil, moral, or rational: to these, her adepts, she sends priests, attendants, and comforters of various kinds; confers on them orders and degrees; and then dismissing them with a speech, confirming to each his privileges, and telling what she expects from each, concludes with a yawn of extra ordinary virtue; the progress and effects whereof on all orders o men, and the consummation of all, in the restoration of Night and Chaos, conclude the poem.

YET, yet a moment, one dim ray of light
Indulge, dread Chaos and eternal Night!
Of darkness visible so much be lent,
As half to shew, half veil, the deep intent.
Ye powers! whose mysteries restored I sing,
To whom time bears me on his rapid wing,
Suspend a while your force inertly strong,
Then take at once the poet and the song.
Now flamed the dog-star's unpropitious ray,
Smote every brain, and withered every bay;
Sick was the sun, the owl forsook his bower,
The moon-struck prophet felt the madding hour:
Then rose the seed of Chaos, and of Night,
To blot out order, and extinguish light,
Of dull and venal a new world to mould,
And bring Saturnian days of lead and gold.
She mounts the throne: her head a cloud conceal'd,
In broad effulgence all below reveal'd,
('Tis thus aspiring Dulness ever shines,)
Soft on her lap her laureate son reclines.
Beneath her footstool science groans in chains,
And wit dreads exile, penalties and pains.
There foamed rebellious logic, gagg'd and bound;
There, stripp'd, fair rhetoric languished on the ground;
His blunted arms by sophistry are borne
And shameless Billingsgate her robes adorn.
Morality, by her false guardians drawn,
Chicane in furs, and casuistry in lawn,
Gasps, as they straighten at each end the cord,
And dies when Dulness gives her Page the word.
Mad Mathesis alone was unconfined,
Too mad for mere material chains to bind:
Now to pure space lifts her ecstatic stare,
Now running round the circle, finds it square.
But held in tenfold bonds the muses lie,
Watched both by envy's and by flatt'ry's eye:
There to her heart sad tragedy address'd
The dagger, wont to pierce the tyrant's breast;
But sober history restrained her rage,
And promised vengeance on a barbarous age.
There sunk Thalia, nerveless, cold, and dead,
Had not her sister Satire held her head:
Nor couldst thou, Chesterfield! a tear refuse,
Thou wep'st, and with thee wept each geutle muse.
When lo! a harlot form soft sliding by,
With mincing step, small voice, and lanquid eye:

Foreign her air, her robe's discordant pride
In patch-work fluttering, and her head aside;
By singing peers upheld on either hand,
She tripp'd and laugh'd, too pretty much to stand;
Cast on the prostrate Nine a scornful look,
Then thus in quaint recitativo spoke:
'O Cara! Cara! silence all that train;
Joy to great Chaos! let division reign·
Chromatic tortures soon shall drive them hence,
Break all their nerves, and fritter all their sense:
One trill shall harmonize joy, grief, and rage,
Wake the dull church, and lull the ranting stage;
To the same notes thy son shall hum or snore,
And all thy yawning daughters cry, *encore.*
Another Phœbus, thy own Phœbus reigns,
Joys in my jigs, and dances in my chains.
But soon, ah soon, rebellion will commence,
If music meanly borrows aid from sense:
Strong in new arms, lo! giant Handel stands,
Like bold Briareus, with a hundred hands;
To stir, to rouse, to shake the soul he comes,
And Jove's own thunders follow Mars's drums.
Arrest him, empress, or you sleep no more'—
She heard, and drove him to the Hibernian shore.
And now had Fame's posterior trumpet blown,
And all the nations summoned to the throne:
The young, the old, who feel her inward sway,
One instinct seizes, and transports away.
None need a guide, by sure attraction led,
And strong impulsive gravity of head:
None want a place, for all their centre found,
Hung to the goddess, and cohered around,
Not closer, orb in orb. conglobed are seen
The buzzing bees about their dusky queen.
The gathering number, as it moves along,
Involves a vast involuntary throng,
Who, gently drawn, and struggling less and less,
Roll in her vortex, and her power confess.
Not those alone who passive own her laws,
But who weak rebels, more advance her cause.
Whate'er of dunce, in college or in town,
Sneers at another in toupee or gown;
Whate'er of mongrel no one class admits,
A wit with dunces, and a dunce with wits.
Nor absent they, no members of her state,
Who pay her homage in her sons, the great;
Who, false to Phœbus, bow the knee to Baal,
Or impious, preach his word without a call.
Patrons, who sneak from living worth to dead,
Withold the pension, and set up the head;

Or vest dull flattery in the sacred gown,
Or give from fool to fool the laurel crown;
And (last and worst) with all the cant of wit,
Without the soul, the muses' hypocrite
There marched the bard and blockhead side by side,
Who ryhmed for hire, and patronized for pride.
Narcissus, praised with all a parson's power,
Looked a white lily sunk beneath a shower.
There moved Montalto with superior air;
His stretched out arm displayed a volume fair;
Courtiers and patriots in two ranks divide,
Through both he passed, and bowed from side to side;
But as in graceful act, with awful eye,
Composed he stood, bold Benson thrust him by:
On two unequal crutches propp'd he came,
Milton's on this, on that one Johnson's name.
The decent knight retired with sober rage,
Withdrew his hand, and closed the pompous page:
But (happy for him as the times went then)
Appeared Apollo's mayor and aldermen,
On whom three hundred gold-capp'd youths await,
To lug the ponderous volume off in state.
When Dulness, smiling—'Thus revive the wits!
But murder first, and mince them all to bits;
As erst Medea (cruel, so to save!)
A new edition of old Æson gave;
Let standard authors thus, like trophies borne,
Appear more glorious as more hacked and torn.
And you, my critics! in the chequered shade,
Admire new light through holes yourselves have made.
Leave not a foot of verse, a foot of stone,
A page, a grave, that they can call their own;
But spread, my sons, your glory thin or thick,
On passive paper, or on solid brick.
So by each bard an alderman shall sit,
A heavy lord shall hang at every wit,
And while on fame's triumphal car they ride,
Some slave of mine be pinioned to their side.'
Now crowds on crowds around the goddess press,
Each eager to present the first address.
Dunce scorning dunce beholds the next advance,
But fop shows fop superior complaisance.
When lo! a spectre rose, whose index-hand
Held forth the virtue of the dreadful wand;
His beavered brow a birchen garland wears,
Dropping with infant's blood and mothers' tears,
O'er every vein a shuddering horror runs,
Eton and Winton shake through all their sons.
All flesh is humbled, Westminster's bold race
Shrink, and confess the genius of the place:

The pale-boy senator yet tingling stands,
And holds his breeches close with both his hands.
Then thus: since man from beast by words is known,
Words are man's province, words we teach alone.
When reason doubtful, like the Samian letter,
Points him two ways, the narrower is the better.
Placed at the door of learning, youth to guide,
We never suffer it to stand too wide.
To ask, to guess, to know, as they commence,
As fancy opens the quick springs of sense,
We ply the memory, we load the brain,
Bind rebel wit, and double chain on chain,
Comfine the thought, to exercise the breath
And keep them in the pale of words till death.
Whate'er the talents, or howe'er designed,
We hang one jingling padlock on the mind:
A poet the first day he dips his quill;
And what the last? a very poet still.
Pity! the charm works only in our wall,
Lost, lost too soon in yonder house or hall.
There truant Windham every muse gave o'er;
There Talbot sunk, and was a wit no more!
How sweet an Ovid, Murray was our boast!
How many Martials were in Pulteney lost!
Else sure some bard, to our eternal praise,
In twice ten thousand rhyming nights and days,
Had reached the work, the all that mortal can,
And South beheld that masterpiece of man.
'Oh,' cried the Goddess, 'for some pedant reign!
Some gentle James, to bless the land again:
To stick the doctor's chair into the throne,
Give law to words, or war with words alone,
Senates and courts with Greek and Latin rule,
And turn the council to a grammar school!
For sure if Dulness sees a grateful day,
'Tis in the shade of arbitrary sway.
O! if my sons may learn one earthly thing,
Teach but that one, sufficient for a king;
That which my priests, and mine alone, maintain,
Which, as it dies, or lives, we fall, or reign:
May you, my Cam and Isis, preach it long!
'The right divine of kings to govern wrong.'
Prompt at the call, around the goddess roll
Broad hats, and hoods, and caps, a sable shoal:
Thick and more thick the black blockade extends,
A hundred head of Aristotle's friends
Nor wert thou, Isis! wanting to the day,
[Thou Christ-church long kept prudishly away.]
Each staunch polemic, stubborn as a rock,
Each fierce logician, still expelling Locke,

Came whip and spur, and dashed through thin and thick
On German Crouzaz, and Dutch Burgersdyck.
As many quit the streams, that murmuring fall
To lull the sons of Margaret and Clare-hall,
Where Bently late tempestuous wont to sport
In troubled waters, but now sleeps in port.
Before them marched that awful Aristarch;
Plowed was his front with many a deep remark:
His hat, which never veiled to human pride,
Walker with reverence took, and laid aside.
Low bowed the rest: he, kingly, did but nod;
So upright Quakers please both man and God.
Mistress! dismiss that rabble from your throne:
Avaunt——is Aristarchus yet unknown?
Thy mighty scholiast, whose unwearied pains
Made Horace dull, and humbled Milton's strains.
Turn what they will to verse, their toil is vain,
Critics like me shall make it prose again.
Roman and Greek grammarians! know your better;
Author of something yet more great than letter;
While towering o'er your alphabet, like Saul,
Stands our digamma, and o'ertops them all.
'Tis true, on words is still our whole debate,
Disputes of *me* or *te*, of *aut* or *at*.
To sound or sink in *cano*, O or A,
Or give up Cicero to C or K.
Let Friend affect to speak as Terence spoke,
And Alsop never but like Horace joke:
For me, what Virgil, Pliny may deny,
Manilius or Solinus shall supply:
For Attic phrase in Plato let them seek,
I poach in Suidas for unlicensed Greek.
In ancient sense if any needs will deal,
Be sure I give them fragments, not a meal;
What Gellius or Stobæus hashed before,
Or chewed by blind old Scholiasts o'er and o'er,
The critic eye, that microscope of wit,
Sees hairs and pores, examines bit by bit.
How parts relate to parts, or they to whole,
The body's harmony, the beaming soul,
Are things which Kuster, Burman, Wasse, shall see
When man's whole frame is obvius to a flea.
Ah, think not, Mistress! more true dulness lies
In Folly's cap, then Wisdom's grave disguise.
Like buoys, that never sink into the flood,
On learning's surface we but lie and nod.
Thine is the genuine head of many a house,
And much divinity without a *Nous*.
Nor could a Barrow work on every block,
Nor has one Atterbury spoiled the flock.

See! still thy own, the heavy cannon roll,
And metaphysic smokes involve the pole.
For thee we dim the eyes, and stuff the head
With all such reading as was never read:
For thee explain a thing till all men doubt it,
And write about it, goddess, and about it:
So spins the silk-worm small its slender store,
And labours till it clouds itself all o'er.
What though we let some better sort of fool
Thrid every science, run through every school?
Never by tumbler through the hoops was shown
Such skill in passing all, and touching none.
He may indeed, if sober all this time,
Plague with dispute, or persecute with rhyme.
We only furnish what he cannot use,
Or wed to what he must divorce, a muse:
Full in the midst of Euclid dip at once,
And petrify a genius to a dunce;
Or set on metaphysic ground to prance,
Show all his paces, not a step advance.
With the same cement, ever sure to bind,
We bring to one dead level every mind:
Then take him to develope, if you can,
And hew the block off, and get out the man.
But wherefore waste I words? I see advance
Whore, pupil, and laced governor, from France.
Walker! our hat——nor more he deigned to say,
But stern as Ajax' spectre strode away
In flowed at once a gay embroidered race,
And tittering pushed the pedants off the place
Some would have spoken, but the voice was drowned
By the French horn, or by the opening hound.
The first came forwards with an easy mien,
As if he saw St. James's and the Queen.
When thus the attendant orator begun;
'Receive, great Empress! thy accomplished son:
Thine from the birth, and sacred from the rod,
A dauntless infant! never scared with God.
The sire saw, one by one, his virtues wake;
The mother begged the blessing of a rake.
Thou gavest that ripeness which so soon began,
And ceased so soon, he ne'er was boy nor man;
Through school and college, thy kind cloud o'ercast,
Safe and unseen the young Æneas past:
Thence bursting glorious, all at once let down
Stunn'd with his giddy larum half the town.
Intrepid then, o'er seas and lands he flew;
Europe he saw, and Europe saw him too.
There all thy gifts and graces we display,
Thou, only thou, directing all our way!

To where the Seine, obsequious as she runs,
Pours at great Bourbon's feet her silken sons;
Or Tyber now no longer Roman, rolls,
Vain of Italian arts, Italian souls:
To happy convents, bosom'd deep in vines,
Where slumber abbots, purple as their wines:
To isles of fragrance, lily-silvered vales,
Diffusing languor in the panting gales
To lands of singing or of dancing slaves,
Love-whispering woods, and lute-resounding waves.
But chief her shrine where naked Venus keeps,
And Cupids ride the lion of the deeps;
Where, eased of fleets, the Adriatic main
Wafts the smooth eunuch and enamoured swain.
Led by my hand, he sauntered Europe round,
And gathered every vice on Christian ground·
Saw every court, heard every king declare
His royal sense of operas or the fair;
The stews and palace equally explored,
Intrigued with glory, and with spirit whored;
Tried all *hors-d'œuvres*, all *liqueurs* defined,
Judicious drank, and greatly daring dined;
Dropp'd the dull lumber of the Latin store,
Spoiled his own language, and acquired no more;
All classic learning lost on classic ground;
And last turned air, the echo of a sound!
See now, half-cured, and perfectly well-bred,
With nothing but a solo in his head;
As much estate, and principle, and wit,
As Jansen, Fleetwood, Cibber shall think fit
Stolen from a duel, followed by a nun,
And, if a borough choose him, not undone;
See, to my country happy I restore
This glorious youth, and add one Venus more.
Her too receive, (for her my soul adores;)
So may the sons of sons of sons of whores
Prop thine, O empress! like each neighbour throne,
And make a long posterity thy own.'
Pleased, she accepts the hero, and the dame,
Wraps in her veil, and frees from sense of shame.
  Then looked, and saw a lazy lolling sort,
Unseen at church, at senate, or at court,
Of ever-listless loiterers, that attend
No cause, no trust, no duty, and no friend.
Thee too, my Paridell! she marked thee there,
Stretched on the rack of a too easy chair,
And heard thy everlasting yawn confess
The pains and penalties of idleness.
She pitied! but her pity only shed
Benigner influence on thy nodding head.

But Annius, crafty seer, with ebon wand,
And well-dissembled emerald on his hand,
False as his gems, and cankered as his coins,
Came, crammed with capon, from where Pollio dines.
Soft, as the wily fox is seen to creep,
Where bask on sunny banks the simple sheep,
Walk round and round, now prying here, now there
So he, but pious, whispered first his prayer.
'Grant, gracious goddess! grant me still to cheat!
O may thy cloud still cover the deceit!
Thy choicer mists on this assembly shed,
But pour them thickest on the noble head.
So shall each youth, assisted by our eyes,
See other Cæsars, other Homers rise;
Through twilight ages hunt the Athenian fowl,
Which Chalcis gods, and mortals call an owl.
Now see an Attys now a Cecrops clear
Nay, Mahomet! the pigeon at thine ear;
Be rich in ancient brass, though not in gold,
And keep his Lares, though his house be sold;
To headless Phœbe his fair bride postpone,
Honour a Syrian prince above his own;
Lord of an Otho, if I vouch it true;
Blessed in one Niger, till he knows of two.
Mummius o'erherd him; Mummius, fool renown'd
Who, like his Cheops, stinks above the ground,
Fierce as a startled adder, swelled, and said,
Rattling an ancient sistrum at his head:
'Speakest thou of Syrian princes? traitor base!
Mine, goddess! mine, is all the horned race.
True, he had wit to make their value rise;
From foolish Greeks to steal them, was as wise;
More glorious yet, from barbarous hands to keep,
When Sallee rovers chased him on the deep.
Then, taught by Hermes, and divinely bold,
Down his own throat he risked the Grecian gold,
Received each demigod, with pious care,
Deep in his entrails—I revered them there;
I bought them, shrowded in that living shrine,
And, at their second birth, they issue mine.'
'Witness, great Ammon! by whose horns I swore,'
Replies soft Annius 'this our paunch before
Still bears them, faithful! and that thus I eat,
Is to refund the medals with the meat.
To prove me, goddess! clear of all design,
Bid me with Pollio sup as well as dine:
There all the learned shall at the labour stand,
And Douglas lend his soft obstetric hand.'
The goddess smiling seemed to give consent;
So back to Pollio hand in hand they went.

Then thick as locusts blackening all the ground,
A tribe, with weeds and shells fantastic crowned,
Each with some wondrous gift approached the power,
A nest, a toad, a fungus, or a flower.
But far the foremost, two, with earnest zeal,
And aspect ardent, to the throne appeal.
The first thus opened: 'Hear thy suppliant's call,
Great queen, and common mother of us all!
Fair from its humble bed I reared this flower,
Suckled, and cheered, with air, and sun, and shower.
Soft on the paper ruff its leaves I spread,
Bright with the gilded button tipped its head,
Then throned in glass, and named it Caroline:
Each maid cried, charming! and each youth, divine!
Did nature's pencil ever blend such rays,
Such varied light in one promiscuous blaze?
Now prostrate! dead! behold that Caroline:
No maid cries charming! and no youth divine!
And lo the wretch! whose vile, whose insect lust
Laid this gay daughter of the spring in dust;
Oh punish him, or to the Elysian shades
Dismiss my soul, where no carnation fades.'
He ceased, and wept. With innocence of mien
The accus'd stood forth, and thus address'd the queen:
'Of all the enamelled race, whose silvery wing
Waves to the tepid zephyrs of the spring,
Or swims along the fluid atmosphere,
Once brightest shined this child of heat and air.
I saw, and started from its vernal bower
The rising game, and chased from flower to flower.
It fled, I followed; now in hope, now pain;
It stopped, I stopped; it moved, I moved again.
At last it fixed, 'twas on what plant it pleased,
And where it fixed, the beauteous bird I seized:
Rose or carnation was below my care;
I meddle, goddess! only in my sphere.
I tell the naked fact without disguise,
And, to excuse it, need but show the prize;
Whose spoils this paper offers to your eye
Fair e'en in death! this peerless butterfly.'
'My sons! (she answered) both have done your parts:
Live happy both, and long promote our arts.
But hear a mother, when she recommends
To your fraternal care our sleeping friends;
The common soul, of Heaven's more frugal make,
Serves but to keep fools pert, and knaves awake:
A drowsy watchman, that just gives a knock,
And breaks our rest, to tell us what's a clock.
Yet by some object every brain is stirred,
The dull may waken to a humming-bird;

The most recluse, discreetly opened, find
Congenial matter in the cockle-kind;
The mind, in metaphysics at a loss,
May wander in a wilderness of moss;
The head that turns at superlunar things
Poized with a tail, may steer on Wilkins' wings
O! would the sons of men once think their eyes
And reason given them but to study flies!
See nature in some partial narrow shape,
And let the author of the whole escape:
Learn but to trifle; or, who most observe,
To wonder at their Maker, not to serve.'
'Be that my task' (replies a gloomy clerk,
Sworn foe to mystery, yet divinely dark;
Whose pious hope aspires to see the day
When moral evidence shall quite decay,
And damns implicit faith, and holy lies,
Prompt to impose, and fond to dogmatize;)
'Let others creep by timid steps, and slow,
On plain experience lay foundations low,
By common sense to common knowledge bred,
And last, to nature's cause through nature led.
All seeing in thy mists, we want no guide,
Mother of arrogance, and source of pride?
We nobly take the high priori road,
And reason downward, till we doubt of God:
Make Nature still encroach upon his plan,
And shove him off as far as e'er we can;
Thrust some mechanic cause into his place,
Or bind in matter, or diffuse in space:
Or, at one bound o'er leaping all his laws,
Make God man's image, man the final cause
Fine virtue local, all relation scorn,
She all in self, and but for self be born:
Of nought so certain as our reason still,
Of nought so doubtful as of soul and will.
Oh hide the God still more! and make us see
Such as Lucretius drew, a god like thee:
Wrapp'd up in self, a god without a thought,
Regardless of our merit, or default.
Or that bright image to our fancy draw,
Which Theocles in raptured vision saw,
While through poetic scenes the genius roves,
Or wanders wild in academic groves;
That nature our society adores,
Where Tindal dictates, and Silenus snores.'
Roused at his name, up rose the bowzy sire,
And shook from out his pipe the seeds of fire;
Then snapp'd his box, and stroked his belly down;
Rosy and reverend, though without a gown.

Bland and familiar to the throne he came,
Led up the youth, and called the goddess dame,
Then thus: 'From priestcraft happily set free,
Lo! every finished son returns to thee;
First slave to words, then vassal to a name,
Then dupe to party; child and man the same;
Bounded by nature, narrowed still by art,
A trifling head, and a contracted heart.
Thus bred, thus taught, how many have I seen,
Smiling on all, and smiled on by a queen?
Marked out for honours, honoured for their birth,
To thee the most rebellious things on earth:
Now to thy gentle shadow all are shrunk,
All melted down in pension or in punk!
So K——, so B——, sneaked into the grave,
A monarch's half, and half a harlot's slave.
Poor W**, nipp'd in folly's broadest bloom,
Who praises now? his chaplain on his tomb.
Then take them all, oh take them to thy breast!
Thy Magus, goddess! shall perform the rest.'
With that a wizard old his cup extends,
Which whoso tastes forget his former friends,
Sire, ancestors, himself. One casts his eyes
Up to a star, and like Endymion dies
A feather, shooting from another's head,
Extracts his brain, and principle is fled;
Lost is his God, his country, ev'ry thing,
And nothing left but homage to a king!
The vulgar herd turn off to roll with hogs,
To run with horses, or to hunt with dogs;
But, sad example! never to escape
Their infamy, still keep the human shape.
But she, good goddess, sent to every child
Firm impudence, or stupefaction mild;
And straight succeeded, leaving shame no room,
Cibberian forehead, or Cimmerian gloom.
Kind self-conceit to some her glass applies,
Which no one looks in with another's eyes:
But as the flatterer or dependant paint,
Beholds himself a patriot, chief, or saint.
On others' interest her gay livery flings,
Interest, that waves on party coloured wings:
Turned to the sun, she casts a thousand dyes,
And as she turns, the colours fall or rise.
Others the syren sisters warble round,
And empty heads console with empty sound.
No more, alas! the voice of fame they hear,
The balm of Dulness trickling in their ear.
Great C——, H——, P——, R——, K——,
Why all your toils? your sons have learned to sing.

How quick ambition hastes to ridicule!
The sire is made a peer, the son a fool.
  On some a priest succinct in amice white
Attends; all flesh is nothing in his sight!
Beeves, at his touch, at once to jelly turn,
And the huge boar is shrunk into an urn:
The board with spacious miracles he loads,
Turns hares to larks, and pigeons into toads,
Another (for in all what one can shine?)
Explains the *seve* and *verdeur* of the vine.
What cannot copious sacrifice atone?
Thy truffles, Perigord! thy hams, Bayonne!
With French libation, and Italian strain,
Wash Bladen white, and expiate Hay's stain.
Knight lifts the head; for what are crowds undone,
To three essential partridges in one?
Gone every blush, and silent all reproach,
Contending princes mount them in their coach.
  Next bidding all draw near on bended knees,
The queen confers her titles and degrees.
Her children first of more distinguished sort,
Who study Shakspeare at the inns of court,
Impale a glow-worm, or *vertu* profess,
Shine in the dignity of F.R.S.
Some, deep free-masons, join the silent race,
Worthy to fill Pythagoras's place;
Some botanists, or florists at the least,
Or issue members of an annual feast.
Nor past the meanest unregarded, one
Rose a Gregorian, one a Gormorgon.
The last, no least in honour or applause,
Isis and Cam made doctors of her laws.
  Then, blessing all, Go children of my care!
To practice now from theory repair.
All my commands are easy, short, and full;
My sons! be proud, be selfish, and be dull.
Guard my prerogative, assert my throne:
This nod confirms each privilege your own.
The cap and switch be sacred to his grace;
With staff and pumps the marquis leads the race:
From stage to stage the licensed earl may run,
Pair'd with his fellow-charioteer, the sun
The learned Baron butterflies design,
Or draw to silk Arachne's subtile line;
The judge to dance his brother serjeant call;
The senator at cricket urge the ball;
The bishop stow (pontific luxury!)
An hundred souls of turkeys in a pie;
The sturdy squire to Gallic masters stoop,
And drown his lands and manors in a soup.

Others import yet nobler arts from France,
Teach kings to fiddle, and make senates dance.
Perhaps more high some daring son may soar,
Proud to my list to add one monarch more;
And, nobly conscious, princes are but things
Born for first ministers, as slaves for kings;
Tyrant supreme! shall three estates command,
And make one mighty Dunciad of the land!'
 More she had spoke, but yawn'd—All nature nods:
What mortal can resist the yawn of gods?
Churches and chapels instantly it reached;
(St. James's first, for leaden G— preached:)
Then catched the schools; the hall scarce kept awake;
The convocation gaped, but could not speak:
Lost was the nations sense, nor could be found,
While the long solemn unison went round:
Wide, and more wide, it spread o'er all the realm;
E'en Palinurus nodded at the helm:
The vapour mild o'er each committee crept;
Unfinish'd treaties in each office slept;
And chiefless armies dozed out the campaign;
And navies yawned for orders on the main.
 O Muse! relate, (for you can tell alone,
Wits have short memories, and dunces none,)
Relate who first, who last, resigned to rest;
Whose heads she partly, whose completely, blest;
What charms could faction, what ambition lull,
The venal quiet, and intrance the dull;
Till drown'd was sense, and shame, and right, and wrong
O sing, and hush the nations with thy song!

* * *

 In vain, in vain—the all-composing hour
Resistless falls; the muse obeys the power.
She comes! she comes! the sable throne behold
Of Night primeval, and of Chaos old!
Before her fancy's gilded clouds decay,
And all its varying rainbows die away.
Wit shoots in vain its momentary fires,
The meteor drops, and in a flash expires.
As one by one, at dread Medea's strain,
The sick'ning stars fade off the ethereal plain;
As Argus' eyes, by Hermes' wand oppress'd,
Closed one by one to everlasting rest;
Thus at her felt approach, and secret might,
Art after art goes out, and all is night.
See skulking truth to her old cavern fled,
Mountains of casuistry heap'd o'er her head;
Philosophy, that lean'd on heaven before,
Shrinks to her second cause, and is no more

Physic of metaphysic begs defence,
And metaphysic calls for aid on sense!
See mystery to mathematics fly!
In vain! they gaze, turn giddy, rave, and dies,
Religion, blushing, veils her sacred fires,
And unawares morality expires.
Nor public flame, nor private, dares to shine;
Nor human spark is left nor glimpse divine!
Lo! thy dread empire, Chaos! is restored;
Light dies before thy uncreating word:
Thy hand, great Anarch! lets the curtain fall;
And universal darkness buries all.

ESSAY ON CRITICISM.

[WRITTEN IN THE YEAR 1709.]

PART I.

Introduction. That it is as great a fault to judge ill as to write ill, and a more dangerous one to the public, ver. 1. That a true taste is as rare to be found as a true genius, v. 9 18. That most men are born with some taste, but spoiled by false education, v. 19-25. The multitude of critics, and causes of them, v. 26-45. That we are to study our own taste, and know the limits of it, v. 46-67. Nature the best guide of judgment, v. 68-87; improved by arts and rules, which are but methodized nature, v. 88. Rules derived from the practice of the ancient poets, v. 88-110; that therefore the ancients are necessary to be studied by a critic, particularly Homer and Virgil, v. 118-138. Of licenses, and the use of them, by the ancients, v. 141-180. Reverence due to the ancients, and praise of them, v. 181, &c.

'Tis hard to say if greater want of skill
Appear in writing or in judging ill;
But of the two, less dangerous is the offence
To tire our patience than mislead our sense:
Some few in that, but numbers err in this;
Ten censure wrong for one who writes amiss;
A fool might once himself alone expose;
Now one in verse makes many more in prose.
'Tis with our judgments as our watches, none
Go just alike, but each believes his own.
In poets as true genius is but rare,
True tastes as seldom is the critic's share;
Both must alike from heaven derive their light,
These born to judge as well as those to write.
Let such teach others who themselves excel,
And censure freely who have written well.
Authors are partial to their wit, 'tis true,
But are not critics to their judgment too?
Yet, if we look more closely, we shall find
Most have the seeds of judgment in their mind:

Nature affords at least a glimmering light;
The lines, though touch'd but faintly, are drawn right:
But as the slightest-sketch, if justly traced,
Is by ill-colouring but the more disgraced,
So by false learning is good sense defaced:
Some are bewilder'd in the maze of schools,
And some made coxcombs nature meant but fools:
In search of wit these lose their common sense,
And then turn critics in their own defence:
Each burns alike who can or cannot write,
Or with a rival's or an eunuch's spite.
All fools have still an itching to deride,
And fain would be upon the laughing side.
If Mævius scribble in Apollo's spite,
There are who judge still worse than he can write.
 Some have at first for wits, then poets, pass'd,
Turn'd critics next, and prov'd plain fools at last.
Some neither can for wits nor critics pass,
As heavy mules are neither horse nor ass.
Those half-learn'd witlings, numerous in our isle,
As half-form'd insects on the banks of Nile;
Unfinished things, one knows not what to call,
Their generation's so equivocal:
To tell them would an hundred tongues require,
Or one vain wit's, that might an hundred tire.
 But you who seek to give and merit fame,
And justly bear a critic's noble name,
Be sure yourself and your own reach to known,
How far your genius, taste, and learning, go;
Launch not beyond your depth, but be discreet,
And mark that point where sense and dulness meet.
 Nature to all things fix'd the limits fit,
And wisely curb'd proud man's pretending wit.
As on the land while here the ocean gains,
In other parts it leaves wide sandy plains;
Thus in the soul, while memory prevails,
The solid power of understanding fails;
Where beams of warm imagination play,
The memory's soft figures melt away.
One science only will one genius fit;
So vast is art, so narrow human wit:
Not only bounded to peculiar arts
But oft in those confined to single parts.
Like kings we lose the conquests gained before,
By vain ambition still to make them more:
Each might his sev'ral province well command,
Would all but stoop to what they understand.
 First follow nature, and your judgment frame
By her just standard, which is still the same;

Unerring nature! still divinely bright,
One clear, unchanged and universal light,
Life, force, and beauty, must to all impart,
At once the source, and end, and test, of art.
Art from that fund each just supply provides,
Works without show, and without pomp presides:
In some fair body thus the informing soul
With spirits feeds, with vigour fills the whole;
Each motion guides, and ev'ry nerve sustains;
Itself unseen, but in the effects remains.
Some, to whom Heaven in wit has been profuse,
Want as much more to turn it to its use;
For wit and judgment often are at strife,
Though meant each other's aid, like man and wife.
'Tis more to guide than spur the muse's steed,
Restrain his fury than provoke his speed:
The winged courser, like a generous horse,
Shows most true mettle when you check his course.
Those rules of old, discover'd, not devis'd,
Are nature still, but nature methodiz'd;
Nature, like liberty, is but restrain'd
By the same laws which first herself ordain'd.
Hear how learned Greece her useful rules indites,
When to repress and when indulge our flights:
High on Parnassus' top her sons she show'd,
And pointed out those arduous paths they trod;
Held from afar, aloft the immortal prize,
And urged the rest by equal steps to rise.
Just precepts thus from great examples given,
She drew from them what they deriv'd from Heaven:
The generous critic fann'd the poet's fire,
And taught the world with reason to admire.
Then Criticism the muse's handmaid proved,
To dress her charms, and make her more beloved;
But following wits from that intention stray'd;
Who could not win the mistress woo'd the maid;
Against the poets their own arms they turn'd,
Sure to hate most the men from whom they learn'd.
So modern 'pothecaries, taught the art
By doctors' bills to play the doctors's part.
Bold in the practice of mistaken rules,
Prescribe, apply, and call their masters fools.
Some on the leaves of ancient authors prey;
Nor time nor moths e'er spoil'd so much as they:
Some drily plain, without invention's aid,
Write dull receipts how poems may be made;
These leave the sense their learning to display,
And those explain the meaning quite away.
You then, whose judgment the right course would steer.
Known well each ancient's proper character;

His fable, subjects, scope in ev'ry page;
Religion, country, genius of his age:
Without all these at once before your eyes,
Cavil you may, but never criticise.
Be Homer's works your study and delight,
Read them by day, and meditate by night;
Thence form your judgment, thence your maxims bring,
And trace the muses upward to their spring.
Still with itself compared his text peruse;
And let your comment be the Mantuan muse.
When first young Maro in his boundless mind
A work to outlast immortal Rome design'd,
Perhaps he seemed above the critic's law,
And but from nature's fountains scorned to draw;
But when to examine ev'ry part he came,
Nature and Homer were, he found, the same.
Convinced, amazed, he checks the bold design,
And rules as strict his laboured work confine
As if the Stagyrite o'erlooked each line.
Learn hence from ancient rules a just esteem;
To copy nature is to copy them.
Some beauties yet no precepts can declare,
For there's a happiness as well as care.
Music resembles poetry; in each
Are nameless graces, which no methods teach,
And which a master-hand alone can reach.
If, where the rules not far enough extend,
(Since rules were made but to promote their end,)
Such lucky license answer to the full
The intent proposed, that license is a rule.
Thus Pegasus, a nearer way to take,
May boldly deviate from the common track.
From vulgar bounds with brave disorder part,
And snatch a grace beyond the reach of art,
Which, without passing through the judgment, gains
The heart, and all its end at once attains.
In prospects thus some objects please our eyes,
Which out of nature's common order rise;
The shapeless rock, or hanging precipice.
Great wits sometimes may gloriously offend,
And rise to faults true critics dare not mend;
But though the ancients thus their rules invade,
(As kings dispense with laws themselves hath made,)
Moderns, beware! or, if you must offend
Against the precept, ne'er transgress its end;
Let it be seldom, and compelled by need;
And have at least their precedent to plead;
The critic else proceeds without remorse,
Seizes your fame, and puts his laws in force.

I know there are to whose presumptuous thoughts
Those freer beauties e'en in them see faults.
Some figures monstrous and mis-shaped appear,
Considered singly, or beheld too near,
Which, but proportioned to their light or place,
Due distance reconciles to form and grace
A prudent chief not always must display
His powers in equal ranks and fair array,
But with the occasion and the place comply,
Conceal his force, nay, seem sometimes to fly
These oft are stratagems which errors seem;
Nor is it Homer nods, but we that dream.
Still green with bays each ancient altar stands,
Above the reach of sacrilegious hands,
Secure from flames, from envy's fiercer rage,
Destructive war, and all-involving age.
See from each clime the learned their incense bring!
Hear in all tongues consenting pæans ring!
In praise so just let every voice be join'd,
And fill the general chorus of mankind.
Hail, bards triumphant! born in happier days,
Immortal heirs of universal praise!
Whose honours with increase of ages grow,
As streams roll down, enlarging as they flow;
Nations unborn your mighty name shall sound,
And worlds applaud that must not yet be found;
O may some spark of your celestial fire
The last, the meanest, of your sons inspire,
(That on weak wings, from far, pursues your flights,
Glows while he reads, but trembles as he writes,)
To teach vain wits a science little known,
To admire superior sense, and doubt their own!

PART II.

Causes hindering a true judgment. 1. Pride, v. 209. 2. Imperfect learning, v. 215. 3. Judging by parts, and not by the whole, v. 233-288. Critics in wit, language, versification only, v. 289, 305, 337, &c. 4. Being too hard to please, or too apt to admire, v. 384. 5. Partiality,—too much love to a sect,—to the Ancients or Moderns, v. 394. 6. Prejudice or prevention, v. 408. 7. Singularity, v. 424. 8. Inconstancy, v. 430. 9. Party spirit, v. 452, &c. 10. Envy, v. 466. Against envy, and in praise of good-nature, v. 508, &c. When severity is chiefly to be used by critics, v. 526, &c.

Of all the causes which conspire to blind
Man's erring judgment, and misguide the mind,
What the weak head with strongest bias rules,
Is pride, the never-failing vice of fools.
Whatever nature has in worth denied,
She gives in large recruits of needful pride:
For as in bodies thus in souls we find,
What wants in blood and spirits swelled with wind:
Pride, where wit fails, steps in to our defence,
And fills up all the mighty void of sense:
If once right reason drives that cloud away,
Truth breaks upon us with resistless day.
Trust not yourself; but, your defects to know,
Make use of every friend—and every foe.
A little learning is a dangerous thing;
Drink deep, or taste not the Pierian spring:
There shallow draughts intoxicate the brain,
And drinking largely sobers us again,
Fired at first sight with what the muse imparts,
In fearless youth we tempt the heights of arts,
While from the bounded level of our mind
Short views we take, nor see the lengths behind;
But more advanced, behold, with strange, surprise,
New distant scenes of endless science rise!
So pleased at first the towering Alps we try,
Mount o'er the vales, and seem to tread the sky!
The eternal snows appear already past,
And the first clouds and mountains seem the last;
But those attained, we tremble to survey
The growing labours of the lengthened way:
The increasing prospect tires our wandering eyes
Hills peep o'er hills, and Alps on Alps arise!

A perfect judge will read each work of wit
With the same spirit that its author writ;
Survey the whole, nor seek slight faults to find
Where Nature moves, and rapture warms the mind;
Nor lose, for that malignant dull delight,
The gen'rous pleasure to be charm'd with wit.
But in such lays as neither ebb nor flow,
Correctly cold, and regularly low,
That shunning faults one quiet tenor keep,
We cannot blame indeed—but we may sleep.
In wit, as nature, what affects our hearts
Is not th' exactness of peculiar parts:
'Tis not a lip or eye we beauty call,
But the joint force and full result of all.
Thus when we view some well proportion'd dome,
(The world's just wonder, and e'en thine, O Rome!)
No single parts unequally surprise,
All comes united to th' admiring eyes;
No monstrous height, or breadth, or length appear;
The whole at once is bold and regular.
Whoever thinks a faultless piece to see,
Thinks what ne'er was, nor is, nor e'er shall be.
In every work regard the writer's end,
Since none can compass more than they intend;
And if the means be just, the conduct true,
Applause, in spite of trivial faults, is due.
As men of breeding, sometimes men of wit,
To avoid great errors, must the less commit;
Neglect the rules each verbal critic lays,
For not to know some trifles is a praise.
Most critics, fond of some subservient art,
Still make the whole depend upon a part:
They talk of principles, but notions prize,
And all to one lov'd folly sacrifice.
Once on a time La Mancha's knight, they say
A certain bard encount'ring on the way,
Discours'd in terms as just, with looks as sage,
As e'er could Dennis of the Grecian stage,
Concluding all were desperate sots and fools
Who durst depart from Aristotle's rules.
Our author, happy in a judge so nice,
Produced his play, and begg'd the knight's advice;
Made him observe the subject and the plot,
The manners, passions, unities; what not?
All which, exact to rule, were brought about,
Were but a combat in the lists left out.
'What! leave the combat out?' exclaims the knight.
'Yes, or we must renounce the Stagirite.'
Not so, by Heaven!' he answers in a rage;
Knights, squires, and steeds must enter on the stage.'

'So vast a throng the stage can ne'er contain.'
'Then build a new, or act it in a plain.'
Thus critics of less judgment then caprice,
Curious, not knowing, not exact, but nice,
Form short ideas, and offend in arts
(As most in manners) by a love to parts.
Some to conceit alone their taste confine,
And glitt'ring thoughts struck out at ev'ry line;
Pleas'd with a work where nothing's just or fit,
One glaring chaos and wild heap of wit:
Poets, like painters, thus unskill'd to trace
The naked nature and the living grace,
With gold and jewels cover ev'ry part,
And hide with ornaments their want of art.
True wit is nature to advantage dress'd,
What oft was thought, but ne'er so well express'd;
Something whose truth convinc'd at sight we find,
That gives us back the image of our mind.
As shades more sweetly recommend the light,
So modest plainness sets off sprightly wit:
For works may have more wit than does them good,
As bodies perish through excess of blood.
Others for language all their care express;
And value books, as women men, for dress:
Their praise is still,—'the style is excellent;'
The sense they humbly take upon content.
Words are like leaves, and where they most abound,
Much fruit of sense beneath is rarely found.
False eloquence, like the prismatic glass,
Its gaudy colours spreads on ev'ry place;
The face of nature we no more survey,
All glares alike, without distinction gay;
But true expression, like th' unchanging sun
Clears and improves whate'er it shines upon:
It gilds all objects, but it alters none.
Expression is the dress of thought, and still
Appears more decent as more suitable.
A vile conceit, in pompous words expressed,
Is like a clown in regal purple dressed:
Fo different styles with different subjects sort,
As several garbs with country, town, and court.
Some by old words to fame have made pretence:
Ancients in phrase, mere moderns in their sense:
Such laboured nothings in so strange a style
Amaze the unlearned, and make the learned smile
Unlucky as Fungoso in the play,
These sparks with awkward vanity display
What the fine gentleman wore yesterday;
And but so mimic ancient wits at best,
As apes our grandsires in their doublets dress'd.

In words as fashions the same rule will hold,
Alike fantastic if too new or old:
Be not the first by whom the new are tried,
Nor yet the last to lay the old aside.
But most by numbers judge a poet's song,
And smooth or rough with them is right or wrong:
In the bright muse though thousand charms conspire,
Her voice is all these tuneful fools admire;
Who haunt Parnassus but to please their ear,
Not mend their minds, as some to church repair,
Not for the doctrine, but the music there.
These equal syllables alone require,
Though oft the ear the open vowels tire,
While expletives their feeble aid to join,
And ten low words oft creep in one dull line:
While they ring round the same unvaried chimes,
With sure returns of still expected rhymes;
Where'er you find 'the cooling western breeze,'
In the next line, it 'whispers through the trees:'
If crystal streams 'with pleasing murmurs creep,'
The reader's threaten'd, not in vain, with 'sleep:'
Then, at the last and only couplet, fraught
With some unmeaning thing they call a thought,
A needless Alexandrine ends the song,
That like a wounded snake drags its slow length along:
Leave such to tune their own dull rhymes, and know
What's roundly smooth, or languishingly slow,
And praise the easy vigour of a line
Where Denham's strength and Waller's sweetness join.
True ease in writting comes from art, not chance,
As those move easiest who have learned to dance.
'Tis not enough no harshness gives offence;
The sound must seem an echo to the sense.
Soft is the strain when Zephyr gently blows,
And the smooth stream in smoother numbers flows;
But when loud surges lash the sounding shore,
The hoarse rough verse should like the torrent roar.
When Ajax strives some rock's vast weight to throw,
The line too labours, and the words move slow
Not so when swift Camilla scours the plain,
Flies o'er th' unbending corn, and skims along the main.
Hear how Timotheus' varied lays surprise,
And bid alternate passions fall and rise,
While at each change the son of Lybian Jove
Now burns with glory and then melts with love:
Now his fierce eyes with sparkling fury glow,
Now sighs steal out, and tears begin to flow:
Persians and Greeks like turns of Nature found,
And the world's victor stood subdued by sound!

The power of music all our hearts allow,
And what Timotheus was is Dryden now.
Avoid extremes, and shun the fault of such
Who still are pleased too little or too much.
At every trifle scorn to take offence;
That always shews great pride or little sense:
Those heads, as stomachs, are not sure the best
Which nauseate all, and nothing can digest.
Yet let not each gay turn thy rapture move;
For fools admire, but men of sense approve.
As things seem large which we through mists descry,
Dulness is ever apt to magnify.
Some foreign writers some our own despise;
The ancients only or the moderns prize.
Thus wit, like faith, by each man is applied
To one small sect, and all are damn'd beside.
Meanly they seek the blessing to confine,
And force that sun but on a part to shine,
Which not alone the southern wit sublimes,
But ripens spirits in cold northern climes;
Which from the first has shone on ages past,
Enlights the present, and shall warm the last
Though each may feel increases and decays,
And sees now clearer and now darker days:
Regard not then if wit be old or new;
But blame the false, and value still the true.
Some ne'er advance a judgment of their own,
But catch the spreading notion of the town;
They reason and conclude by precedent,
And old stale nonsense which they ne'er invent.
Some judge of authors' names, not works, and then
Nor praise nor blame the writings, but the men.
Of all this servile herd the worst is he
That in proud dulness joins with quality;
A constant critic at the great man's board,
To fetch and carry nonsense for my lord.
What woeful stuff this madrigal would be
In some starved hackney sonneteer, or me!
But let a lord once own the happy lines,
How the wit brightens! how the style refines!
Before his sacred name flies every fault.
And each exalted stanza teems with thought!
The vulgar thus through imitation err,
As oft the learned by being singular;
So much they scorn the crowd, that if the throng
By chance go right, they purposely go wrong.
So schismatics the plain believers quit,
And are but damned for having too much wit.
Some praise at morning what they blame at night;
But always think the last opinion right.

A muse by these is like a mistress us'd;
This hour she's idolized, the next abus'd;
While their weak heads, like towns unfortified,
'Twixt sense and nonsense daily change their side.
Ask them the cause; they're wiser still they say;
And still to-morrow's wiser than to-day.
We think our fathers fools, so wise we grow;
Our wiser sons, no doubt, will think us so.
Once school-divines this zealous isle o'erspread;
Who knew most sentences was deepest read:
Faith, gospel, all seemed made to be disputed,
And none had sense enough to be confuted.
Scotists and Thomists now in peace remain,
Amidst their kindred comrades in Duck Lane.
If faith itself has dresses different worn,
What wonder modes in wit should take their turn;
Oft leaving what is natural and fit,
The current folly proves the ready wit;
And authors think their reputation safe
Which lives as long as fools are pleased to laugh.
Some, valuing those of their own side or mind,
Still make themselves the measure of mankind:
Fondly we think we honour merit then,
When we but praise ourselves in other men.
Parties in wit attend on those of state,
And public faction doubles private hate.
Pride, malice, folly, against Dryden rose
In various shapes of parsons, critics, beaux:
But sense survived when merry jests were past;
For rising merit will buoy up at last.
Might he return, and bless once more our eyes,
New Blackmores and new Milbourns must arise:
Nay, should great Homer lift his awful head,
Zoilus again would start up from the dead.
Envy will merit as its shade pursue,
But like a shadow proves the substance true;
For envied wit, like Sol eclipsed, makes known
The opposing body's grossness, not its own.
When first that sun too powerful beams displays,
It draws up vapours which obscure its rays;
But e'en those clouds at last adorn its way,
Reflect new glories, and augment the day,
Be thou the first true merit to befriend;
His praise is lost who stays till all commend
Short is the date, alas! of modern rhymes,
And 'tis but just to let them live betimes
No longer now thy golden age appears
When patriarch wits survived a thousand years:
Now length of fame (our second life) is lost,
And bare threescore is all e'en that can boast:

Our sons their fathers' failing language see,
And such as Chaucer is shall Dryden be.
So when the faithful pencil has designed
Some bright idea of the master's mind,
Where a new world leaps out at his command,
And ready nature waits upon his hand;
When the ripe colours soften and unite,
And sweetly melt into just shade and light
When mellowing years their full perfection give,
And each bold figure just begins to live,
The treacherous colours the fair art betray,
And all the bright creation fades away!
Unhappy wit, like most mistaken things,
Atones not for that envy which it brings:
In youth alone its empty praise we boast,
But soon the short-liv'd vanity is lost;
Like some fair flower the early spring supplies,
That gaily blooms, but e'en in blooming dies.
What is this wit which must our cares employ?
The owner's wife, that other men enjoy;
Then most our trouble still when most admired,
And still the more we give, the more required;
Whose fame with pains we guard, but lose with ease,
Sure some to vex, but never all to please;
'Tis what the vicious fear, the virtuouous shun
By fools 'tis hated, and by knaves undone!
If wit so much from ignorance undergo,
Ah, let not learning too commence its foe!
Of old, those met reward who could excel,
And such were praised who but endeavour'd well:
Though triumphs were to generals only due,
Crowns were reserved to grace the soldiers too
Now, they who reach Parnassus' lofty crown,
Employ their pains to spurn some others down;
And while self-love each jealous writer rules,
Contending wits become the sport of fools;
But still the worst with most regret commend;
For each ill author is as bad a friend.
To what base ends, and by what abject ways,
Are mortals urged through sacred lust of praise!
Ah, ne'er so dire a thirst of glory boast;
Nor in the critic let the man be lost.
Good nature and good sense must ever join;
To err is human, to forgive, divine.
But if in noble minds some dregs remain,
Not yet purged off, of spleen and sour disdain,
Discharge that rage on more provoking crimes,
Nor fear a death in these flagitious times.
No pardon vile obscenity should find,
Though wit and art conspire to move your mind:

But dulness with obscenity must prove
As shameful sure as impotence in love.
In the fat age of pleasure, wealth and ease,
Sprang the rank weed, and thrived with large increase
When love was all an easy monarch's care,
Seldom at council, never in a war,
Jilts ruled the state, and statesmen farces writ;
Nay, wits had pensions, and young lords had wit;
The fair sat panting at a courtier's play,
And not a mask went unimproved away;
The modest fan was lifted up no more,
And virgins smiled at what they blush'd before.
The following license of a foreign reign
Did all the dregs of bold Socinus drain;
Then unbelieving priests reform'd the nation,
And taught more pleasant methods of salvation;
Where Heaven's free subjects might their rights dispute,
Lest God himself should seem too absolute:
Pulpits their sacred satire learn'd to spare,
And vice admired to find a flatterer there!
Encouraged thus, wit's Titans braved the skies,
And the press groan'd with licensed blasphemies.
These monsters, critics! with your darts engage:
Here point your thunder, and exhaust your rage!
Yet shun their fault who, scandalously nice,
Will needs mistake an author into vice:
All seems infected that th' infected spy,
As all looks yellow to the jaundiced eye.

PART III.

RULES for the conduct of manners in a critic. 1. Candour, v. 563. Modesty, v. 566. Good breeding, v. 572. Sincerity and freedom of advice, v. 578. 2. When one's counsel is to be restrained, v. 584. Character of an incorrigible poet, v. 600; and of an impertinent critic, v. 610, &c. Character of a good critic, v. 629. The history of criticism, and characters of the best critics. Aristotle, v. 645. Horace, v. 653. Dionysius, v. 665. Petronius, v. 667. Quintilian, v. 669, Longinus, v. 675. Of the decay of criticism, and its revival. Erasmus, v. 693. Vida, v. 705. Boileau, v: 714. Lord Roscommon, &c., v 725 Conclusion.

LEARN then what morals critics ought to show,
For 'tis but half a judge's task to know.
'Tis not enough taste, judgment, learning, join;
In all you speak let truth and candour shine;
That not alone what to your sense is due
All may allow, but seek your friendship too.
Be silent always when you doubt your sense,
And speak, though sure, with seeming diffidence:
Some positive persisting fops we know,
Who if once wrong will needs be always so;
But you with pleasure own your errors past,
And make each day a critique on the last.
'Tis not enough your counsel still be true,
Blunt truths more mischief than nice falsehoods do:
Men must be taught as if you taught them not,
And things unknown proposed as things forgot.
Without good breeding truth is disapproved;
That only makes superior sense beloved.
Be niggards of advice on no pretence,
For the worst avarice is that of sense.
With mean complacence ne'er betray your trust,
Nor be so civil as to prove unjust.
Fear not the anger of the wise to raise;
Those best can bear reproof who merit praise.
'Twere well might critics still this freedom take,
But Appius reddens at each word you speak,
And stares tremendous, with a threatening eye,
Like some fierce tyrant in old tapestry.

Fear most to tax an honourable fool,
Whose right it is, uncensured, to be dull:
Such without wit are poets when they please,
As without learning they can take degrees.
Leave dangerous truths to unsuccessful satires,
And flattery to fulsome dedicators,
Whom, when they praise, the world believes no more
Than when they promise to give scribbling o'er.
'Tis best sometimes your censure to restrain,
And charitably let the dull be vain;
Your silence there is better than your spite,
For who can rail so long as they can write?
Still humming on their drowsy course they keep,
And lash'd so long, like tops are lash'd asleep.
False steps but help them to renew their race,
As after stumbling jades will mend their pace.
What crowds of these, impenitently bold,
In sounds and jingling syllables grown old,
Still run on poets in a raging vein,
E'en to the dregs and squeezings of the brain,
Strain out the last dull droppings of their sense
And rhyme with all the rage of impotence!
  Such shameless bards we have; and yet 'tis true
There are as mad abandon'd critics too.
The bookful blockhead ignorantly read,
With loads of learned lumber in his head,
With his own tongue still edifies his ears,
And always listening to himself appears:
All books he reads, and all he reads assails,
From Dryden's Fables down to Durfey's Tales.
With him most authors steal their works or buy;
Garth did not write his own Dispensary.
Name a new play, and he's the poet's friend;
Nay, show'd his faults—but when would poets mend?
No place so sacred from such fops is barr'd,
Nor is Paul's Church more safe than Paul's Church-yard:
Nay, fly to altars, there they'll talk you dead;
For fools rush in where angels fear to tread.
Distrustful sense with modest caution speaks—
It still looks home, and short excursions makes;
But rattling nonsense in full volleys breaks,
And never shock'd, and never turn'd aside,
Bursts out, resistless, with a thundering tide.
  But where's the man who counsel can bestow,
Still pleased to teach, and yet not proud to know;
Unbiass'd or by favour or by spite,
Not dully prepossess'd nor blindly right!

Tho' learned, well-bred; and tho' well-bred, sincere;
Modesty bold, and humanely severe;
Who to a friend his faults can freely show,
And gladly praise the merit of a foe;
Blessed with a taste exact, yet unconfin'd,
A knowledge both of books and human-kind;
Generous converse; a soul exempt from pride;
And loves to praise with reason on his side?
Such once were critics; such the happy few
Athens and Rome in better ages knew.
The mighty Stagyrite first left the shore,
Spread all his sails, and durst the deeps explore;
He steer'd securely, and discovered far,
Led by the light of the Mæonian star.
Poets, a race long unconfined and free,
Still fond and proud of savage liberty,
Received his laws, and stood convinced 'twas fit,
Who conqured Nature should preside o'er wit.
  Horace still charms with graceful negligence,
And without method talks us into sense;
Will like a friend, familiarly convey
The truest notions in the easiest way.
He who, supreme in judgment as in wit,
Might boldly censure as he boldly writ.
Yet judged with coolness, though he sung with fire·
His precepts teach but what his works inspire.
Our critics take a contrary extreme,
They judge with fury, but they write with phlegm;
Nor suffers Horace more in wrong translations
By wits, than critics in as wrong quotations.
  See Dionysius, Homer's thoughts refine,
And call new beauties forth from every line!
  Fancy and art in gay Petronius please,
The scholar's learning with the courtier's ease.
  In grave Quintilian's copious work we find
The justest rules and clearest method join'd,
Thus useful arms in magizines we place,
All ranged in order, and disposed with grace;
But less to please the eye than arm the hand,
Still fit for use, and ready at command.
  Thee, bold Longinus! all the Nine inspire,
And bless their critic with a poet's fire:
An ardent judge, who zealous in his trust,
With warmth gives sentence, yet is always just;
Whose own example strengthens all his laws,
And is himself that great sublime he draws.
  Thus long succeeding critics justly reign'd,
License repressed, and useful laws ordain'd:

Learning and Rome alike in empire grew,
And arts still followed where her eagles flew;
From the same foes at last both felt their doom
And the same age saw learning fall and Rome.
With tyranny then superstition join'd;
As that the body, this enslaved the mind;
Much was believed, but little understood,
And to be dull was construed to be good,
A second deluge learning thus o'er-ran,
And the monks finished what the Goths began.
At length Erasmus, that great injured name,
(The glory of the priesthood, and the shame!)
Stemmed the wild torrent of a barbarous age,
And drove those holy vandals off the stage.
But see! each muse in Leo's golden days
Starts from her trance, and trims her withered bays,
Rome's ancient genius o'er its ruins spread,
Shakes off the dust, and rears his rev'rend head.
Then sculpture and her sister arts revive;
Stones leaped to form, and rocks began to live;
With sweeter notes each rising temple rung;
A Raphel painted, and a Vida sung:
Immortal Vida! on whose honoured brow
The poet's bays and critic's ivy grow!
Cremona now shall ever boast thy name,
As next in place to Mantua, next in fame!
But soon by impious arms from Latium chased,
Their ancient bounds the banish'd muses passed:
Thence arts o'er all the northern world advance,
But critic learning flourished most in France:
The rules a nation born to serve obeys,
And Boileau still in right of Horace sways.
But we, brave Britons! foreign laws despised,
And kept unconqured and uncivilised;
Fierce for the liberties of wit, and bold,
We still defied the Romans, as of old.
Yet some there were, among the sounder few
Of those who less presumed and better knew,
Who durst assert the juster ancient cause,
And here restored wit's fundamental laws.
Such was the muse whose rules and practice tell,
'Nature's chief masterpiece is writing well.'
Such was Roscommon, not more learn'd than good,
With manners generous as his noble blood;
To him the wit of Greece and Rome was known,
And every author's merit but his own.
Such late was Walsh—the muse's judge and friend,
Who justly knew to blame or to commend!

18*

To failings mild, but zealous for desert
The clearest head and the sincerest heart.
This humble praise, lamented shade! receive;
This praise at least a grateful muse may give:
The muse whose early voice you taught to sing,
Prescribed her heights, and pruned her tender wing,
(Her guide now lost) no more attempts to rise,
But in low numbers short excursions tries;
Content if hence the unlearned their wants may view,
The learn'd reflect on what before they knew:
Careless of censure, nor too fond of fame;
Still pleased to praise, yet not afraid to blame;
Averse alike to flatter or offend;
Not free from faults, nor yet too vain to mend.

THE TEMPLE OF FAME.

[WRITTEN IN THE YEAR 1711.]

ADVERTISEMENT.

THE hint of the following piece was taken from Chaucer's House of Fame. The design is in a manner entirely altered, the descriptions and most of the particular thoughts my own: yet I could not suffer it to be printed without this acknowledgment. The reader who would compare this with Chaucer, may begin with his Third Book of Fame, there being nothing in the two first books that answer to their title.—POPE.

IN that soft season, when descending showers
Call forth the greens, and wake the rising flowers;
When opening buds salute the welcome day,
And earth relenting feels the genial ray;
As balmy sleep had charm'd my cares to rest,
And love itself was banish'd from my breast,
(What time the morn mysterious visions brings,
While purer slumbers spread their golden wings;)
A train of phantoms in wild order rose,
And, join'd, this intellectual scene compose.
  I stood, methought, betwixt earth, seas, and skies;
The whole creation open to my eyes
In air self-balanced hung the globe below,
Where mountains rise, and circling oceans flow;
Here naked rocks, and empty wastes were seen;
There towering cities, and the forests green:
Here sailing ships delight the wandering eyes;
There trees, and intermingled temples rise:
Now a clear sun the shining scene displays;
The transient landscape now in clouds decays.
  O'er the wide prospect as I gazed around,
Sudden I heard a wild promiscuous sound,
Like broken thunders that at distance roar,
Or billows murmuring on the hollow shore:
Then, gazing up, a glorious pile beheld,
Whose towering summit ambient clouds conceal'd,
High on a rock of ice the structure lay;
Steep its ascent, and slippery was the way;

The wondrous rock like Parian marble shone,
And seem'd, to distant sight, of solid stone.
Inscriptions here of various names I view'd,
The greater part by hostile time subdued:
Yet wide was spread their fame in ages past,
And poets once had promised they should last.
Some fresh engraved appear'd of wits renown'd;
I look'd again, nor could their trace be found.
Critics I saw, that other names deface,
And fix their own, with labour, in their place:
Their own, like others, soon their place resign'd;
Or disappear'd, and left the first behind.
Nor was the work impair'd by storms alone,
But felt the approaches of too warm a sun;
For Fame, impatient of extremes, decays
Not more by envy than excess of praise.
Yet part no injuries of heaven could feel,
Like crystal, faithful to the graving steel:
The rocks high summit, in the temple shade,
Nor heat could melt, nor beating storm invade.
Their names inscribed unnumber'd ages past
From time's first birth, with time itself shall last;
These ever new, nor subject to decays,
Spread and grow brighter with the length of days.
So Zembla's rocks, (the beauteous work of frost,)
Rise white in air, and glitter o'er the coast;
Pale suns, unfelt, at distance roll away,
And on th' impassive ice the lightnings play;
Eternal snows the growing mass supply,
Till the bright mountains prop th' incumbent sky;
As Atlas fix'd, each hoary pile appears,
The gather'd winter of a thousand years.
On this foundation fame's high temple stands;
Stupendous pile! not rear'd by mortal hands.
Whate'er proud Rome or artful Greece beheld,
Or elder Babylon, its fame excell'd.
Four faces had the dome, and ev'ry face
Of various structure, but of equal grace.
Four brazen gates, on columns lifted high,
Salute the diff'rent quarters of the sky.
Here fabled chiefs, in darker ages born,
Or worthies old, whom arms or arts adorn,
Who cities rais'd, or tam'd a monstrous race,
The walls in venerable order grace;
Heroes in animated marble frown,
And legislators seem to think in stone.
Westward, a sumptuous frontispiece appear'd
On Doric pillars of white marble rear'd,
Crown'd with an architrave of antique mould,
And sculpture rising on the roughen'd gold.

In shaggy spoils here Theseus was beheld,
And Perseus dreadful with Minerva's shield:
There great Alcides, stooping with his toil,
Rests on his club, and holds th' Hesperian spoil:
Here Orpheus sings; trees moving to the sound,
Start from their roots, and form a shade around:
Amphion there the loud creating lyre
Strikes, and beholds a sudden Thebes aspire!
Cythæron's echoes answer to his call,
And half the mountain rolls into a wall:
There might you see the length'nihg spires ascend
The domes swell up, the wid'ning arches bend,
The growing tow'rs like exhalations rise,
And the huge colums heave into the skies.
The eastern front was glorious to behold,
With diamond flaming, and barbaric gold.
There Ninus shone, who spread the Assyrian fame,
And the great founder of the Persian name;
There in long robes the royal Magi stand,
Grave Zoroaster waves the circling wand;
The Sage Chaldeans rob'd in white appear'd,
And Brachmans, deep in desert woods rever'd.
These stopp'd the moon, and call'd th' unbodied shades
To midnight banquets in the glimm'ring glades;
Made visionary fabrics round them rise,
And airy spectres skim before their eyes;
Of talismans and sigils knew the pow'r,
And careful watch'd the planetary hour.
Superior, and alone, Confucius stood,
Who taught that useful science to be good.
But on the south, a long majestic race
Of Egypt's priests the gilded niches grace,
Who measur'd earth, describ'd the starry spheres
And trac'd the long records of lunar years.
High on his car Sesostris struck my view,
Whom scepter'd slaves in golden harness drew:
His hand a bow and pointed javelin hold;
His giant limbs are arm'd in scales of gold.
Between the statues obelisks were plac'd,
And the learn'd walls with hieroglyphics grac'd.
Of Gothic structure was the northern side,
O'erwrought with ornaments of barb'rous pride.
There huge colosses rose, with trophies crown'd,
And Runic characters were graved around:
There sat Zamolxis with erected eyes,
And Odin here in mimic trances dies.
There on rude iron columns, smear'd with blood,
The horrid forms of Scythian heroes stood,
Druids and bards, their once loud harps unstrung,
And youths that died to be by poets sung.

These and a thousand more of doubtful fame
To whom old fables gave a lasting name,
In ranks adorn'd the temple,s outward face;
The wall in lustre and effect like glass,
Which o'er each object casting various dyes,
Enlarges some, and others multiplies:
Nor void of emblem was the mystic wall,
For thus romantic Fame increases all.
The temple shakes, the sounding gates unfold
Wide vaults appear, and roofs of fretted gold,
Rais'd on a thousand pillars, wreath'd around
With laurel foliage, and with eagles crown,d
Of bright transparent beryl were the walls,
The friezes gold, and gold the capitals
As heav'n with stars, the roof with jewels glows,
And ever-living lamps depend in rows.
Full in the passage of each spacious gate,
The sage historians in white garments wait;
Grav'd o'er their seats the form of Time was found,
His scythe revers'd, and both his pinions bound.
Within stood heroes, who, through loud alarms,
In bloody fields pursu'd renown in arms.
High on a throne, with trophies charg'd, I view'd
The youth that all things but himself subdu'd:
His feet on sceptres and tiaras trod,
And his horn'd head belied the Libyan god.
There Cæsar, grac'd with bold Minervas, shone;
Cæsar, the world's great master, and his own;
Unmov'd, superor still in ev'ry state,
And scarce detested in his country's fate.
But chief were those who not for empire fought,
But with their toils their people's safety bought;
High o'er the rest Epaminondas stood;
Timoleon, glorious in his brother's blood;
Bold Scipio, saviour of the Roman state,
Great in his triumphs, in retirement great;
And wise Aurelius, in whose well-taught mind,
With boundless power unbounded virtue join'd;
His own strict judge, and patron of mankind.
Much suffering heroes next their honours claim,
Those of less noisy, and less guilty fame,
Fair virtue's silent train: supreme of these
Here ever shines the god-like Socrates;
He whom ungrateful Athens could expel,
At all times just, but when he sign'd the shell:
Here his abode the martyr'd Phocion claims,
With Agis, not the last of Spartan names:
Unconquer'd Cato shews the wound he tore,
And Brutus his ill genius meets no more.

But in the centre of the hallow'd choir,
Six pompous columns o'er the rest aspire;
Around the shrine itself of Fame they stand,
Hold the chief honours, and the fane command.
High on the first the mighty Homer shone,
Eternal adamant compos'd his throne;
Father of verse! in holy fillets dress'd,
His silver beard wav'd gently o'er his breast;
Though blind, a boldness in his looks appears;
In years he seem'd, but not impair'd by years.
The wars of Troy were round the pillars seen:
Here fierce Tydides wounds the Cyprian queen:
Here Hector glorious from Patroclus' fall;
Here dragg'd in triumph round the Trojan wall.
Motion and life did ev'ry part inspire;
Bold was the work, and prov'd the masters fire
A strong expression most he seem'd t' affect,
And here and there disclos'd a brave neglect.
A golden column next in rank appear'd,
On which a shrine of purest gold was rear'd;
Finish'd the whole, and labour'd ev'ry part,
With patient touches of unwearied art:
The Mantuan there in sober triumph state,
Compos'd his posture, and his look sedate;
On Homer still he fix'd a rev'rent eye;
Great without pride, in modest majesty.
In living sculpture on the sides were spread
The Latian wars, and haughty Turnus dead;
Eliza stretch'd upon the fun'ral pyre;
Æneas bending with his aged sire:
Troy flam'd in burning gold, and o'er the throne
'*Arms and the man*' in golden cyphers shone.
Four swans sustain a car of silver bright,
With heads advanc'd, and pinions stretch'd for flight:
Here, like some furious prophet, Pindar rode,
And seemed to labour with the inspiring god.
Across the harp a careless hand he flings,
And boldly sinks into the sounding strings.
The figur'd games of Greece the column grace,
Neptune and Jove survey the rapid race.
The youths hang o'er their chariots as they run;
The fiery steeds seem starting from the stone;
The champions in distorted postures threat;
And all appear'd irregularly great.
Here happy Horace tuned the Ausonian lyre
To sweeter sounds, and temper'd Pindar's fire;
Pleas'd with Alcæus' manly rage to infuse
The softer spirit of the Sapphic muse.
The polish'd pillar diff'rent sculptures grace,
A work outlasting monumental brass.

Here smiling Loves and Bacchanals appear,
The Julian star, and great Augustus here:
The doves that round the infant poet spread
Myrtles and bays, hang hov'ring o'er his head.
Here, in a shrine that cast a dazzling light,
Sate fix'd in thought the mighty Stagyrite;
His sacred head a radiant zodiac crown'd,
And various animals his sides surround;
His piercing eyes, erect, appear to view
Superior worlds, and look all nature through.
With equal rays immortal Tully shone,
The Roman rostra deck'd the consul's throne:
Gathering his flowing robe, he seem'd to stand
In act to speak, and graceful stretch'd his hand.
Behind, Rome's Genius waits with civic crowns,
And the great father of his country owns.
These massy columns in a circle rise,
O'er which a pompous dome invades the skies;
Scarce to the top I stretch'd my aching sight,
So large it spread, and swell'd to such a height:
Full in the midst proud Fame's imperial seat
With jewels blaz'd, magnificently great;
The vivid emeralds there revive the eye,
The flaming rubies show their sanguine dye,
Bright azure rays from lively sapphires stream,
And lucid amber casts a golden gleam.
With various colour'd light the pavement shone,
And all on fire appear'd the glowing throne;
The dome's high arch reflects the mingled blaze,
And forms a rainbow of alternate rays.
When on the goddess first I cast my sight,
Scarce seem'd her stature of a cubit's height;
But swell'd to larger size, the more I gaz'd,
Till to the roof her towering front she rais'd.
With her, the temple ev'ry moment grew,
And ampler vistas open'd to my view:
Upwards the columns shoot, the roofs ascend,
And arches widen, and long aisles extend
Such was her form, as ancient bards have told,
Wings raise her arms, and wings her feet infold
A thousand busy tongues the goddess bears,
A thousand open eyes, and thousand list'ning ears.
Beneath, in order rang'd, the tuneful Nine
(Her virgin handmaids) still attend the shrine:
With eyes on Fame for ever fixed, they sing;
For Fame they raise the voice, and tune the string;
With time's first birth began the heav'nly lays,
And last, eternal, through the length of days,
Around these wonders as I cast a look,
The trumpet sounded, and the temple shook,

And all the nations summoned at the call,
From different quarters fill the crowded hall
Of various tongues the mingled sounds were heard
In various garbs promiscuous throngs appear'd;
Thick as the bees, that with the spring renew
Their flow'ry toils, and sip the fragrant dew,
When the wing'd colonies first tempt the sky,
O'er dusky fields and shaded waters fly,
Or settling, seize the sweets the blossoms yield,
And a low murmur runs along the field.
Millions of suppliant crowds the shrine attend,
And all degrees before the goddess bend;
The poor, the rich, the valiant, and the sage,
And boasting youth, and narrative old age,
Their pleas were diff'rent, their request the same:
For good and bad alike are fond of Fame.
Some she disgrac'd, and some with honours crown'd;
Unlike successes equal merits found.
Thus her blind sister, fickle Fortune, reigns
And, undiscerning, scatters crowns and chains.
First at the shrine the learned world appear,
And to the goddess thus prefer their pray'r:
'Long have we sought t' instruct and please mankind,
With studies pale, with midnight vigils, blind;
But thank'd by few, rewarded yet by none,
We here appeal to thy superior throne:
On wit and learning the just prize bestow,
For Fame is all we must expect below.'
The goddess heard, and bade the muses raise
The golden trumpet of eternal praise:
From pole to pole the winds diffuse the sound,
That fills the circuit of the world around;
Not all at once, as thunder breaks the cloud,
The notes at first were rather sweet than loud:
By just degrees they ev'ry moment rise,
Fill the wide earth, and gain upon the skies.
At ev'ry breath were balmy odours shed,
Which still grew sweeter as they wider spread;
Less fragrant scents th' unfolding rose exhales,
Or spices breathing in Arabian gales.
Next these the good and just, an awful train,
Thus on their knees address'd the sacred fane:
'Since living virtue is with envy curs'd,
And the best men are treated like the worst,
Do thou, just goddess, call our merits forth,
And give each deed th' exact intrinsic worth,'
'Not with bare justice shall your act be crown'd:'
Said Fame, 'but high above desert renown'd:
Let fuller notes th' applauding world amaze,
And the loud clarion labour in your praise.'

This band dismiss'd, behold another crowd
Preferr'd the same request, and lowly bow'd;
The constant tenor of whose well-spent days
No less deserv'd a just return of praise.
But straight the direful trump of slander sounds;
Through the big dome the doubling thunder bounds;
Loud as the burst of cannon rends the skies,
The dire report through ev'ry region flies,
In ev'ry ear incessant rumours rung,
And gath'ring scandals grew on ev'ry tongue
From the black trumpet's rusty concave broke
Sulphureous flames, and clouds of rolling smoke:
The pois'nous vapour blots the purple skies,
And withers all before it as it flies.
A troop came next, who crowns and armour wore
And proud defiance in their looks they bore:
'For thee,' they cried, 'amidst alarms and strife,
We sail'd in tempests down the stream of life;
For thee, whole nations fill'd with flames and blood,
And swam to empire through the purple flood.
Those ills we dar'd, thy inspiration own,
What virtue seem'd, was done for thee alone.'
'Ambitious fools!' the queen replied and frown'd,
'Be all your acts in dark oblivion drown'd;
There sleep forgot, with mighty tyrants gone,
Your statues moulder'd, and your names unknown!'
A sudden cloud straight snatch'd them from my sight,
And each majestic phantom sunk in night.
Then came the smallest tribe I yet had seen;
Plain was their dress, and modest was their mien.
'Great idol of mankind! we neither claim
The praise of merit, nor aspire to fame!
But safe in deserts from th' applause of men,
Would die unheard of, as we liv'd unseen:
'Tis all we beg thee, to conceal from sight
Those acts of goodness which themselves requite.
O let us still the secret joys partake,
To follow virtues e'en for virtue's sake.'
'And live there men who slight immortal Fame?
Who then with incense shall adore our name?
But, mortals! know, 'tis still our greatest pride
To blaze those virtues which the good would hide.
Rise! Muses, rise! add all your tuneful breath
These must not sleep in darkness and in death.'
She said: in air the trembling music floats,
And on the winds triumphant swell the notes;
So soft, though high, so loud, and yet so clear,
E'en list'ning angels lean'd from heaven to hear:
To farthest shores th' ambrosial spirit flies,
Sweet to the world, and grateful to the skies.

Next these a youthful train their vows express'd,
With feathers crown'd, with gay embroidery dress'd:
'Hither,' they cried, 'direct your eyes and see
The men of pleasure, dress, and gallantry;
Ours is the place at banquets, balls, and plays;
Sprightly our nights, polite are all our days;
Courts we frequent, where 'tis our pleasing care
To pay due visits, and address the fair:
In fact, 'tis true, no nymph we could persuade,
But still in fancy vanquish'd every maid:
Of unknown duchesses lewd tales we tell,
Yet, would the world believe us, all were well.
The joy let others have, and we the name,
And what we want in pleasure, grant in fame.'
The queen assents; the trumpet rends the skies,
And at each blast a lady's honour dies.
Pleased with the same success, vast numbers press'd
Around the shrine, and made the same request.
'What, you,' she cried, 'unlearn'd in arts to please;
Slaves to yourselves, and e'en fatigu'd with ease,
Who lose a length of undeserving days,
Would you usurp the lover's dear-bought praise?
To just contempt, ye vain pretenders! fall,
The people's fable, and the scorn of all.'
Straight the black clarion sends a horrid sound,
Loud laughs burst out, and bitter scoffs fly round;
Whispers are heard, with taunts reviling loud,
And scornful hisses run through all the crowd.
Last, those who boast of mighty mischiefs done,
Enslave their country, or usurp a throne;
Or who their glory's dire foundation laid
On sovereigns ruin'd, or on friends bretray'd;
Calm, thinking villains, whom no faith could fix,
Of crooked counsels and dark politics;
Of these a gloomy tribe surround the throne,
And beg to make the immortal treasons known.
The trumpet roars, long flaky flames expire,
With sparks that seem'd to set the world on fire.
At the dread sound pale mortals stood aghast,
And startled nature trembled with the blast.
This having heard and seen, some pow'r unknown
Straight chang'd the scene, and snatch'd me from the throne.
Before my view appear'd a structure fair,
Its sight uncertain, if in earth or air;
With rapid motion turn'd the mansion round;
With ceaseless noise the ringing walls resound:
Not less in numbers were the spacious doors,
Than leaves or trees, or sands upon the shores;
Which still unfolded stand, by night, by day,
Pervious to winds, and open ev'ry way.

As flames by nature to the skies ascend,
As weighty bodies to the centre tend,
As to the sea returning rivers roll,
And the touch'd needle trembles to the pole;
Hither, as to their proper place, arise
All various sounds from earth, and seas, and skies,
Or spoke aloud, or whisper'd in the ear;
Nor ever silence, rest or peace is here,
As on the smooth expanse of crystal lakes.
The sinking stone at first a circle makes,
The trembling surface by the motion stirr'd,
Spreads in a second circle, than a third;
Wide, and more wide, the floating rings advance,
Fill all the watery plain, and to the margin dance;
Thus ev'ry voice and sound, when first they break
On neighbouring air, a soft impression make;
Another ambient circle then they move;
That in its turn impels the next above;
Through undulating air the sounds are sent,
And spread o'er all the fluid element.
There various news I heard of love and strife,
Of peace and war, health, sickness, death and life,
Of loss and gain, of famine and of store,
Of storms at sea, and travels on the shore,
Of prodigies, and portents seen in air,
Of fires and plagues, and stars with blazing hair,
Of turns of fortune, changes in the state,
The falls of favorites, projects of the great,
Of old mismanagements, taxations new;
All neither wholly false, nor wholly true
Above, below, without, within, around,
Confus'd, unnumber'd multitudes are found,
Who pass, repass, advance, and glide away,
Hosts raised by fear, and phantoms of a day:
Astrologers, that future fates foreshow
Projectors, quacks, and lawyers not a few;
And priests, and party zealots, nu...'rous bands;
With home-born lies, or tales from foreign lands,
Each talk'd aloud, or in some secret place,
And wild impatience star'd in ev'ry face.
The flying rumours gather'd as they roll'd,
Scarce any tale was sooner heard than told;
And all who told it added something new,
And all who heard it made enlargements too;
In ev'ry ear it spread, on ev'ry tongue it grew.
Thus flying east and west, and north and south,
News travell'd with increase from mouth to mouth.
So from a spark, that kindled first by chance,
With gath'ring force the quick'ning flames advance.

Till to the clouds their curling heads aspire,
And towers and temples sink in floods of fire.
When thus ripe lies are to perfection sprung,
Full grown, and fit to grace a mortal tongue,
Through thousand vents, impatient, forth they flow,
And rush in millions on the world below.
Fame sits aloft, and points them out their course,
Their date determines, and prescribes their force:
Some to remain, and some to perish soon,
Or wane and wax alternate like the moon.
Around a thousand winged wonders fly,
Borne by the trumpet's blast, and scatter'd thro' the sky.
There, at one passage, oft you might survey
A lie and truth contending for the way;
And long 'twas doubtful, though so closely pent,
Which first should issue thro' the narrow vent:
At last agreed, together out they fly,
Inseparable now the truth and lie;
The strict companions are for ever join'd,
And this or that unmix'd no mortal e'er shall find.
While thus I stood, intent to see and hear,
One came, methought, and whisper'd in my ear,
What could thus high thy rash ambition raise?
Art thou, fond youth, a candidate for praise?'
''Tis true,' said I, 'not void of hopes I came,
For who so fond as youthful bards of Fame?
But few, alas! the casual blessing boast,
So hard to gain, so easy to be lost.
How vain that second life in others' breath,
Th' estate which wits inherit after death!
Ease, health, and life, for this they must resign,
(Unsure the tenure, but how vast the fine!)
The great man's curse, without the gains, endure,
Be envied, wretched, and be flatter'd, poor;
All luckless wits their enemies profess'd,
And all successful, jealous friends at best.
Nor Fame I slight, nor for her favours call;
She comes unlooked for, if she comes at all.
But if the purchase costs so dear a price,
As soothing folly, or exalting vice;
Oh! if the Muse must flatter lawless sway,
And follow still where Fortune leads the way;
Or if no basis bear my rising name,
But the fallen ruins of another's fame;
Then teach me, Heaven! to scorn the guilty bays,
Drive from my breast that wretched lust of praise;
Unblemish'd let me live, or die unknown:
Oh; grant an honest fame, or grant me none!'

MORAL ESSAYS,

IN FOUR EPISTLES.

TO SEVERAL PERSONS.

ADVERTISEMENT.

THE Essay on Man was intended to have been comprised in Four Books.

The First of which the Author has given us under that title in Four Epistles.

The Second was to have consisted of the same number: 1. Of the extent and limits of human reason. 2. Of those arts and sciences, and of the parts of them, which are useful, and therefore attainable; together with those which are unuseful, and therefore unattainable. 3. Of the nature, end, use, and application, of the different capacities of men. 4. Of the use of learning, of the science of the world, and of wit; concluding with a satire against the misapplication of them, illustrated by pictures, characters, and examples.

The Third Book regarded civil regimen, or the science of politics, in which the several forms of a republic were to be examined and explained; together with the several modes of religious worship, as far forth as they effect society: between which the Author always supposed there was the most interesting relation and closest connection; so that this part would have treated of civil and religious society in their full extent.

The Fourth and last Book concerned private ethics, or practical morality, considered in all the circumstances, orders, possessions, and stations, of human life.

The scheme of all this had been maturely digested, and communicated to Lord Bollingbroke, Dr. Swift, and one or two more, and was intended for the only work of his riper years; but was, partly through ill health, partly through discouragements from the depravity of the times, and partly on prudential and other considerations, interrupted, postponed, and, lastly, in a manner laid aside.

But as this was the Author's favourite work, which more exactly reflected the image of his strong capacious mind, and as we can have but a very imperfect idea of it from the *disjecta membra poetæ* that now remain, it may not be amiss to be a little more particular concerning each of these projected Books.

The First, as it treats of Man in the abstract, and considers him in general under every of his relations, becomes the foundation, and furnishes out the subjects of the three following: so that

The Second Book was to take up again the first and second Epistles of the First Book, and treats of Man in his intellectual capacity at large, as has been explained above. Of this only a small part of the conclusion (which, as we said, was to have contained a satire against the misapplication of wit and learning) may be found in the Fourth Book of the Dunciad, and up and down, occasionally, in the other Three.

The Third Book, in like manner, was to reassume the subject of the Third Epistle of the First, which treats of Man in his social, political, and religious capacity. But this part the Poet afterwards conceived might be best executed in an epic poem, as the action would make it more animated, and the fable less invidious; in which all the great principles of true and false governments and religions should be chiefly delivered in feigned examples.

The Fourth and last Book was to pursue the subject of the Fourth Epistle of the First, and treats of ethics, or practical morality, and would have consisted of many members; of which the Four following Epistles were detached portions: the two first, on the characters of Men and Women, being the introductory part of this concluding Book.

EPISTLE I.

TO SIR RICHARD TEMPLE, LORD COBHAM

OF THE KNOWLEDGE AND CHARACTERS OF MEN.

ARGUMENT.

I. THAT it is not sufficient for this knowledge to consider Man in the abstract: books will not serve the purpose, nor yet our own experience singly. General maxims, unless they be formed upon both will be but notional. Some peculiarity in every man, characteristic to himself, yet varying from himself. Difficulties arising from our own passions, fancies, faculties, &c. The shortness of life to observe in, and the uncertainty of the principles of action in Men to observe by, &c. Our own principle of action often hid from ourselves. Some few characters plain, but in general confounded, dissembled, or inconsistent. The same man utterly different in different places and seasons. Unimaginable weaknesses in the greatest, &c. Nothing constant and certain but God and Nature. No judging of the motives from the actions; the same actions proceeding from contrary motives, and the same motives influencing contrary actions. II. Yet to form characters we can only take the strongest actions of a man's life, and try to make them agree: the utter uncertainty of this, from Nature itself, and from policy. Characters given according to the rank of men of the world; and some reason for it. Education alters the nature, or at least character, of many. Actions, passions, opinions, manners, humours, or principles, all subject to change. No judging by Nature. III. It only remains to find (if we can) his ruling passion: that will certainly influence all the rest, and can reconcile the seeming or real inconsistency of all his actions. Instanced in the extraordinary character of Clodio. A caution against mistaken second qualities for first, which will destroy all possibility of the knowledge of mankind. Examples of the strength of the ruling passion, and its continuation to the last breath.

PART I.

YES, you despise the man to books confin'd,
Who from his study rails at human kind;
Tho' what he learns he speaks, and may advance
Some gen'ral maxims, or be right by chance.
The coxcomb bird, so talkative and grave,
That from his cage cries cuckhold, whore, and knave,
Though many a passenger he rightly call,
You hold him no philospher at all.
And yet the fate of all extremes is such,
Men may be read, as well as books, too much.

To observations which ourselves we make
We grow more partial for th' observer's sake
To written wisdom, as another's, less:
Maxims are drawn from notions, these from guess,
There's some peculiar in each leaf and grain,
Some unmark'd fibre, or some varying vein.
Shall only man be taken in the gross?
Grant but as many sorts of mind as moss.
That each from other differs first confess,
Next, that he varies from himself no less;
Add nature's, custom's, reason's passion's strife,
And all opinion's colours cast on life.
Our depths who fathoms, or our shallows finds?
Quick whirls and shifting eddies of our minds.
On human actions reason though you can,
It may be reason, but it is not man:
His principle of action once explore,
That instant 'tis his principle no more.
Like following life through creatures you dissect,
You lose it in the moment you detect.
Yet more; the diff'rence is as great between
The optics seeing as the objects seen.
All manners take a tincture from our own,
Or come discolour'd through our passions shown;
Or fancy's beam enlarges, multiplies,
Contracts, inverts, and gives ten thousand dyes.
Nor will life's stream for observation stay,
It hurries all too fast to mark their way:
In vain sedate reflections we would make,
When half our knowledge we must snatch, not take.
Oft in the passions' wild rotation toss'd,
Our spring of action to ourselves is lost:
Tir'd not determin'd, to the last we yield,
And what comes then is master of the field.
As the last image of that troubled heap,
When sense subsides, and fancy sports in sleep
(Tho' past the recollection of the thought)
Becomes the stuff of which our dream is wrought
Something as dim to our internal view
Is thus, perhaps, the cause of most we do.
True, some are open, and to all men known;
Others so very close they're hid from none;
(So darkness strikes the sense no less than light;)
Thus gracious Chandos is belov'd at sight,
And ev'ry child hates Shylock, though his soul
Still sits at squat, and peeps not from its hole.
At half mankind when gen'rous Manly raves.
All know 'tis virtue, for he thinks them knaves
When universal homage Umbra pays,
All see 'tis vice, and itch of vulgar praise.

When flatt'ry glares, all hate it in a queen,
While one there is who charms us with his spleen.
 But these plain characters we rarely find;
Though strong the bent, yet quick the turns of mind:
Or puzzling contraries confound the whole
Or affectations quite reverse the soul.
The dull flat falsehood serves for policy;
And in the cunning truth itself's a lie:
Unthought-of frailities cheat us in the wise;
The fool lies hid in inconsistencies.
 See the same man in vigour, in the gout,
Alone, in company, in place or out,
Early at bus'ness and at hazard late,
Mad at a fox-chase, wise at a debate,
Drunk at a borough, civil at a ball,
Friendly at Hackney, faithless at Whitehall,
 Catius is ever moral, ever grave,
Thinks who endures a knave is next a knave,
Save just at dinner—then prefers, no doubt
A rogue with ven'son to a saint without.
 Who would not praise Patricio's high desert,
His hand unstain'd, his uncorrupted heart,
His comprehensive head! all int'rests weigh'd,
All Europe sav'd, yet Britain not betray'd.
He thanks you not, his pride is in picquet,
Newmarket fame, and judgment at a bet.
 What made (say, Montaigne, or more sage Charron!)
Otho a warrior, Cromwell a buffoon?
A perjur'd prince a leaden saint revere,
A godless regent tremble at a star?
The throne a bigot keep, a genius quit,
Faithless through piety, and dup'd through wit?
Europe a woman, child, or dotard, rule,
And just her wisest monarch made a fool!
 Known, God and Nature only are the same.
In man the judgment shoots at flying game;
A bird of passage, gone as soon as found:
Now in the moon, perhaps now under ground.

PART II.

 In vain the sage, with retrospective eye,
Would from th' apparent what conclude the why,
Infer the motive from the deed, and show
That what we chanc'd was what we meant to do.
Behold! if fortune or a mistress frowns,
Some plunge in bus'ness, others shave their crowns:

To ease the soul of one oppressive weight
This quits an empire, that embroils a state.
The same adust complexion has impell'd
Charles to the convent, Philip to the field.
  Not always actions shew the man! we find
Who does a kindness is not therefore kind:
Perhaps porsperity becalm'd his breast;
Perhaps the wind just shifted from the east:
Not therefore humble he who seeks retreat;
Pride guides his steps, and bids him shun the great.
Who combats bravely is not therefore brave;
He dreads a death-bed like the meanest slave.
Who reasons wisely is not therefore wise;
His pride in reas'ning, not in acting, lies.
  But grant that actions best discover man;
Take the most strong, and sort them as you can;
The few that glare each character must mark;
You balance not the many in the dark.
What will you do with such as disagree?
Suppress them, or miscall them policy?
Must then at once (the character to save)
The plain rough hero turn a crafty knave?
Alas! in truth, the man but chang'd his mind;
Perhaps was sick, in love, or had not din'd.
Ask why from Britain Cæsar would retreat?
Cæsar himself might whisper, he was beat.
Why risk the world's great empire for a punk?
Cæsar perhaps might answer, he was drunk.
But, sage historians! 'tis your task to prove
One action conduct, one heroic love.
  'Tis from high life high characters are drawn;
A saint in crape is twice a saint in lawn;
A judge is just, a chanc'llor juster still;
A gownman learn'd; a bishop what you will:
Wise if a minister; but if a king,
More wise, more learn'd, more just, more ev'ry thing.
Court-virtues bear, like gems, the highest rate,
Born where Heaven's influence scarce can penetrate.
In life's low vale, the soil the virtues like,
They please as beauties, here as wonders strike.
Though the same sun with all-diffusive rays
Blush in the rose, and in the diamond blaze,
We prize the stronger effort of his power,
And justly set the gem above the flower.
  'Tis education forms the common mind;
Just as the twig is bent the tree's inclined.
Boastful and rough, your first son is a 'squire;
The next a tradesman, meek, and much a liar:
Tom struts a soldier, open, bold, and brave;
Will sneaks a scrivener, an exceeding knave;

Is he a Churchman? then he's fond of power:
A Quaker? sly: a Presbyterian? sour:
A smart free-thinker? all things in an hour.
Ask mens' opinions: Scoto now shall tell,
How trade increases and the world goes well:
Strike off his pension by the setting sun,
And Britain, if not Europe, is undone.
That gay free thinker, a fine talker once
What turns him now a stupid silent dunce?
Some god or spirit he has lately found,
Or chanced to meet a minister that frowned
Judge we by nature? habit can efface,
Interest o'ercome, or policy take place.
By actions? those uncertainty divides.
By passions? these dissimulation hides.
Opinions? they still take a wider range.
Find, if you can, in what you cannot change.
Manners with fortunes, humours turn with climes,
Tenets with books, and principles with times.

PART III.

Search then the ruling passion: there, alone,
The wild are constant, and the cunning known
The fool consistent, and the false sincere;
Priests, princes, women, no dissemblers here.
This clue once found unravels all the rest,
The prospect clears, and Wharton stands confess'd.
Wharton! the scorn and wonder of our days,
Whose ruling passion was the lust of praise:
Born with whate'er could win it from the wise,
Women and fools must like him, or he dies:
Though wondering senates hung on all he spoke,
The club must hail him master of the joke,
Shall parts so various aim at nothing new?
He'll shine a Tully and a Wilmot too:
Then turns repentant, and his God adores
With the same spirit that he drinks and whores:
Enough if all around him but admire,
And now the punk applaud and now the friar.
Thus with each gift of nature and of art,
And wanting nothing but an honest heart;
Grown all to all, from no one vice exempt,
And most contemptible to shun contempt;
His passion still to covet general praise,
His life to forfeit it a thousand ways;
A constant bounty which no friend has made;
An angel tongue which no man can persuade;

A fool with more of wit than half mankind;
Too rash for thought, for action too refined;
A tyrant to the wife his heart approves;
A rebel to the very king he loves;
He dies, sad outcast of each church and state,
And, harder still! flagitious, yet not great!
Ask you why Wharton broke through every rule?
'Twas all for fear the knaves should call him fool.
Nature well known no prodigies remain;
Comets are regular, and Wharton plain.
Yet in this search the wisest may mistake,
If second qualities for first they take.
When Cataline by rapine swelled his store,
When Cæsar made a noble dame a whore,
In this the lust, in that the avarice,
Were means, not ends; ambition was the vice.
That very Cæsar, born in Scipio's days,
Had aimed, like him, by chastity, at praise.
Lucullus, when frugality could charm,
Had roasted turnips in the Sabine farm.
In vain th' observer eyes the builder's toil,
But quite mistakes the scaffold for the pile
In this one passion man can strength enjoy,
As fits give vigour just when they destroy.
Time, that on all things lays his lenient hand,
Yet tames not this; it sticks to our last sand.
Consistent in our follies and our sins,
Here honest Nature ends as she begins.
Old politicians chew on wisdom past,
And totter on in business to the last;
As weak, as earnest, and as gravely out
As sober Lanesborow dancing in the gout.
Behold a reverend sire, whom want of grace
Has made the father of a nameless race,
Shoved from the wall perhaps, or rudely pressed
By his own son, that passes by unblessed;
Still to his wench he crawls on knocking knees,
And envies every sparrow that he sees.
A salmon's belly, Helluo, was thy fate;
The doctor called, declares all help too late.
'Mercy!' cries Helluo, 'mercy on my soul!
Is there no hope (—Alas!—then bring the jowl.'
The frugal Crone, whom praying priests attend,
Still strives to save the hallowed taper's end,
Collects her breath, as ebbing life retires,
For one puff more, and in that puff expires.
'Odious! in woollen! 'twould a saint provoke
(Were the last words that poor Narcissa spoke!)
No, let a charming chintz and Brussels lace
Wrap my cold limbs, and shade my lifeless face.

One would not, sure, be frightful when one's dead—
And—Betty—give this cheek a little red.'
The courtier smooth, who forty years had shined
An humble servant to all human-kind,
Just brought out this, when scarce his tongue could stir,
'If—where I am going—I could serve you, sir?'
'I give and I devise,' old Euclio said,
And sigh'd, 'my lands and tenements to Ned.'
'Your money, sir,?'—'My money, sir, what, all
Why—if I must—' then wept, 'I give it Paul.'
'The manor, sir?'—The manor! hold,' he cried;
'Not that—I cannot part with that,'—and died.
And you, brave Cobham! to the latest breath,
Shall feel your ruling passion strong in death;
Such in those moments as in all the past;
Oh! save my country, Heaven! shall be your last.

EPISTLE II.

TO A LADY.

OF THE CHARACTERS OF WOMEN.

THE ARGUMENT.

THAT the particular characters of women are not so strongly marked as those of men, seldom so fixed, and still more inconsistent with themselves, v. 1, &c. Instances of contrarieties given, even from such characters as are more strongly marked, and seemingly, therefore, most consistent: I. In the affected, v. 21, &c. II. In the soft-natured, v. 29 and 37. III In the cunning and artful, v. 45. IV. In the whimsical, v. 53. V. In the lewd and vicious, v. 69. VI. In the witty and refined, v. 87. VII. In the stupid and simple, v. 101. The former part having shown that the particular characters of women are more various than those of men, it is nevertheless observed, that the general characteristic of the sex, as to the ruling passion, is more uniform, v. 207. This is occasioned partly by their nature, partly by their education, and in some degree by necessity, v. 211. What are the aims and the fate of this sex. I. As to power, v. 219. II. As to pleasure, v. 231. Advice for their true interest, v. 249. The picture of an inestimable woman, with the best kind of contrarieties, v. 269.

NOTHING so true as what you once let fall,
Most women have no characters at all;
Matter too soft a lasting mark to bear,
And best distinguished by black, brown, or fair.
  How many pictures of one nymph we view,
All how unlike each other, all how true!
Arcadia's countess here, in ermined pride,
Is there Pastora by a fountain side:
Here Fannia leering on her own good man,
And there a naked Leda with a swan.
Let then the fair one beautifully cry,
In Magdalene's loose hair and lifted eye,
Or dressed in smiles of sweet Cecilia shine,
With simpering angels, palms, and harps divine,
Whether the charmer sinner it or saint it,
If folly grow romantic, I must paint it.
  Come then, the colours and the ground prepare!
Dip in the rainbow, trick her off in hair;
Choose a firm cloud before it fall, and in it
Catch, ere she change, the Cynthia of this minute.

Rufa, whose eye, quick glancing o'er the park,
Attracts each light gay meteor of a spark,
Agrees as ill with Rufa studying Locke
As Sappho diamonds with her dirty smock·
Or Sappho at her toilette's greasy task
With Sappho fragrant at an evening mask:
So morning insects, that in muck begun,
Shine, buzz, and fly-blow in the setting sun.
How soft is Silia! fearful to offend;
The frail one's advocate, the weak one's friend:
To her Calista proved her conduct nice,
And good Simplicius asks of her advice.
Sudden she storms! she raves! you tip the wink;
But spare your censure; Silia does not drink.
All eyes may see from what the change arose;
All eyes may see—a pimple on her nose.
Papilia, wedded to her amorous spark,
Sighs for the shades—How charming is a park!
A park is purchased; but the fair he sees
All bathed in tears—Oh, odious, odious trees!
Ladies, like variegated tulips, show,
'Tis to their changes half their charms we owe
Fine by defect, and delicately weak,
Their happy spots the nice admirer take.
'Twas thus Calypso once each heart alarm'd,
Awed without virtue, without beauty charm'd;
Her tongue bewitched as oddly as her eyes;
Less wit than mimic, more a wit than wise:
Strange graces still, and stranger flights, she had:
Was just not ugly, and was just not mad;
Yet ne'er so sure our passion to create
As when she touch'd the brink of all we hate.
Narcissa's nature, tolerably mild,
To make a wash would hardly stew a child;
Has e'en been proved to grant a lover's prayer,
And paid a tradesman once to make him stare;
Gave alms at Easter in a Christian trim,
And made a widow happy for a whim.
Why then declare good nature is her scorn,
When 'tis by that alone she can be borne?
Why pique all mortals, yet affect a name,
A fool to pleasure, yet a slave to fame?
Now deep in Taylor and the Book of Martyrs,
Now drinking citron with his Grace and Chartres:
Now conscience chills her, and now passion burns,
And atheism and religion take their turns;
A very heathen in the carnal part,
Yet still a sad good Christian at her heart.
See sin in state, majestically drunk,
Proud as a peeress, prouder as a punk;

Chaste to her husband, frank to all beside;
A teeming mistress, but a barren bride.
What then? let blood and body bear the fault,
Her head's untouched, that noble seat of thought
Such this day's doctrine—in another fit
She sins with poets through pure love of wit.
What has not fired her bosom or her brain?
Cæsar and Tallboy, Charles and Charlemagne.
As Helluo, late dictator of the feast,
The nose of haut-gout, and the tip of taste,
Critiqued your wine, and analyzed your meat,
Yet on plain pudding deigned at home to eat;
So Philomede, lecturing all mankind
On the soft passion, and the taste refin'd,
The address, the delicacy—stoops at once,
And makes a hearty meal upon a dunce.
Flavia's a wit, has too much sense to pray:
To toast our wants and wishes is her way;
Nor asks of God, but of her stars, to give
The mighty blessing, while we live to live.
Then all for death, that opiate of the soul!
Lucretia's dagger, Rosamonda's bowl.
Say, what can cause such impotence of mind?
A spark too fickle, or a spouse too kind.
Wise wretch! with pleasures too refined to please:
With too much spirit to be e'er at ease;
With too much quickness ever to be taught;
With too much thinking to have common thought;
You purchase pain with all that joy can give,
And die of nothing but a rage to live.
Turn then from wits, and look on Simo's mate;
No ass so meek, no ass so obstinate;
On her that owns her faults, but never mends,
Because she's honest, and the best of friends;
Or her whose life the church and scandal share,
For ever in a passion or a prayer;
Or her who laughs at hell, but, like her grace,
Cries, 'Ah! how charming if there's no such place!'
Or who in sweet vicissitude appears
Of mirth and opium, ratafie and tears,
The daily anodyne and nightly draught,
To kill those foes to fair ones, time and thought,
Woman and fool are too hard things to hit;
For true no meaning puzzles more than wit.
But what are those to great Atossa's mind?
Scarce once herself, by turns all womankind?
Who with herself, or others, from her birth,
Finds all her life one warfare upon earth;
Shines in exposing knaves and painting fools,
Yet is whate'er she hates and ridicules:

No thought advances, but her eddy brain
Whisks it about, and down it goes again.
Full sixty years the world has been her trade;
The wisest fool much time has ever made;
From loveless youth to unrespected age,
No passion gratified, except her rage:
So much the fury still out-ran the wit,
The pleasure missed her, and the scandal hit.
Who breaks with her, provokes revenge from hell,
But he's a bolder man who dares be well.
Her every turn with violence pursued,
Nor more a storm her hate than gratitude:
To that each passion turns or soon or late;
Love if it makes her yield must make her hate.
Superiors? death! and equals? what a curse!
But an inferior not dependant? worse.
Offend her, and she knows not to forgive;
Oblige her, and she'll hate you while you live;
But die, and she'll adore you—then the bust
And temple rise—then fall again to dust.
Last night her lord was all t at's good and great;
A knave this morning, and his will a cheat.
Strange! by the means defeated of the ends,
By spirit robbed of power, by warmth of friends,
By wealth of followers! without one distress,
Sick of herself through very selfishness!
Atossa, cursed with every granted prayer,
Childless with all her children, wants an heir:
To heirs unknown descends the unguarded store,
Or wanders, Heaven directed, to the poor.
  Pictures like these, dear Madam! to design,
Asks no firm hand and no unerring line;
Some wandering touches, some reflected light,
Some flying stroke, alone can hit them right:
For how should equal colours do the knack?
Chameleons who can paint in white and black?
  'Yet Chloe sure was formed without a spot.'—
Nature in her then erred not, but forgot.
'With every pleasing, every prudent part,
Say, what can Chloe want?'—She wants a heart.
She speaks, behaves, and acts, just as she ought,
But never, never, reachéd one generous thought.
Virtue she finds too painful an endeavour,
Content to dwell in decencies for ever.
So very reasonable, so unmoved,
As never yet to love or to be loved.
She while her lover pants upon her breast,
Can mark the figures on an Indian chest;
And when she sees her friend in deep despair,
Observes how much a chintz exceeds mohair

Forbid it, Heaven! a favour or a debt
She e'er should cancel!—but she may forget.
Safe is your secret still in Chloe's ear;
But none of Chloe's shall you ever hear
Of all her dears she never slandered one,
But cares not if a thousand are undone.
Would Chloe know if you're alive or dead?
She bids her footman put it in her head.
Chloe is prudent—Would you too be wise?
Then never break your heart when Chloe dies.
  One certain portrait may (I grant) be seen,
Which Heaven has varnished out, and made a queen,
The same for ever! and described by all
With truth and goodness as with crown and ball.
Poets heap virtues, painters gems, at will,
And shew their zeal, and hide their want of skill.
'Tis well—but, artists! who can paint or write
To draw the naked is your true delight.
That robe of quality so struts and swells,
None see what parts of nature it conceals.
The exactest traits of body or of mind
We owe to models of an humble kind.
If Queensbury to strip there's no compelling,
'Tis from a handmaid we must take a Helen.
From peer or bishop 'tis no easy thing
To draw the man who loves his God or king.
Alas! I copy (or my draught would fail)
From honest Mahomet or plain Parson Hale.
  But grant in public, men sometimes are shown,
A woman's seen in private life alone:
Our bolder talents in full light displayed,
Your virtues open fairest in the shade.
Bred to disguise, in public 'tis you hide;
There none distinguish 'twixt your shame or pride,
Weakness or delicacy; all so nice,
That each may seem a virtue or a vice.
  In men we various ruling passions find;
In women two almost divide the kind;
Those only fixed the first or last obey,
The love of pleasure and the love of sway.
  That nature gives; and where the lesson taught
Is but to please, can pleasure seem a fault?
Experience this: by man's oppression curs'd,
They seek the second not to lose the first.
  Men some to business some to pleasure take,
But every women is at heart a rake:
Men some to quiet, some to public strife,
But every lady would be queen for life.
  Yet mark the fate of a whole sex of queens.
Power all their end, but beauty all the means.

In youth they conquer with so wild a rage
As leaves them scarce a subject in their age:
For foreign glory, foreign joy, they roam;
No thought of peace or happiness at home.
But wisdom's triumph is well timed retreat,
As hard a science to the fair as great!
Beauties, like tyrants, old and friendless grown,
Yet hate repose, and dread to be alone;
Worn out in public, weary every eye,
Nor leave one sigh behind them when they die.
Pleasures the sex as children birds pursue,
Still out of reach, yet never out of view;
Sure if they catch to spoil the toy at most,
To covet flying, and regret when lost:
At last to follies youth could scarce defend,
It grows their age's prudence to pretend;
Ashamed to own they gave delight before,
Reduced to feign it when they give no more.
As hags hold sabbaths less for joy than spite,
So these there merry miserable night;
Still round and round the ghosts of beauty glide,
And haunts the places where their honour died.
See how the world its veterans rewards
A youth of frolics, an old age of cards;
Fair to no purpose, artful to no end,
Young without lovers, old without a friend;
A fop their passion, but their prize a sot,
Alive ridiculous, and dead forgot!
Ah! friend! to dazzle let the vain design;
To raise the thought and touch the heart be thine!
That charm shall grow, while what fatigues the ring
Flaunts and goes down an unregarded thing.
So when the sun's broad beam has tired the sight,
All mild ascends the moon's more sober light,
Serene in virgin modesty she shines,
And unobserved the glaring orb declines.
Oh! blessed with temper, whose unclouded ray
Can make to-morrow cheerful as to-day;
She who can love a sister's charms, or hear
Sighs for a daughter with unwounded ear;
She who ne'er answers till a husband cools,
Or if she rules him never shows she rules;
Charms by accepting, by submitting sways,
Yet has her humour most when she obeys;
Let fops or fortune fly which way they will,
Disdains all loss of tickets or codille;
Spleen, vapours, or small-pox, above them all,
And mistress of herself though china fall.
And yet believe me, good as well as ill,
Woman's at best a contradiction still.

Heaven, when it strives to polish all it can,
Its last best work, but forms a softer man;
Picks from each sex, to make the favourite bless'd,
Your love of pleasure, our desire of rest;
Blends, in exception to all general rules,
Your taste of follies with our scorn of fools;
Reserve with frankness, art with truth allied,
Courage with softness, modesty with pride;
Fixed principles, with fancy, ever new,
Shakes all together, and produces—you.
  Be this a woman's fame; with this unbless'd,
Toasts live a scorn, and queens may die a jest.
This Phœbus promised (I forget the year)
When those blue eyes first opened on the sphere;
Ascendant Phœbus watched that hour with care,
Averted half your parent's simple prayer,
And gave you beauty, but denied the pelf
That buys your sex a tyrant o'er itself.
The generous god who wit and gold refines,
And ripens spirits as he ripens mines,
Kept dross for duchesses; the world shall know it,
To you gave sense, good humour, and a poet.

EPISTLE III.

TO ALLEN LORD BATHURST.

OF THE USE OF RICHES.

THE ARGUMENT.

THAT it is known to few, most falling into one of the extremes, avarice or profusion, v. 1, &c. The point discussed, whether the invention of money has been more commodious or pernicious to mankind, v. 21 to 77. That riches, either to the avaricious or the prodigal, cannot afford happiness, scarcely necessaries, v. 89 to 160. That avarice is an absolute frenzy, without an end or purpose, v. 113 and 152. Conjectures about the motives of avaricious men, v. 121 to 153. That the conduct of men, with respect to riches, can only be accounted for by the order of Providence, which works the general good out of extremes, and brings all to its great end by perpetual revolutions, v. 161 to 178. How a miser acts upon principles which appear to him reasonable, v. 179. How a prodigal does the same, v. 199. The true medium and true use of riches, v. 219. The Man of Ross, v. 250. The fate of the profuse and the covetous, in two examples; both miserable in life and in death, v. 300, &c. The story of Sir Balaam, v. 339 to the end.

P. WHO shall decide when doctors disagree,
And soundest casuists doubt, like you and me?
You hold the world from Jove to Momus giv'n,
That man was made the standing jest of heaven,
And gold but sent to keep the fools in play,
For some to heap and some to throw away.
But I, who think more highly of our kind,
(And surely Heaven and I are of a mind.)
Opine that nature, as in duty bound,
Deep hid the shining mischief under ground:
But, when by man's audacious labour won,
Flamed forth this rival to its sire the Sun,
Then careful Heaven supplied two sorts of men,
To squander these, and those to hide again.
Like doctors thus, when much dispute has pass'd,
We find our tenets just the same at last;
Both fairly owning riches, in effect,
No grace of Heaven, or token of the elect;
Given to the fool, the mad, the vain, the evil,
To Ward, to Waters, Chartres, and the devil.

B. What nature wants commodius gold bestows;
'Tis thus we eat the bread another sows.
P. But how unequal it bestows observe;
Tis thus we riot while who sow it starve:
What nature wants (a phrase I much destrust)
Extends to luxury, extends to lust:
Useful I grant, it serves what life requires,
But dreadful too, the dark assassin hires.
B. Trade it may help, society extend:
P. But lures the pirate, and corrupts the friend.
B. It raises armies in a nation's aid:
P. But bribes a senate, and the land's betray'd
In vain may heroes fight and patriot's rave,
If secret gold sap on from knave to knave.
Once, we confess, beneath the patriot's cloack,
From the crack'd bag the dropping guinea spoke,
And, jingling down the back-stairs, told the crew,
'Old Cato is as great a rogue as you.'
Bless'd paper credit! last and best supply
That lends corruption lighter wings to fly!
Gold imp'd by thee can compass hardest things,
Can pocket states, can fetch or carry kings;
A single leaf shall waft an army o'er,
Or ship off senates to some distant shore;
A leaf, like Sibyl's, scatter to and fro
Our fates and fortunes as the winds shall blow;
Pregnant with thousands flits the scrap unseen,
And silent sells a king or buys a queen.
Oh! that such bulky bribes as all might see
Still, as of old, encumbered villainy!
Could France or Rome divert our brave designs
With all their brandies or with all their wines?
What could they more than knights and 'squires
Or water all the quorum ten miles round? [confound,
A statesman's slumbers how this speech would spoil!
'Sir, Spain has sent a thousand jars of oil;
Hugh bales of British cloth blockade the door;
A hundred oxen at your levee roar.'
Poor avarice one torment more would find,
Nor could profusion squander all in kind;
Astride his cheese Sir Morgan might we meet,
And Worldly crying coals from street to street,
Whom with a wig so wild and mien so maz'd
Pity mistakes for some poor tradesman craz'd.
Had Colepepper's whole wealth been hops and hogs,
Could he himself have sent it to the dogs?
His grace will game; to White's a bull be led,
With spurning heels and with a butting head:
To White's be carried, as to ancient games,
Fair coursers, vases, and alluring dames.

Shall then Uxorio, if the stakes be sweep,
Bear home six whores, and make his lady weep?
Or soft Adonis, so perfumed and fine,
Drive to St. James's a whole herd of swine?
Oh! filthy check on all industrious skill,
To spoil the nation's last great trade, Quadrille!
Since then, my lord, on such a world we fall,
What say you? B. Say? Why, take it, gold and all.
P, What riches give us let us then inquire:
Meat, fire, and clothes? B. What more? P. Meat, clothes, [and fire.
Is this too little? would you more than live?
Alas! 'tis more than Turner finds they give;
Alas! 'tis more than (all his visions pass'd)
Unhappy Wharton, waking, found at last!
What can they give? To dying Hopkins heirs?
To Chartres vigour? Japhet nose and ears?
Can they in gems bid pallid Hippia glow?
In Fulvia's buckle ease the throbs below?
Or heal, old Narses, thy obscener ail
With all the embroidery plastered at thy tail?
They might (were Harpax not too wise to spend)
Give Harpax' self the blessing of a friend;
Or find some doctor that would save the life
Of wretched Shylock spite of Shylock's wife.
But thousands die without or this or that,
Die, and endow a college or a cat.
To some indeed heaven grants the happier fate
To enrich a bastard, or a son they hate.
Perhaps you think the poor might have their part:
Bond damns the poor, and hates them from his heart.
The grave Sir Gilbert holds it for a rule,
That ev'ry man in want is knave or fool.
'God cannot love (says Blunt, with tearless eyes)
The wretch he starves'—and piously denies:
But the good bishop, with a meeker air.
Admits and leaves them Providence's care.
Yet to be just to these poor men of pelf,
Each does but hate his neighbour as himself:
Damned to the mines, an equal fate betides
The slave that digs it and the slave that hides.
B. Who suffer thus, mere charity should own,
Must act on motives powerful though unknown.
P. Some war, some plague or famine, they forsee,
Some revelation hid from you and me.
Why Shylock wants a meal the cause is found;
He thinks a loaf will rise to fifty pound.
What made directors cheat in South-sea year?
To live on ven'son when it sold so dear.
Ask you why Phryne the whole auction buys?
Phryne forsees a general excise.

Why she and Sappho raise that monstrous sum?
Alas! they fear a man will cost a plum.
  Wise Peter sees the world's respect for gold,
And therefore hopes this nation may be sold.
Glorious ambition! Peter, swell thy store,
And be what Rome's great Didius was before.
  The crown of Poland, venal twice an age,
To just three millions stinted modest Gage.
But nobler scenes Maria's dreams unfold,
Hereditary realms, and worlds of gold.
Congenial soul! whose life one av'rice joins,
And one fate buries in the Asturian mines.
  Much-injured Blunt! why bears he Britain's hate?
A wizard told him in these words our fate:
'At length corruption, like a general flood,
(So long by watchful ministers withstood)
Shall deluge all, and av'rice creeping on,
Spread like a low-born mist and blot the sun;
Statesman and patriot ply alike the stocks,
Peeress and butler share alike the box,
And judges job, and bishops bite the town,
And mighty dukes pack cards for half-a-crown:
See Britain sunk in lucre's sorded charms,
And France revenged of Anne's and Edward's arms!
'Twas no court badge, great scriv'ner! fir'd thy brain
Nor lordly luxury, nor city gain:
No, 'twas thy righteous end ashamed to see
Senates degenerate, patriots disagree,
And nobly wishing party-rage to cease,
To buy both sides, and give thy country peace.
  'All this is madness,' cries a sober sage:
'But who, my Friend! has reason in his rage?
The ruling passion, be it what it will,
The ruling passion conquers reason still.'
Less mad the wildest whimsy we can frame,
Than e'en that passion if it has no aim;
For though such motives folly you may call,
The folly's greater to have none at all.
  Hear then the truth: ''Tis Heaven each passion sends,
And different men directs to different ends.
Extremes in nature equal good produce;
Extremes in man concur to general use.'
Ask we what makes one keep and one bestow?
That Power who bids the ocean ebb and flow,
Bids seed-time, harvest, equal course maintain
Through reconciled extremes of drought and rain;
Builds life on death, on change duration founds,
And gives the eternal wheels to know their rounds.
  Riches, like insects, when concealed they lie,
Wait but for wings, and in their season fly.

Who sees pale Mammon pine amidst his store,
Sees but a backward steward for the poor;
This year a reservior to keep and spare,
The next a fountain spouting through his heir
In lavish streams to quench a country's thirst,
And men and dogs shall drink him till they burst,
 Old Cotta sham'd his fortune and his birth,
Yet was not Cotta void of wit or worth:
What though (the use of barbarous spits forgot)
His kitchen vied in coolness with his grot?
His court with nettles, moats with cresses stored,
With soups unbought, and sallads, blessed his board?
If Cotta lived on pulse, it was no more
Than Brahmins, saints, and sages, did before:
To cram the rich was prodigal expense;
And who would take the poor from Providence?
Like some lone Chartreux stands the good old hall,
Silence without, and fasts within the wall;
No raftered roofs with dance and tabor sound,
No noontide bell invites the country round;
Tenants with sighs the smokeless towers survey,
And turn the unwilling steeds another way;
Benighted wanderers the forest o'er
Curse the saved candle and unopening door;
While the guant mastiff, growling at the gate,
Affrights the beggar whom he longs to eat.
 Not so his son; he marked this oversight,
And then mistook reverse of wrong for right:
(For what to shun will no great knowledge need,
But what to follow is a task indeed!)
Yet sure of qualities deserving praise,
More go to ruin fortunes than to raise,
What slaughtered hecatombs, what floods of wine,
Fill the capacious 'squire and deep divine!
Yet no mean motive this profusion draws;
His oxen perish in his country's cause;
'Tis George and liberty that crowns the cup,
And zeal for that great house which eats him up.
The woods recede around the naked seat,
The Sylvans groan—no matter—for the fleet:
Next goes his wool—to clothe our valiant bands;
Last, for his country's love, he sells his lands.
To town he comes, completes the nation's hope,
And heads the bold trainbands, and burns a pope:
And shall not Britain now reward his toils,
Britain! that pays her patriots with her spoils?
In vain at court the bankrupt pleads his cause;
His thankless country leaves him to her laws.
 The sense to value riches, with the art
To enjoy them, and the virtue to impart,

Not meanly or ambitiously pursued,
Not sunk by sloth, nor raised by servitude;
To balance fortune by a just expense,
Join with economy magnificence;
With splendour charity, with plenty health;
Oh! teach us Bathurst! yet unspoiled by wealth!
That secret rare, between the extremes to move
Of mad good-nature and of mean self-love.
B. To worth or want well-weighed be bounty giv'n,
And ease or emulate the care of heaven;
(Whose measure full o'erflows on human race)
Mend fortune's fault, and justify her grace.
Wealth in the gross is death, but life diffused,
As poison heals in just proportion used:
In heaps, like ambergris, a stink it lies;
But well dispersèd, is incense to the skies.
P. Who starves by nobles, or with nobles eats?
The wretch that trusts them and the rogue that cheats.
Is there a lord who knows a cheerful noon,
Without a fiddler, flatterer, or buffoon?
Whose table wit or modest merit share,
Unelbowed by a gamester, pimp, or play'r?
Who copies your's or Oxford's better part,
To ease the oppress'd, and raise the sinking heart?
Where'er he shines, oh, fortune! gild the scene,
And angels guard him in the golden mean!
There English bounty yet awhile may stand,
And honour linger ere it leaves the land.
But all our praises why should lords engross?
Rise, honest muse! and sing the Man of Ross:
Pleas'd Vaga echoes through her winding bounds,
And rapid Severn hoarse applauds resounds.
Who hung with woods yon mountain's sultry brow?
From the dry rock who bade the waters flow?
Not to the skies in useless columns toss'd,
Or in proud falls magnificently lost,
But clear and artless, pouring through the plain
Health to the sick, and solace to the swain.
Whose causeway parts the vale with shady rows?
Whose seats the weary traveller repose?
Who taught that heaven directed spire to rise?
'The Man of Ross,' each lisping babe replies.
Behold the market place with poor o'erspread!
The Man of Ross divides the weekly bread:
He feeds yon almshouse, neat, but void of state,
Where age and want sat smiling at the gate:
Him portioned maids, apprenticed orphans bless'd,
The young who labour, and the old who rest.
Is any sick? The Man of Ross relieves,
Prescribes, attends, the medicine makes and gives.

Is there a variance? enter but his door,
Balk'd are the courts, and contest is no more:
Despairing quacks with curses fled the place,
And vile attornies now an useless race
B. Thrice happy man! enabled to pursue
What all so wish, but want the power to do;
Oh! say what sums that generous hand supply?
What mines to swell that boundless charity?
P. Of debts and taxes, wife and children, clear,
This man possess'd—five hundred pounds a-year.
Blush, grandeur! blush; proud courts! withdraw your blaze,
Ye little stars! hide your diminish'd rays.
B. And what? no monument, inscription, stone,
His race, his form his name, almost unknown?
P. Who builds a church to God, and not to fame,
Will never mark the marble with his name.
Go! search it there, where to be born and die
Of rich and poor makes all the history;
Enough that virtue fill'd the space between,
Proved by the ends of being to have been.
When Hopkins dies, a thousand lights attend
The wretch who living saved a candle's end:
Shouldering God's altar a vile image stands,
Belies his features, nay, extends his hands;
That live-long wig, which Gorgon's self might own,
Eternal buckle takes in Parian stone.
Behold what blessings wealth to life can lend!
And see what comfort it affords our end.
In the worst inn's worst room, with mat half-hung,
The floors of plaster, and the walls of dung,
On once a flock-bed, but repair'd with straw,
With tape-tied curtains, never meant to draw,
The George and Garter dangling from that bed
Where tawdry yellow strove with dirty red,
Great Villiers lies—alas! how changed from him,
That life of pleasure and that soul of whim!
Gallant and gay, in Cliveden's proud alcove,
The bower of wanton Shrewsbury and Love;
Or just as gay at council, in a ring
Of mimic'd statesmen and their merry king;
No wit to flatter, left of all his store!
No fool to laugh at, which he valued more;
There, victor of his health, of fortune, friends,
And fame, this lord of useless thousands ends!
His grace's fate sage Cutler could foresee,
And well (he thought) advised him, 'Live like me.'
As well his grace replied, 'Like you, Sir John?
That I can do when all I have is gone!'
Resolve me, reason, which of these is worse,
Want with a full or with an empty purse?

Thy life more wretched, Cutler! was confess'd;
Arise and tell me, was thy death more bless'd?
Cutler saw tenants break and houses fall;
For very want he could not build a wall.
His only daughter in a stranger's power;
For very want he could not pay a dower.
A few grey hairs his reverend temples crown'd;
'Twas very want that sold them for two pound.
What! e'en denied a cordial at his end,
Banish'd the doctor, and expell'd the friend?
What but a want which you perhaps think mad,
Yet numbers feel the want of what he had!
Cutler and Brutus dying, both exclaim,
'Virtue! and Wealth! what are ye but a name?'
  Say, for such worth are other worlds prepared?
Or are they both, in this, their own reward?
A knotty point! to which we now proceed.
But you are tired—I'll tell a tale—B. agreed.
  P. Where London's column, pointing at the skies,
Like a tall bully, lifts the head and lies,
There dwelt a citizen of sober fame,
A plain good man, and Balaam was his name;
Religious, punctual, frugal, and so forth;
His word would pass for more than he was worth.
One solid dish his week-day meal affords,
An added pudding solemnized the Lord's:
Constant at church and 'Change: his gains were sure
His givings rare, save farthings to the poor.
  The devil was piqued such saintship to behold,
And long'd to tempt him like good Job of old;
But Satan now is wiser than of yore,
And tempts by making rich, not making poor.
  Roused by the Prince of Air, the whirlwinds sweep
The surge, and plunge his father in the deep;
Then full against his Cornish lands they roar,
And two rich shipwrecks bless'd the lucky shore.
  Sir Balaam now he lives like other folks,
He takes his chirping pint and cracks his jokes.
'Live like yourself,' was soon my lady's word;
And, lo! two puddings smoked upon the board.
  Asleep and naked as an Indian lay,
An honest factor stole a gem away:
He pledged it to the knight; the knight had wit,
So kept the diamond, and the rogue was bit.
Some scruple rose, but thus he eased his thought,
'I'll now give sixpence where I gave a groat:
Where once I went to church I'll now go twice—
And am so clear too of all other vice!'
  The tempter saw his time, the work he plied;
Stocks and subscriptions pour on every side,

Till all the demon makes his full descent
In one abundant shower of cent. per cent.
Sinks deep within him, and possesses whole,
Then dubs director, and secures his soul.
  Behold Sir Balaam, now a man of spirit,
Ascribes his gettings to his parts and merit;
What late he call'd a blessing now was wit,
And God's good providence a lucky hit.
Things change their titles as our manners turn;
His compting-house employ'd the Sunday morn;
Seldom at church, ('twas such a busy life,)
But duly sent his family and wife.
There, so the devil ordain'd, one Christmas-tide
My good old lady catch'd a cold and died.
  A nymph of quality admires our knight;
He marries, bows at court, and grows polite;
Leaves the dull Cits, and joins (to please the fair)
The well-bred cuckolds in St. James's air:
First for his son a gay commission buys,
Who drinks, whores, fights, and in a duel dies:
His daughter flaunts a viscount's tawdry wife;
She bears a coronet and p—x for life.
In Britain's senate he a seat obtains,
And one more pensioner St. Stephen gains.
My lady falls to play; so bad her chance,
He must repair it; takes a bribe from France.
The House impeach him; Coningsby harangues;
The Court forsake him, and Sir Balaam hangs.
Wife, son, and daughter, Satan! are thy own;
His wealth, yet dearer, forfeit to the crown:
The devil and the king divide the prize;
And sad Sir Balaam curses God and dies.

EPISTLE IV.

TO RICHARD BOYLE, EARL OF BURLINGTON.

OF THE USE OF RICHES

THE ARGUMENT.

THE vanity of expense in people of wealth and quality. The abuse of the word taste, v. 13. That the first principles and foundation in this, as in everything else, is good sense, v. 40. The chief proof of it is to follow nature, even in works of mere luxury and elegance. Instanced in architecture and gardening, where all must be adapted to the genius and use of the place, and the beauties not forced into it, but resulting from it, v. 50. How men are disappointed in their most expensive undertakings for want of this true foundation, without which nothing can please long, if at all; and the best examples and rules will be but perverted into something burthensome and ridiculous, v. 65 to 92. A description of the false taste of magnificence; the first grand error of which is to imagine that greatness consists in the size and dimension, instead of the proportion and harmony, of the whole, v. 97; and the second, either in joining together parts incoherent, or too minutely resembling, or, in the repetition of the same, too frequently. v. 105, &c. A word or two of false taste in books, in music, in painting, even in preaching and prayer: and, lastly, in entertainments; v. 133, &c. Yet Providence is justified in giving wealth to be squandered in this manner, since it is dispersed to the poor and laborious part of mankind, v. 169, (recurring to what is laid down in the First Book, Epistle ii. and in the Epistle preceding this, v. 159, &c.) What are the proper objects of magnificence. and a proper field for the expense of great men, v. 177, &c. And, finally, the great and public works which become a prince, v. 191, to the end.

'TIS strange the miser should his cares employ
To gain tho e riches he can ne'er enjoy:
Is it less strange the prodigal should waste
His wealth to purchase what he ne'er can taste
Not for himself he sees, or hears, or eats;
Artists must choose his pictures, music, meats.
He buys for Topham drawings and designs,
For Pembroke statues, dirty gods, and coins;
Rare monkish manuscripts for Hearne alone,
And books for Mead, and butterflies for Sloane.
Think we all these are for himself? no more
Than his fine wife, alas! or finer whore.
  For what has Virro painted, built, and planted?
Only to show how many tastes he wanted.

What brought Sir Visto's ill-got wealth to waste?
Some demon whisper'd, 'Visto! have a taste.'
Heaven visits with a taste the wealthy fool,
And needs no rod but Ripley with a rule.
See! sportive fate, to punish awkward pride,
Bids Bubo build, and sends him such a guide:
A standing sermon at each year's expense,
That never coxcomb reach'd magnificence!
You shew us Rome was glorious, not profuse,
And pompous buildings once were things of use;
Yet shall, my lord, your just, your noble rules
Fill half the land with imitating fools,
Who random drawings from your sheets shall take
And of one beauty many blunders make;
Load some vain church with old theatric state,
Turn arcs of triumph to a garden gate;
Reverse your ornaments, and hang them all
On some patch'd doghole eked with ends of wall,
Then clap four slices of pilaster on't,
That laced with bits of rustic makes a front;
Shall call the winds through long arcades to roar
Proud to catch cold at a Venetian door,
Conscious they act a true Palladian part,
And if they starve, they starve by rules of art.
  Oft have you hinted to your brother peer
A certain truth, which many buy too dear:
Something there is more needful than expense,
And something previous e'en to taste—'tis sense;
Good sense, which only is the gift of Heaven,
And though no science, fairly worth the seven;
A light which in yourself you must perceive;
Jones and Le Notre have it not to give.
  To build, to plant, whatever you intend,
To rear the column, or the arch to bend,
To swell the terrace, or to sink the grot,
In all let Nature never be forgot;
But treat the goddess like a modest fair,
Nor overdress, nor leave her wholly bare;
Let not each beauty everywhere be spied,
Where half the skill is decently to hide.
He gains all points who pleasingly confounds,
Surprises, varies, and conceals the bounds.
  Consult the genius of the place in all,
That tells the waters or to rise or fall:
Or helps the ambitious hill the heavens to scale,
Or scoops in circling theatres the vale;
Calls in the country, catches opening glades,
Joins willing woods, and varies shades from shades
Now breaks, or now directs, the intending lines,
Paints as you plant, and as you work designs.

Still follow sense, of every art the soul,
Parts answering parts shall slide into a whole,
Spontaneous beauties all around advance,
Start e'en from difficulty, strike from chance:
Nature shall join you; time shall make it grow
A work to wonder at—perhaps a Stow.
Without it, proud Versailles! thy glory falls,
And Nero's terraces desert their walls:
The vast parterres a thousand hands shall make,
Lo! Cobham comes, and floats them with a lake:
Or cut wide views through mountains to the plain,
You'll wish your hill or shelter'd seat again.
E'en in an ornament its place remark,
Nor in an hermitage set Dr. Clarke.
Behold Villario's ten years' toil complete,
His quincunx darkens, his espaliers meet,
The wood supports the plains, the parts unite,
And strength of shade contends with strength of light;
A waving glow the bloomy beds display,
Blushing in bright diversities of day,
With silver quivering rills meander'd o'er—
Enjoy them you! Villario can no more:
Tired of the scene parterres and fountains yield,
He finds at last he better likes a field.
Through his young woods how pleased Sabinus stray'd,
Or sat delighted in the thickening shade,
With annual joy the reddening shoots to greet,
Or see the stretching branches long to meet!
His son's fine taste an opener vista loves,
Foe to the Dryads of his father's groves;
One boundless green or flourish'd carpet views,
With all the mournful family of yews;
The thriving plants, ignoble broomsticks made,
Now sweep those alleys they were born to shade.
At Timon's villa let us pass a day;
Where all cry out, 'What sums are thrown away!'
So proud, so grand; of that stupendous air
Soft and agreeable come never there.
Greatness with Timon dwells in such a draught
As brings all Brobdingnag before your thought;
To compass this his building is a town,
His pond an ocean, his parterre a down:
Who but must laugh the master when he sees
A puny insect shivering at a breeze:
Lo, what huge heaps of littleness around!
The whole a labour'd quarry above ground.
Two Cupids squirt before; a lake behind
Improves the keenness of the northern wind.
His gardens next your admiration call;
On every side you look behold the wall!

No pleasing intricacies intervene,
No artful wildness to perplex the scene;
Grove nods at grove, each alley has a brother,
And half the platform just reflects the other.
The suffering eye inverted nature sees,
Trees cut to statues, statues thick as trees;
With here a fountain never to be play'd,
And there a summer-house that knows no shade;
Here Amphitrite sails through myrtle bowers,
There gladiators fight or die in flowers;
Unwater'd see the drooping seahorse mourn,
And swallows roost in Nilus' dusty urn.
My lord advances with majestic mien,
Smit with the mighty pleasure to be seen.
But soft—by regular approach—not yet--
First through the length of yon hot terrace sweat
And when up ten steep slopes you've dragged your thighs,
Just at his study door he'll bless your eyes.
His study! with what authors is it stored!
In books, not authors, curious is my lord;
To all their dated backs he turns you round;
These Aldus printed, those Du Sueil has bound!
Lo, some are vellum, and the rest as good,
For all his lordship knows, but they are wood!
For Locke or Milton 'tis in vain to look;
These shelves admit not any modern book.
And now the chapel's silver bell you hear,
That summons you to all the pride of prayer:
Light quirks of music, broken and uneven,
Make the soul dance upon a jig to heaven.
On painted ceilings you devoutly stare,
Where sprawl the saints of Verrio or Laguerre,
Or gilded clouds in fair expansion lie,
And bring all Paradise before your eye.
To rest, the cushion and soft dean invite,
Who never mentions hell to ears polite.
But, hark! the chiming clocks to dinner call;
A hundred footsteps scrape the marble hall:
The rich buffet well-colour'd serpents grace,
And gaping Tritons spew to wash your face.
Is this a dinner? this a genial room?
No, it's a temple and a hecatomb;
A solemn sacrifice perform'd in state;
You drink by measure, and to minutes eat.
So quick retires each flying course, you'd swear
Sancho's dread doctor and his wand were there.
Between each act the trembling salvers ring,
From soup to sweet wine, and God bless the king.
In plenty starving, tantalized in state,
And complaisantly help'd to all I hate,

Treated, caress'd, and tired, I take my leave,
Sick of his civil pride from morn to eve;
I curse such lavish cost and little skill,
And swear no day was ever pass'd so ill.
Yet hence the poor are clothed, the hungry fed;
Health to himself and to his infants bread
The labourer bears: what his hard heart denies
His charitable vanity supplies.
Another age shall see the golden ear
Imbrown the slope, and nod on the parterre;
Deep harvests bury all his pride has plann'd,
And laughing Ceres reassume the land.
Who then shall grace or who improve the soil?
Who plants like Bathurst, or who builds like Boyle?
'Tis use alone that sanctifies expense,
And Splendour borrows all her rays from Sense.
His father's acres who enjoys in peace,
Or makes his neighbours glad if he increase;
Whose cheerful tenants bless their yearly toil,
Yet to their lord owe more than to the soil;
Whose ample lawns are not ashamed to feed
The milky heifer and deserving steed;
Whose rising forests not for pride or show,
But future buildings, future navies, grow;
Let his plantations stretch from down to down,
First shade a country, and then raise a town.
You, too, proceed! make falling arts your care,
Erect new wonders, and the old repair;
Jones and Palladio to themselves restore,
And be whate'er Vitruvius was before:
Till kings call forth the ideas of your mind,
(Proud to accomplish what such hands design'd,)
Bid harbours open, public ways extend,
Bid temples worthier of the God ascend;
Bid the broad arch the dangerous flood contain,
The mole projected break the roaring main;
Back to his bounds their subject sea command,
And roll obedient rivers through the land:
These honours peace to happy Britain brings;
These are imperial works, and worthy kings.

EPISTLE V.

TO MR. ADDISON.

[OCCASIONED BY HIS DIALOGUES ON MEDALS.]

SEE the wild waste of all-devouring years!
How Rome her own sad sepulchre appears,
With nodding arches, broken temples, spread!
The very tombs now vanish'd like their dead;
Imperial wonders raised on nations spoil'd,
Where mix'd with slaves the groaning martyr toil'd:
Huge theatres, that now unpeopled woods,
Now drain'd a distant country of her floods;
Fanes, which admiring gods with pride survey,
Statues of men scarce less alive than they!
Some felt the silent stroke of mouldering age,
Some hostile fury, some religious rage:
Barbarian blindness, Christian zeal conspire,
And papal piety and gothic fire.
Perhaps, by its own ruins saved from flame,
Some buried marble half preserves a name;
That name the learn'd with fierce disputes pursue,
And gives to Titus old Vespasian's due.
Ambition sigh'd; she found it vain to trust
The faithless column and the crumbling bust;
Huge moles, whose shadows stretch'd from shore to shore,
Their ruins perish'd, and their place no more:
Convinced she now contracts her vast design,
And all her triumphs shrinks into a coin.
A narrow orb each crowded conquest keeps,
Beneath her palm here sad Judea weeps.
Now scantier limits the proud arch confine,
And scarce are seen the prostrate Nile or Rhine;
A small Euphrates through the piece is roll'd,
And little eagles wave their wings in gold.
The medal, faithful to its charge of fame,
Through climes and ages bears each form and name:
In one short view subjected to our eye,
Gods, emperors, heroes, sages, beauties, lie.

With sharpened sight pale antiquaries pore,
The inscription value, but the rust adore.
This the blue varnish, that the green endears,
The sacred rust of twice ten hundred years!
To gain Pescennius one employs his schemes,
One grasps a Cecrops in ecstatic dreams.
Poor Vadius, long with learned spleen devoured,
Can taste no pleasure since his shield was scoured;
And Curio, restless by the fair-one's side,
Sighs for an Otho, and neglects his bride.
  Theirs is the vanity, the learning thine:
Touched by thy hand again Rome's glories shine;
Her gods and godlike heroes rise to view,
And all her faded garlands bloom anew.
Nor blush these studies thy regard engage;
These pleased the fathers of poetic rage;
The verse and sculpture bore an equal part,
And art reflected images to art.
  Oh! when shall Britain, conscious of her claim,
Stand emulous of Greek and Roman fame?
In living medals see her walls enrolled,
And vanquished realms supply recording gold?
Here, rising bold, the patriot's honest face,
There warriors frowning in historic brass;
Then future ages with delight shall see
How Plato's, Bacon's, Newton's, looks agree;
Or in fair series laurelled bards be shown,
A Virgil there, and here an Addison:
Then shall thy Craggs (and let me call him mine)
On the cast ore another Pollio shine;
With aspect open shall erect his head,
And round the orb in lasting notes be read,
'Statesmen, yet friend to truth! of soul sincere,
In action faithful, and in honour clear;
Who broke no promise, served no private end,
Who gained no title, and who lost no friend
Ennobled by himself, by all approved,
And praised unenvied by the muse he loved.

SATIRES, EPISTLES, AND ODES,

OF

HORACE IMITATED.

[PUBLISHED IN 1737.]

ADVERTISEMENT.

THE occasion of publishing these Imitations was the clamour raised on some of my Epistles. An answer from Horace was both more full and of more dignity than any I could have made in my own person; and the example of much greater freedom in so eminent a divine as Dr. Donne, seemed a proof with what indignation and contempt a Christian may treat vice or folly in ever so low or ever so high a station. Both these authors were acceptable to the princes and ministers under whom they lived. The satires of Dr. Donne I versified at the desire of the Earl of Oxford, while he was Lord Treasurer, and of the Duke of Shrewsbury, who had been Secretary of State, neither of whom looked upon a satire on vicious courts as any reflection on those they served in. And indeed there is not in the world a greater error than that which fools are so apt to fall into, and knaves with good reason to encourage, the mistaking a satirist for a libeller: whereas to a true satirist nothing is so odious as a libeller; for the same reason as to a man truly virtuous, nothing is so hateful as a hypocrite.—POPE.

BOOK II. SATIRE I.

TO MR. FORTESCUE.

P. THERE are (I scarce can think it, but am told,)
There are to whom my satire seems too bold;
Scarce to wise Peter complaisant enough,
And something said of Chartres much too rough.
The lines are weak, another's pleas,d to say;
Lord Fanny spins a thousand such a day.
Tim'rous by nature, of the rich in awe,
I come to council learned in the law:

You'll give me, like a friend both sage and free,
Advice; and (as you used) without a fee.
F. I'd write no more.
P. Not write? But then I think,
And for my soul I cannot sleep a wink.
I nod in company, I wake at night,
Fools rush into my head, and so I write.
F. You could not do a worse thing for your life.
Why, if the night seems tedious—take a wife:
Or rather, truly, if your point be rest,
Lettuce and cowslip wine: probatum est.
But talk with Celsus, Celsus will advise
Hartshorn, or something that shall close your eyes
Or if you needs must write, write Cæsar's praise;
You ll gain at least a knighthood or the bays.
P. What? like Sir Richard, rumbling, rough and fierce,
With arms, and George, and Brunswick, crowd the verse,
Rend with tremendous sound your ears asunder,
With gun, drum, trumpet, blunderbuss, and thunder?
Or nobly wild, with Budgell's fire and force,
Paint angels trembling round his falling horse?
F. Then all your muse's softer art display,
Let Carolina smooth the tuneful lay;
Lull with Amelia's liquid name the nine,
And sweetly flow through all the royal line.
P. Alas! few verses touch their nicer ear;
They scarce can bear their laureat twice a-year;
And justly Cæsar scorns the poets' lays;
It is to history he trusts for praise.
F. Better be Cibber, I'll maintain it still,
Than ridicule all taste, blaspheme quadrille,
Abuse the city's best good men in metre,
And laugh at peers that put their trust in Peter.
E'en those you touch not hate you.
P. What should ail 'em?
F. A hundred smart in Timon and in Balaam:
The fewer still you name you wound the more;
Bond is but one, but Harpax is a score.
P. Each mortal has his pleasure: none deny
Scarsdale his bottle, Darty his ham-pie:
Ridotto sips and dances till she see
She doubling lustres dance as fast as she:
F—loves the senate, Hockleyhole his brother,
Like in all else as one egg to another.
I love to pour out all myself as plain
As downright Shippen or as old Montaigne:
In them, as certain to be loved as seen,
The soul stood forth, nor kept a thought within;
In me what spots, for spots I have, appear,
Will prove at least the medium must be clear.

In this impartial glass my muse intends
Fair to expose myself, my foes, my friends;
Publish the present age; but where my text
Is vice too high, reserve it for the next;
My foes shall wish my life a longer date,
And every friend the less lament my fate.
My head and heart thus flowing through my quill,
Verseman or Proseman, term me which you will,
Papist or Protestant, or both between,
Like good Erasmus, in an honest mean,
In moderation placing all my glory,
While Tories call me Whig, and Whigs a Tory.
Satire's my weapon, but I'm too discreet
To run a-muck, and tilt at all I meet;
I only wear it in a land of Hectors,
Thieves, supercargoes, sharpers, and directors.
Save but our army! and let Jove incrust
Swords, pikes, and guns, with everlasting rust!
Peace is my dear delight—not Fleury's more;
But touch me, and no minister so sore.
Whoe'er offends, at some unlucky time
Slides into verse, and hitches in a rhyme,
Sacred to ridicule his whole life long,
And the sad burthen of some merry song.
Slander or poison dread from Delia's rage;
Hard words or hanging, if your judge be Page:
From furious Sappho scarce a milder fate,
P-x'd by her love, or libelled by her hate.
Its proper power to hurt each creature feels;
Bulls aim their horns, and asses lift their heels;
'Tis a bear's talent not to kick, but hug;
And no man wonders he's not stung by pug.
So drink with Walters, or with Chatres eat,
They'll never poison you, they'll only cheat.
Then, learned Sir! to cut the matter short,
Whate'er my fate, or well or ill at court,
Whether old age, with faint but cheerful ray
Attends to gild the evening of my day,
Or death's black wing already be displayed,
To wrap me in the universal shade;
Whether the darkened room to muse invite,
Or whitened wall provoke the skewer to write;
In durance, exile, Bedlam, or the Mint,
Like Lee or Budgell, I will rhyme and print.
F. Alas, young man, your days can ne'er be long;
In flower of age you perish for a song!
Plums and directors, Shylock and his wife,
Will club their testors now to take your life.
P. What? armed for virtue when I point the pen
Brand the bold front of shameless guilty men,

Dash the proud gamester in his gilded car,
Bare the mean heart that lurks beneath a star;
Can there be wanting, to defend her cause,
Lights of the church or guardians of the laws?
Could pensioned Boileau lash in honest strain
Flatt'rers and bigots e'en in Louis' reign?
Could Laureat Dryden pimp and friar engage,
Yet neither Charles nor James be in a rage?
And I not strip the gilding off a knave,
Unplaced, unpensioned, no man's heir or slave?
I will, or perish in the generous cause:
Hear this and tremble! you who 'scape the laws.
Yes, while I live, no rich or noble knave
Shall walk the world in credit to his grave:
To virtue only and her friends a friend,
The world beside may murmur or commend.
Know, all the distant din that world can keep,
Rolls o'er my grotto, and but sooths my sleep:
 There my retreat the best companions grace,
Chiefs out of war, and statesmen out of place.
There St. John mingles with my friendly bowl,
The feast of reason and the flow of soul:
And he whose lightning pierced the Iberian lines,
Now forms my quincunx, and now ranks my vines;
Or tames the genius of the stubborn plain
Almost as quickly as he conquered Spain.
 Envy must own I live among the great,
No pimp of pleasure, and no spy of state;
With eyes that pry not, tongue that ne'er repeats,
Fond to spread friendships, but to cover heats:
To help who want, to forward who excel;
This all who know me know, who love me, tell;
And who unknown defame me, let them be
Scribblers or peers, alike are mob to me,
This is my plea, on this I rest my cause—
What saith my counsel learned in the laws?
 F. Your plea is good; but still I say beware!
Laws are explained by men—so have a care.
It stands on record, that in Richard's times,
A man was hanged for very honest rhymes.
Consult the Statue; quart. I think it is,
Edward sext. or prim. et quint. Eliz.
See libels, satires—here you have it—read.
 P. Libels and satires! lawless things indeed!
But grave epistles, bringing vice to light,
Such as a king might read, a bishop write,
Such as Sir Robert would approve—F. Indeed!
The case is altered—you may then proceed:
In such a case the plaintiff will be hissed,
My lords the judges laugh, and you're dismissed.

BOOK II. SATIRE II.

TO MR. BETHEL.

What, and how great, the virtue and the art
To live on little with a cheerful heart!
(A doctrine sage, but truly none of mine:)
Let's talk, my friends, but talk before we dine;
Not when a gilt buffet's reflected pride
Turns you from sound philosophy aside;
Not when from plate to plate your eyeballs roll,
And the brain dances to the mantling bowl.
Hear Bethel's sermon, one not versed in schools,
But strong in sense, and wise without the rules.
'Go work, hunt, exercise,' he thus began;
'Then scorn a homely dinner if you can.
Your wine locked up, your butler strolled abroad,
Or fish denied, (the river yet unthawed,)
If then plain bread and milk will do the feat,
The pleasure lies in you and not the meat.
Preach as I please, I doubt our curious men
Will choose a pheasant still before a hen;
Yet hens of Guinea full as good I hold,
Except you eat the feathers green and gold.
Of carps and mullets why prefer the great,
(Though cut in pieces ere my lord can eat,)
Yet for small turbots such esteem profess?
Because God made these large, the other less.
Oldfield, with more than Harpy throat endued,
Cries, Send me, gods a whole hog barbecued!'
Oh blast it, south-winds! till a stench exhale
Rank as the ripeness of a rabbit's tail.
By what criterion do you eat, d'ye think,
If this be prized for sweetness, that for stink?
When the tired glutton labours through a treat,
He finds no relish in the sweetest meat;
He calls for something bitter, something sour,
And the rich feast concludes extremely poor.
Cheap eggs, and herbs, and olives, still we see;
Thus much is left of old simplicity!
The robin redbreast till of late had rest,
And children sacred held a martin's nest,

Till beccaficos sold so devilish dear
To one that was, or would have been, a peer.
Let me extol a cat on oysters fed,
I'll have a party at the Bedford-head;
Or e'en to crack live crawfish recommend;
I'd never doubt at court to make a friend.
'Tis yet in vain, I own, to keep a pother
About one vice and fall into the other:
Between excess and famine lies a mean;
Plain, but not sordid; though not splendid, clean.
  Avidien, or his wife, (no matter which,
For him you'll call a dog, and her a bitch,)
Sell their presented partridges and fruits,
And humbly live on rabbits and on roots;
One half-pint bottle serves them both to dine,
And is at once their vinegar and wine:
But on some lucky day, (as when they found
A lost bank-bill, or heard their son was drowned,)
At such a feast, old vinegar to spare,
Is what two souls so generous cannot bear:
Oil, though it stink, they drop by drop impart,
But souse the cabbage with a bounteous heart.
  He knows to live who keeps the middle state,
And neither leans on this side nor on that;
Nor stops for one bad cork his butler's pay,
Swears, like Albutius, a good cook away;
Nor lets, like Nævius, every error pass,
The musty wine, foul cloth, or greasy glass.
  Now hear what blessings temperance can bring:
(Thus said our friend, and what he said I sing.)
First health: the stomach (crammed from every dish
A tomb of boiled and roast, and flesh and fish,
Where bile, and wind, and phlegm, and acid, jar,
And all the man is one intestine war)
Remembers oft the schoolboy's simple fare,
The temperate sleeps, and spirits light as air.
  How pale each worshipful and reverend guest
Rise from a clergy or a city feast!
What life in all that ample body say?
What heavenly particle inspires the clay?
The soul subsides, and wickedly inclines
To seem but mortal e'en in sound divines.
  On morning wings how active springs the mind
That leaves the load of yesterday behind!
How easy every labour it pursues!
How coming to the poet every Muse!
Not but we may exceed some holy time,
Or tired in search of truth or search of rhyme:
Ill health some just indulgence may engage,
And more the sickness of long life, old age.

For fainting age what cordial drop remains,
If our intemperate youth the vessel drains?
  Our fathers praised rank vension. You suppose,
Perhaps, young men! our fathers had no nose.
Not so: a buck was then a week's repast,
And 'twas their point, I ween, to make it last;
More pleased to keep it till their friends could come,
Than eat the sweetest by themselves at home.
Why had not I in those good times my birth,
Ere coxcomb pies or coxcombs were on earth?
  Unworthy be the voice of fame to hear,
That sweetest music to an honest ear,
(For faith, Lord Fanny! you are in the wrong,
The world's good word is better than a song,)
Who has not learned fresh sturgeon and ham-pie
Are no rewards for want and infamy!
When luxury has lick'd up all thy pelf,
Curs'd be thy neighbours, thy trustees, thyself;
To friends, to fortune, to mankind, a shame.
Think how posterity will treat thy name;
And by a rope, that future times may tell
Thou hast at least bestowed one penny well.'
  'Right,' cries his lordship; 'for a rogue in need
To have a taste is insolence indeed.
In me 'tis noble, suits my birth and state,
My wealth unwieldly, and my heap too great,
Then, like the sun, let bounty spread her ray,
And shine that superfluity away.
Oh impudence of wealth! with all thy store,
How dar'st thou let one worthy man be poor?
Shall half the new-built churches round thee fall?
Make quays, build bridges, or repair Whitehall;
Or to the country let that heap be lent,
As M**o's was, but not at five per cent.
  Who thinks that fortune cannot change her mind,
Prepares a dreadful jest for all mankind.
And who stands safest? Tell me, is it he
That spreads and swells in puff'd prosperity;
Or, bless'd with little, whose preventing care
In peace provides fit arms against a war?'
  Thus Bethel spoke, who always speaks his thought,
And always thinks the very thing he ought;
His equal mind I copy what I can,
And as I love would imitate the man.
In South-sea days, not happier, when surmis'd
The lord of thousands, than if now excis'd;
In forest planted by a father's hand,
Than in five acres now of rented land.
Content with little, I can piddle here
On brocoli and mutton round the year;

But ancient friends, (though poor, or out of play),
That touch my bell, I cannot turn away.
'Tis true, no turbots dignify my boards,
But gudgeons, flounders, what my Thames affords:
To Hounslow-heath I point, and Bansted down,
Thence comes your mutton, and these chicks my own;
From yon old walnut tree a shower shall fall,
And grapes, long lingering on my only wall,
And figs from standard and espalier join;
The devil is in you, if you cannot dine:
 Then cheerful healths (your mistress shall have place)
And, what's more rare, a poet shall say grace.
Fortune not much of humbling me can boast;
Though double tax'd, how little have I lost!
My life's amusements have been just the same
Before and after standing armies came,
My lands are sold, my father's house is gone;
I'll hire another's; is not that my own,
And yours, my friends? through whose free-opening gate
None comes too early, none departs too late;
(For I, who hold sage Homer's rule the best,
Welcome the coming, speed the going, guest.)
'Pray Heaven it last!' cries Swift, 'as you go on;
I wish to God this house had been your own!
Pity to build without a son or wife:
Why, you'll enjoy it only all your life.'
'Well, if the use be mine, can it concern one
Whether the name belong to Pope or Vernon?
What's property? dear Swift! you see it alter
From you to me, from me to Peter Walter;
Or in a mortgage prove a lawyer's share,
Or in a jointure vanish from the heir;
Or in pure equity, the case not clear,
The chancery takes your rents for twenty year:
At best it falls to some ungracious son,
Who cries 'My fathers,s damned, and all's my own,'
Shades that to Bacon could retreat afford,
Becomes the portion of a booby lord;
And Hemsley, once proud Buckingham's delight
Slides to a scrivener or a city knight.
Let lands and houses have what lords they will,
Let us be fixed, and our own masters still.'

BOOK II. SATIRE VI.

[THE FIRST PART IMITATED IN THE YEAR 1714, BY DR. SWIFT; THE LATTER PART, BY MR. POPE, ADDED AFTERWARDS.]

I'VE often wished that I had clear
For life six hundred pounds a-year,
A handsome house to lodge a friend,
A river at my garden's end,
A terrace walk, and half a rood
Of land set out to plant a wood.
  Well, now I have all this, and more,
I ask not to increase my store;
But here a grievance seems to lie,
All this is mine but till I die;
I can't but think 't would sound more clever
To me and to my heirs for ever.
  If I ne'er got or lost a groat,
By any trick or any fault;
And if I pray by reason's rules,
And not like forty other fools,
As thus, 'Vouchsafe, oh, gracious Maker!
To grant me this and t' other acre;
Or, if it be thy will and pleasure,
Direct my plough to find a treasure;
But only what my station fits,
And to be kept in my right wits,
Preserve, Almighty Providence!
Just what you gave me, competence;
And let me in these shades compose
Something in verse as true as prose,
Removed from all the ambitious scene,
Nor puffed by pride, nor sunk by spleen.'
  In short, I'm perfectly content,
Let me but live on this side Trent,
Nor cross the channel twice a year,
To spend six months with statesmen here.
  I must by all means come to town,
'Tis for the service of the crown;
Lewis, the Dean will be of use;
Send for him up, take no excuse.

The toil, the danger, of the seas,
Great ministers ne'er think of these;
Or, let it cost five hundred pound,
No matter where the money 's found,
It is but so much more in debt,
And that they ne'er considered yet.
'Good Mr. Dean, go change your gown'
Let my lord know you 're come to town.'
I hurry me in haste away,
Not thinking it is levee-day,
And find his honour in a pound,
Hemm'd by a triple circle round,
Chequered with ribbons blue and green,
How should I thrust myself between?
Some wag observes me thus perplex'd,
And, smiling, whispers to the next:
'I thought the Dean had been too proud,
To jostle here among a crowd.'
Another, in a surly fit,
Tells me I have more zeal than wit;
'So eager to express your love,
You ne'er consider who you shove,
But rudely press before a duke.'
I own I am pleas'd with this rebuke,
And take it kindly meant, to show
What I desire the world should know.
I get a whisper and withdraw,
When twenty fools, I never saw,
Come with petitions, fairly penn'd,
Desiring I would stand their friend
This humbly offers me his case—
That begs my interest for a place—
A hundred other men's affairs,
Like bees, are humming in my ears.
To-morrow my appeal comes on;
Without your help the cause is gone.—
The duke expects my lord and you,
About some great affair, at two.
Put my Lord Bolinbroke in mind
To get my warrant quickly sign'd:
'Consider, 'tis my first request.'—
'Be satisfied, I'll do my best:'
Then presently he falls to tease,
'You may for certain, if you please;
I doubt not, if his lordship knew.—
And, Mr. Dean, one word from you.'—
'Tis (let me see) three years and more,
(October next it will be four,)

Since Harley bid me first attend,
And chose me for an humble friend;
Would take me in his coach to chat,
And question me of this and that:
As, 'What's o'clock?' and 'How's the wind?
'Whose chariot's that we left behind?'
Or gravely try to read the lines
Writ underneath the country signs;
Or 'Have you nothing new to-day,
From Pope, from Parnell, or from Gay?
Such tattle often entertains
My lord and me as far as Staines,
As once a week we travel down
To Windsor and again to town,
Where all that passes inter nos,
Might be proclaim'd at Charing-cross.
Yet some I know with envy swell,
Because they see me used so well.
'How think you of our friend the dean?
I wonder what some people mean:
My lord and he are grown so great,
Always together tête a tête.
What! they admire him for his jokes—
See but the fortune of some folks!'
There flies about a strange report
Of some express arrived at court;
I'm stopped by all the fools I meet,
And catechised in every street.
'You, Mr. Dean, frequent the great;
Inform us, will the emperor treat?
Or do the prints and papers lie?'
'Faith, sir, you know as much as I.'
'Ah! Doctor, how you love to jest;
'Tis now no secret.' 'I protest
'Tis one to me.'—'Then tell us, pray?
When are the troops to have their pay?'
And though I solemnly declare
I know no more than my lord mayor,
They stand amazed, and think me grown
The closest mortal ever known.
Thus in a sea of folly toss'd,
My choicest hours of life are lost,
Yet always wishing to retreat:
Oh, could I see my country-seat!
There leaning near a gentle brook,
Sleep, or peruse some ancient book,
And there in sweet oblivion drown
Those cares that haunt the court and town.

Oh charming noons! and nights divine!
Or when I sup, or when I dine,
My friends above, my folks below.
Chatting and laughing all-a-row,
The beans and bacon set before 'em,
The grace-cup served with all decorum
Each willing to be pleased, and please,
And e'en the very dogs at ease:
Here no man prates of idle things,
How this or that Italian sings,
A neighbour's madness, or his spouse's,
Or what's in either of the Houses;
But something much more our concern,
And quite a scandal not to learn:
Which is the happier or the wiser,
A man of merit or a miser?
Whether we ought to choose our friends
For their own worth or our own ends?
What good, or better, we may call,
And what the very best of all?
  Our friend, Dan Prior, told (you know)
A tale extremely à-propos:
Name a town life, and in a trice
He had a story of two mice.
Once on a time (so runs the fable)
A country mouse, right hospitable,
Received a town mouse at his board,
Just as a farmer might a lord;
A frugal mouse, upon the whole,
Yet loved his friend, and had a soul;
Knew what was handsome, and would do't,
On just occasion, coute qui coute.
He brought him bacon, (nothing lean!)
Pudding that might have pleased a dean;
Cheese such as men in Suffolk make,
But wished it Stilton for his sake;
Yet to his guest, though no way sparing,
He ate himself the rind and paring.
Our courtier scarce could touch a bit,
But showed his breeding and his wit;
He did his best to seem to eat,
And cried, 'I vow you're mighty neat:
But, lord, my friend, this savage scene!
For God's sake come and live with men:
Consider mice, like men, must die,
Both small and great, both you and I;
Then spend your life in joy and sport:
(This doctrine, friend, I learned at court.')
  The veriest hermit in the nation
May yield, God knows, to strong temptation.

Away they came, through thick and thin,
To a tall house near Lincoln's-inn:
('Twas on the night of a debate,
When all their lordships had sat late.)
Behold the place where if a poet
Shined in description, he might show it;
Tell how the moon-beam trembling falls,
And tips with silver all the walls;
Palladian walls, Venetian doors,
Grotesco roofs, and stucco floors:
But let it (in a word) be said,
The moon was up, and men a-bed;
The napkins white, the carpet red:
The guests withdrawn had left the treat,
And down the mice sat tête a tête.
Our courtier walks from dish to dish,
Tastes for his friend of fowl and fish;
Tells all their names, lays down the law,
'Que ça est bon! Ah gouter ça!
That jelly's rich, this malmsey healing;
Pray, dip your whiskers and your tail in.'
Was ever such a happy swain!
He stuffs and swills, and stuffs again.
'I'm quite ashamed—'tis mighty rude
To eat so much—but all's so good!
I have a thousand thanks to give—
My lord alone knows how to live.'
No sooner said, but from the hall
Rush chaplain, butler, dogs, and all.
'A rat, a rat! clap to the door'—
The cat comes bouncing on the floor.
O for the heart of Homer's mice,
Or gods to save them in a trice!
(It was by Providence they think,
For your damned stucco has no chink.)
'An't please your honour,' quoth the peasant,
'This same dessert is not so pleasant:
Give me again my hollow tree,
A crust of bread and liberty!'

BOOK I. EPISTLE I.

TO LORD BOLINGBROKE.

St. John whose love indulged my labours past,
Mature my present, and shall bound my last!
Why will you break the sabbath of my days?
Now sick alike of envy and of praise.
Public too long, ah! let me hide my age;
See modest Cibber now has left the stage:
Our generals now, retired to their estates,
Hang their old trophies o'er the garden gates,
In life's cool evening, satiate of applause,
Nor fond of bleeding e'en in Brunswick's cause.
  A voice there is, that whispers in my ear,
('Tis reason's voice, which sometimes one can hear,)
Friend Pope! be prudent; let your muse take breath,
And never gallop Pegasus to death;
Let stiff and stately, void of fire or force,
You limp, like Blackmore, on a lord mayor's horse.
  Farewell then verse, and love, and ev'ry toy,
The rhymes and rattles of the man or boy;
What right, what true, what fit, we justly call,
Let this be all my care—for this is all:
To lay this harvest up, and hoard with haste
What ev'ry day will want, and most the last.
  But ask not to what doctors I apply?
Sworn to no master, of no sect am I:
As drives the storm, at any door I knock,
And house with Montaigne now, or now with Locke.
Sometimes a patriot, active in debate,
Mix with the world, and battle for the state:
Free as young Lyttleton, her cause pursue,
Still true to virtue, and as warm as true:
Sometimes with Aristippus or St. Paul,
Indulge my candour, and grow all to all;
Back to my native moderation slide,
And win my way by yielding to the tide.

Long as to him who works for debt the day,
Long as the night to her whose love's away,
Long as the year's dull circle seems to run,
When the brisk minor pants for twenty-one;
So slow the unprofitable moments roll,
That lock up all the functions of my soul;
That keep me from myself, and still delay
Life's instant business to a future day;
That task which, as we follow or despise,
The eldest is a fool, the youngest wise;
Which done, the poorest can no wants endure;
And which, not done, the richest must be poor.
Late as it is, I put myself to school,
And feel some comfort not to be a fool.
Weak though I am of limb, and short of sight,
Far from a lynx, and not a giant quite,
I'll do what Mead and Cheselden advise,
To keep these limbs, and to preserve these eyes.
Not to go back is somewhat to advance,
And men must walk at least before they dance.
Say, does thy blood rebel, thy bosom move
With wretched avarice, or a wretched love?
Know there are words and spells which can control,
Between the fits, this fever of the soul;
Know there are rhymes which, fresh and fresh applied,
Will cure the arrant'st puppy of his pride.
Be furious, envious, slothful, mad, or drunk,
Slave to a wife, or vassal to a punk,
A Switz, a High-Dutch, or a Low-Dutch bear;
All that we ask is but a patient ear.
'Tis the first virtue, vices to abhor,
And the first wisdom to be fool no more:
But to the world no bugbear is so great
As want of figure and a small estate.
To either India see the merchant fly,
Scar'd at the spectre of pale poverty!
See him with pains of body, pangs of soul,
Burn through the tropic, freeze beneath the pole!
Wilt thou do nothing for a nobler end,
Nothing to make philosophy thy friend?
To stop thy foolish views, thy long desires,
And ease thy heart of all that it admires?
Here wisdom calls, 'Seek virtue first, be bold!
As gold to silver, virtue is to gold.'
There London's voice, 'Get money, money still!
And then let virtue follow if she will.'
This, this the saving doctrine preach'd to all,
From low St. James's up to high St. Paul!

From him whose quills stand quivered at his ear,
From him who notches sticks at Westminister.
Barnard, in spirit, sense, and truth, abounds;
'Pray then what wants he?' fourscore thousand pounds:
A pension, or such harness for a slave
As Bug now has, and Dorimont would have.
Barnard, thou art a cit, with all thy worth,
But Bug and D—l, their honours, and so forth.
Yet every child another song will sing,
Virtue, brave boys! 'tis virtue makes a king.
True conscious honour is to feel no sin,
He's armed without that's innocent within:
Be this thy screen, and this thy wall of brass;
Compared to this, a minister's an ass.
And say, to which shall our applause belong,
This new court-jargon, or the good old song?
The modern language of corrupted peers,
Or what was spoke at Cressy or Poitiers?
Who counsels best? who whispers, 'Be but great,
With praise or infamy leave that to fate;
Get place and wealth, if possible with grace;
If not, by any means get wealth and place.'
For what? to have a box where eunuchs sing,
And foremost in the circle eye a king.
Or he who bids thee face with steady view
Proud fortune, and look shallow greatness through,
And while he bids thee sets the example too?
If such a doctrine, in St. James's air,
Should chance to make the well-dressed rabble stare;
If honest S——z take scandal at a spark
That less admires the palace than the park;
Faith I shall give the answer Reynard gave;
'I cannot like, dread sire! your royal cave;
Because I see, by all the tracts about,
Full many a beast goes in, but none come out.'
Adieu to virtue if you're once a slave:
Send her to court, you send her to her grave.
Well, if a king's a lion, at the least
The people are a many-headed beast:
Can they direct what measures to pursue,
Who know themselves so little what to do?
Alike in nothing but one lust of gold,
Just half the land would buy, and half be sold:
Their country's wealth our mighter misers drain,
Or cross, to plunder provinces, the main:
The rest, some farm the poor-box, some the pews:
Some keep assemblies, and would keep the stews;

Some with fat bucks on childless dotards fawn,
Some win rich widows by their chine and brawn.
While with the silent growth of ten per cent.
In dirt and darkness hundreds stink content.
Of all these ways, if each pursues his own,
Satire be gone, and let the wretch alone:
But show me one who has it in his power,
To act consistent with himself an hour.
Sir Job sail'd forth, the evening bright and still,
'No place on earth,' he cried, 'like Greenwich hill!'
Up starts a palace; lo, the obedient base
Slopes at its foot, the woods its sides embrace,
The silver Thames reflects its marble face.
Now let some whimsey, or that devil within,
Which guides all those who know not what they mean,
But give the knight (or give his lady) spleen,
'Away, away! take all your scaffolds down,
For Snug's the word: my dear! we'll live in town.
 At amorous Flavio is the stocking thrown?
That very night he longs to live alone.
The fool whose wife elopes some thrice a quarter,
For matrimonial solace dies a martyr.
Did ever Proteus, Merlin, any witch,
Transform themselves so strangely as the rich?
Well, but the poor—the poor have the same itch:
They change their weekly barber, weekly news,
Prefer a new japanner to their shoes,
Discharge their garrets, move their beds, and run
(They know not whither) in a chaise and one;
They hire their sculler, and when once abroad
Grow sick, and damn the climate like a lord.
You laugh half-beax, half-sloven, if I stand,
My wig all powder, and all snuff my band;
You laugh if coat and breeches strangely vary,
White gloves, and linen worthy Lady Mary!
But when no prelate's lawn, with hair-shirt lined,
Is half so incoherent as my mind,
When (each opinion with the next at strife,
One ebb and flow of follies all my life)
I plant, root up; I build, and then confound;
Turn round to square, and square again to round;
You never change one muscle of your face,
You think this madness but a common case,
Nor once to Chancery nor to Hale apply,
Yet hang your lip to see a seam awry!
Careless how ill I with myself agree,
Kind to my dress, my figure, not to me.

Is this my guide, philosopher, and friend?
This he who loves me, and who ought to mend?
Who ought to make me what he can, or none.
That man divine whom wisdom calls her own,
Great without title, without fortune bless'd;
Rich e'en when plundered, honoured while oppress'd;
Loved without youth, and followed without power:
At home though exiled; free though in the tower:
In short that reasoning, high, immortal thing,
Just less than Jove, and much above a king:
Nay, half in heaven—except (what's mighty odd)
A fit of vapours clouds this demigod!

BOOK I. EPISTLE VI.

TO MR. MURRAY.

'Not to admire, is all the art I know,
To make men happy, and to keep them so.'
Plain truth, dear Murray, needs no flowers of speech,
So take it in the very words of Creech.
This vault of air, this congregated ball,
Self-centered sun, and stars that rise and fall,
There are, my friend! whose philosophic eyes
Look through, and trust the Ruler with his skies;
To him commit the hour, the day, the year,
And view this dreadful all without a fear.
Admire we then what earth's low entrails hold,
Arabian shores, or Indian seas infold;
All the made trade of fools and slaves for gold?
Or popularity? or stars and strings?
The mob's applauses, or the gifts of kings?
Say with what eyes we ought at courts to gaze,
And pay the great our homage of amaze?
If weak the pleasure that from these can spring,
The fear to want them is as weak a thing:
Whether we dread, or whether we desire,
In either case, believe me, we admire:
Whether we joy or grieve, the same the curse,
Surprised at better, or surprised at worse.
Thus good or bad, to one extreme betray
The unbalanced mind, and snatch the man away;
For virtue's self may too much zeal be had;
The worst of madmen is a saint run mad.
Go then, and, if you can, admire the state.
Of beaming diamonds and reflected plate;
Procure a taste to double the surprise,
And gaze on Parian charms with learned eyes;
Be struck with bright brocade or Tyrian dye,
Our birth-day nobles' splendid livery.
If not so pleased, at council-board rejoice
To see their judgments hang upon thy voice;
From morn to night, at senate, Rolls, and hall,
Plead much, read more, dine late, or not at all.

But wherefore all this labour, all this strife?
For fame, for riches, for a noble wife?
Shall one whom nature, learning. birth, conspired
To form, not to admire, but be admired,
Sigh while his Chloe, blind to wit and worth,
Weds the rich dulness of some son o' earth?
Yet time ennobles or degrades each line;
It brightened Craggs's, and may darken thine.
And what is fame? the meanest have their day;
The greatest can but blaze and pass away.
Graced as thou art with all the power of words,
So known, so honoured, at the house of lords:
Conspicuous scene! another yet is nigh,
(More silent far) where kings and poets lie;
Where Murray (long enough his country's pride)
Shall be no more than Tully or than Hyde!
Racked with sciatics, martyred with the stone,
Will any mortal let himself alone?
See Ward, by battered beaux invited over,
And desperate misery lays hold on Dover.
The case is easier in the mind's disease;
There all men may be cured whene'er they please.
Would ye be bless'd? despise low joys, low gains:
Disdain whatever Cornbury disdains;
Be virtuous, and be happy for your pains.
But art thou one whom new opinions sway,
One who believes as Tindal leads the way,
Who virtue and a church alike disowns,
Thinks that but words, and this but brick and stones?
Fly then on all the wings of wild desire,
Admire whate'er the maddest can admire.
Is wealth thy passion? hence! from pole to pole,
Where winds can carry, or where waves can roll;
For Indian spices, for Peruvian gold,
Prevent the greedy, or outbid the bold:
Advance thy golden mountain to the skies:
On the broad base of fifty thousand rise;
Add one round hundred, and (if that's not fair)
Add fifty more and bring it to a square:
For, mark the advantage; just so many score
Will gain a wife with half as many more,
Procure her beauty, make that beauty chaste,
And then such friends—as cannot fail to last.
A man of wealth is dubbed a man of worth;
Venus shall give him form, and Anstis birth.
Believe me many a German prince is worse,
Who proud of pedigree is poor of purse.
His wealth brave Timon gloriously confounds;
Ask for a groat, he gives a hundred pounds:

Or, if three ladies like a luckless play,
Takes the whole house upon the poet's day.
Now, in such exigences not to need,
Upon my word you must be rich indeed:
A noble superfluity it craves,
Not for yourself, but for your fools and knaves;
Something which for your honour they may cheat,
And which it much becomes you to forget.
If wealth alone then make and keep us bless'd,
Still, still be getting, never, never rest.
But if to power and place your passion lie,
If in the pomp of life consist the joy,
Then hire a slave, or (if you will) a lord,
To do the honours, and to give the word;
Tell at your levee, as the crowds approach,
To whom to nod, whom take into your coach,
Whom honour with your hand; to make remarks,
Who rules in Cornwall, or who rules in Berks:
'This may be troublesome, is near the chair;
That makes three members, this can choose a may'r
Instructed thus, you bow, embrace, protest,
Adopt him son, or cousin at the least,
Then turn about, and laugh at your own jest.
Or if your life be one continued treat,
If to live well means nothing but to eat;
Up, up! cries gluttony, 'tis break of day,
Go drive the deer, and drag the finny prey;
With hounds and horns go hunt an appetite—
So Russel did, but could not eat at night;
Called happy dog the beggar at his door,
And envied thirst and hunger to the poor.
Or shall we ev'ry decency confound,
Through taverns, stews, and bagnois, take our round?
Go dine with Chartres, in each vice outdo
K—l's lewd cargo, or Ty—y's crew,
From Latian sirens, French Circæan feasts,
Returned well travelled, and transformed to beasts;
Or for a title punk or foreign flame
Renounce our country, and degrade our name?
If, after all, we must with Wilmot own,
The cordial drop of life is love alone,
And Swift cry wisely *Vive la bagatelle!*
The man that loves and laughs must sure do well.
Adieu—if this advice appear the worst,
E'en take the counsel which I gave you first;
Or better precepts if you can impart;
Why do, I'll follow them with all my heart.

BOOK I. EPISTLE VII.

[IMITATED IN THE MANNER OF DOCTOR SWIFT.]

'Tis true, my lord, I gave my word,
I would be with you June the third;
Changed it to August, and, in short,
Have kept it—as you do at court.
You humour me when I am sick;
Why not when I am splenetic?
In town what objects could I meet?
The shops shut up in every street,
And funerals blackening all the doors,
And yet more melancholy whores:
And what a dust in ev'ry place!
And a thin court that wants your face,
And fevers raging up and down,
And W— and H—— both in town!
 'The dog-days are no more the case,'
'Tis true, but winter comes apace:
Then southward let your bard retire,
Hold out some months 'twixt sun and fire,
And you shall the first warm weather
Me and the butterflies together.
 My lord, your favours well I know;
'Tis with distinction you bestow,
And not to ev'ry one that comes,
Just as a Scotchman does his plums.
'Pray take them, Sir—enough's a feast:
Eat some, and pocket up the rest.'—
'What rob your boys? those pretty rogues!
'No, Sir, you'll leave them to the hogs.'
Thus fools with compliments besiege ye,
Contriving never to oblidge ye.
Scatter your favours on a fop,
Ingratitude's the certain crop;
And 'tis but just, I'll tell you wherefore,
You give the things you never care for.
A wise man always is or should
Be mighty ready to do good;

But makes a difference in his thought
Betwixt a guinea and a groat.
Now this I'll say, you'll find in me
A safe companion, and a free;
But if you'd have me always near—
A word, pray, in your honour's ear:
I hope it is your resolution
To give me back my constitution!
The sprightly wit, the lively eye,
The engaging smile, the gaiety
That laughed down many a summer sun,
And kept you up so oft till one;
And all that voluntary vein,
As when Belinda raised my strain.
A weasel once made shift to slink
In at a corn loft through a chink;
But having ample stuffed his skin,
Could not get out as he got in;
Which one belonging to the house
('Twas not a man, it was a mouse)
Observing, cried, 'You 'scape not so:
Lean as you came, sir, you must go.
Sir, you may spare your application,
I'm no such beast, nor his relation,
Nor one that temperance advance,
Cramm'd to the throat with ortolons;
Extremely ready to resign
All that may make me none of mine.
South-sea subscriptions take who please,
Leave me but liberty and ease.
'Twas what I said to Craggs and Child,
Who praised my modesty, and smiled,
'Give me,' I cried, 'enough for me,
My bread and independancy!'
So bought an annual rent or two,
And lived—just as you see I do;
Near fifty, and without a wife,
I trust that sinking-fund my life.
Can I retrench? Yes, mighty well,
Shrink back to my paternal cell,
A little house with trees a-row,
And, like its master, very low:
There died my father, no man's debtor,
And there I'll die, nor worse nor better.
To set this matter full before ye,
Our old friend Swift will tell his story.
'Harley, the nation's great support'—
But you may read it, I stop short.

* * *

BOOK II. EPISTLE I.

ADVERTISEMENT.

The reflections of Horace, and the judgments passed in his Epistle to Augustus, seemed so seasonable to the present times, that I could not help applying them to the use of my own country. The author thought them considerable enough to address them to his prince, whom he paints with all the great and good qualities of a monarch upon whom the Romans depended for the increase of an absolute empire: but to make the poem entirely English, I was willing to add one or two of those which contribute to the happiness of a free people, and are more consistent with the welfare of her neighbours.—Pope.

TO AUGUSTUS.

While you, great patron of mankind! sustain
The balanced world, and open all the main,
Your country, chief in arms, abroad defend,
At home with morals, arts, and laws amend;
How shall the muse, from such a monarch, steal
An hour, and not defraud the public weal?
Edward and Henry, now the boast of fame,
And virtuous Alfred, a more sacred name,
After a life of generous toils endured,
The Gaul subdued, or property secured,
Ambition humbled, mighty cities stormed,
Or laws established, and the world reformed,
Closed their long glories with a sigh to find
The unwilling gratitude of base mankind!
All human virtue, to its latest breath,
Finds envy never conquered but by death.
The great Alcides, every labour past,
Had still this monster to subdue at last:
Sure fate of all, beneath whose rising ray
Each star of meaner merit fades away!
Oppressed we feel the beam directly beat;
Those suns of glory please not till they set.
To thee the world its present homage pays,
The harvest early, but mature the praise:
Great friend of liberty! in kings a name
Above all Greek, above all Roman, fame;

Whose word is trutl as sacred and revered
As heaven's own oracles from altars heard.
Wonder of kings! like whom, to mortal eyes,
None e'er has risen, and none e'er shall rise.
Just in one instance; be it yet confessed,
Your people, Sir, are partial in the rest;
Foes to all living worth, except your own,
And advocates for folly dead and gone.
Authors, like coins, grow dear as they grow old;
It is the rust we value, not the gold.
Chaucer's worst ribaldry is learned by rote,
And beastly Skelton heads of houses quote.
One likes no language but the Faery Queen;
A Scot will fight for Christ's Kirk of the Green;
And each true Briton is to Ben so civil,
He swears the muses met him at the devil.
Though justly Greece her eldest sons admires,
Why should not we be wiser than our sires?
In every public virtue we excel;
We build, we paint, we sing, we dance, as well;
And learned Athens to our art must stoop,
Could she behold us tumbling through a hoop.
If time improve our wits as well as wine,
Say at what age a poet grows divine?
Shall we, or shall we not, account him so
Who died, perhaps, an hundred years ago?
End all dispute; and fix the year precise
When British bards began to immortalise!
'Who lasts a century can have no flaw;
I hold that wit a classic good in law.'
Suppose he wants a year, will you compound?
And shall we deem him ancient, right, and sound,
Or damn to all eternity at once;
At ninety-nine, a modern and a dunce?
'We shall not quarrel for a year or two;
By courtesy of England he may do.'
Then by the rule that made the horse-tail bare,
I pluck out year by year, as hair by hair,
And melt down ancients like a heap of snow,
While you, to measure merits, look in Stowe,
And estimating authors by the year,
Bestow a garland only on a bier.
Shakspeare (whom you and every play-house bill
Style the divine, the matchless, what you will)
For gain, not glory, winged his roving flight,
And grew immortal in his own despite.
Ben old and poor, as little seemed to heed
The life to come in every poet's creed.
Who now reads Cowley? if he pleases yet,
His moral pleases, not his pointed wit;

Forgot his epic, nay, Pindaric art;
But still I love the language of his heart.
'Yet surely, surely, these were famous men!
What boy but hears t e sayings of old Ben?
In all debates, where critics bear a part,
Not one but nods, and talks of Jonson's art,
Of Shakspeare's nature, and of Cowle,'s wit;
How Beaumont's judgment check'd what Fletcher writ;
How Shadwell hasty, Wycherly was slow;
But for the passion, Southern, sure, and Rowe.
These, only these, support the crowded stage,
From eldest Heywood down to Cibber's age.'
All this may be; the people's voice is odd;
It is, and it is not, the voice of God.
To Gammer Gurton if it give the bays,
And yet deny the Careless Husband praise,
Or say our fathers never broke a rule,
Why then, I say, the public is a fool.
But let them own that greater faults than we
They had, and greater virtues I'll agree.
Spenser himself affects the obsolete,
And Sydney's verse halts ill on Roman feet;
Milton's strong pinion now not heaven can bound,
Now serpent-like, in prose he sweeps the ground;
In quibbles angel and archangel join,
And God the Father turns a school divine.
Not that I'd lop the beaties from his book,
Like slashing Bentley with his desperate hook;
Or damn all Shakspeare, like the affected fool
At court, who hates whate'er he read at school.
But for the wits of either Charles's days,
The mob of gentlemen, who wrote with ease;
Sprat, Carew, Sedley, and a hundred more,
(Like twinkling stars, the miscellanies o'er,)
One simile, that solitary shines
In the dry desert of a thousand lines,
Or lengthen'd thought, that gleams through many a page,
Has sanctified whole poems for an age.
I lose my patience, and I own it too,
When works are censured, not as bad, but new;
While if our elders break all reason's laws,
These fools demand not pardon, but applause.
On Avon's bank, where flowers eternal blow,
If I but ask if any weed can grow,
One tragic sentence if I dare deride,
Which Betterton's grave action dignified,
Or well-mouthed Booth with emphasis proclaims,
(Though but perhaps a muster-roll of names,)
How will our fathers rise up in a rage,
And swear all shame is lost in George's age!

You'd think no fools disgraced the former reign,
Did not some grave examples yet remain,
Who scorn a lad should teach his father skill,
And having once been wrong, will be so still.
He who, to seem more deep than you or I,
Extols old bards, or Merlin's prophecy,
Mistake him not: he envies, not admires—
And to debase the sons, exalts the sires.
Had ancient times conspired to disallow
What then was new, what had been ancient now?
Or what remained so worthy to be read
By learned critics of the mighty dead?
In days of ease, when now the weary sword
Was sheathed, and luxury with Charles restored,
In every taste of foreign courts improved,
'All by the king's example lived and loved;'
Then peers grew proud in horsemanship to excel,
Newmarket's glory rose as Britain's fell;
The soldier breathed the gallantries of France,
And every flowery courtier writ romance.
Then marble, softened into life, grew warm,
And yielding metal flowed to human form;
Lely on animated canvass stole
The sleepy eye, that spoke the melting soul.
No wonder then, when all was love and sport,
The willing muses were debauched at court;
On each enervate string they taught the note
To pant or tremble through an eunuch's throat.
But Britain, changeful as a child at play,
Now calls in princes, and now turns away.
Now Whig, now Tory, what we loved we hate;
Now all for pleasure, now for church and state;
Now for prerogative, and now for laws:
Effects unhappy! from a noble cause.
Time was, a sober Englishman would knock
His servants up, and rise by five o'clock;
Instruct his family in every rule,
And send his wife to church, his son to school.
To worship like his fathers was his care;
To teach their frugal virtues to his heir;
To prove that luxury could never hold,
And place on good security his gold.
Now times are changed, and one poetic itch
Has seized the court and city, poor and rich.
Sons, sires, and grandsires, all will wear the bays
Our wives read Milton, and our daughters plays;
To theatres and to rehearsals throng,
And all our grace at table is a song.
I, who so oft renounce the muse's lie,
Not ***'s self e'er tells more fibs than I.

When sick of muse our follies we deplore,
And promise our best friends to rhyme no more;
We wake next morning in a raging fit,
And call for pen and ink to show our wit.
He served a 'prenticeship who sets up shop;
Ward tried on puppies and the poor his drop;
E'en Radcliff's doctors travel first to France,
Nor dare to practise till they've learned to dance.
Who builds a bridge that never drove a pile?
(Should Ripley venture, all the world would smile:)
But those who cannot write, and those who can,
All rhyme, and scrawl, and scribble to a man.
Yet, Sir, reflect; the mischief is not great:
These madmen never hurt the church or state:
Sometimes the folly benefits mankind,
And rarely avarice taints the tuneful mind.
Allow him but his plaything of a pen,
He ne'er rebels, or plots, like other men:
Flight of cashiers, or mobs, he'll never mind,
And knows no losses while the muse is kind.
To cheat a friend or ward he leaves to Peter;
The good man heaps up nothing but mere metre,
Enjoys his garden and his book in quiet,
And then—a perfect hermit in his diet.
Of little use, the man you may suppose,
Who says in verse what others say in prose;
Yet let me show a poet's of some weight,
And, though no soldier, useful to the state.
What will a child learn sooner than a song?
What better teach a foreigner the tongue?
What's long or short, each accent where to place?
And speak in public with some sort of grace?
I scarce can think him such a worthless thing,
Unless he praise some monster of a king;
Or virtue or religion turn to sport,
To please a lewd or unbelieving court.
Unhappy Dryden!—In all Charles's days
Roscommon only boasts unspotted bays;
And in our own, excuse some courtly stains,
No whiter page than Addison remains:
He from the taste obscene reclaims our youth,
And sets the passions on the side of truth,
Forms the soft bosom with the gentlest art,
And pours each human virtue in the heart.
Let Ireland tell how wit upheld her cause,
Her trade supported, and supplied her laws,
And leave on Swift this grateful verse engraved,
'The rights a court attacked—a poet saved.'
Behold the hand that wrought a nation's cure,
Stretched to relieve the idiot and the poor,

Proud vice to brand, or injured worth adorn,
And stretch the ray to ages yet unborn.
Not but there are who merit other palms;
Hopkins and Sternhold glad the heart with psalms;
The boys and girls whom charity maintains
Implore your help in these pathetic strains:
How could devotion touch the country pews
Unless the gods bestowed a proper muse?
Verse cheers their leisure, verse assists their work;
Verse prays for peace, or sings down pope and Turk.
The silenced preacher yields to potent strain,
And feels that grace his prayer besought in vain;
The blessing thrills through all the labouring throng,
And heaven is won by violence of song.
Our rural ancestors, with little blest,
Patient of labour when the end was rest,
Indulged the day that housed their annual grain
With feasts, and offerings, and a thankful strain:
The joy their wives, their sons, and servants, share,
Ease of their toil and partners of their care:
The laugh, the jest, attendants on the bowl,
Smoothed every brow, and opened every soul:
With growing years the pleasing licence grew,
And taunts alternate innocently flew.
But times corrupt, and nature ill-inclined,
Produced the point that left a sting behind;
Till friend with friend, and families at strife,
Triumphant malice raged through private life,
Who felt the wrong, or feared it, took the alarm,
Appealed to law, and justice lent her arm.
At length by wholesome dread of statutes bound,
The poets learned to please, and not to wound:
Most warped to flattery's side; but some, more nice,
Preserved the freedom, and forbore the vice.
Hence satire rose, that just the medium hit,
And heals with morals what it hurts with wit.
We conquered France, but felt our captive's charms,
Her arts victorious triumphed o'er our arms;
Britain to soft refinements less a foe,
Wit grew polite, and numbers learned to flow.
Waller was smooth; but Dryden taught to join
The varying verse, the full-resounding line,
The long majestic march, and energy divine,
Though still some traces of our rustic vein
And splayfoot verse remained, and will remain.
Late, very late, correctness grew our care,
When the tired nation breathed from civil war.
Exact Racine and Corneille's noble fire
Showed us that France had something to admire.

Not but the tragic spirit was our own,
And full in Shakspeare, fair in Otway, shone;
But Otway failed to polish or refine,
And fluent Shakspeare scarce effaced a line.
E'en copious Dryden wanted, or forgot,
The last and greatest art, the art to blot.
  Some doubt if equal pains or equal fire
The humbler muse of comedy require.
But in known images of life I guess
The labour greater as the indulgence less.
Observe how seldom e'en the best succeed;
Tell me if Congreve's fools are fools indeed?
What pert, low dialogue has Farquhar writ!
How Van wants grace, who never wanted wit!
The stage how loosely does Astrea tread,
Who fairly puts all characters to bed!
And idle Cibber, how he breaks the laws,
To make poor Pinkey eat with vast applause!
But fill their purse, our poet's work is done;
Alike to them by pathos or by pun.
O you! whom vanity's light bark conveys
On fame's mad voyage by the wind of praise,
With what a shifting gale your course you ply,
For ever sunk too low, or borne too high!
Who pants for glory finds but short repose;
A breath revives him, or a breath o'erthrows.
Farewell the stage! if just as thrives the play
The silly bard grows fat or falls away.
There still remains, to mortify a wit,
The many-headed monster of the pit;
A senseless, worthless, and unhonoured crowd,
Who, to disturb their betters mighty proud,
Clattering their sticks before ten lines are spoke,
Call for the farce, the bear, or the black-joke.
What dear delight to Britons farce affords!
Ever the taste of mobs, but now of lords;
(Taste! that eternal wanderer, which flies
From heads to ears, and now from ears to eyes.)
The play stands still; damn action and discourse;
Back fly the scenes, and enter foot and horse;
Pageants on pageants, in long order drawn,
Peers, heralds, bishops, ermine, gold and lawn;
The champion too! and, to complete the jest,
Old Edward's armour beams on Cibber's breast,
With laughter sure Democritus had died
Had he beheld an audience gape so wide.
Let bear or elephant be e'er so white,
The people, sure, the people are the sight!
Ah, luckless poet! stretch thy lungs and roar
That bear or elephant shall heed thee more;

While all its throats the gallery extends,
And all the thunder of the pit ascends!
Loud as the wolves on Oreas's stormy steep
Howl to the roarings of the northern deep;
Such is the shout, the long-applauding note,
At Quin's high plume, or Oldfield's petticoat;
Or when from court a birth-day suit bestowed
Sinks the lost actor in the tawdry load.
Booth enters—hark! the universal peal!
'But has he spoken?' Not a syllable.
'What shook the stage, and made the people stare?'
Cato's long wig, flowered gown, and lackered chair
Yet, lest you think I rally more than teach,
Or praise malignly arts I cannot reach,
Let me once presume to instruct the times,
To know the poet from the man of rhymes.
'Tis he who gives my breast a thousand pains,
Can make me feel each passion that he feigns;
Enrage, compose, with more than magic art,
With pity and with terror tear my heart,
And snatch me o'er the earth, or through the air,
To Thebes, to Athens, when he will and where.
But not this part of the poetic state
Alone deserves the favour of the great.
Think of those authors, Sir, who would rely
More on a reader's sense than gazer's eye.
Or who shall wander where the muses sing?
Who climb their mountain, or who taste their spring?
How shall we fill a library with wit,
When Merlin's cave is half-unfurnished yet?
My liege! why writers little claim your thought
I guess, and with their leave will tell the fault.
We poets are (upon a poet's word)
Of all mankind the creatures most absurd:
The season when to come and when to go,
To sing, or cease to sing, we never know;
And if we will recite nine hours in ten,
You lose your patience just like other men.
Then, too, we hurt ourselves when, to defend
A single verse, we quarrel with a friend;
Repeat unasked; lament the wit's too fine
For vulgar eyes, and point out every line:
But most when straining with too weak a wing,
We needs will write epistles to the king;
And from the moment we oblige the town,
Expect a place or pension from the crown;
Or, dubb'd historians, by express command,
To enrol your triumphs o'er the seas and land
Be called to court to plan some work divine,
At once for Louis, Boileau, and Racine.

Yet think, great Sir! (so many virtues shown,)
Ah! think what poet best may make them known;
Or choose at least some minister of grace,
Fit to bestow the laureat's weighty place.
Charles, to late times to be transmitted fair,
Assigned his figure to Bernini's care;
And great Nassau to Kneller's hand decreed
To fix him graceful on the bounding steed:
So well in paint and stone they judged of merit;
But kings in wit may want discerning spirit.
The hero William, and the martyr Charles,
One knighted Blackmore, and one pensioned Quarles,
Which made old Ben and surly Dennis swear,
'No lord 's anointed, but a Russian bear.'
Not with such majesty, such bold relief,
The forms august of king, or conquering chief,
E'er swelled on marble, as in verse have shined
(In polished verse) the manners and the mind.
Oh! could I mount on the Mæonian wing,
Your arms, your actions, your repose, to sing!
What seas you traversed, and what fields you fought!
Your country's peace how oft, how dearly bought!
How barbarous rage subsided at your word,
And nations wondered while they dropped the sword!
How when you nodded, o'er the land and deep
Peace stole her wing, and wrapped the world in sleep,
Till earth's extremes your mediation own,
And Asia's tyrants tremble at your throne.
But verse, alas! your majesty disdains:
And I'm not used to panegyric strains.
The zeal of fools offends at any time,
But most of all the zeal of fools in rhyme.
Besides, a fate attends on all I write,
That when I aim at praise they say I bite.
A vile encomium doubly ridicules;
There's nothing blackens like the ink of fools.
If true, a woeful likeness; and if lies,
'Praise undeserved is scandal in disguise.'
Well may he blush who gives it, or receives;
And when I flatter, let my dirty leaves,
Like journals, odes, and such forgotten things,
As Eusden, Philips, Settle, writ of kings,
Clothe spice, line trunks, or, fluttering in a row,
Befringe the rails of Bedlam and Soho.

BOOK II. EPISTLE II.

Ludentis speciem dabit, et torquebitur. HOR.

DEAR colonel, Cobham's and your country's friend!
You love a verse; take such as I can send.
A Frenchman comes, presents you with his boy,
Bows and begins—'This lad, sir, is of Blois:
Observe his shape, how clean! his locks how curl'd!
My only son; I'd have him see the world.
His French is pure; his voice too—you shall hear.
Sir, he's your slave for twenty pounds a year.
Mere wax as yet, you fashion him with ease;
Your barber, cook, upholsterer; what you please:
A perfect genius at an opera song—
To say too much might do your honour wrong.
Take him with all his virtues, on my word;
His whole ambition was to serve a lord.
But, sir, to you with what would I not part?
Though, faith, I fear, 'twill break his mother's heart.
Once and but once, I caught him in a lie,
And then, unwhipp'd, he had the grace to cry:
The fault he has I fairly shall reveal,
Could you o'erlook but that, it is—to steal.'
  If, after this, you took the graceful lad,
Could you complain, my friend, he proved so bad?
Faith, in such case, if you should prosecute,
I think Sir Godfrey should decide the suit,
Who sent the thief that stole the cash away,
And punished him that put it in his way.
  Consider then, and judge me in this light;
I told you when I went I could not write;
You said the same; and are you discontent
With laws to which you gave your own assent?
Nay, worse, to ask for verse at such a time!
D'ye think we good for nothing but to rhyme?
  In Anna's wars, a soldier, poor and old,
Had dearly earned a little purse of gold:
Tired with a tedious march, one luckless night
He slept, poor dog! and lost it to a doit.

This put the man in such a desperate mind,
Between revenge, and grief, and hunger joined,
Against the foe, himself, and all mankind,
He leaped the trenches, scaled a castle wall,
Tore down a standard, took the port and all.
'Prodigious well!' his great commander cried;
Gave him much praise, and some reward beside
Next pleased his excellence a town to batter,
(Its name I know not, and 'tis no great matter.)
'Go on, my friend,' he cried; 'see yonder walls!
Advance and conquer! go where glory calls!
More honours, more rewards, attend the brave.'
'Don't you remember what reply he gave?'
'D'ye think me, noble general! such a sot?
Let him take castles who has ne'er a groat.'
  Bred up at home, full early I begun
To read in Greek the wrath of Pelus' son:
Besides, my father taught me from a lad
The better art, to know the good from bad;
(And little sure imported to remove,
To hunt for truth in Maudlin's learned grove).
But knottier points, we know not half so well,
Deprived us soon of our paternal cell;
And certain laws, by sufferers thought unjust,
Denied all posts of profit or of trust;
Hopes after hopes of pious papists fail'd,
While mighty William's thundering arm prevail'd.
For right hereditary tax'd and fin'd,
He stuck to poverty with peace of mind;
And me, the muses help to undergo it;
Convict a papist he, and I a poet.
But, thanks to Homer, since I live and thrive.
Indebted to no prince or peer alive.
Sure I should want the care of ten Monroes,
It I should scribble rather than repose.
  Years following years steal something every day,
At last they steal us from ourselves away;
In one our frolics, one amusements end;
In one a mistress drops, in one a friend.
This subtle thief of life, this paltry time,
What will it leave me if it snatch my rhyme?
If every wheel of that unwearied mill,
That turned ten thousand verses now stands still?
  But, after all, what would you have me do,
When out of twenty I can please not two?
When this heroics only deigns to praise,
Sharp satire that, and that Pindaric lays?
One likes the pheasant's wing, and one the leg;
The vulgar boil, the learned roast, an eg

Hard task to hit the palates of such guests,
When Oldfield loves what Dartineuf detests!
But grant I may relapse, for want of grace,
Again to rhyme, can London be the place?
Who there his muse, or self, or soul, attends,
In crowds, and courts, law, business, feasts, and friends?
My counsel sends to execute a deed;
A poet begs me I will hear him read.
In Palace-yard at nine you'll find me there—
At ten, for certain, sir, in Bloomsbury-square—
Before the lords at twelve my cause comes one—
There's a rehearsal, sir, exact at one—
'Oh! but a wit can study in the streets,
And raise his mind above the mob he meets.'
Not quite so well, however, as one ought;
A hackney-coach may chance to spoil a thought;
And then a nodding beam, or pig of lead,
God knows, may hurt the very ablest head.
Have you not seen, at Guildhall's narrow pass,
Two aldermen dispute it with an ass?
And peers give way, exalted as they are,
E'en to their own s-r-v—nce in a car?
Go, lofty poet! and in such a crowd
Sing thy sonorous verse—but not aloud.
Alas! to grottoes and to groves we run,
To ease and silence every muse's son:
Blackmore himself, for any grand effort,
Would drink and dose at Tooting or Earl's-court.
How shall I rhyme in this eternal roar?
How match the bards whom none e'er match'd before?
The man who, stretch'd in Isis' calm retreat,
To books and study gives seven years complete,
See! strew'd with learned dust, his nightcap on,
He walks an object new beneath the sun!
The boys flock round him, and the people stare:
So stiff, so mute! some statue you would swear
Stept from its pedestal to take the air!
And here, while town, and court, and city roars,
With mobs, and duns, and soldiers at their doors,
Shall I in London act this idle part,
Composing songs for fools to get by heart?
The Temple late two brother serjeants saw,
Who deem'd each other oracles of law;
With equal talents these congenial souls,
One lull'd the Exchequer, and one stunn'd the Rolls;
Each had a gravity would make you split
And shook his head at Murray as a wit.
'Twas, 'Sir, your law'—and, 'Sir, your eloquence;'
'Yours Cowper's manner'—'and yours Talbot's sense.'

Thus we dispose of all poetic merit;
Your Milton's genius, and mine Homer's spirit.
Call Tibbald Shakspeare, and he'll swear the Nine,
Dear Cibber, never match'd one ode of thine.
Lord! how we strut through Merlin's cave, to see
No poets there but Stephen, you, and me!
Walk with respect behind, while we at ease
Weave laurel crowns, and take what names we please.
'My dear Tibullus! if that will not do,
Let me be Horace, and be Ovid to:
Or, I'm content, allow me Dryden's strains,
And you shall rise up Otway for your pains.
Much do I suffer, much, to keep in peace
This jealous, waspish, wrong-head, rhyming race;
And much must flatter, if the whim should bite,
To court applause by printing what I write:
But let the fit pass o'er; I'm wise enough
To stop my ears to their confounded stuff.
In vain bad rhymers all mankind reject,
They treat themselves with most profound respect:
'Tis no small purpose that you hold your tongue,
Each, praised within, is happy all day long:
But how severely with themselves proceed
The men who write such verse as we can read!
Their own strict judges, not a word they spare,
That wants of force, or light, or weight, or care:
Howe'er unwillingly it quits its place,
Nay, though at court, perhaps it may find grace,
Such they'll degrade; and sometimes, in its stead,
In downright charity revive the dead;
Mark where a bold expressive phrase appears,
Bright through the rubbish of some hundred years;
Command old words that long have slept, to wake;
Words that wise Bacon or brave Raleigh spake;
Or bid the new be English, ages hence,
For use will father what's begot by sense;
Pour the full tide of eloquence along,
Serenely pure, and yet divinely strong,
Rich with the treasures of each foreign tongue
Prune the luxuriant, the uncouth refine,
But show no mercy to an empty line;
Then polish all, with so much life and ease,
You think 'tis nature, and a knack to please:
But ease in writing flows from art, not chance;
As those move easiest who have learn'd to dance.
If such the plague and pains to write by rule
Better, say I, be pleased, and play the fool:
Call, if you will, bad rhyming a disease,
It gives men happiness, or leaves them ease.

There lived *in primo Georgii*, they record,
A worthy member, no small fool, a lord;
Who, though the house was up, delighted sate,
Heard, noted, answer'd, as in full debate:
In all but this a man of sober life,
Fond of his friend, and civil to his wife;
Not quite a madman though a pasty fell;
And much too wise to walk into a well.
Him, the damn'd doctors and his friends immured;
They bled, they cupp'd, they purged; in short, they cured:
Whereat the gentleman began to stare:
'My friends!' he cried, 'pox take you for your care!
That from a patriot of distinguish'd note,
Have bled and purged me to a simple vote.'
Well, on the whole, plain prose must be my fate:
Wisdom, curse on it! will come soon or late.
There is a time when poets will grow dull:
I'll ev'n leave verses to the boys at school:
To rules of poetry no more confined,
I'll learn to smoothe and harmonise my mind,
Teach every thought within its bounds to roll,
And keep the equal measure of the soul.
Soon as I enter at my country door,
My mind resumes the thread it dropp'd before;
Thoughts, which at Hyde-park-corner I forgot,
Meet and rejoin me in the pensive grot:
There all alone, and compliments apart,
I ask these sober questions of my heart:—
If, when the more you drink, the more you crave,
You tell the doctor; when the more you have,
The more you want, why not with equal ease
Confess as well your folly, as disease?
The heart resolves this matter in a trice;—
'Men only feel the smart, but not the vice.'
When golden angels cease to cure the evil,
You give all royal witchcraft to the devil;
When servile chaplains cry, that birth and place
Indue a peer with honour, trnth, and grace;
Look in that breast, most dirty D—! be fair;
Say, can you find out one such lodger there?
Yet still, not heeding what your heart can teach,
You go to church to hear these flatterers preach.
Indeed, could wealth bestow or wit or merit,
A grain of courage, or a spark of spirit,
The wisest man might blush, I must agree,
If D——— loved sixpence more than he.
If there be truth in law, and use can give
A property, that's yours on which you live:
Delightful Abscourt, if its fields afford
Their fruits to you, confesses you its lord:

All Worldly s hens, nay, partridge, sold to town;
His vension too, a guinea makes your own;
He bought at thousands, what with better wit
You purchase as you want, and bit by bit.
Now, or long since, what difference will be found?
You pay a penny, and he paid a pound.
Heathcote himself, and such large-acred men,
Lords of fat E'sham, or of Lincoln-fen,
Buy every stick of wood that lends them heat;
Buy every pullet they afford to eat;
Yet these are wights, who fondly call their own
Half that the devil o'erlooks from Lincoln town.
The laws of God, as well as of the land,
Abhor a perpetuity should stand:
Estates have wings, and hang in fortune's power
Loose on the point of every wavering hour,
Ready, by force, or of your own accord,
By sale, at least by death, to change their lord.
'Man?' and 'for ever?' wretch! what wouldst thou [have?
Heir urges heir, like wave impelling wave.
All vast possessions, (just the same the case,
Whether you call them villa, park, or chase)
Alas, my Bathurst! what will they avail?
Join Cotswood hills to Saperton's fair dale;
Let rising granaries and temples here,
There mingled farms and pyramids appear;
Link towns to towns with avenues of oak,
Enclose whole downs in walls; 'tis all a joke
Inexorable death shall level all,
And trees, and stones, and farms, and farmer fall.
Gold, silver, ivory, vases sculptured high,
Paint, marble, gems, and robes of Persian die,
There are who have not,—and, thank Heaven, there are,
Who, if they have not, think not worth their care.
Talk what you will of taste, my friend, you'll find
Two of a face, as soon as of a mind.
Why, of two brothers, rich and restless, one
Ploughs, burns, manures, and toils from sun to sun;
The other slights, for women, sports, and wines,
All Townsend's turnips, and all Grosvenor's mines;
Why one like Bu—, with pay and scorn content,
Bows and votes on, in court and parliament;
One, driven by strong benevolence of soul,
Shall fly, like Oglethorpe, from pole to pole;—
Is known alone to that directing Power,
Who forms the genius in the natal hour;
That God of nature, who, within us still,
Inclines our action, not constrains our will;
Various of temper, as of face or frame,
Each individual: his great end the same.

Yes, sir, how small soever be my heap,
A part I will enjoy as well as keep.
My heir may sigh, and think it want of grace
A man so poor should live without a place:
But sure no statute in his favour says,
How free or frugal I shall pass my days:
I, who at some times spend, at others spare,
Divided between carelessness and care.
'Tis one thing madly to disperse my store;
Another, not to heed to treasure more;
Glad, like a boy, to snatch the first good day
And pleased, if sordid want be far away.
What is 't to me, (a passenger, God wot!)
Whether my vessel be first-rate or not?
The ship itself may make a better figure;
B   am neither less nor bigger.
I neither strut with every favouring breath,
Nor strive with all the tempest in my teeth:
In power, wit, figure, virtue, fortune, placed
Behind the foremost, and before the last.
'But why all this of avarice? I have none.
I wish you joy, sir, of a tyrant gone:
But does no other lord it at this hour,
As wild and mad? the avarice of power?
Does neither rage inflame, nor fear appal?
Not the black fear of death, that saddens all?
With terrors round, can reason hold her throne,
Despise the known, nor tremble at the unknown?
Survey both worlds, intrepid and intire,
In spite of witches, devils, dreams, and fire?
Pleased to look forward, pleased to look behind,
And count each birth day with a grateful mind?
Has life no sourness, drawn so near its end?
Canst thou endure a foe, forgive a friend?
Has age but melted the rough parts away,
As winter fruits grow mild ere they decay?
Or will you think, my friend, your business done,
When, of a hundred throns, you pull out one?
Learn to live well, or fairly make your will;
You've play'd, and loved, and eat, and drunk your fill
Walk sober off, before a sprightlier age
Comes tittering on, and shoves you from the stage;
Leave such to trifle with more grace and ease,
Whom folly pleases, and whose follies please.

BOOK IV. ODE I.

TO VENUS.

Again? new tumults in my breast?
  Ah, spare me, Venus! let me, let me rest
I am not now, alas! the man
  As in the gentle reign of my queen Anne.
Ah, sound no more thy soft alarms,
  Nor circle sober fifty with thy charms.
Mother too fierce of dear desires!
  Turn, turn to willing hearts your wanton fires;
To number five direct your doves;
  There spread round Murray all your blooming loves;
Noble and young, who strikes the heart
  With every sprightly, every decent part,
Equal, the injured to defend,
  To charm the mistress, or to fix the friend.
He, with a hundred arts refined,
  Shall stretch thy conquests over half the kind:
To him each rival shall submit,
  Make but his riches equal to his wit.
Then shall thy form the marble grace,
  (Thy Grecian form) and Chloe lend the face:
His house, embosom'd in the grove,
  Sacred to social life and social love,
Shall glitter o'er the pendent green,
  Where Thames reflects the visionary scene:
Thither the silver-sounding lyres
  Shall call the smiling Loves, and young Desires;
There, every Grace and Muse shall throng,
  Exalt the dance, or animate the song:
There youths and nymphs, in consort gay,
  Shall hail the rising, close the parting day.
With me, alas! those joys are o'er;
  For me, the vernal garlands bloom no more.
Adieu, fond hope of mutual fire,
  The still-believing, still-renew'd desire!

Adieu, the heart-expanding bowl,
  And all the kind deceivers of the soul!
But why? ah, tell me, ah, too dear!
  Steals down my cheek the involuntary tear?
Why words so flowing, thoughts so free,
  Stop, or turn nonsense, at one glance of thee?
Thee, dress'd in fancy's airy beam,
  Absent I follow through the extended dream;
Now, now I seize, I clasp thy charms,
  And now you burst, ah, cruel! from my arms;
And swiftly shoot along the Mall,
  Or softly glide by the canal;
Now shown by Cynthia's silver ray,
  And now on rolling waters snatch'd away.

PART OF BOOK IV. ODE IX.

A FRAGMENT.

Lest you should think that verse shall die,
Which sounds the silver Thames along,
Taught on the wings of truth to fly
Above the reach of vulgar song;

Though daring Milton sits sublime,
In Spenser native Muses play;
Nor yet shall Waller yield to time,
Nor pensive Cowley's moral lay—

Sages and chiefs long since had birth,
Ere Cæsar was, or Newton named;
Those raised new empires o'er the earth,
And these new heavens and systems framed

Vain was the chief's, the sage's pride:
They had no poet, and they died.
In vain they schemed, in vain they bled:
They had no poet, and are dead.

STATIUS HIS THEBAIS.

BOOK I.

[TRANSLATED IN THE YEAR 1703.]

THE ARGUMENT.

Œdipus, king of Thebes, having by mistake slain his father Laius, and married his mother Jocasta, put out his own eyes, and resigned the realm to his sons, Eteocles and Polynices: being neglected by them, he makes his prayer to the fury Tisiphone, to sow debate betwixt the brothers: they agree at last to reign singly, each a year by turns, and the first lot is obtained by Eteocles. Jupiter, in a council of the gods, declares his resolution of punishing the Thebans, and Argives also, by means of a marriage betwixt Polynices and one of the daughters of Adrastus, king of Argos. Juno opposes, but to no effect: and Mercury is sent on a message to the Shades, to the ghost of Laius, who is to appear to Eteocles, and provoke him to break the agreement. Polynices in the mean time departs from Thebes by night, is overtaken by a storm, and arrives at Argos; where he meets with Tydeus, who had fled from Calydon, having killed his brother. Adrastus entertains them, having received an oracle from Apollo that his daughters should be married to a boar and a lion, which he understands to be meant of these strangers, by whom the hides of these beasts were worn, and who arrived at the time when he kept an annual feast in honour of that god: the rise of this solemnity he relates to his guests, the loves of Phœbus and Psamathe, and the story of Chorœbus. He inquires, and is made acquainted with their descent and quality: the sacrifice is renewed, and the book concludes with a hymn to Apollo.

Fraternal rage, the guilty Thebes' alarms,
The alternate reign destroyed by impious arms,
Demand our song; a sacred fury fires
My ravished breast, and all the Muse inspires.
O goddess, say, shall I deduce my rhymes
From the dire nation in its early times,
Europa's rape, Agenor's stern decree,
And Cadmus searching round the spacious sea?
How with the serpent's teeth he sowed the soil,
And reaped an iron harvest of his toil?
Or how from joining stones the city sprung,
While to his harp divine Amphion sung?

Or shall I Juno's hate to Thebes resound,
Whose fatal rage the unhappy monarch found?
The sire against the son his arrows drew;
O'er the wide fields the furious mother flew;
And while her arms a second hope contain,
Sprung from the rocks and plunged into the main.
 But wave whate'er to Cadmus may belong,
And fix, O Muse! the barrier of thy song
At Œdipus—from his disasters trace
The long confusions of his guilty race:
Nor yet attempt to stretch thy bolder wing,
And mighty Cæsar's conquering eagles sing;
How twice he tamed proud Ister's rapid flood,
While Dacian mountains streamed with barbarous blood;
Twice taught the Rhine beneath his laws to roll,
And stretched his empire to the frozen pole;
Or, long before, with early valour strove
In youthful arms to assert the cause of Jove.
And thou, great heir of all thy father's fame,
Increase of glory to the Latian name!
Oh! bless thy Rome with an eternal reign,
Nor let desiring worlds intreat in vain.
What though the stars contract their heavenly space,
And crowd their shining ranks to yield thee place;
Though all the skies, ambitious of thy sway,
Conspire to court thee from our world away;
Though Phœbus longs to mix his rays with thine,
And in thy glories more serenely shine;
Though Jove himself no less content would be
To part his throne and share his heaven with thee;
Yet stay, great Cæsar! and vouchsafe to reign
O'er the wide earth, and o'er the watery main;
Resign to Jove his empire of the skies,
And people heaven with Roman deities.
 The time will come when a diviner flame
Shall warm my breast to sing of Cæsar's fame!
Meanwhile permit that my preluding muse
In Theban wars a humbler theme may choose:
Of furious hate surviving death she sings,
A fatal throne to two contending kings,
And funeral flames that, parting wide in air,
Express the discord of the souls they bear:
Of towns dispeopled, and the wandering ghosts
Of kings unburied in the wasted coasts;
When Dirce's fountain blushed with Grecian blood,
And Thetis, near Ismenos' swelling flood,
With dread beheld the rolling surges sweep
In heaps his slaughtered sons into the deep.
 What hero, Clio! wilt thou first relate?
The rage of Tydeus, or the prophet's fate?

Or how, with hills of slain on every side,
Hippomedon repelled the hostile tide?
Or how the youth, with every grace adorned,
Untimely fell, to be for ever mourned?
Then to fierce Capaneus thy verse extend,
And sing with horror his prodigious end.
  Now wretched Œdipus, deprived of sight,
Led a long death in everlasting night;
But while he dwells where not a cheerful ray
Can pierce the darkness, and abhors the day,
The clear reflecting mind presents his sin
In frightful views, and makes it day within;
Returning thoughts in endless circles roll,
And thousand furies haunt his guilty soul:
The wretch then lifted to the unpitying skies
Those empty orbs from whence he tore his eyes,
Whose wounds, yet fresh, with bloody hands he struck,
While from his breast these dreadful accents broke:
  'Ye Gods! that o'er the gloomy regions reign,
Where guilty spirits feel eternal pain;
Thou, sable Styx! whose livid streams are rolled
Through dreary coasts, which I, though blind, behold;
Tisiphone! that oft hast heard my prayer,
Assist, if Œdipus deserve thy care.
If you received me from Jocasta's womb,
And nursed the hope of mischiefs yet to come;
If, leaving Polybus, I took my way
To Cyrrha's temple, on that fatal day
When by the son the trembling father died,
Where the three roads the Phocion fields divide;
If I the Sphinx's riddle durst explain,
Taught by thyself to win the promised reign;
If wretched I, by baleful furies led,
With monstrous mixture stained my mother's bed,
For hell and thee begot an impious brood,
And with full lust those horrid joys renewed;
Then, self-condemned, to shades of endless night,
Forced from these orbs the bleeding balls of sight;
Oh, hear! and aid the vengeance I require,
If worthy thee, and what thou mightst inspire.
My sons their old unhappy sire despise,
Spoiled of his kingdom, and deprived of eyes;
Guileless I wander, unregarded mourn,
While these exalt their sceptres o'er my urn;
These sons, ye gods! who, with flagitious pride,
Insult my darkness and my groans deride.
Art thou a father, unregarding Jove!
And sleeps thy thunder in the realms above?
Thou fury! then some lasting curse entail,
Which o'er their children's children shall prevail

Place on their heads that crown, distained with gore,
Which these dire hands from my slain father tore;
Go, and a parent's heavy curses bear,
Break all the bonds of nature, and prepare
Their kindred souls to mutual hate and war.
Give them to dare, what I might wish to see,
Blind as I am, some glorious villany!
Soon shalt thou find, if thou but arm their hands,
Their ready guilt preventing thy commands:
Couldst thou some great proportioned mischief frame,
They'd prove the father from whose loins they came.'
  The fury heard, while on Cocytus' brink
Her snakes untied sulphureous waters drink;
But at the summons rolled her eyes around,
And snatched the starting serpents from the ground:
Not half so swiftly shoots along in air,
The gliding lightning or descending star.
Through crowds of airy shades she winged her flight,
And dark dominions of the silent night;
Swift as she passed the flitting ghosts withdrew,
And the pale spectres trembled at her view;
To the iron gates of Tenarus she flies,
There spreads her dusky pinions to the skies,
The day beheld, and, sickening at the sight,
Veiled her fair glories in the shades of night.
Affrighted Atlas, on the distant shore,
Trembled, and shook the heavens and gods he bore.
Now from beneath Malea's airy height,
Aloft she sprung, and steered to Thebes her flight;
With eager speed the well-known journey took,
Nor here regrets the hell she late forsook.
A hundred snakes her gloomy visage shade,
A hundred serpents guard her horrid head;
In her sunk eyeballs dreadful meteors glow;
Such rays from Phœbe's bloody circles flow,
When lab'ring with strong charms she shoots from high
A fiery gleam, and reddens all the sky.
Blood stained her cheeks, and from her mouth there
Blue streaming poisons, and a length of flame. [came
From ev'ry blast of her contagious breath,
Famine and drought proceed, and plagues and death.
A robe obscene was o'er her shoulders thrown,
A dress by fates and furies worn alone.
She tossed her meagre arms; her better hand
In waving circles whirled a funeral brand:
A serpent from her left was seen to rear
His flaming crest, and lash the yielding air.
  But when the fury took her stand on high,
Where vast Cithæron's top salutes the sky,

A hiss from all the snaky tire went round,
The dreadful signal all the rocks rebound;
And through the Achaian cities send the sound.
Œte, with high Parnassus, heard the voice,
Eurotus' banks remurmur'd to the noise;
Again Leucothoe shook at these alarms,
And pressed Palæmon closer in her arms.
Headlong from thence the glowing fury springs,
And o er the Theban palace spreads her wings,
Once more invades the guilty dome, and shrouds
Its bright pavilions in a veil of clouds.
Straight with the rage of all their race possessed,
Stung to the soul, the brothers start from rest,
And all their furies wake within their breast.
Their tortured minds repining envy tears,
And hate engendered by suspicious fears;
And sacred thirst of sway, and all the ties
Of nature broke, and royal purjuries;
And impotent desire to reign alone,
That scorns the dull reversion of a throne.
Each would the sweets of sov'reign rule devour,
While discord waits upon divided power.
  As stubborn steers, by brawny ploughmen broke,
And join reluctant to the galling yoke,
Alike disdain with servile necks to bear
The unwonted weight, or drag the crooked share,
But rend the reins, and bound a different way,
And all the furrows in confusion lay;
Such was the discord of the royal pair
Whom fury drove precipitate to war.
In vain the chiefs contrived a specious way
To govern Thebes by their alternate sway:
Unjust decree! while this enjoys the state,
That mourns in exile his unequal fate,
And the short monarch of a hasty year
Foresees with anguish his returning heir.
Thus did the league their impious arms restrain
But scarce subsisted to the second reign.
  Yet then no proud aspiring piles were raised,
No fretted roofs with polished metals blazed:
No laboured columns in long order placed,
No Grecian stone the pompous arches graced;
No nightly bands in glittering armour wait
Before the sleepless tyrant's guarded gate;
No chargers then were wrought in burnished gold,
Nor silver vases took the forming mould;
Nor gems on bowls embossed were seen to shine,
Blaze on the brims, and sparkle in the wine.
Say, wretched rivals! what provokes your rage?
Say to what end your impious arms engage?

Not all bright Phœbus' views in early morn,
Or when his evening beams the west adorn,
When the south glows with his meridian ray,
And the cold north receives a fainter day;
For crimes like these not all those realms suffice,
Were all those realms the guilty victor's prize!
But fortune now (the lots of empire thrown)
Decrees to proud Eteocles the crown.
What joys, oh, tyrant! swell'd thy soul that day,
When all were slaves thou couldst around survey,
Pleased to behold unbounded power thy own,
And singly fill a feared and envied throne!
But the vile vulgar, ever discontent,
Their growing fear in secret murmurs vent;
Still prone to change, though still the slaves of state,
And sure the monarch whom they have to hate;
New lords they madly make, then tamely bear,
And softly curse the tyrants whom they fear:
And one of those who groan beneath the sway
Of kings imposed, and grudgingly obey,
(Whom envy to the great, and vulgar spite,
With scandal armed, the ignoble mind's delight,)
Exclaimed—'O Thebes! for thee what fates remain,
What woes attend this inauspicious reign!
Must we, alas! our doubtful necks prepare
Each haughty master's yoke by turns to bear,
And still to change whom changed we still must fear?
These now control a wretched people's fate,
These can divide and these reverse the state:
E'en fortune rules no more—O servile land,
Where exiled tyrants still by turns command!
Thou sire of gods and men, imperial Jove!
Is this the eternal doom decreed above?
On thy own offspring hast thou fixed this fate
From the first birth of our unhappy state,
When banished Cadmus, wand'ring o'er the main,
For lost Europa searched the world in vain,
And fated in Bœotian fields to found
A rising empire on a foreign ground,
First raised our walls on that ill-omened plain
Where earth-born brothers were by brothers slain?
What lofty looks the unrivalled monarch bears!
How all the tyrant in his face appears!
What sullen fury clouds his scornful brow!
Gods! how his eyes with threatening ardour glow
Can this imperious lord forget to reign,
Quit all his state, descend, and serve again?
Yet who before more popularly bow'd?
Who more propitious to the suppliant crowd?

Patient of right, familiar in the throne,
What wonder then? he was not then alone.
O wretched we! a vile submissive train,
Fortune's tame fools, and slaves in every reign!
As when two winds with rival force contend,
This way and that the wavering sails they bend,
While freezing Boreas and black Eurus blow,
Now here, now there, the reeling vessel throw;
Thus on each side, alas! our tottering state
Feels all the fury of resistless fate,
And doubtful still, and still distracted stands,
While that prince threatens, and while this commands.
And now the almighty father of the gods
Convenes a counsel in the blessed abodes.
Far in the bright recesses of the skies,
High o'er the rolling heavens a mansion lies,
Whence, far below, the gods at once survey
The realms of rising and declining day,
And all the extended space of earth, and air, and sea.
Full in the midst, and on a starry throne,
The majesty of heaven superior shone:
Serene he looked, and gave an awful nod,
And all the trembling spheres confessed the god.
At Jove's assent the deities around
In solemn state the consistory crowned.
Next a long order of inferior powers
Ascend from hills, and plains, and shady bowers;
Those from whose urns the rolling rivers flow,
And those that give the wandering winds to blow:
Here all their rage and e'en their murmurs cease,
And sacred silence reigns, and universal peace.
A shining synod of majestic gods
Gilds with new lustre the divine abodes;
Heaven seems improved with a superior ray,
And the bright arch reflects a double day.
The monarch then his solemn silence broke,
The still creation listened while he spoke;
Each sacred accent bears eternal weight,
And each irrevocable word is fate.
'How long shall man the wrath of heaven defy,
And force unwilling vengeance from the sky!
Oh! race confederate into crimes, that prove
Triumphant o'er th' eluded rage of Jove!
This wearied arm can scarce the bolt sustain,
And unregarded thunder rolls in vain:
The o'erlaboured Cyclop from his task retires,
The Æolian forge exhausted of its fires.
For this I suffered Phœbus' steeds to stray,
And the mad ruler to misguide the day,

When the wide earth to heaps of ashes turned,
And heaven itself the wandering chariot burned
For this my brother of the watery reign
Released th' impetuous sluices of the main;
But flames consumed, and billows raged in vain.
Two races now, allied to Jove, offend;
To punish these see Jove himself descend.
The Theban kings their line from Cadmus trace,
From godlike Perseus those of Argive race.
Unhappy Cadmus' fate, who does not know,
And the long series of succeeding woe?
How oft the furies from the deeps of night
Arose, and mixed with men in mortal fight;
The exulting mother stained with filial blood,
The savage hunter and the haunted wood?
The direful banquet why should I proclaim,
And crimes that grieve the trembling gods to name?
Ere I recount the sins of these profane,
The sun would sink into the western main,
And, rising, gild the radiant east again.
Have we not seen (the blood of Laius shed)
The murdering son ascend his parent's bed,
Through violated nature force his way,
And stain the sacred womb where once he lay?
Yet now in darkness and despair he groans,
And for the crimes of guilty fate atones;
His sons with scorn their eyeless father view,
Insult his wounds, and make them bleed anew.
Thy curse, oh, Œdipus! just Heaven alarms,
And sets th' avenging Thunderer in arms.
I from the root thy guilty race will tear,
And give the nations to the waste of war.
Adrastus soon, with gods averse, shall join
In dire alliance with the Theban line;
Hence strife shall rise, and mortal war succeed;
The guilty realms of Tantalus shall bleed:
Fixed is their doom. This all-remembering breast
Yet harbours vengeance for the tyrant's feast.'
He said; and thus the queen of Heaven returned;
(With sudden grief her lab'ring bosom burned:)
'Must I, whose cares Phoroneus' towers defend,
Must I, oh Jove! in bloody wars contend?
Thou knowest those regions my protection claim,
Glorious in arms, in riches, and in fame:
Though there the fair Egyptian heifer fed,
And there deluded Argus slept and bled;
Though there the brazen tower was stormed of old,
When Jove descended in almighty gold;
Yet I can pardon those obscurer rapes,
Those bashful crimes disguised in borrowed shapes;

But Thebes, where, shining in celestial charms,
Thou cam'st triumphant to a mortal's arms,
When all my glories o'er her limbs were spread,
And blazing lightnings danced around her bed;
Cursed Thebes the vengeance it deserves may prove—
Ah! why should Argos feel the rage of Jove?
Yet since thou wilt thy sister-queen controul,
Since still the lust of discord fires thy soul,
Go, raise my Samos, let Mycene fall,
And level with the dust the Spartan wall;
Nor more let mortals Juno's power invoke,
Her fanes no more with eastern incense smoke
Nor victims sink beneath the sacred stroke;
But to your Isis all my rights transfer,
Let altars blaze and temples smoke for her;
For her, through Egypt's fruitful clime renowned,
Let weeping Nilus hear the timbrel sound.
But if thou must reform the stubborn times,
Avenging on the sons the fathers' crimes,
And from the long records of distant age
Derive incitements to renew thy rage;
Say, from what period then has Jove designed
To date his vengeance? to what bounds confined?
Begin from thence, where first Alpheus hides
His wandering stream, and through the briny tides
Unmixed to his Sicilian river glides.
Thy own Arcadians there the thunder claim,
Whose impious rites disgrace thy mighty name;
Who raise thy temples where the chariot stood
Of fierce Œnomaus, defiled with blood;
Where once his steeds their savage banquet found,
And human bones yet whiten all the ground.
Say, can those honours please? and canst thou love
Presumptuous Crete, that boasts the tomb of Jove?
And shall not Tantalus's kingdom share
Thy wife and sister's tutelary care?
Reverse, O Jove! thy too severe decree,
Nor doom to war a race derived from thee;
On impious realms and barbarous kings impose
Thy plagues, and curse them with such sons as those.'
  Thus in reproach and prayer the queen express'd
The rage and grief contending in her breast.
Unmoved remained the ruler of the sky,
And from his throne returned this stern reply:
''Twas thus I deemed thy haughty soul would bear
The dire though just revenge which I prepare
Against a nation thy peculiar care:
No less Dione might for Thebes contend,
Nor Bacchus less his native town defend;

Yet these in silence see the fates fulfil
Their work, and reverence our superior will:
For by the black infernal Styx I swear
(That dreadful oath that binds the Thunderer)
'Tis fixed; the irrevocable doom of Jove;
No force can bend me, no persuasion move.
Haste then, Cyllenius, through the liquid air,
Go mount the winds, and to the shades repair;
Bid hell's black monarch my commands obey,
And give up Laius to the realms of day,
Whose ghost yet shivering on Cocytus' sand,
Expects its passage to the farther strand:
Let the pale sire revisit Thebes, and bear
These pleasing orders to the tyrant's ear;
That from his exiled brother, swelled with pride
Of foreign forces and his Argive bride,
Almighty Jove commands him to detain
The promised empire, and alternate reign.
Be this the cause of more than mortal hate;
The rest succeeding times shall ripen into fate.'
  The god obeys, and to his feet applies
Those golden wings that cut the yielding skies:
His ample hat his beamy locks o'erspread,
And veiled the starry glories of his head.
He seized the wand that causes sleep to fly,
Or in soft slumbers seals the wakeful eye;
That drives the dead to dark Tartarean coasts,
Or back to life compels the wandering ghosts.
Thus through the parting clouds the son of May
Wings on the whistling winds his rapid way;
Now smoothly steers through air his equal flight,
Now springs aloft, and towers the ethereal height;
Then wheeling down the steep of heaven he flies,
And draws a radiant circle o'er the skies.
  Meantime the banished Polynices roves,
His Thebes abandoned, through the Aonian groves,
While future realms his wandering thoughts delight,
His daily vision, and his dream by night;
Forbidden Thebes appears before his eye,
From whence he sees his absent brother fly,
With transport views the airy rule his own,
And swells on an imaginary throne:
Fain would he cast a tedious age away,
And live out all in one triumphant day:
He chides the lazy progress of the sun,
And bids the year with swifter motion run:
With anxious hopes his craving mind is toss'd,
And all his joys in length of wishes lost.

The hero then resolves his course to bend
Where ancient Danaus' fruitful fields extend,
And famed Mycene's lofty towers ascend,
(Where late the sun did Atreus' crimes detest,
And disappeared in horror of the feast.)
And now by chance, by fate, or furies, led,
From Bacchus' consecrated caves he fled,
Where the shrill cries of frantic matrons sound,
And Pentheus' blood enriched the rising ground,
Then sees Cithæron towering o'er the plain,
And thence declining gently to the main.
Next to the bounds of Nisus' realm repairs,
Where treacherous Sylla cut the purple hairs;
The hanging cliffs of Scyron's rock explores,
And hears the murmur of the different shores;
Passes the strait that parts the foaming seas,
And stately Corinth's pleasing site surveys.
'Twas now the time when Phœbus yields to night,
And rising Cynthia sheds her silver light;
Wide o'er the world in solemn pomp she drew
Her airy chariot, hung with pearly dew:
All birds and beasts lie hushed: Sleep steals away
The wild desires of men, and toils of day,
And brings, descending through the silent air,
A sweet forgetfulness of human care.
Yet no red clouds, with golden borders gay,
Promise the skies the bright return of day;
No faint reflections of the distant light
Streak with long gleams the scattering shades of night:
From the damp earth impervious vapours rise,
Increase the darkness, and involve the skies.
At once the rushing winds with roaring sound
Burst from the Æolian caves, and rend the ground,
With equal rage their airy quarrel try,
And win by turns the kingdom of the sky:
But with a thicker night black Auster shrouds
The heavens, and drives on heaps the rolling clouds,
From whose dark womb a rattling tempest pours,
Which the cold north congeals to haily showers.
From pole to pole the thunder roars aloud,
And broken lightnings flash from every cloud.
Now smokes with showers the misty mountain ground,
And floated fields lie undistinguished round:
The Inachian streams with headlong fury run,
And Erasinus rolls a deluge on;
The foaming Lerna swells above its bounds,
And spreads its ancient poisons o'er the grounds:
Where late was dust, now rapid torrents play,
Rush through the mounds, and bear the dams away

Old limbs of trees, from crackling forests torn,
Are whirl'd in air, and on the winds are borne:
The storm the dark Lycæan groves displayed,
And first to light exposed the sacred shade.
The intrepid Theban hears the bursting sky,
Sees yawning rocks in massy fragments fly,
And views astonished, from the hills afar,
The floods descending, and the watery war
That, driven by storms, and pouring o'er the plain,
Swept herds, and hinds, and houses, to the main.
Through the brown horrors of the night he fled,
Nor knows, amazed, what doubtful path to tread;
His brother's image to his mind appears, [fears.
Inflames his heart with rage, and wings his feet with
So fares the sailor on the stormy main,
When clouds conceal Boötes' golden wain,
When not a star its friendly lustre keeps,
Nor trembling Cynthia glimmers on the deeps:
He dreads the rocks, and shoals, and seas, and skies,
While thunder roars, and lightning round him flies.
Thus strove the chief, on every side distress'd,
Thus still his courage with his toils increas'd;
With his broad shield opposed, he forced his way
Through thickest woods, and rous'd the beasts of prey;
Till he beheld where from Larissa's height
The shelving walls reflect a glancing light:
Thither with haste the Theban hero flies;
On this side Lerna's poisonous water lies;
On that Prosymna's grove and temple rise.
He passed the gates, which then unguarded lay,
And to the regal palace bent his way;
On the cold marble, spent with toil, he lies,
And waits till pleasing slumber seals his eyes.
Adrastus here his happy people sways,
Bless'd with calm peace in his declining days.
By both his parents of descent divine,
Great Jove and Phœbus graced his noble line:
Heaven had not crown'd his wishes with a son,
But two fair daughters heir'd his state and throne.
To him Apollo (wondrous to relate!
But who can pierce into the depths of Fate?)
Had sung—'Expect thy sons on Argos' shore,
A yellow lion and a bristly boar.'
This long revolved in his paternal breast,
Sat heavy on his heart, and broke his rest;
This, great Amphiarus, lay hid from thee,
Though skill'd in fate and dark futurity.
The father's care and prophet's art were vain,
For thus did the predicting god ordain.

Lo, hapless Tydeus, whose ill-fated hand
Had slain his brother, leaves his native land,
And, seized with horror in the shades of night,
Through the thick deserts headlong urged his flight:
Now by the fury of the tempest driven,
He seeks a shelter from the inclement heaven,
Till, led by fate, the Theban's steps he treads,
And to fair Argos' open court succeeds.
When thus the chiefs from different lands resort
To Adrastus' realms and hospitable court,
The king surveys his guests with curious eyes,
And views their arms and habit with surprise.
A lion's yellow skin the Theban wears,
Horrid his mane, and rough with curling hairs;
Such once employed Alcides' youthful toils,
Ere yet adorned with Nemea's dreadful spoils.
A boar's stiff hide, of Calydonian breed,
Œnides' manly shoulders overspread;
Oblique his tusks, erect his bristles stood,
Alive, the pride and terror of the wood.
Struck with the sight, and fixed in deep amaze,
The king the accomplished oracle surveys,
Reveres Apollo's vocal caves, and owns
The guiding godhead and his future sons.
O'er all his bosom secret transports reign,
And a glad horror shoots through every vein.
To heaven he lifts his hands, erects his sight,
And thus invokes the silent queen of night!
'Goddess of shades! beneath whose gloomy reign
Yon spangled arch glows with the starry train;
You who the cares of heaven and earth allay,
Till nature, quickened by the inspiring ray,
Wakes to new vigour with the rising day:
Oh! thou who freest me from my doubtful state,
Long lost and wildered in the maze of fate!
Be present still, oh goddess! in our aid;
Proceed, and 'firm those omens thou hast made.
We to thy name our annual rites will pay,
And on thy altar sacrifices lay;
The sable flock shall fall beneath the stroke,
And fill thy temples with a grateful smoke.
Hail! faithful Tripos! hail! ye dark abodes
Of awful Phœbus! I confess the gods!'
Thus, seized with sacred fear, the monarch prayed
Then to his inner court the guests conveyed,
Where yet thin fumes from dying sparks arise
And dust yet white upon each altar lies,
The relics of a former sacrifice.
The king once more the solemn rites requires,
And bids renew the feasts and wake the fires.

His train obey, while all the courts around
With noisy care and various tumult sound.
Embroidered purple clothes the golden beds;
This slave the floor and that the table spreads;
A third dispels the darkness of the night,
And fills depending lamps with beams of light;
Here loaves in canisters are piled on high,
And there in flames the slaughtered victims fly.
Sublime in regal state Adrastus shone,
Stretched on rich carpets on his ivory throne;
A lofty couch receives each princely guest;
Around, at awful distance, wait the rest.
  And now the king, his royal feast to grace,
Acestis calls, the guardian of his race,
Who first their youth in arts of virtue trained,
And their ripe years in modest grace maintained;
Then softly whispered in her faithful ear,
And bade his daughters at the rites appear.
When from the close apartments of the night
The royal nymphs approach divinely bright,
Such was Diana's, such Minerva's, face;
Nor shine their beauties with superior grace!
But that in these a milder charm endears,
And less of terror in their looks appears.
As on the heroes first they cast their eyes,
O'er their fair cheeks the glowing blushes rise;
Their downcast looks a decent shame confess'd,
Then on their father's reverend features rest.
  The banquet done, the monarch gives the sign
To fill the goblet high with sparkling wine,
Which Danaus used in sacred rites of old,
With sculpture graced, and rough with rising gold.
Here to the clouds victorious Perseus flies,
Medusa seems to move her languid eyes,
And, e'en in gold, turns paler as she dies.
There from the chase Jove's towering eagle bears,
On golden wings, the Phrygian to the stars:
Still as he rises in the ethereal height,
His native mountains lessen to his sight;
While all his sad companions upward gaze,
Fixed on the glorious scene in wild amaze;
And the swift hounds, affrighted as he flies,
Run to the shade, and bark against the skies.
  This golden bowl with generous juice was crown'd,
The first libation sprinkled on the ground;
By turns on each celestial power they call,
With Phœbus name resounds the vaulted hall.
The courtly train, the strangers, and the rest,
Crowned with chaste laurel, and with garlands dress'd,

While with rich gums the fuming altars blaze,
Salute the god in numerous hymns of praise.
Then thus the king: 'Perhaps, my noble guests!
These honoured altars, and these annual feasts,
To bright Apollo's awful name design'd,
Unknown, with wonder may perplex your mind.
Great was the cause: our old solemnities
From no blind zeal or fond tradition rise;
But saved from death, our Argives yearly pay
These grateful honours to the god of day.
When by a thousand darts the Python slain
With orbs unrolled lay covering all the plain,
(Transfixed as o'er Castalia's streams he hung,
And sucked new poisons with his triple tongue,)
To Argos' realms the victor god resorts,
And enters old Crotopos' humble courts.
This rural prince one only daughter blessed,
That all the charms of blooming youth possessed;
Fair was her face, and spotless was her mind,
Where filial love with virgin sweetness joined:
Happy! and happy still she might have proved
Were she less beautiful, or less beloved!
But Phœbus loved, and on the flowery side
Of Nemea's stream the yielding fair enjoyed!
Now, ere ten moons that orb with light adorn,
The illustrious offspring of the god was born;
The nymph, her father's anger to evade,
Retires from Argos to the sylvan shade;
To woods and wilds the pleasing burden bears
And trusts her infant to a shepherd's cares.
How mean a fate, unhappy child! is thine!
Ah! how unworthy those of race divine!
On flowery herbs in some green covert laid,
His bed the ground, his canopy the shade,
He mixes with the bleeting lambs his cries,
While the rude swain his rural music tries,
To call soft slumber on his infant eyes.
Yet e'en in those obscure abodes to live
Was more, alas! than cruel fate would give;
For on the grassy verdure as he lay,
And breathed the freshness of the early day,
Devouring dogs the helpless infant tore,
Fed on his trembling limbs, and lapp'd the gore.
The astonished mother, when the rumour came,
Forgets her father, and neglects her fame;
With loud complaints she fills the yielding air,
And beats her breast, and rends her flowing hair
Then wild with anguish to her sire she flies,
Demands the sentence, and contented dies.

But, touched with sorrow for the dead too late,
The raging god prepares to avenge her fate.
He sends a monster, horrible and fell,
Begot by furies in the depths of hell.
The pest a virgin's face and bosom bears;
High on her crown a rising snake appears,
Guards her black front, and hisses in her hairs.
About the realm she walks her dreadful round,
When night with sable wing o'erspreads the ground,
Devours young babes before their parents' eyes,
And feeds and thrives on public miseries.
But generous rage the bold Chorœbus warms,
Chorœbus! famed for virtue as for arms;
Some few like him, inspired with martial flame,
Thought a short life well lost for endless fame.
These, where two ways in equal parts divide,
The direful monster from afar descried,
Two bleeding babes depending at her side;
Whose panting vitals, warm with life, she draws,
And in their hearts imbrues her cruel claws.
The youths surround her with extended spears,
But brave Chorœbus in the front appears;
Deep in her breast he plung'd his shining sword,
And hell's dire monster back to hell restored.
The Inachians view the slain with vast surprise,
Her twisting volumes, and her rolling eyes,
Her spotted breast and gaping womb imbrued
With livid poison and our children's blood.
The crowd in stupid wonder fix'd appear,
Pale e'en in joy, nor yet forget to fear.
Some with vast beams the squalid corpse engage,
And weary all the wild efforts of rage.
The birds obscene, that nightly flocked to taste,
With hollow screeches fled the dire repast;
And rav'nous dogs, allured by scented blood,
And starving wolves, ran howling to the wood.
But, fired with rage, from cleft Parnassus' brow
Avenging Phœbus bent his deadly bow,
And hissing slew the feathered fates below:
A night of sultry clouds involved around
The towers, the fields, and the devoted ground:
And now a thousand lives together fled,
Death with his scythe cut off the fatal thread,
And a whole province in his triumph led.
But Phœbus, ask'd why noxious fires appear,
And raging Sirius blasts the sickly year?
Demands their lives by whom his monster fell,
And dooms a dreadful sacrifice to hell.
'Bless'd be thy dust, and let eternal fame
Attend thy manes, and preserve thy name,

Undaunted hero! who divinely brave,
In such a cause disdained thy life to save,
But view'd the shrine with a superior look,
And its upbraided godhead thus bespoke:
'With piety, the soul's securest guard,
And conscious virtue, still its own reward,
Willing I come, unknowing how to fear;
Nor shalt thou, Phœbus, find a suppliant here:
Thy monster's death to me was ow'd alone,
And 'tis a deed too glorious to disown.
Behold him here for whom so many days
Impervious clouds concealed thy sullen rays;
For whom, as man no longer claimed thy care,
Such numbers fell by pestilential air!
But if the abandoned race of human kind
From gods above no more compassion find,
If such inclemency in heaven can dwell,
Yet why must unoffending Argos feel
The vengeance due to this unlucky steel?
On me, on me, let all thy fury fall,
Nor err from me, since I deserve it all:
Unless our desert cities please thy sight,
Or funeral flames reflect a grateful light.
Discharge thy shafts, this ready bosom rend,
And to the shades a ghost triumphant send:
But for my country let my fate atone;
Be mine the vengeance as the crime my own.'
Merit distressed impartial heaven relieves:
Unwelcome life relenting Phœbus gives;
For not the vengeful power, that glowed with rage,
With such amazing virtue durst engage.
The clouds dispersed, Apollo's wrath expired,
And from the wond'ring god the unwilling youth retir'd.
Thence we these altars in his temple raise,
And offer annual honours, feasts and praise:
Those solemn feasts propitious Phœbus please;
These honours still renewed his ancient wrath appease.
'But say, illustrious guest?' adjoined the king,
'What name you bear, from what high race you spring?
The noble Tydeus stands confessed, and known
Our neighbour prince, and heir of Calydon.
Relate your fortunes, while the friendly night
And silent hours to various talk invite.'
The Theban bends on earth his gloomy eyes,
Confused, and sadly thus at length replies:
'Before these altars how shall I proclaim
(O generous Prince!) my nation or my name,
Or through what veins our ancient blood has roll'd?
Let the sad tale for ever rest untold!

Yet if, propitious to a wretch unknown,
You seek to share in sorrows not your own,
Know then, from Cadmus I derive my race,
Jocasta's son, and Thebes my native place.'
To whom the king (who felt his generous breast
Touched with concern for his unhappy guest)
Replies:—'Ah! why forbears the son to name
His wretched father, known too well by fame?
Fame, that delights around the world to stray,
Scorns not to take our Argos in her way.
E'en those who dwell where suns at distance roll,
In northern wilds and freeze beneath the pole,
And those who tread the burning Lybian lands,
The faithless Syrtes, and the moving sands;
Who view the western sea's extremest bounds,
Or drink of Ganges in their eastern grounds;
All these the woes of Œdipus have known,
Your fates, your furies, and your haunted town.
If on the sons the parents' crimes descend,
What prince from those his lineage can defend?
Be this thy comfort, that 'tis thine to efface,
With virtuous acts, thy ancestor's disgrace,
And be thyself the honour of thy race.
But see! the stars begin to steal away,
And shine more faintly at approaching day:
Now pour the wine; and in your tuneful lays
Once more resound the great Apollo's praise.'
'Oh, father Phœbus! whether Lycia's coast
And snowy mountains thy bright presence boast:
Whether to sweet Castalia thou repair,
And bathe in silver dews thy yellow hair;
Or pleased to find fair Delos float no more,
Delight in Cynthus and the shady shore;
Or choose thy seat in Ilion's proud abodes,
The shining structures raised by labouring gods:
By thee the bow and mortal shafts are borne;
Eternal charms thy blooming youth adorn:
Skill'd in the laws of secret fate above,
And the dark counsels of almighty Jove,
'Tis thine the seeds of future war to know,
The change of sceptres and impending woe;
When direful meteors spread through glowing air
Long trails of light, and shake their blazing hair.
Thy rage the Phrygian felt, who durst aspire
To excel the music of thy heavenly lyre;
Thy shafts avenged lewd Tityus' guilty flame,
The immortal victim of thy mother's fame;
Thy hand slew Python, and the dame who lost
Her numerous offspring for a fatal boast.

In Phlegyas' doom thy just revenge appears,
Condemned to furies and eternal fears;
He views his food, but dreads, with lifted eye,
The mouldering rock that trembles from on high.
  Propitious hear our prayer, O power divine!
And on thy hospitable Argos shine;
Whether the style of Titan please thee more,
Whose purple rays the Achæmenes adore;
Or great Osiris, who first taught the swain
In Pharian fields to sow the golden grain;
Or Mithra, to whose beams the Persian bows,
And pays, in hollow rocks, his awful vows;
Mithra! whose head the blaze of light adorns,
Who grasps the struggling heifer's lunar horns.'

VERTUMNUS AND POMONA.

FROM THE

FOURTEENTH BOOK

OF

OVID'S METAMORPHOSES.

THE fair Pomona flourished in his reign:
Of all the virgins of the sylvan train
None taught the trees a nobler race to bear,
Or more improved the vegetable care.
To her the shady grove, the flowery field,
The streams and fountains, no delights could yield;
'Twas all her joy the ripening fruits to tend,
And see the boughs with happy burthens bend.
The hook she bore instead of Cynthia's spear,
To lop the growth of the luxuriant year,
To decent forms the lawless shoots to bring,
And teach the obedient branches where to spring.
Now the cleft rind inserted graffs receives,
And yields an off'pring more than nature gives;
Now sliding streams the thirsty plants renew,
And feed their fibres with reviving dew.
These cares alone her virgin breast employ,
Averse from Venus and the nuptial joy.
Her private orchards walled on every side,
To lawless sylvans all access denied.
How oft the satyrs and the wanton fawns,
Who haunt the forests, or frequent the lawns,
The god whose ensign scares the birds of prey,
And old Silenus, youthful in decay,
Employed their wiles and unavailing care
To pass the fences, and surprise the fair!
Like these Vertumnus owned his faithful flame
Like these rejected by the scornful dame.

To gain her sight a thousand forms he wears,
And first a reaper from the field appears:
Sweating he walks, while loads of golden grain
O'ercharge the shoulders of the seeming swain.
Oft o'er his back a crooked scythe is laid,
And wreaths of hay his sunburnt temples shade
Oft in his hardened hand a goad he bears,
Like one who late unyoked the sweating steers.
Sometimes his pruning-hook corrects the vines,
And the loose stragglers to their ranks confines
Now gathering what the bounteous year allows
He pulls ripe apples from the bending boughs.
A soldier now, he with his sword appears;
A fisher next, his trembling angle bears;
Each shape he varies, and each art he tries,
On her bright charms to feast his longing eyes,
A female form at last Vertumnus wears,
With all the marks of reverend age appears,
His temples thinly spread with silver hairs:
Propped on his staff, and stooping as he goes,
A painted mitre shades his furrowed brows.
The god, in this decrepit form arrayed,
The gardens entered, and the fruit surveyed;
And, 'Happy you,' he thus addressed the maid,
'Whose charms as far all other nymphs outshine
As other gardens are excelled by thine!'
Then kissed the fair; (his kisses warmer grow
Than such as women on their sex bestow;)
Then, placed beside her on the flowery ground,
Beheld the trees with autumn's bounty crowned
An elm was near, to whose embraces led,
The curling vine her swelling clusters spread;
He viewed her twining branches with delight,
And prais'd the beauty of the pleasing sight.
'Yet this tall elm, but for this vine,' he said,
'Had stood neglected, and a barren shade;
And this fair vi .e, but that her arms surround
Her married elm, had crept along the ground.
Ah! beauteous maid! let this example move
Your mind, averse from all the joys of love.
Deign to be loved, and every heart subdue!
What nymph could e'er attract such crowds as you
Not she whose beaut. urged the Centaur's arms,
Ulysses' queen, nor Helen's fatal charms.
E'en now, when silent scorn is all they gain,
A thousand court you, though they court in vain,
A thousand sylvans, demi-gods, and gods,
That haunt our mountains and our Alban woods.
But if you'll prosper, mark what I advise,
Whom age and long experience render wise,

And one whose tender care is far above
All that these lovers ever felt of love,
(Far more than e'er can by yourself be guess'd ;)
Fixed on Vertumnus, and reject the rest:
For his firm faith I dare engage my own;
Scarce to himself, himself is better known.
To distant lands Vertumnus never roves;
Like you, contented with his native groves;
For at first sight, like most, admires the fair;
For you he lives; and you alone shall share
His last affection as his early care.
Besides, he's lovely far above the rest,
With youth immortal, and with beauty bless'd.
Add, that he varies every shape with ease,
And tries all forms that may Pomona please.
But what should most excite a mutual flame,
Your rural cares and pleasures are the same.
To him your orchard's early fruit are due;
(A pleasing offering when 'tis made by you:)
He values these; but yet, alas! complains
That still the best and dearest gift remains.
Not the fair fruit that on yon branches glows
With that ripe red the autumnal sun bestows;
Nor tasteful herbs, that in these gardens rise,
Which the kind soil with milky sap supplies;
You, only you, can move the god's desire;
Oh! crown so constant and so pure a fire!
Let soft compassion touch your gentle mind;
Think 'tis Vertumnus begs you to be kind:
So may no frost, when early buds appear,
Destroy the promise of the youthful year;
Nor winds, when first your florid orchard blows,
Shake the light blossoms from their blasted boughs!'
  This when the various god had urged in vain,
He straight assumed his native form again:
Such, and so bright an aspect now he bears,
As when through clouds the emerging sun appears,
And thence exerting his refulgent ray,
Dispels the darkness, and reveals the day.
Force he prepared, but checked the rash design;
For when, appearing in a form divine,
The nymph surveys him, and beholds the grace
Of charming features and a youthful face,
In her soft breast consenting passions move,
And the warm maid confessed a mutual love.

JANUARY AND MAY:

OR,

THE MERCHANT'S TALE.

FROM CHAUCER.

THERE liv'd in Lombardy, as authors write,
In days of old, a wise and worthy knight;
Of gentle manners, as of gen'rous race,
Bless'd with much sense, more riches, and some grace
Yet, led astray by Venus' soft delights,
He scarce could rule some idle appetites:
For long ago, let priests say what they could,
Weak sinful laymen were but flesh and blood.
But in due time, when sixty years were o'er,
He vow'd to lead this vicious life no more:
Whether pure holiness inspir'd his mind,
Or dotage turn'd his brain, is hard to find;
But his high courage prick'd him forth to wed,
And try the pleasures of a lawful bed.
This was his nightly dream, his daily care,
And to the heav'nly pow'rs his constant prayer,
Once, ere he died, to taste the blissful life
Of a kind husband and a loving wife.
These thoughts he fortified with reasons still,
(For none want reasons to confirm their will.)
Grave authors say, and witty poets sing,
That honest wedlock is a glorious thing:
But depth of judgment most in him appears,
Who wisely weds in his maturer years.
Then let him choose a damsel young and fair,
To bless his age, and bring a worthy heir;
To soothe his cares, and, free from noise and strife,
Conduct him gently to the verge of life.
Let sinful bachelors their woes deplore,
Full well they merit all they feel and more:

Unaw'd by precepts, human or divine,
Like birds and beasts, promiscuously they join;
Nor know to make the present blessing last,
To hope the future, or esteem the past:
But vainly boast the joys they never tried,
And find divulg'd the secrets they would hide.
The married man may bear his yoke with ease,
Secure at once himself and Heav'n to please;
And pass his inoffensive hours away,
In bliss all night, and innocence all day:
Though fortune change, his constant spouse remains,
Augments his joys, or mitigates his pains.
But what so pure, which envious tongues will spare?
Some wicked wits have libell'd all the fair;
With matchless impudence they style a wife,
The dear-bought curse, and lawful plague of life;
A bosom serpent, a domestic evil,
A night invasion, and a mid-day devil.
Let not the wise these sland'rous words regard
But curse the bones of ev'ry lying bard.
All other goods by fortune's hand are given,
A wife is the peculiar gift of Heaven.
Vain fortune's favours, never at a stay,
Like empty shadows, pass and glide away;
One solid comfort, our eternal wife
Abundantly supplies us all our life:
This blessing lasts (if those who try say true)
As long as heart can wish—and longer too.
Our grandsire Adam, ere of Eve possess'd,
Alone, and e'en in Paradise unbless'd,
With mournful looks the blissful scene survey'd,
And wander'd in the solitary shade.
The Maker saw, took pity, and bestow'd
Woman, the last, and best reserv'd of God.
A wife! ah, gentle deities! can he
That has a wife e'er feel adversity?
Would men but follow what the sex advise,
All things would prosper, all the world grow wise.
'Twas by Rebecca's aid that Jacob won
His father's blessing from an elder son:
Abusive Nabal ow'd his forfeit life
To the wise conduct of a prudent wife:
Heroic Judith, as old Hebrews show,
Preserved the Jews, and slew th' Assyrian foe:
At Esther's suit the persecuting sword
Was sheath'd, and Israel liv'd to bless the Lord.
These weighty motives, January the sage
Maturely ponder'd in his riper age;
And, charm'd with virtuous joys, and sober life,
Would try that Christian comfort, call'd a wife.

His friends were summon'd on a point so nice
To pass their judgment, and to give advice;
But fix'd before, and well resolv'd was he,
(As men that ask advice are wont to be.)
'My friends,' he cries, (and cast a mournful look
Around the room, and sigh'd before he spoke;)
'Beneath the weight of threescore years I bend,
And, worn with cares, and hast'ning to my end:
How I have liv'd, alas! you know too well,
In worldly follies, which I blush to tell;
But gracious Heav'n has oped my eyes at last,
With due regret I view my vices past,
And, as the precept of the Church decrees,
Will take a wife, and live in holy ease:
But since by counsel all things should be done,
And many heads are wiser still than one,
Choose you for me, who best shall be content
When my desire 's approv'd by your consent.
'One caution yet is needful to be told
To guide your choice: this wife must not be old.
There goes a saying, and 'twas shrewdly said,
Old fish at table, but young flesh in bed.
My soul abhors the tasteless, dry embrace
Of a stale virgin with a winter face:
In that cold season love but treats his guest
With bean straw, and tough forage at the best.
No crafty widows shall approach my bed;
Those are too wise for bachelors to wed.
As subtle clerks by many schools are made,
Twice-married dames are mistresses of the trade:
But young and tender virgins, ruled with ease,
We form like wax, and mould them as we please.
'Conceive me, Sirs, nor take my sense amiss;
'Tis what concerns my soul's eternal bliss;
Since if I found no pleasure in my spouse,
As flesh is frail, and who (God help me) knows?
Then should I live in lewd adultery,
And sink downright to Satan when I die:
Or were I curs'd with an unfruitful bed,
The righteous end were lost for which I wed;
To raise up seed to bless the powers above,
And not for pleasure only, or for love.
Think not I dote; 'tis time to take a wife,
When vigorous blood forbids a chaster life:
Those that are blest with store of grace divine,
May live like saints by Heaven's consent and mine.
'And since I speak of wedlock, let me say,
(As, thank my stars, in modest truth I may,)
My limbs are active, still I'm sound at heart,
And a new vigour springs in ev'ry part.

Think not my virtue lost, though time has shed
These rev'rend honours on my hoary head:
Thus trees are crown'd with blossoms white as snow,
The vital sap then rising from below.
Old as I am, my lusty limbs appear
Like winter greens, that flourish all the year.
Now, Sirs, ye know to what I stand inclin'd,
Let ev'ry friend with freedom speak his mind.'
He said; the rest in diff'rent parts divide;
The knotty point was urg'd on either side:
Marriage, the theme on which they all declaimed,
Some praised with wit, and some with reason blam'd,
Till, what with proofs, objections, and replies,
Each wondrous positive, and wondrous wise,
There fell between his brothers a debate;
Placebo this was called, and Justin that.
First to the knight, Placebo thus begun:
(Mild were his looks, and pleasing was his tone.)
'Such prudence, Sir, in all your words appears,
As plainly proves experience dwells with years!
Yet you pursue sage Solomon's advice,
To work by counsel when affairs are nice:
But, with the wise man's leave, I must protest,
So may my soul arrive at ease and rest,
As still I hold your own advice the best.
Sir, I have lived a courtier all my days,
And studied men, their manners, and their ways;
And have observ'd this useful maxim still,
To let my betters always have their will.
Nay, if my lord affirm'd that black was white,
My word was this, 'Your Honour's in the right.
Th' assuming wit, who deems himself so wise,
As his mistaken patron to advise,
Let him not dare to vent his dangerous thought;
A noble fool was never in a fault.
This, Sir, affects not you, whose ev'ry word
Is weighed with judgment, and befits a lord:
Your will is mine; and is (I will maintain)
Pleasing to God, and should be so to man;
At least, your courage all the world must praise,
Who dare to wed in your declining days.
Indulge the vigour of your mounting blood,
And let gray fools be indolently good,
Who, past all pleasure, damn the joys of sense
With rev'rend dulness and grave impotence.'
Justin, who silent sate, and heard the man,
Thus, with a philosophic frown, began:
'A heathen author, of the first degree,
(Who, though not faith, had sense as well as we,)

Bids us be certain our concerns to trust
To those of generous principles and just.
The venture 's greater, I'll persume to say,
To give your person than your goods away:
And therefore, Sir, as you regard your rest,
First learn your lady's qualities at least:
Whether she's chaste or rampant, proud or civil,
Meek as a saint, or haughty as the devil;
Whecher an easy, fond, familiar fool,
Or such a wit as no man e'er can rule.
'Tis true, perfection none must hope to find
In all this world, much less in womankind;
But if her virtues prove the larger share,
Bless the kind fates, and think your fortune rare
Ah, gentle Sir, take warning of a friend,
Who knows too well the state you thus commend;
And, spite of all his praises, must declare,
All he can find is bondage, cost, and care.
Heaven knows I shed full many a private tear,
And sigh in silence, lest the world should hear;
While all my friends applaud my blissful life,
And swear no mortal 's happier in a wife;
Demure and chaste as any vestal nun,
The meekest creature that beholds the sun!
But, by th' immortal Powers, I feel the pain,
And he that smarts has reason to complain.
Do what you list for me: you must be sage,
And cautious sure; for wisdom is in age:
But at these years to venture on the fair!
By him who made the ocean, earth and air,
To please a wife, when her occasions call,
Would busy the most vig'rous of us all.
And trust me, Sir, the chastest you can choose
Will ask observance, and exact her dues.
If what I speak my noble lord offend,
My tedious sermon here is at an end.'
'Tis well, 'tis wondrous well,' the knight replies,
'Most worthy kinsman, faith you're mighty wise!
We, Sirs, are fools; and must resign the cause
To heathenish authors, proverbs, and old saws.'
He spoke with scorn, and turn'd another way:—
'What does my friend, my dear Placebo, say?'
'I say,' quoth he, 'by Heaven the man 's to blame,
To slander wives, and wedlock's holy name.'
At this the council rose, without delay;
Each, in his own opinion, went his way;
With full consent, that, all disputes appeas'd,
The knight should marry, when and where he pleas'd.
Who now but January exults with joy?
The charms of wedlock all his soul employ:

Each nymph by turns his wav ring mind possess'd,
And reign'd the short-lived tyrant of his breast;
While fancy pictured ev'ry lively part,
And each bright image wandered o'er his heart.
Thus, in some public forum fix'd on high,
A mirror shows the figures moving by;
Still one by one, in swift succession, pass
The gliding shadows o'er the polish'd glass.
This lady's charms the nicest could not blame,
But vile suspicions had aspersed her fame;
That was with sense, but not with virtue, blest;
And one had grace, that wanted all the rest.
Thus doubting long what nymph he should obey,
He fix'd at last upon the youthful May.
Her faults he knew not, love is always blind,
But ev'ry charm revolv'd within his mind:
Her tender age, her form divinely fair,
Her easy motion, her attractive air,
Her sweet behaviour, her enchanting face,
Her moving softness, and majestic grace.
  Much in his prudence did our knight rejoice,
And thought no mortal could dispute his choice.
Once more in haste he summon'd every friend,
And told them all their pains were at an end.
'Heaven, that (said he) inspir'd me first to wed,
Provides a consort worthy of my bed:
Let none oppose th' election, since on this
Depends my quiet, and my future bliss.
  A dame there is, the darling of my eyes,
Young, beauteous, artless, innocent, and wise;
Chaste, though not rich; and, though not nobly born
Of honest parents, and may serve my turn.
Her will I wed, if gracious Heaven so please,
To pass my age in sanctity and ease;
And, thank the powers, I may possess alone
The lovely prize, and share my bliss with none!
If you, my friends, this virgin can procure,
My joys are full, my happiness is sure.
  One only doubt remains: full oft, I've heard,
By casuists grave, and deep divines, averr'd,
That 'tis too much for human race to know
The bliss of heaven above, and earth below:
Now should the nuptial pleasures prove so great,
To match the blessings of the future state,
Those endless joys were ill exchang'd for these;
Then clear this doubt, and set my mind at ease.'
  This Justin heard, nor could his spleen control,
Touch'd to the quick, and tickled at the soul.
'Sir knight,' he cried, 'if this be all your dread.
Heaven put it past your doubt whene'er you wed

And to my fervent prayers so far consent,
That ere the rites are o'er, you may repent!
Good Heaven, no doubt, the nuptial state approves,
Since it chastises still what best it loves.
Then be not, sir, abandon'd to despair;
Seek, and perhaps you'll find among the fair
One that may do your business to a hair;
Not e'en in wish your happiness delay,
But prove the scourge to lash you on your way:
Then to the skies your mounting soul shall go,
Swift as an arrow soaring from the bow!
Provided still you moderate your joy,
Nor in your pleasures all your might employ,
Let reason's rule your strong desires abate,
Nor please too lavishly your gentle mate.
Old wives there are, of judgment most acute,
Who solve these questions beyond all dispute;
Consult with those, and be of better cheer;
Marry, do penance, and dismiss your fear.'
  So said, they rose, nor more the work delay'd;
The match was offered, the proposals made.
The parents, you may think, would soon comply;
The old have int'rest ever in their eye.
Nor was it hard to move the lady's mind;
When fortune favours, still the fair are kind.
  I pass each previous settlement and deed,
Too long for me to write, or you to read;
Nor will with quaint impertinence display
The pomp, the pageantry, the proud array.
The time approach'd, to church the parties went,
At once with carnal and devout intent:
Forth came the priest, and bade th' obedient wife
Like Sarah or Rebecca lead her life:
Then prayed the powers the fruitful bed to bless,
And made all sure enough with holiness.
  And now the palace-gates are open d wide.
The guests appear in order, side by side,
And, plac'd in state, the bridegroom and the bride.
The breathing flute's soft notes are heard around,
And the shrill trumpets mix their silver sound;
The vaulted roofs with echoing music ring;
These touch the vocal stops, and those the trembling
Not thus Amphion turn'd the warbling lyre, [string.
Nor Joab the sounding clarion could inspire,
Nor fierce Theodamas, whose sprightly strain
Could swell the soul to rage, and fire the martial train.
  Bacchus himself, the nuptial feast to grace,
(So poets sing) was present on the place:

And lovely Venus, goddess of delight,
Shook high her flaming torch in open sight,
And danc'd around, and smil'd on ev'ry knight:
Pleas'd her best servant would his courage try,
No less in wedlock than in liberty.
Full many an age old Hymen had not spied
So kind a bridegroom, or so bright a bride.
Ye bards! renown'd among the tuneful throng
For gentle lays, and joyous nuptial song,
Think not your softest numbers can display
The matchless glories of the blissful day;
The joys are such as far transcend your rage,
When tender youth has wedded stooping age.
The beauteous dame sate smiling at the board,
And darted am'rous glances at her lord.
Not Hester's self, whose charms the Hebrews sing,
E'er looked so lovely on her Persian king;
Bright as the rising sun in summer's day,
And fresh and blooming as the month of May;
The joyful knight surveyed her by his side,
Nor envied Paris with the Spartan bride.
Still as his mind revolved, with vast delight,
Th' entrancing raptures of th' approaching night,
Restless he sate, invoking every pow'r
To speed his bliss, and haste the happy hour.
Meantime the vigorous dancers beat the ground,
And songs were sung, and flowing bowls went round.
With odorous spices they perfum'd the place,
And mirth and pleasure shone in every face.
Damian alone, of all the menial train,
Sad in the midst of triumphs, sighed for pain;
Damian alone, th' knight's obsequious 'squire,
Consum'd at heart, and fed a secret fire,
His lovely mistress all his soul possess'd;
He look'd, he languish'd, and could take no rest:
His task perform'd, he sadly went his way,
Fell on his bed, and loathed the light of day.
There let him lie till his relenting dame
Weep in her turn, and waste in equal flame.
The wearied sun, as learned poets write,
Forsook th' horizon, and rolled down the light;
While glitt'ring stars his absent beams supply,
And night's dark mantle overspread the sky.
Then rose the guests, and, as the time required,
Each paid his thanks, and decently retired.
The foe once gone, our knight prepar'd t' undress,
So keen he was, and eager to possess;
But first thought fit th' assistance to receive
Which grave physicians scruple not to give

Satyrion near, with hot eringoes stood,
Cantharides, to fire the lazy blood,
Whose use old bards describe in luscious rhymes,
And critics learn'd explain to modern times.
By this the sheets were spread, the bride undress'd,
The room was sprinkled, and the bed was bless'd.
What next ensued beseems not me to say;
'Tis sung, he laboured till the dawning day,
Then briskly sprung from bed, with heart so light,
As all were nothing he had done by night,
And sipped his cordial as he sat upright.
He kissed his balmy spouse with wanton play,
And feebly sung a lusty roundelay:
Then on the couch his weary limbs he cast;
For every labour must have rest at last.
But anxious cares the pensive 'squire oppress'd,
Sleep fled his eyes, and peace forsook his breast;
The raging flames that in his bosom dwell,
He wanted art to hide, and means to tell:
Yet hoping time th' occasion might betray,
Composed a sonnet to the lovely May;
Which, writ and folded with the nicest art,
He wrapp'd in silk, and laid upon his heart.
When now the fourth revolving day was run,
('Twas June, and Cancer had received the sun,)
Forth from her chamber came the beauteous bride,
The good old knight moved slowly by her side.
High mass was sung; they feasted in the hall;
The servants round stood ready at their call.
The 'squire alone was absent from the board,
And much his sickness grieved his worthy lord,
Who prayed his spouse, attended with her train,
To visit Damian, and divert his pain.
The obliging dames obey'd with one consent;
They left the hall, and to his lodging went.
The femal tribe surround him as he lay,
And close beside him sat the gentle May:
Where, as she tried his pulse, he softly drew
A heaving sigh, and cast a mournful view!
Then gave his bill, and brib'd the powers divine,
With secret vows, to favour his design.
Who studies now but discontented May?
On her soft couch uneasily she lay:
The lumpish husband snor'd away the night,
'Till coughs awak'd him near the morning light.
What then he did, I'll not presume to tell,
Nor if she thought herself in heav'n or hell:
Honest and dull in nuptial bed they lay,
Till the bell toll'd, and all arose to pray.

Were it by forceful destiny decreed,
Or did from chance or nature's power proceed;
Or that some star, with aspect kind to love,
Shed its selectest influence from above;
Whatever was the cause, the tender dame
Felt the first motions of an infant flame;
Receiv'd the impressions of the love-sick 'squire,
And wasted in the soft infectious fire.
Ye Fair, draw near, let May's example move
Your gentle minds to pity those who love!
Had some fierce tyrant in her stead been found,
The poor adorer sure had hang'd or drown'd;
But she, your sex's mirror, free from pride,
Was much too meek to prove a homicide.
But to my tale: Some sages have defin'd
Pleasure the sov'reign bliss of humankind:
Our knight (who studied much, we may suppose
Deriv'd his high philosophy from those;
For, like a prince, he bore the vast expense
Of lavish pomp, and proud magnificence;
His house was stately, his retinue gay,
Large was his train, and gorgeous his array.
His spacious garden, made to yield to none,
Was compass'd round with walls of solid stone;
Priapus could not half describe the grace
(Though god of gardens) of this charming place
A place to tire the rambling wits of France
In long descriptions, and exceed romance:
Enough to shame the gentlest bard that sings
Of painted meadows, and of purling springs.
Full in the centre of the flowery ground
A crystal fountain spread its streams around,
The fruitful banks with verdant laurels crown'd
About this spring (if ancient Fame say true)
The dapper elves their moonlight sports pursue.
Their pigmy king, and little fairy queen,
In circling dances gambol'd on the green,
While tuneful sprites a merry concert made,
And airy music warbled through the shade.
Hither the noble knight would oft repair,
(His scene of pleasure, and peculiar care;)
For this he held it dear, and always bore
The silver key that lock'd the garden-door.
To this sweet place, in summer's sultry heat,
He us'd from noise and business to retreat,
And here in dalliance spend the live-long day,
Solus cum sola, with his sprightly May:
For whate'er work was undischarg'd a-bed
The duteous knight in this fair garden sped.

But, ah! what mortal lives of bliss secure?
How short a space our worldly joys endure!
O Fortune, fair, like all thy treach'rous kind,
But faithless still, and wav'ring as the wind!
O painted monster, form'd mankind to cheat
With pleasing poison, and with soft deceit!
This rich, this am'rous, venerable knight,
Amidst his ease, his solace, and delight,
Struck blind by thee, resigns his days to grief,
And calls on death, the wretch's last relief.
The rage of jealousy then seized his mind,
For much he feared the faith of womankind.
His wife not suffered from his side to stray,
Was captive kept; he watched her night and day,
Abridged her pleasures, and confined her sway.
Full oft in tears did hapless May complain,
And sighed full oft; but sighed and wept in vain:
She looked on Damian with a lover's eye;
For, oh, 'twas fix'd; she must possess or die!
Nor less impatience vexed her amorous 'squire,
Wild with delay, and burning with desire.
Watched as she was, yet could he not refrain
By secret writing to disclose his pain:
The dame by signs revealed her kind intent,
Till both were conscious what each other meant.
Ah! gentle knight, what would thy eyes avail,
Though they could see as far as ships can sail?
'Tis better, sure, when blind, deceived to be,
Than be deluded when a man can see!
Argus himself, so cautious and so wise,
Was over-watched, for all his hundred eyes:
So many an honest husband may, 'tis known,
Who, wisely, never thinks the case his own.
The dame at last, by diligence and care,
Procured the key her knight was wont to bear;
She took the wards in wax before the fire,
And gave the impression to the trusty 'squire.
By means of this some wonder shall appear,
Which, in due place and season, you may hear.
Well sung sweet Ovid, in the days of yore,
What slight is that which love will not explore?
And Pyramus and Thisbe plainly show
The feats true lovers, when they list, can do:
Though watched and captive, yet, in spite of all,
They found the art of kissing through a wall.
But now no longer from our tale to stray,
It happened, that once, upon a summer's day,
Our reverend knight was urged to amorous play:
He raised his spouse ere matin-bell was rung,
And thus his morning canticle he sung;

'Awake, my love, disclose thy radiant eyes:
Arise, my wife, my beauteous lady, rise!
Hear how the doves with pensive notes complain,
And in soft murmurs tell the trees their pain.
The winter's past; the clouds and tempests fly;
The sun adorns the fields, and brightens all the sky.
Fair without spot, whose every charming part
My bosom wounds, and captivates my heart;
Come, and in mutual pleasures let's engage,
Joy of my life, and comfort of my age'
This heard, to Damian straight a sign she made,
To haste before; the gentle 'squire obeyed:
Secret and undescried he took his way,
And ambushed close behind an arbour lay.
It was not long ere January came,
And hand in hand with him his lovely dame;
Blind as he was, not doubting all was sure,
He turned the key, and made the gate secure.
'Here let us walk,' he said, 'observed by none,
Conscious of pleasures to the world unknown:
So may my soul have joy, as thou, my wife,
Art far the dearest solace of my life:
And rather would I choose, by Heaven above
To die this instant, than to lose thy love.
Reflect what truth was in my passion shown,
When, unendowed, I took thee for my own,
And sought no treasure but thy heart alone.
Old as I am, and now deprived of sight,
Whilst thou art faithful to thy own true knight,
Nor age, nor blindness, rob me of delight.
Each other loss with patience I can bear;
The loss of thee is what I only fear.
Consider then, my lady and my wife,
The solid comforts of a virtuous life.
At first the love of Christ himself you gain;
Next, your own honour undefil'd maintain;
And, lastly, that which sure your mind must move
My whole estate shall gratify your love:
Make your own terms, and ere to-morrow's sun
Displays his light, by Heaven it shall be done.
I seal the contract with a holy kiss,
And will perform, by this—my dear, and this—
Have comfort, spouse, nor think thy lord unkind;
'Tis love, not jealousy, that fires my mind:
For when thy charms my sober thoughts engage,
And join'd to them my own unequal age,
From thy dear side I have no power to part,
Such secret transports warm my melting heart.
For who that once possess'd those heav'nly charms,
Could live one moment absent from thy arms?

He ceas'd, and May with modest grace replied;
(Weak was her voice, as while she spoke she cried,)
'Heav'n knows, (with that a tender sigh she drew)
I have a soul to save as well as you;
And, what no less you to my charge commend,
My dearest honour will to death defend.
To you in holy church I gave my hand,
And join'd my heart in wedlock's sacred band:
Yet after this, if you distrust my care,
Then hear, my lord, and witness what I swear:
First may the yawning earth her bosom rend,
And let me hence to hell alive descend;
Or die the death I dread no less than hell,
Sewed in a sack, and plunged into a well;
Ere I my fame by one lewd act disgrace,
Or once renounce the honour of my race.
For know, Sir Knight, of gentle blood I came;
I loathe a whore, and startle at the name.
But jealous men on their own crimes reflect,
And learn from thence their ladies to suspect:
Else why these needless cautions, Sir, to me?
These doubts and fears of female constancy?
This chime still rings in every lady's ear,
The only strain a wife must hope to hear.'
Thus while she spoke, a sidelong glance she cast,
Where Damian, kneeling, worship'd as she past.
She saw him watch the motions of her eye,
And singled out a pear-tree planted nigh:
'Twas charg'd with fruit that made a goodly show,
And hung with dangling pears was every bough.
Thither th' obsequious 'squire address'd his pace,
And climbing, in the summit took his place:
The knight and lady walk'd beneath in view,
Where let us leave them and our tale pursue.
'Twas now the season when the glorious sun
His heav'nly progress through the Twins had run;
And Jove, exalted, his mild influence yields,
To glad the glebe, and paint the flowery fields:
Clear was the day, and Phœbus, rising bright,
Had streaked the azure firmament with light;
He pierced the glittering clouds with golden streams,
And warm'd the womb of earth with genial beams.
It so befel, in that fair morning-tide,
The fairies sported on the garden-side,
And in the midst their monarch and his bride.
So featly tripp'd the light-foot ladies round,
The knights so nimbly o'er the greensward bound,
That scarce they bent the flow'rs, or touch'd the ground.
The dances ended, all the fairy train
For pinks and daisies searched the flowery plain

While on a bank reclined of rising green,
Thus, with a frown, the king bespoke his queen.
'Tis too apparent, argue what you can,
The treachery you women use to man:
A thousand authors have this truth made out,
And sad experience leaves no room for doubt.
Heaven rest thy spirit, noble Solomon,
A wiser monarch never saw the sun:
All wealth, all honours, the supreme degree
Of earthly bliss was well bestowed on thee!
For sagely hast thou said, Of all mankind,
One only just, and righteous, hope to find:
But shouldst thou search the spacious world around,
Yet one good woman is not to be found.
Thus says the king, who knew your wickedness;
The Son of Sirach testifies no less.
So may some wildfire on your bodies fall,
Or some devouring plague consume you all;
As well you view the lecher in the tree,
And well this honourable knight you see:
But since he's blind and old, (a helpless case)
His 'squire shall cuckold him before your face.
Now by my own dread majesty I swear,
And by this awful sceptre which I bear,
No impious wretch shall 'scape unpunished long
That in my presence offers such a wrong.
I will this instant undeceive the knight,
And, in the very act, restore his sight:
And set the strumpet here in open view,
A warning to these ladies, and to you,
And all the faithless sex, for ever to be true.'
'And will you so,' replied the queen, 'indeed?
Now, by my mother's soul, it is decreed,
She shall not want an answer at her need.
For her, and for her daughters, I'll engage,
And all the sex in each succeeding age;
Art shall be theirs to varnish an offence,
And fortify their crimes with confidence.
Nay, were they taken in a strict embrace,
Seen with both eyes, and pinion'd on the place;
All they shall need is to protest and swear,
Breathe a soft sigh, and drop a tender tear;
Till their wise husbands, gull'd by arts like these
Grow gentle, tractable, and tame as geese.
What though this slanderous Jew, this Solomon,
Call'd women fools, and knew full many a one?
The wiser wits of later times declare
How constant, chaste, and virtuous, women are.
Witness the martyrs, who resigned their breath,
Serene in torments, unconcerned in death;

And witness next what Roman authors tell,
How Arria, Portia, and Lucretia fell.
  But since the sacred leaves to all are free,
And men interpret texts, why should not we?
By this no more was meant, than to have shown,
That sovereign goodness dwells in him alone,
Who only is, and is but only One.
But grant the worst; shall women then be weigh'd
By ev'ry word that Solomon hath said?
What though this king (as ancient story boasts)
Built a fair temple to the Lord of Hosts?
He ceased at last his Maker to adore,
And did as much for idol gods, or more.
Beware what lavish praises you confer
On a rank lecher and idolater;
Whose reign indulgent God, says holy writ,
Did but for David's righteous sake permit;
David, the Monarch after Heaven's own mind,
Who lov'd our sex and honour'd all our kind.
  Well, I'm a woman, and as such must speak;
Silence would swell me, and my heart would break.
Know then, I scorn your dull authorities,
Your idle wits, and all their learned lies.
By Heaven, those authors are our sex's foes,
Whom in our right, I must and will oppose.'
'Nay,' quoth the king, 'dear madam, be not wroth;
I yield it up; but since I gave my oath,
That this much-injured knight again should see,
It must be done—I am a king,' said he,
'And one whose faith has ever sacred been—'
  'And so has mine,' she said—'I am a queen:
Her answer she shall have, I undertake;
And thus an end of all dispute I make.
Try when you list; and you shall find, my lord
It is not in our sex to break our word.'
  We leave them here in this heroic strain,
And to the knight our story turns again;
Who in the garden, with his lovely May,
Sung merrier than the cuckow or the jay:
This was his song—'Oh, kind and constant be,
Constant and kind I'll ever prove to thee.'
  Thus singing as he went, at last he drew,
By easy steps, to where the pear-tree grew:
The longing dame looked up, and spied her love
Full fairly perch'd among the boughs above.
She stoop'd, and sighing, 'Oh, good gods!' she cried,
'What pangs, what sudden shoots distend my side!
O for that tempting fruit, so fresh, so green;
Help, for the love of Heaven's immortal queen;

Help, dearest lord, and save at once the life
Of thy poor infant, and thy longing wife!'
  Sore sighed the knight to hear his lady's cry,
But could not climb, and had no servant nigh:
Old as he was, and void of eyesight too,
What could, alas! a helpless husband do?
'And must I languish then,' she said, 'and die,
Yet view the lovely fruit before my eye?
At least, kind sir, for Charity's sweet sake,
Vouchsafe the trunk between your arms to take;
Then from your back I might ascend the tree:
Do you but stoop, and leave the rest to me.'
  'With all my soul,' he thus replied, again;
'I'd spend my dearest blood to ease thy pain.'
With that his back against the trunk he bent;
She seized a twig, and up the tree she went.
  Now prove your patience, gentle ladies all,
Nor let on me your heavy anger fall:
'Tis truth I tell, though not in phrase refin'd;
Though blunt my tale, yet honest is my mind.
What feats the lady in the tree might do,
I pass, as gambols never known to you;
But sure it was a merrier fit, she swore,
Than in her life she ever felt before.
  In that nice moment, lo! the wond'ring knight
Looked out, and stood restored to sudden sight.
Straight on the tree his eager eyes he bent,
As one whose thoughts were on his spouse intent;
But when he saw his bosom-wife so dress'd,
His rage was such as cannot be express'd:
Not frantic mothers, when their infants die,
With louder clamours rend the vaulted sky:
He cried, he roared, he stormed, he tore his hair;
'Death! hell! and furies! what dost thou do there?'
  'What ails my lord?' the trembling dame replied;
'I thought your patience had been better tried:
Is this your love, ungrateful and unkind,
This my reward for having cured the blind?
Why was I taught to make my husband see
By struggling with a man upon a tree?
Did I for this the power of magic prove?
Unhappy wife, whose crime was too much love!'
  'If this be struggling, by this holy light,
'Tis struggling with a vengeance,' quoth the knight
'So Heaven preserve the sight it has restored,
As with these eyes I plainly saw thee whored;
Whored by my slave—perfidious wretch! may hell
As surely seize thee, as I saw too well.'
'Guard me, good angels,' cried the gentle May;
'Pray Heaven this magic work the proper way!

Alas, my love! 'tis certain, could you see,
You ne'er had used these killing words to me:
So help me, Fates! as 'tis no perfect sight,
But some faint glimmering of a doubtful light.'
'What I have said,' quoth he, 'I must maintain,
For by the immortal powers it seemed too plain—'
'By all those powers, some frenzy seized your mind,'
Replied the dame: 'are these the thanks I find?
Wretch that I am, that e'er I was so kind!'
She said, a rising sigh expressed her woe;
The ready tears apace began to flow,
And as they fell she wip'd from either eye
The drops; (for women, when they list, can cry.)
The knight was touch'd; and in his looks appear'd
Signs of remorse, while thus his spouse he cheer'd:
'Madam, 'tis past, and my short anger o'er!
Come down, and vex your tender heart no more:
Excuse me, dear, if aught amiss was said,
For, on my soul, amends shall soon be made:
Let my repentance your forgiveness draw;
By Heaven, I swore but what I thought I saw.'
'Ah, my lov'd lord! 'twas much unkind,' she cried,
'On bare suspicion thus to treat your bride.
But till your sight's established, for a while,
Imperfect objects may your sense beguile.
Thus, when from sleep we first our eyes display,
The balls are wounded with the piercing ray,
And dusky vapours rise, and intercept the day:
So just recovering from the shades of night,
Your swimming eyes are drunk with sudden light,
Strange phantoms dance around, and skim before your sight.
Then, sir, be cautious, nor too rashly deem;
Heaven knows how seldom things are what they seem!
Consult your reason, and you soon shall find
'Twas you were jealous, not your wife unkind:
Jove ne'er spoke oracle more true than this;
None judge so wrong as those who think amiss.'
With that she leap'd into her lord's embrace,
With well-dissembled virtue in her face.
He hugged her close, and kissed her o'er and o'er,
Disturbed with doubts and jealousies no more:
Both, pleased and blessed, renewed their mutual vows:
A fruitful wife, and a believing spouse.
Thus ends our tale, whose moral next to make,
Let all wise husbands hence example take;
And pray, to crown the pleasure of their lives,
To be so well deluded by their wives.

THE WIFE OF BATH.

HER PROLOGUE. FROM CHAUCER.

BEHOLD the woes of matrimonial life,
And hear with reverence an experienced wife;
To dear-bought wisdom give the credit due,
And think for once a woman tells you true.
In all these trials I have borne a part;
I was myself the scourge that caused the smart;
For since fifteen in triumph have I led
Five captive husbands from the church to bed.
  Christ saw a wedding once, the Scripture says,
And saw but one, 'tis thought, in all his days;
Whence some infer, whose conscience is too nice,
No pious Christian ought to marry twice.
  But let them read, and solve me, if they can,
The words address'd to the Samaritan:
Five times in lawful wedlock she was joined;
And sure the certain stint was ne'er defined.
  'Increase and multiply' was Heaven's command,
And that 's a text I clearly understand.
This too, 'Let men their sires and mothers leave,
And to their dearer wives for ever cleave.'
More wives than one by Solomon were tried,
Or else the wisest of mankind 's belied.
I've had myself full many a merry fit,
And trust in heaven I may have many yet;
For when my transitory spouse, unkind,
Shall die, and leave his woeful wife behind,
I'll take the next good Christian I can find.
  Paul, knowing one could never serve our turn,
Declared 'twas better far to wed than burn.
There's danger in assembling fire and tow;
I grant them that; and what it means you know.
The same apostle, too, has elsewhere own'd,
No precept for virginity he found:

'Tis but a counsel--and we women still
Take which we like, the counsel or our will.
I envy not their bliss, if he or she
Think fit to live in perfect chastity;
Pure let them be, and free from taint of vice;
I for a few slight spots am not so nice.
Heaven calls us different ways; on these bestows
One proper gift, another grants to those;
Not every man 's obliged to sell his store,
And give up all his substance to the poor:
Such as are perfect may, I can't deny;
But, by your leaves, Divines! so am not I.
Full many a saint, since first the world began,
Liv'd an unspotted maid in spite of man:
Let such (a-God's name) with fine wheat be fed.
And let us honest wives eat barley bread.
For me, I'll keep the post assigned by Heaven,
And use the copious talent it has given:
Let my good spouse pay tribute, do me right,
And keep an equal reckoning every night:
His proper body is not his, but mine;
For so said Paul, and Paul 's a sound divine.
Know then, of those five husbands I have had,
Three were just tolerable, two were bad.
The three were old, but rich, and fond beside,
And toiled most piteously to please their bride;
But since their wealth the best they had, was mine,
The rest without much loss I could resign:
Sure to be loved, I took no pains to please,
Yet had more pleasure far than they had ease.
Presents flowed in apace: with showers of gold
They made their court, like Jupiter of old:
If I but smiled, a sudden youth they found,
And a new palsy seiz'd them when I frown'd.
Ye sovereign wives! give ear, and understand,
Thus shall ye speak, and exercise command;
For never was it given to mortal man
To lie so boldly as we women can:
Forswear the fact, though seen with both his eyes,
And call your maids to witness how he lies.
'Hark,' old Sir Paul; 'twas thus I used to say,
'Whence is our neighbour's wife so rich and gay?
Treated, caress'd, where'er she 's pleas'd to roam—
I sit in tatters, and immured at home.
Why to her house dost thou so oft repair?
Art thou so amorous? and is she so fair?
If I but see a cousin or a friend,
Lord! how you swell and rage like any fiend!
But you reel home, a drunken beastly bear,
Then preach till midnight in your easy chair;

Cry wives are false, and ev'ry woman evil,
And give up all that 's female to the devil.
  If poor (you say) she drains her husband's purse;
If rich, she keeps her priest, or something worse;
If highly born, intolerably vain,
Vapours and pride by turns possess her brain;
Now gaily mad, now sourly splenetic,
Freakish when well, and fretful when she's sick;
If fair, then chaste she cannot long abide,
By pressing youth attack'd on ev'ry side;
If foul, her wealth the lusty lover lures,
Or else her wit some fool-gallant procures,
Or else she dances with becoming grace,
Or shape excuses the defects of face.
There swims no goose so grey, but soon or late,
She finds some honest gander for her mate.
  Horses (thou say'st) and asses men may try,
And ring suspected vessels ere they buy;
But wives, a random choice, untried they take;
They dream in courtship, but in wedlock wake;
Then, nor till then, the veil 's removed away,
And all the woman glares in open day.
  You tell me, to preserve your wife's good grace,
Your eyes must always languish on my face,
Your tongue with constant flatteries feed my ear,
And tag each sentence with, My life! My dear!
If by strange chance a modest blush be raised,
Be sure my fine complexion must be praised.
My garments always must be new and gay,
And feasts still kept upon my wedding-day;
Then must my nurse be pleased, and favourite maid;
And endless treats and endless visits paid
To a long train of kindred friends, allies:
All this thou say'st, and all thou say'st are lies.
  On Jenkin, too, you cast a squinting eye:
What? can your 'prentice raise your jealousy?
Fresh are his ruddy cheeks, his forehead fair,
And like the burnished gold his curling hair:
But clear thy rinkled brow, and quit thy sorrow,
I'd scorn thy 'prentice, should you die to-morrow.
  Why are thy chests all lock'd? on what design?
Are not thy worldly goods and treasure mine?
Sir, I'm no fool; nor shall you by St. John,
Have goods and body to yourself alone.
One you shall quit in spite of both your eyes—
I heed not, I, the bolts, the locks, the spies.
If you had wit, you'd say, 'Go where you will,
Dear spouse! I credit not the tales they tell:

Take all the freedom of a married life;
I know thee for a virtuous, faithful wife.
Lord! when you have enough, what need you care
How merrily soever others fare?
Though all the day I give and take delight,
Doubt not sufficient will be left for night.
'Tis but a just and rational desire
To light a taper at a neighbour's fire.
There's danger too, you think, in rich array,
And none can long be modest that are gay.
The cat, if you but singe her tabby skin,
The chimney keeps, and sits content within;
But once grown sleek, will from her corner run,
Sport with her tail, and wanton in the sun:
She licks her fair round face, and frisks abroad
To show her fur, and to be caterwaw'd.'
Lo thus, my friends, I wrought to my desires
These three right ancient venerable sires.
I told them, thus you say, and thus you do;
I told them false, but Jenkin swore 't was true.
I, like the dog, could bite as well as whine,
And first complain'd whene'er the guilt was mine.
I tax'd them oft with wenching and amours,
When their weak legs scarce dragg'd them out of doors;
And swore the rambles that I took by night
Were all to spy what damsels they bedight:
That colour brought me many hours of mirth;
For all this wit is giv'n us from our birth.
Heaven gave to woman the peculiar grace
To spin, to weep, and cully human race.
By this nice conduct, and this prudent course,
By murm'ring, wheedling, stratagem, and force,
I still prevail'd, and would be in the right,
Or curtain lectures made a restless night.
If once my husband's arm was o'er my side,
What! so familiar with your spouse? I cried:
I levied first a tax upon his need;
Then let him—'t was a nicety indeed!
Let all mankind this certain maxim hold,
Marry who will, our sex is to be sold.
With empty hands no tassels you can lure,
But fulsome love for gain we can endure;
For gold we love the impotent and old,
And heave, and pant, and kiss, and cling for gold.
Yet with embraces curses oft I mix'd;
Then kissed again, and chid, and rail'd betwixt.
Well, I may make my will in peace, and die,
For not one word in man's arrears am I

To drop a dear dispute I was unable,
E'en though the pope himself had sat at table;
But when my point was gain'd, then thus I spoke:
'Billy, my dear! how sheepishly you look!
Approach, my spouse! and let me kiss thy cheek;
Thou shouldst be always thus, resigned and meek.
Of Job's great patience since so oft you preach,
Well should you practise who so well can teach.
'T is difficult to do, I must allow;
But I, my dearest! will instruct you how.
Great is the blessing of a prudent wife,
Who puts a period to domestic strife.
One of us two must rule, and one obey!
And since in man right reason bears the sway,
Let that frail thing, weak woman, have her way.
The wives of all my family have ruled
Their tender husbands and their passions cooled.
Fie! 't is unmanly thus to sigh and groan;
What! would you have me to yourself alone?
Why, take me, love! take all and every part!
Here's your revenge! you love it at your heart.
Would I vouchsafe to sell what nature gave,
You little think what custom I could have.
But see! I'm all your own—nay, hold—for shame!
What means my dear?—indeed—you are to blame.
Thus with my first three lords I passed my life,
A very woman and a very wife.
What sums from these old spouses I could raise,
Procured young husbands in my riper days.
Though past my bloom, not yet decay'd was I,
Wanton and wild, and chattered like a pie.
In country dances still I bore the bell,
And sang as sweet as evening Philomel.
To clear my quail-pipe, and refresh my soul,
Full oft I drained the spicy nut-brown bowl;
Rich luscious wines, that youthful blood improve,
And warm the swelling veins to feats of love:
For 'tis as sure as cold engenders hail,
A liquorish mouth must have a lecherous tail:
Wine lets no lover unrewarded go,
As all true gamesters by experience know.
But oh, good gods! whene'er a thought I cast
On all the joys of youth and beauty past,
To find in pleasures I have had my part,
Still warms me to the bottom of my heart.
This wicked world was once my dear delight;
Now all my conquests, all my charms, good night!
The flour consumed, the best that now I can,
Is e'en to make my market of the bran.

My fourth dear spouse was not exceeding true;
He kept, 't was thought, a private miss or two:
But all that score I paid.—As how? you'll say;
Not with my body, in a filthy way;
But I so dress'd, and danced, and drank, and din'd,
And view'd a friend with eyes so very kind
As stung his heart, and made his marrow fry
With burning rage and frantic jealousy.
His soul, I hope, enjoys eternal glory,
For here on earth I was his purgatory.
Oft when his shoe the most severely wrung,
He put on careless airs, and sat and sung.
How sore I galled him only Heaven could know,
And he that felt, and I that caused the woe.
He died when last from pilgrimage I came,
With other gossips, from Jerusalem;
And now lies buried underneath a rood,
Fair to be seen, and rear'd of honest wood:
A tomb, indeed, with fewer sculptures graced
Than that Mausolus' pious widow placed,
Or where enshrined the great Darius lay;
But cost on graves is merely thrown away.
The pit filled up, with turf we covered o'er;
So bless the good man's soul! I say no more.
Now for my fifth loved lord, the last and best;
(Kind Heaven afford him everlasting rest!)
Full hearty was his love, and I can show
The tokens on my ribs in black and blue;
Yet with a knack my heart he could have won,
While yet the smart was shooting in the bone.
How quaint an appetite in woman reigns!
Free gifts we scorn, and love what costs us pains:
Let men avoid us, and on them we leap;
A glutted market makes provisions cheap.
In pure good-will I took this jovial spark;
Of Oxford he, a most egregious clerk.
He boarded with a widow in the town,
A trusty gossip, one Dame Alison;
Full well the secrets of my soul she knew,
Better than e'er our parish priest could do.
To her I told whatever could befall;
Had but my husband piss'd against a wall,
Or done a thing that might have cost his life,
She—and my niece—and one more worthy wife,
Had known it all: what most he could conceal,
To these I made no scruple to reveal.
Oft has he blushed from ear to ear for shame,
That e'er he told a secret to his dame.

It so befel, in holy time of Lent,
That oft a day I to this gossip went;
(My husband, thank my stars, was out of town;)
From house to house we rambled up and down;
This clerk, myself, and my good neighbour Alse,
To see, be seen, to tell and gather tales.
Visits to every church we daily paid,
And marched in every holy masquerade;
The stations duly and the vigils kept;
Not much we fasted, but scarce ever slept.
At sermons, too, I shone in scarlet gay:
The wasting moth ne'er spoiled my best array;
The cause was this, I wore it every day.
'T was when fresh May her early blossoms yields,
This clerk and I were walking in the fields.
We grew so intimate, I can't tell how,
I pawn'd my honour, and engaged my vow,
If e'er I laid my husband in his urn,
That he, and only he, should serve my turn.
We straight struck hands, the bargain was agreed;
I still have shifts against a time of need.
The mouse that always trusts to one poor hole
Can never be a mouse of any soul.
I vow'd I scarce could sleep since first I knew him,
And durst be sworn he had bewitch'd me to him;
If e'er I slept,—I dreamed of him alone,
And dreams foretell, as learned men have shown.
All this I said; but dreams, sirs, I had none:
I followed but my crafty cronies lore,
Who bid me tell this lie—and twenty more.
Thus day by day, and month by month we pass'd;
It pleased the Lord to take my spouse at last.
I tore my gown, I soiled my locks with dust,
And beat my breasts, as wretched widows—must.
Before my face my handkerchief I spread,
To hide the flood of tears I did—not shed.
The good man's coffin to the church was borne:
Around, the neighbours, and my clerk too, mourn:
But as he marched, good gods, he show'd a pair
Of legs and feet so clean, so strong, so fair!
Of twenty winters' age he seem'd to be;
I (to say truth) was twenty more than he:
But vigorous still, a lively buxom dame,
And had a wondrous gift to quench a flame.
A conjurer once, that deeply could divine,
Assured me Mars in Taurus was my sign.
As the stars ordered, such my life has been:
Alas, alas! that ever love was sin!

Fair Venus gave me fire and sprightly grace,
And mars assurance and a dauntless face.
By virtue of this powerful constellation
I followed always my own inclination.
But to my tale. A month scarce passed away,
With dance and song we kept the nuptial day;
All I possess'd I gave to his command,
My goods and chattels, money, house, and land!
But oft repented and repent it still;
He proved a rebel to my sovereign will:
Nay once, by Heaven! he struck me on the face,
Hear but the fact, and judge yourselves the case.
Stubborn as any lioness was I,
And knew full well to raise my voice on high;
As true a rambler as I was before,
And would be so in spite of all he swore.
He against this right sagely would advise,
And old examples set before my eyes;
Tell how the Roman matrons led their life,
Of Gracchus' mother, and Duilius' wife;
And close the sermon, as beseemed his wit,
With some grave sentence out of Holy Writ.
Oft would he say, Who builds his house on sands,
Pricks his blind horse across the fallow lands,
Or lets his wife abroad with pilgrims roam,
Deserves a fool's-cap and long ears at home.
All this availed not; for whoe'er he be
That tells my faults, I hate him mortally;
And so do numbers more I'll boldly say,
Men, women, clergy, regular and lay.
My spouse, who was, you know, to learning bred,
A certain treatise oft at ev'ning read,
Where divers authors (whom the devil confound
For all their lies!) were in one volume bound:
Valerius, whole; and of St. Jerome, part;
Chrycippus and Tertullian, Ovid's Art,
Solomon's Proverbs, Eloisa's loves,
And many more than sure the Church approves.
More legends were there here of wicked wives
Than good in all the Bible and Saints' Lives.
Who drew the lion vanquish'd? 'T was a man;
But could we women write as scholars can,
Men should stand marked with far more wickedness
Than all the sons of Adam could redress.
Love seldom haunts the breast where learning lies,
And Venus sets ere Mercury can rise.
Those play the scholars who can't play the men,
And use that weapon which they have, their pen:

When old, and past the relish of delight,
Then down they sit, and in their dotage write,
That not one woman keeps her marriage-vow.
(This by the way, but to my purpose now.)
It chanced my husband, on a winter's night,
Read in this book aloud with strange delight,
How the first female, as the Scriptures show,
Brought her own spouse and all his race to woe;
How Samson fell; and he whom Dejanire
Wrapped in th' envenom'd shirt, and set on fire;
How curs'd Eriphyle her lord betrayed,
And the dire ambush Clytemnestra laid;
But what most pleased him was the Cretan dame
And husband-bull—Oh, monstrous! fie for shame!
He had by heart the whole detail of woe
Xantippe made her good man undergo;
How oft she scolded in a day he knew,
How many pisspots on the sage she threw.
Who took it patiently, and wiped his head:
'Rain follows thunder;' that was all he said.
He read how Arius to his friend complained
A fatal tree was growing on his land,
On which three wives successively had twined
A sliding noose, and wavered in the wind.
Where grows this plant, replied the friend, oh! where?
For better fruit did never orchard bear:
Give me some slip of this most blissful tree,
And in my garden planted shall it be.
Then how two wives their lord's destruction prove;
Through hatred one, and one through too much love;
That for her husband mixed a poisonous draught,
And this for lust an amorous philtre bought:
The nimble juice soon seized his giddy head,
Frantic at night, and in the morning dead.
How some with swords their sleeping lords have slain,
And some have hammered nails into their brain,
And some have drenched them with a deadly potion:
All this he read, and read with great devotion.
Long time I heard, and swelled, and blushed, and frown'd:
But when no end to these vile tales I found,
When still he read, and laughed, and read again,
And half the night was thus consumed in vain,
Provoked to vengeance, three large leaves I tore,
And with one buffet felled him on the floor.
With that my husband in a fury rose,
And down he settled me with hearty blows.
I groaned, and lay extended on my side;
'Oh! thou hast slain me for my wealth,' I cried:

'Yet I forgive thee—take my last embrace—'
He wept, kind soul! and stooped to kiss my face:
I took him such a box as turned him blue,
Then sighed and cried, 'Adieu, my dear, adieu!'
But after many a hearty struggle past,
I condescended to be pleased at last.
Soon as he said, My mistress and my wife!
Do what you list the term of all your life,
I took to heart the merits of the cause,
And stood content to rule by wholesome laws;
Received the reins of absolute command,
With all the government of house and land,
And empire o'er his tongue and o'er his hand.
As for the volume that reviled the dames,
'Twas torn to fragments, and condemned to flames.
Now Heaven on all my husbands gone bestow
Pleasures above for tortures felt below;
That rest they wished for grant them in the grave,
And bless those souls my conduct helped to save.

THE FABLE OF DRYOPE.

FROM THE NINTH BOOK OF

OVID'S METAMORPHOSES.

SHE said, and for her lost Galanthias sighs,
When the fair consort of her son replies:
"Since you a servant's ravished form bemoan,
And kindly sigh for sorrows not your own,
Let me (if tears and griefs permit) relate
A nearer woe, a sister's stranger fate.
No nymph of all Oechalia could compare
For beauteous form with Dryope the fair,
Her tender mother's only hope and pride,
(Myself the offspring of a second bride.)
This nymph, compressed by him who rules the day
Whom Delphi and the Delian aisle obey,
Andræmon loved; and blessed in all those charms
That pleased a god, succeeded to her arms.
"A lake there was with shelving banks around,
Whose verdant summit fragrant myrtles crown'd:
These shades, unknowing of the Fates, she sought
And to the Naiads flowery garlands brought;
Her smiling babe, a pleasing charge, she press'd
Within her arms, and nourished at her breast.
Not distant far a watery lotos grows;
The spring was new, and all the verdant boughs
Adorned with blossoms, promised fruits that vie
In glowing colours with the Tyrian dye:
Of these she cropp'd to please her infant son,
And I myself the same rash act had done:
But, lo! I saw, as near her side I stood,
The violated blossoms drop with blood.
Upon the tree I cast a frightful look;
The trembling tree with sudden horror shook.
Lotis, the nymph, if rural tales be true,
As from Priapus' lawless lust she flew,

Forsook her form, and, fixing here, became
A flowery plant, which still preserves her name.
This change unknown, astonished at the sight,
My trembling sister strove to urge her flight;
And first the pardon of the nymphs implor'd,
And those offended sylvan powers ador'd:
But when she backward would have fled, she found
Her stiffening feet were rooted in the ground;
In vain to free her fastened feet she strove,
And as she struggles only moves above;
She feels the encroaching bark around her grow
By quick degrees, and cover all below.
Surprised at this, her trembling hand she heaves
To rend her hair; her hand is filled with leaves:
Where late was hair, the shooting leaves are seen
To rise, and shade her with a sudden green.
The child Amphissus, to her bosom press'd,
Perceived a colder and a harder breast,
And found the springs, that ne'er till then denied
Their milky moisture, on a sudden dried.
I saw, unhappy, what I now relate,
And stood the helpless witness of thy fate,
Embraced thy boughs, thy rising bark delay'd,
There wished to grow, and mingle shade with shade.
Behold Andræmon and the unhappy sire
Appear, and for their Dryope inquire!
A springing tree for Dryope they find,
And print warm kisses on the panting rind,
Prostrate, with tears their kindred plant bedew,
And close embrace as to the roots they grew.
The face was all that now remained of thee;
No more a woman, nor yet quite a tree;
Thy branches hung with humid pearls appear,
From every leaf distils a trickling tear;
And straight a voice, while yet a voice remains,
Thus through the trembling boughs in sighs complains:
"If to the wretched any faith be given,
I swear by all the unpitying powers of heaven,
No wilful crime this heavy vengeance bred;
In mutual innocence our lives we led:
If this be false, let these new greens decay,
Let sounding axes lop my limbs away,
And crackling flames on all my honours prey.
But from my branching arms this infant bear,
Let some kind nurse supply a mother's care;
And to his mother let him oft be led,
Sport in her shades, and in her shades be fed;
Teach him, when first his infant voice shall frame
Imperfect words, and lisp a mother's name,

To hail this tree; and say, with weeping eyes,
Within this plant my hapless parent lies:
And when in youth he seeks the shady woods,
Oh! let him fly the crystal lakes and floods,
Nor touch the fatal flowers; but, warned by me,
Believe a goddess shrined in every tree.
My sire, my sister, and my spouse, farewell!
If in your breasts or love or pity dwell,
Protect your plant, nor let my branches feel
The browsing cattle or the piercing steel.
Farewell! and since I cannot bend to join
My lips to yours, advance at least to mine.
My son, thy mother's parting kiss receive,
While yet thy mother has a kiss to give.
I can no more; the creeping rind invades
My closing lips, and hides my head in shades:
Remove your hands; the bark shall soon suffice,
Without their aid, to seal those dying eyes."
She ceased at once to speak and ceased to be,
And all the nymph was lost within the tree;
Yet latent life through her new branches reign'd,
And long the plant a human heat retain'd.

IMITATIONS OF ENGLISH POETS.

[DONE BY THE AUTHOR IN HIS YOUTH.]

CHAUCER

WOMEN ben full of ragerie,
Yet swinken nat sans secresie.
Thilke moral shall ye understond,
From schoole-boy's tale of fayre Irelond;
Which to the fennes hath him betake,
To filche the gray ducke fro the lake.
Right then, there passen by the way,
His aunt, and eke her daughters tway:
Ducke in his trowses hath he hent,
Not to be spied of ladies gent.
'But ho! our nephew!' crieth one:
'Ho!' quoth another, 'cozen John!'
And stoppen, and lough, and callen out,
This sely clerk full low doth lout:
They asken that, and talken this;—
'Lo, here is coz, and here is miss.'
But, as he glozeth with speeches soote,
The ducke sore tickleth his erse roote:
Forepiece and buttons all-to brest,
Forth thrust a white neck, and red crest.
'Te-he!' cry'd ladies: clerke not spake:
Miss stared; and gray ducke cried quaake.
'O moder, moder,' quoth the daughter,
'Be thilke same thing maids long a'ter?
Bette is to pyne on coals and chalke,
Than trust on mon, whose yerde can talke.

SPENSER.

THE ALLEY.

In every town, where Thamis rolls his tyde,
A narrow pass there is, with houses low;
Where ever and anon the stream is eyed,
And many a boat soft gliding to and fro.
There oft are heard the notes of infant woe,
The short thick sob, loud scream, and shriller squall:
How can ye, mothers, vex your children so?
Some play, some eat, some cack against the wall
And, as they crouchen low, for bread and butter call:

And on the broken pavement, here and there,
Doth many a stinking sprat and herring lie;
A brandy and tobacco-shop is near,
And hens and dogs and hogs are feeding by;
And here a sailor's jacket hangs to dry.
At every door are sun-burnt matrons seen,
Mending old nets to catch the scaly fry;
Now singing shrill, and scolding eft between:
Scolds answer foul-mouth'd scolds; bad neighbourhood
I ween!

The snappish cur, the passengers annoy,
Close at my heel, with yelping treble, flies;
The whimpering girl, and hoarser-screaming boy,
Join to the yelping treble shrilling cries:
The scolding quean to louder notes doth rise,
And her full pipes those shrilling cries confound:
To her full pipes the grunting hog replies;
The grunting hogs alarm the neighbours round,
And curs, girls, boys, and scolds, in the deep bass are
drown'd.

Hard by a stye, beneath a roof of thatch,
Dwelt Obloquy, who in her early days
Baskets of fish at Billingsgate did watch,
Cod, whiting, oyster, mackerel, sprat, or plaice:
There learn'd she speech from tongues that never cease.
Slander beside her, like a magpie, chatters,
With Envy, spitting cat, dread foe to peace:
Like a cursed cur, Malice before her clatters,
And, vexing every wight, tears clothes and all to tatters.

Her dugs were mark'd by every collier's hand;
Her mouth was black as bull-dog's at the stall:
She scratched, bit, and spared ne lace ne band;
And bitch and rogue her answer was to all;
Nay, ev'n the parts of shame by name would call:
Yea, when she passes by or lane or nook,
Would greet the man who turn'd him to the wall,
And by his hand obscene the porter took,
Nor ever did askance like modest virgin look.

Such place hath Deptford, navy-building town;
Woolwich and Wapping, smelling strong of pitch:
Such Lambeth, envy of each band and gown;
And Twickenham such, which fairer scenes enrich,
Grots, statues, urns, and Jo—n's dog and bitch:
Ne village is without, on either side,
All up the silver Thames, or all adown;
Ne Richmond's self, from whose tall front are eyed
Vales, spires, meandering streams, and Windsor's
towery pride.

WALLER.

ON A LADY SINGING TO HER LUTE.

Fair charmer, cease! nor make your voice's prize,
A heart, resign'd, the conquest of your eyes:
Well might, alas! that threaten'd vessel fail,
Which winds and lightning both at once assail.
We were too bless'd with these enchanting lays,
Which must be heavenly when an angel plays:
But killing charms your lover's death contrive,
Lest heavenly music should be heard alive.
Orpheus could charm the trees; but thus a tree,
Taught by your hand, can charm no less than he
A poet made the silent wood pursue;
This vocal wood had drawn the poet too.

ON A FAN

Of the Author's design, on which was printed the story of Cephalus and Procris, with the motto—*Aura, Veni.*

'Come, gentle air!' the Æolian shepherd said,
While Procris panted in the secret shade:
'Come, gentle air!' the fairer Delia cries,
While at her feet her swain expiring lies.
Lo, the glad gales o'er all her beauties stray,
Breathe on her lips, and in her bosom play!
In Delia's hand this toy is fatal found,
Nor could that fabled dart more surely wound:
Both gifts destructive to the givers prove;
Alike both lovers fall by those they love.
Yet guiltless too this bright destroyer lives;
At random wounds, nor knows the wound she gives:
She views the story with attentive eyes;
And pities Procris, while her lover dies.

COWLEY.

THE GARDEN.

Fain would my Muse the flowery treasure sing,
And humble glories of the youthful spring;
Where opening roses breathing sweets diffuse,
And soft carnations shower their balmy dews;
Where lilies smile in virgin robes of white,
The thin undress of superficial light,
And varied tulips show so dazzling gay,
Blushing in bright diversities of day.
Each painted floweret in the lake below
Surveys its beauties, whence its beauties grow;
And pale Narcissus, on the bank in vain
Transformed, gazes on himself again.
Here aged trees cathedral walks compose,
And mount the hill in venerable rows;
There the green infants in their beds are laid,
The garden's hope, and its expected shade.

Her orange trees with blooms and pendant shine,
And vernal honours to their autumn join;
Exceed their promise in their ripen'd store,
Yet in the rising blossom promise more.
There in bright drops the crystal fountains play,
By laurels shielded from the piercing day:
Where Daphne, now a tree as once a maid,
Still from Apollo vindicates her shade;
Still turns her beauties from the invading beam,
Nor seeks in vain for succour to the stream.
The stream at once preserves her virgin leaves,
At once a shelter from her boughs receives,
Where summer's beauty midst of winter stays,
And winter's coolness spite of summer's rays.

WEEPING.

While Celia's tears make sorrow bright,
Proud grief sits swelling in her eyes;
The sun, next those the fairest light,
Thus from the ocean first did rise:
And thus through mists we see the sun,
Which else we durst not gaze upon.

These silver drops, like morning dew,
Foretell the fervour of the day:
So from one cloud soft showers we view,
And blasting lightnings burst away.
The stars that fall from Celia's eye
Declare our doom is drawing nigh.

The baby in that sunny sphere
So like a Phaeton appears,
That Heaven, the threatened world to spare,
Thought fit to drown him in her tears;
Else might the ambitious nymph aspire
To set, like him, heaven too on fire.

EARL OF ROCHESTER.

ON SILENCE.

SILENCE! coeval with eternity,
Thou wert ere Nature's self began to be;
'Twas one vast nothing all, and all slept fast in thee.

Thine was the sway ere heaven was formed, or earth—
Ere fruitful thought conceived Creation's birth,
Or midwife word gave aid, and spoke the infant forth.

Then various elements against thee join'd,
In one more various animal combin'd,
And framed the clamorous race of busy human-kind.

The tongue moved gently first, and speech was low,
Till wrangling science taught it noise and show,
And wicked wit arose, thy most abusive foe.

But rebel wit deserts thee oft in vain:
Lost in the maze of words, he turns again,
And seeks a surer state, and courts thy gentle reign.

Afflicted sense thou kindly dost set free,
Oppressed with argumental tyranny,
And routed reason finds a safe retreat in thee.

With thee in private modest dulness lies,
And in thy bosom lurks in thought's disguise:
Thou varnisher of fools, and cheat of all the wise!

Yet thy indulgence is by both confess'd;
Folly by thee lies sleeping in the breast,
And 'tis in thee at last that wisdom seeks for rest.

Silence! the knave's repute, the whore's good name,
The only honour of the wishing dame;
Thy very want of tongue makes thee a kind of fame.

But couldst thou seize some tongues that now art free,
How church and state should be obliged to thee!
At senate and at bar how welcome wouldst thou be!

Yet speech e'en there submissively withdraws
From rights of subjects, and the poor man's cause:
Then pompous silence reigns, and stills the noisy laws.

Past services of friends, good deeds of foes,
What favourites gain, and what the nation owes,
Fly the forgetful world, and in thy arms repose.

The country wit, religion of the town,
The courtier's learning, policy of the gown,
Are best by thee expressed, and shine in thee alone.

The parson's cant, the lawyer's sophystry,
Lord's quibble, critic's jest, all end in thee;
All rest in peace at last, and sleep eternally.

EARL OF DORSET.

ARTEMISSIA.

Though Artemissia talks by fits
Of counsels, classics, fathers, wits,
  Reads Malbranche, Boyle, and Locke;
Yet in some things methinks she fails:
'Twere well if she would pare her nails,
  And wear a cleaner smock.

Haughty and huge as high Dutch bride,
Such nastiness and so much pride
  Are oddly joined by fate.
On her large squab you find her spread,
Like a fat corpse upon a bed,
  That lies and stinks in state.

She wears no colours (sign of grace)
On any part, except her face;
  All white and black beside;
Dauntless her look, her gesture proud,
Her voice theatrically loud,
  And masculine her stride.

So have I seen, in black and white,
A prating thing, a magpie hight,
  Majestically stalk;
A stately worthless animal,
That plies the tongue, and wags the tail,
  All flutter, pride, and talk.

PHRYNE.

Phryne had talents for mankind;
Open she was and unconfin'd,
  Like some free port of trade:
Merchants unloaded here their freight,
And agents from each foreign state
  Here first their entry made.

Her learning and good breeding such,
Whether the Italian or the Dutch,
  Spaniards or French came to her;
To all obliging she'd appear:
'Twas "Si, Signior;" twas "Yaw, Mynheer;"
  'Twas "S'il vous plait, Monsieur."

Obscure by birth, renown'd by crimes,
Still changing names, religion, climes,
  At length she turns a bride:
In diamonds, pearls, and rich brocades,
She shines the first of batter'd jades,
  And flutters in her pride.

So have I known those insects fair
(Which curious Germans hold so rare)
  Still vary shapes and dyes;
Still gain new titles with new forms;
First grubs obscene, then wriggling worms
  Then painted butterflies

DR. SWIFT.

THE HAPPY LIFE OF A COUNTRY PARSON.

Parson! these things in thy possessing
Are better than the bishop's blessing:
A wife that makes conserves; a steed
That carries double when there's need;
October store and best Virginia,
Tithe pig, and mortuary guinea;
Gazettes sent gratis down and frank'd,
For which thy patron's weeklv thank'd;
A large Concordance, bound long since;
Sermons to Charles the First, when prince•
A Chronicle of ancient standing;
A Chrysostom to smooth thy band in.
The Polyglott—three parts—my text,
Howbeit—likewise—now to my next.
Lo here the Septuagint—and Paul,
To sum the whole—the close of all.
He that has these may pass his life,
Drink with the 'squire, and kiss his wife;
On Sundays preach, and eat his fill,
And fast on Fridays—if he will;
Toast church and queen, explain the news,
Talk with churchwardens about pews,
Pray heartily for some new gift,
And shake his head at Doctor S***t.

THE

SATIRES OF DR. JOHN DONNE,

DEAN OF ST. PAUL'S,

VERSIFIED.

Quid vetat et nosmet Lucili scripta legentes
Quærere, num illius, num rerum dura negarit
Versiculos natura magis factos, et euntes
Mollius? HOR.

SATIRE II.

YES! thank my stars, as early as I knew
This town, I had the sense to hate it too;
Yet here, as e'en in hell, there must be still
One giant vice so excellently ill,
That all beside one pities, not abhors,
As who knows Sappho smiles at other whores.
I grant that poetry 's a crying sin;
It brought, no doubt, the excise and army in:
Catched like the plague, or love, the Lord knows how,
But that the cure is starving all allow.
Yet like the papist's is the poet's state,
Poor and disarmed, and hardly worth your hate.

SATIRE II.

SIR, though (I thank God for it) I do hate
Perfectly all this town, yet there 's one state
In all ill things so excellently best,
That hate towards them breeds pity towards the rest.
Though poetry, indeed, be such a sin
As I think that brings dearth and Spaniards in;
Though, like the pestilence and old-fashioned love,
Ridlingly it catch men, and doth remove
Never till it be starved out; yet their state
Is poor, disarmed, like papists, not worth hate.

Here a lean bard, whose wit could never give
Himself a dinner, makes an actor live:
The thief condemned, in law already dead,
So prompts, and saves a rogue who cannot read.
Thus as the pipes of some carved organ move,
The gilded puppets dance and mount above:
Heaved by the breath the inspiring bellows blow,
The inspiring bellows lie and pant below.
  One sings the fair; but songs no longer move;
No rat is rhymed to death, nor maid to love:
In love's, in nature's spite the siege they hold,
And scorn the flesh, the devil, and all but gold.
  These write to lords, some mean reward to get,
As needy beggars sing at doors for meat:
Those write because all write, and so have still
Excuse for writing, and for writing ill.
  Wretched, indeed! but far more wretched yet
Is he who makes his meal on others' wit:
'Tis changed, no doubt, from what it was before;
His rank digestion makes it wit no more:
Sense passed through him no longer is the same;
For food digested takes another name.
  I pass over all those confessors and martyrs
Who live like S—tt—n, or who die like Chartres—

  One (like a wretch, which at bar judged as dead,
Yet prompts him which stands next, and cannot read,
And saves his life) gives idiot actors means,
(Starving himself) to live by 's laboured scenes.
As in some organs puppets dance above,
And bellows pant below which them do move,
One would move love by rhymes; but witchcraft's charms
Bring not now their old fears nor their old harms;
Rams and slings now are silly battery,
Pistolets are the best artillery:
And they who write to lords rewards to get,
Are they not like singers at doors for meat?
And they who write, because all write, have still
That 'scuse for writing, and for writing ill.
  But he is worst who, beggarly, doth chaw
Others' wits-fruits, and in his ravenous maw
Rankly digested, doth those things opt-spue
As his own things: and they 're his own, 'tis true;
For if one eat my meat, though it be known
The meat was mine, the excrement 's his own.
  But these do me no harm, nor they which use,
. . . . to out-usure Jews,

Out-cant old Esdras, or out-drink his heir,
Out-usure Jews, or Irishmen out-swear;
Wicked as pages, who in early years
Act sins which Prisca's confessor scarce hears.
E'en those I pardon, for whose sinful sake
Schoolmen new tenements in hell must make;
Of whose strange crimes no canonist can tell
In what commandment's large contents they dwell.
  One, one man only breeds my just offence,
Whom crimes gave wealth, and wealth gave impudence:
Time, that at last matures a clap to pox,
Whose gentle progress makes a calf an ox,
And brings all natural events to pass,
Hath made him an attorney of an ass.
No young divine, new-beneficed, can be
More pert, more proud, more positive, than he.
What further could I wish the fop to do
But turn a wit, and scribble verses too?
Pierce the soft labyrinth of a lady's ear
With rhymes of this per cent. and that per year?
Or court a wife, spread out his wily parts,
Like net, or lime-twigs, for rich widows' hearts;
Call himself barrister to every wench,
And woo in language of the Pleas and Bench?
Language which Boreas might to Auster hold,
More rough than forty Germans when they scold.

To out-drink the sea, to out-swear the letanie,
Who with sins all kinds as familiar be
As confessors, and for whose sinful sake
Schoolmen new tenements in hell must make;
Whose strange sins canonists could hardly tell
In which commandment's large receit they dwell.
  But these punish themselves. The insolence
Of Coscus, only, breeds my just offence,
Whom time, (which rots all, and makes botches pox,
And plodding on, must make a calf an ox,)
Hath made a lawyer, which, alas! of late,
But scarce a poet! jollier of this state
Than are new-beneficed ministers: he throws,
Like nets or lime-twigs, whereso'er he goes,
His title of barrister on every wench,
And wooes in language of the Pleas and Bench * *
. . . . . . Words, words which would tear
The tender labyrinth of a maid's soft ear,
More, more than ten Sclavonians scolding, more
Than when winds in our ruined abbeys roar.

Cursed be the wretch, so venal and so vain,
Paltry and proud as drabs in Drury-Lane.
'Tis such a bounty as was never known,
If Peter deigns to help you to your own;
What thanks, what praise, if Peter but supplies!
And what a solemn face if he denies!
Grave, as when prisoners shake the head and swear
'Twas only suretyship that brought them there.
His office keeps your parchment fates entire,
He starves with cold to save them from the fire;
For you he walks the streets through rain or dust,
For not in chariots Peter puts his trust:
For you he sweats and labours at the laws,
Takes God to witness he affects your cause,
And lies to every lord in every thing,
Like a king's favourite—or like a king.
These are the talents that adorn them all,
From wicked Waters e'en to godly * *
Not more of simony beneath black gowns,
Not more of bastardy in heirs to crowns.
In shillings and in pence at first they deal,
And steal so little, few perceive they steal;
Till, like the sea, they compass all the land,
From Scotts to Wight, from Mount to Dover strand;
And when rank widows purchase luscious nights,
Or when a Duke to Jansen punts at White's,
Or city-heir in mortgage melts away,
Satan himself feels far less joy than they.

Then sick with poetry, and possessed with muse
Thou wast and mad, I hoped; but men which chuse
Law practice for mere gain, bold soul repute
Worse than imbrothelled strumpets prostitute.
Now like an owl-like watchman he must walk,
His hand still at a bill; now he must talk
Idly, like pris'ners, which whole months will swear
That only suretyship hath brought them there,
And to every suitor lie in every thing,
Like a king's favourite, or like a king:
Like a wedge in a block wring to the barre,
Bearing like asses, and more shameless farre
Than carted whores, lie to the grave judge; for
Bastardy abounds not in kings' titles, nor
Simony and sodomy in churchmen's lives,
As these things do in him; by these he thrives.
Shortly (as the sea) he'll compass all the land,
From Scots to Wight, from Mount to Dover strand;
And spying heirs melting with luxury,
Satan will not joy at their sins as he:

Piecemeal they win this acre first, then that,
Glean on, and gather up the whole estate;
Then strongly fencing ill-got wealth by law,
Indentures, covenants, articles, they draw,
Large as the fields themselves, and larger far
Than civil codes, with all their glosses, are;
So vast, our new divines, we must confess,
Are fathers of the church for writing less.
But let them write, for you each rogue impairs
The deeds, and dexterously omits *ses heires:*
No commentator can more slily pass
O'er a learned unintelligible place;
Or in quotation shrewd divines leave out
Those words that would against them clear the doubt.
  So Luther thought the Pater-noster long,
When doomed to say his beads and even song;
But having cast his cowl, and left those laws,
Adds to Christ's prayer the power and glory clause.
  The lands are bought: but where are to be found
Those ancient woods that shaded all the ground?
We see no new-built palaces aspire,
No kitchens emulate the vestal fire.

For (as a thrifty wench scrapes kitchen-stuffe,
And barrelling the droppings and the snuffe
Of wasting candles, which in thirty year,
(Reliquely kept) perchance buys wedding chear)
Piece-meal he gets lands, and spends as much time
Wringing each acre as maids pulling prime.
In parchment then, large as the fields, he draws
Assurances big as gloss'd civil laws;
So huge, that men (in our time's forwardness)
Are fathers of the church for writing less.
These he writes not, nor for these written payes,
Therefore spares no length; (as in those first dayes
When Luther was profess'd, he did desire
Short Pater-nosters, saying as a fryer
Each day his beads: but having left those laws,
Adds to Christ's prayer the power and glory clause;)
But when he sells or changes land, he impairs
The writings, and (unwatch'd) leaves out *ses heires,*
And slily, as any commentator, goes by
Hard words or sense; or in divinity,
As controverters in vouched texts leave out
Shrewd words, which might against them clear the doubt.
Where are these spread woods which clothed heretofore
Those bought lands? nor built, nor burnt within door.

Where are those troops of poor that thronged of yore
The good old landlord's hospitable door?
Well, I could wish that still, in lordly domes,
Some beasts were killed, though not whole hecatombs
That both extremes were banished from their walls,
Carthusian fasts and fulsome bacchanals;
And all mankind might that just mean observe,
In which none e'er could surfeit, none could starve.
These as good works, 'tis true, we all allow,
But oh! these works are not in fashion now:
Like rich old wardrobes, things extremely rare,
Extremely fine, but what no man will wear.
  Thus much I've said, I trust without offence;
Let no court sycophant pervert my sense,
Nor sly informer watch, these words to draw
Within the reach of treason or the law.

Where the old landlord's troopes and almes? In halls
Carthusian fasts and fulsome bacchanals
Equally I hate. Means blest. In rich men's homes
I bid kill some beasts, but no hecatomb
None starve, none surfeit so. But (oh!) we allow
Good works as good, but out of fashion now,
Like old rich wardrobes. But words none draws
Within the vast reach of the huge statutes-jaws.

SATIRE IV

Well; if it be my time to quit the stage,
Adieu to all the follies of the age!
I die in charity with fool and knave,
Secure of peace at least beyond the grave.
I've had my purgatory here betimes,
And paid for all my satires, all my rhymes.
The poet's hell, its tortures, fiends, and flames,
To this were trifles, toys, and empty names.
With foolish pride my heart was never fired,
Nor the vain itch to admire or be admired:
I hoped for no commission from his grace;
I bought no benefice, I begged no place;
Had no new verses nor new suit to show,
Yet went to court!—the devil would have it so,
But as the fool that in reforming days
Would go to mass in jest (as story says),
Could not but think to pay his fine was odd,
Since 'twas no form'd design of serving God,
So was I punished, as if full as proud,
As prone to ill, as negligent of good,
As deep in debt, without a thought to pay,
As vain, as idle, and as false, as they
Who live at court, for going once that way!

SATIRE IV.

Well; I may now receive and die. My sin
Indeed is great, but yet I have been in
A purgatory, such as feared hell is
A recreation, and scant map of this.
My mind neither with pride's itch, nor hath been
Poisoned with love to see or to be seen.
I had no suit there, nor new suit to show,
Yet went to court: but as Glare, which did go
To mass in jest, catched, was fain to disburse
Two hundred marks, which is the statute's curse,
Before he 'scaped; so it pleased my destiny
(Guilty of my sin of going) to think me
As prone to all ill, and of good as forget-
ful, as proud, lustful, and as much in debt,
As vain, as witless, and as false as they
Which dwell in court, for once going that way.

Scarce was I entered, when, behold! there came
A thing which Adam had been posed to name;
Noah had refused it lodging in his ark,
Where all the race of reptiles might embark:
A verier monster than on Afric's shore
The sun e'er got, or slimy Nilus bore,
Or Sloane or Woodward's wondrous shelves contain;
Nay, all that lying travellers can feign.
The watch would hardly let him pass at noon,
At night would swear him dropp'd out of the moon:
One whom the mob, when next we find or make
A popish plot, shall for a Jesuit take,
And the wise justice, starting from his chair,
Cry, By your priesthood, tell me what you are?
 Such was the wight: the apparel on his back,
Tho' coarse, was reverend, and tho' bare, was black:
The suit, if by the fashion one might guess,
Was velvet in the youth of good Queen Bess,
But mere tufftaffety what now remained;
So time, that changes all things, had ordained!
Our sons shall see it leisurely decay,
First turn plain rash, then vanish quite away.
This thing has travelled, speaks each language too,
And knows what's fit for every state to do;
Of whose best phrase and courtly accent joined
He forms one tongue, exotic and refined.

 Therefore I suffered this. Towards me did run
A thing more strange than on Nile's slime the sun
E'er bred, or all which into Noah's ark came;
A thing which would have posed Adam to name:
Stranger than seven antiquaries' studies,
Than Africk monsters, Guianaes rarities;
Stranger than strangers; one who, for a Dane,
In the Danes' massacre had sure been slain,
If he had lived then, and without help dies
When next the 'prentices 'gainst strangers rise:
One whom the watch at noon lets scarce go by;
One to whom the examining justice sure would cry,
Sir, by your priesthood, tell me what you are?
His cloaths were strange, though coarse, and black,
 though bare;
Sleeveless his jerkin was, and it had been
Velvet, but 'twas now (so much ground was seen)
Become tufftaffety; and our children shall
See it plain rash a while, then nought at all.
The thing hath travail'd, and, faith, speaks all tongues,
And only knoweth what to all states belongs;
Made of the accent and best phrase of all these,
He speaks one language. If strange meats displease,

Talkers I've learned to bear; Morteux I knew,
Henley himself I've heard, and Budgell too,
The doctor's wormwood style, the hash of tongues
A pedant makes, the storm of Gonson's lungs,
The whole artillery of the terms of war,
And (all those plagues in one) the bawling bar:
These I could bear; but not a rogue so civil
Whose tongue will compliment you to the devil—
A tongue that can cheat widows, cancel scores,
Make Scots speak treason, cozen subtlest whores,
With royal favourites in flattery vie,
And Oldmixon and Burnet both outlie.
He spies me out; I whisper, 'Gracious God!
What sin of mine could merit such a rod?
That all the shot of dulness now must be
From this thy blunderbuss discharged on me?'
'Permit,' he cries, 'no stranger to your fame,
To crave your sentiment, if —— 's your name.
What speech esteem you most?' 'The king's,' said I.
'But the best words?'—'O, Sir, the dictionary.'
'You miss my aim; I mean the most acute,
And perfect speaker.'—'Onslow, past dispute.'
'But, Sir, of writers?'—'Swift for closer style,
But Hoadly for a period of a mile.'
'Why, yes, 'tis granted, these indeed may pass;
Good common linguists, and so Panurge was;

Art can deceive or hunger force my taste;
But pedants' motley tongue, soldiers' bombast,
Mountebanks' drug-tongue, nor the terms of law,
Are strong enough preparatives to draw
Me to hear this; yet I must be content
With his tongue, in his tongue called complement;
In which he can win widows, and pay scores,
Make men speak treason, cozen subtlest whores,
Out-flatter favourites, or outlie either
Jovius or Surius, or both together.
He names me, and comes to me: I whisper, 'God!
How have I sinned, that thy wrath's furious rod,
This fellow chooseth me?' He saith, 'Sir,
I love your judgment; whom do you prefer
For the best linguist?' and I seelily
Said, that I thought Calepine's Dictionary.
'Nay, but of men? most sweet Sir!' Beza, then,
Some Jesuits, and two reverend men
Of our two academies, I named. Here
He stopp'd me, and said: 'Nay, your apostles were
Good pretty linguists; so Panurgus was,
Yet a poor gentleman; all these may pass

Nay, troth, the apostles (though perhaps too rough)
Had once a pretty gift of tongues enough:
Yet these were all poor gentlemen! I dare
Affirm 'twas travel made them what they were.'
  Thus others' talents having nicely shown,
He came by sure transition to his own;
Till I cried out, 'You prove yourself so able,
Pity you was not Druggerman at Babel:
For had they found a linguist half so good,
I make no question but the tower had stood.'
  'Obliging Sir! for courts you sure were made,
Why then for ever buried in the shade?
Spirits like you should see and should be seen;
The king would smile on you—at least the queen.'
'Ah, gentle Sir! your courtiers so cajole us—
But Tully has it, Nunquam minus solus:
And as for courts, forgive me if I say,
No lessons now are taught the Spartan way.
Though in his pictures lust be full displayed,
Few are the converts Aretine has made;
And though the court show vice exceeding clear,
None should, by my advice, learn virtue there.'
  At this entranced, he lifts his hands and eyes,
Squeaks like a high-stretched lutestring, and replies:
'Oh, 'tis the sweetest of all earthly things
To gaze on princes, and to talk of kings!'
'Then happy man who shows the tombs!' said I;
'He dwells amidst the royal family;
He every day from king to king can walk—
Of all our Harries, all our Edwards talk,

By travail.' Then, as if he would have sold
His tongue he praised it, and such wonders told,
That I was fain to say, 'If you had lived, Sir,
Time enough to have been interpreter
To Babel's bricklayers, sure the tower had stood.'
He adds, 'If of court-life you knew the good,
You would leave loneness.' I said, 'Not alone
My loneness is; but Spartanes fashion;
To teach by painting drunkards, doth not last
Now; Aretine's pictures have made few chaste;
No more can princes' courts, though there be few
Better pictures of vice, teach me virtue.'
He, like to a high-stretched lutestring squeaks, 'O, Sir
'Tis sweet to talk of kings.' 'At Westminster,'
Said I, 'the man that keeps the abbey tombs,
And for his price doth, with whoever comes,
Of all our Harrys and our Edwards talk,
From king to king, and all their kin, can walk:

And yet, by speaking truth of monarchs dead,
What few can of the living, ease and bread.'
'Lord, Sir, a mere mechanic! strangely low,
And coarse of phrase—your English all are so.
How elegant your Frenchmen!' 'Mine, d'ye mean
I have but one, I hope the fellow's clean.'
'Oh! Sir, politely so! nay, let me die,
Your only wearing is your paduasoy.'
'Not, Sir, my only; I have better still,
And this you see is but my deshabille—'
Wild to get loose, his patience I provoke,
Mistake, confound, object at all he spoke:
But as coarse iron, sharpened, mangles more,
And itch most hurts when angered to a sore;
So when you plague a fool, 'tis still the curse,
You only make the matter worse and worse.
He passed it o'er; affects an easy smile
At all my peevishness, and turns his style.
He asks, 'What news?' I tell him of new plays,
New eunuchs, harlequins, and operas.
He hears, and has a still, with simples in it,
Between each drop it gives, stays half a minute;
Loath to enrich me with too quick replies,
By little and by little drops his lies.
Mere household trash! of birthnights, balls, and shows
More than ten Holinsheds, or Halls, or Stows.

Your ears shall hear nought but kings; your eyes meet
Kings only, the way to it is King-street.'
He smacked and cried, 'He's base, mechanique coarse,
So are all your Englishmen in their discourse.
Are not your Frenchmen neat?' 'Mine, as you see,
I have but one, Sir; look, he follows me.'
'Certes, they're neatly cloathed. I of this mind am,
Your only wearing is your grogaram.'
'Not so, Sir; I have more.' Under this pitch
He would not fly. I chaffed him; but as itch
Scratched into smart, and as blunt iron ground
Into an edge hurts worse; so I (fool!) found
Crossing hurt me. To fit my sullenness,
He to another key his style doth dress,
And asks, 'What news?' I tell him of new playes:
He takes my hand, and as a still, which stayes
A sembrief 'twixt each drop, he niggardly,
As loath to enrich me, so tells many a ly.
More than ten Holinsheds, or Halls, or Stows,
Of trivial household trash he knows. He knows

When the queen frowned or smiled he knows, and what
A subtle minister may make of that:
Who sins, with whom; who got his pension rug,
Or quickened a reversion by a drug;
Whose place is quartered out three parts in four,
And whether to a bishop or a whore:
Who having lost his credit, pawned his rent,
Is therefore fit to have a government:
Who in the secret deals in stocks secure,
And cheats the unknowing widow and the poor:
Who makes a trust of charity a job,
And gets an act of parliament to rob:
Why turnpikes rise, and now no cit nor clown
Can gratis see the country or the town:
Shortly no lad shall chuck or lady vole,
But some excising courtier will have toll:
He tells what strumpet places sells for life,
What 'squire his lands, what citizen his wife:
At last (which proves him wiser still than all)
What lady's face is not a whited wall.
As one of Woodward's patients, sick and sore,
I puke, I nauseate—yet he thrusts in more;
Trims Europe's balance, tops the statesman's part,
And talks gazettes and postboys o'er by heart.
Like a big wife, at sight of loathsome meat,
Ready to cast, I yawn, I sigh, I sweat;

When the queen frowned or smiled; and he knows what
A subtle stateman may gather of that;
He knows who loves whom, and who by poison
Hastes to an officer's reversion:
Who wastes in meat, in cloaths, in horse he notes;
Who loves whores . . . .
He knows who hath sold his land, and now doth beg
A licence, old iron, boots, shoes, and egge-
Shells to transport. Shortly boys shall not play
At span-counter, or blow point, but shall pay
Toll to some courtier; and, wiser than all us,
He knows what lady is not painted. Thus
He with home meats cloyes me. I belch, spue, spit,
Look pale and sickly like a patient, yet
He thrusts on more; and as he had undertook
To say Gallo-Belgicus without book,
Speaks of all states and deeds that have been since
The Spaniards came to the loss of Amyens.
Like a big wife, at sight of loathed meat,
Ready to travail, so I sigh and sweat

Then as a licensed spy, whom nothing can
Silence or hurt, he libels every man;
Swears every place entailed for years to come
In sure succession to the day of doom:
He names the price for every office paid,
And says our wars thrive ill because delayed:
Nay, hints 'tis by connivance of the court
That Spain robs on, and Dunkirk's still a port.
Not more amazement seized on Circe's guests,
To see themselves fall headlong into beasts,
Than mine, to find a subject, stayed and wise,
Already half-turned traitor by surprise.
I felt the infection slide from him to me,
As in the pox some give it to get free;
And quick to swallow me methought I saw
One of our giant statutes ope its jaw.

To hear this makaron talk in vain; for yet,
Either my humour or his own to fit,
He, like a privileged spy, whom nothing can
Discredit, libels now 'gainst each great man.
He names a price of every office paid:
He saith, our wars thrive ill, because delaid;
That offices are entail'd, and that there are
Perpetuities of them lasting as far
As the last day, and that great officers
Do with the Spaniards share and Dunkirkers.
I, more amazed than Circe's prisoners, when
They felt themselves turn beasts, felt myself then
Becoming traytor, and methought I saw
One of our giant statutes ope its jaw
To suck me in for hearing him: I found,
That as burnt venomous leachers do grow sound
By giving others their sores, I might grow
Guilty, and he free: therefore I did show
All signs of loathing; but since I am in,
I must pay mine and my forefathers' sin
To the last farthing: therefore to my power
Toughly and stubbornly I bear this cross: but the hower
Of mercy now was come: he tries to bring
Me to pay a fine to 'scape a torturing,
And says, 'Sir, can you spare me?'—I said, 'Willingly.'
'Nay, Sir, can you spare me a crown?' Thankfully I
Gave it as ransom. But as fiddlers still,
Though they be paid to be gone, yet needs will
Thrust one more jigg upon you; so did he
With his long complimental thanks vex me

In that nice moment as another lie
Stood just a-tilt, the minister came by.
To him he flies, and bows, and bows again,
Then, close as Umbra, joins the dirty train.
Not Fannius' self more impudently near,
When half his nose is in his prince's ear.
I quaked at heart; and, still afraid to see
All the court filled with stranger things than he,
Ran out as fast as one that pays his bail,
And dreads more actions, hurries from a gaol.
Bear me, some god! oh! quickly bear me hence
To wholesome solitude, the nurse of sense,
Where Contemplation prunes her ruffled wings,
And the free soul looks down to pity kings!
There sober thought pursued the amusing theme,
Till fancy coloured it, and formed a dream.
A vision hermits can to hell transport,
And forced e'en me to see the damned at court.
Not Dante, dreaming all the infernal state,
Beheld such scenes of envy, sin, and hate.
Base fear becomes the guilty, not the free—
Suits tyrants, plunderers, but suits not me.
Shall I, the terror of this sinful town,
Care if a liveried lord or smile or frown?
Who cannot flatter, and detest who can,
Tremble before a noble-serving man?
O, my fair mistress, Truth! shall I quit thee,
For huffing, braggart, puft nobility?
Thou who, since yesterday, hast rolled o'er all
The busy idle blockheads of the ball,

But he is gone, thanks to his needy want,
And the prerogative of my crown. Scant
His thanks were ended, when I (which did see
All the court filled with more strange things than he)
Ran from thence with such or more haste than one
Who fears more actions doth haste from prison.
At home in wholesale solitariness
My piteous soul began the wretchedness
Of suitors at court to mourn, and a trance
Like his, who dreamt he saw hell, did advance
Itself o'er me: such men as he saw there
I saw at court, and worse, and more. Low fear
Becomes the guilty, not the accuser; then
Shall I, none's slave, of high-born or raised men
Fear frowns, and, my mistress, Truth! betray thee
For the huffing, bragart, puft nobility?
No, no; thou which since yesterday hast been
Almost about the whole world, hast thou seen,

Hast thou, oh sun! beheld an emptier sort
Than such as swell this bladder of a court?
Now pox on those that show a court in wax!
It ought to bring all courtiers on their backs;
Such painted puppets! such a varnished race
Of hollow gewgaws, only dress and face!
Such waxen noses, stately staring things—
No wonder some folks bow, and think them kings.
See! where the British youth, engaged no more
At Fig's, at White's, with felons, or a whore,
Pay their last duty to the court, and come
All fresh and fragrant to the drawing-room,
In hues as gay, and odours as divine,
As the fair fields they sold to look so fine.
'That's velvet for a king!' the flatterer swears;
'Tis true, for ten days hence 'twill be King Lear's.
Our court may justly to our stage give rules,
That helps it both to fools'-coats and to fools.
And why not players strut in courtiers' clothes?
For these are actors too as well as those.
Wants reach all states; they beg but better dress'd,
And all is splendid poverty at best.
Painted for sight, and essenced for the smell,
Like frigates fraught with spice and cochineal,
Sail in the ladies: how each pirate eyes
So weak a vessel and so rich a prize!

O Sun! in all thy journey, vanity,
Such as swells the bladder of our court? I
Think he which made your waxen garden, and
Transported it from Italy, to stand
With us at London, flouts our courtiers; for
Just such gay painted things, which no sap nor
Taste have in them, ours are; and natural
Some of the stocks are, their fruits bastard all.
'Tis ten a clock, and past: all whom the mues,
Baloun, or tennis, diet, or the stews
Had all the morning held, now the second
Time made ready, that day in stocks are found
In the presence, and I (God pardon me!)
As fresh and sweet their apparels be, as be
Their fields they sold to buy them. For a king
Those hoes are, cries the flatterer; and bring
Them next week to the theatre to sell,
Wants reach all states. Me seems they do as well
At stage, as courts: all are players. Whoe'er looks
(For themselves dare not go) o'er Cheapside books,
Shall .nd their wardrobes inventory. Now
The ladies come. As pirates, (which do know

Top-gallant he and she in all her trim,
He boarding her, she striking sail to him.
'Dear countess! you have charms all hearts to hit!
And, 'Sweet Sir Fopling! you have so much wit!'
Such wits and beauties are not praised for nought,
For both the beauty and the wit are bought.
'Twould burst e'en Heraclitus with the spleen
To see those antics, Fopling and Courtin:
The presence seems, with things so richly odd,
The mosque of Mahound, or some queer pagod.
See them survey their limbs by Durer's rules,
Of all beau kind the best-proportioned fools!
Adjust their clothes, and to confession draw
These venial sins, an atom, or a straw:
But, oh! what terrors must distract the soul
Convicted of that mortal crime, a hole?
Or should one pound of powder less bespread
Those monkey tails that wag behind their head;
Thus finished, and corrected to a hair,
They march, to prate their hour before the fair.
So first to preach a white-gloved chaplain goes,
With band of lily, and with cheek of rose,
Sweeter than Sharon, in immaculate trim,
Neatness itself impertinent in him.

That there came weak ships fraught with cutchanel)
The men board them, and praise (as they think) well,
Their beauties; they the mens wits: both are bought.
Why good wits ne'er wear scarlet gowns I thought
This cause, these men, mens wits for speeches buy,
And women buy all red which scarlets dye.
He call'd her beauty lime-twigs, her hair net:
She fears her drugs ill laid, her hair loose set.
Wouldn't Heraclitus laugh to see Macrine
From hat to shoe, himself at door refine,
As if the presence were a mosque; and lift
His skirts and hose, and call his clothes to shrift,
Making them confess not only mortal
Great stains and holes in them, but venial
Feathers and dust, wherewith they fornicate?
And then by Durer's rules survey the state
Of his each limb, and with strings the odds tries
Of his neck to his leg, and waist to thighs.
So in immaculate clothes and symmetry
Perfect as circles, with such nicety
As a young preacher at his first time goes
To preach, he enters, and a lady, which o

Let but the ladies smile, and they are bless'd:
Prodigious! how the things protest, protest,
Peace, fools! or Gonson will for papists seize you,
If once he catch you at your Jesu! Jesu!
  Nature made every fop to plague his brother,
Just as one beauty mortifies another.
But here 's the captain that will plague them both,
Whose air cries, Arm! whose very look's an oath.
The captain's honest, Sirs, and that's enough,
Though his soul's bullet, and his body buff:
He spits fore-right; his haughty chest before,
Like battering rams, beats open every door;
And with a face as red, and as awry,
As Herod's hang-dogs in old tapestry,
Scarecrows to boys, the breeding woman's curse,
Has yet a strange ambition to look worse;
Confounds the civil, keeps the rude in awe,
Jests like a licensed fool, commands like law.
  Frighted, I quit the room, but leave it so
As men from gaols to execution go;
For hung with deadly sins I see the wall,
And lined with giants deadlier than them all:
Each man an Askapart, of strength to toss
For quoits, both Temple-bar and Charing-cross.

Him not so much as good-will, he arrests,
And unto her, protests, protests, protests;
So much as at Rome would serve to have thrown
Ten cardinals into the Inquisition,
And whispers by Jesu so oft, that a
Persuevant would have ravished him away
For saying of Our Lady's Psalter. But 'tis fit
That they each other plague; they merit it.
But here comes glorious, that will plague 'em both,
Who in the other extreme only doth
Call a rough carelessness good fashion;
Whose cloak his spurs tear, or whom he spits on,
He cares not, he. His ill words do not harm
To him; he rushes in, as if Arm, arm!
He meant to cry; and though his face be as ill
As theirs which in old hangings whip Christ, still
He strives to look worse: he keeps all in awe;
Jests like a licensed fool, commands like law.
  Tired, now, I leave this place, and but pleased so
As men from gaols to execution go;
Go, through the great chamber, (why is it hung
With the seven deadly sins?) being among
Those Askaparts, men big enough to throw
Charing-cross for a bar, men that do know

Scared at the grisly forms, I sweat, I fly,
And shake all o'er, like a discovered spy.
Courts are too much for wits so weak as mine:
Charge them with Heaven's artillery, bold divine!
From such alone the great rebukes endure,
Whose satire 's sacred, and whose rage secure:
'Tis mine to wash a few light stains, but theirs
To deluge sin, and drop a court in tears.
Howe'er, what 's now Apocrypha, my wit,
In time to come, may pass for holy writ.

No token of worth but queen's man and fine
Living; barrels of beef and flagons of wine.
I shook like a spied spie. Preachers! which are
Seas of wit and art, you can, then dare
Drown the sins of this place; but as for me,
Which am but a scant brook, enough shall be
To wash the stains away. Although I yet
(With Maccabees' modesty) the known merit
Of my work lessen, yet some wise man shall,
I hope, esteem my writs Canonical.

EPILOGUE TO THE SATIRES.

IN TWO DIALOGUES.

[WRITTEN IN THE YEAR 1738.

DIALOGUE I.

Fr. Not twice a twelvemonth you appear in print
And when it comes the court see nothing in 't.
You grow correct that once with rapture writ,
And are, besides, too moral for a wit.
Decay of parts, alas! we all must feel!—
Why now, this moment, don't I see you steal?
'Tis all from Horace; Horace long before ye
Said 'Tories called him Whig, and Whigs a Tory;'
And taught his Romans, in much better metre,
'To laugh at fools who put their trust in Peter.'
But Horace, Sir, was delicate, was nice;
Bubo observes he lashed no sort of vice:
Horace would say, Sir Billy served the crown,
Blunt could do business, Higgins knew the town;
In Sappho touch the failings of the sex,
In reverend bishops note some small neglects,
And own the Spaniard did a waggish thing,
Who cropped our ears, and sent them to the king
His sly, polite, insinuating style
Could please at court, and make Augustus smile:
An artful manager, that crept between
His friend and shame, and was a kind of screen.
But faith, your very friends will soon be sore;
Patriots there are who wish you'd jest no more—
And where's the glory? 'twill be only thought
The great man never offered you a groat.
Go, see Sir Robert--

P. See Sir Robert! hum—
And never laugh—for all my life to come?
See him I have; but in his happier hour
Of social pleasure, ill-exchanged for power;
Seen him, uncumbered with a venal tribe,
Smile without art, and win without a bribe.
Would he oblige me? let me only find
He does not think me what he thinks mankind.
Come, come, at all I laugh he laughs, no doubt;
The only difference is—I dare laugh out.
F. Why, yes: with scripture still you may be free,
A horse-laugh, if you please, at honesty,
A joke on Jekyll, or some odd old Whig,
Who never changed his principle or wig.
A patriot is a fool in every age,
Whom all lord chamberlains allow the stage:
These nothing hurts; they keep their fashion still
And wear their strange old virtue as they will.
If any ask you, 'Who's the man so near
His prince that writes in verse, and has his ear?'
Why, answer Lyttleton! and I'll engage
The worthy youth shall ne'er be in a rage;
But were his verses vile, his whisper base,
You'd quickly find him in lord Fanny's case.
Sejanus, Wolsey, hurt not honest Fleury,
But well may put some statesman in a fury.
Laugh then at any but at fools or foes:
These you but anger, and you mend not those.
Laugh at your friends, and if your friends are sore,
So much the better, you may laugh the more.
To vice and folly to confine the jest
Sets half the world, God knows, against the rest,
Did not the sneer of more impartial men
At sense and virtue balance all again.
Judicious wits spread wide the ridicule,
And charitably comfort knave and fool.
P. Dear Sir, forgive the prejudice of youth:
Adieu distinction, satire, warmth, and truth!
Come, harmless characters that no one hit;
Come, Henley's oratory, Osborne's wit!
The honey dropping from Favonia's tongue,
The flowers of Bubo, and the flow of Young!
The gracious dew of pulpit eloquence,
And all the well-whipped cream of courtly sense;
The first was H—vy's, F—'s next, and then
The S—te's, and then H—vy's once again.
O come! that easy Ciceronian style,
So Latin, yet so English all the while.
As, though the pride of Middleton and Bland,
All boys may read and girls may understand!

Then might I sing without the least offence,
And all I sung should be the nation's sense;
Or teach the melancholy muse to mourn,
Hang the sad verse on Carolina's urn,
And hail her passage to the realms of rest.
All parts performed, and all her children bless'd,
So—satire is no more—I feel it die—
No gazetteer more innocent than I,
And let, a God's name! ev'ry fool and knave
Be graced through life, and flattered in his grave.
F. Why so? if satire knows its time and place,
You still may lash the greatest—in disgrace;
For merit will by turns forsake them all;
Would you know when? exactly when they fall.
But let all satire in all changes spare
Immortal S—k, and grave De—re.
Silent and soft, as saints remove to heaven,
All ties dissolved, and ev'ry sin forgiven,
These may some gentle ministerial wing
Receive, and place for ever near a king!
There, where no passion, pride or shame, transport,
Lulled with the sweet nepenthe of a court;
There, where no father's, brother's, friend's disgrace
Once break their rest, or stir them from their place;
But past the sense of human miseries,
All tears are wiped for ever from all eyes;
No cheek is known to blush, no heart to throb,
Save when they lose a question, or a job.
P. Good heaven forbid, that I should blast their glory,
Who know how like Whig ministers to Tory,
And when three sovereigns died could scarce be vex'd,
Considering what a gracious prince was next.
Have I, in silent wonder, seen such things
As pride in slaves and avarice in kings?
And at a peer or peeress shall I fret,
Who starves a sister, or forswears a debt!
Virtue, I grant you, is an empty boast;
But shall the dignity of vice be lost?
Ye Gods! shall Cibber's son, without rebuke,
Swear like a lord, or Rich outwhore a duke?
A favourite porter with his master vie,
Be bribed as often, and as often lie?
Shall Ward draw contracts with a statesman's skill?
Or Japhet pocket, like his grace, a will?
Is it for Bond or Peter (paltry things)
To pay their debts, or keep their faith like kings?
If Blount dispatched himself, he played the man,
And so mayst thou, illustrious Passeran!
But shall a printer, weary of his life,
Learn, from their books, to hang himself and wife?

This, this, my friend, I cannot, must not, bear;
Vice thus abused demands a nation's care;
This calls the church to deprecate our sin,
And hurls the thunder of the laws on gin.
Let modest Foster, if he will, excel
Ten metropolitans in preaching well;
A simple Quaker, or a Quaker's wife,
Outdo Landaffe in doctrine—yea, in life:
Let humble Allen, with an awkward shame,
Do good by stealth, and blush to find it fame.
Virtue may choose the high or low degree,
'Tis just alike to Virtue and to me;
Dwell in a monk, or light upon a king,
She 's still the same beloved contented thing.
Vice is undone if she forgets her birth,
And stoops from angels to the dregs of earth:
But 'tis the fall degrades her to a whore;
Let greatness own her, and she 's mean no more:
Her birth, her beauty, crowds and courts confess,
Chaste matrons praise her, and grave bishops bless;
In golden chains the willing world she draws,
And hers the gospel is, and hers the laws;
Mounts the tribunal, lifts her scarlet head,
And sees pale virtue carted in her stead.
Lo! at the wheels of her triumphal car
Old England's Genius, rough with many a scar,
Dragged in the dust! his arms hang idly round.
His flag inverted trails along the ground!
Our youth, all liveried o'er with foreign gold,
Before her dance; behind her crawl the old!
See thronging millions to the pagod run,
And offer country, parent, wife, or son!
Hear her black trumpet through the land proclaim,
That not to be corrupted is the shame.
In soldier, churchman, patriot, man in power,
'Tis av'rice all, ambition is no more.
See all our nobles begging to be slaves!
See all our fools aspiring to be knaves!
The wit of cheats, the courage of a whore,
Are what ten thousand envy and adore:
All, all look up, with reverential awe,
At crimes that 'scape or triumph o'er the law:
While truth, worth, wisdom, daily they decry—
'Nothing is sacred now but villany.'
Yet may this verse (if such a verse remain,
Show there was one who held it in disdain

DIALOGUE II.

Fr. 'Tis all a libel--Paxton, sir, will say.
P. Not yet, my friend! to-morrow, 'faith it may,
And for that very cause I print to-day.
How should I fret to mangle every line
In reverence to the sins of thirty-nine?
Vice with such giant strides comes on amain,
Invention strives to be before in vain;
Feign what I will, and paint it e'er so strong,
Some rising genius sins up to my song.
F. Yet none but you by name the guilty lash;
E'en Guthry saves half Newgate by a dash.
Spare then the person, and expose the vice.
P. How, sir! not damn the sharper, but the dice
Come on then, satire! general, unconfined,
Spread thy broad wing, and souse on all the kind.
Ye statesmen, priests, of one religion all!
Ye tradesmen, vile in army, court, or hall!
Ye reverend atheists. F. Scandal! name them; who?
P. Why that's the thing you bid me not to do.
Who starved a sister, who forswore a debt,
I never named; the town 's inquiring yet.
The poisoning dame—F. You mean—P. I don't—F.
You do.
P. See now I keep the secret, and not you!
The bribing statesman—F. Hold, too high you go!
P. The bribed elector—F. There you stoop too low.
P. I fain would please you if I knew with what:
Tell me which knave is lawful game, which not?
Must great offenders, once escaped the Crown,
Like royal harts, be never more run down?
Admit your law to spare the knight requires,
As beasts of nature may we hunt the squires?
Suppose I censure—you know what I mean—
To save a bishop may I name a dean?
F. A dean, sir? no: his fortune is not made;
You hurt a man that's rising in the trade
P. If not the tradesman, who set up to-day,
Much less the 'prentice, who to-morrow may.
Down, down, proud satire! though a realm be spoil'd,
Arraign no mightier thief than wretched Wild;
Or, if a court or country 's made a job,
Go drench a pickpocket, and join the mob.

But, sir, I beg you (for the love of vice!)
The matter 's weighty, pray consider twice:
Have you less pity for the needy cheat,
The poor and friendless villain, than the great?
Alas! the small descredit of a bribe
Scarce hurts the lawyer, but undoes the scribe.
Then better sure it charity becomes
To tax directors, who (thank God!) have plums;
Still better ministers, or if the thing
May pinch e'en there—Why lay it on a king.
F. Stop! stop!
P. Must satire then nor rise nor fall?
Speak out, and bid me blame no rogues at all.
F. Yes, strike that Wild, I'll justify the blow.
P. Strike? why, the man was hanged ten years ago:
Who now that obsolete example fears?
E'en Peter trembles only for his ears.
F. What, always Peter? Peter thinks you mad:
You make men desperate if they once are bad,
Else might he take to virtue some years hence—
P. As S—k, if he lives, will love the prince.
F. Strange spleen to S—k!
P. Do I wrong the man?
God knows, I praise a courtier where I can.
When I confess there is who feels for fame,
And melts to goodness, need I Scarb'row name?
Pleased let me own, in Esher's peaceful grove,
(Where Kent and nature vie for Pelham's love,)
The scene, the master opening to my view,
I sit and dream I see my Craggs anew!
E'en in a bishop I can spy desert;
Secker is decent, Rundel has a heart;
Manners with candour are to Benson given,
To Berkley every virtue under heaven.
But does the court a worthy man remove?
That instant I declare he has my love:
I shun his zenith, court his mild decline;
Thus Somers once and Halifax were mine.
Oft, in the clear still mirror of retreat,
I studied Shrewsbury, the wise and great;
Carleton's calm sense and Stanhope's noble flame
Compared, and knew their generous end the same:
How pleasing Atterbury's softer hour!
How shined the soul, unconquered, in the tower!
How can I Pulteney, Chesterfield, forget,
While Roman spirit charms, and Attic wit?
Argyle, the state's whole thunder born to wield,
And shake alike the senate and the field?
Or Wyndham, just to freedom and the throne,
The master of our passions and his own?

Names which I long have loved, nor loved in vain,
Ranked with their friends, nor numbered with their
train;
And if yet higher the proud list should end,
Still let me say, no follower, but a friend.
Yet think nor friendship only prompts my lays;
I follow virtue; where she shines I praise,
Point she to priest or elder, Whig or Tory,
Or round a Quaker's beaver cast a glory.
I never, to my sorrow I declare,
Dined with the Man of Ross or my lord mayor.
Some in their choice of friends—nay, look not grave,
Have still a secret bias to a knave:
To find an honest man I beat about,
And love him, court him, praise him, in or out.
F. Then why so few commended?
P. Not so fierce:
Find you the virtue, and I'll find the verse.
But random praise—the task can ne'er be done;
Each mother asks it for her booby son,
Each widow asks it for the best of men,
For him she weeps, for him she weds again.
Praise cannot stoop, like satire, to the ground;
The number may be hanged, but not be crowned.
Enough for half the greatest of these days
To escape my censure, not expect my praise.
Are they not rich? what more can they pretend?
Dare they to hope a poet for their friend?
What Richelieu wanted Louis scarce could gain,
And what young Ammon wished, but wished in vain.
No power the muse's friendship can command;
No power, when virtue claims it, can withstand.
To Cato, Virgil paid one honest line;
O let my country's friends illumine mine!
—What are you thinking? F. Faith, the thought 's no
I think your friends are out, and would be in. [sin;
P. If merely to come in, sir, they go out,
The way they take is strangely round about.
F. They too may be corrupted, you'll allow?
P. I only call those knaves who are so now.
Is that too little? come, then, I'll comply—
Spirit of Arnall! aid me while I lie.
Cobham 's a coward, Polwarth is a slave,
And Lyttleton a dark designing knave;
St. John has ever been a wealthy fool—
But let me add, Sir Robert's mighty dull,
Has never made a friend in private life,
And was, besides, a tyrant to his wife.
But pray, when others praise him do I blame?
Call Verres, Wolsey, any odious name?

Why rail they then if but a wreath of mine,
Oh, all-accomplished St. John! deck thy shrine!
What! shall each spur-galled hackney of the day,
When Paxton gives him double pots and pay,
Or each new-pensioned sycophant pretend
To break my windows if I treat a friend,
Then wisely plead to me they meant no hurt,
But 'twas my guest at whom they threw the dirt?
Sure if I spare the minister, no rules
Of honour bind me not to maul his tools;
Sure if they cannot cut, it may be said,
His saws are toothless, and his hatchets lead.
It ang'red Turenne, once upon a day,
To see a footman kicked that took his pay;
But when he heard the affront the fellow gave,
Knew one a man of honour, one a knave,
The prudent general turned it to a jest,
And begged he'd take the pains to kick the rest;
Which not at present having time to do—
F. Hold, sir! for God's sake; where's the affront to you?
Against your worship when had S—k writ?
Or P—ge poured forth the torrent of his wit?
Or grant the bard whose distich all commend
[In power a servant, out of power a friend]
To W—le guilty of some venial sin,
What's that to you, who ne'er was out nor in
The priest whose flattery bedropped the crown,
How hurt he you? he only stained the gown.
And how did, pray, the florid youth offend,
Whose speech you took, and gave it to a friend?
P. Faith, it imports not much from whom it came;
Whoever borrowed could not be to blame,
Since the whole house did afterwards the same
Let courtly wits to wits afford supply,
As hog to hog in huts of Westphaly:
If one, through nature's bounty, or his lord's,
Has what the frugal dirty soil affords,
From him the next receives it, thick or thin,
As pure a mess almost as it came in;
The blessed benefit, not there confined,
Drops to the third, who nuzzles close behind;
From tail to mouth they feed and they carouse;
The last full fairly gives it to the house.
F. This filthy similie, this beastly line,
Quite turns my stomach—P. So does flattery mine;
And all your courtly civet-cats can vent,
Perfume to you, to me is excrement.
But hear me further—Japhet, 'tis agreed,
Writ not, and Chartres scarce could write or read;

I all the courts of Pindus guiltless quite;
But pens can forge, my friend, that cannot write;
And must no egg in Japhet's face be thrown,
Because the deed he forged was not my own?
Must never patriot then declaim at gin,
Unless, good man! he has been fairly in?
No zealous pastor blame a failing spouse
Without a staring reason on his brows?
And each blasphemer quite escape the rod,
Because the insult 's not on man, but God?
Ask you what provocation I have had?
The strong antipathy of good to bad.
When truth or virtue an affront endures,
The affront is mine, my friend, and should be yours
Mine, as a foe professed to false pretence,
Who think a coxcomb's honour like his sense
Mine, as a friend to every worthy mind;
And mine as man, who feel for all mankind.
F. You're strangely proud.
P. So proud, I am no slave;
So impudent, I own myself no knave:
So odd, my country's ruin makes me grave.
Yes, I am proud; I must be proud to see
Men not afraid of God, afraid of me;
Safe from the bar, the pulpit, and the throne,
Yet touched and shamed by ridicule alone.
O sacred weapon! left for truth's defence,
Sole dread of folly, vice, and insolence!
To all but heaven-directed hands denied,
The muse may give thee, but the gods must guide.
Reverend I touch thee! but with honest zeal,
To rouse the watchmen of the public weal,
To virtue's work provoke the tardy hall,
And goad the prelate slumbering in his stall.
Ye tinsel insects! whom a court maintains,
That counts your beauties only by your stains,
Spin all your cobwebs o'er the eye of day,
The muse's wing shall brush you all away:
All his grace preaches, all his lordship sings,
All that makes saints of queens and gods of kings;
All, all but truth, drops dead-born from the press,
Like the last Gazette or the last address.
When black ambition stains a public cause,
A monarch's sword when mad vain glory draws,
Not Waller's wreath can hide the nation's scar,
Not Boileau turn the feather to a star.
Not so when diademed with rays divine,
Touched with the flame that breaks from virtue's shrine,
Her priestess muse forbids the good to die,
And opes the temple of eternity.

There other trophies deck the truly brave
Than such as Anstis casts into the grave;
Far other stars than * and ** wear,
And may descend to Mordington from Stair!
[Such as on Hough's unsullied mitre shine,
Or beam, good Digby, from a heart like thine,]
Let envy howl, while heaven's whole chorus sings,
And bark at honour not conferred by kings;
Let flattery sickening see the incense rise,
Sweet to the world, and grateful to the skies:
Truth guards the poet, sanctifies the line,
And makes immortal verse as mean as mine.
Yes, the last pen for freedom let me draw,
When truth stands trembling on the edge of law.
Here, last of Britons! let your names be read:
Are none, none living! let me praise the dead;
And for that cause which made your fathers shine,
Fall by the votes of their degenerate line.
F. Alas! alas! pray end what you began,
And write next winter more Essays on Man.

EPISTLES.

EPISTLE TO DR. ARBUTHNOT,

BEING THE PROLOGUE TO THE SATIRES.

ADVERTISEMENT.

THIS paper is a sort of bill of complaint, begun many years since and drawn up by snatches as the several occasions offered. I had no thoughts of publishing it, till it pleased some persons of rank and fortune [the authors of Verses to the Imitator of Horace, and of an Epistle to a Doctor of Divinity from a Nobleman at Hampton-Court] to attack in a very extraordinary manner, not only my writings (of which being public, the public is judge), but my person, morals, and family; whereof, to those who know me not, a truer information may be requisite. Being divided between the necessity to say something of myself, and my own laziness to undertake so awkward a task, I thought it the shortest way to put the last hand to this Epistle. If it have anything pleasing, it will be that by which I am most desirous to please, the truth and the sentiment; and if anything offensive, it will be only to those I am least sorry to offend, the vicious or the ungenerous

Many will know their own pictures in it, there being not a circumstance but what is true; but I have, for the most part, spared their names, and they may escape being laughed at if they please.

I would have some of them to know it was owing to the request of the learned and candid friend to whom it is inscribed, that I make not as free use of theirs as they have done of mine. However, I shall have this advantage and honour on my side, that whereas, by their proceeding, any abuse may be directed at any man, no injury can possibly be done by mine, since a nameless character can never be found out but by its truth and likeness.—POPE.

P. SHUT, shut the door, good John! fatigued, I said;
Tie up the knocker; say I'm sick, I'm dead.
The dog-star rages! nay, 'tis past a doubt,
All Bedlam or Parnassus is let out:
Fire in each eye, and papers in each hand,
They rave, recite, and madden round the land.
What walls can guard me, or what shades can hide?
They pierce my thickets, through my grot they glide;

By land, by water, they renew the charge,
They stop the chariot and they board the barge.
No place is sacred, not the church is free,
E'en Sunday shines no sabbath-day to me.
Then from the Mint walks forth the man of rhyme,
Happy to catch me just at dinner-time.
Is there a parson much bemused in beer
A maudlin poetess, a rhyming peer,
A clerk foredoomed his father's soul to cross
Who pens a stanza when he should engross?
Is there who, locked from ink and paper, scrawls
With desperate charcoal round his darkened walls?
All fly to Twit'nam, and in humble strain
Apply to me to keep them mad or vain.
Arthur, whose giddy son neglects the laws,
Imputes to me and my damned works the cause:
Poor Cornus sees his frantic wife elope,
And curses wit, and poetry, and Pope.
Friend to my life! (which, did not you prolong,
The world had wanted many an idle song,)
What drop or nostrum can this plague remove?
Or which must end me, a fool's wrath or love?
A dire dilemma! either way I'm sped:
If foes, they write; if friends, they read me dead.
Seized and tied down to judge, how wretched I!
Who can't be silent, and who will not lie.
To laugh, were want of goodness and of grace;
And to be grave, exceeds all power of face.
I sit with sad civility, I read
With honest anguish, and an aching head,
And drop at last, but in unwilling ears,
This saving council, "Keep your peace nine years.'
"Nine years!" cries he, who high in Drury Lane
Lulled by soft zephyrs through the broken pane,
Rhymes ere he wakes, and prints before term ends,
Obliged by hunger and request of friends:
"The piece, you think, is incorrect? why take it;
I'm all submission; what you have it—make it."
Three things another's modest wishes bound,
My friendship, and a prologue, and ten pound.
Pitholeon sends to me; "You know his grace;
I want a patron; ask him for a place."
Pitholeon libelled me—"But here's a letter
Informs you, Sir, 'twas when he knew no better.
Dare you refuse him? Curll invite to dine;
He'll write a journal, or he'll turn divine."
Bless me! a packet.—"'Tis a stranger sues,
A virgin tragedy, an orphan muse."
If I dislike it, "Furies, death and rage!"
If I approve, "Commend it to the stage."

There (thank my stars) my whole commission ends;
The players and I are, luckily, no friends.
Fired that the house rejects him, "'Sdeath, I'll print it,
And shame the fools—Your interest, Sir, with Lintot."
Lintot, dull rogue! will think your price too much:
"Not, Sir, if you revise it, and retouch."
All my demurs but double his attacks;
At last he whispers, "Do, and we go snacks."
Glad of a quarrel, straight I clap the door;
"Sir, let me see your works and you no more."
'Tis sung, when Midas' ears began to spring,
(Midas, a sacred person and a king,)
His very minister, who spied them first,
(Some say his queen,) was forced to speak or burst.
And is not mine, my friend, a sorer case,
When every coxcomb perks them in my face? [things,
A Good friend! forbear; you deal in dangerous
I'd never name queens, ministers, or kings;
Keep close to ears, and those let asses prick,
'Tis nothing.—P. Nothing! if they bite and kick?
Out with it, Dunciad! let the secret pass,
That secret to each fool, that he's an ass:
The truth once told, (and wherefore should we lie?)
The Queen of Midas slept, and so may I.
You think this cruel? take it for a rule,
No creature smarts so little as a fool.
Let peals of laughter, Codrus, round thee break,
Thou unconcerned canst hear the mighty crack:
Pit, box, and gallery in convulsions hurl'd,
Thou stand'st unshook amidst a bursting world.
Who shames a scribbler? break one cobweb through,
He spins the slight self-pleasing thread anew:
Destroy his fib, or sophistry, in vain;
The creature's at his dirty work again,
Throned on the centre of his thin designs,
Proud of a vast extent of flimsy lines!
Whom have I hurt? has poet yet or peer
Lost the arch'd eyebrow or Parnassian sneer?
And has not Colly still his lord and whore?
His butchers Henley, his free-masons Moore?
Does not one table Bavius still admit?
Still to one Bishop Phillips seem a wit?
Still Sappho—A. Hold! for God's sake, you'll offend;
No names—be calm—learn prudence of a friend
I too could write, and I am twice as tall;
But foes like these—P. One flatterer 's worse than all.
Of all mad creatures, if the learned are right,
It is the slaver kills, and not the bite.
A fool quite angry is quite innocent:
Alas! 'tis ten times worse when they repent.

One dedicates in high heroic prose,
And ridicules beyond a hundred foes:
One from all Grub Street will my fame defend,
And more abusive calls himself my friend.
This prints my letters, that expects a bribe,
And others roar aloud, "Subscribe, subscribe!"
There are who to my person pay their court:
I cough like Horace, and, though lean, am short
Ammon's great son one shoulder had too high,
Such Ovid's nose, and, "Sir, you have an eye—"
Go on, obliging creatures! make me see
All that disgraced my betters met in me.
Say, for my comfort, languishing in bed,
"Just so immortal Maro held his head:"
And when I die, be sure you let me know
Great Homer died three thousand years ago.
Why did I write? what sin to me unknown
Dipped me in ink, my parents', or my own?
As yet a child, nor yet a fool to fame,
I lisped in numbers, for the numbers came:
I left no calling for this idle trade,
No duty broke, no father disobeyed:
The muse but served to ease some friend, not wife—
To help me through this long disease, my life,
To second, Arbuthnot! thy art and care,
And teach the being you preserved to bear.
But why then publish? Granville, the polite,
And knowing Walsh, would tell me I could write;
Well-natured Garth inflamed with early praise,
And Congreve loved, and Swift endured, my lays;
The courtly Talbot, Somers, Sheffield, read,
E'en mitred Rochester would nod the head,
And St. John's self (great Dryden's friend before)
With open arms received one poet more.
Happy my studies when by these approved!
Happier their author, when by these beloved!
From these the world will judge of men and books;
Not from the Burnets, Oldmixons, and Cooks.
Soft were my numbers; who could take offence,
While pure description held the place of sense?
Like gentle Fanny's was my flowery theme,
A painted mistress, or a purling stream.
Yet then did Gildon draw his venal quill;
I wish'd the man a dinner, and sat still:
Yet then did Dennis rave in furious fret;
I never answered; I was not in debt.
If want provoked, or madness made them print,
I waged no war with Bedlam or the Mint.
Did some more sober critic come abroad;
If wrong, I smiled; if right, I kiss the rod.

Pains, reading, study, are their just pretence,
And all they want is spirit, taste, and sense.
Commas and points they set exactly right,
And 'twere a sin to rob them of their mite;
Yet ne'er one sprig of laurel graced these ribbalds,
From flashing Bentley down to piddling Tibbalds:
Each wight who reads not, and but scans and spells,
Each word-catcher, that lives on syllables,
E'en such small critics some regard may claim,
Preserved in Milton's or in Shakespeare's name.
Pretty! in amber to observe the forms
Of hairs, or straws, or dirt, or grubs, or worms!
The things, we know, are neither rich nor rare,
But wonder how the devil they got there.
Were others angry; I excused them too;
Well might they rage, I gave them but their due.
A man's true merit 'tis not hard to find;
But each man's secret standard in his mind,
That casting weight pride adds to emptiness
This who can gratify? for who can guess?
The bard whom pilfered pastorals renown,
Who turns a Persian tale for half-a-crown,
Just writes to make his barrenness appear,
And strains from hard-bound brains eight lines a-year
He who still wanting, though he lives on theft,
Steals much, spends little, yet has nothing left;
And he who now to sense, now nonsense, leaning,
Means not, but blunders round about a meaning;
And he whose fustian 's so sublimely bad,
It is not poetry, but prose run mad:
All these my modest satire bade translate,
And owned that nine such poets made a Tate.
How did they fume, and stamp, and roar, and chafe!
And swear not Addison himself was safe.
Peace to all such! But were there one whose fires
True genius kindles, and fair fame inspires,
Blessed with each talent, and each art to please,
And born to write, converse, and live with ease;
Should such a man, too fond to rule alone,
Bear, like the Turk, no brother near the throne;
View him with scornful yet with jealous eyes,
And hate for arts that caused himself to rise;
Damn with faint praise, assent with civil leer,
And without sneering teach the rest to sneer;
Willing to wound, and yet afraid to strike;
Just hint a fault, and hesitate dislike;
Alike reserved to blame, or to commend;
A timorous foe, and a suspicious friend;
Dreading e'en fools; by flatterers besieged,
And so obliging that he ne'er obliged;

Like Cato give his little senate laws,
And sit attentive to his own applause;
While wits and templars every sentence raise,
And wonder with a foolish face of praise—
Who but must laugh if such a man there be!
Who would not weep if Atticus were he!
What though my name stood rubric on the walls
Or plastered posts, with claps, in capitals?
Or smoking forth, a hundred hawkers' load,
On wings of winds came flying all abroad?
I sought no homage from the race that write;
I kept, like Asian monarchs, from their sight:
Poems I heeded (now berhymed so long)
No more than thou, great George; a birthday song;
I ne'er with wits or witlings passed my days,
To spread about the itch of verse and praise;
Nor like a puppy daggled through the town
To fetch and carry sing-song up and down;
Nor at rehearsals sweat, and mouthed, and cried,
With handkerchief and orange at my side;
But, sick of fops, and poetry, and prate,
To Bufo left the whole Castalian state.
Proud as Apollo on his forked hill
Sat full-blown Bufo, puffed by every quill;
Fed with soft dedication all day long,
Horace and he went hand in hand in song
His library (where busts of poets dead
And a true Pindar stood without a head)
Received of wits an undistinguished race,
Who first his judgment asked, and then a place:
Much they extolled his pictures, much his seat,
And flattered every day, and sometimes ate;
Till grown more frugal in his riper days,
He paid some bards with port, and some with praise,
To some a dry rehearsal was assigned,
And others (harder still) he paid in kind.
Dryden alone (what wonder?) came not nigh;
Dryden alone escaped this judging eye:
But still the great have kindness in reserve,
He helped to bury whom he helped to starve.
May some choice patron bless each grey-goose quill!
May every Bavius have his Bufo still!
So when a statesman wants a day's defence,
Or envy holds a whole week's war with sense,
Or simple pride for flattery makes demands,
May dunce by dunce be whistled off my hands!
Blessed be the great! for those they take away,
And those they left me—for they left me Gay;
Left me to see neglected genius bloom,
Neglected die, and tell it on his tomb:

Of all thy blameless life the sole return
My verse, and Queensberry weeping o'er thy urn
Oh! let me live my own, and die so too!
(To live and die is all I have to do;)
Maintain a poet's dignity and ease,
And see what friends, and read what books, I please;
Above a patron, though I condescend
Sometimes to call a minister my friend.
I was not born for courts or great affairs;
I pay my debts, believe, and say my prayers;
Can sleep without a poem in my head,
Nor know if Dennis be alive or dead.
Why am I asked what next shall see the light?
Heavens! was I born for nothing but to write?
Has life no joys for me? or (to be grave)
Have I no friend to serve, no soul to save?
'I found him close with Swift'—'Indeed? no doubt,'
Cries prating Balbus, 'something will come out.'
'Tis all in vain, deny it as I will;
'No such a genius never can lie still;'
And then for mine obligingly mistakes,
The first lampoon Sir Will or Bubo makes.
Poor guiltless I! and can I choose but smile,
When every coxcomb knows me by my style?
Cursed be the verse, how well soe'er it flow,
That tends to make one worthy man my foe,
Give virtue scandal, innocence a fear,
Or from the soft-eyed virgin steal a tear!
But he who hurts a harmless neighbour's peace
Insults fallen worth, or beauty in distress,
Who loves a lie, lame slander helps about,
Who writes a libel, or who copies out;
That fop whose pride affects a patron's name,
Yet absent wounds an author's honest fame;
Who can your merit selfishly approve,
And show the sense of it without the love;
Who has the vanity to call you friend,
Yet wants the honour, injured, to defend;
Who tells whate'er you think, whate'er you say,
And if he lie not, must at least betray;
Who to the dean and silver bell can swear,
And sees at Cannons what was never there;
Who reads but with a lust to misapply,
Makes satire a lampoon, and fiction lie;
A lash like mine no honest man shall dread,
But all such babbling blockheads in his stead.
Let Sporus tremble—A. What? that thing of silk,
Sporus! that mere white curd of ass's milk?
Satire or sense, alas! can Sporus feel!
Who breaks a butterfly upon a wheel?

P. Yet let me flap this bug with gilded wings,
This painted child of dirt, that stinks and stings;
Whose buzz the witty and the fair annoys,
Yet wit ne'er tastes, and beauty ne'er enjoys.
So well-bred spaniels civilly delight
In mumbling of the game they dare not bite.
Eternal smiles his emptiness betray,
As shallow streams run dimpling all the way.
Whether in florid impotence he speaks,
And as the prompter breathes, the puppet squeaks;
Or at the ear of Eve, familiar toad,
Half froth, half venom, spits himself abroad,
In puns, or politics, or tales, or lies,
Or spite, or smut, or rhymes, or blasphemies:
His wit all see-saw, between that and this,
Now high, now low, now master up, now miss,
And he himself one vile antithesis.
Amphibious thing! that acting either part,
The trifling head or the corrupted heart;
Fop at the toilette, flatterer at the board,
Now trips a lady, and now struts a lord.
Eve's tempter thus the Rabbins have expressed,
A cherub's face, a reptile all the rest;
Beauty that shocks you, parts that none will trust
Wit that can creep, and pride that licks the dust.
  Not fortune's worshipper nor fashion's fool,
Not lucre's madman nor ambition's tool,
Not proud nor servile, be one poet's praise,
That if he pleased he pleased by manly ways;
That flattery, e'en to kings, he held a shame,
And thought a lie in verse or prose the same;
That not in fancy's maze he wandered long,
But stooped to truth, and moralised his song;
That not for fame, but virtue's better end,
He stood the furious foe, the timid friend,
The damning critic, half-approving wit,
The coxcomb hit, or fearing to be hit;
Laughed at the loss of friends he never had,
The dull, the proud, the wicked, and the mad
The distant threats of vengeance on his head,
The blow unfelt, the tear he never shed;
The tale revived, the lie so oft o'erthrown,
The imputed trash and dulness not his own;
The morals blackened when the writings 'scape,
The libelled person, and the pictured shape;
Abuse on all he loved, or loved him spread,
A friend in exile, or a father dead;
The whisper that, to greatness still too near,
Perhaps yet vibrates on his sovereign's ear—

Welcome for thee, fair virtue! all the past;
For thee, fair virtue! welcome e'en the last!
A. But why insult the poor, affront the great?
P. A knave 's a knave to me in ev'ry state;
Alike my scorn if he succeed or fail,
Sporus at court, or Japhet in a jail;
A hireling scribbler or a hireling peer,
Knight of the post corrupt, or of the shire,
If on a pillory, or near a throne,
He gain his prince's ear, or lose his own.
Yet soft by nature, more a dupe than wit,
Sappho can tell you how this man was bit:
This dreaded satirist Dennis will confess
Foe to his pride, but friend to his distress:
So humble, he has knocked at Tibbald's door,
Has drunk with Cibber; nay, has rhymed for Moore.
Full ten years slandered, did he once reply?
Three thousand suns went down on Welsted's lie.
To please a mistress one aspersed his life;
He lashed him not, but let her be his wife:
Let Budgell charge low Grub Street on his quill,
And write whate'er he pleased, except his will;
Let the two Curlls of town and court abuse
His father, mother, body, soul, and muse:
Yet why? that father held it for a rule
It was a sin to call our neighbour fool;
That harmless mother thought no wife a whore;
Hear this, and spare his family, James Moore!
Unspotted names, and memorable long!
If there be force in virtue or in song.
Of gentle bloods (part shed in honour's cause,
While yet in Britain honour had applause)
Each parent sprung—A. What fortune, pray?—
P. Their own;
And better got than Bestia's from the throne.
Born to no pride, inheriting no strife,
Nor marrying discord in a noble wife,
Stranger to civil and religious rage,
The good man walked innoxious through his age:
No courts he saw, no suits would ever try,
Nor dared an oath, nor hazarded a lie.
Unlearned, he knew no schoolman's subtle art,
No language but the language of the heart.
By nature honest, by experience wise,
Healthy by temp'rance and by exercise;
His life, though long, to sickness past unknown;
His death was instant, and without a groan.
O grant me thus to live, and thus to die!
Who sprung from kings shall know less joy than I.

Oh, friend! may each domestic bliss be thine!
Be no unpleasing melancholy mine:
Me let the tender office long engage
To rock the cradle of reposing age,
With lenient arts extend a mother's breath,
Make languor smile, and smooth the bed of death,
Explore the thought, explain the asking eye,
And keep a while one parent from the sky!
On cares like these, if length of days attend,
May Heaven, to bless those days, preserve my friend,
Preserve him social, cheerful and serene,
And just as rich as when he served a queen.
A. Whether that blessing be denied or given,
Thus far was right, the rest belongs to Heaven.

EPISTLE TO ROBERT EARL OF OXFORD

AND LORD MORTIMER.

Sent to the Earl of Oxford, with Dr. Parnell's Poems, published by our Author, after the said Earl's Imprisonment in the Tower and Retreat into the Country, in the Year 1721.

Such were the notes thy once-loved poet sung,
Till death untimely stopp'd his tuneful tongue.
Oh, just beheld and lost! admired and mourn'd!
With softest manners, gentlest heart, adorn'd!
Bless'd in each science! bless'd in every strain!
Dear to the muse! to Harley dear—in vain!
For him thou oft hast bid the world attend,
Fond to forget the statesman in the friend;
For Swift and him despised the farce of state,
The sober follies of the wise and great;
Dexterous the craving, fawning crowd to quit
And pleased to 'scape from flattery to wit.
Absent or dead, still let a friend be dear,
(A sigh the absent claims, the dead a tear,)
Recall those nights that closed thy toilsome days,
Still hear thy Parnell in his living lays,
Who, careless now of interest, fame, or fate,
Perhaps forgets that Oxford e'er was great;

Or, deeming meanest what we greatest call,
Beholds thee glorious only in thy fall.
  And sure, if aught below the seats divine
Can touch immortals, 'tis a soul like thine;
A soul supreme, in each hard instance tried,
Above all pain, and passion, and all pride,
The rage of power, the blast of public breath,
The lust of lucre, and the dread of death.
  In vain to deserts thy retreat is made,
The muse attends thee to thy silent shade:
'Tis hers the brave man's latest steps to trace,
Rejudge his acts, and dignify disgrace.
When interest calls off all her sneaking train,
And all the obliged desert, and all the vain,
She waits, or to the scaffold or the cell,
When the last lingering friend has bid farewell.
E'en now she shades thy evening walk with bays,
(No hireling she, no prostitute to praise,)
E'en now, observant of the parting ray,
Eyes the calm sunset of thy various day;
Through fortune's cloud one truly great can see
Nor fears to tell that Mortimer is he.

EPISTLE TO JAMES CRAGGS, ESQ.

SECRETARY OF STATE, IN THE YEAR 1720.

A SOUL as full of worth as void of pride,
Which nothing seeks to shew or needs to hide,
Which nor to guilt nor fear its caution owes,
And boasts a warmth that from no passion flows;
A face untaught to feign; a judging eye,
That darts severe upon a rising lie,
And strikes a blush through frontless flattery.
All this thou wert; and being this before,
Know, kings and fortune cannot make thee more.
Then scorn to gain a friend by servile ways,
Nor wish to lose a foe these virtues raise;
But candid, free, sincere, as you began,
Proceed—a minister, but still a man.
Be not (exalted to whate'er degree)
Ashamed of any friend, not e'en of me:
The patriot's plain but untrod path pursue;
If not, 'tis I must be ashamed of you.

EPISTLE TO MR. JERVAS

WITH MR. DRYDEN'S TRANSLATION OF FRESNOY'S ART OF PAINTING.

This verse be thine, my friend! nor thou refuse
This, from no venal or ungrateful muse.
Whether thy hand strike out some free design,
Where life awakes, and dawns at every line,
Or blend in beauteous tints the colour'd mass,
And from the canvass call the mimic face;
Read these instructive leaves, in which conspire
Fresnoy's close art, and Dryden's native fire;
And reading, wish, like theirs, our fate and fame,
So mix'd our studies, and so join'd our name;
Like them to shine through long-succeeding age;
So just thy skill, so regular thy rage.
Smit with the love of sister arts we came,
And met congenial, mingling flame with flame;
Like friendly colours found them both unite,
And each from each contract new strength and light.
How oft in pleasing tasks we wear the day,
While summer suns roll unperceived away—
How oft our slowly-growing works impart,
While images reflect from art to art!
How oft review, each finding, like a friend,
Something to blame, and something to commend!
What flattering scenes our wandering fancy wrought
Rome's pompous glories rising to our thought!
Together o'er the Alps, methinks we fly,
Fired with ideas of fair Italy.
With thee on Raphael's monument I mourn
Or wait inspiring dreams at Maro's urn;
With thee repose where Tully once was laid,
Or seek some ruin's formidable shade.
While fancy brings the vanish'd piles to view,
And builds imaginary Rome anew,
Here thy well-studied marbles fix our eye,
A fading fresco here demands a sigh:
Each heavenly piece unwearied we compare,
Match Raphael's grace with thy loved Guido's air,
Caracci's strength, Corregio's softer line,
Paulo's free stroke, and Titian's warmth divine.
How finish'd with illustrious toil appears
This small well-polish'd gem, the work of years!

Yet still how faint by precept is express'd
The living image in the painter's breast!
Thence endless streams of fair ideas flow,
Strike in the sketch, or in the picture glow;
Thence beauty, waking all her forms, supplies
An angel's sweetness, or Bridgewater's eyes.
  Muse! at that name thy sacred sorrow shed,
Those tears eternal that embalm the dead;
Call round her tomb each object of desire,
Each purer frame inform'd with purer fire;
Bid her be all that cheers or softens life,
The tender sister, daughter, friend, and wife;
Bid her be all that makes mankind adore,
Then view this marble, and be vain no more!
  Yet still her charms in breathing paint engage,
Her modest cheek shall warm a future age.
Beauty, frail flower! that every season fears,
Blooms in thy colours for a thousand years.
Thus Churchill's race shall other arts surprise,
And other beauties envy Worsley's eyes;
Each pleasing Blount shall endless smiles bestow
And soft Belinda's blush for ever glow.
  Oh! lasting as those colours may they shine!
Free as thy stroke, yet faultless as thy line;
New graces yearly like thy works display,
Soft without weakness, without glaring gay;
Led by some rule that guides, but not constrains,
And finish'd more through happiness than pains:
The kindred arts shall in their praise conspire,
One dip the pencil, and one string the lyre.
Yet should the graces all thy figures place,
And breathe an air divine on every face;
Yet should the muses bid my numbers roll
Strong as their charms, and gentle as their soul;
With Zeuxis' Helen thy Bridgewater vie,
And these be sung till Granville's Myra die:
Alas! how little from the grave we claim!
Thou but preserves a face, and I a name.

EPISTLE TO MISS BLOUNT

WITH THE WORKS OF VOITURE, 1717.

In these gay thoughts the loves and graces shine,
And all the writer lives in every line;
His easy art may happy nature seem;
Trifles themselves are elegant in him.
Sure to charm all was his peculiar fate,
Who without flattery pleased the fair and great;
Still with esteem no less conversed than read;
With wit well-natured, and with books well-bred:
His heart, his mistress and his friend did share;
His time, the muse, the witty, and the fair.
Thus wisely careless, innocently gay,
Cheerfully he play'd the trifled life away,
Till fate scarce felt his gentle breath suppress'd,
As smiling infants sport themselves to rest.
E'en rival wits did Voiture's death deplore,
And the gay mourn'd, who never mourn'd before;
The truest hearts for Voiture heaved with sighs;
Voiture was wept by all the brightest eyes:
The smiles and loves had died in Voiture's death,
But that for ever in his lines they 've breath.
  Let the strict life of graver mortals be
A long, exact, and serious comedy;
In every scene some moral let it teach,
And, if it can, at once both please and preach:
Let mine an innocent gay farce appear,
And more diverting still than regular;
Have humour, wit, a native ease and grace,
Though not too strictly bound to time and place.
Critics in wit or life are hard to please;
Few write to those, and none can live to these.
  Too much your sex is by their forms confined,
Severe to all, but most to womankind;
Custom, grown blind with age, must be your guide;
Your pleasure is a vice, but not your pride:
By nature yielding, stubborn but for fame,
Made slaves by honour, and made fools by shame.
Marriage may all those petty tyrants chase,
But sets up one, a greater, in their place:
Well might you wish for change by those accursed,
But the last tyrant ever proves the worst.
Still in constraint your suffering sex remains,
Or bound in formal or in real chains:

Whole years neglected for some months adored,
The fawning servant turns a haughty lord.
Ah! quit not the free innocence of life
For the dull glory of a virtuous wife;
Nor let false shews nor empty titles please:
Aim not at joy, but rest content with ease.
The gods, to curse Pamelia with her prayers,
Gave the gilt coach and dappled Flanders mares,
The shining robes, rich jewels, beds of state,
And, to complete her bliss, a fool for mate.
She glares in balls, front boxes, and the ring,
A vain, unquiet, glittering, wretched thing!
Pride, pomp, and state, but reach her outward part;
She sighs, and is no duchess at her heart.
But, Madam, if the fates withstand, and you
Are destined Hymen's willing victim too,
Trust not too much your now resistless charms,—
Those, age or sickness, soon or late, disarms;
Good humour only teaches charms to last,
Still makes new conquests, and maintains the past.
Love raised on beauty will, like that, decay;
Our hearts may bear its slender chain a day,
As flowery bands in wantonness are worn,
A morning's pleasure, and at evening torn;
This binds in ties more easy, yet more strong,
The willing heart, and only holds it long.
Thus Voiture's early care still shone the same,*
And Monthausier was only changed in name:
By this e'en now they live, e'en now they charm,
Their wit still sparkling, and their flames still warm.
Now crown'd with myrtle on the Elysian coast,
Amid those lovers, joys his gentle ghost;
Pleased while with smiles his happy lines you view,
And finds a fairer Rambouillet in you.
The brightest eyes in France inspired his muse;
The brightest eyes in Britain now peruse;
And dead, as living, 'tis our author's pride
Still to charm those who charm the world beside.

* Mademoiselle Paulet.

EPISTLE TO THE SAME,

ON HER LEAVING THE TOWN AFTER THE CORONATION, 1715.

As some fond virgin, whom her mother's care
Drags from the town to wholesome country air,
Just when she learns to roll a melting eye,
And hear a spark, yet think no danger nigh,
From the dear man unwilling she must sever,
Yet takes one kiss before she parts for ever;
Thus from the world fair Zephalinda flew,
Saw others happy, and with sighs withdrew;
Not that their pleasures caused her discontent;
She sigh'd not that they stay'd, but that she went.
She went to plain work, and to purling brooks,
Old-fashion'd halls, dull aunts, and croaking rooks:
She went from opera, park, assembly, play,
To morning walks, and prayers three hours a-day;
To part her time 'twixt reading and bohea,
To muse, and spill her solitary tea,
Or o'er cold coffee trifle with the spoon,
Count the slow clock, and dine exact at noon;
Divert her eyes with pictures in the fire,
Hum half a tune, tell stories to the squire;
Up to her godly garret after seven,
There starve and pray, for that 's the way to heaven.
Some squire, perhaps, you take delight to rack,
Whose game is whist, whose treat a toast in sack;
Who visits with a gun, presents you birds,
Then gives a smacking buss, and cries—No words!
Or with his hounds comes hallooing from the stable,
Makes love with nods, and knees beneath a table;
Whose laughs are hearty, though his jests are coarse,
And loves you best of all things—but his horse.
In some fair evening, on your elbow laid,
You dream of triumphs in the rural shade;
In pensive thought recall the fancied scene,
See coronations rise on every green;
Before you pass the imaginary sights
Of lords, and earls, and dukes, and garter'd knights,
While the spread fan o'ershades your closing eyes,
Then give one flirt, and all the vision flies.
Thus vanish sceptres, coronets and balls,
And leave you in lone woods or empty walls!

So when your slave, at some dear idle time,
(Not plagued with headaches or the want of rhyme,
Stands in the streets abstracted from the crew,
And while he seems to study, thinks of you;
Just when his fancy paints your sprightly eyes,
Or sees the blush of soft Parthenia rise,
Gay pats my shoulder, and you vanish quite,
Streets, chairs, and coxcombs, rush upon my sight
Vex'd to be still in town, I knit my brow,
Look sour, and hum a tune, as you may now

EPISTLE TO MR. MOORE.

AUTHOR OF THE CELEBRATED WORM-POWDER.

How much, egregious Moore! are we
  Deceived by shows and forms!
Whate'er we think, whate'er we see,
  All human-kind are worms.

Man is a very worm by birth,
  Vile reptile, weak, and vain!
Awhile he crawls upon the earth,
  Then shrinks to earth again

That woman is a woman we find
  E'er since our grandam's evil;
She first conversed with her own kind,
  That ancient worm the devil.

The learn'd themselves we book-worms name,
  The blockhead is a slow-worm;
The nymph whose tail is all on flame,
  Is aptly term'd a glow-worm.

The fops are painted butterflies,
  That flutter for a day;
First from a worm they take their rise,
  And in a worm decay.

The flatterer an ear-wig grows;
  Thus worms suit all conditions;
Misers are muck-worms, silkworms beaus,
  And death-watches physicians.

34*

That statesmen have the worm, is seen
  By all their winding play;
Their conscience is a worm within,
  That gnaws them night and day.

Ah, Moore! thy skill were well employ'd,
  And greater gain would rise,
If thou couldst make the courtier void
  The worm that never dies!

O learned friend of Abchurch-lane,
  Who sett'st our entrails free;
Vain is thy art, thy powder vain,
  Since worms shall eat e'en thee.

Our fate thou only canst adjourn
  Some few short years, no more!
E'en Button's wits to worms shall turn,
  Who maggots were before

EPISTLE TO MRS M. B.

ON HER BIRTHDAY.

Oh! be thou bless'd with all that Heaven can send,
Long health, long youth, long pleasure, and a friend;
Not with those toys the female world admire,
Riches that vex, and vanities that tire.
With added years, if life bring nothing new,
But like a sieve let every blessing through,
Some joys still lost, as each vain year runs o'er,
And all we gain, some sad reflection more:
Is that a birthday? 'tis, alas! too clear,
'Tis but the funeral of the former year.
  Let joy or ease, let affluence or content,
And the gay conscience of a life well spent,
Calm every thought, inspirit every grace,
Glow in thy heart, and smile upon thy face.
Let day improve on day, and year on year,
Without a pain, a trouble, or a fear,
Till death, unfelt, that tender frame destroy
In some soft dream, or ecstasy of joy,
Peaceful sleep out the sabbath of the tomb,
And wake to raptures in a life to come.

EPISTLE TO MR. THOMAS SOUTHERN,

ON HIS BIRTHDAY, 1742.

RESIGN'D to live, prepared to die,
With not one sin but poetry,
This day Tom's fair account has run
(Without a blot) to eighty-one.
Kind Boyle, before his poet, lays
A table with a cloth of bays;
And Ireland, mother of sweet singers,
Presents her harp still to his fingers.
The feast his towering genius marks
In yonder wild-goose and the larks!
The mushrooms show his wit was sudden!
And for his judgment, lo, a pudden!
Roast beef, though old, proclaims him stout
And grace, although a bard, devout.
May Tom, whom Heaven sent down to raise
The price of prologues and of plays,
Be every birthday more a winner,
Digest his thirty-thousandth dinner;
Walk to his grave without reproach,
And scorn a rascal and a coach.

PASTORALS;

WITH A

DISCOURSE ON PASTORAL POETRY.

[WRITTEN IN THE YEAR 1704; POPE BEING THEN 16.]

THERE are not, I believe, a greater number of any sort of verses than of those which are called Pastorals, nor a smaller than of those which are truly so. It therefore seems necessary to give some account of this kind of Poem; and it is my design to comprise, in this short paper, the substance of those numerous dissertations the critics have made on the subject, without omitting any of their rules in my own favour: you will also find some points reconciled about which they seem to differ, and a few remarks which I think have escaped their observation.

The original of poetry is ascribed to that age which succeeded the creation of the world; and as the keeping of flocks seems to have been the first employment of mankind, the most ancient sort of poetry was probably Pastoral. It is natural to imagine, that the leisure of those ancient shepherds admitting and inviting some diversion, none was so proper to that solitary and sedentary life as singing; and that in their songs they took occasion to celebrate their own felicity. From hence a poem was invented, and afterwards improved to a perfect image of that happy time; which, by giving us an esteem for the virtues of a former age, might recommend them to the present. And since the life of shepherds was attended with more tranquillity than any other rural employment, the poets chose to introduce their persons, from whom it received the name of Pastoral.

A Pastoral is an imitation of the action of a shepherd, or one considered under that character. The form of this imitation is dramatic, or narrative, or mixed of both; the fable is simple; the manners not too polite nor too rustic: the thoughts are plain, yet admit a little quickness and passion, but that short and flowing: the expression humble, yet as pure as the language will afford; neat, but not florid; easy, and yet lively. In short, the fable, manners, thoughts, and expressions, are full of the greatest simplicity in nature.

The complete character of this Poem consists in simplicity, brevity, and delicacy; the two first of which render an eclogue natural, and the last delightful.

If we could copy Nature, it may be useful to take this idea along with us, that Pastoral is an image of what they call the Golden Age: so that we are not to describe our shepherds as shepherds at this day really are, but as they may be conceived then to have been, when the best of men followed the employment. To carry this resemblance yet further, it would not be amiss to give these shepherds some skill in astronomy, as far as it may be useful to that sort of life: and an air of piety to the gods should shine through the poem, which so visibly appears in all the works of antiquity; and it ought to preserve some relish of the old way of writing: the connexion should be loose, the narrations and descriptions short, and the periods concise. Yet it is not sufficient that the sentences only be brief; the whole eclogue should be so too: for we cannot suppose poetry in those days to have been the business of men, but their recreation at vacant hours.

But, with a respect to the present age, nothing more conduces to make these composures natural, than when some knowledge in rural affairs is discovered. This may be made to appear rather done by chance than on design, and sometimes is best shown by inference; lest, by too much study to seem natural, we destroy that easy simplicity from whence arises the delight. For what is inviting in this sort of poetry, proceeds not so much from the idea of that business, as of the tranquillity of a country life.

We must therefore use some illusion to render a Pastoral delightful; and this consists in exposing the best side only of a shepherd's life, and in concealing its miseries. Nor is it enough to introduce shepherds discoursing together in a natural way; but a regard must be had to the subject; that it contains some particular beauty in itself, and that it be different in every eclogue. Besides, in each of them a designed scene or prospect is to be presented to our view, which should likewise have its variety. This variety is obtained, in a great degree, by frequent comparisons, drawn from the most agreeable objects of the country; by interrogations to things inanimate; by beautiful digressions, but those short; sometimes by insisting a little on circumstances; and lastly, by elegant turns on the words, which render the numbers extremely sweet and pleasing. As for the numbers themselves, though they are properly of the heroic measure, they should be the smoothest, the most easy and flowing imaginable.

It is by rules like these that we ought to judge of Pastoral: and since the instructions given for any art are to be delivered as that art is in perfection, they must of necessity be derived from those in whom it is acknowledged so to be. It is therefore from the practice of Theocritus and Virgil (the only undisputed authors of Pastoral) that the critics have drawn the foregoing notions concerning it.

Theocritus excels all others in nature and simplicity. The subjects of his Idyllia are purely Pastoral; but he is not so exact in his persons, having introduced reapers and fishermen as well as shepherds. He is apt to be too long in his descriptions, of which that of the Cup, in the first Pastoral, is a remarkable instance. In the manners he seems a little defective; for his swains are sometimes abusive and immodest, and perhaps too much inclining to rusticity: for instance, in his Fourth and Fifth Idyllia. But it is enough that all others learned their excellencies from him, and that his dialect alone has a secret charm in it, which no other could ever attain.

Virgil, who copies Theocritus, refines upon his original; and in all points where judgment is principally concerned, he is much superior to his master. Though some of his subjects are not pastoral in themselves, but only seem to be such, they have a wonderful variety in them, which the Greek was a stranger to. He exceeds him in regularity and brevity, and falls short of him in nothing but simplicity and propriety of style; the first of which, perhaps, was the fault of his age, and the last, of his language.

Among the moderns, their success has been greatest who have most endeavoured to make these ancients their pattern. The most considerable genius appears in the famous Tasso and our Spenser. Tasso, in his Aminta, has as far excelled all the pastoral writers, as, in his Gierusalemme, he has outdone the epic poets of his country. But as this piece seems to have been the original of a new sort of poem, the Pastoral Comedy, in Italy, it cannot so well be considered as a copy of the ancients. Spenser's Calendar, in Mr. Dryden's opinion, is the most complete work of this kind which any nation has produced ever since the time of Virgil. Not but that he may be thought imperfect in some few points. His eclogues are somewhat too long, if we compare them with the ancients: he is sometimes too allegorical, and treats of matters of religion in a pastoral style, as the Mantuan had done before him. He has employed the Lyric measure, which is contrary to the practice of the old poets. His stanza is not still the same, nor always well chosen. This last may be the reason his expression is sometimes not concise enough; for the Tetrastic has obliged him to extend his sense to the length of four lines, which would have been more closely confined in the couplet.

In the manners, thoughts, and characters, he comes near to Theocritus himself; though, notwithstanding all the care he has taken, he is certainly inferior in his dialect: for the Doric had its beauty and propriety in the time of Theocritus; it was used in part of Greece, and frequent in the mouths of many of the greatest persons: whereas the old English and country phrases of Spenser were either entirely obsolete, or spoken only by people of the lowest condition. As there is a difference betwixt simplicity and rusticity, so the expression of simple thoughts should be plain, but not clownish. The addition he has made of a calendar to his eclogues is very beautiful; since by this, besides the general moral of innocence and simplicity, which is common to other authors of Pastoral, he has one peculiar to himself: he compares human life to the several seasons, and at once exposes to his readers a view of the great and little worlds, in their various changes and aspects. Yet the scrupulous division of his Pastorals into months, has obliged him either to repeat the same description in other words, for three months together; or, when it was exhausted before, entirely to omit it: whence it comes to pass that some of his eclogues (as the sixth, eighth, and tenth, for example) have nothing but their titles to distinguish them. The reason is evident, because the year has not that variety in it to furnish every month with a particular description, as it may every season.

Of the following eclogues I shall only say, that these four comprehend all the subjects which the critics upon Theocritus and Virgil will allow to be fit for Pastoral; that they have as much variety of description, in respect of the several seasons, as Spenser's; that, in order to add to this variety, the several times of the day are observed, the rural employments in each season or time of day, and the rural scenes or places proper to such employments; not without some regard to the several ages of man, and the different passions proper to each age.

But, after all, if they have any merit, it is to be attributed to some good old authors, whose works, as I had leisure to study, so, I hope, I have not wanted care to imitate.

PASTORALS.

'RING.

TO SIR WILLIAM TRUMBALL.

First in these fields I try the sylvan strains,
Nor blush to sport on Windsor's blissful plains:
Fair Thames! flow gently from thy sacred spring,
While on thy banks Sicilian muses sing;
Let vernal airs through trembling osiers play,
And Albion's cliffs resound the rural lay.
You that, too wise for pride, too good for pow'r,
Enjoy the glory to be great no more,
And carrying with you all the world can boast
To all the world illustriously are lost!
O let my Muse her slender reed inspire,
Till in your native shades you tune the lyre:
So when the nightingale to rest removes,
The thrush may chant to the forsaken groves,
But charm'd to silence, listens while she sings,
And all the aërial audience clap their wings.
Soon as the flocks shook off the nightly dews,
Two swains, whom love kept wakeful, and the muse,
Pour'd o'er the whitening vale their fleecy care,
Fresh as the morn, and as the season fair:
The dawn now blushing on the mountain's side,
Thus Daphnis spoke, and Strephon thus replied:
Daph. Hear how the birds on every bloomy spray
With joyous music wake the dawning day!
Why sit we mute, when early linnets sing,
When warbling Philomel salutes the spring?
Why sit we sad, when Phosphor shines so clear,
And lavish Nature paints the purple year?
Streph. Sing then, and Damon shall attend the strain,
While yon slow oxen turn the furrow'd plain.
Here the bright crocus and blue vi'let glow;
Here western winds on breathing roses blow.
I'll stake yon lamb, that near the fountain plays,
And from the brink his dancing shade surveys.

DAPH. And I this bowl, where wanton ivy twines,
And swelling clusters bend the curling vines:
Four figures rising from the work appear,
The various seasons of the rolling year;
And what is that which binds the radiant sky,
Where twelve fair signs in beauteous order lie?
DAM. Then sing by turns, by turns the Muses sing,
Now hawthorns blossom, now the daisies spring;
Now leaves the trees, and flow'rs adorn the ground;
Begin, the vales shall ev'ry note rebound.
STREPH. Inspire me, Phœbus! in my Delia's praise,
With Waller's strains, or Granville's moving lays:
A milk white bull shall at your altar stand
That threats a fight, and spurns the rising sand.
DAPH. O Love! for Sylvia let me gain the prize,
And make my tongue victorious as her eyes:
No lambs or sheep for victims I'll impart;
Thy victim, Love, shall be the shepherd's heart.
STREPH. My gentle Delia beckons from the plain—
Then, hid in shades, eludes her eager swain;
But feigns a laugh to see me search around,
And by that laugh the willing fair is found.
DAPH. The sprightly Sylvia trips along the green;
She runs, but hopes she does not run unseen;
While a kind glance at her pursuer flies,
How much at variance are her feet and eyes!
STREPH. O'er golden sands let rich Pactolus flow,
And trees weep amber on the banks of Po;
Blest Thames' shores the brightest beauties yield:
Feed here my lambs, I'll seek no distant field.
DAPH. Celestial Venus haunts Idalia's groves;
Diana Cynthus, Ceres Hybla, loves:
If Windsor shades delight the matchless maid,
Cynthus and Hybla yield to Windsor shade.
STREPH. All nature mourns, the skies relent in show'rs,
Hush'd are the birds, and closed the drooping flow'rs;
If Delia smile, the flow'rs begin to spring,
The skies to brighten, and the birds to sing.
DAPH. All nature laughs, the groves are fresh and fair,
The sun's mild lustre warms the vital air;
If Sylvia smiles, new glories gild the shore,
And vanquish'd nature seems to charm no more.
STREPH. In spring the fields, in autumn hills, I love;
At morn the plains, at noon the shady grove:
But Delia always; absent from her sight,
Nor plains at morn nor groves at noon delight.
DAPH. Sylvia 's like autumn ripe, yet mild as May,
More bright than noon, yet fresh as early day:

E'en spring displeases when she shines not here;
But bless'd with her, 'tis spring throughout the year.
STREPH. Say, Daphnis, say, in what glad soil appears,
A wondrous tree, that sacred monarch bears?
Tell me but this, and I'll disclaim the prize,
And give the conquest to thy Sylvia's eyes.
DAPH. Nay, tell me first, in what more happy fields
The thistle springs, to which the lily yields;
And then a nobler prize I will resign;
For Sylvia, charming Sylvia, shall be thine.
DAM. Cease to contend: for, Daphnis, I decree
The bowl to Strephon, and the lamb to thee.
Blest swains, whose nymphs in ev'ry grace excel;
Blest nymphs, whose swains those graces sing so well!
Now rise, and haste to yonder woodbine bow'rs,
A soft retreat from sudden vernal show'rs;
The turf with rural dainties shall be crown'd,
While op'ning blooms diffuse their sweets around.
For see! the gath'ring flocks to shelter tend,
And from the Pleiads fruitful show'rs descend.

SUMMER.

TO DR. GARTH.

A SHEPHERD'S boy (he seeks no better name)
Led forth his flocks along the silver Thame,
Where dancing sun-beams on the waters play'd,
And verdant alders form'd a quiv'ring shade.
Soft as he mourn'd, the streams forgot to flow,
The flocks around a dumb compassion show,
And Naiads wept in ev'ry wat'ry bow'r,
And Jove consented in a silent show'r.
Accept, O Garth, the Muse's early lays,
That adds this wreath of ivy to thy bays;
Hear what from love unpractised hearts endure,
From love, the sole disease thou canst not cure.
Ye shady beeches, and ye cooling streams,
Defence from Phœbus', not from Cupid's, beams,
To you I mourn; nor to the deaf I sing;
The woods shall answer, and their echo ring.
The hills and rocks attend my doleful lay;
Why art thou prouder and more hard than they?

The bleating sheep with my complaints agree,
They parch'd with heat, and I inflamed by thee;
The sultry Sirius burns the thirsty plains,
While in thy heart eternal Winter reigns.
Where stray ye, Muses! in what lawn or grove,
While your Alexis pines in hopeless love?
In those fair fields where sacred Isis glides,
Or else where Cam his winding vales divides?
As in the crystal spring I view my face,
Fresh rising blushes paint the wat'ry glass;
But since those graces please thy eyes no more,
I shun the fountains which I sought before.
Once I was skill'd in ev'ry herb that grew,
And ev'ry plant that drinks the morning dew;
Ah, wretched shepherd, what avails thy art,
To cure thy lambs, but not to heal thy heart!
Let other swains attend the rural care,
Feed fairer flocks, or richer fleeces shear:
But nigh yon mountain let me tune my lays,
Embrace my love, and bind my brows with bays.
That flute is mine which Colin's tuneful breath
Inspired when living, and bequeath'd in death.
He said, Alexis, take this pipe, the same
That taught the groves my Rosalinda's name:
But now the reeds shall hang on yonder tree,
For ever silent, since despised by thee.
Oh! were I made, by some transforming power,
The captive bird that sings within thy bow'r!
Then might my voice thy list'ning ears employ,
And I those kisses he receives enjoy.
And yet my numbers please the rural throng;
Rough satyrs dance, and Pan applauds the song
The nymphs, forsaking every cave and spring,
Their early fruit and milk-white turtles bring!
Each am'rous nymph prefers her gifts in vain;
On you their gifts are all bestow'd again.
For you the swains the fairest flow'rs design,
And in one garland all their beauties join:
Accept the wreath which you deserve alone,
In whom all beauties are comprised in one.
See what delights in sylvan scenes appear!
Descending gods have found Elysium here.
In woods bright Venus with Adonis stray'd,
And chaste Diana haunts the forest-shade.
Come, lovely nymph, and bless the silent hours,
When swains from shearing seek their nightly bow'rs,
When weary reapers quit the sultry field,
And, crown'd with corn, their thanks to Ceres yield.
This harmless grove no lurking viper hides,
But in my breast the serpent Love abides.

Here bees from blossoms sip the rosy dew
But your Alexis knows no sweets but you.
Oh, deign to visit our forsaken seats,
The mossy fountains, and the green retreats!
Where'er you walk, cool gales shall fan the glade;
Trees, where you sit, shall crowd into a shade:
Where'er you tread, the blushing flow'rs shall rise,
And all things flourish where you turn your eyes.
Oh! how I long with you to pass my days,
Invoke the muses, and resound your praise!
Your praise the birds shall chant in ev'ry grove,
And winds shall waft it to the powers above.
But would you sing, and rival Orpheus' strain,
The wond'ring forest soon should dance again,
The moving mountains hear the pow'rful call,
And headlong streams hang list'ning in their fall!
 But see, the shepherds shun the noon-day heat,
The lowing herds to murm'ring brooks retreat,
To closer shades the panting flocks remove;
Ye Gods! and is there no relief for love?
But soon the sun with milder rays descends
To the cool ocean, where his journey ends:
On me Love's fiercer flames for ever prey;
By night he scorches, as he burns by day.

AUTUMN.

TO MR. WYCHERLEY.

Beneath the shade a spreading beech displays,
Hylas and Ægon sung their rural lays:
This mourn'd a faithless, that an absent love;
And Delia's name and Doris' fill'd the grove.
Ye Mantuan Nymphs, your sacred succour bring;
Hylas and Ægon's rural lays I sing.
 Thou whom the Nine with Plautus' wit inspire,
The art of Terence, and Menander's fire;
Whose sense instructs us, and whose humour charms,
Whose judgment sways us, and whose spirit warms;
Oh, skill'd in Nature! see the hearts of swains,
Their artless passions, and their tender pains.
 Now setting Phœbus shone serenely bright,
And fleecy clouds were streak'd with purple light;
When tuneful Hylas, with melodious moan,
Taught rocks to weep, and made the mountains groan

Go, gentle Gales, and bear my sighs away!
To Delia's ear the tender notes convey.
As some sad turtle his lost love deplores,
And with deep murmurs fills the sounding shores,
Thus, far from Delia, to the winds I mourn,
Alike unheard, unpitied, and forlorn.
Go, gentle Gales, and bear my sighs along!
For her, the feather'd choirs neglect their song;
For her, the limes their pleasing shades deny;
For her, the lilies hang their heads and die.
Ye flow'rs that droop, forsaken by the spring;
Ye birds that, left by summer, cease to sing;
Ye trees, that fade when autumn heats remove,
Say, is not absence death to those who love?
Go, gentle Gales, and bear my sighs away!
Cursed be the fields that cause my Delia's stay:
Fade ev'ry blossom, wither ev'ry tree,
Die ev'ry flow'r, and perish all but she.—
What have I said? Where'er my Delia flies,
Let spring attend, and sudden flow'rs arise!
Let op'ning roses knotted oaks adorn,
And liquid amber drop from ev'ry thorn.
Go, gentle Gales, and bear my sighs along!
The birds shall cease to tune their ev'ning song,
The winds to breathe, the waving woods to move,
And streams to murmur, ere I cease to love.
Not bubbling fountains to the thirsty swain,
Not balmy sleep to lab'rers faint with pain,
Not show'rs to larks, or sunshine to the bee,
Are half so charming as thy sight to me.
Go, gentle Gales, and bear my sighs away!
Come, Delia, come; ah, why this long delay?
Through rocks and caves the name of Delia sounds
Delia, each cave and echoing rock rebounds.
Ye Pow'rs, what pleasing frenzy soothes my mind!
Do lovers dream, or is my Delia kind?
She comes, my Delia comes!—Now cease my lay,
And cease, ye Gales, to bear my sighs away!
Next Ægon sung, while Windsor groves admired:
Rehearse, ye Muses, what yourselves inspired.
Resound, ye Hills, resound my mournful strain!
Of perjured Doris, dying I complain:
Here where the mountains, less'ning as they rise,
Lose the low vales, and steal into the skies;
While lab'ring oxen, spent with toil and heat,
In their loose traces from the field retreat;
While curling smokes from village-tops are seen,
And the fleet shades glide o'er the dusky green.
Resound, ye Hills, resound my mournful lay!
Beneath yon poplar oft we pass'd the day:

Oft on the rind I carved her am'rous vows,
While she with garlands hung the bending boughs:
The garlands fade, the vows are worn away;
So dies her love, and so my hopes decay.
 Resound, ye Hills, resound my mournful strain!
Now bright Arcturus glads the teeming grain;
Now golden fruits on loaded branches shine,
And grateful clusters swell with floods of wine;
Now blushing berries paint the yellow grove:
Just Gods! shall all things yield returns but love?
 Resound, ye Hills, resound my mournful lay!
The shepherds cry, "Thy flocks are left a prey."
Ah! what avails it me the flocks to keep,
Who lost my heart while I preserved my sheep?
Pan came, and ask'd, What magic caused my smart,
Or what ill eyes malignant glances dart?
What eyes but hers, alas, have pow'r to move!
And is there magic but what dwells in love!
 Resound, ye Hills, resound my mournful strains!
I'll fly from shepherds, flocks, and flow'ry plains;
From shepherds, flocks, and plains, I may remove,
Forsake mankind, and all the world—but Love!
I know thee, Love! on foreign mountains bred,
Wolves gave thee suck, and savage tigers fed;
Thou wert from Ætna's burning entrails torn,
Got by fierce whirlwinds, and in thunder born!
 Resound, ye Hills, resound my mournful lay!
Farewell, ye Woods; adieu the light of day!
One leap from yonder cliff shall end my pains:
No more, ye Hills, no more resound my strains!
 Thus sung the shepherds till th' approach of night
The skies yet blushing with departing light,
When falling dews with spangles deck'd the glade,
And the low sun had lengthen'd ev'ry shade.

WINTER.

TO THE MEMORY OF MRS. TEMPEST.

Lycidas. Thyrsis, the music of that murm'ring spring
Is not so mournful as the strains you sing;
Nor rivers, winding through the vales below,
So sweetly warble, or so smoothly flow.
Now sleeping flocks on their soft fleeces lie,
The moon, serene in glory, mounts the sky,
Whilst silent birds forget their tuneful lays,
Oh sing of Daphne's fate and Daphne's praise
Thyr. Behold the groves that shine with silver frost,
Their beauty wither'd, and their verdure lost.
Here shall I try the sweet Alexis' strain,
That call'd the list'ning Dryads to the plain?
Thames heard the numbers, as he flow'd along,
And bade his willows learn the moving song.
Lyc. So may kind rains their vital moisture yield,
And swell the future harvest of the field.
Begin; this charge the dying Daphne gave,
And said, "Ye shepherds, sing around my grave!"
Sing, while beside the shaded tomb I mourn,
And with fresh bays her rural shrine adorn.
Thyr. Ye gentle Muses, leave your crystal spring;
Let nymphs and sylvans cypress garlands bring:
Ye weeping loves, the stream with myrtles hide,
And break your bows, as when Adonis died;
And with your golden darts, now useless grown,
Inscribe a verse on this relenting stone:
"Let nature change, let heav'n and earth deplore;
Fair Daphne's dead, and love is now no more!"
'Tis done; and Nature's various charms decay;
See gloomy clouds obscure the cheerful day!
Now hung with pearls the dropping trees appear,
Their faded honours scatter'd on her bier.
See where on earth the flow'ry glories lie;
With her they flourish'd, and with her they die.
Ah! what avail the beauties Nature wore?
Fair Daphne's dead, and beauty is no more!
For her the flocks refuse their verdant food,
The thirsty heifers shun the gliding flood;
The silver swans her hapless fate bemoan,
In notes more sad than when they sing their own;
In hollow caves sweet echo silent lies,
Silent, or only to her name replies:

Her name with pleasure once she taught the shore;
Now Daphne's dead, and pleasure is no more!
No grateful dews descend from ev'ning skies,
Nor morning odours from the flow'rs arise;
No rich perfumes refresh the fruitful field,
Nor fragrant herbs their native incense yield.
The balmy zephyrs, silent since her death,
Lament the ceasing of a sweeter breath;
Th' industrious bees neglect their golden store;
Fair Daphne's dead, and sweetness is no more!
No more the mountain larks, while Daphne sings,
Shall, list'ning in mid air, suspend their wings;
No more the birds shall imitate her lays,
Or, hush'd with wonder, hearken from the sprays:
No more the streams their murmurs shall forbear,
A sweeter music than their own to hear,
But tell the reeds, and tell the vocal shore,
Fair Daphne's dead, and music is no more!
Her fate is whisper'd by the gentle breeze,
And told in sighs to all the trembling trees;
The trembling trees, in ev'ry plain and wood,
Her fate remurmur to the silver flood;
The silver flood, so lately calm, appears
Swell'd with new passion, and o'erflows with tears;
The winds, and trees, and floods, her death deplore,
Daphne, our grief, our glory now no more!
But see! where Daphne wond'ring mounts on high
Above the clouds, above the starry sky!
Eternal beauties grace the shining scene,
Fields ever fresh, and groves for ever green!
There while you rest in amaranthine bow'rs,
Or from those meads select unfading flow'rs,
Behold us kindly, who your name implore,
Daphne, our goddess, and our grief no more!
LYC. How all things listen while thy muse complains!
Such silence waits on Philomela's strains,
In some still ev'ning, when the whisp'ring breeze
Pants on the leaves, and dies upon the trees.
To thee, bright Goddess, oft a lamb shall bleed,
If teeming ewes increase my fleecy breed.
While plants their shade, or flow'rs their odours give,
Thy name, thy honour, and thy praise shall live!
THYR. But see, Orion sheds, unwholesome dews
Arise, the pines a noxious shade diffuse;
Sharp Boreas blows, and nature feels decay;
Time conquers all, and we must time obey.
Adieu, ye vales, ye mountains, streams and groves;
Adieu, ye shepherds' rural lays and loves;
Adieu, my flocks; farewell, ye sylvan crew;
Daphne, farewell; and all the world adieu.

MESSIAH:

A SACRED ECLOGUE,

IN IMITATION OF VIRGIL'S POLLIO.

ADVERTISEMENT.

In reading several passages of the prophet Isaiah, which foretell the coming of Christ, and the felicities attending it, I could not but observe a remarkable parity between many of the thoughts and those in the Pollio of Virgil. This will not seem surprising, when we reflect that the Eclogue was taken from a Sibylline prophecy on the same subject. One may judge that Virgil did not copy it line by line, but selected such ideas as best agreed with the nature of pastoral poetry, and disposed them in that manner which served most to beautify his piece. I have endeavoured the same in this imitation of him, though without admitting anything of my own; since it was written with this particular view, that the reader, by comparing the several thoughts, might see how far the images and descriptions of the prophet are superior to those of the poet. P.

Ye Nymphs of Solyma! begin the song:
To heav'nly themes sublimer strains belong.
The mossy fountains, and the sylvan shades,
The dreams of Pindus, and th' Aonian maids,
Delight no more—O thou my voice inspire,
Who touch'd Isaiah's hallow'd lips with fire!
  Rapt into future times, the bard begun:
A Virgin shall conceive, a Virgin bear a Son!
From Jesse's root behold a branch arise,
Whose sacred flow'r with fragrance fills the skies:
Th' etherial Spirit o'er its leaves shall move,
And on its top descends the mystic dove.
Y Heav'ns! from high the dewy nectar pour,
And in soft silence shed the kindly show'r!
The sick and weak the healing plant shall aid,
From storm a shelter, and from heat a shade.
All crimes shall cease, and ancient fraud shall fail;
Returning Justice lift aloft her scale;
Peace o'er the world her olive wand extend,
And white-robed Innocence from heav'n descend.
Swift fly the years, and rise the expected morn!
Oh spring to light, auspicious Babe! be born.

See Nature hastes her earliest wreaths to bring,
With all the incense of the breathing spring;
See lofty Lebanon his head advance,
See nodding forests on the mountains dance;
See spicy clouds from lowly Saron rise,
And Carmel's flow'ry top perfume the skies!—
Hark! a glad voice the lonely desert cheers;
Prepare the way! a God, a God appears!
A God, a God! the vocal hills reply;
The rocks proclaim th' approaching deity.
Lo, earth receives him from the bending skies!
Sink down, ye mountains, and ye valleys rise;
With heads declined, ye cedars, homage pay;
Be smooth, ye rocks; ye rapid floods, give way;
The Saviour comes! by ancient bards foretold;
Hear him, ye deaf, and all ye blind behold!
He from thick films shall purge the visual ray,
And on the sightless eyeball pour the day:
'Tis he th' obstructed paths of sound shall clear,
And bid new music charm th' unfolding ear:
The dumb shall sing, the lame his crutch forego
And leap exulting like the bounding roe.
No sigh, no murmur the wide world shall hear;
From ev'ry face he wipes off ev'ry tear.
In adamantine chains shall death be bound,
And hell's grim tyrant feel th' eternal wound.
As the good shepherd tends his fleecy care,
Seeks freshest pasture and the purest air,
Explores the lost, the wand'ring sheep directs,
By day o'ersees them, and by night protects;
The tender lambs he raises in his arms,
Feeds from his hand, and in his bosom warms·
Thus shall mankind his guardian care engage,
The promised father of the future age.
No more shall nation against nation rise,
Nor ardent warriors meet with hateful eyes,
Nor fields with gleaming steel be cover'd o'er,
The brazen trumpets kindle rage no more;
But useless lances into scythes shall bend,
And the broad falchion in a ploughshare end.
Then palaces shall rise; the joyful son
Shall finish what his short-lived sire begun;
Their vines a shadow to their race shall yield,
And the same hand that sow'd shall reap the field.
The swain in barren deserts with surprise
Sees lilies spring, and sudden verdure rise;
And starts amidst the thirsty wilds to hear
New falls of water murm'ring in his ear.
On rifted rocks, the dragon's late abodes,
The green reed trembles, and the bulrush nods.

Waste sandy valleys, once perplex'd with thorn,
The spiry fir and shapely box adorn!
To leafless shrubs the flowery palms succeed,
And od'rous myrtle to the noisome weed
The lambs with wolves shall graze the verdant mead,
And boys in flow'ry bands the tiger lead;
The steer and lion at one crib shall meet,
And harmless serpents lick the pilgrim's feet
The smiling infant in his hand shall take
The crested basilisk and speckled snake,
Pleased the green lustre of the fields survey,
And with their forky tongue shall innocently play.
Rise, crown'd with light, imperial Salem, rise!
Exalt thy tow'ry head, and lift thy eyes!
See a long race thy spacious courts adorn;
See future sons and daughters, yet unborn,
In crowding ranks on every side arise,
Demanding life, impatient for the skies!
See barb'rous nations at thy gates attend,
Walk in thy light, and in thy temple bend;
See thy bright altars throng'd with prostrate kings,
And heap'd with products of Sabæan springs!
For thee Idume's spicy forests blow,
And seeds of gold in Ophir's mountains glow.
See heav'n its sparkling portals wide display,
And break upon thee in a flood of day.
No more the rising sun shall gild the morn,
Nor ev'ning Cynthia fill her silver horn;
But lost, dissolved in thy superior rays,
One tide of glory, one unclouded blaze
O'erflow thy courts: the Light himself shall shine
Reveal'd, and God's eternal day be thine!
The seas shall waste, the skies in smoke decay,
Rocks fall to dust, and mountains melt away;
But fix'd his word, his saving power remains;
Thy realm for ever lasts, thy own MESSIAH reigns!

ELEGY

TO THE MEMORY OF

AN UNFORTUNATE LADY.

WHAT beck'ning ghost, along the moonlight shade,
Invites my steps, and points to yonder glade?
'Tis she!—but why that bleeding bosom gored!
Why dimly gleams the visionary sword?
Oh ever beauteous, ever friendly! tell,
Is it in heaven a crime to love too well?
To bear too tender or too firm a heart,
To act a lover's or a Roman's part?
Is there no bright reversion in the sky
For those who greatly think or bravely die?
Why bade ye else, ye pow'rs, her soul aspire
Above the vulgar flight of low desire?
Ambition first sprung from your blest abodes,
The glorious fault of angels and of gods;
Thence to their images on earth it flows,
And in the breasts of kings and heroes glows.
Most souls, 'tis true, but peep out once an age,
Dull, sullen pris'ners in the body's cage;
Dim lights of life, that burn a length of years
Useless, unseen, as lamps in sepulchres;
Like Eastern kings, a lazy state they keep,
And, close confined to their own palace, sleep.
From these, perhaps, (ere nature bade her di,
Fate snatch'd her early to the pitying sky.
As into air the purer spirits flow,
And sep'rate from their kindred dregs below;
So flew the soul to its congenial place,
Nor left one virtue to redeem her race.
But thou, false guardian of a charge too good,
Thou, mean deserter of thy brother's blood!
See on these ruby lips the trembling breath,
These cheeks now fading at the blast of death
Cold is that breast which warm'd the world before,
And those love-darting eyes must roll no more.

Thus, if eternal justice rules the ball,
Thus shall your wives, and thus your children fall:
On all the line a sudden vengeance waits,
And frequent hearses shall besiege your gates;
There passengers shall stand, and pointing say,
(While the long funerals blacken all the way,)
"Lo! these were they whose souls the furies steel'd,
And cursed with hearts unknowing how to yield."
Thus unlamented pass the proud away,
The gaze of fools, and pageant of a day!
So perish all whose breast ne'er learn'd to glow
For other's good, or melt at others' woe.
　What can atone (O ever-injured shade!)
Thy fate unpitied, and thy rites unpaid?
No friend's complaint, no kind domestic tear,
Pleased thy pale ghost, or graced thy mournful bier.
By foreign hands thy dying eyes were closed,
By foreign hands thy decent limbs composed,
By foreign hands thy humble grave adorn'd:
By strangers honour'd, and by strangers mourn'd!
What though no friends in sable weeds appear,
Grieve for an hour, perhaps, then mourn a year,
And bear about the mockery of woe
To midnight dances, and the public show?
What though no weeping loves thy ashes grace,
Nor polish'd marble emulate thy face?
What though no sacred earth allow thee room,
Nor hallow'd dirge be mutter'd o'er thy tomb?
Yet shall thy grave with rising flow'rs be dress'd,
And the green turf lie lightly on thy breast:
There shall the morn her earliest tears bestow,
There the first roses of the year shall blow;
While angels with their silver wings o'ershade
The ground now sacred by thy relics made.
　So, peaceful rests, without a stone, a name,
What once had beauty, titles, wealth, and fame.
How loved, how honour'd once, avails thee not,
To whom related, or by whom begot;
A heap of dust alone remains of thee;
'Tis all thou art, and all the proud shall be!
　Poets themselves must fall, like those they sung,
Deaf the praised ear, and mute the tuneful tongue.
E'en he, whose soul now melts in mournful lays,
Shall shortly want the gen'rous tear he pays!
Then from his closing eyes thy form shall part,
And the last pang shall tear thee from his heart;
Life's idle business at one grasp be o'er,
The muse forgot, and thou beloved no more!

TWO CHORUSES

TO

THE TRAGEDY OF BRUTUS.

CHORUS OF ATHENIANS.

STROPHE I.

Ye shades, where sacred truth is sought;
Groves, where immortal sages taught;
Where heav'nly visions Plato fired,
And Epicurus' lay inspired!
In vain your guiltless laurels stood
Unspotted long with human blood.
War, horrid war, your thoughtful walks invades,
And steel now glitters in the muses' shades.

ANTISTROPHE I.

O heav'n-born sisters! source of art!
Who charm the sense, or mend the heart;
Who lead fair virtue's train along,
Moral truth and mystic song!
To what new clime, what distant sky,
Forsaken, friendless, shall ye fly?
Say, will ye bless the bleak Atlantic shore?
Or bid the furious Gaul be rude no more?

STROPHE II.

When Athens sinks by fates unjust,
When wild barbarians spurn her dust;
Perhaps e'en Britain's utmost shore
Shall cease to blush with strangers' gore:
See arts her savage sons control,
And Athens rising near the pole!
Till some new tyrant lifts his purple hand,
And civil madness tears them from the land.

ANTISTROPHE II.

Ye gods! what justice rules the ball!
Freedom and arts together fall;
Fools grant whate'er ambition craves,
And men, once ignorant, are slaves.
Oh, cursed effects of civil hate,
In ev'ry age, in ev'ry state!
Still, when the lust of tyrant pow r succeeds,
Some Athens perishes, some Tully bleeds.

CHORUS OF YOUTHS AND VIRGINS.

SEMICHORUS.

O TYRANT Love! hast thou possess'd
The prudent, learn'd, and virtuous breast?
Wisdom and wit in vain reclaim,
And arts but soften us to feel thy flame.
Love, soft intruder, enters here,
But ent'ring learns to be sincere.
Marcus with blushes owns he loves,
And Brutus tenderly reproves.
Why, virtue, dost thou blame desire,
Which nature hath imprest?
Why, nature, dost thou soonest fire
The mild and gen'rous breast?

CHORUS.

Love's purer flames the gods approve;
The gods and Brutus bend to love;
Brutus for absent Porcia sighs,
And sterner Cassius melts at Junia's eyes.
What is loose love? a transient gust,
Spent in a sudden storm of lust,
A vapour fed from wild desire—
A wand'ring, self-consuming fire.
But Hymen's kinder flames unite,
And burn for ever one;
Chaste as cold Cinthia's virgin light,
Productive as the sun.

SEMICHORUS.

Oh, source of ev'ry social tie,
United wish, and mutual joy!

What various joys on one attend,
As son, as father, brother, husband, friend!
Whether his hoary sire he spies,
While thousand grateful thoughts arise;
Or meets his spouse's fonder eye,
Or views his smiling progeny;
What tender passions take their turns,
What home-felt raptures move!
His heart now melts, now leaps, now burns,
With rev'rence, hope, and love.

CHORUS.

Hence guilty joys, distastes, surmises;
Hence false tears, deceits, disguises,
Dangers, doubts, delays, surprises—
Fires that scorch, yet dare not shine.
Purest love's unwasting treasure,
Constant faith, fair hope, long leisure
Days of ease, and nights of pleasure;
Sacred Hymen! these are thine.

PROLOGUE

TO

MR. ADDISON'S TRAGEDY OF CATO.

To wake the soul by tender strokes of art,
To raise the genius, and to mend the heart;
To make mankind in conscious virtue bold,
Live o'er each scene, and be what they behold;
For this the tragic muse first trod the stage,
Commanding tears to stream through ev'ry age,
Tyrants no more their savage nature kept,
And foes to virtue wonder'd how they wept.
  Our author shuns by vulgar springs to move
The hero's glory, or the virgin's love;
In pitying love we but our weakness show,
And wild ambition well deserves its woe.
Here tears shall flow from a more generous cause,
Such tears as patriots shed for dying laws:
He bids your breasts with ancient ardour rise,
And calls forth Roman drops from British eyes
Virtue confess'd in human shape he draws;
What Plato thought, and godlike Cato was:
No common object to your sight displays,
But what with pleasure Heav'n itself surveys;
A brave man struggling in the storms of fate,
And greatly falling with a falling state.
While Cato gives his little senate laws,
What bosom beats not in his country's cause?
Who sees him act, but envies every deed?
Who hears him groan, and does not wish to bleed?
E'en when proud Cæsar, midst triumphal cars,
The spoils of nations, and the pomp of wars,
Ignobly vain, and impotently great,
Show'd Rome her Cato's figure drawn in state,
As her dead father's rev'rend image past
The pomp was darken'd, and the day o'ercast;
The triumph ceased, tears gush'd from ev'ry eye
The world's great victor pass'd unheeded by;
Her last good man dejected Rome adored,
And honour'd Cæsar's less than Cato's sword.
  Britons! attend: be worth like this approved,
And show you have the virtue to be moved.

With honest scorn the first famed Cato view'd
Rome learning arts from Greece, whom she subdued
Your scenes precariously subsist too long
On French translations, and Italian song:
Dare to have sense yourselves; assert the stage;
Be justly warm'd with your own native rage;
Such plays alone should win a British ear,
As Cato's self had not disdain'd to hear.

PROLOGUE TO SOPHONISBA.

BY POPE AND MALLET.*

When learning, after the long Gothic night,
Fair, o'er the western world renew'd its light,
With arts arising, Sophonisba rose:
The tragic muse, returning, wept her woes.
With her the Italian scene first learn'd to glow,
And the first tears for her were taught to flow.
Her charms the Gallic muses next inspired:
Corneille himself saw, wonder'd, and was fired.
  What foreign theatres with pride have shown,
Britain, by juster title, makes her own.
When Freedom is the cause, 'tis hers to fight;
And hers, when Freedom is the theme, to write.
For this a British author bids again
The heroine rise, to grace the British scene.
Here, as in life, she breathes her genuine flame:
She asks, what bosom has not felt the same?
Asks of the British youth—Is silence there?
She dares to ask it of the British fair.
  To night our home-spun author would be true,
At once, to nature, history, and you.
Well pleased to give our neighbours due applause,
He owns their learning, but disdains their laws.
Not to his patient touch or happy flame,
'Tis to his British heart he trusts for fame.
If France excel him in one free-born thought,
The man, as well as poet, is in fault.
  Nature! informer of the poet's art,
Whose force alone can raise or melt the heart,
Thou art his guide: each passion, every line,
Whate'er he draws to please, must all be thine.
Be thou his judge: in every candid breast,
Thy silent whisper is the sacred test.

* "I have been told by Savage, that of the Prologue to Sophonisba the first part was written by Pope, who could not be persuaded to finish it; and that the concluding lines were written by Mallet."—Dr Johnson.

EPILOGUE

TO MR. ROWE'S JANE SHORE.

DESIGNED FOR MRS. OLDFIELD.

Prodigious this! the frail-one of our play
From her own sex should mercy find to-day!
You might have held the pretty head aside,
Peep'd in your fans, been serious, thus, and cried,
"The play may pass—but that strange creature, Shore,
I can't—indeed now—I so hate a whore!"—
Just as a blockhead rubs his thoughtless skull,
And thanks his stars he was not born a fool;
So from a sister sinner you shall hear,
"How strangely you expose yourself, my dear!"
But let me die, all raillery apart,
Our sex are still forgiving at their heart;
And did not wicked custom so contrive,
We'd be the best good-natured things alive.
  There are, 'tis true, who tell another tale,
That virtuous ladies envy while they rail:
Such rage without betrays the fire within;
In some close corner of the soul they sin;
Still hoarding up, most scandalously nice,
Amidst their virtues, a reserve of vice.
The godly dame, who fleshly failings damns,
Scolds with her maid, or with her chaplain crams,
Would you enjoy soft nights, and solid dinners?
Faith, gallants, board with saints, and bed with sinners.
  Well, if our author in the wife offends,
He has a husband that will make amends:
He draws him gentle, tender, and forgiving;
And sure such kind, good creatures may be living.
In days of old, they pardon'd breach of vows;
Stern Cato's self was no relentless spouse:
Plu—Plutarch, what's his name, that writes his life?
Tells us, that Cato dearly loved his wife;

Yet if a friend, a night or so, should need her,
He'd recommend her as a special breeder.
To lend a wife, few here would scruple make;
But, pray, which of you all would take her back?
Though with the stoic chief our stage may ring,
The stoic husband was the glorious thing.
The man had courage, was a sage, 'tis true,
And loved his country—but what's that to you?
Those strange examples ne'er were made to fit ye,
But the kind cuckold might instruct the City:
There many an honest man may copy Cato,
Who ne'er saw naked sword, or look'd in Plato.
If, after all, you think it a disgrace,
That Edward's miss thus perks it in your face;
To see a piece of failing flesh and blood,
In all the rest so imprudently good;
Faith, let the modest matrons of the town
Come here in crowds, and stare the strumpet down.

ODES.

ON ST. CECILIA'S DAY

[WRITTEN IN THE YEAR 1708.]

DESCEND, ye Nine! descend and sing,
The breathing instruments inspire;
Wake into voice each silent string,
And sweep the sounding lyre!
In a sadly-pleasing strain
Let the warbling lute complain;
Let the loud trumpet sound
Till the roofs all around
The shrill echoes rebound;
While in more lengthen'd notes, and slow,
The deep, majestic, solemn organs blow.
Hark! the numbers soft and clear
Gently steal upon the ear;
Now louder and yet louder rise,
And fill with spreading sounds the skies.
Exulting in triumph now swell the bold notes
In broken air trembling the wild music floats
Till by degrees, remote and small,
The strains decay,
And melt away
In a dying, dying fall.

By music minds an equal temper know,
Nor swell too high nor sink too low.
If in the breast tumultuous joys arise,
Music her soft assuasive voice applies;
Or when the soul is press'd with cares,
Exalts her in enlivening airs.
Warriors she fires with animated sounds,
Pours balm into the bleeding lover's wounds
Melancholy lifts her head,
Morpheus rouses from his bed

Sloth unfolds her arms and wakes,
Listening Envy drops her snakes;
Intestine War no more our passions wage,
And giddy Factions bear away their rage.

But when our country's cause provokes to arms,
How martial music every bosom warms!
So when the first bold vessel dared the seas,
High on the stern the Thracian raised his strain,
While Argo saw her kindred trees
Descend from Pelion to the main:
Transported demigods stood round,
And men grew heroes at the sound,
Inflamed with glory's charms:
Each chief his sevenfold shield display'd,
And half unsheath'd the shining blade;
And seas, and rocks, and skies rebound,
To arms, to arms, to arms!

But when through all the infernal bounds,
Which flaming Phlegethon surrounds,
Love, strong as death, the poet led
To the pale nations of the dead,
What sounds were heard,
What scenes appear'd,
O'er all the dreary coasts!
Dreadful gleams
Dismal screams,
Fires that glow,
Shrieks of woe,
Sullen moans,
Hollow groans,
And cries of tortured ghosts!—
But, hark! he strikes the golden lyre,
And, see! the tortured ghosts respire;
See shady forms advance!
Thy stone, O Sisyphus! stands still,
Ixion rests upon his wheel,
And the pale spectres dance;
The Furies sink upon their iron beds,
And snakes uncurl'd hang listening round their heads.

By the streams that ever flow,
By the fragrant winds that blow
O'er the Elysian flowers;
By those happy souls who dwell
In yellow meads of asphodel,
Or amaranthine bowers;
By the heroes' armed shades
Glittering through the gloomy glades;

By the youths that died for love,
Wandering in the myrtle grove,
Restore, restore Eurydice to life;
Oh, take the husband, or restore the wife!
He sung, and hell consented
To hear the poet's prayer;
Stern Proserpine relented,
And gave him back the fair.
Thus song could prevail
O'er death and o'er hell,
A conquest how hard and how glorious!
Though fate had fast bound her,
With Styx nine times round her,
Yet music and love were victorious.

But soon, too soon, the lover turns his eyes;
Again she falls, again she dies, she dies!
How wilt thou now the fatal sisters move?
No crime was thine, if 'tis no crime to love.
Now under hanging mountains,
Beside the falls of fountains,
Or where Hebrus wanders,
Rolling in meanders,
All alone,
Unheard, unknown,
He makes his moan;
And calls her ghost,
For ever, ever, ever, lost!
Now with furies surrounded,
Despairing, confounded,
He trembles, he glows,
Amidst Rhodope's snows:
See, wild as the winds o'er the desert he flies;
Hark! Hæmus resounds with the Bacchanals' cries—
Ah! see, he dies!
Yet e'en in death Eurydice he sung,
Eurydice still trembled on his tongue;
Eurydice the woods,
Eurydice the floods,
Eurydice the rocks and hollow mountains, rung.

Music the fiercest grief can charm,
And fate's severest rage disarm:
Music can soften pain to ease,
And make despair and madness please:
Our joys below it can improve,
And antedate the bliss above.
This the divine Cecilia found,
And to her Maker's praise confined the sound.

When the full organ joins the tuneful quire,
The immortal powers incline their ear;
Borne on the swelling notes our souls aspire,
While solemn airs improve the sacred fire,
And angels lean from heaven to hear.
Of Orpheus now no more let poets tell;
To bright Cecilia greater power is given:
His numbers raised a shade from hell,
Hers lift the soul to heaven.

ON SOLITUDE.

[WRITTEN WHEN THE AUTHOR WAS ABOUT TWELVE YEARS OLD.]

Happy the man whose wish and care
A few paternal acres bound,
Content to breathe his native air
In his own ground:

Whose herbs with milk, whose fields with bread,
Whose flocks supply him with attire—
Whose trees in summer yield him shade,
In winter fire.

Bless'd, who can unconcern'dly find
Hours, days, and years slide soft away,
In health of body, peace of mind;
Quiet by day—

Sound sleep by night; study and ease
Together mix'd; sweet recreation;
And innocence, which most does please,
With meditation.

Thus let me live, unseen, unknown—
Thus unlamented let me die;
Steal from the world, and not a stone
Tell where I lie.

THE DYING CHRISTIAN TO HIS SOUL.

Vital spark of heavenly flame!
Quit, oh quit this mortal frame!
Trembling, hoping, lingering, flying;
Oh the pain, the bliss of dying!
Cease, fond nature! cease thy strife,
And let me languish into life.

Hark! they whisper; angels say,
Sister Spirit, come away.
What is this absorbs me quite!
Steals my senses, shuts my sight,
Drowns my spirits, draws my breath?
Tell me, my soul! can this be death?

The world recedes; it disappears!
Heaven opens on my eyes! my ears
With sounds seraphic ring:
Lend, lend your wings! I mount! I fly!
O Grave! where is thy victory?
O Death! where is thy sting?

THE UNIVERSAL PRAYER.

DEO OPT. MAX.

FATHER of all! in every age,
  In every clime, adored,
By saint, by savage, and by sage,
  Jehovah, Jove, or Lord!

Thou Great First Cause, least understood,
  Who all my sense confined,
To know but this, that thou art good,
  And that myself am blind:

Yet gave me, in this dark estate,
  To see the good from ill;
And, binding nature fast in fate,
  Left free the human will.

What conscience dictates to be done,
  Or warns me not to do,
This teach me more than hell to shun,
  That more than heaven pursue.

What blessings thy free bounty gives
  Let me not cast away;
For God is paid when man receives:
  To enjoy is to obey.

Yet not to earth's contracted span
  Thy goodness let me bound,
Or think thee Lord alone of man,
  When thousand worlds are round.

Let not this weak unknowing hand
  Presume thy bolts to throw,
And deal damnation round the land
  On each I judge thy foe.

If I am right, thy grace impart
  Still in the right to stay;
If I am wrong, oh! teach my heart
  To find that better way.

Save me alike from foolish pride,
  Or impious discontent,
At aught thy wisdom has denied,
  Or aught thy goodness lent.

Teach me to feel another's woe,
  To hide the fault I see;
That mercy I to others show,
  That mercy show to me.

Mean though I am, not wholly so,
  Since quicken'd by thy breath:
O lead me, wheresoe'er I go,
  Through this day's life or death!

This day be bread and peace my lot;
  All else beneath the sun
Thou know'st if best bestow'd or not,
  And let thy will be done.

To Thee, whose temple is all space;
  Whose altar, earth, sea, skies;
One chorus let all being raise!
  All nature's incense rise!

EPITAPHS.

His saltem accumulem donis, et fungar inani
Munere! VIRG.

ON CHARLES EARL OF DORSET,

In the Church of Withyam, in Sussex.

DORSET, the grace of courts, the muse's pride,
Patron of arts, and judge of nature, died;
The scourge of pride, though sanctified or great,
Of fops in learning, and of knaves in state;
Yet soft his nature, though severe his lay—
His anger moral, and his wisdom gay.
Bless'd satirist! who touch'd the mean so true,
As show'd vice had his hate and pity too.
Bless'd courtier! who could king and country please,
Yet sacred keep his friendships and his ease.
Bless'd peer! his great forefathers' every grace
Reflecting, and reflected in his race;
Where other Buckhursts, other Dorsets, shine,
And patrons still, or poets, deck the line.

ON SIR WILLIAM TRUMBALL,

One of the Principal Secretaries of State to King William III., who, having resigned his place, died in his retirement at Easthamstead, in Berkshire, 1716.

A PLEASING form, a firm yet cautious mind;
Sincere, though prudent—constant, yet resign'd;
Honour unchanged, a principle profess'd—
Fix'd to one side, but moderate to the rest;

An honest courtier, yet a patriot too—
Just to his prince, and to his country true;
Fill'd with the sense of age, the fire of youth—
A scorn of wrangling, yet a zeal for truth;
A generous faith, from superstition free—
A love to peace, and hate of tyranny:
Such this man was, who now from earth removed,
At length enjoys that liberty he loved.

ON THE HON. SIMON HARCOURT,

Only Son of the Lord Chancellor Harcourt, at the Church of Stanton-Harcourt, in Oxfordshire, 1720.

To this sad shrine, whoe'er thou art, draw near;
Here lies the friend most loved, the son most dear;
Who ne'er knew joy but friendship might divide,
Or gave his father grief but when he died.
How vain his reason, eloquence how weak,
If Pope must tell what Harcourt cannot speak!
Oh! let thy once-loved friend inscribe thy stone,
And with a father's sorrows mix his own!

ON JAMES CRAGGS, ESQ.

In Westminster Abbey.

JACOBUS CRAGGS
REGI MAGNÆ BRITANNIÆ A SECRETIS
ET CONCILIIS SANCTIORIBUS,
PRINCIPIS PARITER AC POPULI AMOR ET
DELICIÆ:
VIXIT, TITULIS ET INVIDIA MAJOR
ANNOS, HEU PAUCOS, XXXV.
OB. FEB. XVI. MDCCXX.

Statesman, yet friend to truth! of soul sincere,
In action faithful, and in honour clear!
Who broke no promise, served no private end;
Who gain'd no title, and who lost no friend:
Ennobled by himself, by all approved;
Praised, wept, and honour'd by the muse he loved.

INTENDED FOR MR. ROWE,

In Westminster Abbey.

THY reliques, Rowe! to this fair urn we trust,
And sacred place by Dryden's awful dust:
Beneath a rude and nameless stone he lies,
To which thy tomb shall guide inquiring eyes
Peace to thy gentle shade, and endless rest!
Bless'd in thy genius, in thy love too bless'd!
One grateful woman to thy fame supplies
What a whole thankless land to his denies.

ON MRS. CORBET,

Who died of a Cancer in her Breast.

HERE rests a woman, good without pretence,
Bless'd with plain reason and with sober sense:
No conquest she but o'er herself desired,
No arts essay'd but not to be admired.
Passion and pride were to her soul unknown,
Convinced that virtue only is our own.
So unaffected, so composed a mind,
So firm yet soft, so strong yet so refined,
Heaven, as its purest gold, by tortures tried;
The saint sustain'd it, but the woman died.

ON THE MONUMENT OF THE

HONOURABLE ROBERT DIGBY,

AND OF HIS SISTER MARY,

Erected by their Father the Lord Digby, in the Church of Sherborne in Dorsetshire, 1727.

Go! fair example of untainted youth,
Of modest wisdom and pacific truth:
Composed in sufferings, and in joy sedate;
Good without noise, without pretension great:
Just of thy word, in every thought sincere,
Who knew no wish but what the world might hear:

Of softest manners, unaffected mind,
Lover of peace, and friend of human-kind!
Go live; for Heaven's eternal year is thine;
Go and exalt thy moral to divine.
And thou, bless'd maid! attendant on his doom,
Pensive hast follow'd to the silent tomb,
Steer'd the same course to the same quiet shore,
Not parted long, and now to part no more!
Go then, where only bliss sincere is known!
Go where to love and to enjoy are one!
Yet take these tears, mortality's relief,
And till we share your joys forgive our grief:
These little rites, a stone, a verse, receive;
'Tis all a father, all a friend, can give!

ON SIR GODFREY KNELLER,

In Westminster Abbey, 1723.

Kneller by Heaven, and not a master, taught,
Whose art was nature, and whose pictures thought;
Now for two ages having snatch'd from fate
Whate'er was beauteous or whate'er was great,
Lies crown'd with princes' honours, poets' lays,
Due to his merit and brave thirst of praise.
Living, great Nature fear'd he might outvie
Her works; and, dying, fears herself may die.

ON GENERAL HENRY WITHERS,

In Westminster Abbey, 1729.

Here, Withers! rest; thou bravest, gentlest mind;
Thy country's friend, but more of human-kind.
O, born to arms! O worth in youth approved!
O soft humanity, in age beloved!
For then the hardy veteran drops a tear,
And the gay courtier feels the sigh sincere.
Withers! adieu; yet not with thee remove
Thy martial spirit or thy social love!
Amidst corruption, luxury, and rage,
Still leave some ancient virtues to our age;
Nor let us say (those English glories gone)
The last true Briton lies beneath this stone.

ON MR. ELIJAH FENTON,

At Easthamstead, in Berkshire, 1730.

THIS modest stone, what few vain marbles can,
May truly say, "Here lies an honest man."
A poet bless'd beyond the poet's fate,
Whom Heaven kept sacred from the proud and great,
Foe to loud praise, and friend to learned ease,
Content with science in the vale of peace;
Calmly he look'd on either life, and here
Saw nothing to regret, or there to fear—
From Nature's temperate feast rose satisfied,
Thank'd Heaven that he had lived, and that he died.

ON MR. GAY,

In Westminster Abbey, 1732.

OF manners gentle, of affections mild;
In wit a man, simplicity a child:
With native humour tempering virtuous rage,
Form'd to delight at once and lash the age:
Above temptation in a low estate,
And uncorrupted e'en among the great:
A safe companion and an easy friend,
Unblamed through life, lamented in thy end.
These are thy honours! not that here thy bust
Is mix'd with heroes, or with kings thy dust;
But that the worthy and the good shall say,
Striking their pensive bosoms—Here lies Gay.

ANOTHER.

WELL, then! poor Gay lies under ground,
So there 's an end of honest Jack:
So little justice here he found,
'Tis ten to one he 'll ne'er come back.

INTENDED FOR SIR ISAAC NEWTON,

In Westminster Abbey.

ISAACUS NEWTONUS:
Quem Immortalem
Testantur Tempus, Natura, Cœlum:
Mortalem
Hoc Marmor Fatetur.

NATURE and Nature's laws lay hid in night;
God said, Let Newton be! and all was light.

ON DR. FRANCIS ATTERBURY,

BISHOP OF ROCHESTER,

Who died in exile in Paris, 1732,

[His only daughter having expired in his arms, immediately after she arrived in France to see him.]

DIALOGUE.

SHE. Yes, we have lived—One pang, and then we part!
May Heaven, dear father! now have all thy heart.
Yet, ah! how once we loved, remember still,
Till you are dust like me.
HE. Dear shade! I will:
Then mix this dust with thine—O spotless ghost!
O more than fortune, friends, or country lost!
Is there on earth one care, one wish beside?
Yes—"Save my country, Heaven!" he said, and died

ON EDMUND DUKE OF BUCKINGHAM,

Who died in the nineteenth year of his age, 1735.

IF modest youth, with cool reflection crown'd,
And every opening virtue blooming round,
Could save a parent's justest pride from fate,
Or add one patriot to a sinking state,

This weeping marble had not ask'd thy tear,
Or sadly told how many hopes lie here!
The living virtue now had shone approved!
The senate heard him, and his country loved
Yet softer honours and less noisy fame
Attend the shade of gentle Buckingham,
In whom a race, for courage famed and art,
Ends in the milder merit of the heart;
And chiefs or sages long to Britain given,
Pay the last tribute of a saint to Heaven.

FOR ONE WHO WOULD NOT BE BURIED IN WESTMINSTER ABBEY.

Heroes and kings! your distance keep
In peace let one poor poet sleep,
Who never flatter'd folks like you
Let Horace blush, and Virgil too.

ANOTHER ON THE SAME.

Under this marble, or under this sill,
Or under this turf, or e'en what they will,
Whatever an heir, or a friend in his stead,
Or any good creature shall lay o'er my head,
Lies one who ne'er cared, and still cares not, a pin
What they said, or may say, of the mortal within;
But who, living and dying, serene still and free,
Trusts in God that as well as he was he shall be

MISCELLANIES.

THE BASSET TABLE—AN ECLOGUE.

CARDELIA, SMILINDA, LOVET.

CARDELIA. The basset table spread, the tallier come,
Why stays Smilinda in the dressing-room?
Rise, pensive nymph! the tallier waits for you.
SMIL. Ah, madam! since my Sharper is untrue,
I joyless make my once-adored Alpheu.
I saw him stand behind Ombrelia's chair,
And whisper with that soft deluding air,
And those feign'd sighs which cheat the listening fair
CARD. Is this the cause of your romantic strains?
A mightier grief my heavy heart sustains;
As you by love, so I by fortune cross'd;
One, one bad deal three septlevas have lost.
SMIL. Is that the grief which you compare with mine?
With ease the smiles of fortune I resign:
Would all my gold in one bad deal were gone,
Were lovely Sharper mine, and mine alone.
CARD. A lover lost is but a common care,
And prudent nymphs against that change prepare:
The knave of clubs thrice lost—oh! who could guess
This fatal stroke—this unforeseen distress?
SMIL. See Betty Lovet! very à-propos,
She all the cares of love and play does know
Dear Betty shall the important point decide;
Betty! who oft the pain of each has tried;
Impartial, she shall say who suffers most,
By cards' ill usage, or by lovers lost.
LOV. Tell, tell your griefs; attentive will I stay,
Though time is precious, and I want some tea.
CARD. Behold this equipage, by Mathers wrought,
With fifty guineas (a great penn'worth bought.

See on the toothpick Mars and Cupid strive,
And both the struggling figures seem alive.
Upon the bottom shines the queen's bright face;
A myrtle foliage round the thimble-case.
Jove, Jove himself, does on the scissars shine,
The metal and the workmanship divine—
SMIL. This snuff-box—once the pledge of Sharper's love,
When rival beauties for the present strove:
At Corticelli's he the raffle won;
Then first his passion was in public shown:
Hazardia blush'd, and turn'd her head aside,
A rival's envy (all in vain) to hide:—
This snuff-box—on the hinge see brilliants shine
This snuff-box will I stake: the prize is mine.
CARD. Alas! far lesser losses than I bear
Have made a soldier sigh, a lover swear.
And, oh! what makes the disappointment hard,
'Twas my own lord that drew the fatal card.
In complaisance I took the queen he gave,
Though my own secret wish was for the knave:
The knave won sonica, which I had chose,
And the next pull my septleva I lose.
SMIL. But, ah! what aggravates the killing smart,
The cruel thought that stabs me to the heart;
This cursed Ombrelia, this undoing fair,
By whose vile arts this heavy grief I bear;
She, at whose name I shed these spiteful tears,
She owes to me the very charms she wears.
An awkward thing when first she came to town,
Her shape unfashion'd, and her face unknown:
She was my friend; I taught her first to spread
Upon her sallow cheeks enlivening red;
I introduced her to the park and plays,
And by my interest Cozens made her stays.
Ungrateful wretch! with mimic airs grown pert,
She dares to steal my favourite lover's heart.
CARD. Wretch that I was, how often have I swore
When Winnall tallied I would punt no more!
I know the bite, yet to my ruin run,
And see the folly which I cannot shun
SMIL. How many maids have Sharper's vows deceived—
How many cursed the moment they believed!
Yet his known falsehoods could no warning prove:
Ah! what is warning to a maid in love?
CARD. But of what marble must that breast be form'd
To gaze on Basset and remain unwarm'd?
When kings, queens, knaves, are set in decent rank
Exposed in glorious heaps the tempting bank,

Guineas, half-guineas, all the shining train,
The winner's pleasure, and the loser's pain,
In bright confusion open rouleaus lie—
They strike the soul, and glitter in the eye:
Fired by the sight, all reason I disdain,
My passions rise, and will not bear the rein.
Look upon Basset, you who reason boast,
And see if reason must not there be lost.
SMIL. What more than marble must that heart compose,
Can hearken coldly to my Sharper's vows?
Then, when he trembles! when his blushes rise!
When awful love seems melting in his eyes!
With eager beats his Mechlin cravat moves;
He loves—I whisper to myself, He loves!
Such unfeign'd passion in his looks appears,
I lose all memory of my former fears;
My panting heart confesses all his charms—
I yield at once, and sink into his arms.
Think of that moment, you who prudence boast;
For such a moment, prudence well were lost.
CARD. At the Groom-porter's batter'd bullies play,
Some dukes at Marybone bowl time away;
But who the bowl or rattling dice compares
To Basset's heavenly joys and pleasing cares?
SMIL. Soft Simplicetta dotes upon a beau;
Prudina likes a man, and laughs at show:
Their several graces in my Sharper meet—
Strong as the footman, as the master sweet.
LOV. Cease your contention, which has been too long
I grow impatient, and the tea 's too strong.
Attend, and yield to what I now decide:
The equipage shall grace Smilinda's side;
The snuff-box to Cardelia I decree.
Now leave complaining, and begin your tea.

VERBATIM FROM BOILEAU.

UN JOUR, DIT UN AUTEUR, ETC.

ONCE, (says an author, where I need not say,)
Two travellers found an oyster in their way:
Both fierce, both hungry, the dispute grew strong,
While, scale in hand, Dame Justice pass'd along.
Before her each with clamour pleads the laws,
Explain'd the matter, and would win the cause.

Dame Justice, weighing long the doubtful right,
Takes, opens, swallows it before their sight.
The cause of strife removed so rarely well,
There, take, (says Justice,) take ye each a shell.
We thrive at Westminster on fools like you:
'Twas a fat oyster—live in peace—adieu.

ANSWER TO THE FOLLOWING QUESTION OF MRS. HOWE.

What is prudery?
'Tis a beldam,
Seen with wit and beauty seldom.
'Tis a fear that starts at shadows;
'Tis (no, 'tisn't) like Miss Meadows;
'Tis a virgin hard of feature,
Old, and void of all good-nature;
Lean and fretful; would seem wise,
Yet plays the fool before she dies.
'Tis an ugly, envious shrew,
That rails at dear Lepell and you.

OCCASIONED BY SOME VERSES OF HIS GRACE THE DUKE OF BUCKINGHAM.

Muse, 'tis enough, at length thy labour ends.
And thou shalt live, for Buckingham commends.
Let crowds of critics now my verse assail;
Let Dennis write, and nameless numbers rail;
This more than pays whole years of thankless pain,—
Time, health, and fortune are not lost in vain.
Sheffield approves, consenting Phœbus bends,
And I and malice from this hour are friends.

A PROLOGUE, BY MR. POPE,

To a Play for Mr. Dennis's Benefit, in 1733, when he was old, blind, and in great distress, a little before his death.

As when that hero, who, in each campaign,
Had braved the Goth, and many a Vandal slain,

Lay fortune-struck a spectacle of woe!
Wept by each friend, forgiven by every foe;
Was there a generous, a reflecting mind,
But pitied Belisarius, old and blind?
Was there a chief but melted at the sight?
A common soldier, but who clubb'd his mite?
Such, such emotions should in Britons rise,
When, press'd by want and weakness, Denis lies;
Dennis, who long had warr'd with modern Huns,
Their quibbles routed, and defied their puns;
A desperate bulwark, sturdy, firm, and fierce,
Against the Gothic sons of frozen verse:
How changed from him who made the boxes groan,
And shook the stage with thunders all his own!
Stood up to dash each vain pretender's hope,
Maul the French tyrant, or pull down the pope!
If there 's a Briton then, true bred and born,
Who holds dragoons and wooden shoes in scorn—
If there 's a critic of distinguish'd rage,
If there 's a senior who contemns this age,
Let him to-night his just assistance lend,
And be the critic's, Briton's, old man's, friend.

MACER: A CHARACTER.

When simple Macer, now of high renown,
First sought a poet's fortune in the town,
'Twas all the ambition his high soul could feel,
To wear red stockings, and to dine with Steele:
Some ends of verse his betters might afford,
And gave the harmless fellow a good word.
Set up with these, he ventured on the town,
And with a borrow'd play outdid poor Crown.
There he stopp'd short, nor since has writ a tittle,
But has the wit to make the most of little;
Like stunted hide-bound trees, that just have got
Sufficient sap at once to bear and rot.
Now he begs verse, and what he gets commends,
Not of the wits his foes, but fools his friends.
So some coarse country wench, almost decay'd,
Trudges to town, and first turns chambermaid:
Awkward and supple each devoir to pay,
She flatters her good lady twice a-day;
Thought wondrous honest, though of mean degree,
And strangely liked for her simplicity:
In a translated suit, then tries the town,
With borrow'd pins, and patches not her own:

But just endured the winter she began,
And in four months a batter'd harridan.
Now nothing left, but wither'd, pale, and shrunk,
To bawd for others, and go shares with punk.

SONG, BY A PERSON OF QUALITY.

[WRITTEN IN THE YEAR 1733.]

FLUTTERING spread thy purple pinions,
  Gentle Cupid! o'er my heart;
I a slave in thy dominions:
  Nature must give way to art.

Mild Arcadians, ever blooming,
  Nightly nodding o'er your flocks,
See my weary days consuming
  All beneath yon flowery rocks.

Thus the Cyprian goddess, weeping,
  Mourn'd Adonis, darling youth;
Him the boar, in silence creeping,
  Gored with unrelenting tooth.

Cynthia! tune harmonious numbers:
  Fair Discretion! string the lyre;
Soothe my ever-waking slumbers:
  Bright Apollo! lend thy choir.

Gloomy Pluto! king of terrors,
  Arm'd in adamantine chains,
Lead me to the crystal mirrors,
  Watering soft Elysian plains.

Mournful cyprus, verdant willow,
  Gilding my Aurelia's brows,
Morpheus hovering o'er my pillow,
  Hear me pay my dying vows.

Melancholy smooth Mæander
  Swiftly purling in a round,
On thy margin lovers wander
  With thy flowery chaplets crown'd.

Thus when Philomela, drooping,
  Softly seeks her silent mate,
See the bird of Juno stooping;
  Melody resigns to fate.

ON A CERTAIN LADY AT COURT.

I KNOW the thing that 's most uncommon;
  (Envy, be silent and attend!)
I know a reasonable woman,
  Handsome and witty, yet a friend.

Nor warp'd by passion, awed by rumour,—
  Not grave through pride, nor gay through folly,—
An equal mixture of good humour,
  And sensible soft melancholy.

"Has she no faults then, (envy says,) Sir?"
  Yes, she has one, I must aver:
When all the world conspires to praise her,
  The woman 's deaf, and does not hear.

ON HIS GROTTO AT TWICKENHAM,

Composed of Marbles, Spars, Gems, Ores, and Minerals.

THOU who shalt stop where Thames' translucent wave
Shines a broad mirror through the shadowy cave;
Where lingering drops from mineral roofs distil,
And pointed crystals break the sparkling rill;
Unpolish'd gems no ray on pride bestow,
And latent metals innocently glow:
Approach. Great nature studiously behold!
And eye the mine without a wish for gold.
Approach: but awful! lo! the Ægerian grot,
Where nobly pensive St. John sat and thought,
Where British sighs from dying Wyndham stole,
And the bright flame was shot through Marchmont's
  soul.
Let such, such only, tread this sacred floor,
Who dare to love their country, and be poor.

ON RECEIVING FROM THE

RIGHT HON. LADY FRANCES SHIRLEY A STANDISH AND TWO PENS.

Yes, I beheld the Athenian queen
  Descend in all her sober charms!
And "Take," she said, and smiled serene,
  "Take at this hand celestial arms:

Secure the radiant weapons wield;
  This golden lance shall guard desert,
And if a vice dares keep the field,
  This steel shall stab it to the heart."

Awed, on my bended knees I fell,
  Received the weapons of the sky,
And dipp'd them in the sable well,
  The fount of fame or infamy.

"What well? what weapon?" Flavia cries;
  "A standish, steel, and golden pen!
It came from Bertram's, not the skies;
  I gave it you to write again.

But, friend! take heed whom you attack;
  You'll bring a house, (I mean of peers,)
Red, blue, and green—nay, white and black,
  L***** and all, about your ears.

You'd write as smooth again on glass,
  And run on ivory so glib,
As not to stick at fool or ass,
  Nor stop at flattery or fib.

Athenian queen! and sober charms!
  I tell ye, fool! there 's nothing in't:
'Tis Venus, Venus gives these arms;
  In Dryden's Virgil see the print.

Come, if you'll be a quiet soul,
  That dares tell neither truth nor lies,
I'll list you in the harmless roll
  Of those that sing of these poor eyes."

TO LADY MARY WORTLEY MONTAGUE.

In beauty or wit,
No mortal, as yet,
To question your empire has dared;
But men of discerning
Have thought that in learning,
To yield to a lady was hard.

Impertinent schools,
With musty dull rules,
Have reading to females denied!
So papists refuse
The Bible to use,
Lest flocks should be wise as their guide.

'Twas a woman at first
(Indeed she was cursed)
In knowledge that tasted delight;
And sages agree,
The laws should decree
To the first of possessors the right.

Then bravely, fair dame,
Resume the old claim,
Which to your whole sex does belong;
And let men receive,
From a second bright Eve,
The knowledge of right and of wrong.

But if the first Eve
Hard doom did receive,
When only one apple had she,
What a punishment new
Shall be found out for you,
Who, tasting, have robb'd the whole tree!

THE FOURTH EPISTLE OF THE FIRST BOOK OF HORACE'S EPISTLES.

A MODERN IMITATION.

Say, St. John, who alone peruse
With candid eye the mimic muse,

What schemes of politics, or laws,
In Gallic lands the patriot draws!
Is then a greater work in hand,
Than all the tomes of Haine's band?
'Or shoots he folly as it flies?
Or catches manners as they rise?'
Or, urged by unquench'd native heat,
Does St. John Greenwich sports repeat?
Where (emulous of Chartres' fame)
E'en Chartres' self is scarce a name.
To you (the all-envied gift of Heaven)
The indulgent gods, unask'd, have given
A form complete in every part,
And, to enjoy that gift, the art.
What could a tender mother's care
Wish better to her favourite heir,
Than wit, and fame, and lucky hours—
A stock of health, and golden showers,
And graceful fluency of speech,
Precepts before unknown to teach?
Amidst thy various ebbs of fear,
And gleaming hope, and black despair,
Yet let thy friend this truth impart,
A truth I tell with bleeding heart
(In justice for your labours past),
That every hour shall be your last—
That every hour you life renew
Is to your injured country due.
In spite of fears, of mercy spite,
My genius still must rail, and write.
Haste to thy Twickenham's safe retreat,
And mingle with the grumbling great:
There, half devour'd by spleen, you'll find
The rhyming bubbler of mankind;
There (objects of our mutual hate)
We'll ridicule both church and state.

EPIGRAM ON MRS. TOFTS,

A handsome Woman with a fine voice, but very covetous and proud.

So bright is thy beauty, so charming thy song,
As had drawn both the beasts and their Orpheus along;
But such is thy avarice, and such is thy pride,
That the beasts must have starved, and the poet have died.

A DIALOGUE.

POPE. SINCE my old friend is grown so great
As to be minister of state,
I'm told (but 'tis not true, I hope)
That Craggs will be ashamed of Pope.

CRAGGS. Alas! if I am such a creature,
To grow the worse for growing greater,
Why, faith, in spite of all my brags,
'Tis Pope must be ashamed of Craggs.

TO SIR GODFREY KNELLER,

On his painting for me the Statues of Apollo, Venus, and Hercules.

WHAT god, what genius, did the pencil move
When Kneller painted these?
'Twas friendship—warm as Phœbus, kind as love,
And strong as Hercules.

A FAREWELL TO LONDON.

In the Year 1715.

DEAR, d—d, distracting town, farewell!
Thy fools no more I'll tease:
This year in peace, ye critics, dwell—
Ye harlots, sleep at ease!

Soft B*** and rough C*****, adieu!
Earl Warwick, make your moan—
The lively H*****k and you
May knock up whores alone.

To drink and droll be Rowe allow'd
Till the third watchman toll;
Let Jervis gratis paint, and Frowde
Save three-pence and his soul.

Farewell Arbuthnot's raillery
  On every learned sot,
And Garth, the best good Christian he,
  Although he knows it not.

Lintot, farewell! thy bard must go;
  Farewell, unhappy Tonson!
Heaven gives thee, for thy loss of Rowe,
  Lean Philips, and fat Johnson.

Why should I stay? Both parties rage;
  My vixen mistress squalls;
The wits in envious feuds engage;
  And Homer (d—n him!) calls.

The love of art lies cold and dead
  In Halifax's urn;
And not one muse of all he fed
  Has yet the grace to mourn.

My friends, by turns, my friends confound,—
  Betray, and are betray'd:
Poor Y***rs sold for fifty pound,
  And B******ll is a jade.

Why make I friendship with the great,
  When I no favour seek?—
Or follow girls seven hours in eight?—
  I need but once a week.

Still idle, with a busy air,
  Deep whimsies to contrive;
The gayest valetudinaire,
  Most thinking rake alive.

Solicitous for others' ends,
  Though fond of dear repose;
Careless or drowsy with my friends,
  And frolic with my foes.

Luxurious lobster-nights, farewell,
  For sober, studious days!
And Burlington's delicious meal,
  For salads, tarts, and pease!

Adieu to all but Gay alone,
  Whose soul, sincere and free,
Loves all mankind, but flatters none,
  And so may starve with me.

EPIGRAM

On one who made long Epitaphs.

FRIEND, for your epitaphs I'm grieved,
Where still so much is said:
One half will never be believed,
The other never read.

EPIGRAM,

Engraved on the Collar of a Dog which I gave to his Royal Highness.

I AM his Highness' dog at Kew:
Pray tell me, sir, whose dog are you?

EPIGRAM,

Occasioned by an Invitation to Court.

In the lines that you sent are the Muses and Graces:
You've the nine in your wit, and the three in your faces.

ON AN OLD GATE,

Erected in Chiswick Gardens

O GATE, how camest thou here?
GATE. I was brought from Chelsea last year,
Battered with wind and weather
Inigo Jones put me together.
Sir Hans Sloane
Let me alone:
Burlington brought me hither

A FRAGMENT.

WHAT are the falling rills, the pendent shades,
The morning bowers, the even colonnades,
But soft recesses for the uneasy mind
To sigh unheard in, to the passing wind!
So the struck deer, in some sequester'd part,
Lies down to die, the arrow in his heart;
There hid in shades, and wasting day by day,
Inly he bleeds, and pants his soul away.

VERSES LEFT BY MR. POPE,

On his lying in the same bed which Wilmot the celebrated Earl of Rochester slept in, at Adderbury, then belonging to the Duke of Argyle, July 9th, 1739

WITH no poetic ardour fired,
  I press'd the bed where Wilmot lay:
That here he loved, or here expired,
  Begets no numbers grave and gay.

But in thy roof, Argyle, are bred
  Such thoughts as prompt the brave to lie
Stretch'd out in honour's nobler bed,
  Beneath a nobler roof—the sky:

Such flames as high in patriots burn,
  Yet stoop to bless a child or wife;
And such as wicked kings may mourn,
  When freedom is more dear than life.

VERSES TO MR. C.

St. James's Place, London, October 22.

FEW words are best; I wish you well;
  Bethel, I'm told, will soon be here:
Some morning walks along the Mall,
  And evening friends, will end the year.

If, in this interval, between
  The falling leaf and coming frost,
You please to see, on Twit'nam Green,
  Your friend, your poet, and your host;

For three whole days you here may rest,
  From office, business, news, and strife;
And (what most folks would think a jest)
  Want nothing else, except your wife.

NOTES.

NOTES.

P. 76. THE RAPE OF THE LOCK.

It appears by the following motto, prefixed in some of the earlier editions, that this poem was written or published at the lady's request:—

> " Nolueram, Belinda, tuos violare capillos;
> Sed juvat, hoc precibus me tribuisse tuis."—MART.

But there are some further circumstances not unworthy of being related. Mr. Caryl (a gentleman who was secretary to Queen Mary, wife of James II., whose fortunes he followed into France, author of the comedy of "Sir Solomon Single," and of several translations in Dryden's Miscellanies) originally proposed the subject, with a view of putting an end, by this piece of ridicule, to a quarrel that had arisen between two noble families—those of Lord Petre and of Mrs. Fermor—on the trifling occasion of his having cut off a lock of her hair. The author sent it to the lady, with whom he was acquainted; and she took it so well as to give about copies of it. That first sketch, we learn from one of his letters, was written in less than a fortnight, in 1711, in two cantos only, and it was so printed, first, in a Miscellany of Bern. Lintot's, without the name of the author. But it was received so well, that he made it more considerable the next year by the addition of the machinery of the Sylphs, and extended it to five cantos. These additions were inserted so as to seem not to be added, but to grow out of the poem; and which our author always esteemed, and justly, the greatest effort of his skill and art as a poet.

P. 76, line 19. *Belinda still*, &c.

All the verses from hence to the end of this canto were added afterwards.

P. 78, line 26. *In the clear mirror*, &c.

The language of the Platonists, the writers of the intelligible world of spirits, &c.

P. 78, line 39. *And now, unveil'd*, &c.

The translation of these verses, containing the description of the toilette, by our author's friend Dr. Parnell, deserve, for their humour, a place among these Notes.

> Et nunc dilectum speculum, pro more retectum,
> Emicat in mensa, quæ splendet pyxide densa:
> Tum primum lympha, se purgat candida Nympha,
> Jamque sine menda, cœlestis imago videnda,
> Nuda caput, bellos retinet, regit, implet ocellos.
> Hæc stupet explorans, seu cultûs numen adorans.
> Inferior claram Pythonissa apparet ad aram,
> Fertque tibi caute, dicatque Superbia! laute,

Dona venusta; oris, quæ cunctis, plena laboris,
Excerpta explorat, dominamque deamque decorat.
Pyxide devota, se pandit hic India tota,
Et tota ex ista transpirat Arabia cista;
Testudo hic flectit, dum se mea Lesbia pectit;
Atque elephas lente, te pectit Lesbia dente;
Hunc maculis noris, nivei jacet ille coloris.
Hic jacet et munde, mundus muliebris abunde;
Spinula resplendens æris longo ordine pendens,
Pulvis suavis odore, et epistola suavis amore.
Induit arma ergo Veneris pulcherrima virgo;
Pulchrior in præsens tempus de tempore crescens;
Jam reparat risus, jam surgit gratia visus,
Jam promit cultu, mirac'la latentia vultu;
Pigmina jam miscet, quo plus sua Purpura gliscet,
Et geminans bellis splendet mage fulgor ocellis.
Stant Lemures muti, Nymphæ intentique saluti,
Hic figit Zonam, capiti locat ille Coronam,
Hæc manicis formam, plicis dat et altera normam;
Et tibi vel *Betty*, tibi vel nitidissima *Letty!*
Gloria factorum temere conceditur horum.

P. 79, line 13. *The busy sylphs*, &c.

Ancient traditions of the Rabbis relate, that several of the fallen angels became amorous of women, and particularly some; among the rest Asael, who lay with Naamah, the wife of Noah, or of Ham, and who continuing impenitent, still presides over the women's toilettes.—Bereshi Rabbi in Genes. vi. 2.

P. 80, line 4. *Launch'd on the bosom*, &c.

From hence the poem continues, in the first edition, to line 46—

The rest the winds dispersed in empty air—

all after, to the end of the canto, being additional.

P. 85, line 32. .... *and think of Scylla's fate!*

Vide Ovid. Metam. viii.

P. 86, line 12. *But airy substance*, &c.

See Milton, book vi. of Satan cut asunder by the Archangel Michael.

P. 86, line 25. *Atalantis.*

A famous book written about that time by a woman—full of court and party scandal, and in a loose effeminacy of style and sentiment, which well suited the debauched taste of the better vulgar.

P. 88, line 12. *And there a goose-pie talks.*

Alludes to a real fact: a lady of quality imagined herself in this condition.

P. 89, line 31. .... *Sir Plume repairs.*

Sir George Brown. He was the only one of the party who took the thing seriously. He was angry that the poet should make him talk nothing but nonsense; and, in truth, one could not well blame him.

P. 93, 2nd line from bottom. *This Partridge soon*, &c.

John Partridge was a ridiculous star-gazer, who in his Almanacks every year never failed to predict the downfall of the Pope, and the King of France, then at war with the English.

P. 97. ESSAY ON MAN.

The opening of this poem, in fifteen lines, is taken up in giving an account of the subject, which, agreeably to the title, is an Essay on Man, or a philosophical inquiry into his nature and end, his passions and pursuits.

The exordium relates to the whole work, of which the Essay on Man was only the first book. The sixth, seventh, and eighth lines allude to the subjects of this Essay, viz. the general order and design of Providence; the constitution of the human mind; the origin, use, and end of the passions and affections, both selfish and social; and the wrong pursuits of power, pleasure, and happiness. The tenth, eleventh, twelfth, &c. have relation to the subjects of the books intended to follow, viz. the characters and capacities of men, and the limits of learning and ignorance; the thirteenth and fourteenth, to the knowledge of mankind, and the various manners of the age.

P. 97, lines 7, 8. *A wild .... Or garden.*

The wild relates to the human passions, productive (as he explains in the Second Epistle) both of good and evil; the garden, to human reason, so often tempting us to transgress the bounds God has set to it, and wander in fruitless inquiries.

P. 98, line 18. *The strong connexions, nice dependencies.*

The thought is very noble, and expressed with great philosophic beauty and exactness. The system of the universe is a combination of natural and moral fitnesses, as the human system is of body and spirit. By the "strong connexions," therefore, the poet alluded to the natural part; and by the "nice dependencies, to the moral. For the Essay on Man is not a system of naturalism, but of natural religion. Hence it is that, where he supposes that disorders may tend to some greater good in the natural world, he supposes they may tend likewise to some greater good in the moral, as appears from these sublime images in the following lines:—

"If plagues or earthquakes break not Heav'n's design,
Why then a Borgia, or a Catiline?
Who knows, but He whose hand the lightning forms,
Who heaves old ocean, and who wings the storms,
Pours fierce ambition in a Cæsar's mind,
Or turns young Ammon loose to scourge mankind?"

P. 100, line 23. *Ask for what end,* &c.

If there be any fault in these lines, it is not in the general sentiment, but a want of exactness in expressing it. It is the highest absurdity to think that earth is man's footstool, his canopy the skies, and the heavenly bodies lighted up principally for his use; yet not so, to suppose fruits and minerals given for this end.

P. 101, line 28. *Here with degrees of swiftness,* &c.

It is a certain axiom in the anatomy of creatures, that in proportion as they are formed for strength, their swiftness is lessened; or as they are formed for swiftness, their strength is abated.

P. 101, last line. *And stunn'd him with the music of the spheres.*

This instance is poetical and even sublime, but misplaced. He is arguing philosophically in a case that required him to employ the *real* objects of sense only: and, what is worse, he speaks of this as a *real* object—"If Nature thunder'd," &c. The case is different where (p. 103) he speaks of the motion of the heavenly bodies under the sublime imagery of "ruling angels:" for whether there be ruling angels or not, there is real *motion*, which was all his argument wanted; but if there be no "music of the spheres," there was no real sound, which his argument could not do without.

P. 102, line 11. ...... *the headlong lioness.*

The manner of the lions hunting their prey in the deserts of Af ica is this:—At their first going out in the night-time, they set up a loud roar, and then listen to the noise made by the beasts in their flight, pursuing them by the ear, and not by the nostril. It is probable that the story of the jackal's hunting for the lion was occasioned by observation of this defect of scent in that terrible animal.

Page 103, line 3. *Let rulin' angels*, &c.

The poet, throughout this poem, with great art, uses an advantage which his employing a Platonic principle for the foundation of his Essay had afforded him; and that is, the expressing himself (as here) in Platonic notions, which, luckily for his purpose, are highly poetical, at the same time that they add a grace to the uniformity of his reasoning.

P. 104, line 2. *The proper study*, &c.

The poet having shown, in the First Epistle, that the ways of God are too high for our comprehension, rightly draws this conclusion, and methodically makes it the subject of his introduction to the Second, which treats of the nature of man.

P. 105, line 13. *Who saw its fires here rise*, &c.

Sir Isaac Newton, in calculating the velocity of a comet's motion, and the course it describes, when it becomes visible, in its descent to and ascent from the sun, conjectured, with the highest appearance of truth, that comets revolve perpetually round the sun, in ellipses vastly eccentrical, and very nearly approaching to parabolas; in which he was greatly confirmed, in observing between two comets a coincidence in their perihelions, and a perfect agreement in their velocities.

P. 105, line 23. *Mere curious pleasure, or ingenious pain.*

That is, when admiration sets the mind on the rack.

P. 106, line 36. *Nor God alone*, &c.

These words are only a simple affirmation in the poetic dress of a similitude, to this purpose—Good is not only produced by the subdual of the passions, but by the turbulent exercise of them; a truth conveyed under the most sublime imagery that poetry could conceive or paint: for the author is here only showing the providential issue of the passions, and how, by God's gracious disposition, they are turned away from their natural bias, to promote the happiness of mankind. As to the method in which they are to be treated by man, in whom they are found, all that he contends for in favour of them is only this, that they should not be quite rooted up and destroyed, as the Stoics, and their followers in all religions, foolishly attempted. For the rest, he constantly repeats this advice:—

"The action of the stronger to suspend,
Reason still use, to reason still attend."

P. 107, line 29. *We, wretched subjects,* &c.

St. Paul himself did not choose to employ other arguments, when disposed to give us the highest idea of the usefulness of Christianity (Rom. vii.) But, it may be, the poet finds a remedy in natural religion. Far from it. He here leaves reason unrelieved. What is this, then, but an intimation that we ought to seek for a cure in that religion which only dares profess to give it?

P. 109, lines 33, 34. *Wants, frailties, passions, closer still ally*
The common interest, &c.

As these lines have been misunderstood, I shall give the reader their plain and obvious meaning. To these frailties, says he, we owe all the endearments of private life; yet, when we come to that age which generally disposes men to think more seriously of the true value of things, and consequently of their provision for a future state, the consideration, that the grounds of those joys, loves, and friendships, are wants, frailties, and passions, proves the best expedient to wean us from the world; a disengagement so friendly to that provision we are now making for another. The observation is new, and would in any place be extremely beautiful, but has here an infinite grace and propriety, as it so well confirms, by an instance of great moment, the general thesis—That God makes ill, at every step, productive of good.

P. 111, line 1. *Here then we rest,* &c.

It having been shown, in explaining the origin, use, and end of the passions, in the Second Epistle, that man has social as well as selfish passions, that doctrine naturally introduces the Third, which treats of man as a social animal, and connects it with the Second, which considered him as an individual: and as the conclusion from the subject of the First Epistle made the introduction to the Second, so here, again, the conclusion of the Second

("Ev'n mean self-love becomes, by force divine,
The scale to measure others' wants by thine")

forms the introduction to the Third.

P. 111, 2nd line from bottom. ...... *greatest with the least.*

As acting more strongly and immediately in beasts, whose instinct is plainly an external reason; which made an old schoolman say, with great elegance, "Deus est anima brutorum:"

"In this 'tis God directs......"

P. 112, 7th line from bottom. ...... *than favour'd Man,* &c.

Several of the ancients, and many of the Orientals since, esteemed those who were struck by lightning as sacred persons, and the particular favourites of Heaven.

P. 114, line 30. *Man walk'd with beast, joint-tenant of the shade.*

The poet still takes his imagery from Platonic ideas. Plato had said, from old tradition, that during the golden age, and under the reign of Saturn, the primitive language then in use was common to man and beasts. Moral philosophers took this in the popular sense, and so invented those fables which give speech to the whole brute creation. The naturalists understood the tradition to signify, that, in the first ages, men used inarticulate sounds like beasts to express their wants and sensations, and that it was by slow degrees they came to the use of speech.

P. 115, line 3. *Learn from the birds*, &c.

It is a common practice among navigators, when thrown upon a desert coast and in want of refreshments, to observe what fruits have been touched by the birds, and to venture on these without further hesitation.

P. 115, line 7. *Learn of the little nautilus to sail.*

Oppian describes this fish in the following manner:—"They swim on the surface of the sea, on the back of their shells, which resemble the hulk of a ship: they raise two feet like masts, and extend a membrane between, which serves as a sail; the other two feet they employ as oars at the side. They are usually seen in the Mediterranean."

P. 116, line 7. *Then, looking up*, &c.

The poet here makes their more serious attention to religion to have arisen, not from their gratitude amidst abundance, but from their helplessness in distress; by showing that, during the former state, they rested in second causes, the immediate authors of their blessings, whom they revered as God; but that, in the other, they reasoned up to the First:

"Then, looking up from sire to sire," &c.

This, I am afraid, is but too true a representation of human nature.

P. 116, line 13. *Ere wit oblique*, &c.

A beautiful allusion to the effects of the prismatic glass on the rays of light.

P. 116, 7th line from bottom. .... *and heaven on pride.*

This might be very well said of those times, when no one was content to go to heaven without being received there on the footing of a god.

P. 117, line 35. *For forms of government*, &c.

The author of these lines was far from meaning that no one form of government is itself better than another (as, that mixed or limited monarchy, for example, is not preferable to absolute), but that no form of government, however excellent or preferable in itself, can be sufficient to make a people happy, unless it be administered with integrity. On the contrary, the best sort of government, when the form of it is preserved and the administration corrupt, is most dangerous.

P. 117, line 37. *For modes of faith*, &c.

These latter ages have seen so many scandalous contentions for "modes of faith," to the violation of Christian charity and dishonour of Sacred Scripture, that it is not at all strange they should become the object of so benevolent and wise an author's resentment. But that which he here seemed to have more particularly in his eye, was the long and mischievous squabble between W——d and Jackson, on a point confessedly above reason, and amongst those adorable mysteries which it is the honour of our religion to find unfathomable.

P. 118, line 1. *O Happiness!* &c.

The two foregoing Epistles having considered man with regard to the *means*, (that is, in all his relations, whether as an individual or a member of society,) this last comes to consider him with regard to the *end*—that is, happiness.

P. 118, line . *O'erlook'd, seen double.*

"O'erlook'd" by those who place happiness in anything exclusive of virtue; "seen double" by those who admit anything else to have a share with virtue in procuring happiness; these being the two general mistakes that this Epistle is employed in confuting.

P. 119, line 33. *Order is Heav'n's first law.*

That is, the first law made by God relates to order; which is a beautiful allusion to the Scripture history of the creation, when God first appeased the disorders of chaos, and separated the light from the darkness.

P. 120, line 34. *See godlike Turenne.*

This epithet has a peculiar justness; the great man to whom it is applied not being distinguished from other generals for any of his superior qualities so much as for his providential care of those whom he led to war; which was so extraordinary, that his chief purpose in taking on himself the command of armies seems to have been the preservation of mankind. In this "godlike" care he was more distinguishably employed throughout the whole course of that famous campaign in which he lost his life.

P. 120, 7th line from bottom. *Lent Heaven a parent*, &c.

This last instance of the poet's illustration of the ways of Providence, the reader sees, has a peculiar elegance; where a tribute of piety to a parent is paid in a return of thanks to, and made subservient of his vindication of, the Great Giver and Father of all things. The mother of the author, a person of great piety and charity, died the year this poem was finished, viz. 1733.

P. 121, line 5. *Think we, like some weak prince*, &c.

Agreeably hereunto, Holy Scripture, in its account of things under the common providence of Heaven, never represents miracles as wrought for the sake of him who is the object of them, but in order to give credit to some of God's extraordinary dispensations to mankind.

P. 121, line 7. *Shall burning Etna*, &c.

Alluding to the fate of those two great naturalists, Empedocles and Pliny, who both perished by too near an approach to Etna and Vesuvius, while they were exploring the cause of their eruptions.

P. 122, line 11. *Go, like the Indian*, &c.

Alluding to the example of the Indian in Ep. I. p. 99, and showing that that example was not given to discredit any rational hopes of future happiness, but only to reprove the folly of separating them from charity; as when

...... "zeal, not charity, became the guide,
And hell was built on spite, and heav'n on pride."

P. 123, line 3. *Heroes are much the same*, &c.

This character might have been drawn with much more force, and deserved the poet's care. But Milton supplies what is here wanting

"They err who count it glorious to subdue
By conquest far and wide, to overrun
Large countries, and in field great battles win,

Great cities by assault. What do these worthies,
But rob and spoil, burn, slaughter, and enslave
Peaceable nations, neighb'ring or remote,
Made captive, yet deserving freedom more
Than those their conqu'rors; who leave behind
Nothing but ruin wheresoe'er they rove,
And all the flourishing works of peace destroy?
Then swell with pride, and must be titled gods;
Till conqu'ror Death discovers them scarce men,
Rolling in brutish vices, and deform'd,
Violent or shameful death their due reward."

Par. Reg. book iii.

Eloisa to Abelard.

P. 136, line 5. *You rais'd these hallow'd walls.*

He founded the monastery.

P. 140, line 15. *May one kind grave,* &c.

Abelard and Eloisa were interred in the same grave, or in monuments adjoining, in the monastery of the Paraclete. He died in the year 1142, she in 1163.

P. 141. Windsor Forest.

This poem was written at two different times; the first part of it, which relates to the country, in the year 1704, at the same time with the Pastorals: the latter part was not added till the year 1713, when it was published.

P. 142, line 29. *The fields are ravish'd,* &c.

Alluding to the destruction made in the New Forest, and the tyrannies exercised there by William I.

P. 142, 7th line from bottom. .... *himself denied a grave!*

The place of his interment at Caen in Normandy was claimed by a gentleman, as his inheritance, the moment his servants were going to put him in his tomb: so that they were obliged to compound with the owner before they could perform the king's obsequies.

P. 142, 6th line from bottom. .... *second hope.*

Richard, second son of William the Conqueror.

P. 144, line 26. .... *and as chaste a queen.*

Queen Anne.

P. 145, line 21. *Still bears the name,* &c.

The River Loddon.

P. 146, l. 36. *There the last numbers flow'd from Cowley's tongue.*

Cowley died at Chertsey, on the borders of the forest, and was from thence conveyed to Westminster.

P. 147, line 5. *Here noble Surrey,* &c.

Henry Howard, Earl of Surrey, one of the first refiners of English poetry, who flourished in the time of Henry VIII.

P. 147, line 17. ... *Edward's acts* ....

Edward III. born here.

P 147, line 25. .... *Henry mourn*

Henry VI.

P. 147, line 28. .... *once-fear'd Edward sleeps.*

Edward IV.

P. 148, 9th line from bottom. *And temples rise.*

The fifty new churches.

P. 149, line 4. *Where clearer flames glow round the frozen pole.*

The poet is here recommending the advantages of commerce, and therefore the extremities of heat and cold are not represented in a forbidding manner: as again,

> "Or under southern skies exalt their sails,
> Led by new stars, and borne by spicy gales."

But in the "Dunciad," where the mischief of Dulness is described, they are painted in all their inclemencies:—

> "See round the poles, where keener spangles shine—
> Where spices smoke beneath the burning line."

P. 149, line 12. *Unbounded Thames,* &c.

A wish that London might be made a free port.

P. 152. THE DUNCIAD.

This poem was written in the year 1726. In the next year an imperfect edition was published at Dublin, and reprinted at London in 12mo.; another at Dublin, and another at London in 8vo.; and three others in 12mo. the same year. But there was no perfect edition before that of London in 4to., which was attended with notes. We are willing to acquaint posterity that this poem was presented to King George the Second and his queen by the hands of Sir Robert Walpole, on the 12th of March, 1728-9.—SCHOL. VET.

It was expressly confessed in the preface to the first edition, that this poem was not published by the author himself. It was printed originally in a foreign country. And what foreign country? Why, one notorious for blunders; where finding blanks only instead of proper names, these blunderers filled them up at their pleasure.

The very hero of the poem hath been mistaken to this hour; so that we are obliged to open our notes with a discovery who he really was. We learn from the former editor, that this piece was presented by the hands of Sir Robert Walpole to King George the Second. Now, the author directly tells us, his hero is the man

> .... "who brings
> The Smithfield muses to the ear of kings:"

and it is notorious who was the person on whom this prince conferred the honour of the Laurel.

It appears as plainly from the apostrophe to the great in the third verse that Tibbald could not be the person, who was never an author in fashion, or caressed by the great; whereas this single characteristic is sufficient to point out the true hero, who, above all other poets of his time, was the peculiar delight and chosen companion of the nobility of England, and wrote, as he himself tells us, certain of his works at the "earnest desire of persons of quality."

Lastly, the sixth verse affords full proof; this poet being the only one who was universally known to have had a *son* so exactly like him, in his poetical, theatrical, political, and moral capacities, that it could justly be said of him,

> "Still Dunce the second reign'd like Dunce the first."

BENTL.

P. 152, line 2. *The Smithfield muses, &c.*

Smithfield is the place where Bartholomew Fair was kept, whose shows, machines, and dramatic entertainments, formerly agreeable only to the taste of the rabble, were, by the hero of this poem and others of equal genius, brought to the Theatres of Covent Garden, Lincoln's-inn Fields, and the Haymarket, to be the reigning pleasures of the court and town. This happened in the reigns of King George I. and II. See Book iii.

P. 152, line 4. .... *by Dulness, Jove, and Fate.*

That is, by their judgments, their interests, and their inclinations.

P. 153, line 6. *Dean, Drapier, Bickerstaff, or Gulliver!*

The several names and characters he assumed in his ludicrous, his splenetic, or his party writings; which take in all his works.

P. 153, line 9. *Or praise the court, or magnify mankind.*

Ironically—alluding to Gulliver's representations of both. The next line relates to the papers of the Drapier against the currency of Wood's copper coin in Ireland, which, upon the great discontent of the people, his Majesty was graciously pleased to recal.

P. 153, line 17. .... *by his famed father's hand.*

Mr. Caius Gabriel Cibber, father of the Poet-laureate. The two statues of the lunatics over the gates of Bedlam Hospital were done by him;—as the son justly says of them, no ill monuments of his fame as an artist.

P. 154, line 22. *Like Cimon, &c.*

The procession of a Lord Mayor is made partly by land, and partly by water. Cimon, the famous Athenian general, obtained a victory by sea, and another by land, on the same day, over the Persians and Barbarians.

P. 154, line 26. *But liv'd in Settle's numbers one day more.*

Settle was poet to the City of London. His office was to compose yearly panegyrics upon the Lord Mayors, and verses to be spoken in the pageants. But that part of the shows being at length frugally abolished, the employment of City Poet ceased; so that upon Settle's demise there was no successor to that place.

P. 154, 11th line from bottom. *And Eusden eke out, &c.*

Laurence Eusden, poet-laureate. Mr. Jacob gives a catalogue of some few only of his works, which were very numerous. Mr. Cook, in his "Battle of Poets," says of him,

> "Eusden, a laurel'd bard, by fortune raised,
> By very few was read, by fewer praised."

P. 154, 10th line from bottom. .... *like Tate's poor page.*

Nahum Tate was poet laureate—a cold writer, of no invention, but sometimes translated tolerably when befriended by Mr. Dryden. In his second part of Absalom and Achitophel are above two hundred admirable lines together of that great hand, which strongly shine through the insipidity of the rest. Something parallel may be observed of another author here mentioned.

P. 154, 6th line from bottom. *Bayes, formed by nature*, &c.

It is hoped the poet here hath done full justice to his hero's character, which it were a great mistake to imagine was wholly sunk in stupidity: he is allowed to have supported it with a wonderful mixture of vivacity. This character is heightened according to his own desire, in a letter he wrote to our author. "Pert and dull at least you might have allowed me. What! am I only to be dull, and dull still, and again, and for ever?" He then solemnly appealed to his own conscience, that "he could not think himself so, nor believe that our poet did; but that he spoke worse of him than he could possibly think, and concluded it must be merely to show his wit, or for some profit or lucre to himself." And to show his claim to what the poet was so unwilling to allow him, of being pert as well as dull, he declares he will have the last word; which occasioned the following epigram:—

"Quoth Cibber to Pope, Though in verse you foreclose,
I'll have the last word; for, by ——, I'll write prose.
Poor Colly, thy reas'ning is none of the strongest;
For know, the last word is the word that lasts longest."

P. 155, line 19. *There hapless Shakspeare*, &c.

It is not to be doubted but Bayes was a subscriber to Tibbald's Shakspeare. He was frequently liberal in this way, and, as he tells us, "subscribed to Mr. Pope's Homer out of pure generosity and civility; but when Mr. Pope did so to his Nonjuror, he concluded it could be nothing but a joke."

This Tibbald, or Theobald, published an edition of Shakspeare, of which he was so proud himself as to say, in one of Mist's Journals, "that to expose any errors in it was impracticable;" and in another, "that whatever care might for the future be taken by any other editor, he would still give above five hundred emendations, that *shall* escape them all."

P. 155, line 27. .... *Ogilby the great.*

"John Ogilby was one who, from a late initiation into literature, made such a progress as might well style him the prodigy of his time, sending into the world so many large volumes; his translations of Homer and Virgil done to the life, and with such excellent sculptures: and, what added great grace to his works, he printed them all on special good paper, and in a very good letter."—WINSTANLY.

P. 155, line 28. .... *Newcastle shines complete.*

"The Duchess of Newcastle was one who busied herself in the ravishing delights of poetry, leaving to posterity in print three ample volumes of her studious endeavours."—WINSTANLY. Langbaine reckons up *eight* folios of her Grace's; which were usually adorned with gilded covers, and had her coat of arms upon them.

P. 155, line 32. .... *Settle, Banks, and Broome.*

The poet has mentioned these three authors in particular, as they are parallel to our hero in his three capacities:—1. Settle was his

Brother Laureate; only indeed upon half-pay, for the City instead of the Court; but equally famous for unintelligible flights in his poems on public occasions, such as shows, birthdays, &c. 2. Banks was his rival in tragedy (though more successful) in one of his tragedies, the "Earl of Essex," which is yet alive; "Anna Boleyn," the "Queen of Scots," and "Cyrus the Great," are dead and gone. These he drest in a sort of beggars' velvet, or a happy mixture of the thick fustian and thin prosaic; exactly imitated in "Perolla and Isidora," "Cæsar in Egypt," and the "Heroic Daughter." 3. Broome was a serving man of Ben Jonson, who once picked up a comedy from his betters, or from some cast scenes of his master, not entirely contemptible.

P. 155, line 35. *Caxton.*

A printer in the time of Edw. IV., Rich. III., and Hen. VII.; Wynkyn de Word, his successor, in that of Hen. VII. and VIII. The former translated into prose Virgil's "Æneis," as a history; of which he speaks, in his "Proeme," in a very singular manner, as of a book hardly known.

P. 155, line 39. *Nich de Lyra, or Harpsfield.*

A very voluminous commentator, whose works, in five vast folios, were printed in 1472.

P. 155, line 40. *Philemon.*

Philemon Holland, Doctor in Physic. "He translated so many books, that a man would think he had done nothing else; insomuch that he might be called Translator General of his age. The books alone of his turning into English are sufficient to make a country gentleman a complete library."—WINSTANLY.

P. 156, line 3. *E'er since Sir Fopling's Periwig.*

The first visible cause of the passion of the town for our hero, was a fair flaxen full-bottom'd periwig, which, he tells us, he wore in his first play of the "Fool in Fashion." It attracted, in a particular manner, the friendship of Col. Brett, who wanted to purchase it.

P. 156, line 17. *As forc'd from wind guns, &c.*

The thought of these four verses is found in a poem of our Author's of a very early date (namely written at fourteen years old, and soon after printed) to the Author of a poem called "Successio."

P. 156, line 35. *My Fletcher.*

A familiar manner of speaking, used by modern critics, of a favourite author. Bays might as justly speak thus of Fletcher, as a French wit did of Tully, seeing his works in a library, "Ah! mon cher Ciceron! je le connois bien; c'est le même que Marc Tulle." But he had a better title to call Fletcher his own, having made so free with him.

P. 156, line 36. *Take up the Bible, once my better guide?*

When, according to his father's intention, he had been a clergyman, or (as he thinks himself) a bishop of the church of England.

P. 156, line 39. *At White's amidst the Doctors.*

These Doctors had a modest and upright appearance, no air of over-bearing; but, like true Masters of Arts, were only habited in black and white. They were justly styled subtiles and graves, but not always irrefragabiles, being sometimes examined, and, by a nice distinction, divided and laid open.—SCRIBL.

This learned critic is to be understood allegorically: the doctors in this place mean no more than false dice, a cant phrase used amongst gamesters. So the meaning of these four sonorous lines is only this, "Shall I play fair, or foul?"

P. 156, line 44. *Ridpath—Mist.*

George Ridpath, author of a Whig paper, called the "Flying Post;" Nathanael Mist, of a famous Tory journal.

P. 156, line 47. *Or rob Rome's ancient geese of all their glories.*

Relates to the well-known story of the geese that saved the Capitol; of which Virgil, Æneid. viii.

> "Atque hic auratis volitans argenteus anser
> Porticibus, Gallos in limine adesse canebat:"

A passage I have always suspected. Who sees not the antithesis of *auratis* and *argenteus* to be unworthy the Virgilian majesty? And what absurdity to say a goose sings? canebat.

P. 156, line 48. *And cackling save the Monarchy of Tories?*

Not out of any preference or affection to the Tories. For what Hobbes so ingenuously confesses of himself, is true of all party-writers whatsoever: "That he defends the supreme powers, as the geese by their cackling defended the Romans, who held the Capitol; for they favoured them no more than the Gauls, their enemies; but were as ready to have defended the Gauls, if they had been possessed of the Capitol." Epist. Dedic. to the "Leviathan."

P. 157, line 1. *Gazetteers.*

A band of ministerial writers, hired at the price mentioned in the note on book ii. ver. 316, who, on the very day their patron quitted his post, laid down their paper, and declared they would never more meddle in politics.

P. 157, line 4. *Cibberian forehead.*

So indeed all the MSS. read, but I make no scruple to pronounce them all wrong, the laureate being elsewhere celebrated by our poet for his great modesty—modest Cibber—read, therefore, at my peril, Cerberian forehead. This is perfectly classical, and, what is more, Homerical; the dog was the ancient, as the bitch is the modern, symbol of impudence; (Κυνὸς ὄμματ' ἔχων, says Achilles to Agamemnon) which, when in a superlative degree, may well be denominated from Cerberus, the dog with three heads.—But as to the latter part of this verse, Cibberian brain, that is certainly the genuine reading.

P. 157, line 11. *O born in sin*, &c.

This is a tender and passionate apostrophe to his own works, which he is going to sacrifice, agreeable to the nature of man in great affliction; and reflecting, like a parent, on the many miserable fates to which they would otherwise be subject.

P. 157, line 14. *My better and more Christian progeny!*

"It may be observable, that my muse and my spouse were equally prolific; that the one was seldom the mother of a child, but in the same year the other made me the father of a play. I think we had a dozen of each sort between us; of both which kinds some died in their infancy," &c. Life of C. C. p. 217, 8vo. edit.

P. 157, line 17. *Gratis-given Bland—sent with a Pass.*

It was a practice so to give the "Daily Gazetteer" and ministerial pamphlets (in which this B was a writer), and to send them post-free to all the towns in the kingdom.

P. 157, line 19. *With Ward, to Ape and Monkey climes.*

"Edward Ward, a very voluminous poet in Hudibrastic verse, but best known by the "London Spy," in prose. He has of late years kept a public house in the city (but in a genteel way), and with his wit, humour, and good liquor (ale), afforded his guests a pleasurable entertainment, especially those of the high-church party."—JACOB, "Lives of Poets," vol. ii. p. 225. Great number of his works were yearly sold into the Plantations. Ward, in a book called "Apollo's Maggot," declared this account to be a great falsity, protesting that his public-house was not in the City, but in Moorfields.

P. 157, lines 24, 26. *Tate—Shadwell.*

Two of his predecessors in the Laurel.

P. 157, line 29. *With that, a Tear, (portentous sign of Grace!)* &c.

It is to be observed that our poet hath made his hero, in imitation of Virgil's, obnoxious to the tender passions. He was indeed so given to weeping, that he tells us, when Goodman the player swore, if he did not make a good actor, he'd be damned; "the surprise of being commended by one, who had been himself so eminent on the stage, and in so positive a manner, was more than he could support. In a word (says he) it almost took away my breath, and (laugh if you please) fairly drew tears from my eyes." P. 149 of his Life, 8vo. W.

P. 157, line 36. *Now flames the Cid,* &c.

In the first notes on the "Dunciad" it was said, that this author was particularly excellent at tragedy. "This (says he) is as unjust as to say I could not dance on a rope." But certain it is that he had attempted to dance on this rope, and fell most shamefully, having produced no less than four tragedies (the names of which the poet preserves in these few lines) the three first of them were fairly printed, acted, and damned; the fourth suppressed in fear of the like treatment.

P. 157, line 39. *The dear Nonjuror—Molière's old stubble.*

A comedy threshed out of Moliere's "Tartuffe," and so much the translator's favourite, that he assures us all our author's dislike to it could only arise from disaffection to the government:

"Qui meprise Cotin, n'estime point son Roi,
Et n'a, selon Cotin, ni Dieu, ni foi, ni loi.—BOILEAU.

He assures us, that "when he had the honour to kiss his Majesty's hand upon presenting his dedication of it, he was graciously pleased, out of his royal bounty, to order him two hundred pounds for it. And this, he doubts not, grieved Mr. P."

P. 157, line 42. *When the last blaze sent Ilion to the skies.*

See Virgil, Æn. ii., where I would advise the reader to peruse the story of Troy's destruction, rather than in Wynkyn. But I caution him alike in both to beware of a most grievous error, that of thinking he was brought about by I know not what Trojan Horse; there never having been any such thing. For, first, it was not Trojan, being made by the Greeks; and, secondly, it was not a horse, but a mare. This is clear from many verses in Virgil:—

—— "Uterumque armato milite complent."

"Inclusos utero Danaos" ——

Can a horse be said utero gerere? Again,

"Uteroque recusso,
Insonuere cavæ."

—— "Atque utero sonitum quater arma dedere."

Nay, is it not expressly said

"Scandit fatalis machina muros
Fœta armis?" ——

How is it possible the word fœta can agree with a horse? And indeed can it be conceived that the chaste and virgin Goddess Pallas would employ herself in forming and fashioning the male of that species? But this shall be proved to a demonstration in our Virgil restored.—SCRIBL.

P. 157, line 44. *Thulè.*

An unfinished poem of that name, of which one sheet was printed many years ago, by Amb. Philips, a northern author. It is an usual method of putting out a fire, to cast wet sheets upon it. Some critics have been of opinion that this sheet was of the nature of the Asbestos, which cannot be consumed by fire. But I rather think it an allegorical allusion to the coldness and heaviness of the writing.

P. 158, line 1. *Sacred Dome.*

Where he no sooner enters, but he reconnoitres the place of his original; as Plato says the spirits shall, at their entrance into the celestial regions.

P. 158, line 5. *Great Mother.*

Magna mater, here applied to dulness. The Quidnuncs, a name given to the ancient members of certain political clubs, who were constantly inquiring quid nunc? What news?

P. 158, line 22. *Tibbald.*

Lewis Tibbald (as pronounced) or Theobald (as written) was bred an attorney, and son to an attorney (says Mr. Jacob) of Sittenburn, in Kent. He was author of some forgotten plays, translations, and other pieces. He was concerned in a paper called the "Censor," and a translation of Ovid. "There is a notorious idiot, one hight Whachum, who, from an underspur-leather to the law, is become an under-strapper to the playhouse, who hath lately burlesqued the Metamorphoses of Ovid by a vile translation, &c. This fellow is concerned in an impertinent paper called the 'Censor.'"—DENNIS'S "Rem. on Pope's Hom." p. 9, 10

Ibid. *Ozell.*

"Mr. John Ozell (if we credit Mr. Jacob) did go to school in Leicestershire, where somebody left him something to live on, when he shall retire from business. He was designed to be sent to Cambridge, in order for priesthood; but he chose rather to be placed in an office of accounts, in the City, being qualified for the same by his skill in arithmetic, and writing the necessary hands. He has obliged the world with many translations of French plays."—JACOB, "Lives of Dram. Poets," p. 198.

P. 158, line 26. *A Heideggre.*

A strange bird from Switzerland, and not (as some have supposed) the name of an eminent person who was a man of parts, and, as was said of Petronius, arbiter elegantiarum.

P. 158, line 32. *Withers.*

See on P. 155, line 32.

Ibid. *Gildon.*

Charles Gildon, a writer of criticisms and libels of the last age, bred at St. Omer's with the Jesuits; but renouncing popery, he published Blount's books against the divinity of Christ, the "Oracles of Reason," &c. He signalized himself as a critic, having written some very bad plays; abused Mr. P. very scandalously in an anonymous pamphlet of the "Life of Mr. Wycherley," printed by Curl; in another, called the "New Rehearsal," printed in 1714; in a third, entitled the "Complete Art of English Poetry," in two volumes; and others.

P. 158, line 33. *Howard.*

Hon. Edward Howard, author of the "British Princes," and a great number of wonderful pieces, celebrated by the late Earls of Dorset and Rochester, Duke of Buckingham, Mr. Waller, &c.

P. 158, line 45. .... *under Archer's wing—Gaming*, &c.

When the statute against gaming was drawn up, it was represented that the king, by ancient custom, plays at hazard one night in the year; and therefore a clause was inserted, with an exception as to that particular. Under this pretence, the groom-porter had a room appropriated to gaming all the summer the court was at Kensington, which his Majesty accidentally being acquainted of, with a just indignation prohibited. It is reported, the same practice is yet continued wherever the court resides, and the hazard table there open to all the professed gamesters in town.

"Greatest and justest sov'reign! know you this?
Alas! no more, than Thames' calm head can know
Whose meads his arms drown, or whose corn o'erflow."

DONNE TO QUEEN ELIZ

P. 159, line 5. *Chapel Royal.*

The voices and instruments used in the service of the Chapel Royal being also employed in the performance of the Birthday and New Year Odes.

P. 159, line 10. *But pious Needham.*

A matron of great fame, and very religious in her way; whose constant prayer it was, that she might "get enough by her profession to leave it off in time, and make her peace with God." But her fate was not so happy; for being convicted, and set in the pillory, she was (to the lasting shame of all her great friends and votaries) so ill used by the populace, that it put an end to her days.

P. 159, line 11. *Back to the Devil.*

The Devil Tavern in Fleet Street, where these odes are usually rehearsed before they are performed at court: upon which a wit of these times made this epigram:

"When laureates make odes, do you ask of what sort?
Do you ask if they 're good, or are evil?
You may judge—from the devil they come to the court,
And go from the court to the devil."

P. 159, line 14. *Ogilby. God save king Log!*

See Ogilby's "Æsop's Fables," where, in the story of the Frogs and their King, this excellent hemistic is to be found.

P. 160, line 2. *Henley's gilt tub.*

The pulpit of a dissenter is usually called a tub; but that of Mr. Orator Henley was covered with velvet, and adorned with gold. He had also a fair altar, and over it is this extraordinary inscription, "The Primitive Eucharist." See the history of this person, Book iii.

Ibid. *Or Flecknoe's Irish throne.*

Richard Flecknoe was an Irish priest, but had laid aside (as himself expressed it) the mechanic part of priesthood. He printed some plays, poems, letters, and travels. I doubt not our author took occasion to mention him in respect to the poem of Mr. Dryden, to which this bears some resemblance, though of a character more different from it than that of the "Æneid" from the "Iliad," or the "Lutrin" of Boileau from the "Defait de Bouts rime of Sarazin."

P. 160, line 3. *Or that where on her Curls the public pours.*

Edmund Curl stood in the pillory at Charing Cross, in March, 1727-8. "This (saith Edmund Curl) is a false assertion—I had indeed the corporal punishment of what the gentlemen of the long robe are pleased jocosely to call mounting the rostrum for one hour: but that scene of action was not in the month of March, but in February." ("Curliad," 12mo, p. 19.) And of the History of his being tossed in a blanket, he saith, "Here, Scriblerus! thou leeseth in what thou assertest concerning the blanket: it was not a blanket, but a rug," p. 25. Much in the same manner Mr. Cibber remonstrated that his brothers, at Bedlam, mentioned Book i. were not brazen, but blocks; yet our author let it pass unaltered, as a trifle that no way altered the relationship.

P. 160, line 15. *Rome in her Capitol saw Querno sit.*

Camillo Querno was of Apulia, who hearing the great encouragement which Leo X. gave to poets, travelled to Rome with a harp in his hand, and sung to it twenty thousand verses of a poem called "Alexias." He was introduced as a buffoon to Leo, and promoted to the honour of the laurel; a jest which the court of Rome and the Pope himself entered into so far, as to cause him to ride on an elephant to the Capitol, and to hold a solemn festival on his coronation at which it is recorded the poet himself was so transported as to wee for joy. He was ever after a constant frequenter of the Pope's table drank abundantly, and poured forth verses without number.—PAULUS JOVIUS, "Elog. Vir. doct." chap lxxxii. Some idea of his poetry is given by Fam. Strada, in his "Prolusions."

P. 161, line 14. *And gentle dulness ever loves a joke.*

This species of mirth called a joke, arises from a mal-entendu; and therefore may be well supposed to be the delight of dulness.

P. 161, line 24. *A brain of feathers, and a heart of lead;* i. e.

"A trifling head, and a contracted heart,"

As the poet, Book iv. describes the accomplished sons of dulness; of whom this is only an image, or scarecrow, and so stuffed out with these corresponding materials.—SCRIBL.

P. 161, line 27. *Never was dashed out, at one lucky hit.*

Our author here seems willing to give some account of the possibility of dulness making a wit (which could be done no other way than by chance). The fiction is the more reconciled to probability, by the known story of Apelles, who being at a loss to express the foam of Alexander's horse, dashed his pencil in despair at the picture, and happened to do it by that fortunate stroke.

P. 161, line 30. *And called the phantom More.*

Curl, in his key to the "Dunciad," affirmed this to be James More Smith, Esq., and it is probable (considering what is said of him in the "Testimonies") that some might fancy our author obliged to represent this gentleman as a plagiary, or to pass for one himself. His case indeed was like that of a man I have heard of, who, as he was sitting in company, perceived his next neighbour had stolen his handkerchief. "Sir (said the thief, finding himself detected), do not expose me, I did it for mere want; be so good but to take it privately out of my pocket again, and say nothing." The honest man did so, but the other cried out, "See, gentlemen, what a thief we have among us—look, he is stealing my handkerchief!"

Ibid. *The phantom More.*

It appears from hence, that this is not the name of a real person, but fictitious. More from μῶρος, stultus, μωρία, stultitia, to represent the folly of a plagiary. Thus Erasmus, Admonuit me Mori, cognomen tibi, quod tam ad Moriæ vocabulum accedit quam es ipse à re alienus. Dedication of Moriæ Encomium to Sir Thos. Moore the farewell of which may be our author's to his plagiary, Vale,; More! et moriam tuam gnaviter defende. Adieu, More! and be sure strongly to defend thy own folly.—SCRIBL.

P. 161, line 33. *But lofty Lintot.*

We enter here upon the episode of the booksellers: persons, whose names being more known and famous in the learned world than those of the authors in this poem, do therefore need less explanation. The action of Mr. Lintot here imitates that of Dares in Virgil, rising just in this manner to lay hold on a bull. This eminent bookseller printed the " Rival Modes " before-mentioned.

P. 161, line 38. *Stood dauntless Curl.*

We come now to a character of much respect, that of Mr. Edmund Curl. As a plain repetition of great actions is the best praise of them, we shall only say of this eminent man, that he carried the trade many lengths beyond what it ever before had arrived at; and that he was the envy and admiration of all his profession. He possessed himself of a command over all authors whatever; he caused them to write what he pleased; they could not call their very names their own. He was not only famous among these; he was taken notice of by the state, the church, and the law, and received particular marks of distinction from each.

P. 161, last line. *Curl's Corinna.*

This name, it seems, was taken by one Mrs. T——, who procured some private letters of Mr. Pope, while almost a boy, to Mr. Cromwell, and sold them without the consent of either of those gentlemen to Curl, who printed them in 12mo, 1727. He discovered her to be the publisher, in his Key, p. 11. We only take this opportunity of mentioning the manner in which those letters got abroad, which the author was ashamed of as very trivial things, full not only of levities, but of wrong judgments of men and books, and only excusable from the youth and inexperience of the writer.

P. 162, line 5. *Obscene with filth*, &c.

Though this incident may seem too low and base for the dignity of an epic poem, the learned very well know it to be but a copy of Homer and Virgil; the very words ὄνθος and fimus are used by them, though our poet (in compliance to modern nicety) has remarkably enriched and coloured his language, as well as raised the versification, in this episode, and in the following one of Eliza.

P. 162, line 12. *Down with the Bible, up with the Pope's Arms.*

The Bible, Curl's sign; the Cross Keys, Lintot's.

P. 162, line 13.

See Lucian's Icaro-Menippus; where this fiction is more extended.

P. 162, 5 lines from bottom. *Evans, Young, and Swift.*

Some of those persons, whose writings, epigrams, or jests he had owned.

P. 163, line 4. .... *like Congreve, Addison, and Prior.*

These authors being such whose names will reach posterity, we shall not give any account of them, but proceed to those of whom it is necessary. Besaleel Morris was author of satires on the translators of Homer, with many other things printed in newspapers. " Bond writ a satire against Mr. P——. Capt. Breval was author of ' The Confederates,' an ingenious dramatic performance to expose Mr. P., Mr. Gay, Dr. Arb, and some ladies of quality," says Curl, Key, p. 11.

P. 163, line 5. *Mears, Warner, Wilkins.*

Booksellers, and printers of much anonymous stuff.

P. 163, line 6. *Breval, Bond, Besaleel.*

I foresee it will be objected from this line, that we were in an error in our assertion on v. 50 of this book, that More was a fictitious name, since these persons are equally represented by the poet as phantoms. So at first sight it may seem; but be not deceived, reader; these also are not real persons. 'Tis true, Curl declares Breval, a Captain, author of a piece called "The Confederates;" but the same Curl first said it was written by Joseph Gay: is his second assertion to be credited any more than his first? He likewise affirms Bond to be one who writ a satire on our poet. But where is such a satire to be found; where was such a writer ever heard of? As for Besaleel, it carries forgery in the very name; nor is it, as the others are, a surname. Thou may'st depend upon it, no such authors ever lived; all phantoms.—SCRIBL.

P. 163, line 8. *Joseph Gay.*

A fictitious name put by Curl before several pamphlets, which made them pass with many for Mr. Gay's.

P. 163, line 17. .... *this magic gift.*

In verity (saith Scriblerus) a very bungling trick. How much better might our worthy brethren of Grub Street be taught (as in many things they have already been) by the modern master of Polemics, who when they make free with their neighbours, seize upon their good works rather than their good name; as knowing that those will produce a name of their own.

P. 163, line 18. *Cook shall be Prior.*

The man here specified writ a thing called "The Battle of Poets," in which Philips and Welsted were the heroes, and Swift and Pope utterly routed. He also published some malevolent things in the British, London, and Daily Journals; and at the same time wrote letters to Mr. Pope, protesting his innocence. His chief work was a translation of Hesiod, to which Theobald writ notes and half-notes, which he carefully owned.

Ibid. .... *and Concanen, Swift.*

In the first edition of this poem there were only asterisks in this place, but the names were since inserted, merely to fill up the verse, and give ease to the ear of the reader.

P. 163, line 20. *And we too boast our Garth and Addison.*

Nothing is more remarkable than our author's love of praising good writers He has in this very poem celebrated Mr. Locke, Sir Isaac Newton, Dr. Barrow, Dr. Atterbury, Mr. Dryden, Mr. Congreve, Dr. Garth, Mr. Addison; in a word, almost every man of his time that deserved it; even Cibber himself (presuming him to be author of the "Careless Husband"). It was very difficult to have that pleasure in a poem on this subject, yet he has found means to insert their panegyric, and has made even Dulness out of her own mouth pronounce it.

P. 163, line 24. *On Codrus' old, or Dunton's modern bed.*

Of Codrus the poet's bed, see Juvenal, describing his poverty very copiously, Sat. iii. v. 103, &c.

John Dunton was a broken bookseller, and abusive scribbler; he writ "Neck or Nothing," a violent satire on some ministers of state; a libel on the Duke of Devonshire and the Bishop of Peterborough, &c.

P. 163, line 28. *And Tutchin flagrant from the scourge.*

John Tutchin, author of some vile verses, and of a weekly paper called the "Observator." He was sentenced to be whipped through several towns in the west of England, upon which he petitioned King James II. to be hanged. When that prince died in exile, he wrote an invective against his memory, occasi ned by some humane elegies on his death. He lived till the time of Queen Anne.

P. 163, line 29. *There Ridpath, Roper.*

Authors of the "Flying Post," and "Post-boy," two scandalous papers on different sides, for which they equally and alternately deserved to be cudgelled, and were so.

P. 163, line 37. *Eliza.*

Eliza Haywood. This woman was authoress of those most scandalous books, called "The Court of Carimania," and the "New Utopia."

P. 163, line 40. *Kirkall.*

The name of an engraver: some of this lady's works were printed in four volumes in 12mo, with her picture thus dressed up before them.

P. 163, 4th line from bottom. *Osborne.*

Thomas Osborne, a bookseller in Gray's-inn, very well qualified by his impudence to act this part; therefore placed here instead of a less deserving predecessor. This man published advertisements for a year together, pretending to sell Mr. Pope's subscription books of Homer's Iliad at half the price; of which books he had none; but cut to the size of them, which was quarto, the common books in folio, without copper-plates, on a worse paper, and never above half the value.

P. 164, line 31. *Rolli.*

Paulo Antonio Rolli, an Italian poet, and writer of many operas in that language, which, partly by the help of his genius, prevailed in England nearly twenty years. He taught Italian to some fine gentlemen, who affected to direct the operas.

P. 164, line 33. *Bentley his mouth, &c.*

Not spoken of the famous Dr. Richard Bentley, but of one Thomas Bentley, a small critic, who aped his uncle in a little Horace. The great one was intended to be dedicated to the Lord Halifax; but, on a change of the ministry, was given to the Earl of Oxford; for which reason the little one was dedicated to his son, the Lord Harley.

P. 164, line 39. *Welsted.*

Leonard Welsted, author of the "Triumvirate," or a letter in verse from Palemon to Celia at Bath, which was meant for a satire on Mr. P. and some of his friends, about the year 1718.

P. 165, line 18. *J. Durant Breval.*

Author of a very extraordinary book of travels, and some poems

P. 165, line 38. *Whitfield.*

The preacher.

P. 165, line 40. *Bray back to him again.*

The poet here celebrated, Sir R. B., delighted much in the word "bray," which he endeavoured to ennoble by applying it to the sound of armour, war, &c.

P. 165, last line. *Who sings so loudly, and who sings so long.*

A just character of Sir Richard Blackmore, knight, who, as Mr. Dryden expresseth it,

Writ to the rumbling of his coach's wheels;

and whose indefatigable Muse produced no less than six epic poems: "Prince and King Arthur," twenty books; "Eliza," ten; "Alfred," twelve; "The Redeemer," six; besides "Job," in folio; the whole "Book of Psalms;" "The Creation," seven books; "Nature of Man," three books; and many more. It is in this sense he is styled afterwards "the everlasting Blackmore." Notwithstanding all which

Mr. Gildon seems assured, that "this admirable author did not think himself on the same footing with Homer."—Compare Art of Poetry, vol. i. p. 108.

P. 166, line 15. *In naked majesty Oldmixon stands.*

Mr. John Oldmixon, next to Mr. Dennis, the most ancient critic of our nation. He was all his life a virulent party-writer for hire, and received his reward in a small place, which he enjoyed to his death.

P. 166, line 23. *Next, Smedley dived.*

The person here mentioned, an Irishman, was author and publisher of many scurrilous pieces; a weekly Whitehall Journal in the year 1722, in the name of Sir James Baker; and particularly whole volumes of Billingsgate against Dr. Swift and Mr. Pope, called "Gulliveriana" and "Alexandriana," printed in 8vo.

P. 166, line 31. *Concanen.*

Matthew Concanen, an Irishman, bred to the law.

P. 166, 11th line from bottom. *With each a sickly brother at his back: Sons of a day!* &c.

These were daily papers, a number of which, to lessen the expense, were printed one on the back of another.

P. 166, 5th line from bottom. *Osborne.*

A name assumed by the eldest and gravest of these writers, who at last, being ashamed of his pupils, gave his paper over, and in his age remained silent.

P. 166, 2nd line from bottom. *Arnall.*

William Arnall, bred an attorney, was a perfect genius in this sort of work. He began under twenty with furious party-papers; then succeeded Concanen in the "British Journal."

P. 167, line 34. *And Milbourn.*

Luke Milbourn, a clergyman, the fairest of critics; who, when he wrote against Mr. Dryden's Virgil, did him justice in printing at the same time his own translations, which were intolerable.

P. 168, line 35. *Toland and Tindal.*

Two persons, not so happy as to be obscure, who wrote against the religion of their country. Toland, the author of the Atheist's Liturgy, called "Pantheisticon," was a spy in pay to Lord Oxford. Tindal was author of the "Rights of the Christian Church," and "Christianity as Old as the Creation."

P. 169, line 2. *Morgan.*

A writer against religion, distinguished no otherwise from the rabble of his tribe, than by the pompousness of his title,—"a moral philosopher."

P. 169, line 3. *Norton.*

Norton De Foe, said to be the natural offspring of the famous Daniel De Foe, one of the authors of the "Flying Post."

P. 171, line 8. *And Shadwell nods the poppy,* &c.

Shadwell took opium for many years, and died of too large a dose in the year 1692.

P. 181, line 7. *Narcissus praised.*

Lord Hervey, extravagantly lauded in Middleton's dedication of the "Life of Cicero."

P. 181, line 9. *Montalto.*

Sir Thomas Hanmer, editor of the rival Shakspeare.

P. 181, line 14. *Bold Benson.*

This man endeavoured to raise himself to fame by erecting monu ments, striking coins, setting up heads, and procuring translations, of Milton.

P. 182, last line. *Still expelling Locke.*

In the year 1703 there was a meeting of the heads of the University of Oxford to censure Mr. Locke's "Essay on Human Understanding," and to forbid the reading it.

P. 183, line 2. *Crousaz.*

Author of the commentary on the "Essay on Man."

P. 183, line 22. *While, towering o'er your alphabet, like Saul,—Stands our digamma.*

Alludes to the boasted restoration of the Æolic digamma, in his long-projected edition of Homer.

P. 184, line 27. *Walker! our hat.*

A well-known expression of Bentley to one of the fellows of his college, whose constant attendance on him was charged to sycophancy.

P. 186, line 7. *Annius.*

The name taken from Annius, the monk of Viterbo, famous for many impositions and forgeries of ancient manuscripts and inscriptions, which he was prompted to by mere vanity; but our Annius had a more substantial motive.
Annius, Sir Andrew Fountaine.

P. 186, 3rd line from bottom. *Douglas.*

A physician of great learning and no less taste; above all, curiou in what related to Horace; of whom he collected every edition, translation, and comment, to the number of several hundred volumes.

P. 188, line 6. *Wilkins' wings.*

One of the first projectors of the Royal Society; who, among many enlarged and useful notions, entertained the extravagant hope of a possibility to fly to the moon; which has put some volatile geniuses on making wings for that purpose.

P. 188, 5th line from bottom. *Silenus.*

Mr. Thomas Gordon. Silenus was an Epicurean philosopher, as appears from Virgil, Eclogue vi. where he sings the principles of that philosophy in his drink.

P. 189, line 17. *Poor W**.*

Philip, Duke of Wharton, who died an exile and an outlaw in 1731.

P. 192, last line. *And universal darkness buries all.*

If the last line of a poem ought to be the most forcible, the tautology here is peculiarly unfortunate. Of the fourth book in general, Gray expressed himself, that it was masterly, adding, "That the genii of the operas and schools, with their attendants, were as fine as any thing Pope had ever written; but that the metaphysician's part was, to him, the worst; and that there were a few ill-expressed lines, and even some hardly intelligible."

P. 193, line 6 from bottom. *Let such teach others.*

The inadequacy of all but artists to judge of an art is a maxim of ancient origin. "De pictore, sculptore, fictore, nisi artifex, judicare non potest," says Pliny.

P. 194, line 12. *All fools have still an itching to deride.*

Warburton conceives this "to allude to idiots and natural fools, who are observed to be ever on the grin." It more obviously alludes to the foolish jealousy which tempts inferior writers to ridicule those whom they cannot hope to equal. One of the well known absurdities of Hobbes was his attributing laughter to pride!

P. 194, line 21. *Insects on the banks of Nile.*

Fenton amusingly, and with sufficient truth, pronounces "the Nile to be as fruitful of English similes as the sun;" compassionately adding, "that it would be as hard to restrain a young poet from either, as forbidding fire and water was esteemed among the Romans."

P. 194, line 10 from bottom. *One science only will one genius fit.*

Warton vindicates this maxim; but adduces only the weak examples:—that La Fontaine wrote clever tales, but was hissed in comedy; that Terence made no attempt in tragedy; that Rowe's "Biter" was wretched; that Heemskirk and Teniers could never have succeeded in the sublime of painting; that Tully made bad verses, &c.

P. 195, line 13 from bottom. *Sure to hate most, &c.*

It is amusing to see the picture of criticism, as sketched by Swift, himself the most unsparing of critics:—"Momus, fearing the worst, and calling to mind an ancient prophecy, which bore no very good face to his children the moderns, bent his flight to the regions of a malignant deity, called Criticism. She dwelt on the top of a snowy mountain in Nova Zembla: there Momus found her extended in her den, on the spoils of numberless volumes, half devoured. At her right hand sat Ignorance, her father and husband, blind with age; at her left, Pride, her mother, dressing her up in the scraps of paper herself had torn. There was Opinion, her sister, light of foot, hoodwinked and headstrong, yet giddy, and perpetually turning. About her played her children, Noise and Impudence, Dulness and Vanity, Positiveness, Pedantry and Ill Manners. The goddess herself had claws like a cat," &c. &c.—Tale of a Tub.

P. 195, line 10 from bottom. *Bold in the practice of mistaken rules.*

The Abbé d'Aubignac, patronised by Richelieu, wrote a treatise on the Aristotelic rules of the drama; but this did not prevent his writing a tragedy, which was hissed off the stage.

P. 196, line 4. *Cavil you may, but never criticise.*

The author, after this verse, originally inserted the following, which he has however omitted in all the later editions:—

Zoilus, had these been known, without a name
Had died, and Perault ne'er been damn'd to fame;
The sense of sound antiquity had reign'd,
And sacred Homer yet been unprofaned.
None e'er had thought his comprehensive mind
To modern customs, modern rules confined;
Who for all ages writ, and all mankind.

P. 198, line 4. *Pride, the never-failing vice of fools.*

The evil of false confidence to the poet is, that it makes him contemptuous of advice; the evil of excessive correction is, that it substitutes exactness for vigour, and replaces the impulses of the imagination by the labours of the judgment The chief hazard of correction in poetry arises from the tameness which use throws over the noblest idea; a portion of its original brilliancy is lost at every new contemplation; until at last the mind becomes completely disqualified for a true estimate of its value; the force of words supersedes the force of sentiment; the clear, free, and salient stream of thought runs dry; and all is first, smoothness, and next, stagnation.

P. 198, last line. *Hills peep o'er hills, and Alps on Alps arise!*

Johnson lavishes panegyric on this simile, as "the most apt, the most proper, and the most sublime of any in the English language:" he omits to mention that the simile, and of course the panegyric, belong to another. Warton gives the passage almost word for word from Drummond:—

All as a pilgrim who the Alpes doth passe
* * * * * * * *
Till mounting some tall mountaine, he doth finde
More hights before him thann he left behinde.

P. 199, line 16 from bottom. *Once on a time La Mancha's knight.*

An allusion to a story in the "Second Part of Don Quixote," written by Alonzo Avellanada, and translated by Le Sage.

P. 200, line 9 from bottom. *Some by old words to fame have made pretence.*

The adoption of obsolete phrases must be injurious to poetry; for that which is not capable of being understood is not capable of being felt: but Gray, a true critic, pronounces that "the language of the age is never the language of poetry:" he might have added, nor is the language of vulgarity the language of nature; though this dogma has been stoutly fought for.

P. 200, line 5 from bottom. *Fungoso.*

Ben Jonson's "Every Man out of his Humour."

P. 201, line 17. *The sound must seem an echo to the sense.*

Johnson, in the "Rambler," justly controverts this principle; denies that Pope's examples exemplify any thing but the failure of his theory; and contemptuously asks, why the speed of Camilla should be pictured by the slowest line in our language? The obvious source of the error in the text exists in the supposition that the Greek and Roman quantities can be transferred to English Poetry. The genius of the classic and the English tongues is totally distinct; and all attempts to mould English syllables into ancient harmony have only given additional evidence of the hopelessness of the enterprise.

P. 203, line 13. *Scotists.*

The disciples of Johannes Duns Scotus, the great unintelligible doctor, the Kant of his day. "Thomists," the disciples of Thomas Aquinas, celebrated for his singular subtlety, and his "Summa Summæ," containing comments on Aristotle, &c.

P. 203, line 14. *Kindred cobwebs.*

Bale narrates, as a miracle of the seventh century, that, at the sixth general council of Constantinople, where the mass was established and the clergy were forbidden to marry, a vast quantity of cobwebs were seen suddenly to fall on the heads of the people.

P. 203, line 14. *Duck Lane.*

A place where old and second-hand books were sold formerly, near Smithfield.—POPE.

P. 203, line 27 *Against Dryden rose.*

Dryden unhappily exposed himself too much to the censure of the moralist: living in a loose day, he submitted to the general habit, and increased the degeneracy which his powerful mind was given to reclaim. The person here carelessly alluded to, was Jeremy Collier, a rough critic, but an honest writer: the critic was the Duke of Buckingham, who ridiculed with memorable pleasantry the extravagances of Dryden's plays.

P. 203, line 32. *Milbourns.*

Luke Milbourn, a clergyman, and a tolerable critic; but, unluckily for his fame, opposed to Pope in his comments on Shakspeare.

P. 203, line 34. *Zoilus.*

A lesson to criticism in both his life and death: a general trafficker in abuse, he wrote against all the highest names of Greek literature, Homer, Aristotle, Plato, Demosthenes, &c.: having thus rendered himself obnoxious to his countrymen, he fled to Egypt, where, according to the narrative of Vitruvius, he was seized by Ptolemy Philadelphus, who, in his abhorrence of critical libel, ordered him to be stoned to death.

P. 204, line 1. *Our sons their fathers' failing language see.*

This is one of the fantastic sorrows of poetry: the language of Dryden is still as fresh as it was on the day when it flowed from his powerful pen.

P. 204, line 27. *If wit so much from ignorance undergo.*

Warton refers to the amusing anecdote of Boileau's presenting the order for his pension to the French treasurer The order was expressed, "in satisfaction for his works;" the treasurer, who may be supposed to have been buried from his infancy in the dust of his office, asked "what kind of works?"—"Masonry," replied the contemptuous bard; "I am a builder."

A still more curious example of this species of ignorance lately occurred even in our own stirring country. An opulent banker in the west of England was requested to receive subscriptions for the testimonial to the memory of Sir Walter Scott: the banker gravely replied, "that he had no objection to receive the subscriptions, except his never having heard the name before; and he wished previously to know to what firm it belonged."

P. 205, line 10. *And not a mask, &c.*

Alluding to the custom in that age of ladies going in masks to the play.

P. 205, line 13. *Foreign reign.*

The reign of William III.

P. 207, line 11 from bottom. *Nay, fly to altars, &c.*

A passage imitated from Boileau's "Il n'est temple si saint, des anges respecté." Du Perrier, a French scribbler, had followed Boileau to church, and insisted on his listening to a newly written Ode during the elevation of the host; desiring also his opinion, "whether it were not a rival of Malherbe!"

P. 208, line 11. *The mighty Stagyrite, &c.*

Aristotle, the first and the best of critics.

P. 208, line 14 from bottom. *Grave Quintilian, &c.*

The manuscripts of Quintilian, complete, were found by the learned Poggio, in 1417, in the dust at the bottom of a tower of the monastery of St. Gal, near Constance.

P. 209, line 23. *Immortal Vida!* &c.

A rare instance of poetry leading to the highest honours of professional life. Vida was the son of a Cremonese peasant, but of an ancient Italian line.

P. 209, line 8 from the bottom. *Such was the Muse,* &c.

The Duke of Buckingham's rank, opulence, and love of literature, intitled him to more distinction than he deserved by his ability: but he was the object of panegyric to the whole living generation of poets. Yet not to all with equal success. Pope's insertion of this couplet in his second edition, touched the feeling or the vanity, which had been so often wooed in vain; and from that period this powerful nobleman was his friend.

P. 209, line 6 from bottom. *Such was Roscommon,* &c.

An "Essay on Translated Verse" seems, at first sight, to be a barren subject; yet Roscommon has decorated it with many precepts of utility and taste, and enlivened it with a tale in imitation of Boileau.

P. 211, line 2 from bottom. *High on a rock of ice,* &c.

In Milton's poem on the fifth of November, a description of the tower of Fame is given from the twelfth book of the "Metamorphoses." The icy ascent to the temple in the text implies the insecurity and chillness of the first efforts for human distinction. The image, like all the principal features of the poem, is from Chaucer.

P. 212, line 25. *So Zembla's rocks,* &c.

It gives some insight into the nature of poetical impression, to observe that nearly all those passages in our greater authors which have come popular, are distinguished by beauty of epithet.

P. 212, line 14 from bottom. *Four faces had the dome,* &c.

The temple is described to be square, the four fronts with open gates facing the different quarters of the world, as an intimation that all nations of the earth may alike be received into it. The western front is of Grecian architecture: the Doric order was peculiarly sacred to heroes and worthies. Those whose statues are after mentioned, were the first names of old Greece in arms, and arts.—Pope.

P. 213, line 3. *There great Alcides,* &c.

This figure of Hercules is drawn with an eye to the position of the famous statue of Farnese.—Pope.

P. 213, line 18. *And the great founder of the Persian name.*

Cyrus was the beginning of the Persian, as Ninus was of the Assyrian monarchy.

P. 213, line 31. *Egypt's priests,* &c.

The learning of the old Egyptian priests consisted for the most part in geometry and astronomy: they also preserved the history of their nation. The greatest hero on record is Sesostris, whose actions and conquests may be seen at large in Diodorus, &c.

P. 214, line 24. *The youth that all things but himself subdued.*

Alexander the Great.

P. 214, line 16 from bottom. *Timoleon, glorious in his brother's blood.*

Timoleon had saved the life of his brother Timophanes in the battle between the Argives and Corinthians; but afterwards killed him when he affected the tyranny, preferring his duty to his country to all the obligations of blood.—Pope.

P. 214, line 6 from bottom. *He whom ungrateful Athens*, &c.

Aristides, who for his great integrity was distinguished by the appellation of "the Just."

P. 214, line 4 from bottom. *Martyr'd Phocion.*

Who, when he was about to drink the hemlock, charged his son to forgive his enemies, and not to revenge his death on those Athenians who had decreed it.—WARTON.

P. 215, line 18 from bottom. *Four swans sustain*, &c.

Pindar being seated in a soaring chariot, alludes to the chariot-races he celebrated in the Grecian games: the swans are emblems of poetry, their posture intimates the sublimity and activity of his genius. Neptune presided over the Isthmian, and Jupiter over the Olympian games.—POPE.

P. 225, line 4 from bottom. *Manly raves.*

The principal character in the "Plain Dealer" of Wycherley. The epithet "generous" seems but ill applied to that harsh and crude libe.ler of human nature.

P. 226, line 1. *Hate it in a queen.*

Supposed to be Queen Caroline, who was frequently laughed at for an idle pedantry, and a pretended love of science.

P. 226, line 9. *Unthought-of frailties cheat us in the wise.*

Warton tells us, that the night before the battle of Blenheim, Prince Eugene, having occasion to return to Marlborough's tent, soon after the council held on the operations of the forthcoming day had broken up, found the great duke giving orders to his aide-de-camp, Colonel Selwyn (who narrated the circumstance), by the light of a single candle, all the others having been put out the moment the council was over. "What a man is this," said the Prince, "who at such a time can think of saving candle-ends!"

P. 226, line 21. *Patricio's high desert.*

Lord Godolphin.

P. 226, line 27. *Charron.*

Author of the celebrated treatise "De la Sagesse," and friend of Montaigne.

P. 226, line 29. *A perjured prince*, &c.

Louis XI. of France wore in his hat a leaden image of the Virgin Mary, which, when he swore by, he feared to break his oath.—POPE.

P. 226, line 30. *A godless regent tremble at a star.*

Philip, Duke of Orleans, Regent in the minority of Louis XV. superstitious enough to be a believer in judicial astrology, though an unbeliever in all religion.

P. 226, line 31. *The throne a bigot keep, a genius quit.*

Philip V. of Spain, who, after renouncing the throne for religion, resumed it to gratify his Queen: and Victor Amadeus II., king of Sardinia, who resigned the crown, and, trying to reassume it, was imprisoned till his death.

P. 226, line 12 from bottom. *Europe a woman, child, or dotard, rule.*

The Czarina, the French King, the Pope, and her wisest monarch, the King of Sardinia.

P. 227, line 3. *The same adust complexion* &c.

Philip II. of Spain was atrabilaire: Charles V. suffered much from bile. Melancholy drove Charles to the cloister, and Philip to war.

P. 227, line 20 from bottom. *'Tis from high life*, &c.

The sarcasm of this well-known passage, more than its soundness, has assisted its celebrity.

P. 228, line 21 from bottom. *Wharton stands confess'd.*

One of the most remarkable instances on record of the abuse of nature, fortune, of great talents turned into contempt, of high rank degraded, of vast opulence made useless, and of memorable opportunities perverted into disaster, shame, and ruin.

P. 228, line 13 from bottom. *Wilmot.*

John Wilmot, Earl of Rochester, famous for his wit and extravagances in the time of Charles II.

P. 229, line 14. *When Cæsar made a noble dame*, &c.

Servilia: She was the sister of Cato and mother of Brutus.

P. 229, line 19 from bottom. *Sober Lanesborow*, &c.

Lord Lanesborow, who danced when a cripple from the gout

P. 229, line 5 from bottom. *And in that puff expires.*

Told by Lady Bolingbroke of an old Parisian Countess.

P. 230, line 2. *And—Betty—give this cheek a little red.*

The mistress was the celebrated Mrs. Oldfield; the maid Mrs. Saunders, her friend, also a clever actress.

P. 230, line 5 from bottom. *I cannot part with that*, &c.

The words of Sir William Bateman in his last moments. Warton justly observes, that the realities of avarice and gluttony defy all exaggeration.

P. 232, line 17 from bottom. *Hardly stew a child.*

It was said, that some monstrous use of a dead body for this purpose was made by a woman of rank at the time. The rest of the character was designed for the Duchess of Hamilton.

P. 233, line 13 from bottom. *Cries, 'Ah! how charming,'* &c.

The Duchess of Montague.

P. 235, line 9. *Chloe is prudent*, &c.

Lady Suffolk. Pope dining at her table heard her tell one of the footmen to remind her to send to know how Mrs. Blount, who was ill, had passed the night.

P. 235, line 23 from bottom. *Mahomet.*

Servant to the late King, said to be the son of a Turkish Bassa, whom he took at the siege of Buda, and constantly kept about his person.—Pope.

P. 238. Epistle III.

This Epistle was written after a violent outcry against our author, on suspicion that he had ridiculed a worthy nobleman merely for his wrong taste. He justified himself on that article in a letter to the Earl of Burlington.

P. 238, line 1. *Who shall decide, &c.*

The speakers are Pope and the old and witty Lord Bathurst.

P. 238, last line. *Ward, Waters.*

John Ward of Hackney, Esq. member of parliament, being prosecuted by the Duchess of Buckingham, and convicted of forgery, was first expelled the house, and then stood on the pillory on the 17th of March, 1727. The Waters here mentioned is the same person who is introduced under the character of "Wise Peter," whose name was Walter, though sometimes called Waters.

P. 239, line 16. *Beneath the patriot's cloak.*

This is a true story, which happened in the reign of William III. to an unsuspected old patriot, who coming out at the back-door from having been closeted by the king, where he had received a large bag of guineas, the bursting of the bag discovered his business there.—Pope.

P. 239, line 6 from bottom. *Colepepper's.*

Sir William Colepepper, Bart.

P. 240, line 12. *Turner.*

One, who being possessed of £300,000, laid down his coach, because interest was reduced from five to four per cent., and then put £70,000 into the Charitable Corporation for better interest; which sum having lost, he took it so much to heart, that he kept his chamber ever after. It is thought he would not have outlived it, but that he was heir to another estate, which he daily expected; and that by this course of life he saved both clothes and all other expenses.—Pope.

P. 240, line 14. *Unhappy Wharton, &c.*

A nobleman of great qualities; but as unfortunate in the application of them, as if they had been vices and follies.—Pope.

P. 240, line 15. *Hopkins.*

A citizen, whose rapacity obtained him the name of Vulture Hopkins.

P. 240, line 16. *Japhet nose and ears?*

Japhet Crook, alias Sir Peter Stranger.

P. 240, line 26. *Endow a college, or a cat.*

"La belle Stuart," of Grammont's Memoirs, was the endower.

P. 240, line 30. *Bond damns the poor, &c.*

This Epistle was written in the year 1730, when a corporation was established to lend money to the poor on pledges, by the name of the Charitable Corporation.

P. 241, line 3. *Wise Peter, &c.*

Peter Walter, a person not only eminent in the wisdom of his profession, as a dexterous attorney, but allowed to be a good, if not a safe conveyancer; extremely respected by the nobility of this land, though free from all manner of luxury and ostentation.

P. 241, line 6. *Rome's great Didius.*

A Roman lawyer, so rich as to purchase the empire when it was set to sale on the death of Pertinax.—Pope.

P. 241, line 7. *The crown of Poland, &c.*

The two persons here mentioned, Mr. Gage, and lady Mary Herbert, daughter of William, Marquis of Powis, in the Mississippi despised to realize above £300,000; the gentleman with a view to the purchase of the crown of Poland, the lady on a vision of the like royal nature.—Pope.

P. 241, line 9. *Maria's dreams*, &c.

Lady Mary Herbert, daughter of William, Marquis of Powis.—Pope.

P. 241, line 13. *Much-injured Blunt*, &c.

Sir John Blunt, originally a scrivener, was one of the first projectors of the South Sea Company, and afterwards one of the directors and chief managers of the famous scheme in 1720. He was also one of those who suffered most severely by the bill of pains and penalties on the said directors.—Pope.

P. 243, line 23. *Oxford's better part.*

Edward Harley, Earl of Oxford.—Pope.

P. 243, line 9 from bottom. *The Man of Ross*, &c.

Kyrle possessed about £500 a year: by his union of activity, intelligence, and character, he promoted many of those improvements, whose utility is felt in every neighbourhood.

P. 244, line 16 from bottom. *Great Villiers lies*, &c.

This lord, yet more famous for his vices than his misfortunes, having been possessed of about £50,000 a year, and passed through many of the highest posts in the kingdom, died in the year 1687, in a remote inn in Yorkshire, reduced to the utmost misery.—Pope.

P. 244, line 13 from bottom. *Shrewsbury.*

The Countess of Shrewsbury, a woman abandoned to gallantries. The earl, her husband, was killed by the Duke of Buckingham in a duel; and it has been said, that during the combat she held the Duke's horses in the habit of a page.—Pope.

P 247, line 8 from bottom. *Topham.*

A gentleman famous for a judicious collection of drawings.

P. 248, line 4. *Ripley.*

This man was a carpenter, employed by a first minister, who raised him to an architect, without any genius in the art; and, after some wretched proofs of his insufficiency in public buildings, made him comptroller of the Board of Works.—Pope.

P. 248, line 6. *Bubo.*

Bubb Duddington, who had just built a fine house at Eastbury, near Blandford.

P. 248, line 19 from bottom. *Le Nôtre.*

The architect of the groves and grottoes of Versailles: he came hither on a mission to improve our taste. He planted St. James's and Greenwich-parks.—Pope.

P. 250, line 19 from bottom. *Verrio or Laguerre.*

Verrio (Antonio) painted many ceilings, &c. at Windsor, Hampton Court, &c. and Laguerre at Blenheim Castle, and other places.—Pope.

P. 252, line 1. *See the wild waste*, &c.

Pope's remarks on this Epistle seem contradicted by the fact, that Addison died on the 17th of June, 1719, and consequently Pope could not, in 1720, request to share with him in the friendship of Craggs. The explanation is, that the six concluding lines were written on a former occasion, and while both Addison and Craggs were living.

P. 253, line 3. *This the blue varnish, that the green.*

This a collector of silver, that of brass coins.—WARBURTON.

P. 253, line 7. *Poor Vadius.*

From the Memoirs of Scriblerus. Vadius was Dr. Woodward.

P. 253, line 10. *Neglects his bride.*

If Dio be a true chronicler, a noble Roman in the time of Tiberius distinguished himself by an extraordinary taste for antiques. This personage, whose name was Vibius Rufus, boasted that he possessed the two noblest pieces of antiquity in the world; one was Cicero's widow, Terentia, whom he had married in her third widowhood, and who had arrived at the mature age of a hundred years; the other was the chair in which Cæsar was assassinated.—WARBURTON.

P. 253, line 13. *Her gods and godlike heroes*, &c.

Winkelman's History of the Ancient Arts was once the standard of all knowledge and criticism: it has since fallen to its level, and is considered to be little beyond a laborious catalogue; but it gives some amusing details of the fates of statues, &c. When the Austrians took Madrid, Lord Galloway made a search for a celebrated bust of Caligula, which one of the Colonnas had carried to Spain; it was at length found in the Escurial, as the weight to a church-clock.

P. 253, last line. *And praised, unenvied*, &c.

Those six lines form Craggs's epitaph. Warton remarks, that though Pope was attached to Bolingbroke's party, he had seen enough of both sides to trust neither too far: he regarded them both when in power as nearly the same. On this subject he wrote,—

"Our ministers like gladiators live:
'Tis half their business blows to ward or give.
The good their virtue would effect, or sense,
Dies between exigents and self-defence."

P. 254, line 3 from bottom. *Lord Fanny spins*, &c.

Those were the lines by which Pope struck the first blow in the battle with Lord Hervey. Lord Hervey's appearance was effeminate; and he was said to improve a peculiarly pale complexion by the unmanly aid of rouge.

P. 255, line 16. *What? like Sir Richard*, &c.

Johnson describes Blackmore as a man, who destroyed a good reputation as a physician by a bad one as a poet.

P. 255, line 21. *Falling horse.*

The horse on which his Majesty charged at the battle of Oudenard; when the Pretender and the princes of the blood of France fled before him.—WARTON.

P. 255, line 11 from bottom. *Darty his ham-pie.*

Darteneuf, a contemptible fellow, who made a ridiculous reputation by his gluttony. On reading this passage he acknowledged the application; but said, that if Pope had given him "sweet-pie instead of ham-pie, he could never have forgiven him."

P. 255, line 5 from the bottom. *Downright Shippen.*

A member of parliament in opposition to Sir Robert Walpole, a frequent speaker, and supposed to be conspicuous for sense, integrity, and love of liberty; yet, in contradiction to the whole three, a rank *jacobite.*

P. 256, line 14. *To run a-muck*

Alludes to a practice among the Malayans, who are great gamesters;

which is, that when a man has lost all his property, he intoxicates himself with opium, works himself up to a fit of frenzy, rushes into the streets, and attacks and murders all he meets.—WARTON.

P. 256, line 17. *Save but our army!*

It is a curious instance of the blindness of politicians, that the standing army of England, from which the overthrow of our liberties had been so violently predicted, has been uniformly the protector of those liberties.

P. 256, line 25. *Delia's rage.*

A Miss Mackenzie was, at this time, presumed to have died of poison, administered by a rival. The suspected Delia's name is given in the old edition, "Lady D—ne."

P. 256, line 26. *Page.*

A brutal judge, whose conduct on Savage's trial is given down to ignominy by Johnson.

P. 257, line 23. *And he, whose lightning,* &c.

Charles Mordaunt, Earl of Peterborough, who in 1705 took Barcelona, and in the winter following, with only 280 horse and 900 foot, accomplished the conquest of Valencia.

P. 258, line 9. *Bethel.*

Bethel, a frequent and familiar correspondent of Pope: he performs in this Epistle the part of the Horatian Ofellus.

P. 258, line 18. *Will choose a pheasant,* &c.

In the original a peacock, a stronger contrast. The peacock was among the most costly dishes of Roman epicurism: its price was sometimes fifty denarii, about a guinea and a half. The rearing of peacocks for the table was a trade: a flock of a hundred has been rated at £322 of our money. Aufidius Lurco, according to Varro, made an income of nearly £500 a year by peacocks alone.

P. 258, line 25. *Oldfield.*

A fool, who ate himself out of his fortune.

P. 258, line 26. *Hog barbecued,* &c.

A West Indian term of gluttony; a hog roasted whole, stuffed with spice, and basted with Madeira wine.—POPE.

P. 259, line 4. *Bedford-head.*

A famous eating-house.

P. 260, line 6 from bottom. *In South Sea days,* &c.

Pope had South Sea stock, valued in the day of national madness at between £20,000 and £30,000. He kept it until it vanished into air.

P. 260, line 3 from bottom. *Than in five acres,* &c.

Pope's villa at Twickenham was rented from a Mrs. Vernon.

P. 261, line 6 from bottom. *Shades, that to Bacon,* &c.

Gorhambury, near St. Albans.

P. 261, line 3 from bottom. *Proud Buckingham's delight*

Villiers, Duke of Buckingham.

Page 262, line 1. *I've often wish'd.*

Pope's part of this poem begins at the hundred and twenty-fifth line; but such is his dexterity of imitation, that the change is scarcely discoverable.

P. 262, line 22. *In my right wits.*

Swift for some years had laboured under an apprehension of insanity. His abruptness, eccentricity, and singular fondness for looking on the repulsive side of human nature, might have justified the alarm, from the beginning of his career.

P. 262, line 6 from bottom. *Nor cross the channel twice a year.*

Swift held himself so strongly aggrieved by being fixed in Ireland, that he was continually soliciting an exchange of his preferment for an English benefice. Notwithstanding his old and open hostility to Sir R. Walpole, he appears to have, at one time, been on the point of obtaining an English deanery. But his love of political bustle was not to be resisted: and he had but just arrived in London, *for the purpose of concluding the arrangement;* when he plunged into a newspaper with Bolingbroke, and commenced a course of vigorous libel on the only man who could effect his object.

P. 264, line 12. *My lord and me,* &c.

Harley. The premier's intimacy with Swift naturally promised a share in that official overthrow which pours from the fountains of the treasury; and Swift clearly calculated on being a bishop. But "The Tale of the Tub" stood in his way; and the queen honourably refused to suffer its writer to take his place among the heads of the church. Swift's adherence to Mrs. Howard, justly obnoxious as she was to the queen, might have not slightly assisted the royal determination.

P. 265, line 24. *He had a story of two mice.*

Warton observes that this story "belongs to Æsop, though not inserted in the collection which bears his name." His authority is Babrius, probably himself too late to be an authority: but Warton, from his silence on the subject, might seem to be unaware of the curious controversy on Æsop, which put the world of scholarship in commotion about the beginning of the century; threw Sir William Temple's rash panegyric of antiquity into ridicule; and produced the "bellum plusquam civile" of Boyle, Atterbury, Freind, Bentley, &c. Literary quarrel never adopted a more promising topic, for all its features were contestable. It was thus disputed, and may be disputed still,—whether the Fables were originally Greek or Indian;—whether they were written in the most remote antiquity, or were as recent as the day of Socrates, or were chiefly the production of yet more recent times;—whether they were originally in prose or in verse;—whether a syllable of the life of Æsop by Planudes is true or false; whether Æsop were a slave and deformed, or free and straight-backed;—whether he were a Greek, an Egyptian, or a Phrygian;—whether he lived in the sixth century before our era, or whether he ever existed. The fate of the Fables is equally curious in point of change. The first known collection was made by Phalereus of Athens about the fourth century, B.C.; (perhaps originally translated from some oriental dialect;) their first Greek shape was prose, for Socrates employed his prison hours in turning some of them into verse: the example was followed, and the chief fables were thrown into elegiac metre. They were again either collected, or versified, by Babrius, about the close of the Augustan age. Again, the monk Planudes, in the fourteenth century, broke down the verse into prose, and gave us the Æsop of modern times. A learned paper by Tyrrwhit, "Dissertatio de Babrio," renewed the subject in 1776, and supplied all the facts that are now capable of being ascertained.

P. 268, line 17. *I'll do what Mead.*

The celebrated physician.

P. 268, line 17. *Cheselden.*

The most adventurous, but the most successful surgical operator of his day: a friend of Pope.

P. 269, line 2. *Who notches sticks at Westminster.*

Exchequer tallies.

P. 269, line 3. *Barnard.*

Sir John Barnard, Knight, was born at Reading, and brought up at a school at Wandsworth in Surrey: his parents were Quakers. In 1703, he quitted the Society of Quakers, was received into the church by Compton, Bishop of London, and continued a member of it. He became a celebrated member of parliament, and an eminent merchant and magistrate of London.

P. 269, line 6. *As Bug now has, and Dorimant,* &c.

The industry of the commentators has been unable to apply those names.

P. 270, line 13 from bottom. *Linen worthy lady Mary.*

Pope could never forgive Lady Mary's at once laughing at his passion, and libelling his poetry. This celebrated woman, though a beauty, and vain of her charms, was supposed to be singularly negligent of her person. Walpole says, "that when she left Florence, after a three weeks' stay in one of the archduke's palaces, they were obliged to fumigate the rooms." And this in Italy!

P. 273, line 8. *It brighten'd Craggs's.*

The secretary was the son of a man originally in a menial situation, yet who by industry and character rose to be postmaster-general.

P. 273, line 19. *See Ward by batter'd beaux,* &c.

Ward and Dover, well-known quacks.

P. 273, line 24. *Disdain whatever Cornbury disdains.*

Lord Cornbury, a man of talents and virtue.

P. 273, line 5 from bottom. *Anstis birth.*

Garter king-at-arms.

P. 274, line 8 from bottom. *Wilmot.*

The Earl of Rochester.

P. 276, line 18 from bottom. *Child.*

Sir Francis Child, the banker.

P. 276, line 18 from bottom. *Craggs and Child.*

Pope had some South Sea Stock, which he kept until it sank to nothing. Warburton, to the credit of the poet's equanimity, informs us, that he used to say,—"It was a satisfaction to him that he did not grow rich by the public calamity."

P. 278, line 12. *And beastly Skelton,* &c.

Poet laureate to Henry VIII.

P. 278, line 14. *Christ's Kirk of the Green.*

A ballad written by James I. of Scotland.

P. 279, line 15. *Gammer Gurton*, &c.

One of the first printed plays in English, written by Still of Christ's College, Cambridge; afterwards bishop of Bath and Wells.

P. 279, line 5 from bottom. *Betterton's grave action.*

This celebrated actor was one of the earliest friends of Pope.

P. 281, line 10. *Should Ripley venture*, &c.

Ripley was the government architect; and, with the usual ill fate of favourites, contrived to please none but his employers.

P. 283, line 12. *Congreve.*

He alludes to the characters of Brisk and Witwood.

P. 283, line 15. *Astrea.*

A name taken by Mrs. Behn, authoress of several gross plays, &c.

P. 283, line 38. *From heads to ears, and now from ears to eyes.*

The course of theatrical degeneracy, as Warburton says, "from plays to operas, and from operas to pantomimes."

P. 293, line 1. *Again? new tumults*, &c.

Pope has here adopted the metre of Ben Jonson, in his translation.

P. 293, line 9. *Number five*, &c.

Murray's Chambers, in King's Bench Walks.

P. 293, line 18. *Make but his riches*, &c.

Bowles quotes Seward for the anecdote of Mansfield's early life; that he told his friend, Lord Foley, that, from the slenderness of his income, he must give up the bar, and take orders:—a resolution which Lord Foley prevented, by giving him two hundred pounds a year.

P. 295, line 6. *In Spenser native Muse play.*

This praise is not of either the most discriminating or the loftiest order: yet Spenser was an established favourite of Pope. Spence records his saying,—"There is something in Spenser that pleases one as strongly in age as in youth: I read the 'Faery Queen' when I was about twelve, with a vast deal of delight; and I think it gave me as much when I read it over about a year or two ago."

P. 375, line 9. *Much better metre.*

From Boileau:—

"Avant lui, Juvénal avait dit en Latin,
Qu'on est assis à l'aise aux sermons de Cotin."

P. 375, line 12. *Bubo.*

Bubb Doddington.

P. 375, line 13. *Sir Billy.*

Sir William Young, of use to the minister, as a talker against time.

P. 375, line 14. *H—ggins.*

Formerly gaoler of the Fleet prison, who enriched himself by many exactions, for which he was tried and expelled.—POPE.

P. 375, line 10. *Who cropp'd our ears.*

Said to be executed by the captain of a Spanish ship on one Jenkins, a captain of an English one. He cut off his ears, and bid him carry them to the king his master.—POPE. The whole story was afterwards said to be a fiction.

P. 376, line 3. *But in his happier hour.*

Pope here forgets his party to compliment the minister: but this slight tergiversation may be forgiven, when we are told that it was in return for a favour conferred, not on himself, but on his friend, the Abbé Southcote.

Walpole's private life was gross, his personal manners were rough, and his ministerial principles were avowedly and undeniably formed on the corruptibility of the human character: but his management of England, during the doubtful period of the Hanover succession, was masterly. Even Burke gives him all the praise that can be awarded to a successful statesman. Bowles quotes the sufficiently characteristic description from the pen of Lady M. W. Montague:—

On seeing a portrait of Sir Robert Walpole.

"Such were the lively eyes and rosy hue
Of Robin's face, when Robin first I knew,
The gay companion, and the favourite guest,
Loved without awe, and without fear caress'd,
His cheerful smile, and open, honest look
Added new graces to the truths he spoke."

P. 376, line 9. *He laughs, no doubt.*

Walpole's general remark that "every man has his price," has been diluted by his biographer, Archdeacon Coxe, into a particular sneer at the patriots of his day, "All those have their price." But the phrase was only too characteristic of Walpole's rough dealing with mankind, his habitual contempt for all professions of public virtue, and his personal experience. Corruption, in his day, was a notorious agent, and an agent on all sides alike: the ministerialist was corrupted by possession, the oppositionist was corrupted in prospect. The purse was the notorious instrument of political conversion.

Practices thus alien to the natural honesty of the British mind, were to be accounted for only by the rapid changes of party, which exhibited all things as saleable; the anxious revolutions of government for the last fifty years, which exhibited all things as uncertain; and the result of both, and more powerful than either, the irreligion which had begun to usurp all men's minds. In Walpole's day, England was hurrying down into the infidelity of the continent; and, but for the sudden awakening of her church to a sense of her danger, she might have shared the fearful punishment which, before the close of the century, was to cover the continent with such unexampled devastation.

Warton mentions, to the credit of Walpole's placability, that, during Atterbury's confinement in the Tower, a fine of a thousand pounds falling to him as Dean of Westminster, which could not be received, except by setting the seal to the lease in full chapter; Walpole strongly interested himself to have the chapter held in the Tower, that the bishop might have the benefit of the fine. The chapter was held in the Tower, and Atterbury received the thousand pounds, immediately before his banishment.

P. 376, line 13. *A joke on Jekyl.*

Sir Joseph Jekyl, master of the rolls, a true Whig in his principles, and a man of the utmost probity.—POPE.

P. 376, line 21. *Why, answer, Littleton.*

George Littleton, secretary to the Prince of Wales, distinguished for both his writings and speeches in the spirit of liberty.—POPE.

P. 376, line 25. *Sejanus.*

This minister, delivered down to "immortal shame" by the pen of Tacitus, burned the panegyric of Crematius Cordus on Brutus and

Cassius: the book immediately became popular. Bacon says, with his quaint force,—"The punishing of wits enhances their authority: a forbidden writing is thought to be a certain spark of truth, that flies up in the faces of them that seek to tread it out."

P. 376, line 25. *Fleury.*

Cardinal; and minister to Louis XV.

P. 376, line 11 from bottom.—*Henley—Osborn.*

See them in their places in the Dunciad.—POPE.

P. 376, line 2 from bottom. *The pride of Middleton.*

Middleton's "Life of Cicero," which appeared in 1741, was once regarded as a standard of English writing. Middleton, though an accomplished scholar and able man, yet disingenuous by habit, and discontented on principle, unfortunately signalized his career by attacking nearly all the eminent ecclesiastical names of his day, and is still remembered as the defeated assailant of Sherlock and Waterland. His latest work of notoriety, the "Free Inquiry into the Miraculous Powers," brought down on him the resentment of his profession; and, as he lived useless, he died dishonoured. He was acute without judgment, zealous without sincerity, and learned without knowledge.

P. 377, line 4. *Carolina.*

Consort to King George II. She died in 1737. Queen Caroline had been charged with severity of temper; and it was openly said, that even on her death bed, she had refused pardon to the prince, her son, who had entreated that he might receive her blessing. Coxe says, on this point,—"I am happy to have it in my power to remove the stigma from the memory of this great princess: she sent her blessing to her son, with a message of forgiveness, and told Sir R. Walpole "she would have seen him with pleasure, but prudence forbade the interview, as it might embarrass and irritate the king." This may be vindication; but it must be limited to the *queen*. Courtiership on the death bed!—prudence preventing a mother from seeing her son at the last glance that she was to give to this world. The genius of etiquette was probably never so honoured before.

P. 377, line 16. *Immortal S—k.*

Charles Hamilton, third son of the Duke of Hamilton, who was created Earl of Selkirk in 1687.

P. 377, line 20 from bottom. *Three sovereigns died.*

Mary, William, and Anne: the gracious prince was George I.

P. 377, line 16 from bottom. *Or peeress shall I fret.*

Bowles says this alludes to Lady M. Montague, who was reported to have suffered her sister, the Countess of Mar, to sink into destitution in Paris. But he denies the destitution, chiefly on the ground that the earl's Scotch estate was given to his wife and daughter by George I. for their maintenance. Yet the Scotch estate might not be large; the rents paid to an exile are not always of the most punctual order; and Lady Mary's personal profligacy was the natural school for hardness of heart.

P. 377, line 12 from bottom. *Cibber's son—Rich.*

Two players: look for them in the Dunciad.—POPE.

P. 377, line 4 from bottom. *If Blount despatch'd himself.*

He was the younger son of Sir Henry Blount, who wrote an admirable account of a Voyage to the Levant, 1636; and younger brother of Sir Thomas Pope Blount, who wrote the "Censura Authorum;" and this Charles Blount was not only the author of the "Oracles of Reason," but of an infidel treatise, intitled "Anima Mundi," and of the "Life of Apollonius Tyanæus," in folio, 1680; with notes said to be taken from the manuscript of Lord Herbert of Cherbury. It was his sister-in-law with whom he was in love, when he destroyed himself.

P. 377, line 3 from bottom. *Passeran.*

A Piedmontese nobleman, who wrote a "Philosophical Discourse on Death," in defence of suicide. He was banished from Piedmont for his excesses, and lived long in misery; but at length recanted his philosophical absurdities, and died in penitence.

P. 377, line 2 from bottom. *But shall a printer.*

A fact that happened in London a few years past. The unhappy man left behind him a paper justifying his action by the reasonings of some of these authors.—POPE.

P. 377, last line. *Learn, from their books, to hang.*

The circumstance alluded to in the preceding note excited much commiseration at the time. It was the case of an unfortunate debtor of the name of Smith, a bookbinder, who with his wife was found hanging in his room in the King's Bench: they were within a few yards of each other, both dead; and their infant, two years old, lay, shot dead, in its cradle. The suicide had evidently been of the most deliberate kind: the husband and wife were dressed with peculiar neatness; a curtain was drawn between them, as if to conceal their dying struggles from each other; and a loaded pistol lay at the foot of the man, and a knife near the woman, apparently to complete the catastrophe if the rope should fail. Two letters lay on the table, one to their landlord relative to his rent, and the other to a Mr. Brindley, attempting to justify their suicide.

P. 378, line 3. *This calls the church to deprecate our sin.*

Alluding to the forms of prayer composed in the times of public calamity and distress.

P. 378, line 4. *Gin.*

A spirituous liquor, the exorbitant use of which had almost destroyed the lowest rank of the people, till it was restrained by an act of parliament in 1736.—POPE.

P. 378, line 5. *Foster.*

A preacher of celebrity among the Dissenters; he wrote a "Defence of Christianity" against Toland. Warburton, angry for once with Pope, quotes Hobbes, "that there are very few bishops that can act a sermon so well as divers Presbyterians and fanatic preachers can do."

P. 378, line 7. *Quaker's wife.*

A Mrs. Drummond, a preacher.

P. 378, line 8. *Outdo Llandaff.*

A prelate of irreproachable character, who is said never to have offended Pope; and whose son is no small ornament to his profession, Dr. Harris, of Doctors' Commons.—WARTON.

P. 378, line 9. *Humble Allen.*

Allen of Bath. Pope, in the first edition of this poem, had written "low-born," a depth to which Allen's humility did not descend: the epithet was therefore changed, and an apologetical letter sent in explanation. It seems probable that the rich man was not much more captivated by his new epithet than his old. The affair was obviously too delicate even for Pope's dexterity; and he found that there are virtues for which even their possessors are not too willing to be praised.

P. 378, line 18. *Let greatness own her.*

Warburton, who, if not the depository of Pope's secrets, was at least the instrument by which he conveyed his intentions to the public, affirms that all this bold and highly wrought passage alluded only to Theodora, the profligate empress of Justinian. But a moral drawn from an oriental libertine, and drawn through the dreary lapse of a thousand years, is too unlike the author's keen sense of living incidents, to be taken as his object. The court, in his day, offered more than one Theodora; or, if England were unproductive, France teemed. The last century, on the continent, was the reign of mistresses.

P. 378, line 22. *And hers the Gospel.*

An unbecoming phrase; but meant merely to signify that the disposal of honours in church as well as state rested in impure hands.

P. 378, line 11 from bottom. *'Tis avarice all.*

Warton quotes Bolingbroke's antithetical expression,—"so far from having the virtues, we have not even the vices of our ancestors." Bolingbroke himself the living example of specious degeneracy!

P. 379, line 1. *Paxton.*

Solicitor to the treasury, whose office was to denounce attacks on the government.

P. 379, line 11. *Ev'n Guthrie.*

The ordinary of Newgate, who publishes the "Memoirs of the Malefactors," and is often prevailed on to be so tender of their reputation, as to set down no more than the initials of their names.—Pope.

P. 379, line 21. *The town's inquiring yet.*

Swift says,—"I have long observed, that twenty miles from London nobody understands hints, initial letters, or town-facts and passages:" but this was written a hundred years ago. The communication of intelligence of this order is more extensive in the nineteenth century.

P. 379, line 3 from bottom. *Wretched Wild.*

Jonathan Wild, a famous thief, and thief-impeacher, who was at last caught in his own train, and hanged.—Pope.

P. 380, line 26. *Scarborough.*

Earl of, and Knight of the Garter, whose personal attachments to the king appeared from his steady adherence to the royal interest, after his resignation of his great employment of master of the horse; and whose known honour and virtue made him esteemed by all parties.—Pope.

P. 380, line 27. *Esher's peaceful grove.*

The house and gardens of Esher, in Surrey, belonging to the Honourable Mr. Pelham, brother of the Duke of Newcastle.

P. 380, line 32. *Secker is decent.*

A great deal of Pope's unhappy style of alluding to the heads of the establishment must be referred to his own prejudices; some to the pert freethinking fashion of the day. Secker, the archbishop, was an honest, learned, and useful divine. Benson was a man of general esteem, and who would probably have been a bishop, but for the interference of Gibson, the Bishop of London, who charged him with unscriptural notions on the subject of sacrifice—an objection perfectly sufficient; for what can be more pernicious than error armed with authority?

P. 380, line 34. *To Berkley, every virtue.*

The Bishop of Cloyne, memorable for his zeal, his learning, and his metaphysical fancies. He mounted a paradox, and rode it, till he left common sense out of sight, and was flung: the common fate of all who hope to succeed in a science, of which nature has denied us access to the first principles. Until we know what spirit is, metaphysics must be a dream.

P. 380, line 13 from bottom. *Somers.*

John, Lord Somers, died in 1716. He had been lord keeper in the reign of William III., who took from him the seals in 1700. The author had the honour of knowing him in 1706. A faithful, able, and incorrupt minister, who, to the qualities of a consummate statesman, added those of a man of learning and politeness.—POPE.

P. 380, line 13 from bottom. *Halifax.*

A peer, no less distinguished by his love of letters than his abilities in parliament. He was disgraced in 1710, on the change of Queen Anne's ministry.—POPE.

P. 380, line 11 from bottom. *Shrewsbury.*

Charles Talbot, Duke of Shrewsbury, had been secretary of state, ambassador in France, lord lieutenant of Ireland, lord chamberlain, and lord treasurer. He several times quitted his employments, and was often recalled. He died in 1718.—POPE.

P. 380, line 10 from bottom. *Carleton.*

Henry Boyle, Lord Carleton, nephew of the famous Robert Boyle, who was secretary of state under William III. and president of the council under Queen Anne.—POPE.

P. 380, line 10 from bottom. *Stanhope.*

James, Earl Stanhope; a nobleman of equal courage, spirit, and learning; general in Spain, and secretary of state.—POPE.

P. 380, line 6 from bottom. *Pulteney, Chesterfield.*

Warton tells us, that he heard "a lady of exquisite wit and judgment say of those two celebrated men, that the latter was always striving to be witty, the former could not help being so." If this were the case, Pulteney has reason to complain of biography; for while Chesterfield has left us many happy *jeux d'esprit*, Pulteney has left nothing but the dry pages of the "Craftsman," and even there his possession has been more than disputed. Warton rather maliciously adds, that the lines on Argyll were inserted, after the duke's declaring in the House of Lords, "on occasion of some of Pope's satires," that if any man dared to use his name in an invective, he would run him through the body, and throw himself on the mercy of his peers, who, he trusted, would weigh the provocation. Argyll's well-known character might justify the poet's prudence in passing him by, but scarcely justifies his volunteering a panegyric.

P. 381, line 11. *My Lord Mayor.*

Sir John Barnard, mayor in this year, 1738; a man respected for his integrity, activity, and intelligence: he was a member of parliament. In 1747, the city voted him a statue.

P. 381, line 29. *What Richelieu, &c.*

The arrogant, but the able minister of France, As he had raised the monarchy to its height by violence, he laboured to keep it there by corruption: his first object had been accomplished in the ruin of Protestantism; his next, in the purchase of the whole literary body of France. He is said also to have expended eighty thousand crowns a year in public pensions to writers of all countries;—an immense sum in his day: but his private bribes were probably much more lavish, and much more effectual.

P. 381, line 9 from bottom. *Arnall! aid me while I lie.*

One of the writers for the Walpole ministry: a shrewd and sensible man; but latterly wasteful; and, after undergoing great distress, closing his career by the still more unhappy fate of suicide.—Bowles.

P. 382, line 6. *To break my windows.*

Pope had become obnoxious to the street politicians; and they broke his windows, one day, when Lords Bolingbroke and Bathurst were at dinner with him

P. 382, lines 21, 22. *S——k.—P—ge.*

Sherlock and Page

P. 382, line 24. *In power.*

A line in an epistle to Sir R. Walpole, by Lord Melcombe.

P. 382, line 28. *He only stain'd.*

The priest alluded to in the preceding line, notwithstanding Pope's denying note, was Dr. Allured Clarke, who wrote a panegyric on Queen Caroline.

P. 382, line 29. *Florid youth.*

Lord Hervey, alluding to his painting himself.

P. 394, line 16.

This Epistle was sent to the Earl of Oxford, with Dr. Parnell's Poems published by our author, after the said earl's imprisonment in the Tower, and retreat into the country, in the year 1721.—Pope.

P. 395, line 18 from bottom.

Craggs was made secretary at war in 1717, when the Earl of Sunderland and Mr. Addison were appointed secretaries of state: this Epistle appears to have been written soon after he was made one of the secretaries of state. He was deeply implicated in the famous South Sea scheme: he died soon after the detection of it, and would most probably have been called to a severe account had he lived. He died of the small-pox, February 16, 1721.

P. 396, line 10. *So mix'd our studies.*

Pope's fondness for painting, an art in which he was not born to excel, led him into frequent intercourse with Jervas. The painter was an intelligent and accomplished man, who probably returned the poet's attentions by his anecdotes of high life. He was the most fashionable portrait-painter of his day, though Walpole boldly pronounces him defective in the three great points of his art—drawing, colouring, and composition. Jervas was remarkable for vanity of person: Lady Bridgewater was sitting to him; and after paying her some rapturous compliment on her beauty (for he conceived himself to be in love with her), he said, that "she had not a handsome ear."—"And pray, Mr. Jervas," said she, "what is a handsome ear?" Jervas turned up his cap, and showed her his own.

P. 396, line 17. *In pleasing tasks, &c.*

A head of Betterton by Pope is in Lord Mansfield's possession; another is in the collection at Arundel Castle.

P. 396, line 3 from bottom. *Paulo's free stroke.*

Warton says that Reynolds told him, "he did not think the epithets of the various painters well applied:" but they are unquestionably the epithets which criticism has applied to them from their first days of fame; and if Pope thus loses the merit of originality, at least he has the value of precedent.

P. 396, last line. *The work of years!*

Fresnoy employed above twenty years in finishing his poem.

P. 397, line 19. *Thus Churchill's race.*

Churchill's race were the four beautiful daughters of John, the great Duke of Marlborough: Henrietta, Countess of Godolphin, afterwards Duchess of Marlborough; Anne, Countess of Sunderland; Elizabeth, Countess of Bridgewater; and Mary, duchess of Montagu.

P. 397, line 20. *Worsley's eyes.*

Frances, Lady Worsley, wife of Sir Robert Worsley, Bart., of Appuldercombe, in the Isle of Wight; mother of Lady Carteret, the wife of John, Lord Carteret, afterwards Earl Granville.

P. 397, line 21. *Each pleasing Blount.*

The two sisters, Teresa and Martha Blount.

P. 398, line 19. *The Smiles and Loves.*

From the pretty epitaph on Voiture:

"Etruscæ Veneres, Camœnæ Iberæ,
Hermes Gallicus, et Latina Siren,
Risus, Deliciæ, et Dicacitates,
Lusus, Ingenium, Joci, Lepores,
Et quicquid unquam fuit elegantiarum,
Quo Vecturius hoc jacent sepulcro."

P. 399, line 12 from bottom. *Thus Voiture's early care.*

Mademoiselle Paulet.

P. 400. *Mrs. Teresa Blount.*

On her leaving town after the coronation of George I. in 1715.

P. 402. *Mrs. Martha Blount.*

Pope's attachment to this woman lasted to the close of his life; but it was less like that of a lover, than of a child to its nurse; and she returned the feeling much in the style of a nurse to a child, alternately fondling, and tyrannizing over, her rather capricious charge. She probably clung to his fame, for her heart seems never to have been interested in the connection. But after a long and intimate intercourse, she suddenly assumed a ridiculous reserve; and, as Wharton, with just contempt at this affectation, remarks:—"When she visited Pope, in his very last illness, and her company seemed to give him fresh spirits, the antiquated prude could not be prevailed on to stay and pass the night at Twickenham, because of her reputation!"

P. 408. *Sir William Trumball.*

Our author's friendship with this gentleman commenced at very unequal years; he was under sixteeen, but Sir William above sixty, and had lately resigned his employment of secretary of state to king William.—P.

P. 408, line 1. *First in these fields.*

"Prima Syracosio dignata est."—VIRGIL.

P. 408, line 12. *In your native shades.*

Sir W. Trumball was born in Windsor-forest, to which he retreated, after he had resigned the post of secretary of state to King William III.—P.

P. 409, line 12. *Granville.*

George Granville, afterwards Lord Lansdowne, known for his

poems, most of which he composed very young; and proposed Waller as his model.—P.

P. 410, line 4. *A wondrous tree, that sacred monarch bears?*

An allusion to the royal oak, in which Charles II. had been hid from the pursuit after the battle at Worcester.—P.

P. 410, line 18 from bottom. *A Shepherd's boy.*

Spenser.

P. 411, line 21. *Colin.*

The name taken by Spenser in his Eclogues, where his mistress is celebrated under that of Rosalinda.—WARTON.

P. 411, line 24. *Rosalinda's.*

This is the lady with whom Spenser fell violently in love, as soon as he left Cambridge, and went into the north; it is uncertain into what family, and in what capacity.—WARTON.

P. 412, line 10. *Your praise the birds.*

Pope had first written the lines,—

" Your praise the tuneful birds to heaven shall bear,
And listening wolves grow milder as they hear . '

but he acknowledges this to have been an oversight; " and the author, young as he was, soon found the absurdity, which Spenser himself had overlooked, of introducing wolves into England."

P. 412, line 9 from bottom *The art of Terence, and Menander's fire.*

" Alluding," says Warburton, " to Cæsar's character of Terence,—O dimidiate Menander !" &c. a sufficiently qualified panegyric of the Roman Comedian; but that any allusion was intended is by no means clear. It is curious to find modern criticism dilating on the " comic power" of Terence, which the character so distinctly denies :—

" Lenibus atque utinam scriptis adjuncta foret *vis Comica.*"

P. 413, line 28. *Not balmy sleep,* &c.

" Quale sopor fessis."—VIRGIL.

Warton attributes this passage to Drummond of Hawthornden's picturesque lines :—

" To virgins flowers, to sun-burnt earth the rain,
To mariners fair winds amid the main,
Cool shades to pilgrims, whom hot glances burn,
Are not so pleasing as thy blest return."

Milton's noble lines concluding with

" Nor glittering starlight without thee is sweet,"

contain the same idea; but expressed, as it could be expressed only, by the golden flow of Milton.

P. 414, line 4 from bottom. *Thus sung.*

To this poem Warton appends a note in praise of the pastorals of Fairfax, whose verse is almost Shaksperian ; and Bowles adds Brown's pastorals, from which even Milton did not disdain to borrow.

P. 415. *Mrs. Tempest.*

This lady was of an ancient family in Yorkshire, and particularly admired by the author's friend, Mr. Walsh; who, having celebrated her in a pastoral elegy, desired his friend to do the same, as appears from one of his letters, dated September 9, 1706 :—" Your last eclogue being on the same subject with mine, on Mrs. Tempest's death, I should take it very kindly in you to give it a little turn, as if it were to the memory of the same lady." Her death having happened on the night of the great storm in 1703, gave a propriety to this eclogue, which in its general turn alludes to it. The scene of the pastoral lies in a grove; the time is midnight.—P.

P. 415, line 22. *Cypress garlands bring.*

Bowles quotes the pretty ballad from "the Maid's Tragedy:"—

"Lay a garland on my brow
  Of the dismal yew.
Maidens, willow branches bear;
  Say, I died true.
My love was false, but I was true,
  From my hour of birth:
Upon my buried body lie
  Softly, gentle earth."

P. 416, line 27. *But see, where Daphne.*

Thus Milton:—

Weep no more, woful shepherds, weep no more
Where other groves and other streams along,
With nectar pure his oozy locks he laves,
And hears the inexpressive nuptial song
In the blest kingdoms meek of joy and love."—*Lycidas.*

P. 416, the four last lines.

These last four lines allude to the several subjects of the four pastorals, and to the several scenes of them particularized before in each.—P.

P. 417, line 8. *A Virgin shall conceive—All crimes shall cease,* &c.—VIRG. Ecl. iv. ver. 6.

P. 418, line 1. *See, Nature hastes,* &c.—VIRG. Ecl. iv. ver. 18.

P. 418, line 7. *Hark! a glad voice,* &c.—VIRG. Ecl. iv. ver. 46.

P. 418, line 6 from bottom. *The lambs with wolves,* &c.—VIRG. Ecl. iv. ver. 21.

P. 419, line 13. *Rise, crowned with light, imperial Salem, rise!*

The thoughts of Isaiah, which compose the latter part of the poem, are wonderfully elevated, and much above those general exclamations of Virgil, which make the loftiest parts of his Pollio.—P.

P. 425, line 7. *Tyrants no more.*

Possibly in allusion to Louis the Fourteenth's saying, that "the Cinna of Corneille made him wish to pardon the Cardinal de Rohan."

P. 425, line 11. *In pitying love.*

Warton contemptuously asks, "Why then did Addison introduce the loves of Juba and Marcia?" The answer may fairly be, that no play can be popular without some touch of nature; and that those loves furnish the only touch of nature in the play. It must, however, be acknowledged, that of all loves, on or off the stage, those are the least qualified to take the heart of the spectator by surprise. Marcia is more frigid than Cato himself, and Juba is as formal as an ambassador. That the haughty daughter of the head of the Roman commonwealth should stoop to the passion of a Lybian leader of savages, was sufficiently improbable; but that *passion* should declaim in the language of either, was an impossibility. Even the love of Desdemona was attributed by her countrymen to witchcraft; yet what incomparably superior ground for passion was laid in the impetuous and fiery vividness of Othello, and the rich romance and exquisite sensibility of his "fair Venetian!" It is said in imperfect apology for Addison, that those scenes were an after thought, in compliment to the habits of the stage: it might more honestly be said, in tribute to the necessities of the stage. No play can ever effectually engage the interest of the audience without passion; and of all the movers of sympathy, the simplest, the most powerful, and the most universal, is love.

P. 425, line 2 from bottom. *Britons, attend.*

It has been already remarked, that the original word was "arise;" but it was thought too inflammatory: such were the delicacies of the time.

P. 443. THE BASSET TABLE.

Pope's claims to this poem are not perfectly clear. He and Lady Wortley Montague wrote six "Town Eclogues," of which four were by her ladyship; but which four, is the difficulty.

The style of this poem was popular. Gay wrote a "Quaker's Eclogue," and Swift a "Footman's Eclogue." It was probably on this occasion, and to the ideas suggested by the latter *jeu d'esprit*, that the "Beggars' Opera" owed its birth. "I think," said Swift, one day to Pope, "the pastoral ridicule is not yet exhausted: what think you of a Newgate pastoral among the thieves there?" Gay was furnished with the design (how far advanced by Swift's vigorous conception, and Pope's subtlety of satire, cannot now be told), and found in it an instant and extraordinary source of emolument and fame.

A pretty poem of Lady Wortlev Montague is preserved (Algaotti, v. 7.):—

"Thou silver deity of secret night,
  Direct my footsteps through the woodland shade;
Thou conscious witness of unknown delight,
  The lover's guardian, and the Muse's aid;
By thy pale beams I solitary rove;
  To thee my tender grief confide:
Serenely sweet, you gild the silent grove,
  My friend, my goddess, and my guide.
Ev'n thee, fair queen, from thy amazing height,
  The charms of young Endymion drew,
Veil'd in the mantle of concealing night,
  With all thy greatness, all thy coldness too."

Her ladyship is recorded to have had a female jealousy of correction. When she occasionally showed a copy of her verses to Pope, she would say,—"Now, Pope, no touching; for then, whatever is good for anything will pass for yours; and the rest for mine."

P. 447, line 5. *Was there a chief, &c.*

The fine figure of the commander, in that capital picture of Belisarius, at Chiswick, supplied the poet with this beautiful idea.—WARBURTON.

P. 447, line 10. *Their quibbles routed, and defied their puns.*

An old gentleman of the last century, who used to frequent Button's coffee-house, told me they had many pleasant scenes of Dennis's indignation and resentment, when Steele and Rowe, in particular, teazed him with a pun.—WARTON.

P. 447, line 24. *When simple Macer, &c.*

This character first appeared in the volume of Pope's and Swift's "Miscellanies" in 1774. Warton conceives Macer to be James Moore Smith, writer of the "Rival Modes," a comedy, and a contributor to a virulent journal, the "Inquisitor," set up by the Duke of Wharton. He had pilfered some verses from Pope.

Bowles, with greater probability, conceives Macer to have been intended for Philips, to whom Pope had taken an early and an inveterate dislike: he is elsewhere called "lean Philips." His first literary acquaintance was with Steele: he borrowed the "Distressed Mother" from Voltaire, and translated the "Persian Tales."

P. 449, line 4. *A reasonable woman.*

The lady was Mrs. Howard, of Marble-hill, bed-chamber woman to Queen Caroline, and afterwards Countess of Suffolk. Pope's panegyric might have been more meritoriously applied.

P. 449, line 6 from bottom. *Egerian grot.*

The retreat where Numa sought counsel of his genius, the nymph Egeria; a fiction almost too fine for his rude age, and ruder country. Juvenal, in some of those lines which signally show the picturesque eloquence of the great poet, exclaims against the artificial taste, which had attempted to decorate the haunt of the king and his living oracle:—

"Quanto præstantius esset
Numen aquæ, viridi si margine clauderet undas
Herba, nec ingenuum violarent marmora tophum!"

P. 449, line 4 from bottom. *British sighs from dying Wyndham.*

Pope's early Jacobitism reconciled even his acute, and rather contemptuous mind, to all the absurdities of party. Sir William Wyndham was a Jacobite; wrong-headed enough to think that a Stuart reign was compatible with liberty; obstinate enough to persevere in his folly to the end of his days; and, with the usual morality of faction, flexible enough to take office under a government, which existed solely on the principle of excluding the Stuarts from the throne. In the reign of Anne, and on the accession of the Oxford cabinet, he thus became successively master of the buck-hounds, secretary at war, and chancellor of the exchequer. But the accession of the Brunswick line brought in a more decided policy; and the prosperous Jacobite was dismissed from all his places, and committed to the Tower. From this confinement, however, he was released on bail; and, exhausting the rest of his days in retirement, died in 1740.

www.ingramcontent.com/pod-product-compliance
Lightning Source LLC
LaVergne TN
LVHW021319110826
845150LV00003B/620

* 9 7 8 1 4 2 5 5 5 6 9 8 3 *